Perspectives on Imitation

Perspectives on Imitation: From Neuroscience to Social Science

Volume 2: Imitation, Human Development, and Culture

edited by Susan Hurley and Nick Chater

A Bradford Book
The MIT Press
Cambridge, Massachusetts
London, England

MIT Press books may be purchased at special quantity discounts for business or sales promotional use. For information, please email special_sales@mitpress.mit.edu or write to Special Sales Department, The MIT Press, 5 Cambridge Center, Cambridge, MA 02142.

This book was set in Stone serif and Stone sans on 3B2 by Asco Typesetters, Hong Kong and was printed and bound in the United States of America.

Library of Congress Cataloging-in-Publication Data

Perspectives on imitation : from neuroscience to social science / Susan Hurley and Nick Chater, editors.
   p.   cm.
Includes bibliographical references and index.
Contents: v. 1. Mechanisms of imitation and imitation in animals—v. 2. Imitation, human development, and culture.
ISBN 0-262-58252-X (set : pbk.)—ISBN 0-262-08335-3 (v. 1 : hc.)—ISBN 0-262-58250-3 (v. 1 : pbk.)—ISBN 0-262-08336-1 (v. 2 : hc.)—ISBN 0-262-58251-1 (v. 2 : pbk.)
1. Imitation. 2. Animal learning. 3. Social psychology. I. Hurley, Susan. II. Chater, Nick.
BF357.P47   2005
302—dc22   200404986

10 9 8 7 6 5 4 3 2 1

Contents of Volume 2

Imitation, Human Development, and Culture

Contents of Volume 1

Mechanisms of Imitation and Imitation in Animals

Volume 2: Imitation, Human Development, and Culture

Introduction: The Importance of Imitation

Susan Hurley and Nick Chater

Imitation is often thought of as a low-level, cognitively undemanding, even childish form of behavior, but recent work across a variety of sciences argues that imitation is a rare ability that is fundamentally linked to characteristically human forms of intelligence, in particular to language, culture, and the ability to understand other minds. This burgeoning body of work has important implications for our understanding of ourselves, both individually and socially. Imitation is not just an important factor in human development, it also has a pervasive influence throughout adulthood in ways we are just starting to understand.

These two volumes present papers by researchers working in disciplines that include neuroscience and brain imaging, psychology, animal behavior, philosophy, computer science, education studies, anthropology, media studies, economics, sociology, and law. Among the authors are many who are leading figures in imitation research and who have produced seminal work on imitation. They also include younger researchers and scholars commenting on work in disciplines other than their own. One of our main aims in these volumes has been to provide a resource that brings together important work on this topic from various disciplines, makes it accessible across disciplines, and fosters interdisciplinary cross-fertilization. In particular, we want to convey why imitation is a topic of such intense current interest in the cognitive sciences and how important this work is for the social sciences and for philosophy, where it has yet to be assimilated.

This introduction surveys the central themes of the volumes, chapter by chapter, and then distills some of the important issues on which they bear, both methodological and substantive. En route, the following questions are addressed:

Which actions count as imitation and which are better understood in other terms?

What is imitated—the goals of action or the movements that are the means to goals, or both?

How is imitation achieved? By what neural mechanisms, in the contexts of what cognitive architectures or social environments?

Who imitates—only human beings, or other animals?

When does imitation occur—only in development, or also in adulthood?

Why does imitation occur—what are its evolutionary and cultural functions?

The structure of this introduction largely follows the structure of the two volumes. In volume 1, part I focuses on the subpersonal mechanisms by which imitation is achieved, and part II on imitation in animals. In volume 2, part I is on the role of imitation in human development and part II is on the role of imitation in human culture. This introduction concludes with a broad view of why imitation matters and highlights themes and questions that unite the two volumes.

Volume 1, Part I Mechanisms of Imitation

What exactly is imitation? Imitation may be presumed to require at least *copying* in a generic sense. The observer's perception of the model's behavior causes similar behavior in the observer, in some way such that the similarity between the model's behavior and that of the observer plays a role, though not necessarily at a conscious level, in generating the observer's behavior.[1] More than that we will not try to say at the outset. As we will explain below, imitation needs to be distinguished from other forms of social learning that may look superficially similar, and there are different accounts, in part motivated by the aims of different disciplines, of what is distinctive about imitation. However, even the generic idea of copying perceived behavior poses a certain immediate problem, which thus provides a natural starting place.

Imitation appears to require the solution to a difficult *correspondence problem*. How is the perceived action of another agent translated into similar performance by the observer? When I imitate your hand movements at least I can see my own hands, even though my visual perspective on the

1. Although even this generic formulation may include controversial elements. See W. Prinz in vol. 1, ch. 5 on how similarity can be functional in imitation, and Meltzoff in vol. 2, ch. 1 cf. Heyes in vol. 1, ch. 6 who questions the role of similarity in generating the observer's response, and Whiten's comments on Heyes in vol. 1, ch. 8.

two actions is different; but when I imitate your facial gestures, I cannot see my own face. How is the perceptual-to-motor mapping achieved? Moreover, when an infant imitates an adult, the two have very different body structures and dynamics. What information and mechanisms are needed to solve this problem?

Striking discoveries in neuroscience suggest a possible answer. Certain neurons appear to constitute a direct link between perception and action; their firing correlates with specific perceptions as well as specific actions. Some of these, *canonical neurons*, can be thought of as reflecting affordances (in Gibson's sense, 1986); they fire when a certain type of action is performed, but are also triggered by perception of objects that afford such actions. Others, *mirror neurons*, fire when a certain type of action is performed, but also when another agent is observed performing the same type of action. That is, mirror neurons are sensitive both to others' actions and to equivalent actions of one's own. They can be very specifically tuned. For example, certain cells fire when a monkey sees an experimenter bring food to her own mouth with her own hand *or* when the monkey brings food to its own mouth (even in the dark, so that the monkey cannot see its hand).

When mirror neurons were discovered by a group of scientists in Parma, Italy, it was tempting to suggest that they enable imitation by avoiding the correspondence problem. If the same neurons code for perceived action and matching performance, it may seem that no neural translation is needed. However, things are not quite that simple. Neuroscientist Giacomo Rizzolatti, one of the Parma group, addresses the relationship between the ability to understand another agent's action and the ability to replicate it, both of which he holds are required for imitation. In his view, action understanding phylogenetically precedes imitation and is subserved by mirror systems, which are necessary but not sufficient for imitation. Indeed, imitation has not been demonstrated in the macaque monkeys in which mirror neurons were discovered (but see Voelkl & Huber 2000). Rizzolatti suggests that the motor resonance set up by mirror neurons makes action observation meaningful by linking it to the observer's own potential actions.

Mirror neurons were discovered in monkeys by single-cell recording. Evidence for human mirror systems includes brain imaging work, as well as demonstrations that observing another agent act primes the muscles the observer would need to do the same thing. Rizzolatti describes mirror neurons in the monkey frontal brain area F5 as part of a neural circuit, including also parietal area PF and the superior temporal sulcus (STS) visual area. In human beings, he suggests, a similar circuit constitutes a comparator system in which an intended imitative movement is controlled by reference to an observed target movement, enabling imitative learning. (Others have postulated similar control systems, although they differ on details; e.g., Rizzolatti locates the comparator site in PF, while Marco Iacoboni locates it in STS.) In monkeys, mirror neurons display *high-level resonance;* they code for the goals or ends of performed or observed actions. By contrast, in human beings, the mirror system displays both high-level resonance and *low-level resonance;* it extends to the specific movements that are the means to achieving goals.

This difference between mirroring the ends of action and mirroring the means of action is important for Rizzolatti's argument that action understanding precedes imitation. His view faces the objection that many animals to whom it would be implausible to attribute action understanding can nonetheless replicate movements. Consider response priming, by which observing a movement "primes" the same movement by the animal, independently of any understanding of the goal of the movement (as in the flocking of birds). In response to this objection Rizzolatti suggests that such low-level mirroring of movements could be present without high-level mirroring of goals, or vice versa. Action understanding requires high-level mirroring of goals, which is found in macaque monkeys. However, genuine imitative learning has not been found in these monkeys and would require the interplay of mirroring for both the ends and the means of action, which is found in human mirror systems (again see and cf. Voelkl & Huber 2000). Rizzolatti's argument here finds an ally in the views of Michael Tomasello, who links the phylogenetically rare capacity for imitative learning to the flexible recombinant means and ends structure of intentional action: the ability to use a given movement for different ends and pursue a given end by a variety of means.

Psychologist Paul Harris has suggested an experimental assessment of the extent to which mirror neurons subserve action understanding in monkeys.[2] Monkey mirror neurons fire when a monkey reaches for an apple, or when it sees the experimenter reach for the apple. The same mirror neurons also fire when a monkey sees a screen come down in front of the apple, so that it is no longer visible, and then sees the experimenter's hand reach behind the screen to where the apple is hidden. But they do not fire when the monkey first sees that there is no apple, and then the screen comes down and the monkey sees the experimenter's hand reach behind

2. This was in a discussion at the Royaumont conference, 2002.

the screen in the same way. The mirror neurons, that is, appear to code for the goal of the action. Harris suggests a variant that would address how insightfully the monkey attributes goals to others. Suppose the monkey and experimenter look at a nut and see the screen come down in front of it. Then the experimenter leaves the room. The monkey is permitted to remove the nut. Now the experimenter returns and the monkey sees the experimenter reach behind the screen for the nut, which the monkey knows is no longer there. Will the monkey's mirror neuron for reaching for the nut fire? If so, this would suggest that the monkey attributes the goal of reaching for the nut to the experimenter, who "doesn't know" that the nut is no longer there. Or will it not fire, because the nut is not there? Does the mirror neuron, that is, code for the *intended goal* of the observed action, or merely its *result?*[3]

Neuroscientist Marco Iacoboni also characterizes the ends-means comparator structure of the neural circuit for imitation, drawing on human brain imaging studies. He suggests a division of labor within the mirror system—that frontal areas of the mirror system code for the ends or goals of action, and parietal areas for movements and means. To enable imitation, both areas generate motor signals relating to a planned imitative action for comparison with the observed action; the motor plan is then adjusted until a match is obtained. Iacoboni compares this neural architecture for imitation to current ideas about functional motor control architectures that combine inverse and forward models. *Inverse models* estimate what motor plan is needed to reach a certain goal from a given state of affairs. They can be adjusted by comparison with real feedback from motor activity, but this is slow. It is often more efficient to use real feedback to train *forward models*, which take copies of motor plans as input and simulate or predict their consequences. Forward models can then be used with inverse models to control goal-directed behavior more efficiently. In particular, forward models can predict the consequences of a planned imitative action for comparison with the observed action, so that the motor plan can be adjusted until a match is obtained. Iacoboni is optimistic that imaging work will contribute to mapping this functional architecture for motor control onto the neural mirror system.

Mirror neurons were discovered in the monkey homologue of part of Broca's area, one of the primary language areas of the human brain. Broca's

3. See Nicholas Rawlins in vol. 1, ch. 8.1 for another means of assessing mind reading by animals, via recordings from hippocampal place cells rather than mirror neurons.

area is among those areas activated when human participants perform imitative tasks, and Iacoboni's group has recently shown that transient lesions of this area made by transcranial magnetic stimulation interfere with imitative tasks. As Iacoboni explains, when imaging techniques are used to morph a chimp brain onto a human brain, the areas that expand most are the perisylvian brain areas occupied by the mirror system, which are extremely important for language. Now a broadly nativist view of language *could* motivate a kind of protectiveness about Broca's area as the best candidate for an innate language module in the brain. However, the discovery that Broca's area is occupied by the mirror system and has an essential role in imitation has underscored questions about how language might depend on the capacity for imitation, either in evolutionary or developmental time frames. To what extent might language acquisition exploit imitative learning mechanisms rather than expressing innate linguistic knowledge? Iacoboni argues that evolution leads from action recognition through imitation to language.

What are the key features of imitation and the human mirror system that language might build on or exploit? First, if imitative learning requires flexible relations between means and ends, such flexibility could be an evolutionary precursor of the arbitrary relations between symbol and referent. Second, as Iacoboni (vol. 1, ch. 2) and Michael Arbib (2002, and in press) argue in different ways, the mirror system provides a common code for the actions of self and other, hence for production and perception of language. By thus enabling action understanding, the mirror system may be the basis for the intersubjective "parity" or sharing of meaning that is essential to language. Third, as Arbib has suggested, the flexible recombinant structure of ends and means in imitation may be a basis for recombinant grammatical structure in language. Here Iacoboni provides an alternative suggestion. He regards actual conversation as more like a dance than a formal structure, an embodied practice of social interaction with essential motor elements, and in this way dependent on action recognition and the mirror system.[4]

Vittorio Gallese, another member of the Parma group who discovered mirror neurons, concurs with Rizzolatti, Iacoboni, and Jean Decety and Thierry Chaminade in hypothesizing that extensions of the mirror system provide a plausible neural basis for emotional understanding and em-

4. See also the comments by Pickering on Pepperberg in vol. 1, ch. 12.4; Donald in vol. 2, ch. 14 and Christiansen's comments in vol. 2, ch. 19.8; Claxton's comments on Kinsbourne in vol. 2, ch. 8.9; and Chater in vol. 2, ch. 18.

pathy.[5] Gallese's *shared manifold hypothesis* generalizes the empathic role of the mirror system, postulating a primitive intersubjective information space that develops out of the modeling of environmental interactions in biological control systems. This shared manifold arises prior to self–other distinctions, both phylogenetically and ontogenetically, softening the contrast between adult human mind reading and mere responses to others' behavior as found in other social animals. Nevertheless, the shared manifold is preserved in human adults. It supports automatic intersubjective identifications, not just across different perceptual modalities and action, but also for sensations and emotions. There is evidence, for example, of mirror mechanisms for pain and disgust, and hearing an expression of anger increases the activation of muscles used to express anger. Gallese argues that the extended mirror system is the neural basis of the shared manifold.

Neuroscientists Decety and Chaminade invoke single-cell, imaging, and behavioral evidence in support of the shared neural coding of action and the perception of action in a mirror system. They also regard such automatic motor resonance as a necessary basis for intersubjectivity in understanding action and in emotional empathy. But while Gallese's focus is on how the blended intersubjective space that precedes the self–other distinction is established, Decety and Chaminade focus on the characteristically human self–other distinction, and the way it is imposed on what is common to the representation of self and other. They report imaging experiments that probe the neural bases of the self–other distinction and reveal the relevance of left-right lateralization.

As Marcel Kinsbourne comments, their work dissects out the neural substrate of the self–other distinction by setting up conditions that differ only in this respect, so that the few nonoverlapping areas of brain activation they observe code for this difference. For example, they compare participants imagining performing an act themselves with participants imagining someone else performing the same act. In addition to the mostly common areas of activation, they find differential left inferior parietal activation for imagining oneself performing an act and differential right inferior parietal activation for imagining someone else performing the same act. Similarly, they compare participants imitating an act with participants being imitated in performing the same act, and again find mostly common activation but also some lateralized differential activation. Left inferior parietal areas enable you to imitate, they suggest, while right inferior parietal

5. Susan Jones in vol. 1, ch. 8.4, likes the idea that mirror neurons underlie intersubjective empathy, but is skeptical about their role in imitation.

areas enable you to recognize that you are being imitated. Decety and Chaminade regard the capacity to identify with others as especially dependent on right hemisphere resources.

Well before mirror neurons were discovered and invoked in neuroscientific arguments for the common coding of perception and action, psychologists argued for common coding from behavioral evidence. Meltzoff and Moore (1977) postulated a common "supramodal" code underlying early imitation (see Meltzoff, vol. 2, ch. 1). Wolfgang Prinz (1990) developed an argument for common coding to explain the reaction time advantage of imitative tasks and imitative interference effects, and related it to William James's views on ideomotor action. Common coding, Prinz reasoned, would facilitate imitation by avoiding the need for sensory-to-motor translation.[6] Here Prinz provides a definitive statement of his common coding view applied to imitation and further behavioral evidence for it from recent experiments.

In imitation, when an observed act *a* leads to performance of a similar act *b*, it seems to be no accident that *a* and *b* are similar. How, Prinz asks, can the similarity of observed and performed acts have a functional role in imitation? An approach that conceives of actions as responses to prior stimuli and of perceptions and actions as separately coded faces the problem of how correspondence between perceptions and similar actions is achieved. By contrast, the *ideomotor approach* Prinz favors conceives of actions as the means to realizing intentions and postulates the common coding of perception and action, so that a representation of movement observed in another agent tends inherently to produce a similar movement by the observer. The regular concurrence of action with perceived effects enables the prediction of the effects of an action (as in a forward model) and the selection of an action, given an intention to produce certain effects (as in an inverse model). As a result, the representation of a regular effect of action, whether proximal or distal, acquires the power to evoke a similar action if it is not inhibited. By explaining how perception and action share representational resources, the ideomotor view avoids the correspondence problem and explains the functionality of similarity in imitation.

6. Prinz argued that we should expect common codes for perception and action to code for distal events rather than for proximal events, such as patterns of activation of sensory receptors or of muscle neurons. Note that the mirror neurons discovered in monkeys appear to code distally, although, as Rizzolatti (vol. 1, ch. 1) and Iacoboni (vol. 1, ch. 2) explain, the human mirror system appears to code for the results or goals of action in some brain areas and the movements that are the behavioral means to such goals in others.

In this view, as Kinsbourne comments, when automatic imitative effects are held covert, inhibition occurs at the level of motor output rather than centrally, between separate perceptual processing and action processing. This point has implications for how we understand failures to inhibit imitation, whether pathological or normal. More generally, the common coding approach challenges standard Humean assumptions about the intrinsic motivational inertness of perception.

The consequences of damage to the mechanisms that normally inhibit automatic imitative tendencies in adults are revealed in classic studies of patients with frontal or prefrontal lesions. Luria's patients[7] found it very difficult not to imitate what the experimenter was doing, even when they were instructed to do something else. Lhermitte's imitation syndrome patients[8] imitated gestures the experimenter made, although they were not instructed to do so, and even when these gestures were socially unacceptable or odd. When asked why they did this, they did not disown their behavior but explained that they felt that the gestures they saw somehow included an order to imitate them; that their response was the reaction called for.

However, there are both theoretical and empirical reasons to hold that the automatic tendency of human adults to imitate is not confined to those with brain damage. The philosopher, and proponent of the idea that we understand other minds by mental simulation, Robert Gordon (1995a) argues that it takes a special containing mechanism to keep the emotion recognition process from reverting to ordinary emotional contagion, and this mechanism is not fail-safe. If simulation theory is right, he holds, there is only a delicate separation between one's own mental life and one's representation of the mental life of another; "offline" representations of other people have an inherent tendency to go "online." Moreover, striking similarities have been observed between the behavior of Lhermitte's patients and that of normal college students in priming experiments by social psychologists.[9]

Normal adults are studied in three experimental paradigms described by Prinz that provide evidence for the ideomotor approach. This work shows how an action by normal adults is spontaneously induced or modulated by the perception of a similar action. Perception has effects on action that are automatic but nevertheless have cognitive depth in that they

7. See Kinsbourne, vol. 2, ch. 7; see also L. Eidelberg (1929).
8. Lhermitte (1986), Lhermitte et al. (1986).
9. As Bargh (in press) comments; see also Dijksterhuis in vol. 2, ch. 9.

depend on the way participants understand what they are perceiving and doing.

First, in imitative interference paradigms, both the initiation and selection of gestures are faster when participants are primed by perception of similar gestures or of their results or goals, even if such primes are logically irrelevant to their task.

Second, induction paradigms examine when spontaneous movements are induced by actions you actually perceive (perceptual induction, or involuntary imitation) as well as when movements are induced by actions you would like to perceive (intentional induction, as when moviegoers or sports fans in their seats make gestures they would like to see made). Both types of induction are found and are modulated by various contextual factors. It is interesting that perceptual induction is stronger than intentional induction when participants observe the results of a task performed by another person, especially when the participants have practiced the task earlier, but it is absent when participants believe that otherwise similar observed results have been generated by a computer rather than a person! Thus, perceptual induction appears to depend in part on background beliefs about whether what is perceived is the result of agency.

Third, coordination paradigms adapt imitative interference paradigms to tasks in which labor is divided and coordinated across two persons. Participants are asked to press the left key when a red cue is given and the right key when a green cue is given, while also observing irrelevant but distracting pointing cues. When a single participant does this task, the responses are faster and the errors less frequent when the irrelevant cues point toward the key called for by the relevant color cues. What happens when two participants sit side by side and one is asked to respond to red, the other to green? The interference effect persists, as if the two participants composed one agent with a unified action plan. The left-right response dimension extends across the two participants, and the irrelevant pointing cues interfere with both participants' responses. Remarkably, the interference effect disappears if the participants sit side-by-side but one is asked to respond to red only and the other to do nothing. While the "red" participant's partial task is unchanged, in the absence of coordination across the two participants, the left-right response dimension is lost and the irrelevant pointer cues no longer produce interference.

These results suggest that the automatic effects of perception on action depend on social context in a strong sense. Whether an individual's action is subject to interference by given perceptions can depend on whether her actions are part of a collective action with which those perceptions interfere. Understanding what you are doing in terms of a team effort can alter the ways in which your actions are automatically influenced by perception (see Bacharach, 1999; Hurley, 1989).

The correspondence problem posed by imitation is also addressed by the psychologist Celia Heyes in her *associative sequence learning model*. By what mechanism are perceptions linked to similar actions in imitation? Must such correspondences be innate? Heyes thinks not, and aims to show how they could be acquired, in the right environment, through general-purpose associative learning mechanisms whereby "neurons that fire together, wire together." In this respect her account allies her with the minority[10] who are skeptical about influential evidence[11] of imitation by human newborns. Her account is compatible with the common coding of perception and action, but regards neural mirror properties as acquired through association rather than based on intrinsic similarity. In effect, from this point of view Humean associationism may be on the right track, even if a Humean view of perception as inert turns out not to be.

A general solution to the correspondence problem must cover imitation of *perceptually opaque* acts such as facial gestures, which cannot be seen by their agent, as well as of *perceptually transparent* acts such as hand gestures, which can be seen by their agent. It must cover imitative learning of novel acts, as well as imitation of acts already in an agent's repertoire. Heyes's account aims to satisfy these demands. It characterizes both direct and indirect routes by which sensorimotor associations can be acquired. Direct associations are formed when someone watches her own hand gesture, for example. But this won't work when the agent cannot perceive her own actions, as in facial gestures. Here the association can be mediated by a third item, such as a mirror, an action word, or a stimulus that evokes the same behavior in the actor and in other agents the actor observes. Moreover, adult imitation of infants is common, and can perform the associative function of a mirror (see also Meltzoff, vol. 2, ch. 1 on the importance of being imitated).

In effect, the associative mechanism that enables opaque imitation extends into the cultural environment. Novel acts can be learned by

10. Including Moshe Anisfeld in vol. 2, ch. 4 and Susan Jones, commenting on Whiten in vol. 1, ch. 12.6.
11. From work by Andrew Meltzoff and others; see Meltzoff, vol. 2, ch. 1. Note that Meltzoff argues that the correspondence between perception and action expressed by mirror neurons may be learned rather than innate, and that it remains an open question what the role of experience is in forming mirror neurons.

observing another agent perform an unfamiliar sequence of familiar elements of an act, where each perception of an element already has a motor association, resulting in a new sequence of motor elements that become linked through repetition to give rise to a novel act. Thus, given interactions with the right environment, imitation emerges.

Heyes sharpens issues faced by other views, but as she recognizes, her account also faces several challenges. If imitation does not require dedicated evolved mechanisms, why is it so rare in the animal kingdom? It is greatly facilitated, she suggests, by cultural environments; enculturated chimps raised like human children are better imitators than other chimps. By arguing that the emergence of imitation from general learning mechanisms may depend on cultural environments, Heyes turns the tables on the view that imitation is the copying mechanism that drives cultural accumulation and evolution.[12] In her view, the similarity of what is perceived and what is done in imitation is emergent rather than functional, in Prinz's sense. But can imitation both emerge from culture in this way and provide its engine in some complex dynamic process? (Does it help in considering this question to consider analogies to genetic copying and evolution?)

Philosopher Susan Hurley's *shared circuits hypothesis* draws together various threads from early chapters and elsewhere, concerning the relationships among control, imitation, and simulation within a complex comparator architecture. Her shared circuits model can be regarded as a dynamic descendent of the common coding theory, and is also a close relative of Gallese's shared manifold hypothesis.

Hurley describes a subpersonal functional architecture in five layers, starting with adaptive feedback control such as that found in a thermostat, where real sensory feedback is compared with a target behavior and motor output is adjusted until feedback and target match. At the second layer, internally simulated motor-to-sensory feedback or "prediction" is added to speed and smooth motor control; affordance neurons with both sensory and motor fields are predicted at this layer. At the third layer, the sensorimotor links between one's own actions and one's observations of them or their consequences are instead activated in reverse, so that one's observation of others' actions results in the priming of similar movements, emulation of similar goals, and imitation. Mirror systems are predicted at this layer, which realizes a version of the primitive intersubjective space

12. For discussion see Sugden (vol. 2, ch. 15), Gil-White (vol. 2, ch. 16), Greenberg (vol. 2, ch. 17), Chater (vol. 2, ch. 18) and comments by Blackmore (vol. 2, chs. 19.9, 19.12, 19.13).

postulated by Gallese (see also Meltzoff, vol. 2, ch. 1 on the fundamental self–other equivalence exploited by early imitation). Via indirect links, associations could also be formed between one's own perceptually opaque acts, such as facial gestures, and similar acts by others. At the fourth layer, the tendency to copy the acts of others can be inhibited or "taken offline," so that observing another's act creates a simulation of that act. Simulation for action understanding requires the system to track whether copying is offline or not, so that a self–other distinction would come to overlay the self–other similarities registered in the more basic intersubjective space.

Finally, at the fifth layer, input can be simulated as well. A distinction between the imagined and the real requires the system to track whether an input is simulated, so that counterfactual situations can be simulatively entertained and assessed in deliberation, planning, and hypothetical and instrumental reasoning. Variations of the specified structure could be re-peatedly implemented in a linked network of such circuits, yielding the flexible recombinant properties characteristic of intentional action.

Hurley is concerned to advance understanding of the way descriptions of the mind at neural, functional, and personal levels can be related to one another while avoiding oversimple assumptions of isomorphism be-tween levels of description. Her midlevel, functional subpersonal architec-ture holds promise here. It lends itself to neural mapping exercises and also raises issues concerning mind reading and higher cognitive abilities. It shows how an intersubjective space can be distilled out of the shared in-formation space for perception and action and used in simulation. More-over, it suggests how the self–other and the imagined/real distinctions, which are essential to the cognitive abilities of persons, can emerge from these prior shared information spaces. Hurley's hypothesis provides a sub-personal parallel to Robert Gordon's[13]; understanding other agents depends at the most fundamental level on multiplying first person information through simulation rather than on building an inferential bridge between first person and third person information. Subpersonal information about persons arrives in the first person plural, without distinction or inference between self and other.

Volume 1, Part II   Imitation in Animals

Vol. 1, part I discusses work in neuroscience and psychology concern-ing what mechanisms could solve the perception-action correspondence

13. Gordon (1995a,b, 2002) and volume 2, chapter 3.

problem for imitation. By contrast, studies of social learning in animals often focus on distinguishing true imitation from other superficially similar behaviors, and in particular on the requirement of novelty for imitative learning. Sophisticated experimental and theoretical work on different kinds of copying behavior in animals helps to clarify the nature and varieties of imitation in human development (see vol. 2, part I) and in human adults, as well as in nonhuman animals. It also sheds light on the role of varieties of imitative behavior in the generation and transmission of culture (see vol. 2, part II) and poses the question of how far imitation can explain what is distinctive about human cultural transmission.

It has proved remarkably difficult to find evidence of true imitation in nonhuman animals, and for a long while sceptics who regarded the capacity for imitation as exclusively human had the upper hand. A new consensus is emerging as a result of painstaking work showing imitation in some great apes and monkeys (see Byrne, vol. 1, ch. 9 and Whiten et al., vol. 1, ch. 11; see also Voelkl & Huber, 2000), dolphins (Herman, 2002), and birds such as some parrots, corvids, and quail (Pepperberg, 1999; G. Hunt & Gray, 2003; Weir et al., 2002; Akins & Zentall, 1996). Cautious moves are being made to describe continuities along a spectrum from the capacities of other social animals to the interrelated capacities for imitation, mind reading, and language that appear to be characteristically human. To understand the significance of this work with animals, it is necessary to understand some of the distinctions that have been drawn between imitation and other forms of social learning.

The concept of "true imitation" is contested, owing in part to the different theoretical aims and methodologies of those concerned with imitation.[14] What matters for present purposes is not what deserves this label, but that relevant distinctions be recognized. The most restrictive understanding of true imitation requires that a novel action be learned by observing another perform it, and in addition to novelty, requires a means/ends structure. You copy the other's means of achieving her goal, not just her goal or just her movements.

A variety of other less cognitively demanding forms of learning in social contexts might look superficially similar. For example, in *stimulus enhancement*, another's action draws your attention to a stimulus that triggers an innate or previously learned response; you do not thereby learn a novel action by observing the other. In *emulation*, by contrast, you observe an-

---

14. See Rizzolatti (vol. 1, ch. 1), Byrne (vol. 1, ch. 9), and Thomas Zentall's comments on Byrne (vol. 1, ch. 12.1); Heyes (2001) and Heyes and Galef (1996).

other achieving a goal in a certain way, find that goal attractive, and attempt to achieve it yourself by whatever means (cf. the very different sense of "emulation" used in Grush, 1995 and forthcoming). Individual trial-and-error learning may then lead you to the other's means of achieving the goal. In both stimulus enhancement and emulation, any coincidence of the movements between learner and model is incidental. A further contrast is with mere *response priming*, as in flocking behavior or contagious yawning, where bodily movements are copied but not as a learned means to a goal.

Goal emulation and response priming can be thought of as the ends and means components, respectively, of full-fledged imitation. The distinction between ends and means is not absolute; a movement can be a means to adopting a posture, for example, which may in turn be a means to bring about an effect on an external object or conspecific. We can understand more complex forms of imitation in terms of a structured sequence of means/ends relationships in which one acquires a goal, learns how to achieve it by achieving several subgoals, learns how to achieve the subgoals by certain means, and so on. More complex forms of imitation are methodologically important for animal research (and, as we will see in part III, for research on imitation in human development) because they reduce the plausibility of explanations of mirroring behaviors in terms of mere stimulus enhancement, emulation, or response priming. For example, the more complex the movements modeled in a goal-directed behavior that is emulated, the more implausible it is that trial-and-error learning would reproduce these specific movements. Similarly, certain complex patterns of movement are unlikely to be reproduced by response priming because the learner is unlikely to have a prespecified matching response that merely needs to be triggered. True imitation can make sense of the copying of such complex patterns of movement as the learned means to an end.

Response priming, goal emulation, and stimulus enhancement are certainly found in nonhuman animals, and careful experiments are needed to obtain evidence of imitation in a more restricted sense. For this purpose, the *two-action* experimental paradigm has become the tool of choice. When two models illustrate two different means of obtaining the same attractive result, will animals who observe one or the other model differentially tend to copy the specific method they have seen demonstrated? If not—if they use either method indifferently to achieve the goal, or converge on one method despite the different methods modeled—they may be displaying mere goal emulation plus trial-and-error learning, or stimulus enhancement, rather than imitative learning.

Psychologist and primatologist Richard Byrne explains some of the limitations of the two-action experimental criterion for imitative learning and in particular questions its usefulness in demonstrating novelty. Success on the two-action criterion, Byrne suggests, is consistent with an alternative account in which a modeled action primes rare preexisting acts in a large repertoire, which may be further amplified by individual trial-and-error learning, so that no imitative learning of a genuinely novel skill has occurred.[15] We may note, in addition, that with merely *two* actions to be distinguished by the learner, even a very partial grasp of the means used by the model may suffice to bias the learner toward that means—and the rest might then be acquired by individual trial-and-error learning.

What naturally occurring examples of imitative learning might resist such an alternative explanation? The persistence of a less efficient method of performing a given task in a particular population, such as apes using one short stick instead of two long sticks to fish out insects, might be evidence for imitative as opposed to trial-and-error learning. But, as Byrne explains, it will be hard to rule out the possibility that environmental differences rather than imitation explain such behavioral differences among populations.

He finds better evidence for imitative learning of novel skills in his field observations of what he calls *program-level imitation*, in which animals imitatively learn a specific organization of a complex process. Gorillas, he argues, learn to prepare particular types of plants for eating using a standardized, complex organization of manual processing stages, despite idiosyncratic lower-level differences among individual gorillas; the standard processing pattern is even learned by gorillas whose hands have been maimed by snares, who might be expected to find different processing techniques through individual trial-and-error learning. Byrne argues that such program-level imitation cannot be explained in terms of socially guided priming, emulation, and trial-and-error learning; it illustrates imitative learning of genuinely novel skills.[16] This capacity to transmit complex techniques for processing food, he suggests, may have helped apes compete with monkeys in exploiting shared food resources, despite the lesser mobility and other feeding disadvantages of apes.

From the question of what behavior distinguishes imitation from other forms of social learning, Byrne returns to the question of subpersonal

15. See and cf. Meltzoff on infant imitation of novel acts in volume 2, chapter 13.
16. See various comments on Byrne and Russon (1998) for assessments of the evidence for program-level imitation in gorillas and orangutans.

mechanisms of imitation. His focus is on the mechanisms needed to enable program imitation rather than those needed to solve the correspondence problem. A mirror mechanism could recognize elements in fluid movements and find corresponding units in the existing action repertoire, which could be strung together in observed new ways. But Byrne argues that for program-level imitation, a further *behavior parsing* mechanism is also needed, which would statistically parse many such observed strings to extract their shared organization or deep structure from the idiosyncratic surface variation. Skilled action has a modular structure that facilitates flexible recombinant functioning. The behavior parsing mechanism could detect module boundaries in observed behavior, the points at which links between behavior strings are weakest, by registering points of smooth resumption after interruption of behavior; clusters of pauses; and patterns of substitution, omission, or repetition. Alternatively, as the developmental psychologist Birgit Elsner suggests on the basis of work with human children, modules might be parsed by reference to subgoals. Byrne sees behavior parsing capacities as an important precursor to more sophisticated human abilities for high-level perception of an underlying structure of intentions and causes in the surface flux of experience.

It is tempting also to regard behavior parsing and the recombinant structure of program-level imitation as precursors of syntactic parsing and the recombinant structure of language. Michael Arbib (2002) explains the neural intertwining of human mirror and language systems along related lines. Moreover, the problem of finding recombinant units of action in apparently smooth streams of bodily movement has many parallels with the problem of finding linguistic units such as words in the apparently continuous acoustic stream of speech.

A quite different slant on the relations between imitation and language is provided by the psychologist Irene Pepperberg's pioneering work with the African Grey parrot Alex. African Greys have walnut-sized brains with very little that resembles primate cortex. Yet Alex does what bigger-brained animals cannot; he acquires significant fragments of English speech by listening in on conversations between human trainers, and he uses it to perform cognitive tasks put to him in English. Alex's well-known accomplishments are described in detail elsewhere (Pepperberg, 1999). He can both comprehend and produce words for fifty objects; seven colors; five shapes; numerals up to 6; the categories of color, shape, material, and number; plus the words "no," "come," "go," "want," etc. He can combine these words in new ways to identify, request, comment, refuse, alter his environment, add objects to categories, or process queries. For example, from an array of red and blue balls and blocks, he can quantify a subarray, such as the set of blue blocks, on request.

Does Alex imitate? He learns the specific vocalizations of another species and uses them functionally. Such exceptional vocalizations are unlikely to occur in normal development and cannot plausibly be explained as the priming or evoking of innate behaviors. Pepperberg locates Alex's vocal abilities in relation to three different levels of imitation and shows that the similarity of African Grey speech to human speech is not an artifact of human perception, but shares acoustic characteristics with human speech. Alex derives new sounds from old ones by babbling, but in ways that respect English rules for building words. Byrne considers whether Alex's copying of the structure of English speech can be regarded as emulation or as program-level imitation comparable to that displayed by human children.

One of the most thought-provoking aspects of Pepperberg's work is the model/rival training method on which Alex's success depends. Standard behavioral training techniques were unsuccessful. Moreover, just being part of a standard referential triangle, in which two participants refer to the same object, does not enable Alex to learn as he does. Rather, what is essential is that Alex be able to eavesdrop on a referential triangle composed of two human English users referring to an object. One plays the role of trainer, the other models the learning process and acts as a rival to Alex for the trainer's attentions and rewards. The trainer gives feedback to the model, scolding for errors such as the bird might make, or providing rewards for correct responses, and the pair demonstrate the referential and functional use of the label. It is essential that the bird observe role reversal between trainer and model; otherwise, the bird does not learn both parts of the interaction, and does not learn to transfer responses to new trainers. Moreover, it is essential that the objects referred to are themselves used as rewards, to avoid confusion between labeled objects and different rewards. When any of these elements of model/rival training are omitted, training is unsuccessful. When such birds are given model/rival training for some labels and other training techniques are used for other labels, the birds practice only the model/rival trained labels when alone! Pepperberg suggests that observing a model responding to a trainer may enable the parrot to represent the required response separately from the "do-as-I-do" command. As she notes, promising work is under way using the model/rival technique to facilitate learning for some autistic children.[17]

---

17. See also Jones's comments on Whiten et al. in volume 1, chapter 12.6 for a different angle on imitation and therapy for autism.

The dependence of Alex's learning on exposure to a very specific training regimen recalls Heyes's view that imitative learning can depend on particular cultural environments. More generally, observations of non-human animals in different environments or using different, apparently reasonable, testing methods may lead to very different estimates of their cognitive abilities. Because of the way environmental structure and input can affect the manifestation of cognitive capacities, great care is needed in determining what capacities are present and how they compare with human capacities.

This point is underscored by the way skepticism about chimp imitation has been overcome, as explained by the psychologists Andrew Whiten, Victoria Horner, and Sarah Marshall-Pescini, as well as by Bennett Galef, a former skeptic. Imitation was regarded through most of the nineteenth century as a low-level ability, characteristic of the mentally weak or childish, and as less rationally demanding than individual trial-and-error learning. But at the end of the nineteenth century Edward Thorndike showed that many animals who could learn through trial and error could not imitate, and argued that imitation is in fact the rarer and more cognitively demanding ability. This view is now generally accepted. While early fieldwork with chimps appeared to provide evidence of their imitative abilities, critics such as Galef, Heyes, and Michael Tomasello challenged this interpretation effectively. Many subsequent experimental studies reported a lack of chimp imitation. Only recently has evidence of chimp imitation won over most critics; the relevant questions now are what, how, and why they imitate, rather than whether they can do so at all.

Whiten and colleagues have played a prominent role in demonstrating chimp imitation and comparing it with imitation in children. Their innovative experiments using ingenious "artificial fruits" extend the two-action method, revealing that chimps sometimes emulate and sometimes imitate. For example, Whiten's pin-apple is a box containing food that can be opened in two ways: by poking or pulling its bolts, and then pulling or twisting a handle. One way of opening it is modeled for one group of chimps, the other way for another group. The chimps imitate the specific means modeled to remove the bolts, but merely emulate using the handle to achieve the goal of reaching the food. Children, by contrast, imitate the specific means modeled for both parts of the task, even when this is less efficient. Using a more complex pin-apple, the two-action method shows that chimps imitate sequential structure but not details of component techniques, suggesting program-level imitation. Yet another artificial fruit, the key-way, is used with the two-action method to contrast imitation of the hierarchical structure of a task with imitation of left-right versus right-left sequence. Here, young chimps, like children, ignore the modeled sequence direction but do imitate hierarchical structure. They organize the multiple moves needed to open the key-way by rows or by columns, according to what they have seen modeled.

Why do chimps sometimes imitate and sometimes emulate? Do they imitate selectively, or do they have only a limited ability to imitate? Whiten and colleagues argue that chimps imitate selectively, selecting aspects of a modeled task to be imitated or not according to their appraisal of the significance of these aspects for achieving their goal. For example, a hierarchical task structure is not transparently irrelevant to success, while left-right sequence direction is. Using a variant of a task used by Paul Harris and Stephen Want to demonstrate selective imitation in children, Whiten and colleagues show that chimps imitate more selectively than 3-year-old children.[18] A model shows chimps how to obtain food in a box by using a tool to stab the food though tunnels in the box. The model first stabs down a tunnel and hits a barrier, which blocks the food from reach, but then stabs through a different tunnel and reaches the food. This "mistake" is modeled using both a transparent box, in which it is obvious that the initial downward stab will not reach the food, and an opaque box, in which it is not obvious. As predicted, chimps imitate the futile first downward stab less when the transparent box is used. Three-year-old children, by contrast, imitate the futile downward stab in both versions of the task, even if they are left alone to remove social pressure to conform.

Even if chimps *can* imitate, children are "imitation machines," as Michael Tomasello (1999, p. 159) has put it and as Andrew Meltzoff also argues (in vol. 2, ch. 1). Children have a stronger tendency than chimps to imitate rather than emulate, even when doing so is transparently inefficient. For example, after seeing a demonstrator use a rake inefficiently, prongs down, to pull in bait, chimps tend to turn the rake over and use it more efficiently, edge down, to pull in the bait. Two-year-old children in a parallel experiment almost never do so; they go right on imitating the inefficient means of obtaining the bait they have seen demonstrated, with prongs down (Nagell et al., 1993; cf. Gergely et al., 2002). Human imitation is flexible, ubiquitous, effortless, and intrinsically rewarding (see Jones, vol. 1, 12.6, p. 298). Chimps may appear to be better off in this comparison, at least in the short run. Why might it be beneficial to humans in the long run to imitate with such determination? Tomasello (1999) explains this in

18. See and cf. Harris and Want in volume 2, chapter 6.

terms of the *ratchet effect*. Imitation preserves rare one-off insights about how to achieve goals, which would not be rediscovered readily by independent trial-and-error learning, and so would be lost without imitation. Imitation spreads these discoveries around, makes them available to all as a platform for further development. Through the ratchet effect, imitation is the mechanism that drives cultural and technological transmission, accumulation, and evolution.[19]

We have discussed the mechanisms that may underlie and enable the strong imitative tendencies that are so characteristically human, and we will go on to consider their possible functions and effects in relation to human culture. But first we turn to the role of imitation in human development, and in particular in the development of another distinctive human capacity, the ability to understand other minds.

Volume 2, Part I   Imitation and Human Development

Human beings are distinctive among animals in their capacities for language and for understanding other minds, or *mind reading*. Whether these are innate as *capacities*, the skilled behavioral expression of these capacities develops over years of interaction between infants and their environments, in well-studied stages during which much learning occurs. The same could be said about a third distinctive human capacity, the ability to imitate. This, however, begins to be manifested very early—indeed, at birth, according to highly influential work by the developmental psychologist Andrew Meltzoff and others on imitation in human infants, including newborns.

The relationships among this trio of capacities—for language, mind reading, and imitation—are of fundamental importance for understanding the transition of human infants into adult persons. Does the development of either language or mind reading depend on imitation? If so, at what levels of description and in what senses of "depend"? Or does dependence run the other way or both ways, dynamically? The answers are controversial, and may of course differ for language and mind reading. Several of the chapters in vol. 2, part I focus on the question of how imitation is related to the understanding of other minds and in particular other *agents*. This question brings into play the further controversy about whether mind reading is best understood as theorizing about other minds or as

19. See and cf. Harris (vol. 2, ch. 6), Sugden (vol. 2, ch. 15), Gil-White (vol. 2, ch. 16), Greenberg (vol. 2, ch. 17), Chater (vol. 2, ch. 18) and Blackmore (vol. 2, ch. 19).

simulating them. How does the theory–simulation controversy concerning the mechanism by which we understand other minds bear on the relationships between imitation and mind reading, or vice versa?

Meltzoff surveys his work on early imitation and draws on it to argue that early imitation and its enabling mechanisms beget the understanding of other agents, not the other way around.[20] In a series of famous experiments, Meltzoff and Moore studied imitation in newborns and infants under 1 month, including facial and manual imitation. Since infants can see others' facial acts but not their own, newborn facial imitation suggests an innate, supramodal correspondence between observed acts and an observer's similar acts.[21] Moreover, very young infants defer imitation across a delay of 24 hours and correct their imitative responses, homing in on a match without external feedback. The *active intermodal mapping* (AIM) hypothesis interprets this evidence in terms of the comparison and matching of proprioceptive feedback from an observer's own acts to an observed target act, where these are coded in common, supramodal terms. Elsewhere, Meltzoff and Moore (1997) explicate this common code as initially coding for relations among bodily organs such as lips and tongue, and developing through experience of body babbling toward more dynamic, complex, and abstract coding.

Meltzoff emphasizes that various further imitative and related behaviors are not present from birth, but are acquired at stages throughout infancy. Infants from 6 weeks to 14 months recognize that they are being imitated,[22] but only older infants act in ways that apparently purposively test whether they are being imitated. Since only people can imitate systematically, an ability to recognize being imitated provides a means of recognizing that an entity is a person. By 14 months, infants imitate a modeled novel act after a week's delay; they turn on a light by touching a touch-sensitive light panel with their foreheads instead of their hands, differentially copying the novel means modeled as well as the result (see Meltzoff, vol. 2, ch. 13, p. 59, and Tomasello and Carpenter, vol. 2, ch. 17, p. 138.) Note that in a follow-up to the Meltzoff's light-pad experiment,

20. In contrast to Rizzolatti (vol. 1, ch. 1) and Tomasello (1999), who argue in their different ways that understanding an action precedes imitation.

21. See Nicholas Humphrey (vol. 2, ch. 8.2) for some intriguing speculations on possible pathological phenomenological manifestations in adulthood of such supramodal mappings.

22. With differential activation of the right inferior parietal lobe; see Decety and Chaminade (vol. 1, ch. 4).

children do use their hands to touch the light-pad when they see a demonstrator whose hands are occupied by doing something else touch it with her head (Gergely et al., 2002). Children *can* emulate as well as imitate. Nevertheless, their tendency to imitate rather than emulate appears to be considerably greater than that of chimps when direct comparisons have been made, as in Nagell et al., 1993. By 15 or 18 months, infants recognize the underlying goal of an unsuccessful act they see modeled and produce it using various means. For example, after seeing an adult try but fail to pull a dumbbell apart in her hands, they succeed in pulling it apart using their knees as well as their hands. However, they do not recognize and attempt to bring about the goals of failed "attempts" from similar movements by inanimate devices.

Thus, in Meltzoff's view, the ability to understand other minds has innate foundations but develops in stages. Imitation plays a critical role in his arguments for a middle ground between Fodorian nativism and Piagetian theory. Infants have a primitive ability to recognize being imitated and to imitate, and hence to recognize people as different from other things and to recognize equivalences between the acts of self and other. The initial bridge between self and other provides a basis for access to people that we do not have to things, which is developed in an early three-stage process.

First, an infant's own acts are linked to others' similar acts supramodally, as evidenced by newborns' imitation of others' facial acts. Second, own acts of certain kinds are linked bidirectionally to own experiences of certain kinds through learning. Third, others' similar acts are linked to others' similar experiences. This process gets mind reading started on understanding agency and the mental states most directly associated with it: desires, intentions, perceptions, and emotions. The ability to understand other minds is not all or nothing, as Meltzoff emphasizes.[23] An understanding of mental states that are further from action, such as false beliefs, comes later in development.

Meltzoff claims here that the early three-stage process he describes is not a matter of formal reasoning, but rather one of processing the other as "like me." Meltzoff is often interpreted as viewing mind reading in terms of theoretical inferences from first-person mind-behavior links to similar third-person links, in an updating of classical arguments from analogy. There are clear elements of first-to-third-person inference in his view of

23. The same point can be made for other animals; see Tomasello (1999) on levels of mind-reading ability.

how mind reading develops. As he states in vol. 2, ch. 1, "the crux of the "like-me" hypothesis is that infants may use their own intentional actions as a framework for interpreting the intentional actions of others" (p. 75). For example, 12-month-old infants follow the "gaze" of a model significantly less often when the model's eyes are closed than when they are open, but do not similarly refrain from following the "gaze" of blindfolded models until they are given first-person experience with blindfolds. Similarly, as Paul Harris comments, giving 3-month-old infants Velcro mittens to enhance their grasping abilities also enhances their ability to recognize others' goals in grasping. Nevertheless, the initial self–other linkage that Meltzoff postulates, expressed in imitation by newborns, is via a supramodal common code for observed acts and the observer's acts, which is direct and noninferential (see Meltzoff & Moore, 1997). In a graded view of mind reading such as Meltzoff's, the role of theoretical inference from the first to the third person in mind reading can enter at later stages and increase significantly with development.

Philosopher Alvin Goldman also considers the relationship between imitation and mind reading, first from the perspective that understands mind reading in terms of theorizing, which he attributes to Meltzoff, and then from his preferred view of mind reading in terms of simulation. The *"theory theory"* approach to mind reading regards commonsense psychology as a kind of protoscientific theory in which knowledge is represented in the form of laws about mental states and behavior; to the degree that these are not innate, they are discovered by testing hypotheses against evidence. People's specific mental states and behaviors are inferred from other mental states and behaviors by means of such laws. No copying is involved. By contrast, *simulation theories* understand mind reading to start with the mind reader taking someone else's perspective and generating pretend mental or behavioral states that match the other person's. These are not made the object of theoretical inference, but rather are used as inputs to the simulator's own psychological processes, including decision-making processes, while these are held offline, producing simulated mental states and behavior as output. The simulated outputs are then assigned to the other person; these may be predicted behaviors by the other, or mental states of the other that explain the observed behaviors. This is an extension of practical abilities rather than a theoretical exercise. The simulator copies the states of the other and uses the copies as inputs to her own psychological equipment, instead of formulating laws and making inferences from them about the other. Within this broad theory versus simulation contrast, many finer distinctions have rightly been drawn among various versions, levels of description, and aims within each category.[24]

Consider the role of imitation in Meltzoff's version of a theory-theory approach to mind reading. One could restate Meltzoff's three-stage process, described earlier, in explicitly theory-theory terms, as follows. At stage one, the innate equivalence between my own acts and others' acts (exploited by early imitation and the recognition of being imitated) makes it possible to recognize that some acts (by myself) are similar to other acts (by another). At stage two, first-person experience provides laws that link one's own acts and mental states. At stage three, it is inferred that another's act that is similar to mine is lawfully linked to the other's mental states in the same way that my act is lawfully linked to my mental states. As Meltzoff points out (personal communication), there is no inference from the first person to the third person at stage one of this account; the initial bridge between the self and other expressed in imitation and recognition of being imitated is bidirectional. However, an inference from the first person to the third person does enter as we proceed through stages two and three of this account. It resembles traditional arguments from analogy in inferring laws linking third-person acts and mental states from laws linking first-person acts and mental states.

Goldman does not object here to the first-to-third-person inference per se. He notes that psychologists could be correct to attribute such an analogical inference to mind readers, even if, as philosophers have often argued, it is epistemologically unsound. Nor does he object to making understanding of other minds depend on direct first-person knowledge of one's own mental states; his own simulationist account does this. However, he regards such dependence as internally incompatible with a theory-theory approach to self-knowledge, according to which knowledge of first-person mental states relies on theoretical inference in the same way that knowledge of third-person mental states does. Thus, he argues that the argument from analogy makes knowledge of one's own mind asymmetrically prior to knowledge of other minds, while a theory-theory of self-knowledge treats them symmetrically, as equally dependent on theoretical inference. Thus, the argument from analogy and the theory-theory of self-knowledge are incompatible.

24. For some of these, and challenges to the distinction, see Davies and Stone (1995a,b), and Carruthers and Smith (1996). See also Millikan (vol. 2, ch. 8.4), who distinguishes ontological, ontogenetic, and epistemological questions about thoughts of other minds, on which theory-theory and simulation theory may differ.

Meltzoff might respond by rejecting this kind of theory-theory for self-knowledge while retaining his account of how mind reading builds on imitation, with its first-to-third-person inference. Philosopher Ruth Millikan argues, referring to Wilfrid Sellars, that theory theorists have other resources to draw on in characterizing self-knowledge, and that a critique of theory-theory needs to go deeper than Goldman's. She traces the theory-theory of mind reading back to a more general philosophical view of Willard Van Orman Quine and Sellars about the nature of thoughts, which was then applied to thoughts about other minds in particular, or mind reading. Undermining the theory-theory of mind reading, she argues, requires showing either that the more general view of thoughts is mistaken, or that thoughts about other minds are peculiar in some way, so that the more general view does not apply straightforwardly to them.

Quine and Sellars held that thoughts acquired their content in the same general way as theoretical terms in a scientific theory: in virtue of their inferential relations to one another, as well as to inputs and outputs. Millikan's own view is that this general view of thought is wrong (Millikan, 2000). But even if we assume that this general view is correct and that thoughts are in general identified by their inferential or functional roles, what should we say about the specific case of thoughts about another's thoughts, that is, mind reading? Surely, Millikan urges, thought about inferential roles and their relations rests on our own inferential dispositions, not on entirely independent beliefs about laws that govern inferential roles. Millikan's suggestion is that thinking about a thought requires me to be able to entertain that thought, which can be regarded as a kind of offline processing, or simulation. However, other mental processes in addition to mind reading, such as imagining and hypothetical thinking, also require offline simulation. She is skeptical that such simulative processes in general, or mind reading in particular, are directly linked to imitation.

Goldman finds a simulationist approach to the links between imitation and mind reading more promising than a theory-theory approach. He considers two compatible proposals: first, that simulationist mechanisms guide some imitation as well as mind reading, and second, that imitation plays a pivotal role in the development of advanced mind reading via simulationist mechanisms.[25]

To motivate the first proposal, Goldman notes that autists tend to be deficient in imitative skills, especially those requiring perspective switching, as well as in mind-reading skills. The two deficits may have a common

25. Compare the links described by Hurley (vol. 1, ch. 7).

cause: dysfunction in simulation mechanisms that normally enable perspective taking and thus underlie both abilities. He regards mirror neurons as a plausible neural substrate of such simulation mechanisms, since by means of them the observation of an action activates a similar goal-related plan (although that activity may be inhibited elsewhere). Thus, dysfunction of the mirror system may be at the root of a cascade of related problems in autism—problems with perspective-taking, imitation, and mind reading (see J. Williams et al., 2001).

Goldman's second proposal is that imitation contributes to advanced mind reading through role-play. Role-play is simulation that can be understood as a kind of extended imitation, in which an action type rather than an action token is copied creatively, with novel embellishments and including the mental states or processes appropriate to the action type. Children who engage in more role-play early on are better at advanced mind-reading tasks later, such as understanding that others may have false beliefs. Goldman sketches a progression in which action imitation extends to role-play, including mental simulation, which in turn contributes to mastery of advanced mind-reading skills.

Unlike Goldman, Wolfgang Prinz objects to the idea that we have direct, privileged access to our own minds, which we use to infer or simulate other minds. Organisms, Prinz argues, are designed to know the world at the expense of knowing themselves; perceptual mechanisms cancel out information deriving from the self in order to distill information about the world from the total information available. While we must, of course, use our own minds to know the world, our privileged access is to the world, not to our own minds. We come to understand ourselves as like others in part as a result of our experience as infants of being imitated by adults; the infant needs such a "mirror" to get to know herself.[26] Being imitated enables the infant to overcome the tendency to cancel out self-information in order to know the world; it allows an infant to perceive her own actions through the other. But, as Prinz admits, this view of self-knowledge does not address the question of how being imitated is recognized (see Decety and Chaminade, vol. 1, ch. 4), or indeed of how other minds are understood in the first place.

Philosopher Robert Gordon's radical version of simulation theory, which is quite different from Goldman's, explicitly rejects the first-to-third-person direction of explanation in understanding other minds. Note that it is a

---

26. Compare the role of being imitated in addressing the correspondence problem, in Heyes's account of imitation (vol. 1, ch. 6).

mistake to associate simulation theories too closely with the first-to-third-person arguments from analogy (Gordon's view is a counterexample) or theory theories with rejection of this type of argument (Meltzoff's view is a counterexample). The theory versus simulation distinction cuts across acceptance or rejection of the first-to-third-person direction of explanation.

Gordon here examines the links between imitation and mind reading from his own simulationist perspective on mind reading. Goldman finds no link between imitation and what he calls the "rationality" or "charity" approach to understanding other minds, versions of which are associated especially with Donald Davidson (1982, 1984) and Daniel Dennett (1987). However, Gordon's version of simulation theory is at the same time a variant of the rationality approach.[27] The role of rationality in Gordon's view of mind reading as simulation turns out to be important for understanding both how he connects imitation with mind reading and how he aims to avoid the first-to-third-person move in his account of mind reading.

In the course of comparing Meltzoff's and Gallese's views, Gordon distinguishes two kinds of mirroring response. In constitutive mirroring, a copied motor pattern is part of the very perception of the other person's action, although the motor pattern may be inhibited and thus not produce overt movement. By contrast, in imitative mirroring, a motor pattern that was active when the other person's action was observed is reactivated without inhibition. The same mirror neurons may be active in both.

Gordon finds constitutive mirroring in Gallese's account of the primitive intersubjective "we" space or shared manifold, which is the basis of empathy and which implicitly expresses the similarity of self and other (but not, as Gallese points out, their distinctness). Gallese understands empathy to involve, not the recognition of others as bodies endowed with minds, but rather the assumption of a common scheme of reasons by reference to which persons, self and others alike, are intelligible (vol. 1, ch. 3; see and cf. Strawson, 1959). Gordon proposes, in more detail, that when constitutive mirroring imposes first-person phenomena, a process of analysis by synthesis occurs in which the other's observed behavior and the self's matching response—part of the very perception of the other's behavior—become intelligible together in the same process. For example, when I see you reach to pick up a ringing phone, your act and my matching response are made sense of together, within a scheme of reasons that is part of the funda-

---

27. See also Gallese (vol. 1, ch. 3), for implied links among imitation, a simulationist approach to mind reading, and rationality assumptions.

mental commonality of persons. I don't infer from the first to the third person, but rather multiply the first person.

Gordon finds the first-to-third-person inference in Meltzoff's account problematic, not because it attributes *similarity* to one's own and others' acts or experiences, but because it requires that they be *identified* and *distinguished*. In the first stage of Meltzoff's account, the similarity between acts of self and other is supposed to be established by their innate equivalence, which is exploited by early imitation; this stage may involve constitutive mirroring, as in Gallese's primitive shared manifold. But the second and third stages of Meltzoff's account, where the analogical inference occurs, requires that self and other also be distinguished. If this kind of act *of mine* is linked to *my* experiences of a certain kind, then a similar (as established in stage one) kind of act *by another person* is also linked to that person's experiences of a similar kind. As Gordon says, if I cannot distinguish *a* and *b*, I cannot make an analogical inference from *a* to *b*. While such an inference may sometimes be a feature of mature imitative mirroring, Gordon regards it as beyond the capacities of infants.

However, a standard charge against pure simulation theories of mind reading has been that they lack the resources to explain how mature mind readers distinguish and identify different people and keep track of which actions and mental states belong to which people. Gordon suggests that multiple first persons are distinguished and tracked in the process of making them intelligible as persons, to avoid incoherence and disunity under the common scheme of reasons (see and cf. Hurley, 1998, part I). Mental states that do not make sense together are assigned to different persons. But can this be done in pure simulation mode, with no overlay of theory and inference? Simulation is supposed to be offline use of practical abilities, in contrast to theorizing about the actions and thoughts of others. But what exactly is the difference between making sense of an action and theorizing about it? When I use practical reason offline in mind reading, I don't formulate normative laws from which I make inferences; rather, I activate my own normative and deliberative dispositions. As Millikan might say, my thought about another's action is not wholly separate from my entertaining that action.

A suggestion worth considering here is this: The fundamental *similarity between self and other* may best be understood, not in terms of theorizing, but rather in terms of simulation (as in Gordon's constitutive mirroring, Gallese's shared manifold, Hurley's level three, or the innate self–other equivalence exploited by early imitation, in Meltzoff's view; a question that needs further attention is whether this fundamental intersubjectivity should be understood to hold at the subpersonal level, at the personal level, or both). Such primitive intersubjectivity may persist into adulthood and remain an essential aspect of mature empathy and mind reading, as Gallese suggests. But as mind reading develops, it also employs a *self–other distinction*, as when an older child attributes to the other false beliefs, different from her own, or distinguishes imitating from being imitated (see Decety and Chaminade in vol. 1, ch. 4 and Hurley's stage 4 in vol. 1, ch. 7). More generally, mature mind reading requires the ability to distinguish, identify, and track different persons and to assign acts and mental states to them. The full range of distinctions and identifications that mature mind reading requires may indeed draw on theoretical and inferential resources, even while the simulative foundation remains essential.

Developmental psychologist Moshe Anisfeld represents a minority (including Celia Heyes and Susan Jones) who remain skeptical about evidence for very early and newborn imitation. He defends here a more extended, Piagetian timetable for representationally mediated imitation (as opposed to mere contagion effects, such as contagious crying by very young infants). Piaget regarded facial imitation as representational, since the imitator cannot see his own act and so must infer its correspondence to the observed act. Anisfeld finds evidence of facial imitation persuasive only for infants more than 6 months old. Work claiming to show earlier facial imitation, he argues, is subject to various methodological criticisms; in his view, there is convincing evidence only for tongue protrusion effects, but these are better understood as arousal effects than as imitation. Piaget regarded deferred imitation as representational when a novel activity is copied after a delay and without any immediate practice having occurred. Anisfeld finds evidence of deferred imitation persuasive only for infants that are more than 11 months old. He argues that work purporting to show earlier deferred imitation suffers from inappropriate controls, or fails to meet the novelty requirement. Moreover, Anisfeld finds support for Piaget's views about the development of representational abilities in work showing how children acquire the ability to generalize deferred imitation in stages: first across different test environments, and then later across different types or colors of stimuli.

The contribution of imitation to understanding other agents is examined in earlier chapters by Gallese, Hurley, Meltzoff, Goldman, and Gordon. By contrast, psychologists Michael Tomasello and Malinda Carpenter, like Rizzolatti, emphasize the contribution of action understanding to imitation. Here Tomasello and Carpenter review work in the past decade on the ways that imitative learning depends on intention reading.

In 1993, Tomasello, Kruger, and Ratner found no convincing evidence of imitative learning in nonhuman animals, and proposed that the understanding of behavior as goal directed or intentional distinguishes human social learning from social learning in other species. In this view, while human beings can either imitate observed means or choose other means to emulate observed goals, other animals do not distinguish means and goals in this way. Animals can copy movements without understanding their relevance to goals, or can learn about the affordances of objects by observing action on them. In neither case, the claim was, do other animals learn about the intentional, means-end structure of the observed action.

Subsequently, Whiten and colleagues obtained results with apes, using artificial fruit in a two-action paradigm, which were described earlier as widely influential in overcoming skepticism about imitation by apes. Tomasello and Carpenter comment here that such results can be interpreted in more than one way. Does a differential tendency to push or pull a rod to open the artificial fruit, in accordance with the model shown, reveal imitative learning with intentional structure or only emulation and affordance learning? They argue that other paradigms developed with children, which they review here, have made a clearer distinction between imitative learning and other forms of social learning (see also Meltzoff, vol. 2, ch. 1.5). It remains to be seen what results these methods will yield with other animals.

In these paradigms, the modeled action is unsuccessful or accidental. If the observer copies what was intended even though it was not shown, as opposed to only the observed movements or the observed though unintended result, that suggests the observer understands the intentional structure of the observed action. For example, an action modeled with an "Oops" indicating it was accidental is copied by 14- to 18-month-olds less than the same action without the "Oops." Eighteen-month-old infants (but not 12-month-olds) copy modeled actions equally whether they are successful or unsuccessful; they read the intended result into the model and produce the successful action even if they have only seen the unsuccessful model. While 14-month-olds copy an unusual means, such as touching the light box described earlier with their heads, they do so more often when the model's hands are free than when she is holding a blanket (Gergely et al., 2002). This suggests that the children infer that the model whose hands are free must have some purpose in adopting this unusual means, even if the purpose is obscure. Moreover, children learn more from an otherwise identical demonstration if they already have information about the model's prior intentions when they watch the demonstration.

Tomasello and Carpenter argue that in recent demonstrations of imitative learning in which the modeled behavior is the same and only the modeled intention varies across conditions, the ability to read intentions is needed to explain what is copied. Given the results from the various imitation paradigms, they regard it as most parsimonious to assume that children use their understanding of intentions to imitate. Further progress in understanding social learning in children and other animals can be made, they suggest, by paradigms that systematically factor the information at the social learner's disposal into information about the demonstrated behavior, its results, its context, and the demonstrator's intention.[28]

How then should we view the relationship between imitation and mind reading? On the one hand, Tomasello and Carpenter emphasize the dependence of full-fledged imitative learning, with an intentional, means-ends structure, on intention reading, and Rizzolatti similarly argues that action understanding precedes imitation. On the other hand, chapters by Hurley, Meltzoff, Goldman, and Gordon argue in various ways that imitation underlies early mind-reading abilities. Are these views in conflict?

Not necessarily, in our view. In order to appreciate their potential compatibility, however, it is important to distinguish various stages or levels in both imitation and mind reading and the ways these could build on one another dynamically in evolutionary and developmental processes. Recall the way Rizzolatti argues that action understanding precedes imitation in evolution: he distinguishes the mirroring of movements (in response priming) from the mirroring of goals (in emulation) and from genuine imitative learning with a flexible intentional structure relating observed means to observed results. He suggests that the capacity to copy observed results via mirror systems may underlie a phylogenetically early understanding of action in terms of goals and intentions, which in turn is needed for phylogenetically later imitative learning with intentional structure, in which the mirroring of means and of ends are linked flexibly in the larger mirror circuit that is characteristic of human beings. Recall also earlier suggestions that recognition of a fundamental self–other similarity via simulation (as in Gallese's primitive shared manifold, Hurley's layer three, Meltzoff's innate self–other equivalence, Gordon's constitutive mirroring) may developmentally precede the registration of a self–other distinction, and more generally precede the inferential abilities, on which more advanced mind reading

28. Recall Harris's suggested experiment with monkeys, described earlier.

depends, to identify and distinguish persons and to keep track of which mental states go with which persons. Very early imitation may express a fundamental self–other similarity, while the distinctive human capacity for imitative learning with its flexible means-ends structure in turn contributes to the development of the self–other distinction and of more advanced mind-reading skills.

Developmental psychologists Paul Harris and Stephen Want focus on the ability to imitate selectively, which they suggest may require a certain level of mind-reading ability. They compare the capacities of 2-year-old and 3-year-old children to learn from observing others correct their own errors in using tools. One series of experiments employs a transparent tube containing a toy that can be pushed out of the tube with a stick; however, if the stick is pushed through the tube in the wrong direction, the toy will be trapped inside.[29] Few 2-year-olds find the solution without demonstration. Some of them are then given a demonstration in which the model extracts the toy correctly, while others observe a model who first makes an incorrect attempt, says "Oops" to register his own mistake, and then goes on to extract the toy correctly. Children in both groups of 2-year-olds learn from the demonstration to use the stick to try to extract the toy, but in neither group do they learn how to do so correctly. They apply the stick in the two directions at random, and extract the toy about half the time. Similarly, 3-year-olds who observe the model are only able to extract the toy about half the time. However, a significantly higher level of success is achieved by 3-year-olds who observe the model correct his own error. (Just observing the incorrect demonstration without subsequent correction does not lead to success at either age.[30])

Harris and Want interpret these results in terms of different capacities for selective imitation. The 2-year-olds learn nonselectively from whatever demonstration they are given: correct, incorrect, or both. But the 3-year-old children have a capacity for selective imitation, which is revealed when they observe both the correct and incorrect variants and differentially select the correct variant. It is interesting that the older children learn more efficiently by observing a model's mistake and immediate self-correction than they do from their own string of trial-and-error attempts. The 3-year-old's greater capacity for selective imitation here may turn on the development of either sufficient intention-reading skills to understand the model's deliberate self-correction after a first unsuccessful attempt, or sufficient

29. Similar results are obtained using a different apparatus.
30. Note the parallels with Pepperberg's training of Alex.

understanding of the causal mechanics of the task. Harris and Want favor the former explanation and suggest a further experiment to address this issue.

They also sketch an intriguing possible connection between the development of selective imitation and the course of cultural evolution. In the upper Paleolithic period, an explosive development of complex tool forms began, after a very long period during which a standardized form of hand axe persisted more or less unchanged. What accounts for this relatively sudden change after such a long period of stasis? If imitation is the mechanism that gives rise to the ratchet effect described earlier, thus enabling culture to accumulate and evolve, could this advance in the development of human tool use be explained by the advent of human imitative learning? Perhaps the neural mirror systems for movements and for goals became linked at around this point into a larger mirror system, enabling characteristically human imitation with its flexible means-ends structure. However, Harris and Want doubt that the advent of imitation per se provides the needed explanation; the standard hand axes that persisted for so long already required a complex and challenging production process that was itself probably guided by imitative learning. Moreover, they argue that nonhuman primates display a capacity for imitative tool use and yet no ratchet effect occurs in their tool culture. Rather, Harris and Want suggest, the spark that set off cumulative progress in human tool use may have been a distinctively human shift from nonselective to selective imitation, not found in other primates, which speeded up the selective transmission of more effective tool variants from one generation to the next. On the other hand, recall that Whiten and colleagues report that chimps imitated selectively, while 3-year-old children did not, in a variant of Harris and Want's task! The jury is still out on how to explain these different results concerning selective imitation in children (see Whiten, vol. 1, ch. 11).

Neurologist Marcel Kinsbourne's hymn to imitation sounds themes from both preceding and following chapters in describing the ways in which human beings can find social entrainment more compelling than reason. The enactive encoding of objects in terms of their affordances for action is a pervasive general phenomenon that underlies imitation in particular: observed action affords imitation. But chasing predators is inadvisable; it is adaptive to inhibit overt imitation in many circumstances. Even infants imitate selectively; recall that they do not copy mechanical devices in the same way as they do people.

Yet the fact that patients with damage to frontal inhibitory areas imitate too widely suggests that overt imitation is just the disinhibited tip of the iceberg of continual covert imitation, which is itself just one aspect of enactive encoding. While covert imitation may function to assist the analysis of speech input through simulative synthesis,[31] Kinsbourne also suggests that it reflects a fundamental motivation of human beings, adults as well as children, to interact synchronously or entrain with one another, which is a mechanism of affiliation as well as of social perception and learning. He regards imitative entrainment as having potent persuasive effects, emotional as much as cognitive, on human beings.

Philosopher Susan Brison comments that Kinsbourne's view of the compelling social influence of imitative entrainment contrasts strikingly with the overrationalist dismissal of imitative influences that is often expressed when freedom of speech is invoked to argue against regulation of violent entertainment. She raises two important questions about what is in effect the ecology of responsibility. First, if a cultural environment entrains imitative violence, are the perpetrators of such violent acts nevertheless responsible for their acts? Second, should citizens take responsibility for doing something about the resulting violence? We can, she argues, answer *both* questions positively. Later chapters by Eldridge and by Huesmann take up related issues. Educationist Guy Claxton is struck by the importance for education of the pervasive although selective tendency to entrain; of the way the intentional stance arises out of the intentional dance, as he puts it. More generally, Kinsbourne's view of the powerful human tendency to entrain through imitation prompts questions about the broader social and cultural effects and functions of imitation. These are the focus of vol. 2, part II.

Volume 2, Part II   Imitation and Culture

Social psychologist Ap Dijksterhuis agrees with Kinsbourne that imitation has important affiliative functions and is the default social behavior for human beings. The results he presents indicate that imitative behavior in human social interactions may be much more common than is generally recognized.

Dijksterhuis distinguishes two imitative pathways. First, he describes a "low road" to the imitation of specific observed behaviors, arguing that we are wired for such imitation by shared representations of our own acts and observed acts, such as those discussed in vol. 1, part I in connection with mirror neurons and ideomotor theory, and in vol. 2, part I in connection

31. See also Gordon (vol. 2, ch. 3), on simulative analysis by synthesis.

with innate self–other equivalences expressed in early imitation. However, his main focus here is on the less direct "high road" to the imitation of complex patterns of behavior. On the high road, imitation is mediated unconsciously by the activation of personality traits and social stereotypes, which lead observers automatically to assimilate their behavior to general patterns of observed behavior. Such imitation, he argues, acts as "social glue," with many beneficial social consequences; in many (though importantly, not all) cases it leads people to coordinate actions, to interact more smoothly, and to like each other.

Dijksterhuis describes an extensive series of experiments that provide striking evidence of heavy travel on the high road to imitation in everyday social life. In these experiments, normal adult participants are primed by exposure to stimuli associated with traits (such as hostility, rudeness, politeness) or with stereotypes (such as elderly persons, college professors, soccer hooligans). Hostility-primed participants deliver more intense "shocks" than control participants in subsequent, ostensibly unrelated experiments based on Milgram's (1963) classic experiments. Rudeness-primed participants spontaneously behave more rudely, and politeness-primed participants more politely, than control participants in subsequent, ostensibly unrelated interactions with experimenters. Youthful participants who are subliminally primed with words associated with the elderly, such as "gray," "bingo," or "sentimental," subsequently walk more slowly, perform worse on memory tasks, and express more conservative attitudes than age-matched control participants. College professor-primed participants perform better and soccer hooligan-primed participants perform worse than control participants on a subsequent, ostensibly unrelated general knowledge quiz. Such priming results are very robust. They hold across a wide range of verbal and visual primes and induced behavior, and when the primes are presented subliminally as well as when participants are conscious of them.[32] Either way, participants are unaware of any influence or correlation between the primes and their behavior.

As Dijksterhuis explains, these results show imitation in a broader sense than we have been considering up to now; traits and stereotypes elicit general patterns of behavior and attitudes, and influence the ways in which behavior is carried out, rather than eliciting specific novel behaviors. These broad imitative influences have been referred to as the *chameleon effect*

32. See also Bargh et al. (1996), Bargh (in press), Bargh and Chartrand (1999), Chartrand and Bargh (1996, 1999, 2002), Carver et al. (1983), Chen and Bargh (1997), Dijksterhuis and Bargh (2001), and Dijksterhuis and van Knippenberg (1998).

(Chartrand & Bargh, 1999). They are rapid, automatic, and unconscious, and do not depend on any conscious goal of the participant, making imitation the default social behavior for normal human adults. Just thinking about or perceiving a certain kind of action automatically increases, in ways participants are not aware of, the likelihood of engaging in that general type of behavior oneself. Nevertheless, these influences are often inhibited, for example, by goals that make conflicting demands; elderly-primed participants don't walk more slowly if they have an independent need to hurry. These influences are also inhibited when participants are focused on themselves. Again, overt imitation is the tip of the iceberg of underlying covert imitation.

Another leading researcher in this area, social psychologist John Bargh, has emphasized elsewhere how very hard it is for people to accept that these broad imitative tendencies apply to themselves, both because they are unconscious and automatic, so that people are not aware of them, and because such external influences threaten their conception of themselves as being in conscious control of their own behavior (Bargh, 1999). Participants are surprised by, and even tend to resist, the experimental findings. We might expect resistance to be especially strong where the high road to imitation would make antisocial behavior more likely, as in exposure to aggressive traits and stereotypes in violent entertainment, discussed by Eldridge, vol. 2, ch. 11 and Huesmann, vol. 2, ch. 12. Nevertheless, it seems plausible to suppose that the power of broad imitative influences on behavior is recognized and exploited by advertising campaigns that expose viewers to traits and stereotypes. As Bargh suggests, recognizing that we are subject to such automatic and unconscious imitative influences may help us to gain control of them and to assimilate behavior patterns more selectively.

In addition to being subject to automatic imitative influences, human beings often deliberately select a pattern of behavior to imitate because it is associated with certain traits and stereotypes, even if they do not actually partake of these traits or stereotypes. This can be benign; perhaps I can become virtuous, as Aristotle suggested, by behaving like a virtuous person. But like automatic imitation, deliberate selective imitation does not always operate benignly. For example, a group of cooperators may develop shared behaviors by means of which members identify one another as cooperators and exclude noncooperators from free riding. Noncooperators may then selectively imitate such behaviors in order to induce cooperative behavior from group members, and then fail to return cooperative behavior, thus deceptively obtaining the benefits of cooperation without paying the costs.

So-called *"greenbeard genes"* could produce genetically determined analogues of such imitative free riding (see Dawkins, 1982, p. 149). However,
the evolution of a general capacity for selective imitation would make it
possible to obtain the advantages of free riding without the need to evolve
genes for specific behaviors (see Hurley, in press).

Sociologist Diego Gambetta examines the deceptive uses of selective imitation to impersonate members of a group or category to which the mimic
does not belong. Adopting the term used in biology, he refers to such
deceptive impersonation as *mimicry*, which he analyzes in terms of the
relations among three roles: the mimic, the model, and the dupe. (Compare the quite different sense of "mimicry" in Call & Carpenter, 2002,
p. 214, and Tomasello et al., 1993: copying modeled behavior without
understanding its goals.) In models, an unobservable property is correlated
with observable signature behaviors. The mimic imitates[33] the model's observable signature behaviors in order to mimic the model's unobservable
property; that is, in order to deceive the dupe into treating the mimic as if
he possessed the model's unobservable property as well as its observable behavior. The model or dupe in turn may develop defenses against mimicry.
Gambetta provides a rich and often amusing set of examples of the relentless semiotic warfare among mimic, model, and dupe as they search for
new ways to "outwit" one another, whether via genetic signs or intentional
signals. The conditions under which mimicry is possible can be analyzed
by means of signaling theory, which specifies equilibrium conditions under
which truth is transmitted even when the signalers have an interest in deception, but Gambetta enriches this abstract analysis in two ways. First, he
provides a set of illustrated semiotic distinctions: *cues* are costless to display
and often mimic-proof; *marks* are lifestyle by-products that are often costly
to mimic; *symbolic signs* are often cheap to display, of low evidential value,
and vulnerable to mimicry. Second, he distinguishes various triangular
relationships among mimic, model, and dupe. For example, is mimic pitted
against dupe, via model, or pitted against model, via dupe? Gambetta calls
for a systematic interdisciplinary extension of the study of mimicry.

Lawyer Harry Litman provides an example of Gambetta's concerns in the
contemporary crime of identity theft. Commenting also on the research
surveyed by Dijksterhuis, Litman notes that its potential public policy
implications are immense, most obviously concerning the protection of
media violence on freedom of speech grounds. However, in his view fur-

---

33. Although mimicry does not always rely on imitation; for example, it can rely on
lying instead.

ther work is needed on the magnitude, selectivity, evolutionary role, and neural basis of high-road imitative effects, especially when the implications for policy about media violence are in question.

Sociologist John Eldridge takes up the question of why disagreement persists about the imitative influences of media violence. The issue has been highly politicized by libertarian, moral right, and feminist agendas and distorted by misleading reporting; some have questioned whether media violence can be identified and its effects researched objectively. Eldridge acknowledges the many studies showing a correlation of exposure to media violence and actual violence, as well as longitudinal studies concluding that causation runs from media violence to actual violence, such as those by Rowell Huesmann, described in vol. 2, ch. 12.

But Eldridge presses the point that causal claims rest on decisions about how the causal relata are identified, and he raises general issues about how images of violence are contextualized and given meaning so as to lead to one response rather than another. Eldridge finds it less fruitful to focus on the imitation of particular episodes of media violence than on the powerful role of the media today, including media violence, in the processes of socialization and transmission of values. For example, he describes a study in which 10-year-olds express a view of killing in the film *Pulp Fiction* as "cool." Yet he also emphasizes the different interpretations given to images of violence, taking images of war as an example. Are they viewed as news, expressions of patriotism, manipulative propaganda, spectacle, history, fictional entertainment, art? The influence of such images can depend significantly on the way they are interpreted. In his view, media violence contributes, along with other influences and subject to many contextual variables, to the vocabulary of motives by which we understand, excuse, and justify conduct.

George Comstock, co-author of a major meta-analysis linking media violence with actual violence (Paik and Comstock, 1994), agrees with many of Eldridge's points about interpretation and context, but is concerned that they may obscure important empirical issues about the imitation and emulation of violence. These issues arise even if, with Eldridge, we focus on broad patterns of behavior mediated by assimilation of stereotypes or values from the media (as in Dijksterhuis' high road to imitation) instead of on the copying of specific behaviors. Comstock argues that the combined weight of many studies makes it "irrefutably clear" that young people exposed to more media violence are more likely to behave aggressively; that there is a strong case for causation, not merely correlation; that the "reverse hypothesis" that aggressiveness leads to viewing of media violence is not supported by the evidence; that effect sizes are significant and comparable to those found in major public health risks; and that the influence of media violence extends to illegal and seriously harmful behavior.

Psychologist Rowell Huesmann concurs that the evidence is compelling that exposure to media violence increases the probability that children will behave aggressively. Huesmann usefully distinguishes short-term processes, which include priming, excitation transfer, and immediate imitation, from long-term influences that operate through observational learning (of schemas for attributing hostile intentions, of scripts linking situations to aggressive responses, and of norms for evaluating such scripts) and desensitization. While the long-term influences are cognitively mediated and lead to broad patterns of behavior, repeated short-term effects contribute to establishing long-term patterns of aggression. Huesmann presents an integrated view of empirical support for the causal influence of media violence on actual aggression from various mutually supporting paradigms. These include well-controlled experiments, robustly replicable correlational studies from various countries, and longitudinal studies and regression analyses showing that exposure to media violence during childhood predicts actual aggression years later, but not vice versa (when other possible explanations are controlled for, including initial aggressiveness, class, education, and so on).

Since 80% of those doing research on media violence conclude from the evidence that this form of violence is causing aggression, why, Huesmann asks, do a minority deny this causal link, and why does public understanding lag so far behind the evidence? Powerful vested interests are at stake; we dislike any suggestion of censorship; and, as social psychologists have emphasized, our conception of ourselves as autonomous is threatened by evidence of imitative influences in general, let alone when they are influences to aggression. But Huesmann suggests that the most powerful explanation is that the general importance of imitation in socialization and the molding of human behavior patterns has not yet been widely appreciated. In particular, he suggests, recent scientific work on the mechanisms and functions of imitation, such as the work reported in these two volumes, has not yet been digested, either by relevant disciplines or by the public. As Hurley comments, the risks associated with media violence may be better and more widely understood when what is being learned about imitation in general has been more widely assimilated and has been applied to the imitation of violence in particular.

Philosopher Jesse Prinz examines the failure of moral emotions to develop in psychopaths and the role of imitation in the normal development of moral motivations. Normally, he argues, moral judgments are intrinsically bound to moral emotions, and hence are intrinsically motivating. This link results from a process of moral development in which emotional mirroring and imitation play critical roles. But in psychopathy, emotional and hence moral development fails.

Psychopaths are often intelligent and can recognize that certain behaviors are conventionally regarded as wrong, but they fail to distinguish actions that would be wrong even if there were no rule against them (such as hitting other students) from actions that are merely against the rules (such as not wearing the correct uniform to school). They show deficits in nonmoral emotions, such as fear and sadness in nonmoral contexts, as well as deficits in moral emotions, such as empathy with others in distress. They are impulsive and find it difficult to inhibit an initial response or default plan of action. Prinz understands this constellation of features in terms of a deficit in the behavioral inhibition system (see Gray, 1987) that underlies many aspects of emotion and motivation. Psychopathic deficits in inhibitory emotions such as sadness and fear, Prinz suggests, may be symptoms of this underlying deficit. A sadness deficit may in turn contribute to lack of empathy with others' sadness, and remove one of the components of more complex emotions such as guilt and shame.

Prinz goes on to argue for the importance of broadly imitative processes in four stages of normal moral development. Moral responsiveness begins with emotional contagion and vicarious distress; young children "catch" emotions from others by imitating observed facial expressions and in other ways.[34] Imitative learning contributes in turn to the development of more active prosocial responses to other's distress, such as consoling; the acquisition of sensitivity to normative rules; and finally the acquisition of moral emotions and the distinguishing of moral from other norms. Moral development can be impaired by bad role models in these imitative processes, as well as by emotional deficits such as those found in psychopaths.

Prinz's account of moral development resembles Adam Smith's eighteenth-century theory of sympathy at certain points, especially with respect to emotional contagion. Smith hypothesizes that when I observe another in a situation that would induce a certain feeling in me, I automatically experience a weaker version of that feeling. Robert Sugden observes the way current work on emotional mirroring, its neural basis and

---

34. See the discussion of emotional mirroring and its neural basis in Rizzolatti (vol. 1, ch. 1), Iacoboni (vol. 1, ch. 2), Gallese (vol. 1, ch. 3), and Decety and Chaminade (vol. 1, ch. 4).

its developmental role, supports Smith's theory. Smith also postulates that human beings are fundamentally motivated to bring their feelings and responses into correspondence with those of others—thus in effect agreeing with Kinsbourne that people love to entrain. Commenting on Prinz's chapter, Huesmann concurs on the importance of emotional contagion in moral development, but also emphasizes the imitative aspect of the cognitive processes by which we learn to evaluate morally the scripts available to govern behavior (which may themselves have been imitatively generated, in his view), and to reject scripts that are morally unacceptable.

Psychologist Merlin Donald views human imitative skills as part of the broader human capacity for *mimesis*: purposeful analog motoric communication that reenacts and creatively modifies complex episodes and behaviors as continuous wholes, without parsing into chunks represented by discrete symbols.[35] He argues that basic mimetic capacities evolved as primarily motoric adaptations in hominids about two million years ago and remain just out of reach for most primates. Mimesis enabled not just imitation but also the rehearsal and refinement of skills, the public motoric display of perceived or remembered episodes, social coordination and ritual, nonlinguistic gesture and pantomime, and reciprocal emotional display or mirroring.

Human mimetic communication preceded symbolic language and provided the fundamental support for the cultural interactions and conformity to norms that eventually led to language. Symbolic language was scaffolded on mimesis, Donald claims; it emerged from stabilized networks in which human beings with mimetic skills and analog brains interacted. Moreover, despite the immense historical overlay of linguistic culture, the human mind and its cultures are still fundamentally mimetic. Mimetic, analog styles of representation operate below the cognitive surface, affecting the way we use linguistically structured symbols and providing the foundation of our mental communities.

Morten Christiansen stresses that even if Donald is right about mimetic culture preceding and scaffolding language, more needs to be said to explain the commonalities of structure across the world's languages. While the usual question is, Why is the human brain so well suited for learning language?, we need to ask, Why is language so well suited to being learned by the human brain? Christiansen argues that natural language has itself adapted to strong selectional pressures provided by specific constraints on

---

35. Compare Byrne (vol. 1, ch. 9) on behavior parsing by gorillas and Arbib (vol. 1, ch. 8.2) on the decompositional structure of imitation and its relationship to syntactic structure.

human learning and processing capacities, in particular, the capacities for processing sequential and hierarchical structures. That is, linguistic universals are not themselves genetically specified, but rather reflect the cultural evolution of language to fit universal but language-independent features of human cognition, and thus to be learnable. Moreover, the pressures operating on language to adapt to human learning capacities are significantly stronger than those operating on humans to be able to use language. Despite the differences among them, Donald, Christiansen, Byrne, Iacoboni, and Arbib agree in suggesting that social learning of the structure of complex actions may provide an essential evolutionary foundation for linguistic capacities.

As Susan Blackmore explains, "mimetic" in Donald's sense should not be confused with "memetic" in the sense of meme theory, as first proposed by Richard Dawkins and developed by herself (Blackmore, 1999), Daniel Dennett (1995), and others. According to meme theory, memes are analogous to genes in that both are replicators that evolve through a process of imperfect copying under selective pressure. Memes are understood to be whatever is copied by imitation, the mechanism that makes memetic evolution possible. So while imitation is just one aspect of mimesis in Donald's sense, it is fundamental to meme theory. While memes need not be representational, mimesis requires intentional, representational action. Donald views imitation as a relatively uncreative aspect of mimesis, while Blackmore argues that copying errors, recombination, and selection among variants makes memetic evolution creative in the same way that genetic evolution is. And while genetic adaptations may explain the emergence of basic mimetic capacities, including the capacity for imitation itself, meme theory explains culture in terms of the comparative reproductive success of memes themselves rather than the comparative reproductive success of genes.

What is the relationship between imitation and rationality? Modern human cultures tend to assume, as well as aspire to, rationality, despite experimental evidence of systematic human irrationality. The assumption that human beings make rationally consistent choices, as if they were maximizing along some single dimension of expected utility, is especially prevalent in economics. Biologists have also modeled animal behavior resulting from blind processes of natural selection as if it were the rational solution to maximizing problems. The gene-meme analogy thus leads to the question, Can a supposed tendency for human beings to act as if they were rational be shown to result from processes of memetic selection? Economist Robert Sugden answers "no." He argues, against an argument made by Ken Binmore (1994), that there is no reason to suppose that the memes that are most successful at being imitated will yield behavior conforming to rational choice theory.

Sugden's central point is that as-if rational behavior by replicators does not necessarily entail as-if rational behavior by the actors who carry those replicators. To make this point, he provides three related models of replicator population dynamics. Replicator types, whether genetic or memetic, replicate at a certain rate and have effects, via the choices made by the actors who carry them, on their own replication rates. For a replicator (as opposed to the actor who carries it) to behave as if it were rational means that it "acts" in such a way that it survives in a stable equilibrium. The three models make different assumptions about the causal loop by which replicators determine choices by the actor who carries them, and such choices in turn determinate rates of replication by replicators. The question then is, Will the as-if rationality of replicators lead the *actors* who carry the replicators to act as if they were rational?

Under unrealistically simplifying assumptions about the causal loop, it will do so: where each replicator type is the cause of one and only one action type, and where replicators reproduce asexually by producing exact copies of themselves. In this first model, decision probabilities exactly reflect the dynamics of the replicator population, and the actors as well as the replicators behave as if they were rational. But under more realistic assumptions, this does not hold. Sugden's second model shows that as-if rationality by genetic replicators does not induce as-if rationality by actors where reproduction is sexual, where each actor has genes from two parents and passes on at random only one of its pair of genes to its offspring, so that actions are determined by a combination of genes and decision probabilities no longer mirror the population of genes.

Nor do actors inherit as-if rationality from memetic replicators that reproduce asexually, but through selective imitation of other agents. In Sugden's third model, when actors meet, one actor compares the consequences of her own meme and the other actor's meme for a particular decision problem and decides accordingly whether to adopt the other actor's meme: whether to imitate. But these pairwise comparisons do not guarantee that the decision probabilities across the population of actors will respect transitivity; the decision probabilities may cycle in a way that is irrational at the level of actors, although they may be explicable at the level of memetic replicators.[36]

---

36. Many readers will no doubt be reminded here of the rational individual preferences and irrationally cycling collective preferences of social choice theory; see Arrow (1963).

As economist Paul Seabright and philosopher Mark Greenberg both emphasize, Sugden shows that rational behavior is not *guaranteed* to develop by genetic or memetic evolution, but leaves quite open whether it may *in fact* have developed by such means, which is a further, empirical question. Sugden's concern is to show that purely a priori approaches to this question are misguided. Just as the theory of biological evolution depends on an empirical understanding of actual genetic mechanisms, so we need to know "messy" facts about the causal loops governing memes and about their human transmitters, in order to know the consequences of memetic selection for the rationality of behavior.

Anthropologist Francisco Gil-White also calls for more empirical study of influences on the transmission of memes. He considers the common characterization of memes as selfish replicators to be mistaken. Nevertheless, he defends the usefulness of understanding cultural change in terms of Darwinian processes operating on memes, which are understood as elements of culture transmitted nongenetically that show inheritance, mutation, and selection. He explains that strict replication is not required by a Darwinian account of memetic evolution and cumulative adaptation, and responds to the objections that memes lack well-defined boundaries and that they change too rapidly for selection to determine cultural evolution. Nor does a Darwinian account of memetic evolution depend only on exact imitation as a copying mechanism; it can countenance other complex cognitive mechanisms of transmission, such as the emulation of a model's inferred goal based on observing a statistical cloud of the model's performances, even if these are unsuccessful. Gil-White emphasizes that the transmission of memes can depend, not just on the information content of the meme, but also on a range of noncontent-related influences described in classic work by Robert Boyd and Peter Richerson (1985), such as the meme's frequency in relation to other memes (*conformity bias*) and its association with high-status persons (*prestige bias*). While Harris and Want suggest in vol. 2, ch. 6 that selective imitation may explain cultural progress, Gil-White stresses the way noncontent biases on meme transmission can explain cultural differences. He sees memetic accounts of cultural change in terms of noncontent biases as rivals to "selfish-meme" accounts inspired by Richard Dawkins's selfish-gene theory. Finally, he criticizes Susan Blackmore's arguments that memetic evolution can drive genetic evolution. Blackmore in response defends her conceptions of memes as "selfish" and of memetic drive. She argues that Gil-White misrepresents meme theory's conception of replication and that meme theory can accommodate noncontent biases.

Mark Greenberg objects that Gil-White's defense of memetic evolution against the rapid-change objection assumes perfect selection: that everyone selects the most attractive variant of a particular type of behavior to copy, thus agreeing in their evaluations of such behavior. But in fact people may differ widely in their goals and hence their evaluations of others' behavior, and so select quite different examples to imitate. Moreover, human goal-seeking can result in radical departures from existing models rather than cumulative change.

Greenberg argues that the selfish-meme theory has the potential to challenge the commonsense goal-based account, but that its success will depend on its doing more explanatory work than competing goal-based accounts. For example, the development and spread of a technological innovation might naturally be understood as a result of deliberate, goal-directed thought and action: research, development, production, marketing, and rational consumer choice. The proliferation of an innovation may indeed reflect the differential imitation and survival of a meme for that innovation, yet human goals appear to explain *why* that meme is selectively imitated and hence spreads. (Greenberg's point here again recalls the suggestion by Harris and Want that *selective* imitation drove progress in tool use.) More generally, even when cultural changes do reflect the accumulation of variation under selective pressure, human goals may explain the selecting and hence the changes. Meme theory needs to show when and why the prima facie plausible goal-based account is inadequate and the deeper or more comprehensive explanation is that some memes are more conducive to their own replication than others are.

Greenberg draws an illuminating threefold distinction among ways in which memes might be selected. First, memes can be deliberately selected because of the relationship of their content to human goals: the commonsense account. Second, memes can be good at getting themselves copied by virtue of their content-related effects but regardless of whether they serve deliberate human goals (say, by exploiting other features of human psychology or society): the selfish-meme theory. Third, memes can be selected by mechanisms that are indifferent to their content, as in conformity or prestige biases: the noncontent bias theory. Noncontent bias accounts, in Greenberg's view, do not undermine content-based selfish-meme accounts. The fundamental issue is not between content-based and noncontent-based accounts of selection. Rather, it is whether either content-based selfish-meme theory or noncontent bias theory, or both in alliance, can do more explanatory work than the content-based, goal-directed, commonsense account.

Psychologist Nick Chater highlights another aspect of the explanatory competition between Darwinian memetics and commonsense, goal-based accounts of cultural change: speed. He distinguishes a Mendelian view of memetics, which he finds promising, from a Darwinian view, about which he is more skeptical than Greenberg. While Mendelian memetics explains cultural change in terms of the differential spread of memes, Darwinian memetics is more ambitious; it aims to explain cultural complexity as the result of blind selection among memes. As a result, he argues, Darwinian memetics faces a serious problem: Blind selection is slow and will be overtaken by fast intentional selection in the production of cultural complexity. Darwinian accounts of the emergence of biological complexity assume that variation is random, not directed, and that selectional forces operate by means of the reproductive success of whole organisms, not directly at the level of individual genes. But neither assumption holds for cultural transmission. We often create deliberate variation and imitate creatively, guided by our goals; we intentionally select particular aspects of models to imitate and decide not to imitate other aspects. Cultural complexity, unlike biological complexity, is largely produced by design; by sighted, not blind, watchmakers.

In response to the related challenges that Greenberg and Chater pose for meme theory, Blackmore agrees that goals are indeed relevant to memetic evolution, but they are just one of many factors contributing to selection processes. Selfish-meme accounts of religious practices do more explanatory work than goal-based accounts, she suggests, since the relevant goals were exploited and redesigned by religious memes.

Viewed in the overall context of these volumes, these last chapters come full circle by emphasizing the role of human goals in guiding deliberate selective imitation and hence cultural evolution. By what cognitive processes, deliberate or otherwise, do human beings acquire and pursue their goals? Other intelligent social animals can acquire goals by emulation, but few if any can learn imitatively novel means by which to achieve their goals. Other social animals do not engage, at least in the way that humans do, in mind reading—which arguably depends on the capacity for imitation and which certainly serves many human goals, along with other forms of simulative thought. However, human beings have a default tendency to imitate, automatically and unconsciously, in ways that their deliberate pursuit of goals can override but not explain. Do the distinctive human capacity and tendency to imitate at some level enable the effective, flexible pursuit of goals, or do goals guide selective human imitation—or both—in a dynamic process? To understand how culture emerges from biology, we should put the cultural roles of imitation into biological and psychological context. The cognitive neuroscience and the evolutionary and developmental psychology of imitation should inform our views of the roles and functions of imitation in human culture.

Why Imitation Matters

In light of the contributions from a variety of disciplinary perspectives that we have surveyed, the importance of imitation can be described in both substantive and methodological terms. Here we briefly sketch how the study of imitation illuminates substantive issues about the links between perception and action and between self and other; the modularity of mind; the relationships among various levels of description of minds in society; the relationship between genetic endowment and social environment in forming human minds; the relationships between cultural evolution, in which imitation is arguably the primary copying mechanism, and biological evolution, which gave rise to the capacity for imitation in the first place. We conclude by suggesting that the study of imitation illustrates promising methodologies for interactive collaboration among the cognitive and social sciences and philosophy.

The study of imitation sheds light on two relationships that are central to understanding minds in general and human minds in particular: the relationship between perception and action and the relationship between self and other. The following paragraph sketches our view of how it does so, drawing on suggestions in various chapters. While there is plenty of room for disagreement about the details, it is hard to doubt the relevance of imitation to these issues.

Hypotheses about the control, imitative, and simulative functions of the mirror system, and evidence from imitation studies for ideomotor and common coding theories, suggest that perception and action share a fundamental information space that is preserved as higher cognitive capacities and that distinctions are built on it (see Gallese, vol. 1, ch. 3; Decety and Chaminade, vol. 1, ch. 4; Prinz, vol. 1, ch. 5; Hurley, vol. 1, ch. 7; and Meltzoff, vol. 2, ch. 1). The distinction between results and the means to those results, on which goal-directed, perceptually guided intentional action as well as imitative learning depend, emerges as a flexible articulation of this shared processing (see Rizzolatti, vol. 1, ch. 1). However, perception remains fundamentally enactive, in a way that challenges orthodox views of perception and action as separate and of perception as motivationally inert (see Kinsbourne, vol. 2, ch. 7; see also and cf. Noë, in press). The intersubjectivity characteristic of human beings, the basis for their innate capacity to understand and empathize with one another, is enabled as a specialization of such enactive perception. Perceiving your action enactively, in a way that immediately engages my own potential similar action, thus enables me to understand, or to imitate, your action. Shared processing of the actions of other and self is a special aspect of the shared processing of perception and action. The problem of "knowledge" of other minds looks quite different from this perspective. It is not so much that intersubjective information bridges an informational gap between self and other as that the self–other distinction is imposed on the fundamental information space that self and other share. As Gordon puts it, the first person is multiplied—though care is needed over whether this multiplication is understood at the level of subpersonal information, at the personal level, or both (see and cf. Gallese, vol. 1, ch. 3; W. Prinz, vol. 1, ch. 5; Hurley, vol. 1, ch. 7; Meltzoff, vol. 2, ch. 1; and Gordon, vol. 2, ch. 3). Simulation theories of mind reading can be right about shared processing for self and other with respect to this fundamental intersubjectivity, even if more advanced aspects of mind reading require theorizing in ways enabled by language.

Imitation is also prime territory in which to investigate issues about the modularity of mind and the relationships among different levels of description: neural, functional, personal, social, and cultural. Does the study of imitation support views of cognition as emerging from layers of dynamic perceptual-motor skills scaffolded by social and cultural environments (horizontal modularity), rather than as embodied in a central module that interfaces between perception and action (vertical modularity; see Hurley, 1998, 2001; Brooks, 1999)? What does the common coding of perception and action in imitation imply about the modularity of mind? How do different levels of description of imitation constrain one another? How, for example, would shared subpersonal processing for self and other be reflected in personal-level understanding of others? What do neural mirror systems imply about imitation and mind reading? Why do some creatures have neural mirror systems but not imitative capacities, and what more is needed for imitation? What do hypotheses about the functional subpersonal architecture that enables imitation imply about neural structures and function (or vice versa)? About the development and nature of our capacities as persons to understand other persons? Do empathy and mind reading at the personal level depend on simulation? Is simulation, in effect, offline imitation? Is simulation a personal-level rival to theorizing, or a subpersonal mechanism, or both? Does cultural evolution depend primarily on blind, automatic mirroring mechanisms or on deliberative, goal-driven, selective imitation?

The study of imitation can contribute to our understanding of broad theoretical issues, such as those between nativists and empiricists about the relative contributions of genetic and environmental influences to psychology and language. These issues arise at various levels in the study of imitation. Why does a special capacity to learn imitatively from social environments evolve genetically—and why so rarely? What does imitation reveal about the relationship between human nature and other animals? Is the correspondence between perception and action that imitation exploits innate, as Meltzoff suggests, or is it acquired in cultural environments, as Heyes suggests? Does the location of mirror neurons in Broca's area suggest that imitative learning plays more of a role in language acquisition than nativists about language acquisition allow? Does imitation structure linguistic competence in some way as well as prompting performance (assuming that a competence/performance distinction is viable)? Do the recombinant ends-means and sequential-hierarchical structures and the self–other parity found in imitative action provide a basis for syntactic structure and shared meanings in linguistic action? If so, should we understand this foundation in evolutionary or developmental terms, or both? If not, what is the relationship between language and imitation? (See Iacoboni, Arbib, Byrne, Pepperberg, Pickering, Donald, Christiansen.)

More generally, imitation is a critical locus for understanding the ecology of human cognition and norms: the dynamic interactions between cognitive processes and sociocultural processes. Once the capacity for imitation has evolved, does it give rise to a new medium of evolution—culture—that can drive genetic evolution, or does genetic evolution remain in the driver's seat? Or do life and culture, brain and language, coevolve? Is automatic or selective imitation the primary engine of cultural evolution? (See Donald, Christiansen, Sugden, Gil-White, Greenberg, and Chater.) Are innate or cultural deficits primarily responsible for autism; for psychopathy; for violent aggression? Can individual responsibility itself be understood, compatibly with an innate human tendency to imitate, in partly ecological terms? (See Donald, Jesse Prinz, Eldridge, Huesmann, and Brison.) As we have seen, the study of imitation connects with practical issues; for example, it may have clinical applications in the treatment of autism (see Pepperberg, Jones), and policy implications in relation to media violence (see Huesmann, Comstock, Litman, and Hurley) and education (see Claxton). How should we respond to the irony of imitation: that the capacity for imitation appears to be a distinctive feature of human nature and may well be part of the basis for other distinctive features of human nature, such as mind reading and language, which together set us apart from other animals? Yet at the same time our innate, automatic tendencies to imitate can also threaten our conception of ourselves as autonomous and deliberative in ways that no other animals are.

Finally, the study of imitation illustrates a promising topic-based, interdisciplinary methodology. We have seen that imitation has important roles in human cognition and society. To seek a fundamental understanding of these, we do best to bring together the discoveries and theories of the various disciplines that study imitation, so that they can constrain, inform, and cross-fertilize one another—though of course we must remain aware of how specific aims and contexts differ across disciplines (see, e.g., Rizzolatti, vol. 1, ch. 1 and Byrne, vol. 1, ch. 9). In particular, these two volumes illustrate the fruitful interaction of techniques across disciplines: the interaction of single-cell brain recording; brain imaging work[37]; behavioral experiments; fieldwork; clinical work; and formal, conceptual, and theoretical arguments. Many new experiments as well as theoretical developments are suggested in these volumes as a result of interdisciplinary thinking.

These volumes also illustrate that there is work for philosophy to do that is often overlooked within a prevalent conception of philosophy as a strictly a priori discipline that addresses conceptual issues and is sharply separated from scientific inquiry about empirical matters. We do not subscribe to that division, but rather to the view that important conceptual and empirical issues are often densely and seamlessly intermingled, as they are in the study of imitation. As many scientists are aware, philosophical questions often grow organically out of scientific work, as again they do from work on imitation: questions that are at once philosophical and empirical and that can be addressed fruitfully by philosophy as well as by the sciences. We do not suggest that such questions should displace philosophy's historically derived traditional questions, but rather that they provide additional areas to which philosophical argument can contribute. Indeed, "natural philosophy" was long understood to include physics as well as metaphysics, logic, and ethics. We propose to revive and revise the term "natural philosophy" to describe the kind of empirically embedded philosophical work illustrated in these volumes.

Progress on some topics of fundamental and broad importance may demand topic-based research that cuts across disciplines, which, unfortu-

37. See the discussion by Iacoboni (vol. 1, ch. 2), Decety (vol. 1, ch. 4), and Kinsbourne (vol. 1, ch. 8.5) on the interaction of brain imaging and other techniques.

nately, contemporary institutional and disciplinary constraints often fail to facilitate. We hope that these volumes will encourage institutions to build opportunities for topic-based interdisciplinary research into their normal infrastructure and operating assumptions.

Acknowledgments

We are grateful to many of the authors in these volumes for their helpful comments. We wish to express our great appreciation and gratitude to Jill Taylor and Ursula Richards; we have relied heavily on their painstaking assistance and tireless work in compiling these volumes. Most of all, we wish to thank the Gatsby Charitable Trust, London (especially Horace Barlow), and the Lifelong Learning Foundation, Manchester (especially Chris Brookes), for sharing our vision and providing the funding that made the 2002 Royaumont conference on imitation possible. These volumes were inspired by the deep intellectual excitement of those few days, and we hope that they have managed to capture some of it.

I   Imitation and Human Development

1 Imitation and Other Minds: The "Like Me" Hypothesis

Andrew N. Meltzoff

1.1 Introduction

Human adults and children effortlessly learn new behaviors from watching others. Parents provide their young with an apprenticeship in how to act as a member of their particular culture long before verbal instruction is possible. A wide range of behaviors—from tool use to social customs—are passed from one generation to another through imitative learning. In western cultures, toddlers hold telephones to their ears and babble into the receivers. The children of Australian aborigines would not do this, one suspects. There is no innate proclivity to treat pieces of plastic in this manner, nor is it due to Skinnerian learning. Imitation is chiefly responsible.

Imitation evolved through Darwinian means but achieves Lamarckian ends. It provides a mechanism for the "inheritance" of acquired characteristics. Imitation is powerful and can lead to rapid learning; it is essentially no-trial learning.

Imitation is rare in the animal kingdom. Many animals watch their conspecifics and engage in similar activities, but this is often mediated by less complex processes than imitation. Definitions of imitation can be tricky, but the canonical case of imitation, at least the most interesting case for theory, occurs when three conditions are met: (1) the observer produces behavior similar to that of the model, (2) the perception of an act causes the observer's response, and (3) the equivalence between the acts of self and other plays a role in generating the response. Equivalence need not be registered at a conscious level, but if it is not used at any level in the system (neurally, cognitively, computationally), the soul of imitation has been snatched away.

1.2   Connecting Imitation, "Like Me," and Understanding Other Minds

Over the past decade, I have developed the thesis that infant imitation is connected with the perception of others as "like me" and understanding others' minds (Meltzoff, 1990b; Meltzoff & Moore, 1995; Meltzoff & Brooks, 2001; Meltzoff, 2002a). There is a growing consensus among philosophers, evolutionary psychologists, and neuroscientists that this trio of concepts fit together (e.g., Goldman, 1992b, 2000; Gordon, 1995a; Tomasello, 1999; Rizzolatti et al., 2002).

My thesis is that imitation and understanding other minds (often referred to as a theory of mind or mind reading) are causally related. But which way does the causal arrow run? Some have argued that understanding other minds, especially judgments of others' intentions, underlies imitation (e.g., Tomasello et al., 1993a). This puts the cart before the horse, in my opinion. I wish to show that imitation, and the neural machinery that underlies it, begets an understanding of other minds, not the other way around. Table 1.1 provides a sketch for how such a developmental pathway might work.

Step 1 is ensured by innate equipment. Imitation by newborns provides evidence that the observation and execution of human acts are innately coupled. We hypothesized that this is mediated by a "supramodal" representation of acts (Meltzoff & Moore, 1977, 1997). Progress has been made in specifying the neural underpinnings of imitation, as will be elaborated later in this chapter.

Step 2 is based on individual experience. Through everyday experience infants map the relation between their own bodily states and mental experiences. For example, there is an intimate relation between striving to

Table 1.1
Emergence of understanding other minds from simpler beginnings—the case for normal human ontogeny

Imitation
Intrinsic connection between observed and executed acts, as manifest by newborn imitation (Meltzoff & Moore, 1997).
↓
First-person experience
Infants experience the regular relationship between their own acts and underlying mental states.
↓
Understanding Other Minds
Others who act "like me" have internal states "like me."

achieve a goal and concomitant facial expression and effortful bodily acts. Infants experience their own unfulfilled desires and the simultaneous facial and postural behavior that accompanies such states. These experiences contribute to a detailed bidirectional map linking mind and behavior, at least in the infant's own case.

Step 3 involves a projection. When infants see others acting similarly to how they have acted in the past, they project onto others the mental state that regularly goes with that behavior. This could not occur if infants saw no equivalence between their acts and those of others (ensured by step 1), nor would it proceed very far if there was no binding between their own internal states and bodily acts (step 2). Infants imbue the acts of others with felt meaning, not through a process of step-by-step formal reasoning, but because the other is processed as "like me."

Clearly, this is only a partial story about understanding other minds. The mental states most amenable to this analysis are purposive action, desires, visual perception, and basic emotions. For these, there is a relatively close coupling between the underlying mental states and their expression in bodily action (step 2). Further developments are needed for understanding false beliefs and other mental states, which are farther from the action, as it were (e.g., Astington & Gopnik, 1991; Bruner, 1999; Flavell, 1999; Harris, 1989; Humphrey, 2002; Meltzoff et al., 1999; Wellman, 1990, 2002; Perner, 1991a). Development is also required to understand that the thoughts and feelings of the self and the other may *diverge*. This crucial human ability is probably beyond the grasp of young infants, but it is central to adult perspective-taking (i.e., being able to mentally "stand in another's shoes" even though those shoes are recognized to be a poor fit for oneself). The proposals offered in this chapter chiefly focus on the initial foothold for interpreting others as bearers of psychological properties commensurate with one's own. This is relevant for philosophical, neurological, and psychological theory building, because if we don't have a valid characterization of the initial state, our models of mentalizing will have a shaky foundation.

1.3   Imitation of Novel Acts

It does not take an experiment to convince us that human adults imitate. The evidence for animal and infant imitation, however, has been more contentious. The debates often come down to two factors: (1) the novelty of the acts copied and (2) the temporal delay between stimulus and response. Suppose an organism only imitates familiar behaviors. One would want to take special care to differentiate this from spontaneous, coincidental production of the act. Similarly, if imitation is restricted to immediate reproduction, if the organism can only mirror synchronously and with no delay, one would need special controls to check whether this can be reduced to lower-level entrainment mechanisms.

It is notoriously difficult to define novelty in imitation by animals and humans. Piaget reported that 1.5-year-old infants imitated novel behaviors such as "hitting my shoulders with my hands (the movement one uses to get warm)" and throwing a temper tantrum after seeing another child do so (Piaget, 1951/1962). One could quibble about whether these are novel. Animal researchers try to approach the problem by testing multistep sequences (often composed of familiar acts); they suggest that particular serial orders can be considered novel and would not arise by chance in the absence of the demonstration (R. Byrne, 2002c; R. Byrne & Russon, 1998; Whiten, 2002a).

The most convincing cases of novel imitation, however, occur when the behavior is not in the subject's repertoire to begin with. For example, if I wanted to test whether adults are capable of imitating a novel act, I might demonstrate touching my bellybutton with my elbow. We are motorically capable of these acts (otherwise failure would be uninformative), but they are not routines. One cannot record an organism's entire lifetime of experience, but sufficiently unusual behaviors with a baseline rate of zero are reasonable tests of the imitation of novelty.[1]

To test whether human infants are capable of imitating novel acts, I used 14-month-old infants. The act chosen was leaning forward to touch a rectangular box with one's forehead. The delay imposed between stimulus and response was 1 week (Meltzoff, 1988a). It was not a matter of the adult's act entraining the infant. Imitation had to occur based on a memory.[2]

---

1. Some behaviorists have argued that there may be no such thing as novel imitation, even in adults. The idea is that unless one has recorded the organism's entire history, there is always a chance that the subject has done (and been reinforced for) the behavior in the past. The more accepted consensus is that the imitation of novelty can be tested using behaviors that are not familiar routines, have a baseline rate of near zero in the absence of modeling them, and are "arbitrary" (no survival value for the species) in and of themselves (see Meltzoff, 1988a, p. 474, for an extended discussion of novelty in imitation).

2. The infants came into the laboratory on day 1 and observed the act. They were not allowed to touch or handle the object and were sent home before returning a week later. In followup studies, the parents were blindfolded or were not initially in the room, so that they were kept completely unaware of the gesture shown to the infant (Hanna & Meltzoff, 1993; Klein & Meltzoff, 1999).

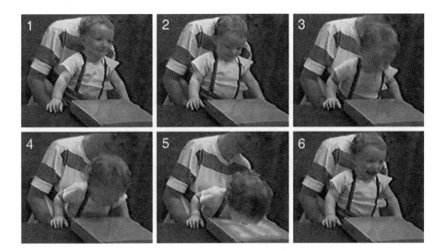

Figure 1.1
Imitation of a novel act by 14-month-old infants. None (0%) of the controls produced this behavior. There is a social-game quality to human imitation. Infants often smile after accurate imitation, as shown in panel 6. (From Meltzoff, 1999b.)

The results showed that infants imitated after the 1-week delay (figure 1.1). Fully 67% of the infants duplicated the act, with a mean latency of 3.1 seconds after they were given the box. The control groups confirmed that 0% of the infants who had not seen the target behavior produced the behavior spontaneously. In the affordance control group, infants were simply given the object. This tested whether the object had visible properties that automatically provoked the response; the data showed it did not. In the stimulus-enhancement control group, an adult manipulated the object but refrained from performing the target act. This tested whether drawing infants' attention to the object led them to produce the behavior; it did not. An independent laboratory replicated this finding and confirmed that head touching was not an automatic response based on the object's properties, because there were conditions under which infants chose to duplicate the adult's behavior and conditions under which they did not (Gergely et al., 2002).

1.3.1 Implications for Theory
These tests have the following implications:

- Infants imitate novel acts.

• Infants imitate from memory and are not restricted to immediate resonance.

• Infants can imitate the means used (head touching); hence they are not limited to emulation.

• Infants use other people to learn about and expand their own actions. The imitation of novelty suggests a bidirectional flow of information—a "like you" as well as a "like me" pathway (probably supported by the same underlying mechanism).

1.4 "Like Me": Recognition of Being Imitated from Behavioral and Neuroscience Perspectives

We have shown that infants imitate novel acts, which demonstrates a linkage from observation to execution. The shorthand is that infants map from the other to the self. The "like me" hypothesis suggests that they also can go in the reverse direction, recognizing when someone acts as they do; in shorthand, mapping from the self to the other. One way of testing this idea is to run imitation in the reverse direction. This entails evaluating whether subjects can recognize that they are being imitated.

The situation of being imitated is a special one. It is not the temporal contingency that makes it special. Physical objects may come under temporal control, but only people who are paying attention to you and acting intentionally can match the form of your acts in a generative fashion. Only people can systematically act "like me." If infants can recognize when an entity is acting "like me," this would allow them to make a distinction between people and all other entities in the world.[3]

I tested whether infants recognize when another acts "like me" and the affective consequences of this experience. A broad range of ages was used, from 6 weeks to 14 months old. One experiment involved 14-month-old infants and two adults. One of the adults imitated everything the baby did; the other adult imitated what the previous baby had done. Although both adults were acting in perfectly infantile ways, and were good controls for one another, the infants reacted differentially. The results showed that

---

3. This does not deny that infants recognize conspecifics by vision and audition, as do other animals. The idea is that over and above this they also register others as acting "like me." This distinction has not been tested in the animal literature. It would be useful to test whether great apes can recognize when others are acting "like me" based on an equivalence in the *form* of the actions (not just the temporal contingencies).

the infants looked longer at the person who was imitating them and also smiled more often at that person (Meltzoff, 1990b).

These results could be based on the detection of temporal contingency, so in the next study both adults acted at the same time. When an infant produced a behavior from a predetermined list, both adults simultaneously sprang into action. One imitated the infant, the other performed a mismatching response. Thus both were temporally contingent. The results showed that the infants looked significantly longer and smiled more at the adult who was imitating them. Evidently infants recognize a deeper commonality between self and other beyond timing alone. I would argue that there are neural mechanisms for recognizing "congruent with me," not just "contingent on me."

We also discovered that infants exhibited what I termed *testing behavior*, as if probing the causal relations between acts of the self and the other. Infants watched the adult imitate them and then made sudden and unexpected movements while staring at the adult. They would suddenly freeze all actions and then switch abruptly from one act to another, while inspecting the adult as if to see if he followed. This seems to go beyond simple resonance and mirror neuron activity, because the subject is purposely acting *differently* from what they observe. This pattern of behavior is exhibited down to about 9 months of age. However, this is not an innate reaction. We set up studies matching the mouth opening and closing of 6-week-olds. The baby's attention was attracted, but it did not lead the baby to systematically switch to tongue protrusion or another gesture. There was no testing. Young infants process specific behavior-to-behavior mapping, whereas the older infants go beyond this and understand the abstraction of a matching game per se, where the notion is "you will do what I do" with substitutable behaviors. Mutual imitation and the question of "who is imitating whom" is not only apparent in toddlers but also in older children (Asendorpf, 2002; Nadel, 2002) and adults.

1.4.1 Neuroscience Findings

We designed a positron emission tomography (PET) study to investigate the neural correlates of adults' recognition of being imitated by another person (Decety et al., 2002). The subject either imitated or was imitated by an experimenter who was visible from inside the scanner. The results indicated that the right inferior parietal lobe was specifically activated when the subjects recognized that they were being imitated by the other, as opposed to performing the action freely or imitating someone else. We hypothesized that the right inferior parietal lobe is involved in sorting out agency and differentiating actions produced by the self from matching actions observed in others: "Did I will that or did he?" Further neuroscience work strongly supports this view (Chaminade & Decety, 2002 and Decety and Chaminade, vol. 1, ch. 4).

1.4.2   Implications for Theory

These tests have the following implications:

- Infants recognize that they are being imitated.
- This "like me" recognition is based on the structural congruence between the self and the other, not simply temporal information.
- Older infants test the self–other correspondence, probing the agency involved.
- The right inferior parietal lobe plays a role in differentiating like-actions generated by the self and the other.

1.5   Understanding Others' Goals and Intentions: Developmental and Neuroscience Perspectives

We have considered evidence about two types of mappings:

Other → self (novel imitation)
Self → other (recognition of being imitated)

Human infants are facile at both forms of imitation, but surely adults do more. A crucial component is the psychological attributions they make. For example, if I see someone struggling to pull an object apart, I do not merely code their movements, I ascribe goals and intentions to the person.

Are we born making these attributions to the actions of others? Does this ability emerge with language? Theory of mind research addresses such questions in 3- and 4-year-old children (e.g., Flavell, 1999; Harris, 1989; M. Taylor, 1996). To begin to examine this issue at the preverbal level, I (Meltzoff, 1995) developed a procedure called the behavioral reenactment technique. The procedure capitalizes on imitation, but it uses this proclivity in a new, more abstract way. It investigates the ability to read below the visible surface behavior to the underlying goals and intentions of the actor.

One study involved showing 18-month-old infants an unsuccessful act (Meltzoff, 1995, experiment 1). For example, an adult "accidentally" under-

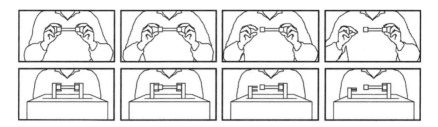

Figure 1.2
The display used to test infants' understanding of intention. The top row shows the unsuccessful attempt to separate the dumbbell by the human demonstrator. The bottom row shows a mechanical device mimicking these same movements. Infants treated the former but not the latter within a psychological framework involving goals or intentions; see the text for details. (From Meltzoff, 1995.)

or overshot a target, or tried to perform an act but his hand slipped several times; thus the goal state was not achieved (figure 1.2, top). To an adult, it was easy to read the actor's intention although he did not fulfill it. The experimental question was whether infants also saw beyond the literal body movements to the underlying goal of the act. The measure of how they interpreted the event was what they chose to reenact. In this case the correct answer was not to imitate the movement that was actually seen, but the actor's goal, which remained unfulfilled.

The study compared infants' tendency to perform the target act in several situations: (1) after they saw the full target act demonstrated, (2) after they saw the unsuccessful attempt to perform the act, and (3) after it was neither shown nor attempted. The results showed that 18-month-olds can infer the unseen goals implied by unsuccessful attempts. Infants who saw the unsuccessful attempt and infants who saw the full target act both produced target acts at a significantly higher rate than controls. Evidently young toddlers can understand our goals even if we fail to fulfill them.

I (Meltzoff, 1999b) sought to determine the earliest age at which infants inferred unfulfilled goals. The results suggest that this capacity is not innate, but first develops between 9 and 15 months of age. Infants that were 15 months old behaved much like the 18-month-olds in the original study. Those that were 9 months old, however, did not respond above baseline levels to the demonstrations of unsuccessful attempt, although they could succeed if the adult demonstrated successful acts. Bellagamba and Tomasello (1999) replicated the effect in 18-month-olds and also found that 12-month-olds were too young to respond in this way, so there is converging evidence for an important developmental change at approximately 1 year of age.

If infants can detect the underlying goal or intention of the human act, they should also be able to achieve the act using a variety of means. I tested this in a study of 18-month-olds using a dumbbell-shaped object that was too big for the infants' hands. An adult grasped the ends of the dumbbell and attempted to yank it apart, but his hands slid off, so he was unsuccessful in carrying out his intention. The dumbbell was then presented to the infants. It is interesting that the infants did not attempt to imitate the surface behavior of the adult. Instead, they used novel ways to struggle to get the gigantic toy apart. They put one end of the dumbbell between their knees and used both hands to pull it upward, or put their hands on inside faces of the cubes and pushed outward, and so on. They used *different means* than the experimenter, but these acts were directed toward the *same end*. This fits with my (Meltzoff, 1995) hypothesis that the infants had determined the goal of the act, differentiating it from the surface behavior that was observed.

Work by Want and Harris (2001, 2002) goes further and shows that 3-year-old children benefit from observing others using multiple means to achieve a goal. They benefit more from watching an adult change a failed attempt into a successful act than from watching the demonstration of successes alone. Other work also underscores the importance of goals in imitation (Bekkering et al., 2000; Gleissner et al., 2000).

In an adult framework, people's acts can be goal directed and intentional, but the motions of inanimate devices are not; they are governed purely by physics, not psychology. Do infants interpret the world in this way? In order to begin to assess this, I designed an inanimate device made of plastic and wood (Meltzoff, 1995; see figure 1.2, bottom). The device had short poles for arms and mechanical pincers for hands. It did not look human, but it traced the same spatiotemporal path that the human actor traced and manipulated the object much as the human actor did. The results showed that infants did not attribute a goal or intention to the movements of the inanimate device when its pincers slipped off the ends of a dumbbell. The infants were no more (or less) likely to pull the toy apart after seeing the unsuccessful attempt of the inanimate device than infants in the baseline condition. This was the case despite the fact that the infants pulled the dumbbell apart if the inanimate device successfully completed this act. Evidently infants make certain attributions to an inanimate device, but not others; they can understand successes, but not failures. (Successes lead to a change in the object, whereas failures leave the object intact and therefore must be interpreted at a deeper level.)[4]

As adults, we can describe the behaviors of others using either physical or psychological terms. Strict behaviorists stick to the former description precisely because they eschew appealing to invisible psychological states. By 18 months of age, infants are no longer behaviorists, if they ever were so. They do not construe the behavior of others simply as, "hold the dumbbell and then remove one hand quickly," but rather construe it as an effort at pulling. And they interpret the actions of people differently than the motions of inanimate devices.

However, finding a surprising competence at 18 months of age does not preclude further development. The adult view about intention is something like this: If another person desires x and believes that doing y will bring about x, he will intend to do y, independently of and perhaps contrary to my own beliefs, desires, and intentions about the matter. Infants are using a simpler construal. The 18-month-olds appreciate the goal-directedness of a human action (an unsuccessful attempt), but this does not mandate that infants ascribe the mature adult notion of intention as a first-person experience in the mind of the actor (see Meltzoff, 1995, pp. 847–848, for a fuller analysis).

1.5.1 Neuroscience Findings

We designed a nonverbal task in which adults processed the goals of actions while they were undergoing PET scanning (Chaminade et al., 2002).

---

4. The line of studies using the dumbbell rule out several alternative interpretations. Although some of the other stimuli used in the original study may contain clues about the affordances of an object (Huang et al., 2002), the dumbbell provides a critical test. The dumbbell remains immobile during the adult's efforts. The object never changes. Thus no affordance is revealed, nor is end-state information shown that can lead to learning by emulation. Moreover, the inanimate device traces the same spatial path as the human movements, so physically following the outward motions does not yield the response. It is therefore important that the dumbbell yielded statistically significant data when the results were analyzed individually (Meltzoff, 1995, p. 843). The effect with this particular object does not lend itself to lower-order interpretations such as those suggested by Huang et al. (2002). It is also worth noting that the distinction between the person and device is not attributable simply to infants being inhibited in the case of the inanimate device (as speculated by Heyes, 2001a) because: (1) infants imitated the device when it performed the action successfully and (2) 100% of the infants approached and picked up the toy after it was manipulated by the inanimate device, and there were no signs of wariness (see Meltzoff, 1995, pp. 844–845, for details).

The subjects watched an adult building a tower out of Lego blocks. In one condition, the subjects had to infer the adult's goal from watching the means used (they saw partial movement of the blocks, but the end state of the construction was obscured). In another condition, they had to infer the means from seeing the end state (the final tower was shown, but the movement of blocks needed to achieve the construction was obscured). The results revealed that the medial prefrontal lobe was specifically activated when the subjects were forced to infer the goal. The medial prefrontal region is known to play a critical role in adult theory-of-mind tasks (e.g., Blakemore & Decety, 2001; C. Frith & Frith, 1999). This fits well with the arguments in this chapter because it supports, at a neural level what we had hypothesized based on the developmental results—a relation between extracting goals from actions in a simple motor task and higher-order attribution of intention.

1.5.2 Implications for Theory
These experiments have the following implications:

- Infants code human acts in terms of goals.
- Infants can infer goals from people's unsuccessful attempts.
- Once infants represent these goals, they can achieve them by multiple means.
- Infants make different attributions to people than to inanimate devices; they make primitive psychological attributions to entities that are "like me."[5]
- The medial prefrontal lobe is involved in discerning the intentions of others.

1.6 Understanding Others' Perception

For adults, certain bodily movements have particular meanings. If a person looks up into the sky, bystanders follow his or her gaze. This is not imitation; the adults are trying to see what the person is looking at. Adults realize that people acquire information from afar, despite the spatial gap between perceiver and object. When do we ascribe perception to others? Is there a stage when head turns are interpreted as purely physical motions

5. We have not isolated the criteria infants use for making these attributions. For example, it could be features (eyes, face), action patterns (articulated limb movements), or other social-communicative cues to the presence of agency (S. Johnson, 2000).

with no notion that they are *directed toward* the external object, no notion of a perceiver?

Some developmental psychologists have taken this conservative stance (Corkum & Moore, 1995). They argue that the infant visually tracks the adult's head as it rotates; this is a physical motion in space and so the infant's own head is dragged to the correct hemi-field. Once it is there, the object is encountered by happenstance. Presto! Infants turn in the direction of adults, but it is all done by the laws of physics and geometry; psychology has nothing to do with it. I believe that infants can do more than this.

A recent study examined whether infants understand the object-directedness of adult attentive movements (Brooks & Meltzoff, 2002). Two identical objects were used, and the adult turned to look at one of them with no other cues. For one group of infants, the adult turned to the target object with *eyes open*, and for the other, the adult turned with *eyes closed*. The adult's head movement was identical in both. The findings showed that 12- to 18-month-old infants turned selectively, seeking out the target significantly more often when the adult turned with eyes open than with eyes closed. Furthermore, a microanalysis showed that the infants fixated on the distal object for a longer time when they followed the adult's open eyes. This visual inspection is important because the object, in itself, is the same whether the adult turns with open or closed eyes. The object takes on special valence because it is looked at by another person. The infants also pointed to the object more when the adult looked at it with open than with closed eyes. This involves a different motor movement than the adult's, indicating that the symmetrical head movement is not purely imitation (figure 1.3).

This is sophisticated behavior, but it is not based on innate knowledge. Recent research shows that 9-month-olds turn just as readily in the direction of an adult's head turn, regardless of whether the adult's eyes are open or closed (Brooks & Meltzoff, 2003). Nine-month-olds do not take into account the status of the adult's perceptual organs, the eyes.

Inanimate obstacles can also block one's view. Brooks and Meltzoff (2002) conducted another experiment, duplicating all aspects of the first, but using a headband and a blindfold. The headband allowed the adult to have visual access to the object, whereas the blindfold blocked the adult's visual access. The results were very different than the eye-closure case. The 12-month-olds turned to follow the adult even when the adult wore a blindfold. This is not just a matter of blindfolds causing some general suppression of activity. Quite the contrary; infants make the mistake of

Figure 1.3
Gaze following by 1-year-old infants. Infants selectively look when the adult turns
with eyes open versus eyes closed, showing they take into account the status of the
adult's eyes, not just the gross direction of head movement.

following the "gaze" of the adult wearing the blindfold. They refrain from
looking when the adult has closed eyes, but do turn to look when the
adult has a blindfold. It is as if they do not understand that blindfolds
block perception.[6] Perhaps they understand eye closure more easily than
blindfolds, because experience with their own eyes teaches them that this
biological movement cuts off visual perception in their own case. Other
explanations are possible, but if it could be substantiated, it would be a
particularly compelling case of "like me" projection.

One way of testing this is to give infants first-person experience with
blindfolds. Meltzoff and Brooks (2004) conducted such a study, and the
results are very provocative. One group of 12-month-old infants was shown
that opaque objects blocked their view. Their view was blocked when the
blindfold was held to *their* eyes, and was restored again when the blindfold
was removed. This experience had nothing to do with the experimenter's
viewpoint; it was a first-person experience. In the critical test, the adult put
the blindfold over her own eyes. This was the first time the infants were
presented with the blindfolded adult. The results showed that infants now

6. The journal paper also considers several other possible interpretations and provides data bearing on them. For example, the infants were not wary of the blindfold
or eye closures.

interpreted the blindfold correctly. They did not turn when the adult wore the blindfold. In further control groups the infants were allowed to familiarize themselves with the blindfold, but without experiencing blocking of the view. This had no effect. They still mistakenly followed the blindfolded adult's "gaze" in this case.

1.6.1 Implications for Theory

This work has the following implications:

- One-year-old infants follow the gaze of adults.
- They understand adult gaze as directed at an object, not as a meaningless body movement.
- One-year-old infants interpret some obstacles to perception (eye closure) differently than others (blindfolds).
- First-person experience with blindfolds changes infants' interpretation of others who wear blindfolds. Crucially, they use first-person experience to make third-person attributions.

1.7 Nature's Share: What Is Innate?

Theorists are drawn to questions about the origins of action coding and seeing others as psychological agents. This question can be addressed from evolutionary, developmental, and neural viewpoints.

1.7.1 Does Experience Play a Role in Mirror Neuron Development?

There is a burgeoning literature in neuroscience concerning the coding of actions and how organisms map observed actions onto their own acts. Mirror neurons are perhaps the most celebrated example (Rizzolatti et al., 1996a; Rizzolatti, vol. 1, ch. 1, and Gallese, vol. 1, ch. 3). Are mirror neurons innate? This may be the case, but the role of experience in forming mirror neurons deserves more consideration than it has been given.

Mirror neurons are activated whether a monkey sees or performs the act of grasping an object. These neurons seem to code the act, regardless of whether it is performed by the self or the other. The developmental question I would ask is whether this is an innately specified coding. It may not be. Adult monkeys have repeatedly watched themselves grasp objects. Mirror neurons could code visuomotor associations forged from such learning experiences. Such gradual learning, if it occurs, would influence the philosophical implications that can be drawn (see e.g., Goldman, vol. 2, ch. 2 and Gordon, vol. 2, ch. 3).

There are two ways of testing whether mirror neurons develop through experience. One is to test newborn monkeys. A second approach is selective rearing in which the experimenter arranges a situation that prevents monkeys from visually monitoring their own grasps, for example, by wearing a collar that blocks the view of their hands. The critical question for theory is whether mirror neurons can be found in the brains of such animals. If both populations have functioning mirror neurons, it would suggest that mirror neurons do not emerge from learned associations of repeatedly seeing oneself grasp an object. It would be widely agreed, I think, that it is uncertain how these results would turn out.

1.7.2 Innate Facial Imitation

If one's question concerns origins, developmental studies are crucial. The philosopher's queries about man's original nature are not directly answered by tests of adult animals and neurologically damaged adult humans. These need to be supplemented with tests of human young. Facial imitation provides such an opportunity. Human infants have a natural collar; they cannot see their own faces. If they are young enough, they will never have had a chance to see themselves in a mirror or to learn the associations in question. Human neonates provide a direct test of the correspondence problem: how we come to relate acts of self and other.

Meltzoff and Moore (1983a, 1989) discovered that newborns imitate facial acts. The mean age of these infants was 32 hours. The youngest child was 42 minutes old at the time of test. Facial imitation suggests an innate mapping between observation and execution in the human case. Moreover, the studies provide information about the nature of the machinery infants use to connect observation and execution. The studies require a little patience to get through, but it is worth it, because the starting state is so vital for theories.

In Meltzoff and Moore (1977), 12- to 21-day-olds were shown to imitate four different gestures, including facial and manual movements. The infants confused neither actions nor body parts. They responded differentially to tongue protrusion with tongue protrusion and not lip protrusion, showing that they can identify the specific *body part*. They also responded differentially to lip protrusion versus lip opening, showing that different *action patterns* can be imitated with the same body part. This is confirmed by research showing that infants differentially imitate two different kinds of movements with the tongue (Meltzoff & Moore, 1994, 1997). Such differential imitation and other evidence cited later suggests that imitation is not a diffuse arousal response of the type suggested by Jones (1996) (for further review and analysis, see Meltzoff, 2002b).

Tongue protrusion is researchers' favorite choice in studies of early imitation. Sometimes this is construed as meaning that tongue protrusion is the only gesture that can be imitated (Anisfeld, 1996). However, "most common" is not the same as "only one." The tongue protrusion gesture is commonly used because it is the most dramatic case, and it is the easiest to score from videotape. However, there are many published studies documenting a range of acts that can be imitated, as the following list shows.

- Mouth opening: Fontaine, 1984; Heimann, 1989, 2002; Heimann et al., 1989; Heimann & Schaller, 1985; Kugiumutzakis, 1999; Legerstee, 1991; Maratos, 1982; Meltzoff & Moore, 1977, 1983a, 1992, 1994
- Hand movements: Meltzoff & Moore, 1977; Vinter, 1986
- Emotional expressions: Field et al., 1983, 1986, 1982
- Head movements: Meltzoff & Moore, 1989
- Lip and cheek movements: Fontaine, 1984; Kugiumutzakis, 1999; Meltzoff & Moore, 1977; Reissland, 1988
- Eye blinking: Fontaine, 1984; Kugiumutzakis, 1999
- Two types of tongue protrusion: Meltzoff & Moore, 1994, 1997

In all, there are more than twenty-four studies of early imitation from thirteen independent laboratories. The empirical evidence from multiple laboratories moves us beyond the "lone" tongue-protrusion notion. Nonetheless, young infants cannot imitate the full range of gestures copied by older children, and there is development in imitation. For example, I have argued that the neonate is less self-conscious about imitating than the older child (Meltzoff & Moore, 1997).

The chief question concerns the neural and psychological processes linking the observation and execution of matching acts. How do infants solve the correspondence problem? Two discoveries are key.

First, early imitation is not restricted to immediate duplication. In one experiment, the infants had a pacifier in their mouths so that they couldn't imitate during the demonstration (Meltzoff & Moore, 1977). The pacifier was then withdrawn. The results were that the infants initiated their imitative response in the subsequent 2.5-minute response period while looking at a passive face. In a more dramatic example, 6-week-olds performed deferred imitation after a 24-hour delay (Meltzoff & Moore, 1994). The infants saw a gesture on one day and returned the next day to see an adult with a passive-face pose. The infants stared at the face and then imitated the gesture from long-term memory.

Second, infants correct their imitative response. They converge on the match without feedback from the experimenter. An infant's first response to seeing a facial gesture is activation of the corresponding body part. For example, when infants see an adult protrude his or her tongue, there is a quieting of other body parts and an activation of the tongue. They do not necessarily protrude their tongue at first, but may elevate it or move it inside the oral cavity. The important point is that the tongue, rather than the lips or fingers, is energized before the movement is isolated. It is as if young infants isolate *what* part of their body to move before knowing *how* to move it. Meltzoff and Moore (1997) call this organ identification. Neurophysiological data show that visual displays of parts of the face and hands activate specific brain sites in monkeys (Desimone, 1991; Gross, 1992; Gross & Sergent, 1992; Jellema et al., 2002; Perrett et al., 1992; Rolls, 1992) and related work is emerging in human studies (Buccino et al., 2001). These new neuroscience findings fit closely with the finding of correct activation of a body part by neonates. Specific body parts could be neurally represented and serve as a foundation for imitation in infants.

1.7.3 Active Intermodal Mapping Hypothesis

Meltzoff and Moore proposed that facial imitation is based on active inter-modal mapping (AIM) (Meltzoff & Moore, 1977, 1994, 1997). Figure 1.4 provides a conceptual schematic of the AIM hypothesis. The key claim is that imitation is a matching-to-target process. The active nature of the matching process is captured by the proprioceptive feedback loop. The loop allows infants' motor performance to be evaluated against the seen target and serves as a basis for correction. AIM proposes that such comparison is possible because the observation and execution of human acts are coded within a common framework. We call it a supramodal act space, because it is not restricted to modality-specific information (visual, tactile, motor, etc.). Metaphorically, we can say that exteroception (perception of others) and proprioception (perception of self) speak the same language from birth; there is no need for "association." AIM does not rule out the existence of certain basic acts that can be imitated on first try without the need for feedback, but it allows proprioceptive feedback and the correction of responses for novel acts. A more detailed analysis of the functional architecture of AIM and its proposed solution to the correspondence problem is provided elsewhere (Meltzoff & Moore, 1997).

This hypothesis of a supramodal framework that emerged from developmental science fits well with proposals from cognitive science (the common coding thesis of W. Prinz, 2002) and discoveries in neuroscience

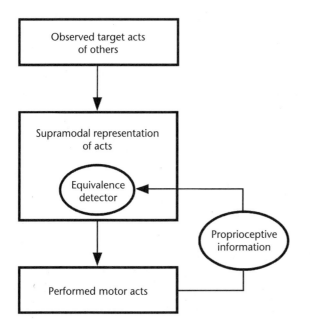

Figure 1.4
The AIM hypothesis for imitation. (From Meltzoff & Moore, 1997.)

concerning shared neural substrates for perception and action (Decety, 2002c; Iacoboni et al., 1999; Rizzolatti et al., 2001; vol. 1, chs. 1 by Rizzolatti, 2 by Iacoboni, 3 by Gallese, and 4 by Decety and Chaminade). An important task for the future is to analyze the commonalities and differences in these proposed mechanisms, and relevant papers are beginning to emerge (e.g., Meltzoff & Decety, 2003; Rizzolatti et al., 2002).

1.7.4 Implications for Theory
The work described in the preceding section has the following implications for theory.

• Newborns imitate facial acts that they have never seen themselves perform.
• In humans there is an innate observation-execution pathway.
• This is mediated by structures that allow infants to defer imitation to another point in time and to correct their imitation without feedback from the experimenter.
• Recent discoveries in developmental psychology, adult cognitive science, and neuroscience are converging to help us specify at multiple levels of analysis the *lingua franca* uniting perception and production.

1.8   The Importance of Development in Understanding Other Minds: A Third Way

Fodor thinks that infants innately assign adult commonsense psychology to people:

Here is what I would have done if I had been faced with this problem in designing Homo sapiens. I would have made a knowledge of commonsense Homo sapiens psychology innate; that way no one would have to spend time learning it.... The empirical evidence that God did it the way I would have isn't, in fact, unimpressive. (Fodor, 1987, p. 132)

The opposing school is that newborns lack any inkling that other humans have psychological properties. It is claimed, for example, that the child is born a "solipsist" (Piaget, 1954) or is in a state of "normal autism" (Mahler et al., 1975), treating people the same as things. It is a long way, probably an impossible path, from there to commonsense psychology.

Modern developmental scientists, including myself, have been trying to develop a third way. It grants far more to the newborn than the second view, while stopping short of the first. In my view, infant imitation and the neural representations that underlie it provide an innate foundation for building adult commonsense psychology, but infants do not possess the adult framework to begin with. Infants imitate at birth, but they do not infer intentions from the unsuccessful efforts of others or understand "perception" in others. This is hardly grounds for Fodorian nativism; God apparently did not give young infants a full-blown commonsense psychology. It is equally true, however, that young infants outstrip Piagetian theory. What we seem to need is a new theory of development, a "starting-state nativism" that includes a rich understanding of people and things but still leaves gaps to be filled in by structured experience.

1.9   "Like Me" Theory: A Developmental Sketch

Imitation indicates that newborns, at some level of processing, no matter how primitive, can map actions they see performed by others onto actions of their own body. Human acts are especially relevant to infants because they look like the infant feels himself to be and because they are events that infants can intend. When a newborn sees a human act, it may be meaningful: "That seen event is like this felt event."

The innate capacity to construe certain movements in the environment as "me relevant" has cascading developmental effects in infants. First, the world of material objects can be divided into those entities that perform these acts (people) and those that do not (things). Second, the *lingua franca* of human acts provides access to other people that is not afforded by things.[7]

The ability of young infants to interpret the bodily acts of others in terms of their own acts and experiences gives them a tool for cracking the problem of other minds (vol. 2, chs. 2 by Goldman, and 3 by Gordon). This idea can be developed further by applying the model from table 1.1 to the examples of following a gaze and understanding the other's intentions.

The crux of the "like me" hypothesis is that infants may use their own intentional actions as a framework for interpreting the intentional actions of others. Consider the goal-directed striving and try-and-try-again behavior used in my behavioral reenactment studies (Meltzoff, 1995). Infants have goals and act intentionally. They have experienced their own failed plans and unfulfilled intentions. Indeed, in the second half-year of life they are obsessed with the success and failure of their plans. They mark such self-failures with special labels. Psycholinguistic research shows that among the toddler's earliest words are "uh-oh," and in England, "oh bugger." They use these terms to comment on a mismatch between their own intentions and real-world outcomes (Gopnik & Meltzoff, 1986). They also experiment with unsuccessful efforts by repeating the solution (and the failure) numerous times until it comes under voluntary control. During such episodes, infants often vary the means and try and try again. When an infant sees another act in this same way, the infant's self-experience could suggest that there is a goal, plan, or intention beyond the surface behavior. Thus, infants would interpret an adult's failed attempts, and the behavioral envelope in which they occur, as a pattern of strivings, rather than ends in themselves. In

7. Infants with sensory or motor deficits, such as blindness or motor paralysis, present an interesting case. Because AIM postulates organ identification and a supramodal framework, the deficits can be compensated for. Development may be slowed, but not blocked. Supramodal representation allows one modality to substitute for another; for example, facial organs and actions may be identified by tactile exploration in the case of blindness. Autism presents another interesting case. Young children with autism have profound deficits in understanding other minds (e.g., Baron-Cohen et al., 1993, 2000), and our own studies of autism reveal deficits in the same imitation tasks we used with typically developing infants (G. Dawson et al., 1998). Others have also reported deficits on other imitation tasks (for a review, see S. Rogers, 1999). These results from autism are highly compatible with the framework presented here (Meltzoff & Gopnik, 1993), but are also open to alternative interpretations.

short, infants could come to understand the goals and intentions of others through experience with their own intentions: "Those acts are intentional, just like mine."

Similarly, understanding another's gaze could benefit from one's own perceptual experiences. Infants in the first year of life imitate head movements and eye blinking (Fontaine, 1984; Meltzoff, 1988a; Meltzoff & Moore, 1989; Piaget, 1951/1962). They thus can register the similarity between their own head movements and those of others and between their own eyelid closures and those of others. The subjective experiences that infants gain from turning in order to see could thus be used to make sense of the similar actions of others. Moreover, the infant's experience is that closing its own eyes cuts off perceptual access. Because infants can map their own eye closures onto the eye closures of others (as shown by the imitation of blinking), there is an elementary foundation for understanding perception in others. This also makes sense of the fact that young infants have more advanced understanding of what it means for others to close their eyes than they do of others wearing blindfolds (Brooks & Meltzoff, 2002). Our intervention experiment gave them first-person experience with blindfolds, and they were immediately able to use this to understand the blindfold-wearing other in a new way (Meltzoff & Brooks, 2004). This seems to be a using first-person experience to interpret others and therefore lends support to the model in table 1.1.

It has long been thought that the equivalence between self and other is integral to our adult commonsense psychology (J. Baldwin, 1906; Hume, 1740/1984; Husserl, 1953/1977; Nietzsche, 1881/1977; Smith, 1759/1976). Empathy, role-taking, and all varieties of putting yourself in someone else's shoes emotionally and cognitively seem to depend on this. The problem has always been that this equivalence was thought to be a late achievement in ontogeny and dependent on language. The findings from developmental science, suggest that infants already register the equivalence between acts of self and other. It is innate. This equivalence colors infants' very first interactions and interpretations of the social world and is foundational for human development.

1.10   Booting Up a Baby to Read Minds

There is a kinship between the problem of understanding other minds and the problem of imitation. This kinship is not merely a surface similarity; the two problems are causally related from the perspective of developmental science and neuroscience.

Philosophers are struck by the fact that we experience our own thoughts and feelings but do not see ourselves from the outside as others see us. We perceive visual and auditory signals emanating from others but do not directly experience their mental states. There seems to be a wide gulf between knowing the self and the other.

Likewise, developmental scientists and neuroscientists are struck by the correspondence problem in imitation. Infants can see an adult's face but cannot see their own faces. They can feel their own face move but have no access to the feeling of movement in others. Facial imitation exposes the gap between self and other most dramatically, but the same issue is posed by other types of imitation in both adults and animals.

Fodor is correct that solipsism and blank-slate empiricism are too impoverished to characterize the human starting state. However, this does not mean that adult commonsense psychology is implanted in the mind at birth or matures independent of experience. Here is an alternative to Fodor's creation myth. Nature designed a baby with an imitative brain; culture immerses the child in social play with psychological agents perceived to be "like me." Adult commonsense psychology is the product.[8]

Acknowledgments

Work on this chapter was supported by a grant from the National Institutes of Health (HD-22514). I thank P. Kuhl and B. Repacholi for comments on an earlier draft and R. Gordon and A. Goldman for feedback on the conference paper, which sharpened my writing about infant social cognition in the absence of their having language and explicit step-by-step reasoning powers. I also gratefully acknowledge the valuable collaboration of J. Decety, R. Brooks, K. Moore, and A. Gopnik, and the assistance of C. Harris and C. Fisher.

8. See comments on this chapter by Harris (vol. 2, ch. 8.1, p. 173) and Humphrey (vol. 2, ch. 8.2, p. 178); see also Goldman, vol. 2, ch. 2, p. 79; Gordon, vol. 2, ch. 3, p. 95; and Anisfeld, vol. 2, ch. 4, p. 107. ED.

2 Imitation, Mind Reading, and Simulation

Alvin I. Goldman

2.1 Imitation and Mind Reading: What Is the Connection?

Two of the most studied phenomena of the social mind are imitation and mind reading. What is the connection between the two, if any? It is not obvious that there is a substantial connection. Imitation is normally defined as some sort of behavior-behavior relationship, whereas mind reading is a mind-mind relationship. Nonetheless, there might be interesting connections between them. One of the phenomena might be a developmental precursor of the other; or proficiency at one task might enhance proficiency at the other. This could go in either direction; imitation might facilitate mind reading, or mind reading might facilitate imitation. A third possibility is that the two phenomena share a common cause; a single underlying process might underpin both imitation and mind reading. This chapter explores some of these possible connections.

2.2 Approaches to Mind Reading

Before turning to the imitation–mind reading connection, we should distinguish three different approaches to mind reading: the *rationality theory*, the *theory theory*, and the *simulation theory*. If there is an imitation–mind reading connection, its specific nature may well hinge on which of these approaches is correct. The so-called rationality approach has been championed by philosophers like Dennett (1987) and Davidson (1984). This approach says that ordinary people assume that their peers are rational and proceed to impute to them those desires and beliefs it would be rational of them to have in their circumstances. I know of no attempt by these or other rationality theorists, however, to draw a connection between imitation and mind reading.[1] Nor do I myself see any natural way of developing

1. See and cf. Gordon 2002 and vol. 2, ch. 3; Hurley, vol. 1, ch. 7. ED.

ɡnore the rationality theory and fix my atten-
ɹor approaches: theory theory (TT) and simula-
ᴨapter will not address the general debate between
ᴄussion will be confined to links between imitation
ᴊ that have been or might be proposed under the aegis of
ᴋelatively greater attention will be given to simulationism,
ᴢ I find ST a generally superior theory (Goldman, 1989, 1992a,
ᴊ1; Gallese & Goldman, 1998) and because the connections be-
ımitation and mind reading seem more promising under ST than
ᴀer TT.

Both TT and ST provide accounts of how ordinary people go about the business of attributing mental states. TT says that attributions of mental states, to both self and others, are guided by a commonsense psychological "theory." A theory, in a strict sense, is a body of propositions that includes (putative) laws or generalizations. Thus, a psychological theory is a body of propositions featuring psychological generalizations. If such generalizations are to be useful in predicting others' mental states, they must be intrapersonal, diachronic generalizations, specifying the transitions that a given psychological system will make from some initial states to successor states. According to TT, a mental attributor is like a scientist who approaches other people's minds—and her own—in the same way she approaches any system. She forms beliefs, or perhaps probability judgments, about the current state or condition of the target system. She extracts from her knowledge base some psychological generalizations and uses them to infer subsequent or prior states of the system. In the case of physics, the contents of a theorizer's beliefs are physical states of the system in question and generalizations about such states. In the case of mind reading, the contents of the attributor's beliefs are mental states and generalizations about mental states. Another feature of the TT approach concerns how the commonsense theory is learned. According to TT (at least the brand of TT of interest here), learning by infants has the same character as scientific learning; it proceeds by testing old theories against new evidence and sometimes creating new theories to replace old ones (Gopnik & Meltzoff, 1997; Wellman, 1990; Perner, 1991a).

What are the distinctive posits of ST? A prototypical mind-reading routine of the simulationist type has three main steps. First, the attributor creates in herself pretend states intended to match those of the target. In other words, the attributor attempts to put herself in the target's "mental shoes" (Gordon, 1986; Heal, 1986; Goldman, 1989). The kinds of mental states that can be pretended range across the mental spectrum and include perceptions, desires, beliefs, hopes, plans, sensations, and emotions. The ond step is to feed these initial pretend states into some mechanism of attributor's own psychology, e.g., a decision-making or emotion-generati mechanism, and allow that mechanism to operate on the pretend states as to generate one or more new states. If the attributor wishes to predict a target's decision, for example, she might create pretend desires and beliefs (which she takes the target to have) and let her decision-making system operate on them so as to produce a (feigned) decision. Third, the attributor assigns the output state to the target as a state the target will undergo (or has already undergone). This three-step routine is the most full-blown simulation heuristic. There might also be shorter versions, however, such as a two-step routine. Here a pretend state is created in the attributor, who simply imputes that state to the target without feeding it into any mechanism for further processing. Clearly, the distinctive idea of ST is that mind reading is subserved by pretense and attempted replication. A mind reader adopts the mental "position" of the target and replicates (or attempts to replicate) mental activity appropriate to that position.

The chief contrast between ST and TT concerns the attributor's attempt to replicate mental states of the target, which includes the initial mental pretense. For ST this is a core part of mind reading; for (pure) TT, it plays no role whatever. According to TT, an attributor uses only descriptions of a target's states and psychological regularities. The attributor does not try to clothe herself in those very states, so as to mentally mimic or "impersonate" the target. All processing in the attributor is purely inferential processing, which moves from beliefs to other beliefs about the states of the target. TT posits no essential use of mental pretense by attributors.

2.3   Theory Theory, Imitation, and Mind Reading

Given these core ideas of TT and ST, let us now ask what stories each might tell about the connection between imitation and mind reading. I start with TT. An early suggestion of an imitation-mind reading connection was floated by Meltzoff and Gopnik (1993) and later pursued by Meltzoff with other collaborators. Since Meltzoff and Gopnik are leading theory theorists, one naturally expects their approach to follow TT contours, and this is realized to some extent in their paper. However, as I will argue, it is not easy to spell out their story so that it is fully compatible with the dominant themes of TT.

As background, recall that Meltzoff and Moore (1977, 1983a) discovered that infants as young as 42 minutes can display facial imitation. How can

copy the facial expressions modeled before
.e is that an infant of this age has never seen her
ner outward facial expression with internally ex-
,. So how can she know which *felt* movements would
,ession *seen* in others? To explain the imitation ability,
,ore postulate an innate crossmodal (or supramodal) match-
visual perceptions of adult facial acts and proprioceptive in-
about their own acts. Given this matching, infants are said to
and, at some level, a correspondence between the self and the

A self–other correspondence is an important part of Meltzoff and Gopnik's story about imitation. In order for a commonsense psychology to
get off the ground, they say, infants must make a basic distinction between
persons and things. Imitation is supposed to be the infant's criterion for
which things are persons. Persons are "entities that can be imitated and
also who imitate me" (Meltzoff & Gopnik, 1993, p. 337). But what else does
the infant associate with persons? If the ability to imitate and be imitated
exhausts the infant's concept of a person, how does identifying something
as a person constitute any progress toward folk psychologizing? Perhaps
"persons" are antecedently understood as things that have, or are capable
of having, mental states. How, then, does the infant know that what she
imitates and what can imitate her is a person, i.e., the bearer of mental
states? Perhaps Meltzoff and Gopnik mean to suggest that the mentality-
imitability relationship is known innately. If so, this piece of innate knowledge is the main source of commonsense psychology, not what is yielded
by imitation per se. Furthermore, even the conjunction of the propositions
"Whatever is imitable has mental states" and "That thing is imitable" goes
nowhere in helping the infant determine which *specific* mental states
another person is in at a given time. Specific mental states, however, are
clearly what mind readers seek to determine, and the way they make such
determinations is what Meltzoff and Gopnik, like all theorists of mentalizing, should hope to explain.

Meltzoff and Gopnik marshall additional resources that might help provide such explanations. They posit innate knowledge of *specific* equivalences between external behavior and internal proprioceptive states or
motor intentions. The infant's "starting-state" theory includes correspondences between the other's observed bodily movements and the infant's
own experienced mental states. It is not immediately clear, however, how
this knowledge can contribute to the assignment of specific mental states
either to the self or to the other. Knowing which specific motor intentions

of mine can produce behavior that matches the behavior of another can explain how I can execute such a matching, but it does not address the question of how I can know, or infer, what mental states the other is in. Does it, perhaps, help me determine what my *own* mental states are? Knowing one of these correspondences would enable me to infer that *if* I match the other's behavior, then I must have had such-and-such a motor intention. But Meltzoff and Gopnik nowhere suggest that the value of imitation is that it helps one determine one's own mental states in this circuitous fashion. In fact, as we will soon see, Meltzoff elsewhere assumes that no such inference is necessary because one has direct knowledge of one's own states.

Meltzoff and Gopnik definitely contend that infants like to imitate and be imitated because they learn things from this activity, things relevant to their growing competence at folk psychology. They argue that imitation is used as a "discovery procedure" in human social development. But exactly how does imitation contribute to the child's development of competence in mind reading? I do not find a clear statement of such a contribution in their 1993 paper, but perhaps it can be found in later writings, especially by Meltzoff and others.

According to Meltzoff, when a child observes a creature that is *behaviorally* "like me," this prompts an inference that the other is also *mentally* "like me," using an analogical argument familiar to philosophers. Since the infant knows what she is mentally like in certain circumstances, this can help her identify the specific mental states of others under similar circumstances. Here are some passages articulating these ideas.

Through experience [infants] may learn that when they act in particular ways, they themselves have certain concomitant internal states (proprioceptions, emotions, intentions, etc.). Having detected this regularity, infants have grounds for making the inference that when they see another person act in the same way that they do, the person has internal states similar to their own. (Meltzoff, 1999a, p. 390)

Similarly, Meltzoff and Moore write:

This grasp of the other as like oneself ... allows the infant to use the self as a framework for enriching its understanding of the other. Having done an action itself, the infant has subjective, experiential knowledge of that act [more precisely, of feelings associated with that act]. When the infant sees another perform an act that he knows is like his own, the infant can interpret the seen act in terms of this subjective experience. (Meltzoff & Moore, 1995, p. 65)

These passages suggest a sequence of inferential steps that might be spelled out as follows:

(1) When I act in way *w*, the action is preceded or accompanied by internal states *x*, *y*, and *z* (proprioceptive sensations, motor intentions, etc.).
(2) Therefore anyone who acts in way *w* will also experience internal states *x*, *y*, and *z*.
(3) This person now before me is acting in way *w*.
(4) Therefore he is now experiencing, or just experienced, internal states *x*, *y*, and *z*.

This formulation clarifies how an infant might apply a psychological law or regularity. Statement (2) articulates the sort of regularity in question. Notice, however, that this is a backward, or correlational, law rather than a forward law. It does not describe transitions from one state to a subsequent state of the system. Nonetheless, it may qualify as a folk-psychological law.

At least two problems may be raised, however, for this analogical approach to the child's thinking about folk psychology. The first is an epistemological problem that philosophers of mind have raised for the analogical approach. Epistemologically speaking, how solid is the inference from (1) to (2)? Can one reasonably project from one's own case to that of others? One's own case, after all, is but a single instance. Can a correlation between action and mental states in a single case really support an inductive inference to an analogous correlation for other people (or bodies), whose internal states cannot—perhaps even in principle—be verified in any other fashion? Although this problem is frequently posed in the philosophical literature, I will not press it. The mere fact that a style of inference is epistemologically problematic does not show that it is psychologically problematic. Infants might be programmed to perform a certain type of inference even if, from an epistemological standpoint, that type of inference is rather shaky. (Similar issues arise in connection with a language learner's "inference" to rules of grammar from a very restricted evidential base.) It is no criticism of a psychological hypothesis that it imputes to children, or even adults, a mode of inference that falls short of some ideal standard of epistemological rationality or justification.

A more serious problem for Meltzoff's approach concerns the status of proposition (1) rather than the inference from (1) to (2). The statement that the child knows (1) is premised on the assumption that she can have direct, experiential knowledge of her own mental states, in the present example, proprioceptive sensations or motor intentions. But how is this direct, experiential knowledge compatible with the TT approach? In fact, the TT approach to self-knowledge is sharply at variance with the postulation of direct knowledge. According to TT, knowledge of first-person mental states strictly parallels knowledge of third-person mental states; both rely on theoretical inference (presumably from premises about behavior). This theoretical-inference approach is emphatically defended by Gopnik (1993), who maintains that people, including children, determine their own mental states in the same theory-driven way by which they determine the mental states of others, via inferences using folk-psychological laws. If this approach is carried through systematically, the child would first have to know (or believe) folk-psychological laws *before* she could determine her own mental states. Meltzoff's story, by contrast, assumes direct, noninferential knowledge of particular first-person mental states. Such direct knowledge is incompatible with a pure, undiluted, version of TT. So it seems to me that Meltzoff and Gopnik do not have an internally consistent *theory-theory* story of how imitation is connected with the development of mind reading.

It should be emphasized that my criticism of Meltzoff's way of connecting imitation to mind reading appeals to internal inconsistency, that is, its lack of consistency with a *pure* form of TT. I am not leveling a general critique of the direct access thesis. We should be skeptical, I think, of Meltzoff's application of such a thesis to young infants, but I do not urge a blanket rejection of all forms of direct access. However, a precise formulation of a tenable direct access thesis, one that includes all needed qualifications, is outside the scope of this chapter. It is worth remarking, moreover, that not all simulationists accept direct knowledge of one's own mental states. Simulation theory is primarily a theory about third-person mental-state attribution, and simulation theorists differ quite strongly on the question of self-knowledge, or self-attribution (e.g., contrast Gordon, 1996 with Goldman, 2000).

2.4 Perspective-Taking, Autism, and Imitation

I now turn to simulationist views of the imitation-mind reading connection. At least two different ST-related ideas have been floated about the imitation-mind reading connection. One says that a simulation-related phenomenon is at the root of imitation. This should not be interpreted as a claim that all imitation is guided by full-fledged mind reading. That would conflict with the fact that neonatal imitation ontogenetically precedes even primitive mind reading. The proposal is best interpreted as the weaker claim that simulational mechanisms guide at least some imitation as well as mind reading (at any rate, a good deal of mind reading, if not all of it). The second idea proposes a quite different connection between imitation and mind reading, essentially reversing the direction of explanation. It says that imitation plays a pivotal role in the development of advanced mind reading, via mechanisms of a simulationist kind.

This section explores the first of these connections (corresponding to the third alternative mentioned in section 2.1). The idea is that mental simulation is a crucial mechanism for both imitation and mind reading. The principal driving force behind this idea consists in the evidence that autism is associated not only with a well-known deficit in mind reading but also a deficit in imitation. This suggests a common cause of these deficits, a dysfunction responsible for both of them. If the root of this dysfunction lies in simulational mechanisms, this would support the idea that there is an important connection between imitation and simulation-driven mind reading.

As explained in section 2.2, the fundamental idea of mental simulation is that mind readers go about their task by putting themselves, imaginatively, in a target's mental "shoes." Many writers speak of taking the other person's "perspective," where this can mean adopting either their specifically perceptual perspective or, more broadly, their nonperceptual perspective as well, e.g., their desires, beliefs, and other mental attitudes. Critical to ST is the idea that in trying to impute mental states to others, an attributor typically has to set aside her own actual mental states, including perceptual states, and substitute those of the target. If one has trouble executing these kinds of mental operations, one will have trouble with many mind-reading tasks. If it can be shown that the same type of subjects who have trouble with mind-reading tasks—as is well known of autistics— also have trouble with imitation tasks requiring perspective reversals, that would tend to support the claim that proficiencies in mind reading and in (certain aspects of) imitation have a certain common source. This is the theme of the present section.

It must be conceded that proponents of TT will deny that mental simulation is the only way of accounting for success or failure at perspective-taking. They would not readily cede this territory to ST. It is not part of this chapter's mission, however, to take up this issue between TT and ST. I only adduce the kind of evidence that advocates of ST have found, or are likely to find, congenial to their approach, without trying to settle the debate that might still be pursued by theory theorists.

DeMyer and colleagues (DeMyer et al., 1972) first described the difficulty that autistic children have with imitation. Another investigator who found imitation deficits in autism was Ohta (1987), whose findings hint at a simulational source. Ohta studied autistic children with an average chrono-logical age of 10 years. In a series of gesture imitation tests, including finger and hand movements, the children were instructed to look at the model and mimic it. In one gesture, the examiner faced the subject and waved the left hand with an open palm facing outward, toward the subject. In this task some autistic children displayed what Ohta called partial imitation, which involved the failure to reproduce the target gesture from the vantage point of the model. These autistic children placed their palms inward, toward themselves, rather than outward, an error that never appeared in control subjects. Similar errors were made by about half the autistic children on each of two other imitation tasks, which corresponded to the competence of 3-year-old normal children. Ohta concluded that partial imitation, which seems to be some sort of failure of perspective-taking, is a disorder in imitation of gestures.

A distinctly simulationist interpretation of Ohta's findings was later proposed by Braten (1998). In face-to-face situations, remarks Braten, the reenactment of gestures by infants depends on perceptual reversal of the model's movements. To imitate properly in the outward-facing palms task, the child must leave his egocentric perspective and adopt that of the model, who sees the back of her hand rather than her palm. Braten says that the imitator must engage in "virtual co-enactment" of the model's movements *as if* he were the co-author of those movements. Although this terminology differs from standard simulationist terminology, Braten's idea is clearly simulationist, as he himself indicates.

Sally Rogers and Bruce Pennington (1991) surveyed the then-existing lit-erature on imitation tests with autistic subjects and proposed for the first time that imitation is a key early foundation in the normal development of mind reading. Early capacities involving imitation, emotion sharing, and theory of mind, they said, are specifically deficient in autism. Rogers and Pennington specifically suggested that autism involves a biological impair-ment of the capacity to coordinate self and other representations, prevent-ing the infant with autism from developing the notion that the other is a template of the self.

Soon after Rogers and Pennington's review, the picture was muddied by apparent nonreplications of imitation deficits in autistic subjects. How-ever, Rogers (1999) revisited the issue and found methodological faults in the nonreplication studies. In several of them, almost all the subjects per-formed at or near ceiling levels, so that possible group differences might have been obscured. These ceiling effects prevented the extraction of any information from the data. Rogers concluded that "every methodologically rigorous study so far published has found an autism-specific deficit in motor imitation" (S. Rogers 1999, p. 262).

Whiten and Brown (1998) pursued the question of imitation problems for autistic subjects. Their samples featured three categories of autistic subjects: autistic adults, autistic children, and what they call "young" autistics, i.e., children with a chronological age of 5. Their overall results did not show the general deficit in imitation implied by the Rogers and Pennington theory, because some imitative competence appears largely intact in all except the young autistic sample. However, imitative deficiencies in the young autistics were very striking. In "do-as-I-do" imitation tests, a group of normal 5–6-year-olds and even a group of children with mild learning difficulties had a median score at ceiling, i.e., 6.0, whereas young autistics had a median score under 1.5. This poor performance suggests that "in early phases of development there could well be the type of imitative barrier that Rogers and Pennington propose as fundamental in the cascade of deficits characterizing autism" (Whiten and Brown, 1998, p. 270). The Whiten-Brown results complement Braten's claims, inasmuch as autistic children had special difficulties with imitation tasks requiring the subject to invert the action from the observer's perspective to that of the actor. One task involved a grasp-thumb action, in which one hand of the model grasps the thumb of the other hand, which faces outward. Imitation errors involved reversals of the direction of either one or both hands.

Additional evidence of difficulties with self-oriented actions comes from a study by Hobson and Lee (1999). They set out to study difficulties autistic subjects might have in imitating the behavioral "style" of an action. Quite serendipitously, two of their tasks required subjects to act upon an object in a manner involving orientation to the self. In these tasks, there were sharp differences between autistic subjects and nonautistic controls. In one task, the experimenter took a wooden pipe rack in his left hand and held it against the upper part of his left shoulder, somewhat as one might position a violin. He took a wooden stick in his right hand and strummed across the ridges and slots of the rack three times, making a staccato sound. All but one autistic participant, out of sixteen, performed the action of running the stick over the pipe rack, so the majority of them had observed and could recall the action and understood that their task was to execute it. However, there was a striking difference in the ways the participants of each group held the pipe rack. Only two of the sixteen participants with autism held the pipe rack against his or her shoulder in the manner demonstrated, whereas a majority of participants without autism (ten out of sixteen) did so. In a second task involving self-oriented action, the experimenter brought a hand-sized cloth frog to his forehead and wiped it with the frog three times. Only five participants with autism, but a large majority of participants without autism (fourteen out of sixteen) spontaneously imitated brow wiping. Hobson and Lee interpret these findings in the manner suggested earlier, as supporting a deficit in perspective-switching in autism.

The participants saw the experimenter perform the action in relation to his own body, but in order to imitate they needed to perform the same action in relation to quite a different body, namely their own. In other words, they needed to *identify* with the experimenter as acting in relation to himself, so that when their turn came, they would emulate not just the action but also the self-orientation with which the agent ... executed the action. It was this identification with the experimenter-as-self-orientated-agent that seemed to be deficient in the participants with autism. (Hobson & Lee, 1999, p. 657)

Leaving the topic of autism, I turn to Braten's (1998) simulationist interpretation of Meltzoff's (1995) finding that 18-month-old children "imitate" the failed actions of adult models with successful actions of their own. For example, when a model tried but failed to pull a dumbbell apart, a toddler successfully pulled it apart. Braten's plausible interpretation is that a child, in watching a model, "virtually" tracks the model's performance from an actor's perspective in his own "companion space." The child then proceeds to "imitate" what he has imagined as the action's goal, not what he has actually observed. It is noteworthy that Meltzoff and Moore (1998, p. 2), in a control demonstration, report that exposure to an *inanimate* model "attempting" to pull the dumbbell apart rarely results in the observer's reenactment. Consistently with ST, seeing a nonbiological entity does not trigger the kind of virtual tracking associated with mind reading.

Neurobiological support for the simulationist interpretation of imitation comes from the discovery of mirror neurons. First discovered in the ventral premotor cortex of macaque monkeys (area F5), mirror neurons constitute an observation-execution matching system (Rizzolatti et al., 1996a; Gallese et al., 1996). These neurons fire when a monkey performs a specific action, such as a precision grip, but also when a monkey is merely watching another individual (monkey or human) perform an equivalent action. Mirror neurons are especially associated with goal-related actions. We may therefore interpret mirror neuron activity as the neural substrate of an intention, or plan, to execute a goal-oriented action.

Observation-driven mirror neuron activity implies that when a monkey watches another individual perform a goal-related action, the observer experiences or undergoes a similar goal-related plan. Thus, observation-driven mirror neuron activity seems to consist in the organism's adopting the mental stance of the observed individual and replicating its goal representation. It is a case of coplanning or imaginatively coenacting the action executed by the observed individual. This does not yet constitute mind reading because the observing organism need not attribute or impute any mental state to the other, and may even lack the psychological concept of a desire or plan. Nonetheless, the phenomenon may be related to simulational mind reading insofar as the emulated state of planning the action in question is a natural launching pad for simulation-style mind reading (Gallese and Goldman, 1998).

Note that observation-driven mirror neuron activation does not generate actual imitative behavior, presumably because the neural activity is inhibited by mechanisms elsewhere in the motor pathway. Nonetheless, the monkey mirror system could represent an evolutionary precursor of the human mechanism for imitation. Such mirror systems have also been established in humans, and could subserve both the human capacity for imitation and the human capacity for mind reading. Other cortical areas that constitute matching or "resonance" mechanisms are doubly activated by observation of an action (e.g., finger movement) and by an instruction to imitate that action (Iacoboni et al., 1999).

Justin Williams et al. (2001) have recently advanced a developmental connection between mirror neurons, imitation, and autism that incorporates all the elements discussed in this section. They speculate that mirror neurons provide a key foundation for the building of imitative and mind-reading competencies. They join Rogers and Pennington (1991) in hypothesizing a developmental link between early imitation and such social abilities as shared attention, recognition of gestures, and language (especially the social and pragmatic aspects of language), as well as empathy and full-fledged mind reading. They propose that autism arises from some dysfunction in the mirror neuron system that lies at the base of the cascade of autistic problems. Endorsing Gallese and Goldman's (1998) simulationist interpretation of mirror neurons, they view this ontogenetic cascade from the perspective of ST rather than TT. The hypothesized mirror neuron dysfunction might affect all mirror areas or might be confined to just certain groups, such as those in the parietal cortex (identified by Fogassi et al., 1998). The dysfunction in question could interfere with early imitation and lead to the impairment of self–other representations, which, according to Rogers and Pennington, underpins autistic problems.

2.5 Imitation, Role Play, and Mind Reading

I turn now to a second sort of connection between imitation and mind reading as viewed from a simulationist perspective. The proposal here is that imitation contributes to advanced mind reading through the intermediate route of role play. Although role playing might be understood in a purely behavioral fashion (i.e., merely acting as if one were a so-and-so), it is here assumed that role play must also involve mental simulation. The role player must also mentally place herself in the shoes of an actual or imagined protagonist. Thus, the idea of role play, at least in the present context, ushers in simulationist ideas.

The first strand in the present proposal is to link role play to imitation by viewing it as a species of *extended imitation*. From the age of 2 years and onward, normal children engage in role play, i.e., acting out the role of a person or creature. Harris (2000) defines role play as a species of pretend play in which a child temporarily acts the part of someone other than herself, e.g., by impersonating a mother, a bus driver, or a soldier. His definition also covers cases in which a child enacts a role but projects it onto a doll or toy that serves as a prop for the role (Harris, 2000, p. 30). I propose that role play be viewed as a kind of extended imitation. Ordinary imitation involves the behavioral duplication of an observed action. An action is typically imitated at the same time that it is observed, but in deferred imitation, the actor imitates behavior that was previously observed and is now recalled. In the case of role play the actor need not imitate any actually observed behavior. There is, however, a *type* of behavior the actor is familiar with and which she imitates in some relevant respects. For example, consider a child playing the role of a bus driver. Although the child may not recall actions of any specific bus driver that she seeks to duplicate, she knows that bus drivers sit at the front of a bus, hold a steering wheel, call out stops as the bus proceeds, and so forth. Thus, when a child plays the role of a bus driver, she selects some such action types (as opposed to tokens) and seeks to copy them.

Another respect in which role play is "extended" is that it is *creative*. Children engaged in role play knowingly embellish a scenario along novel lines not previously witnessed. However, this does not preclude the behavior from being the imitation of a familiar pattern or prototype. If a role-playing child pretends to engage in a telephone conversation, the detailed content of the conversation may be novel, but other features of the telephone transaction will replicate a familiar general pattern.

A third respect in which role play is extended imitation is that it involves more elaborate and intricate acts of intended *mental* imitation, i.e., trying to duplicate in one's own mind the (supposed) mental acts or processes of another. If what we said earlier about imitation and mirror neurons is correct, even primitive behavioral imitation may involve putting oneself in the model's shoes with respect to a motor plan. But in advanced role play, the imitator tries to copy more than just the motor plan of a model. She tries to mentally emulate more complex mental activity. The intended model, of course, need not be an actual person; it can be an imaginary one. But my hypothesis is that a child constructs a model, or uses a prop as an imagined model, and tracks that model's mental activity in her own mind, as evidenced by the verbal and nonverbal behavior that she displays.

These ideas are well illustrated by Harris's discussion of cases in which a child enacts a role but projects it onto a doll or toy that serves as a prop for the role (Harris, 2000, p. 30). Children often immerse themselves in an imaginary role and speak as if they were themselves experiencing it from the point of view of the invented person or creature. They use terms of reference, including deictic terms, appropriate to the adopted role (Harris, 2000, p. 30). They give expression to the emotions, sensations, and needs appropriate to the role. For example, John at 21 months is playing with his Jack-in-the-box, and he often impersonates Jack. If Jack's hand is poking out when John closes the lid, John says "Ouch, ouch. Boo-hoo" (his word for "hurt") (Wolf, 1982, p. 319; paraphrased from Harris, 2000, p. 31). During the period from 2 to 3 years of age, children often conjure up an imaginary person or creature whose identity remains stable over many months—a sort of companion to the child. As Harris indicates, this process is a clear example of simulation. I am hypothesizing that such simulation is an extension of the more primitive phenomenon of imitation, but differs from imitation both in its comparative creativity and in its greater preoccupation with creating the mental life of an imagined character.

Continuing to draw from Harris's summary (2000, pp. 42–45), the next point is that experimental evidence indicates that role play makes a positive contribution toward mind-reading performance. Astington and Jenkins (1995) and Schwebel et al. (1999) found that children who engaged in more joint play, including role play, performed better on mind-reading tasks, but no such connection was found for solitary pretence, which involves just objects and props rather than role play. Taylor and Carlson

(1997) checked whether 3- and 4-year-old subjects had invented an imaginary character. Those 4-year-olds who had previously invented an imaginary character performed better on belief tasks, even when age and verbal ability were controlled for. No effect was found for 3-year-olds, but few of them engaged in this type of role play.

One might object that perhaps skill at role play is an effect of mentalizing ability, not a precursor and cause of it. Youngblade and Dunn (1995) addressed this objection with the following study: A group of toddlers were assessed for pretend play first at approximately 33 months (i.e., before age 3) and then again 7 months later, at about 40 months. A key result was that pretend play at 33 months was linked to better performance in belief tasks at 40 months. Since 33 months is an age at which children usually fail false-belief tasks, it is unlikely that the variation among the children in pretend play at 33 months was a consequence of their preexisting false-belief competence at that age. Note that among the measures of pretend play taken at 33 months, only role enactment was a predictor of understanding false beliefs. Thus involvement in role play, which gives practice at mental simulation, is an advance predictor of later success in belief tasks (Harris, 2000, p. 45).

Putting these pieces together, we have a progression in which behavioral imitation is first enriched and expanded into role play, which includes mental imitation or simulation. Second, practice at such mental simulation makes a contribution toward mastery of mind reading as represented by improved success in belief tasks. Thus, when mind reading is approached in a simulationist mode, a clear pattern emerges in which imitative enrichment featuring role play gradually leads to increased competence at advanced mind reading. Conversely, it is well known that autistic children, who characteristically have serious impairments in advanced mind reading, also show (earlier) deficiencies in role play.

Note, finally, that there is no incompatibility between the two connections I have sketched between simulationist mind reading and imitation. Either link alone could be right, or both could be right. So ST has abundant resources for claiming to find important connections between imitation and mind reading.[2]

2. See comments on this chapter by W. Prinz (vol. 2, ch. 8.3, p. 180) and by Millikan (vol. 2, ch. 8.4, p. 182). ED.

3 Intentional Agents Like Myself

Robert M. Gordon

3.1 Introduction

According to Meltzoff, Tomasello, and Gallese, certain human responses to conspecifics have the following property: although they do not require possession of mental concepts, they nonetheless manifest an implicit "like me" recognition, a recognition of conspecifics as intentional or goal-directed agents like oneself. This is an important idea, one that I think is crucial to understanding how we can bootstrap ourselves into an explicit folk psychology. I don't think it has been developed adequately, however. Meltzoff, I believe, was the originator, and here I will try to point up some inadequacies in the way he conceives this "like me" recognition, namely, in terms of analogical inference. Then I will sketch a very different account, which I think is particularly consonant with some remarks of Gallese's. Lest it appear that I am pitting Gallese against Meltzoff, or indeed myself against Meltzoff, I should note that some of Meltzoff's writings (e.g., Meltzoff, 1995) seem to me quite congenial to the view I am presenting.

I should make it clear that I am not talking about how we "read" other minds or anticipate the behavior of mind-endowed entities. I am concerned only with how, without prior possession of mental concepts, we can implicitly recognize certain entities as intentional agents like ourselves.

3.2 Constitutive versus Imitative Mirroring

Gallese (vol. 1, ch. 3) and Meltzoff (vol. 2, ch. 1) are each concerned with phenomena that fall under the category of *mirroring responses*: roughly speaking, responses brought about by b's perception of a, in which b comes to have property p because a has property p. For example, because a does or did something (of a given description d), b does "the same" (that is, something fitting description *d*); because *a* activates and executes a given motor plan, *b* activates "the same" motor plan; or, because *a* undergoes certain visceral responses (specifically, those characteristic of the emotion expressed on *a*'s face), *b* undergoes "the same" visceral responses (see Adolphs et al., 2000).

It is important to note that whereas Meltzoff is speaking primarily of the *imitative* mirroring of another's behavior, Gallese's discussion is more concerned with mirroring that constitutes part of one's very *representation* of the other's behavior (as explained in the next paragraph). This difference is crucial. If I try to imitate your behavior, I try to copy or match something I have perceived you to be doing, perhaps along with the manner in which you did it. However, for any actions for which I have the corresponding mirror neurons, in perceiving the behavior that I am now trying to match, my brain was already making use of a copying or matching procedure. As I observed you, one or more of my premotor neurons responded as if it were I who was carrying out the behavior. Now, as I imitate you (at least, if I do so successfully), presumably the same neurons that had previously responded *as if* I were carrying out the behavior will be activated again as I actually carry it out. The first response I will call *constitutive mirroring*, in that it was a constitutive part of my representation of your behavior; the second, I will call *imitative mirroring*.

According to the results cited by Gallese, the sight of other (living) human or humanlike bodies deposits in one's brain, not just a visual representation of their behavior, but also internal replicas of, among other things, the motor plans and visceral responses—and possibly even the lower-level intentions—that lie behind the behavior. Although these replicas may be implemented within my brain when I observe your behavior, that does not make them *my* intentions, urges, and motor plans. First, they are not *endogenous*. They are not produced by my own decision-making and emotion-forming processes. Rather, they are *exogenous* states, induced "from the outside" by observation of another's behavior. Second, thanks to processes that are usually automatic and often unconscious, these responses are mapped onto another human or humanlike body, ideally the one whose motor behavior or facial expression elicited the response. For example, I see my son's leg poised to kick a soccer ball, and my own leg involuntarily prepares to kick, but in a way that helps me to anticipate his kick, not my own, and also to recognize it as a kick toward his left, not toward my left. Even though this projection onto my son may emerge into consciousness, it is surely not something I have brought about by analogical reasoning. I do not begin with a belief that something is going on in me, as opposed to in him, and then conclude with a belief that something is going on in him, as opposed to in me. In order for my mirroring to assist me in anticipating my son's kick, I needn't even be aware of my own leg's preparing to kick. And I don't theorize that my son must be intending and preparing to kick. Rather than infer from some intention of my own that my son has a certain intention, I find myself "getting behind" his behavior, as if it were my own.[1]

This phenomenology of "getting behind" is probably the cumulative result of a number of factors. The mirrored motor plan enables me to anticipate what his body will do, within his egocentric space (a kick toward his left), and, equally important, within his explanatory context: I am a defender, the goal I am defending is on the right, and I need to get the ball to the side without crossing it in front of the goal. It is these factors, as well as the resulting phenomenology, that justify calling the mirroring of his motor plans and behavior constitutive of my representation of his behavior.

(Concerning the relationship between constitutive and imitative mirroring, I will offer a hypothesis that is not essential to my argument but may be worth investigating. It seems reasonable to speculate that when I later recall your behavior with the purpose of imitating it, I reactivate not only a visual image but also the pattern of premotor and motor activation that occurred when I first observed your behavior. Then my actual, or overt, imitation will consist in, or at least build on, the now disinhibited reactivation of that pattern. Thus, when I imitate, I do not have to go back to a purely visual memory and then do a crossmodal mapping from visual to motor representations, for I have already captured your action in motor memory. I need only retrieve the pattern from memory and, as I suggested, reactivate it—this time, actually carrying it out rather than inhibiting it from overt expression.)

1. Buccino et al. (2001) establish that the mirror system in humans extends to perceived actions of the foot as well as of the hand and mouth. Beyond the mere replication of motor plans, when we observe object-directed foot actions such as ball-kicking, we engage parietal systems that are probably conducting higher-level analyses of the action. (I thank Vittorio Gallese for the reference.) Strictly speaking, the neuroscientific evidence does not yet show the replication of intentions. However, the phenomenology, as well as some of the research by Wolfgang Prinz (vol. 1, ch. 5), suggests that I replicated my son's *intention* to kick the ball to the left.

3.3 Meltzoff on the Analogy of Self and Other

In volume 2, chapter 1,[2] Meltzoff writes:

Human acts are especially relevant to infants because they look like the infant feels himself to be and because they are events that infants can intend. When a newborn sees a human act, it may be meaningful: "That seen event is like this felt event." (p. 74)

Thus in Meltzoff's view, the infant uses an argument from analogy of the form: When I produce behavior of type x, I feel a certain way f; therefore, when a similar body does x, the behavior was probably produced by another subject—another "I"—that feels the same way f.

According to Meltzoff, such an inferential process is well within the capacity of the human infant. However, the capacity for analogical reasoning is not the only concern. To apply the argument would require the following additional capabilities:

1. being able to identify one's own behavior in a way that allows comparison with the observed behavior of another body and
2. being able to identify one's own feeling or experience *as such* (i.e., interpret it as something that is going "within me," in the appropriate sense; that is, subjectively, as opposed to "out there in the world" or in someone else).

The first capability would be particularly problematic in the imitation of facial expressions, since the infant has no visual perception of its own current facial expression. Even adults have difficulty (I do, in any case) associating their own current facial configuration with a visual image. Therefore, I do not think Meltzoff can be right in asserting, as he does in chapter 1 (vol. 2), that "when infants see others acting similarly to how they have acted in the past, they project onto others the mental experience that regularly goes with that behavior. This could not occur if infants saw no equivalence between their acts and those of others" (p. 57).

More generally, infants would have trouble with the second capability, because it would demand considerable conceptual sophistication to under-

2. Meltzoff has defended the analogical inference account in numerous other publications, including Meltzoff & Gopnik (1993). In personal correspondence, however, he notes that he did not mean that the baby "thought through a step-by-step formal analogy." Rather, as he states later (Meltzoff, 2002a, p. 35), because infants are able to "recognize the similarities between their own acts and those of others," the acts of others are imbued with "felt meaning."

stand that "this"—whether it be a particular sensation of pain or the phenomenological aspect of an action such as sticking out one's tongue—is just something that is going on within me, in the appropriate sense, that is, subjectively, as opposed to out there in the world or in another. Both of these capabilities would be required to make sense of the premise, "*This* is what is going on within me when my body is doing *that*," and thus to get an argument from analogy started.

For a further illustration of the problem, consider another, better-known neonatal tendency to mirror another's behavior: responsive crying. Infants, even neonates, exhibit emotional distress when they cry in response to the crying of other infants. To get an argument from analogy started, the infant would have to conceptualize as follows: "*This* distress (namely, the distress that I am "directly" aware of) lies behind *this* crying, but it is not what lies behind *that other* crying I hear." But does the neonate, does even the older infant, have the sophistication to think herself into such a posture? I think not. What should be problematic for the infant is not *assimilation* (whatever is doing that crying must be undergoing what I am undergoing), but *differentiation* (whatever is doing that crying is something distinct from me).[3] Without the ability to differentiate between *a* and *b*, of course, there can be no analogical inference from *a* to *b*. At the same time, there would be no need for an analogical inference before the infant has begun to individuate minds and to think, "*My* mental state, *my* distress, is not what lies behind *that* crying."

An analogical argument may sometimes be applicable to "mature" imitative mirroring. Arguably, when I imitate your behavior, I may somehow take note of the inner states, such as intentions, urges, and perhaps even motor plans insofar as I am aware of them, that underlie my behavior. (Meltzoff speaks only of "feelings," but that seems an unnecessary limitation.) In imitating what you are doing with a box, I may find myself having the intention, say, to open the box. Then I might speculate, "Something like *this* may have transpired in you when you opened the box."[4] However, even if such an account sometimes applies to mature imitative mirroring, it certainly does not apply to the constitutive mirroring that Gallese is concerned with.

3. For a relevant discussion, see and compare Gallese (vol. 1, ch. 3) on the shared manifold. ED.

4. For the purposes of analogical argument, I would have to disregard some of my intentions. My intention to be imitating you, for example, would be an intention I should not project onto you.

3.4 Constitutive Mirroring and Intentional Explanation

In chapter 3 of volume 1 Gallese emphasizes that "we do not just perceive ... someone to be, broadly speaking, similar to us. We are *implicitly* aware of this similarity because we literally *embody* it" (vol. 1, ch. 3, p. 104, emphasis added). Later, elaborating on the relevant notion of embodiment, he cites Merleau-Ponty: "It is as if the other person's intention inhabited my body and mine his" (1945; English translation 1962, p. 185).

Gallese's discussion of embodiment (and Merleau-Ponty's discussion of habitation) seems to point toward something quite different than an argument from analogy; different, indeed, from any argument at all. His discussion of a shared manifold of intersubjectivity is suggestive, but I will offer what I think is a clearer picture of the way embodiment—*in contrast to* inference, whether analogical or not—might yield an implicit recognition that one's conspecifics are intentional or goal-directed agents like oneself.

For the kind of recognition I have in mind, what is necessary and sufficient is this: that I interpret their behavior under the same scheme that makes my own behavior, along with the intentions, motor plans, and visceral feelings that underlie it, intelligible to me; namely, the intentional scheme of reasons, purposes, and object-directedness. In the case of my endogenous visceral feelings, the brain typically incorporates them automatically into the "emotional coloration" of the eliciting object. Thus, when I gaze at the Grand Canyon beneath me, a large part of its emotional quality evidently comes from my sensory pickup of what is happening in my body. Presumably the brain selects the particular object to which the feelings are to be referred by consulting the emotion-formation system that produced the visceral response in the first place. In the case of endogenous intentions and motor plans, the brain evidently has ways of making their consequences unsurprising to us, probably by using efference copies and forward models. However, it also has ways of making the intentions and motor plans themselves unsurprising, by embedding them within a structure of reasons and purposes; I am running because it is raining, and doing so in order to avoid getting drenched. It seems a plausible hypothesis that these determinations too would generally be made by consulting the same system that produced the decision to run in the first place.

(A brief note on "consulting" the system. I do not mean to refer to a mysterious process of introspection, but rather to a hypothetical mechanism like one of the following: a hypothetical neural capacity to do a "trace" of the pathways and processes that led to a particular outcome, which is of course something we can set an ordinary classical computer to do, except that a neural system would also assess "weights" at various nodes; a hypothetical capacity of decision-making and emotion-formation systems to conduct "what if?" experiments on themselves. For example, a system might subtract a particular input and see if that would make a difference in outcome. The latter hypothesis seems to me to fit with forward models of various kinds, and also with the way we deal consciously with counterfactual questions of the sort, "What would you have done if . . . ?" Generally, we seem to answer such questions by *deciding* what to do. See Gordon, 2002.)

The thesis that draws inspiration from Gallese's discussion of embodiment is this: The brain treats the exogenous replicas of another's motor plans and visceral responses in the same way it treats their like-coded endogenous counterparts. It seeks to make them unsurprising, to make sense of them, by fitting them to the "intentional" scheme of reasons, purposes, and object-directedness. It cannot do so directly, however, because it does not have access to the system that originally motivated them. Instead, it may "attempt," in one way or another, to produce in itself a like-coded *endogenous* response, one that matches the exogenous response it seeks to make unsurprising. Because it does have access to the system that motivates the endogenous response, the brain is able to consult it in assigning an intentional interpretation. Then it might assign the same interpretation, at least tentatively, defeasibly, to the matching exogenous response: a process of analysis by synthesis (see Kinsbourne, vol. 2, ch. 7, p. 168ff).

The general idea—a speculative idea, of course—is that, when a motor plan is induced exogenously, the brain will test various hypothetical ways of embedding it in an intentional scheme of reasons and purposes. This hypothesis testing (or hypothetico-practical reasoning, as I called it in Gordon, 1986) would engage productive processes such as practical reasoning, emotion formation, and decision making. In many cases, the hypotheses would be generated by a search of the shared environment.

I have already set out one instance of this. When I mirror my son's kick to the left, I also supply an explanatory context: I am a defender, the goal I am defending is on the right, and I need to get the ball to the side without crossing it in front of the goal. Within this context, his behavior makes sense; because I take it for granted that he is a smart player, it is even unsurprising. This is a complex case, however. The processing that would make his behavior unsurprising is complicated. It would be more illuminating to discuss a very easy case in which the brain might make sense of an exogenous motor plan by fitting it to the intentional scheme of reasons and purposes.

You see your colleague reaching out and picking up an object. What you observe stirs up your mirror neurons; if it did not, your brain might interpret the motion as it does other observed physical phenomena, calling on a theory or model. Thanks to your mirror neurons, however, visual perception deposits in your premotor cortex the motor plan for reaching out and picking up the same object. However, unlike motor plans that are produced in the normal way by your own decision-making system, this one arrives unmotivated, without reason or purpose. The object you find yourself picking up—or not quite picking up, stopping short of it—is a telephone. Specifically, it is your colleague's office phone.

Suppose that in fact your colleague is picking up the phone because it is ringing. What she is doing is answering the phone. Most of us, hearing a phone ringing nearby, might by habit have an initial impulse to pick it up ourselves. Then memory kicks in and inhibits the impulse. That is, we do not actually reach for the phone, because the phone that is ringing is not ours but another's, and since the other is nearby (and not incapacitated) it would be inappropriate for us to pick it up. Suppose that, as is plausible, your premotor cortex is activated: a motor plan is initiated for picking up an object with the size and location of the phone receiver, and perhaps also for bringing it to your ear. (If one's motor cortex were not activated in this way, I doubt one would report "an impulse to pick up the phone.")

In this case, it is likely that you would be independently activating the very same mirror neurons that were activated by observing your colleague. There would be two pathways to activation, one exogenous and one endogenous. Even though you do not have access to the systems that generated the exogenous, or incoming, motor plan, you do have access to those that are generating the endogenous, or outgoing, motor plan. This access allows you to give reasons and purposes for performing the action you would have performed, had it not been inhibited. It is obvious to you, for example, that you would not have been inclined to pick up the phone just now if it were not ringing, and that your sole purpose was to answer the phone. Then you would have a ready answer if asked why your colleague reached over to pick up that object. Not, of course, an infallibly correct answer, but a good first appoximation, an answer likely enough to be correct that it could serve as a default answer.

Now consider an easy case in which the brain, by producing an endogenous counterpart, might make sense of a facial expression the sight of which induces an exogenous visceral response, representing the expression as directed toward an object. Suppose I am looking at someone whose facial expression induces an exogenous visceral response in me. My brain maps the response onto her face, thereby isolating it to some degree from my endogenous visceral responses: These feelings are hers, not my own. But, as with my own emotion-induced visceral responses, my brain looks for something in the world to which the response is to be referred. Typically, I find myself following the other's direction of gaze, halting at something she is obviously looking at. If the scene is complex, my gaze halts at whatever in her line of gaze *endogenously* produces in me the same or a similar visceral response that her expression is exogenously producing. If, for example, her face shows fright, my gaze halts at something frightening, something that induces in me, at least to a small degree, the visceral disturbances characteristic of fright. Sometimes the search fails to yield such an "objective correlative," and that is where imaginative transformation may come into play—often, an involuntary fleeting transformation, such as one's adoption of a child's perspective, from which, for example, what is not terrifying appears terrifying, or the converse. Sometimes such a transformation will succeed in yielding an endogenous match to the exogenous response induced by the expression. And sometimes not.

Each of these simple cases begins with something I assume the brain would find problematic: a visceral response, motor plan, or intention that is thrust upon it unmotivated. More precisely, the original of which it is a copy was motivated in a decision-making system and emotion-formation system other than its own, as if the brain were "possessed" by alien spirits. To avoid conflict with its endogenous productions, it maps the exogenous response onto an appropriate body. Exogenous plans and feelings need not integrate with those produced by one's own decision-making and emotion-forming processes. Rather, in effect, they will have been separated into distinct "I's," typically one per enduring human body.[5] Not only does it make sense of the behavior of another body to regard it as the expression of an inner mental life, it also makes sense of one's own inner mental life to assign a portion of it to the other body. For it avoids the disunity that would result if one had to "own" every stray motor plan, urge, and feeling that was injected exogenously into one's brain. What the brain does in these cases is, in a manner of speaking, to multiply the first person, so that exogenous plans and feelings are on the one hand assigned to a multiplicity of other bodies and on the other hand interpreted under the same

5. Only by way of this partitioning can one come to understand "I" as a true indexical, referring to one "I" or "self" among possible others; see Millikan (1993).

intentional scheme as their endogenous, truly first-person counterparts. This, according to my account, is what it is to implicitly recognize others as intentional beings like oneself.

I further speculated that in lieu of access to the systems that activate our exogenous responses, the brain might substitute a procedure of analysis by synthesis, producing a similarly coded endogenous response that it *can* analyze. Often, much of the work would be done by our common environment, together with our common biology and our socialization. For example, I respond as you do to the ringing of a telephone, and the same motor plan is independently activated endogenously as well as exogenously. Or I look at something, I see you looking at the same thing, and I get the same visceral response endogenously from the object you are looking at as I do exogenously from looking at your face. However, sometimes, as noted earlier, the exogenous activation initiates a search of the environment that halts when the same visceral response is produced endogenously. Sometimes an imaginative transformation is required for a matching endogenous response; and sometimes nothing does the trick. One way or another, the brain seems to be seeking an endogenous match to the exogenous intruder. Even the process of "getting behind" my son's kick to the left may involve, not only exogenous kicking, but also its endogenous replication. Not only do I automatically make the spatial shift that allows me to interpret my incipient kick to the left as a kick to his left; also automatically, I judge what to do in his "place" (i.e., in the role of a defender so situated) and proceed to do it—in an inhibited sort of way. If what I "do" endogenously is the same as what I "do" exogenously, then I shout, "Good move!" If not, then, perhaps, I criticize later. Aside from the considerable oversimplification, I think it a plausible speculation that something along these lines—the congruence or incongruence of exogenous and endogenous activation—may underlie some aspects of acculturation, such as instruction in a physical task.

3.5   What I Have Been Trying to Show

I have been trying to show how constitutive mirroring responses may manifest an implicit recognition of conspecifics as intentional or goal-directed agents like oneself, without requiring possession of mental concepts. My negative claim is that this implicit recognition is not the conclusion of an inferential leap from self to other. An analogical inference would begin with a premise concerning the states underlying my own behavior; more particularly, those states of which I am aware. However, the mirroring phenomena I have been discussing are not "my own" in the requisite sense. If I am aware of them at all, I am aware of them as underlying the other's behavior, not my own. My positive claim might be put this way. The implicit recognition of conspecifics as intentional agents like oneself is a case of procedural rather than declarative knowledge. Specifically, the human brain will in fact seek the reasons and purposes behind the exogenous motor plan or intention, or the object to which the exogenous visceral feeling refers, just as it would for its own endogenous productions. If the brain does this, then it is treating the corresponding behavior, that is, the behavior that induced the exogenous response, as the behavior of an intentional agent.

I suggested at the outset that this implicit recognition is crucial to understanding how we can bootstrap ourselves into an explicit folk psychology. Bootstrapping is possible because intentional explanations in terms of reasons, purposes, and objects are at least implicitly mental. Even though there is no explicit mention of beliefs in, "I am running because it is raining," or of desires in, "I am running in order to avoid getting drenched," nonetheless these explanations, understood as intentional explanations, are true only if the corresponding mental state ascriptions and explanations are true. If I am indeed running because it is raining, that is, for the reason that it is raining, then I am running because I believe it is raining. And if I am running in order to avoid getting drenched, then I am running because I want not to get drenched. I am fairly confident that one of the principal avenues by which children come to develop the concepts of belief and desire is through the capacity to give such implicitly mental explanations of others' actions as well as their own. It would take several pages to set out how the ability to give these explanations can be parlayed into making explicitly mental (because I believe, because I want) explanations, but at least the seeds of such an account may be found in what I have written about ascent routines (Gordon, 1995b, 1996, 2000).

Mirroring systems probably play a very important role in "mind reading" by simulation (see Gallese & Goldman, 1998). If this is so, then analysis by synthesis may be the way, or at least a way, in which constitutive mirroring plays this role, making up for the fact that the brain lacks access to the systems that produced the responses it is mirroring. However, my main concern here has not been with whether and how constitutive mirroring might contribute to mind reading. What I have tried to show is how the human brain, by forcing exogenous responses into the same intentional scheme that makes our endogenous responses intelligible to ourselves, implicitly recognizes the external sources of these responses as "intentional agents like oneself."[6]

Acknowledgments

The author thanks Susan Hurley, Shaun Gallagher, Vittorio Gallese, and Natika Newton for helpful comments on earlier drafts.

6. For discussion relevant to this chapter, see especially Gallese (vol. 1, ch. 3) and Hurley (vol. 1, ch. 7). ED.

4 No Compelling Evidence to Dispute Piaget's Timetable of the Development of Representational Imitation in Infancy

Moshe Anisfeld

4.1 Introduction

Recent experimental work on imitation in infancy has challenged Piaget's theory and timetable (Piaget, 1951/1962, Part 1). Two aspects of Piaget's work have been criticized: his contention that imitation of invisible gestures (i.e., gestures the imitator cannot see when he or she performs them) could not occur until the third quarter of the first year, and his contention that deferred imitation of novel sequences of actions could not occur until the beginning of the second year.

The critics have marshalled empirical research that they interpret as showing invisible imitation in the neonatal period and deferred imitation at 6–9 months. This chapter argues that in both areas the empirical criticism of Piaget is not well founded. It removes a source of support for theories that attribute mental representation to young infants. In turn, it provides support for Piagetian theories that see mental representation as evolving gradually in the course of the first year.

The chapter starts with a brief summary of Piaget's theory to provide a context for his work on imitation. This summary is followed by an examination of the work on invisible imitation and deferred imitation.

4.2 Piaget's Theory of the Development of Representation

According to Piaget, (1951/1962, 1952/1963, 1954), in the first 6 months infants' functioning is nonrepresentational. The memories that young infants form of the stimuli they encounter are strictly tied to the sensory impressions of the stimuli and the motor adjustments that they elicit. These sensorimotor memories are elicitable by the stimuli that produced them; they are not otherwise available; that is, they are not represented independently.

Sensorimotor functioning, although nonrepresentational, carries within it the seeds from which representational intelligence sprouts. When a 1-month-old baby makes sucking motions on seeing his mother before making contact with her nipple, these motions anticipate the actual activity and thus in a crude sense represent it. More obvious representational activities evolve as babies develop an interest not only in using their schemes (i.e., repeatable patterns of sensorimotor activity) but also in contemplating them. Thus, in the middle of their first year, Piaget's children exhibited a fascination with their hand movements (Piaget, 1954, pp. 231–232).

Sensorimotor intelligence evolves gradually through six stages into symbolic representational intelligence. What the infant knows (and remembers) becomes increasingly separated from the specific encounters that give rise to that knowledge. There is a gradual growth of interest in reflecting on the environment and in understanding it.

In the absence of symbolic language, the infant uses sensorimotor means for representational purposes. For instance, Piaget (1952/1963, p. 186) reports that at 6.39 months when his daughter Lucienne saw her toy parrots suspended from a new place, the chandelier, she briefly shook her legs—an action she often performed in association with her toys. Because Lucienne did not try to reach the parrots or engage in any other action, Piaget interprets her leg shaking as a form of "motor recognition." Lucienne was using a sensorimotor action to take notice of the new location of her parrots. She used sensorimotor means for a representational purpose. (This capsule summary should suffice as background for our study of imitation. For an expanded summary of the emergence of representational intelligence, see, e.g., Anisfeld, 1984, ch. 3.)

Piaget applied his differentiation between representational and nonrepresentational functioning specifically to imitation. He distinguished between early forms of imitation, which are nonrepresentational, and later forms, beginning around 6 months, which become increasingly more representationally sophisticated (Piaget, 1951/1962, chs. 1–3). An example of early imitation is contagious crying, where child *b* starts crying on hearing child *a* crying and stops when *a* stops. In this case, there is no need to assume intervening representational activity to account for *b*'s behavior; the effect is direct and spontaneous. By contrast, representational imitation is characterized by mediating internal activity. The imitator is aware of the self, of the imitatee, and of the act of imitation. Piaget focused on the cognitive function of representational imitation: to improve one's understanding and performance of observed activities and/or to reflect on them. But representational imitation in infancy, like imitation at all levels and all ages, also has a social function: to bond with the imitatee.

In the sections that follow, I examine two categories of representational imitation dealt with by Piaget: imitation of invisible gestures, the less sophisticated form, and deferred imitation, the more sophisticated form. The section on invisible imitation will serve to summarize and update the results of previous critical analyses (Anisfeld, 1979, 1991, 1996; Anisfeld et al., 2001). Deferred imitation will receive a fuller treatment.

4.2.1 An Interlude on Imitation and Language

The Piagetian conceptualization of imitation in infancy as a representational activity can help answer a question raised at the Royaumont conference that produced these volumes. Marco Iacoboni reported that imitation was found to be subserved by Broca's area, the area of the brain responsible for language. He wondered what the connection was between imitation and language.

The answer I am suggesting is that both are primarily representational systems. Although language is used with great effectiveness for communicative and instrumental purposes, its basic function is representational: to afford a conceptual map of the world and to serve as an instrument of thought. The nineteenth-century German philosopher Wilhelm von Humboldt said that the instrumental use of language is derivative and subsidiary, a parasitic overlay on the cognitive function (see Chomsky, 1966, p. 21). Imitation may be viewed in a similar way. Although imitation is used very effectively in the learning of new skills, the formation of social cohesion, and the spread of social norms and fads, its basic function in infancy is representational. It aids infants in their cognitive mastery of their environment.

4.3 Imitation of Invisible Gestures

In invisible imitation (e.g., tongue protrusion) the infant sees the model but does not see the results of her own corresponding action. In the absence of a common visual basis, how does the infant link her action to the model's action? How does a baby know that by sticking out her tongue she will be doing the same thing as the model? In the imitation of gestures in which the infant can see the results of her action (e.g., opening and closing a hand), there is some commonality between what the infant sees the model do and what she sees herself do, although the two sights differ in size and perspective. But in invisible imitation, there is no sensorimotor commonality between the infant's visual image of the model and her own motor response. Piaget argued, therefore, that invisible imitation can occur only at an age when a baby is able to use extraneous cues from which to infer the homologous relation between a model's gesture and her gesture. To do this, the baby has to see stimuli not only as affording opportunities for action but also as sources of information.

4.3.1 Invisible Imitation at 6–12 Months: Piaget's Observations and Experimental Research

Piaget first observed invisible imitations in his own children at the age of 8–12 months (Piaget, 1951/1962, ch. 2). He reports, for instance, how at 8 months Jacqueline learned, over a period of 6 days, to move her lips in imitation of her father's similar movement. The imitation was made possible, according to Piaget (1951/1962, p. 31), by an incident in which Jacqueline made a noise with her saliva while moving her lips, and her father immediately imitated both the movement and the noise. Because father and daughter were habitually engaging in mutual imitation, the common noise led Jacqueline to conclude that her gesture and her father's gesture were the "same." In order to make equivalences between parts of her body invisible to her and other peoples' bodies, the child is dependent on such mediating cues, or, in Piaget's terminology, "indices" (Piaget, 1951/1962, p. 42).

Experimental research (Kaye & Marcus, 1978, 1981) has demonstrated that with systematic training, babies 2–3 months younger than Piaget's children can be induced to imitate some invisible gestures. Specifically, Kaye and Marcus (1981) modeled various behaviors for nine babies every month from the age of 6 to 12 months. The monthly demonstrations lasted for as long as the infant's interest could be sustained—up to 10 minutes. Typically, there were ten to twenty demonstrations over 5 minutes. Kaye and Marcus report that when ear touching was modeled, there were imitative approximations at 6 months; significantly more infants touched their faces following modeling than at baseline. In an earlier study, Kaye and Marcus (1978) found imitation of mouth movements at 6 months. As Kaye and Marcus (1978, p. 141) note, these results are consistent with Piaget's theory.

4.3.2 No Compelling Evidence for Invisible Imitation in the Neonatal Period

Observations of apparent imitation of invisible gestures by babies in the first half of the first year were dismissed by Piaget and others as pseudo-imitation that was due to inadvertent conditioning and other factors (see Anisfeld, 1991; R. Byrne & Russon, 1998). But Piaget's timetable for the occurrence of invisible imitation was challenged in 1977 by Meltzoff and

Moore in experiments with 2 to 3-week-old infants on the imitation of tongue protrusion, mouth opening, and lip protrusion. The experimental work that followed this initial study concentrated mainly on the neonatal period, testing babies from birth to 7 weeks. Various gestures were studied in this research, including the gestures studied by Meltzoff and Moore as well as other gestures, such as blinking and facial emotional expressions. In 1991 I argued on the basis of an exhaustive review of the literature that there was little evidence for neonatal imitation of invisible gestures. Now, more than 10 years later, there is an even stronger basis for skepticism about such imitation.

Experiments with Tongue Protrusion and Mouth Opening   Gestures other than tongue protrusion and mouth opening have been studied only occasionally and the results are inconclusive. Of the two most often studied gestures, tongue protrusion and mouth opening, the results are more positive for tongue protrusion than for mouth opening. This can be clearly seen by an examination of eleven studies in which both tongue protrusion and mouth opening were investigated under the same conditions (eight of these eleven studies were examined in Anisfeld, 1996).

Two of these tongue-protrusion and mouth-opening studies (Meltzoff & Moore, 1977) are hard to interpret because of methodological problems and atypical response rates (Anisfeld, 1996). One study (Ullstadius, 1998) found effects for both tongue protrusion and mouth opening only when comparing them with a no-gesture, passive-face condition, not when comparing them with each other (to be referred to as a cross-condition control), i.e., there were no more tongue protrusions when tongue protrusion was modeled than when mouth opening was modeled, and no more mouth openings when mouth opening was modeled than when tongue protrusion was modeled. Thus, the results of three of the eleven mouth-opening and tongue-protrusion studies are ambiguous and inconclusive.

The results of another group of four studies show an increase in the number of tongue-protrusion responses when tongue protrusion was modeled, but no increase in mouth-opening responses when mouth opening was modeled (Abravanel & DeYong, 1991; Anisfeld et al., 2001; Heimann et al., 1989, observation 2; Heimann & Schaller, 1985). Two studies found an effect for tongue protrusion and inconsistent results for mouth opening (Meltzoff & Moore, 1992, 1994). In one study (Legerstee, 1991) it is not clear whether there was an effect for one or both gestures. Finally, one study (Meltzoff & Moore, 1983a) found a statistical effect for both tongue protrusion and mouth opening, but the mouth-opening effect can be interpreted as a by-product of the tongue-protrusion effect (Anisfeld, 1996).

Matching of Tongue Protrusion Interpreted as an Arousal Response   There is thus little basis for claiming an effect for any gesture other than tongue protrusion. A lone tongue-protrusion effect can be accounted for by an arousal interpretation (see Turkewitz et al., 1984). The arousal interpretation assumes that tongue protrusion displays are particularly arousing to neonates and that when aroused, neonates tend to protrude their tongues.

Most studies investigating tongue protrusion (in conjunction with mouth opening or in conjunction with other gestures) used one of two bases against which they compared the babies' levels of tongue protrusion: a passive-face control and a cross-condition control. It has been clearly recognized that seeing a protruding tongue is more arousing to babies than seeing a passive face (e.g., Meltzoff & Moore, 1983b). Thus, tongue-protrusion effects that rest on comparing the tongue-protrusion condition with a passive-face condition can be accounted for by the arousal interpretation. There are nine such effects in eight studies (Abravanel & DeYong, 1991; Abravanel & Sigafoos, 1984; Heimann et al., 1989; Heimann & Schaller, 1985; Meltzoff & Moore, 1977, second experiment; Ullstadius, 1998; Vinter, 1986-2 effects; Wolff, 1987).

In addition, the common practice in these studies has been to present the passive-face condition first. This is problematic because response rates tend to increase over the course of the experiment (see Anisfeld et al., 2001). Therefore, the babies' higher rate of tongue protrusion when they are exposed to tongue protrusion than when they are exposed to a passive face may be due, not to the modeling of tongue protrusion, but to its being placed later in the sequence.

Five studies (Legerstee, 1991; Meltzoff & Moore, 1977, first experiment, 1983a, 1992, 1994) used mouth opening as a control for tongue protrusion (and vice versa). However, tongue protrusion may be more arousing than mouth opening, as suggested by Jones's (1996) finding that 4-week-old infants looked longer at tongue-protrusion displays than at mouth-opening displays. Thus the results showing a higher rate of tongue protrusion in the tongue-protrusion condition than in the mouth-opening condition can also be accounted for by the arousal hypothesis.

Imitation of Tongue Protrusion to the Side of the Mouth?   One of the tongue-protrusion and mouth-opening studies (Meltzoff & Moore, 1994) included in the preceding discussion had a condition in which the model protruded his tongue (a male served as the model) from the right side of the mouth, in addition to a condition in which he protruded his tongue in the usual way from the middle of the mouth. There were also two nontongue-protrusion conditions in this study: a mouth-opening condition and a passive–face condition. At the Royaumont conference, Meltzoff singled out the results concerning the side modeling as providing strong support for the imitation hypothesis. I focus here on this aspect of the study; other aspects have been criticized in Anisfeld (1996, pp. 156–157).

Ten 6-week-old babies participated in the side condition and in each of the other three conditions. All four groups went through five trials over 3 days, with each trial lasting 90 seconds.

The results that Meltzoff and Moore present are based on the coding of tongue protrusions into four ascending categories: "(a) small nonmidline tongue protrusions (NMT), (b) small tongue protrusions to the side (STS), (c) large tongue protrusions (LTP) [not to the side], and (d) large tongue protrusions to the side (LTPS)" (Meltzoff & Moore, 1994, pp. 90–91).

Meltzoff and Moore endeavor to show that over trials, the participants learned to match the side protrusions modeled. The straightforward way to do this would have been to demonstrate that infants exposed to the side protrusions produced more side protrusions than infants exposed to the other three conditions, over all trials, or specifically in later trials as a result of learning. The dependent variable in this analysis could have been the sum of categories (a) + (b) + (d) or just category (d)—the most prominent side category. But Meltzoff and Moore do not provide any such evidence. Instead, they present a trial-by-trial analysis, using the S statistic (Ferguson, 1965, ch. 3).

In the S analysis, a count was made for each participant of the number of responses in each category in each of four trials. (What about the fifth trial?) The S count compares the order of categories with expectations. The expectation of Meltzoff and Moore was that the maximum number of responses in each of the four categories would be ordered in relation to the four trials, so that the maximum for (a) would be on trial 1, for (b) on trial 2, etc. The conformity of the results to this ideal order was tested by comparing the categories with each other with respect to their ordering, assigning a +1 to an order conforming to expectation, a −1 to an order opposite from expectation, and a 0 when no order could be assigned, as when there were no entries for a category. A participant would be counted as conforming to expectation if the sum of that infant's values was positive, even if it was just +1 (out of a possible +6).

Meltzoff and Moore found that in the side-protrusion condition, but not in the other three conditions, most participants had positive sums. From this finding they concluded that over trials the participants learned to match the side protrusions modeled. This conclusion is unwarranted because the categories progress on two dimensions: sidedness of protrusions and magnitude of protrusions. Thus, category (d), large tongue protrusions to the side, differs from category (a), small nonmidline tongue protrusions, not only in regard to the clarity of the sidedness, but also in the absolute magnitude of the protrusion. An even clearer case for my criticism is made by the comparison of category (c), large tongue protrusions not to the side, and category (b), small tongue protrusions to the side. Category (c) coming after category (b) is ordered in magnitude, but reverses the sidedness order: (c), a nonsided category, coming after (b), a sided category.

Given that the order of the categories confounds magnitude with sidedness, the results Meltzoff and Moore obtained could be due to the increased vigor of the infants' protrusions. A progressive intensification of the vigor of tongue protrusions in the side condition would be consistent with the arousal hypothesis because with increasing trials, the infants might be expected to become more attuned to the peculiarity of the model's action and to the exposure of teeth that it entails. This attunement would produce a larger level of arousal and correspondingly larger tongue protrusions.

In conclusion, Meltzoff and Moore have not provided direct evidence that the participants matched the modeling of side protrusions. They have not shown that the participants produced more side protrusions in the side condition than in the other conditions, specifically the midline condition. The indirect and weak results they have presented are open to reinterpretation.

4.3.3 Invisible Imitation Beyond the Neonatal Period: Up to 6 Months

Considering all the evidence obtained in research with neonates, I am led to conclude that there is little evidence of neonatal matching of any gesture other than tongue protrusion. And the tongue protrusion effect can be parsimoniously interpreted as an arousal response.

Research with infants beyond the neonatal period up to 6 months is also consistent with the arousal interpretation. In this older age there is little evidence of infants matching either mouth opening or tongue protrusion. Six of the studies of tongue protrusion and mouth opening that investigated imitation in the neonatal period also included older ages, 2–6 months. Five of these studies found no matching effect for either gesture (Abravanel & Sigafoos, 1984; Fontaine, 1984; Heimann et al., 1989; Jacobson, 1979—only tongue protrusion was studied; Lewis & Sullivan, 1985). One of the six studies (Meltzoff & Moore, 1992) found a matching effect at the mean age of 2.44 months for tongue protrusion and questionable results for mouth opening (see Anisfeld, 1996).

Furthermore, three of the five studies that failed to find matching effects in the age range of 2–6 months did find matching effects for tongue protrusion in the neonatal period (Abravanel & Sigafoos, 1984; Heimann et al., 1989; Jacobson, 1979). This age-related difference can be accommodated by the arousal hypothesis. For older infants, the sight of a protruding tongue may be less arousing than for younger infants. Also, as infants become skilled in manual and other coordinated activities, the tongue may lose its predominance as an instrument for expressing arousal (see Jones, 1996).

4.3.4 Conclusion
In conclusion, for invisible gestures other than tongue protrusion, there is little evidence of neonatal matching of modeled responses. A lone tongue-protrusion matching effect can be explained by assuming that seeing a model protrude her tongue is more arousing to neonates than the conditions with which this demonstration condition was compared, and that when aroused, neonates tend to increase the rate of their tongue protrusion. Thus, what seems like imitation may actually be an arousal response. Therefore, there is little basis to dispute the Piagetian position that invisible imitation does not occur until the second half of the first year.

4.4 Deferred Imitation

Deferred imitation of unpracticed novel activities entails more elaborate representational processing than does the imitation of invisible gestures. Piaget assumed that deferred imitation could not occur until the first birthday. Critics have produced experimental results which to them indicated deferred imitation as early as 6 months. In the sections that follow, after an exposition of Piaget's position, I will challenge the critics' conclusions.

4.4.1 Piaget's View of Deferred Imitation
Under the heading of deferred imitation Piaget also discussed two immediate imitation phenomena: imitation of complex behaviors without practice and imitation of objects (Piaget, 1951/1962, pp. 62–79). What ties these three phenomena together is that they entail fairly sophisticated mental

activity that occurs without overt aid, and they manifest the child's use of imitation for representational purposes, i.e., to capture interesting observed behavior and to reflect on it. These characteristics are seen in Piaget's anecdotal examples from his children in the three categories.

Deferred Imitation   Piaget's examples of deferred imitation are ones that involve the replication of a complex, coherent sequence of actions without prior practice, for a seemingly representational purpose. Piaget suggests that when an unpracticed sequence of actions is reproduced after a delay, the sequential organization must have been constructed mentally and retained over time. He notes that in his children, deferred imitations of actions and deferred imitations of words or word sequences appeared contemporaneously. Words being representational vehicles par excellence, the contemporaneous appearance of verbal deferred imitation strengthens the representational interpretation of the deferred imitation of actions.

(a) Observation 52: Jacqueline, 16.10 months, saw how a friend threw a temper tantrum.

He screamed as he tried to get out of a play-pen and pushed it backwards, stamping his feet. J. stood watching him in amazement, never having witnessed such a scene before. The next day, she herself screamed in her play-pen and tried to move it, stamping her foot lightly several times in succession. The imitation of the whole scene was most striking. Had it been immediate, it would naturally not have involved representation, but coming as it did after an interval of more than 12 hours, it must have involved some representative or pre-representative element. (Piaget, 1951/1962, p. 63)

Because the "temper tantrum" consisted of a combination of common actions (screaming, foot stamping, and pushing), its immediate reproduction would not have entailed a particularly taxing mental operation. Immediate reproduction may also not have been imitative in purpose; it may have reflected social contagion. Or if Jacqueline had executed the tantrum on seeing her friend again, this could be interpreted as a recognition response, Piaget's "recognitory assimilation" (1952/1963, pp. 185–196). But she executed the temper tantrum spontaneously after a delay, apparently to recall a behavior that had impressed her and to reflect on it. Note that she stamped her foot (not feet) lightly. Jacqueline was not having a temper tantrum; she was representing one through her actions.

(b) Observation 55: Lucienne, 16.76 months, imitated in the bath a behavior sequence she had observed her older sister Jacqueline perform many times, but Jacqueline wasn't there at the time.

She took a towel, rolled it up into a ball, wiped her mouth with it and put it under her chin. (Piaget, 1951/1962, p. 64)

Representation was implied here by the fact that although this was a complex four-part sequential behavior, Lucienne produced it full blown all at once without external practice. Piaget infers that the organization was done internally. And the function of the imitation was apparently to represent Jacqueline's behavior.

Imitation of Complex Behaviors Immediate imitation of complex behaviors that on first try reproduces the modeled behavior faithfully can be as representational as deferred imitation. Here is an example.

(c) Observation 51: Piaget reports that at 16.00 months Jacqueline

watched me quickly crossing and uncrossing my arms and hitting my shoulders with my hands (the movement one uses to get warm). She had never before tried to imitate this action, which I had recently suggested to her two or three times. She succeeded, however, in giving a correct imitation at the first attempt. Her movement was rather short but was perfectly reproduced. (Piaget, 1951/1962, p. 62)

What impressed Piaget about this imitation is that although it involved a coordinated sequence of movements not previously performed by Jacqueline, she imitated it faithfully at once without trial and error. Piaget inferred that there must have been an "internal combination of movements" (p. 62).

Imitation of Objects Imitation of objects is another set of phenomena Piaget grouped with deferred imitation. Here are two examples, at the ages of 12–14 months.

(d) Observation 57: At 13.82 months Lucienne watched with keen interest as her father moved his bicycle back and forth parallel to the cot in which she was sitting. When it stopped, she tried to get it to move by pushing on the saddle. She also looked down to investigate the movement. Finally, she

swayed slowly backward and forwards with the same rhythm as that of the bicycle (which was then motionless). The child's whole behavior seemed to indicate clearly that this imitation ... took place merely for the purpose of representation. (Piaget, 1951/1962, p. 65)

(e) Observation 58: At 12.33 months Laurent, watching with great attention Piaget's opening and closing of a matchbox, opened and closed his right hand, keeping his eyes on the box, said "tff tff" to reproduce the sound, and opened and closed his mouth.

What is remarkable about the imitations of objects cited here is that the children reproduced on their own bodies the postures and movements of inanimate objects. Lucienne and Laurent did not copy the behavior of models, but rather they constructed by themselves representational models of the states and transformations of objects. Imitation of objects appears to be more transparently representational in purpose than the imitation of human models.

Conclusion For Piaget the hallmark of deferred imitation is that it indicates internal organization for a representational purpose without the aid of external practice. To qualify as representational imitation, the child's delayed behavior must not be reducible to other functions. Piaget's two examples of deferred imitation, (a) and (b), were complex three- and four-part sequences of actions. They occurred in the seventeenth month, but he gives examples of representational imitation from the domain of object imitation that occurred as early as 12–14 months. It thus seems clear that Piaget believed that deferred imitation, especially when it involved simpler activities, could occur at the beginning of the second year.

4.4.2 Deferred Imitation: The Experimental Literature

This section reviews the experimental studies on deferred imitation in the period from 6 to 12 months. This research tends to attribute to Piaget the view that deferred imitation could not occur until 18 months (e.g., Barr et al., 1996, p. 167; Klein & Meltzoff, 1999, p. 102), and it sets out to demonstrate that it does occur earlier, as early as 6 months. This review shows that the results obtained do not prove the existence of deferred imitation of novel behaviors before 11–12 months. On the basis of Piaget's discussion of the imitation of his three children, I have derived the expectation that deferred imitation could occur in the beginning of the second year. The experimental research thus provides empirical support for this expectation, pushing the age down by about 1 month.

The work of three groups of investigators (Meltzoff et al.; Barr & Hayne et al.; Mandler & Bauer et al.) is reviewed in the following paragraphs. The first two groups of investigators claim to have demonstrated deferred imitation at 6–9 months. It will be shown that these conclusions are unwarranted.

The basic requirement for deferred imitation to qualify as representational is that an activity the infant has not carried out before be reproduced after a delay without immediate practice. This criterion was not met in experiments with children in the age range of 6–9 months. In some of these experiments the activity that was demonstrated in all its steps was indeed novel, but the participants reproduced only part of the activity. The reproduced part by itself was not novel because it merely entailed the application of a common action (e.g., pulling) to a new object. This is not the type of deferred imitation Piaget thought could not occur until the beginning of the second year. His assignment of deferred imitation to the second year concerned ordered sequences of actions, not the much simpler case of a single familiar action applied to a new object.

In still other experiments, the evidence for deferred imitation of any kind disappears when appropriate controls are used. The appropriate control for the demonstration condition is a nondemonstration condition. My analysis shows that in some experiments there is an imitation effect only when inappropriate control conditions are added to the nondemonstration condition, not when just the nondemonstration condition is used.

Meltzoff et al. Studies Meltzoff and colleagues conducted three studies in the age range of concern here. Two, conducted with 9-month-olds, followed a similar methodology (Meltzoff, 1988b; Heimann & Meltzoff, 1996) while the third, conducted with 12-month-olds, used a somewhat different methodology (Klein & Meltzoff, 1999).

Studies with 9-Month-Olds Both studies with 9-month-olds had an experimental group and a nondemonstration baseline control group, as well as other control groups. The participants in the experimental condition witnessed the demonstration of the target actions, and after a delay were tested to see if they reproduced the target actions. The participants in the baseline condition did not see the demonstration; they took part only in the response phase.

In addition, Heimann and Meltzoff (1996) used an alternative activity control group, and Meltzoff (1988b) used an alternative activity control group and a touching control group. In the alternative activity condition, the experimenter demonstrated a different action with the same object instead of the target action. The purpose of using the alternative activity control was to exclude the possibility that "infants who see that objects have consequences, that they beep or rattle, . . . [would be] more motivated to manipulate them" (Meltzoff, 1988b, p. 219). In the touching condition, the experimenter merely touched each of the objects. "This condition controls for the possibility that infants might somehow be induced into producing the target actions if they see the adult approach and touch the object, even if the exact target action was not modeled" (Meltzoff, 1988b, p. 219).

Three tasks were demonstrated to the experimental and alternative activity participants in the Meltzoff (1988b) and Heimann and Meltzoff (1996) studies. Here is one task as an example. Experimental action: The experimenter shook a plastic egg with metal nuts in it to produce a sound. Alternative action: The experimenter spun the egg to produce the sound.

Each of the three experimental and alternative tasks was demonstrated three times, for a total duration of 20 seconds. In the Meltzoff study, the participants were tested after 24 hours and in the Heimann and Meltzoff study after 10 minutes. In the Meltzoff study, the participants were allowed 20 seconds to respond to each object from the moment it was touched, and in the Heimann and Meltzoff study, they were allowed 30 seconds. (Heimann and Meltzoff report results for both 20 seconds and 30 seconds.)

In both studies, parametric and nonparametric statistical analyses were performed on the data, with similar results. Because the "underlying data are more amenable to nonparametric analysis" (Meltzoff, 1988b, p. 220), our focus here is on the nonparametric results.

In the original analyses performed by the investigators, the two (in Heimann & Meltzoff, 1996) or three (in Meltzoff, 1988b) control groups were combined. Comparing the experimental group with the combined control groups, both studies found higher levels of target behaviors in the experimental group than in the combined control groups. Specifically, using chi-square tests, they found that the proportion of participants who produced two to three of the three target behaviors was higher in the experimental group than in the combined control groups.

The combination of the three groups into a single control group is inappropriate. The baseline condition, which controlled for the possibility that infants will engage in the target behaviors without the benefit of modeling, is the critical condition for determining whether the demonstration resulted in imitation. If the comparison between the experimental group and the baseline group yields significant results, it might be appropriate to try to decompose the effect and ask whether it was due to the adult presentation of the target behaviors (i.e., that it was an imitation effect), or to the adult touching or manipulating the objects. But if there is no effect in the comparison of the imitation group with the baseline group, there is no rationale for the alternative activity and touching groups. These groups become relevant only if a comparison between the experimental group and the baseline group yields an effect. For this reason, I computed chi-square

Table 4.1
Proportion of participants producing two to three target actions (out of three) in the experimental and control conditions (baseline, alternative activity, and touching) in the Meltzoff (1988b) and Heimann and Meltzoff (1996) studies, and chi-square comparisons between the experimental and baseline conditions

	Condition				
Study, Response Time	Experi-mental	Base-line	Alter-native	Touch-ing	$\chi^2(p)$
Meltzoff, 20 seconds	.50	.33	.17	.08	.35 (.55)
Heimann & Meltzoff, 20 seconds	.45	.27	.19	—	.78 (.38)
Heimann & Meltzoff, 30 seconds	.52	.27	.19	—	1.65 (.20)

Notes: The proportions and chi-square tests were calculated on the basis of information provided by Meltzoff (1988b, table 2) and Heimann and Meltzoff (1996, table 2). The continuity correction was used in the present chi-square tests as Meltzoff (1988b) had done in his tests. Meltzoff: Experimental group $N = 24$, baseline group $N = 12$, alternative activity group $N = 12$, touching group $N = 12$. Heimann and Meltzoff: Experimental group $N = 31$, baseline group $N = 15$, alternative activity group $N = 16$.

tests to compare the experimental with the baseline condition. The results of this analysis are presented in table 4.1.

It may be seen in table 4.1 that the nonbaseline control conditions had lower levels of target behaviors than the baseline condition, possibly because the babies' seeing the experimenter perform different actions suppressed their spontaneous inclination to perform the target actions. For instance, shaking being a common action, the babies may have been inclined to shake the egg, but observing the experimenter do something else to the egg (touch or spin it) inhibited this spontaneous inclination.

Whatever the explanation for the lower levels of the nonbaseline groups, their addition to the baseline group in the original analyses lowered the level of target responding in the combined control group and yielded a significant difference between it and the experimental group. Table 4.1 shows that when the experimental group is compared with just the baseline group, the difference ceases to be significant. There is thus no evidence in these studies of deferred imitation in 9-month-olds.

It might be noted that the Heimann and Meltzoff (1996) study also tested the participants when they reached the age of 14 months. At this older age, there was a significant difference between the experimental and baseline groups; chi square $(1, N = 46) = 4.95$, $p = .03$.

A more general criticism of these studies is that they provide no rationale for selecting the alternative activities they used from among a potential array of other alternative activities. Different alternative activities may have different effects on the likelihood of the children performing the target activities.

In conclusion, the claims of Meltzoff (1988b) and Heimann and Meltzoff (1996) that they found deferred imitation in 9-month-olds are based on flawed statistical comparisons. In these studies the experimental condition was compared with a combination of control conditions that included not only a legitimate baseline condition but also other irrelevant conditions that deflated the performance level of the control comparison. When the experimental group is compared with just the baseline group in each of the two studies, no imitation effect is found.

Study with 12-Month-Olds   Klein and Meltzoff (1999) reported a study with 12-month-olds that had an experimental condition in which the target behaviors were demonstrated three times in 20 seconds, and two control conditions, baseline and alternative activity. The experimental participants were exposed to five different action demonstrations, for example, stirring in a box with a stick. One experimental group was tested after 3 minutes (study 1), another after 1 week (study 1), and a third after 4 weeks (study 3). The results are presented in table 4.2.

Table 4.2
Mean number of target actions (out of five) produced by the experimental and control groups in the three delay conditions in Klein and Meltzoff (1999)

Delay	Experimental	Baseline	Alternative activity
3 minutes	3.50[a]	1.56	1.81
1 week	2.80[a]	1.56	1.81
4 weeks	2.56	1.50	Not used

Notes: The same control groups were used for the 3-minute and 1-week conditions. The means of the 3-minute and 1-week experimental groups were significantly higher than the mean of the two control groups combined. The mean of the 4-week experimental group was significantly higher than the mean of the baseline group.
[a] These numbers were obtained from figure 2 in Klein and Meltzoff (1999).

The actions demonstrated—pushing, pulling, putting things in containers, stirring, banging—are normally familiar to babies. Indeed, the finding that the baseline group spontaneously produced 31 percent (1.53/5) of the actions suggests that these actions were in the repertoire of the participants. There is, therefore, little evidence here of learning of new behaviors by sheer viewing without immediate accompanying action. (It does not seem likely that a truly new action could be learned in 20 seconds.) What the demonstration seems to have accomplished was to activate the known behaviors and associate them with the new objects presented. The actions involved are so common and so widely used that it is not surprising that the demonstration facilitated their generalization to new objects. But there is no evidence here of deferred imitation of new activities of the sort described by Piaget.

Barr and Hayne et al. Studies   This section covers six articles contributed by the Barr and Hayne et al. group. The results reported in these articles for children aged 6–12 months are analyzed; the results obtained for older children are not reviewed here. Five of the six articles used a jingling puppet task. Six studies reported in these five articles are discussed together. One article reporting the use of a variety of other tasks, not the puppet task, is analyzed separately.

Jingling Puppet Task with 6- and 12-Month-Olds   In this task the participants watched an experimenter demonstrate taking off a mitten from a rabbit or mouse puppet (step 1), shaking the mitten three times to make a bell inside it ring (step 2), then replacing the mitten onto the puppet (step 3). This three-part demonstration, which took 20–30 seconds, was done three times for the 12-month-olds and (in the successful procedures) six times for the 6-month-olds. After a delay of 24 hours, the participants were allowed to play with the puppet. Their behavior was observed for either 90 or 180 seconds, depending on the experiment.

The performance of the participants who were subjected to the experimental procedure was compared with the performance of participants in one of two control conditions: an alternative activity condition or a baseline condition. In the alternative activity condition, the experimenter shook the puppet and made the bell attached to its back (which was invisible to the child) ring. The alternative activity control was used in five of the studies (Barr et al., 1996; Barr & Hayne, 1999; Hayne et al., 2000; Hayne et al., 1997). In the baseline control, used in one study (Barr et al., 2001),

Table 4.3

Mean number of target actions (out of three) produced by 6- and 12-month-old experimental (E) and control (C) participants in the six puppet studies

Study	6 months		12 months	
	E	C	E	C
BDH, experiment 3 (6 months), experiment 1 (12 months)	1.00	.10	1.00	.05
BH, experiment 1A	—	—	.90	.00
HBB, experiment 2 (6 months), experiment 1 (12 months)	1.30	.20	1.20	.20
HMB, experiment 1	—	—	1.50	.25
HMB, experiment 2	—	—	1.33	.33
BVRC, experiment 1	.85	.07	—	—

Notes: All numbers, except those for HMB-experiment 2, were read from graphs. All differences between experimental and control groups were significant.
BDH = Barr et al. (1996).
BH = Barr and Hayne (1999).
HBB = Hayne et al. (2000).
HMB = Hayne et al. (1997).
BVRC = Barr et al. (2001).

the participants skipped the demonstration phase and merely took part in the response phase.

Although the demonstration involved a sequence of actions, the results in these studies are, surprisingly, presented in terms of mean number of individual actions. However, from the means provided, it is possible to derive some information concerning the participants' performance with regard to sequences. The results obtained are given in table 4.3.

Based on these results, the authors claim that even 6-month-old children can imitate novel behaviors after a delay without immediate practice. This would indeed be the case if the participants had executed the entire sequence of three actions, or at least two of them. But as table 4.3 shows, in two of the three studies with 6-month-olds, the means were 1.00 and .85, indicating that the participants reproduced on the average only about one action or less than one action, pulling off the mitten. In one of the three studies of 6-month-olds, the mean was 1.30, indicating that some participants performed more than one action. It is not clear how much faith one can put in this isolated finding, given that it was not replicated in two other studies in this series. The results are more positive for the 12-month-old groups. In three of five studies, they scored on average above 1 (1.20–1.50).

The finding that almost all the participants in all the studies pulled the mitten off the puppet after a brief demonstration does not indicate that they learned a new action without immediate overt practice, for the simple reason that although the object (the puppet) was novel, the action applied to it was not. What the demonstration seems to have accomplished is to help transfer a response that was in the babies' repertoires (pulling) to a new object (the puppet). It is not surprising that even 6-month-olds readily acquired this kind of extension of an established response even in the absence of direct overt practice. The association of a known behavior with a new object seems to have been sufficiently interesting to the babies for them to perform the behavior 24 hours after having witnessed it. Their reproductions could be interpreted as recognition responses; the child saying gesturally, "Oh, I have seen this interesting thing before." There is no reason to grant the 6-month-old participants deferred imitation of a novel complex activity.

How are we to interpret the three 1+ means for 12-month-olds? These results indicate that some participants did more than just take off the mitten. Unfortunately, the articles do not provide information on whether one or the other or both of the two other actions demonstrated (shaking the mitten and putting it back on) was reproduced by some participants. Let us assume that the participants who contributed to raising the mean above 1 followed the sequence of actions demonstrated; they took off the mitten and shook it. Although each of the two actions is not novel, their sequencing is. This indicates that at 12 months some babies are capable of deferred imitation of novel two-action sequences. They can mentally organize two actions into a sequence and remember it over a period of 24 hours without immediate practice.

There is thus evidence here that rudimentary deferred imitation can occur at 12 months. Piaget's examples of deferred imitation were more complex and they occurred at an older age, between 16 and 17 months. But from his examples of imitation of objects, I have inferred that deferred imitation *can* occur as early as it did here. It should not surprise us that an experimental investigation of 216 babies—the number of 12-month-olds tested in the studies being considered—will uncover a capacity not seen in anecdotal observations of just three babies—the number of children that Piaget observed.

In his discussion of deferred imitation, Piaget highlighted not only representational processing but also representational intent. While the results analyzed provide evidence of representational processing, the presence of representational intent is open to question. Piaget inferred representational intent by excluding other reasonable purposes. For instance, Jacqueline reproduced the temper tantrum in the absence of the model and in the absence of any obvious external triggering stimuli. Piaget therefore inferred that she spontaneously recalled what had happened the day before and acted out her reminiscence, the way an adult would describe an interesting past experience. But in the tasks described, it is less clear that by reproducing the target actions, the participants intended to imitate.

Because the objects on which the actions were modeled were represented, the actions performed could have been produced as elicited recognition responses, not intended as representational imitations. Thus the participants' memory of a novel sequence of actions provides evidence of representational activity, but it is an open question as to whether there was representational intent.

A Study Using a Variety of Tasks with 6- and 9-Month-Olds   Collie and Hayne (1999) reported two experiments with 6- and 9-month-olds. In the first experiment, the infants were presented with six objects designed as three pairs. In one pair, one action was associated with each object, and in the other two pairs two actions were associated with each object. In the second experiment, the participants were presented with twelve objects, designed as six pairs: four single-action pairs and two double-action pairs. An example of a single-action pair is pulling cord on a woman doll (step 1), making her legs jump; spinning a man doll (step 1), turning him upside down. An example of a double-action pair is picking an owl up from a tree (step 1) and pressing its belly (step 2), making its eyes flash; picking the sun up from the sky (step 1) and shaking it (step 2), making it rattle.

For any one participant, one member of each pair was demonstrated and one was not, serving as a control for the demonstrated member of the pair. Each action was modeled six times in succession, for a total of 2–3 minutes. After 24 hours, the participants were presented again with all the objects and a count was made of the number of target actions they performed within 3 minutes of touching an object. Inexplicably, no distinction is made in the reporting of the results—summarized in table 4.4—between the single actions and the two-sequence actions, although the latter can obviously lay a stronger claim to being novel.

The actions involved—such as picking up, shaking, and pulling—are not new. Indeed, the nondemonstrated columns in table 4.4 show that the participants spontaneously produced on their own an average of 1.30

Table 4.4

Mean number of target actions produced by the 6- and 9-month-olds for demonstrated and nondemonstrated objects in Collie and Hayne (1999)

Study	6 months		9 months	
	Demonstrated	Nondemonstrated	Demonstrated	Nondemonstrated
Experiment 1, max = 5[a]	1.38	.62	2.15	1.23
Experiment 2, max = 8[b]	2.88	1.60	3.25	1.75

Note: These figures were read from graphs. All differences between demonstrated and nondemonstrated actions were significant.

[a] One single-action pair + two double-action pairs = five actions.

[b] Four single-action pairs + two double-action pairs = eight actions.

actions. The greater number of actions performed on the demonstrated objects may be due to the enhanced interest in these objects that was created by the demonstration. Moreover, the greater attractiveness of the demonstrated objects may have resulted in less attention to the nondemonstrated objects.

Mandler and Bauer et al. Studies   Two studies are reviewed here: one with 9-month-olds and one with 11-month-olds. These studies have the advantage of focusing on the reproduction of sequences of actions, which are more challenging and are more likely to be novel than individual actions.

Study with 9-Month-Olds (L. Carver & Bauer, 1999)   Six double-action tasks were used in this study with 9-month-olds. An example of a task is opening a book (step 1) and pulling a handle (step 2), making a picture of a duck pop up. Three of the tasks were used in the demonstration part of the experiment and all six were used in the test, the three nondemonstrated tasks serving as controls. In each of the three demonstration tasks, the participants were first allowed to play freely with each object for as long as they wanted. The target sequence was then demonstrated twice, with narration. The demonstration was done two more times after average intervals of 43 hours. Then a week after the third demonstration session, the participants were shown (on slides) the events they had seen, as well as new events. The memory test took place 1 month after the slide presentation. At the memory session, the participants were given each of the three previously demonstrated objects and the three nondemonstrated objects. Table 4.5 presents the results.

Table 4.5

Mean number of target actions and sequences per task in the Carver and Bauer (1999) study in the demonstrated and nondemonstrated tasks

	Demonstrated	Nondemonstrated
Individual actions, max = 2	.87	.58
Sequences of actions, max = 1	.18	.10

Note: The difference between the number of demonstrated and nondemonstrated actions was significant, but the difference between the number of demonstrated and nondemonstrated sequences was not.

The table shows that, as in the other research reviewed, the demonstration led the 9-month-olds in this study to increase the production of individual actions that they were inclined to produce spontaneously (as indicated by the nondemonstrated results). But despite the extensive, repeated demonstrations, they did not acquire the novel sequences of the actions.

Study with 11-Month-Olds (Mandler & McDonough, 1995)   In the first experiment, 11-month-old participants ($M = 11.33$ months) were exposed to two object-based sequences of the sort used by Carver and Bauer (1999), as well as arbitrary sequences, which are not discussed here. One sequence consisted of pushing a button through the hole of a transparent box (step 1) and shaking the box (step 2), producing a rattling noise. The participants were first allowed to manipulate each object for as long as they remained engaged ($M = 57$ seconds) to establish a baseline level of performance. The target sequence was then demonstrated three times in succession. At the test, which took place after a delay of 20 seconds for one object and 24 hours for the other object, the participants were again exposed to each object for as long as they were engaged by it (mean duration of exposure for both delays = 60 seconds). The levels of production of the target actions and sequences at baseline and after demonstration are presented in table 4.6.

As I have noted with respect to other studies, an increase in actions following demonstration does not constitute evidence for Piagetian deferred imitation of novel actions because the actions themselves (e.g., pushing, shaking) were not novel. In fact, the spontaneous baseline level is considerably above 0.

However, the demonstration also facilitated the production of sequences. Only 11% of the participants produced a sequence at baseline

Table 4.6

Results for target actions and sequences during baseline and after 20 seconds and 24 hours in Mandler and McDonough (1995), $N = 18$

	20-second Delay Condition		24-hour Delay Condition	
	At Baseline	After Demonstration	At Baseline	After Demonstration
Mean number of actions, max = 2	.56	.94	.39	1.06
Number of subjects who produced the sequence	2	6	2	8

Note: At both memory delays, the number of target actions produced after demonstration significantly exceeded the number produced at baseline. According to information in the article and clarifications provided by Mandler, the level of sequences at both delays was also significantly higher than at baseline.

(2/18), whereas 33% (6/18) did so 20 seconds after the demonstration, and 44% (8/18) did so 24 hours after the demonstration. The extensive exposure to the sequences seems to have helped a substantial number of 11-month-olds—perhaps the older ones, since the ages ranged up to 11.66 months—learn a truly new sequence of actions. This would be about 1 month earlier than Piaget found complex representational activity in his children.

4.4.3 Generalization of Responses

Piaget's theory holds that the memories of infants become increasingly detached from the specific circumstances of the initial encounter. The broader the generalization of an observed behavior beyond the specific circumstances of initial observation, the higher the assumed level of representation. There is support for this notion in the studies of deferred imitation. Three of the studies already discussed (Hayne et al., 2000, 1997; Klein & Meltzoff, 1999) investigated the effects of changes between demonstration and testing on the production of target behaviors.

In their first and second experiments, Hayne et al. (1997) changed the identity of a puppet (rabbit to mouse, or vice versa) or its color. They found that both changes reduced the performance of their experimental 12-month-olds to that of the control participants, but 18-month-olds whom they studied generalized from one puppet to another puppet and from one color to another color. Similarly, Hayne et al. (2000) found that the puppet change eliminated the effect for the 6-month-olds and 12-month-olds whom they studied.

Hayne et al. (2000) also studied the effects of changes in the testing environment between the demonstration phase and response phase (home to laboratory, laboratory to home). They found that for their 12-month-olds, the environmental change left the experimental effect intact, but for their 6-month-olds, the environmental change undid the effect. Klein and Meltzoff (1999) studied the influence of environmental change on the performance of their 12-month-olds. Their changes, including both home/laboratory changes as well as a tent-laboratory/regular-laboratory change, had no influence on the results. The findings of Hayne et al. (2000) and Klein and Meltzoff (1999) are thus consistent in showing that 12-month-olds generalize between testing environments. The environmental changes made were apparently less salient for babies of this age than the changes made in the stimulus itself, which, as we have seen, eliminated the effect.

The results thus support Piaget's view in showing that as they get older, children become increasingly less bound by an initial sensorimotor experience. Environmental changes inhibit generalization for 6-month-olds, but only changes in the stimulus itself inhibit generalization for 12-month-old infants. It should be noted that these limitations apply only to unaided generalization. We have seen in the previous sections that the experimenter's brief demonstration of the application of a familiar action (e.g., shaking, pulling) to a new object in the new laboratory environment is sufficient for babies to remember it and to perform it on the object on which it was demonstrated. It is only with regard to the additional spontaneous extensions not facilitated by demonstration that the limitations apply.

4.4.4 Conclusions

Piaget thought of deferred imitation of sequences of actions as a representational phenomenon that had two characteristics: mental processing without attendant overt practice and imitative intent. He thought that this type of deferred imitation could not occur until the second year of life, with the more complex imitations not occurring until the beginning of the second quarter of the second year. Experimental investigators have attempted to bring the age down to as low as 6 months. I have reviewed experiments with children in the age range of 6 to 12 months. My detailed examination of the experiments shows that only at 11–12 months do some children exhibit rudimentary deferred imitation of novel sequences of actions. These findings provide experimental evidence for the hypothesis, derived from Piaget's discussion and observations, that deferred imitation can begin to occur at about the age of 1 year. It must be noted, however, that while the results analyzed provide evidence for representational processing without overt practice, it is not clear that the results satisfy Piaget's other criterion, that of imitative intent. The participants may have reenacted the modeled actions after a delay, not to imitate them, but to express their recognition of the objects.

At the younger ages of 6–9 months studied in the experiments reviewed here, there is little evidence of deferred imitation. Three experiments (Barr et al., 1996, 2001; L. Carver & Bauer, 1999) found no evidence for deferred imitation of sequences of action. Only one experiment (Hayne et al., 2000) can be interpreted as indicating that some 6-month-olds reproduced a two-action sequence.

There being little evidence for the deferred imitation of sequences in 6-month-olds, the burden of the claim for deferred representational imitation at this age rests on the assumption that the individual actions were novel. Such an assumption is hard to defend. In all of the experiments that obtained effects, the responses demonstrated were common everyday types of actions (e.g., pulling, picking up, putting in, and shaking). In some of the experiments the objects used by the investigators were selected to be new. However, even if a given object selected to be new was indeed new to the participants (in the sense that they appreciated the difference between it and similar objects in their experience), the most that can be claimed is that the demonstration helped the participants extend to one more object an action they had applied to many objects before. Generalization being such a ubiquitous process (e.g., McDonough & Mandler, 1998), it is hardly surprising that it was facilitated by even a very brief (20 seconds) demonstration. What the demonstration seems to have accomplished was to raise a prepotent response above threshold and link it to the object presented. Then when the object was re-presented after a delay, it activated the target action as a recognition response, the baby acknowledging the new object by gestures.[1]

Acknowledgments

I thank Elizabeth Anisfeld, Shimon Anisfeld, and Allan Goldstein, who read multiple versions of the chapter and contributed significantly to its improvement in substance and style. They have my deep gratitude. I also appreciate the helpful suggestions of Bill Arsenio, Samantha Berkule, Cara Frankel, Tim Lytton, Jean Mandler, Susan Rose, Holly Ruff, and Jaime Zins.

1. See comments on this chapter by Zentall (vol. 2, ch. 8.5, p. 189) and by Elsner (vol. 2, ch. 8.6, p. 191). ED.

5 Intention Reading and Imitative Learning

Michael Tomasello and Malinda Carpenter

5.1 Introduction

Imitation presents very difficult problems for mechanistic theories of human psychology. Behaviorism never knew what to do with imitation, since it represented a kind of learning not easily analyzable into stimuli and responses. Information-processing psychology has basically ignored imitation; virtually no textbook of cognitive psychology or cognitive science even mentions it. Perhaps the main problem is that social learning and imitation are very closely intertwined with processes of social cognition—understanding how other persons work and understanding what a particular person is doing on a specific occasion—and these also have not been given much attention by either behaviorists or mainstream cognitive scientists.

Tomasello et al. (1993a) provided an evolutionary and developmental account of the way human social learning relates to processes of social cognition more generally. The basic proposal was that what differentiates human social learning from that of other animals, including our nearest primate relatives, is that humans understand the behavior of others not just as body movements, but as intentional, goal-directed action. Simply put, humans perceive others not as moving their limbs in particular ways, but as doing such things as opening a drawer, giving a gift to someone, washing the dishes, telling a story, throwing a ball—each of which may be done with many different body movements so long as the same goal in the external world is reached. Thus, when they attempt to reproduce the actions of others, humans—at least in some circumstances—reproduce the actions as they have understood them from the point of view of the intentionality involved, that is, the intended effect on the external world, including the social world.

In the decade since the publication of the paper by Tomasello et al. (1993a), empirical studies of the social learning of various animal species and human children have multiplied severalfold. Consequently, there have been important advances—empirically, theoretically, and methodologically—in the understanding of these topics. In this chapter we review the most important empirical and methodological contributions of the past decade in this field, and we then try to assess what they mean for our understanding of how processes of social learning are shaped, or perhaps even created, by different forms of social cognition—especially those we will call intention reading. First we deal briefly with a few important studies on nonhuman primates and other nonhuman animals, but our attention is primarily directed at the many new studies focused on human children, mainly in the second year of life.

5.2   Imitative Learning in Nonhuman Animals

Tomasello et al. (1993a) claimed that there was no convincing evidence that any nonhuman animals engaged in humanlike imitative learning. They explained humanlike imitative learning in the following way: A child, for example, observes an adult using a knife to open a bottle. The child understands the intentional structure of the action; the adult's goal is to open the bottle and she has chosen one behavioral means, among other possible means, for doing this. The child can then either adopt the adult's means or not, as she chooses. Other animals do not understand intentional action in this way, and so they cannot engage in this kind of social learning process, which Tomasello et al. (1993a) called imitative learning, one form of cultural learning. Around the same time, Whiten and Ham (1992) coined another term, "goal emulation," to describe the case in which the learner parses the observed action into end and means, but then chooses to ignore the means used by the demonstrator and employ a different one instead. Both imitative learning and goal emulation thus require some understanding of the demonstrator's goal or intention.

The claim was that other animals do not perceive or understand the distinction between goals as mental entities representing the desired state of affairs the organism is attempting to bring about, and behavioral means toward goals ("means-ends dissociation" in the terminology of Piaget, 1952/1963). They thus engage in two other forms of social learning instead. One is mimicking. Mimicking refers to the process in which an organism reproduces the body movements of another, without an understanding of any goal that might be structuring those movements. For example, Hayes and Hayes (1952) trained their human-raised chimpanzee Viki to reproduce various body movements and gestures that they performed, for example, blinking their eyes or clapping their hands. They trained her throughout her daily life in their home for a period of more than 17 months before systematic testing began. The training consisted of a human performing a behavior and then using various shaping and molding techniques, with rewards, to get Viki to repeat the behavior ("Do this"). After she had become skillful, some novel behaviors were systematically introduced. In general, she reproduced them faithfully and quickly; she had clearly "gotten the idea" of the mimicking game.

Later, Custance et al. (1995) demonstrated in a more rigorous fashion similar abilities in two nursery-reared chimpanzees after they were trained for 3.5 months in a manner similar to that for Viki. Of the forty-eight novel actions demonstrated after the training period, one subject correctly reproduced thirteen and the other correctly reproduced twenty. Whether the subjects could see their own responses or whether the response was "invisible" (e.g., facial expressions) was not a significant factor. Evidence that this is only mimicking comes from a study by Call and Tomasello (1995), who tested a human-raised orangutan who was trained in similar ways. He was successful in learning body movements, but then when shown how to solve a problem involving an object (a human used a tool and told the orangutan to "Do this"), he could not transfer his mimicking skills to this goal-directed action.

The best mimickers in the animal world are various species of birds (especially, for example, parrots). Birds' skills of vocal mimicry are well known, but recently they have also been shown to reproduce the body movements of others whom they observe solving a task. For example, if they observe a conspecific using its beak to open a container, they will do the same, whereas if they observe the conspecific using its foot to open a container, they will do that (F. Campbell et al., 1999; Zentall et al., 1996; see also a similar behavior by a marmoset species reported by Voelkl & Huber, 2000). But it is not currently known whether these intriguing observations represent cases of imitative learning, in which the learner discerns the intentional structure of the observer's behavior and chooses to reproduce its means to reach the goal, or instead mimicry, in which the observer simply copies body movements relatively blindly. Research with human infants has attempted to distinguish these two cases in various ways, as we will see later, and these could be used to good effect in the studies with birds.

The other major form of social learning that does not depend on reading intentions is called emulation learning. In emulation learning, an observer simply watches the objects with which a demonstrator is interacting and learns something about them. When an organism observes another organism manipulate objects in this way, it learns a lot about those objects and their affordances for action—much more than when it observes those objects sitting idle. Thus, if we give naive chimpanzees a rock and a nut, they may not discover on their own how to crack the nut open. But if they see another do it, they might learn from this observation that nuts can be opened, which creates a new possibility for them, and they might even learn something about the rock's role in the process. In emulation learning, the organism learns new things, some of them quite complex; it is just that they are about the environment, not about behavior. We can say that the observer is attending to the end result in the environment produced by the other—which was, from the human point of view, the behaver's goal. But in emulation learning, as opposed to imitative and other forms of cultural learning, the observer does not attend at all to the behavior of the other, much less to the other's goal.

There are many studies that show that chimpanzees and other apes are good emulators (e.g., Nagell et al., 1993; Call & Tomasello, 1995; see Tomasello, 1996, for a review). One apparently contradictory study is that of Whiten et al. (1996), who presented chimpanzees with a transparent "foraging box" containing fruit. On any given trial, the box could be opened by one of two mechanisms, each of which could be operated in two ways. For each mechanism, a human experimenter demonstrated one way of opening the box to some subjects and the other way to other subjects (with the other mechanism being blocked). The subjects were then given the chance to open the box themselves. The results were that for one mechanism there was no effect of the observed demonstration. For the other mechanism there was some evidence that chimpanzees were more likely to use the manner of opening demonstrated by the experimenter. The authors claimed to have demonstrated imitative learning. However, in the analysis by Tomasello (1996), the chimpanzees could easily have learned to match the manner of opening via emulation. One group of chimpanzees saw that the stick afforded pushing through the clasp, while the other saw that it afforded twisting and pulling. A similar analysis applies to a recent study with marmosets, who were especially skillful at learning a box's affordances through emulation (Bugnyar & Huber, 1997).

Some researchers have claimed that emulation learning is not a useful concept because it can never be distinguished from imitative learning when an organism reproduces some action on an object because the object normally undergoes some kind of transformation from which the learner could be learning (R. Byrne & Russon, 1998). But in research with human children, investigators have created some interesting new paradigms that are potentially capable of distinguishing imitative learning and goal emulation from emulation learning and mimicking. These are elaborated later, but they basically involve the demonstrator either trying unsuccessfully to do something or doing something by accident—the two main cases where the demonstrator's intention does not match the result produced on the object in the real world. In these cases, a learner engaged in imitative learning or goal emulation will reproduce the action she believes the demonstrator intended, whereas a mimicker will produce the body movements only (including the unsuccessful and accidental actions), and an emulator will reproduce the unintended result. There have been two attempts to do these kinds of studies with chimpanzees (Call et al., submitted; Myowa-Yamakoshi & Matsuzawa, 2000), but neither study produced clearly interpretable results.

5.3 Imitative Learning in Human Children

Human neonates can mimic some facial expressions of other persons from very soon after birth (Meltzoff & Moore, 1977, 1989). By the middle of the first year, infants also can learn new things about objects and their affordances via emulation learning (Barr et al., 1996; von Hoftsten & Siddiqui, 1993). But until recently, it was unclear at what age infants were capable of engaging in imitative learning and goal emulation with intention reading. Recently a number of novel experimental techniques have been devised in an effort to determine precisely what kinds of social learning children are employing. The basic problem is that if, for example, an adult takes the top off of a pen and a child then does the same, there are many possible explanations, including emulation, mimicking, and imitative learning, among others. Researchers have therefore employed some of the following techniques for dissociating different components of what the child perceives, understands, and reproduces of the demonstration:

• demonstrations with unusual means to an end that children would be unlikely to use on their own spontaneously, and monitoring children's looking behavior to see if they are concerned with the goal;
• demonstrations of trying or failing or having an accident, in which the adult's surface behavior is not an accurate reflection of what she intends to do; and
• demonstrations that can be interpreted in different ways, depending on the child's understanding of what the adult is intending to do—which is

manipulated in various ways by providing different interpretive contexts before or during the demonstration.

In what follows we look at examples of these different techniques in turn and then at some other interesting cases of intention reading and imitative learning that have interesting theoretical implications but that have been less well researched.

5.3.1 Unusual Means

Meltzoff (1988a) presented 14-month-old infants with a novel demonstration of an adult bending down and touching her head to the top of a box, which then lit up. Although the infants could more easily have solved this task by emulation (e.g., by touching the box with their hand instead of their head), they instead chose to use the same means as the adult, unusual as it was—they too touched their head to the top of the box. These infants could have been either mimicking the adult's unusual action without understanding her goal of turning on the light, or else they could have been copying this action with the same goal in mind—imitative learning. In order to determine which of these two social learning mechanisms the infants were using, Carpenter et al. (1998b) tested 9- to 15-month-old infants on the head touch and other similar tasks. However, they delayed the illumination of the light slightly after the infant's reproduction of the action, and coded whether infants looked in anticipation to the light. They found that 12-month-old and older infants, on average, looked to the light in anticipation (before it came on). If the light did not come on, these infants often repeated their action or looked quizzically at the adults. This suggests that the infants were adopting the adult's means in order to achieve the same goal as the adult—to turn on the light. The infants thus were not just mimicking the adult's action but instead were engaging in imitative learning of her novel action.

5.3.2 Accidents, Trying, and Failing

By 12 months of age it seems that infants are not just mimicking adults but instead can discern their goals and choose to use the same behavioral means the adults used to achieve the same goal. It has been assumed in these studies that the child understands the adult's goal mentalistically— she sees a kind of thought bubble coming from the adult's head containing a picture of the end state the adult is trying to bring about—but this is not necessarily the case. It is possible that what the infants were trying to reproduce was simply the observed result of the adult's action (the illuminated light—the external goal) with no understanding of the adult's mental goal or intention. Two further studies of infants in this age range—in which the observed result of the action differed from the adult's thought-bubble intention or goal—indicate that infants do indeed use their understanding of others' goals and intentions when learning novel actions from them.

In one study, infants were shown the same actions, for the same results, but the adult's intention varied across conditions. The infants could thus only use an understanding of the adult's intentions to solve this problem correctly. Carpenter et al. (1998a) showed 14- to 18-month-olds a series of two actions on objects, in counterbalanced order. For each object, the two actions were followed by an interesting result, for example, the sudden illumination of colored lights. In the key conditions, one of the demonstrator's actions was marked verbally as intentional ("There!") and one was marked verbally as accidental ("Whoops!"), but otherwise the actions looked very similar. Instead of mimicking both actions they saw, even the youngest infants reproduced the actions marked as intentional significantly more often than those marked as accidental. In a third condition, when both actions were marked verbally as intentional, the infants typically reproduced both actions.

In the other study, infants were able to go beyond filtering out unintended actions and achieve results that they never saw in their entirety. Meltzoff (1995) showed 18-month-olds an adult either successfully achieving a result on an object (e.g., pulling apart two halves of a dumbbell) or trying but failing to achieve that result (e.g., the adult's hands slipped off the ends of the dumbbell). The infants produced the completed result equally often in both conditions—whether they had seen the adult produce that result or had only seen the adult's intention but not the completed result. Various control conditions reported by Meltzoff et al. (1999) indicated that infants in the intention condition were not just absorbing lower-level information such as the first part of the action (e.g., grasp the toy here and make pulling movements). When the adult demonstrated the failed action on a small dumbbell and gave infants a giant dumbbell, the infants tried different means to pull the toy apart. Likewise, when infants were given a trick dumbbell that was glued together, their hands slipped off just like the adult's had, but they continued trying to separate it, again using different means. Meltzoff thus concluded that infants understood the adult's unfulfilled intention and produced the result that the adult meant to produce (instead of copying the adult's surface behavior).

Bellagamba and Tomasello (1999) replicated these findings with 18-month-olds, but found that 12-month-olds did not reproduce the adult's intended action when they only saw her trying unsuccessfully to perform it.

A related study with older children is that by Want and Harris (2001). In this study, the adult showed 2.5- and 3.5-year-old children a mistaken action before showing them the correct solution to a problem or showed them the correct solution alone. That is, in the mistake condition, the adult first inserted a tool into the incorrect side of an apparatus, saying "Oops," and then inserted it into the correct side. Three-year-olds but not 2-year-olds performed better in the mistake condition than in the condition in which they saw only the correct solution (although it is unclear whether the children benefited from watching the adult's mistake or simply gained more information than the other children from the extra highlighting of causal information in the incorrect demonstration).

So by 14 to 18 months of age, infants can distinguish between intentional actions and accidental or unfulfilled actions, and choose to reproduce (or produce) the intended actions or results. Instead of copying exactly what others do, infants do what others intend to do. They do this for human actors, but not for machines (Meltzoff, 1995). They thus are not mimicking or emulating in these situations, but instead are engaging in the imitative learning (or goal emulation) of adults' goal-directed actions.

5.3.3   Manipulating Children's Interpretation

Other studies have manipulated the social learning context in an effort to influence children's interpretation of adult intentional action, which should have an influence on what they reproduce if, and only if, they are interpreting the behavior intentionally. Gergely et al. (2002) showed 14-month-olds an adult touching her head to the top of a box to turn on a light (as in Meltzoff, 1988a). However, for half of the infants, the adult's hands were occupied (she was holding a blanket around her shoulders) and for half the adult's hands were free. Infants who saw the hands-free demonstration touched the box with their heads significantly more often than infants who saw the hands-occupied demonstration (all the infants also touched the top of the box with their hands). The infants thus used the context of the situation to interpret the adult's behavior, appearing to assume that if the adult's hands were free and she still chose to use her head, then there must be a good reason for this choice. However, if the adult's hands were occupied, then the use of her head was explained as necessary given her circumstances—not an essential part of her action (and thus the infants did not reproduce this action). These infants' interpretation of the adult's goal probably differed across conditions, depending on the context of the situation (even though the adult's actions were identical). In the hands-occupied condition her goal was "turn on the light," and in the hands-free condition it was "turn on the light with your head." By 14 months, infants thus evidence a deeper understanding of intentional action and how it relates to the surrounding context and what this means for their own choice of a behavioral means in similar circumstances.

A series of studies of older children by Bekkering and colleagues (Bekkering et al., 2000; Gleissner et al., 2000; Wohlschläger et al., in press) extends these findings. For example, Bekkering et al. (2000) showed 3- to 6-year-old children an experimenter touching a table in one of two locations. In one condition, there were dots on the table in those locations and in another condition there were no dots. In the "no dot" condition, the children usually matched the adult's behavior exactly, even copying her crossed or straight arm positions—presumably because there was no other apparent goal to her actions than these arm movements. In the "dot" condition, however, the children touched the same locations as the experimenter, but often did not match her exact arm positions. This is presumably because when there were dots they interpreted the adult's goal as "touching the dots" (by whatever means), whereas when there were no dots the only possible goal was "moving one's arm like this." Bekkering and colleagues concluded that imitation in young children is guided by their understanding of adults' goals; that is, there is a hierarchy of goals and subgoals and children imitate what they perceive adults' main goal to be. Sometimes this involves matching others' actions; sometimes it does not.

A further study also shows that children's use of the context to interpret adults' actions influences what they learn from a demonstration. Carpenter et al. (2002) demonstrated to five groups of children how to pull out a pin and open a box. What differed among groups was what children experienced just prior to this demonstration, with some children receiving information about the adult's "prior intention" (i.e., what she intended to do with the box as she approached it). One group of children watched this demonstration alone; these children thus did not know what the adult's prior intention was. Three other groups received some information about the adult's prior intention before seeing this demonstration. Either the adult tugged unsuccessfully on the door of the box, or showed the box already open, or visited and opened three different boxes before demonstrating how to open the test box. Thus, all children in all four of these conditions saw a full demonstration of how to open the box, but only the children in the three prior intention conditions could know what the adult was about to do before she began this demonstration. The children in a control demonstration group saw a goal-irrelevant action (the adult raked her fingers down the roof of the box) before the full demonstration, and a sixth baseline group received no demonstration at all. Two- and 2.5-year-old children were significantly better at opening the box themselves when they knew the adult's prior intention. This was the case even when the adult's actions on the test box were absolutely identical in the prior and no prior intention groups (i.e., when children gained information about the adult's prior intention through her actions on other boxes). It is interesting that the children who did not know what the adult was about to do per-formed just as poorly as the children who received no demonstration at all. This study demonstrates with special clarity the role of intentional under-standing in children's imitative learning because a child that did not in-terpret the adult's behavior intentionally would have learned the same amount in all the different conditions. Instead, the way that the children interpreted the adult's prior intentions actually enabled them to imitatively learn something that they otherwise could not have learned.

What is remarkable about children's behavior in these studies is this: Children saw the same demonstration in different experimental conditions. What differed across conditions was various contextual factors that led the children to interpret the adult's actions in different ways, that is, under different intentional descriptions: touching a dot or not, trying to open a box or not, trying to turn on a light or trying to turn on a light with the head. As young as 14 months, the children's interpretation of the adult's action was then directly reflected in what they subsequently attempted to reproduce of the adult's behavior.

5.3.4   Imitating Reciprocal Behavior

There are some kinds of actions that children observe and attempt to imi-tate that have a special structure because they involve people having goals toward one another reciprocally. For example, a mother might blow a rasp-berry on her child's arm. If a child wants to imitate this behavior, she is faced with a choice, depending on her interpretation. Thus, she might blow a raspberry on her own arm, in exactly the same place the mother did, or alternatively, she might blow a raspberry back on her mother's arm—interpreting the behavior in this case reciprocally as "blowing on the part-ner's arm." Tomasello (1999) called this role reversal imitation. In a pilot study, Carpenter et al. (submitted) have found that 12- and 18-month-old children are able to employ this reciprocal interpretation in some cases. At both ages, children reciprocated in these kinds of dyadic, body-oriented situations, but 18-month-olds were more likely than 12-month-olds to reciprocate in situations involving interactions around objects.

This same interpretation applies to the learning of a piece of language, since learning to use linguistic symbols is also reciprocal. Thus, when an adult uses a linguistic symbol in a communicative act, the adult intends things toward the child's attentional state; she wants the child to attend to something. Consequently, to learn to use a symbol like an adult, a child must learn to use it toward the adult in the same way the adult used it toward the child (Tomasello, 1999). It is interesting that Rakoczy et al. (2004) have provided evidence that something like this is also going on in children's early symbolic play. Before 2 years of age, children learn symbolic behaviors with objects by imitatively learning them from adults, in much the same way that they learn instrumental actions with artifacts. But from about 2 years of age on, they look to the adult more often, and in some cases smile more often, when producing the symbolic behaviors. This is evidence that children of this age are reproducing a special kind of intentionality, a kind of shared intentionality (mutually reciprocal) in which for the moment we agree to, for example, treat this pencil as if it were a horse.

5.3.5 Learning Words

Given the general ability to learn a linguistic symbol through role-reversal imitation, it is still the case that in learning particular words on particular occasions children often need to read the adult's intentions to connect the word appropriately to its intended referent. Several language acquisition studies show that children as young as 18 months can combine all of the types of intention reading we have discussed earlier while imitatively learning novel words. For example, in a study of 24-month-olds by Tomasello and Barton (1994), an adult announced her (prior) intention to find a target object by saying, "Let's go find the *toma*." She searched through several buckets, extracting and rejecting with a scowl the novel objects inside. She then extracted another novel object with an excited expression and stopped searching. In a later comprehension test, when asked to go get the *toma* themselves, children chose the object the adult had identified as fulfilling her intention. Akhtar and Tomasello (1996) used a modified procedure to show that 24-month-old children could identify the intended referent even when the adult was unable to open the container with the target object inside—that is, when she had an unfulfilled intention. Tomasello et al. (1996) replicated both these studies with 18-month-old children.

Another study investigated children's use of their understanding of intentional versus accidental actions when learning novel words. In a study of 24-month-olds by Tomasello and Barton (1994), the adult announced her (prior) intention to perform a target action by saying "I'm going to *meek* Big Bird!" She then performed one accidental action (saying "Whoops!") and one intentional action (saying "There!"), in counterbalanced order. Later, when the children were asked to *meek* a different character themselves, they performed the action the adult had marked as intentional. Finally, using a preferential-looking paradigm, Poulin-Dubois and Forbes (2002) found that 27- but not 21-month-old children could use an actor's eye-gaze and gestures to learn verbs that differed only in intention (e.g., topple versus knock over). These word-learning studies thus also provide evidence of children's understanding of accidental actions, unfulfilled intentions, and prior intentions by 18–24 months of age.

5.3.6 Children with Autism

Children with autism show mixed results on tests of imitation (see S. Rogers, 1999 and I. Smith & Bryson, 1994, for reviews). They are clearly very good at mimicking—their tendency to engage in echolalia is evidence of that. However, very few studies have attempted to determine what other social learning mechanisms these children are capable of, and in particular how their understanding of intentions (or the lack thereof) might affect the process. Carpenter et al. (2002) found that 3- to 4-year-old children with autism (with nonverbal mental ages ranging from 28 to 50 months) performed at near-ceiling levels on imitation tasks such as the head touch task used by Carpenter et al. (1998a). These children too looked to the light in anticipation (before it came on), as often as did a control group of children with other developmental delays—indicating their appreciation of the goal-directed nature of this action. Two studies that used versions of Meltzoff's (1995) test of understanding of others' unfulfilled intentions also found no impairment for children with autism (Aldridge et al., 2000; Carpenter et al., 2001), again suggesting their appreciation of the goal-directed nature of these unfulfilled actions.

However, there may still be important differences in the way in which children with autism and other children copy others' behavior. For example, Hobson and Lee (1999) found that adolescent children with autism copied the particular style of a demonstrator's actions less often than did developmentally delayed and typically developing children. They interpreted this deficit in terms of autistic children's problems in identifying with the "attitude" of the adult demonstrator, including her intention in using a particular behavioral style.

5.3.7 Criticisms

Recently there have been several studies that have attempted to show that intention understanding is unnecessary for children to show the same pattern of results as that taken as evidence of understanding of others' intentions in some imitation studies. For example, in a follow-up to Meltzoff's (1995) study of understanding of unfulfilled intentions, Huang et al. (2002) found that infants produced the complete target action as often in conditions in which they were provided with information about the objects' affordances or in which the relevant parts of the objects were moved in close proximity to each other as they did in the completed and unfulfilled conditions of Meltzoff (1995). Likewise, Thompson and Russell (in press) found that children who saw a "ghost" condition in which the experimental apparatus moved by itself performed as well as children who saw an adult demonstrate the same actions on the apparatus. These researchers concluded that children could be using nonimitative, nonsocial-cognitive understanding to succeed in the intention imitation (and other imitation) tasks.

However, there are several imitation studies in which these kinds of explanations do not hold because the actions are exactly the same (or very similar) across the different intention conditions. For example, in the study by Carpenter et al. (1998a) of children's understanding of accidental and intentional actions, the actions were performed as similarly as possible across conditions, with the main difference being the verbal labeling ("Whoops" or "There") of the adult's intention. Likewise, in the studies by Gergely et al. (2002) and by Bekkering and colleagues, the only difference between conditions was whether the adult had a blanket around her or whether there were dots on the table. Finally, in the study by Carpenter et al. (2002) of children's understanding of others' prior intentions, in the two most interesting conditions—when the children did not know the adult's prior intention and when they inferred her prior intention from her actions on other boxes—again, the actual demonstrations on the test box were absolutely identical and the children succeeded in imitating only when they knew the adult's prior intention. These studies provide particularly strong evidence of children's understanding of others' intentions because this is the only thing that varied across conditions.

Thus, given the evidence from all of the different imitation paradigms, these alternative explanations are not so likely across the board, and we thus think it is more parsimonious to assume that children do use their understanding of intentional action to reenact the behavior of others. They may also be capable of using other mechanisms, such as an understanding of the affordances of objects or spatial contiguity as well, but we believe that their understanding of the intentions of others is more basic and, in certain situations like language acquisition, is the predominant method used from early on.

5.4   Conclusion

In an admirable attempt at simplicity, some researchers have proposed that we define imitation as "doing what others do" (e.g., R. Byrne, 1995). This is fine as far as it goes, but it takes only a moment's reflection to see that "what others do" can be defined or interpreted in many different ways from an intentional point of view. Is the adult moving her hands around the box in certain ways or trying to open the box? Is the adult moving her arm in a certain way or touching the dot? Is the adult turning on the light or turning on the light with her head? Is an accidental act part of what someone is doing? The point is that social learning and imitation cannot be viewed in isolation from the child's other social-cognitive skills. Children reproduce what they understand others to be doing, and so their social learning and imitation depend crucially on their skills of social cognition, especially those involved in reading the intentions of other people. The different manifestations of intention reading in young children's imitative learning, as reviewed here, are summarized in table 5.1.

Overall, research over the past decade has supported the general view of Tomasello et al. (1993a) with regard to these matters. Although there is some controversy about the skills of great apes in some experiments, there is no doubt that human children are the planet's most skillful imitators (even in the 1996 study by Whiten et al., the children were much better than the chimpanzees). Great apes mostly focus on changes of state in the objects involved in a demonstration, and they pay much less attention to the actual behavior, much less intentions, of the demonstrator. Human children, in contrast, focus on the intentions of the demonstrator to give them a definition of what she is doing, and this manifests itself in the myriad ways reviewed here. However, this does not mean that our knowledge has not advanced. It has in many ways, the most important of which are listed here.

Table 5.1
Development of intention reading in imitation in typically developing children

	0–9 months	12 months	14–15 months	18 months	24 months	36 months
Level of development	No understanding of intentions	Understanding • Goal-directed action	Understanding • Intentions (rational)	Understanding • Unfulfilled intentions • Reciprocal intentions • Commnicative intentions	Understanding • Prior intentions • Symbolic intentions	Understanding • Hierarchy of goals
Form of imitation	Mimicking or emulation	Imitative learning	Imitative learning or goal emulation	Role reversal imitation	All	All

1. We now know much more about how children interpret the intention of a behavior, based on such things as direct behavioral cues (e.g., those indicating effort, failure, or accidents), immediate context (e.g., the presence or absence of a concrete, perceptible goal), and preceding behavioral and perceptual context (e.g., what the demonstrator has been doing just prior to the demonstration).

2. We now know of the theoretical possibility of goal emulation in which the observer understands the demonstration in terms of both its ends and means, but chooses its own means (Whiten & Ham, 1992). And we have begun to investigate some of the factors that determine which behavioral means a child will choose on a given occasion (e.g., Gergely et al., 2002).

3. We also now have begun to think about hierarchies of goals, and the implication of this for imitative learning (Bekkering et al., 2000). For example, is the adult turning on the light or turning on the light with her head? Determining whether a behavior or an aspect of behavior is irrelevant or relevant to a demonstrator's achieving a goal is often far from straightforward.

4. Finally, it seems that we are learning more about the imitative learning skills, and intention-reading skills, of children with autism, who may be less disadvantaged in this domain than previously believed.

We conclude with a possible avenue for theoretical progress in a field that has sometimes been mired in terminological disputes. Call and Carpenter (2002) note that there is just so far one can go by identifying and naming new social learning processes haphazardly. A much more systematic approach is to break down social learning into the sources of information at the observer's disposal, for example, the actions of the demonstrator, the changes of state in the environment (result), the demonstrator's goal or intention, and facts about the immediate context and the immediately preceding behavioral context that affect the observer's interpretations. By breaking down the information in this way, and possibly in other ways, we can identify more precisely exactly what children and other animals are learning when they learn to do what others do.[1]

1. See the comments on this chapter by Claxton (vol. 2, ch. 8.7, p. 194). ED.

6 On Learning What Not to Do: The Emergence of Selective Imitation in Tool Use by Young Children

Paul L. Harris and Stephen Want

6.1 Introduction

Tool use by human beings depends on a process of social transmission. Children rarely invent new tools; rather, they see others use them, and they do likewise. In the study of nonhuman primates, the study of imitative tool use has been a major focus of research. Surprisingly, however, imitative tool use by young children has rarely been studied. Instead, developmental psychologists have focused on the imitation of simple facial gestures in the first year of life (Want & Harris, 2001). In this chapter, we seek to remedy that neglect. We describe an investigation of imitative tool use by 2- and 3-year-old children. To set these studies against a larger backdrop, we first consider the history of human toolmaking and distinguish between two broad types of social transmission: nonselective and selective imitation.

6.2 A Brief History of Human Toolmaking

The earliest-known stone tools date from the beginning of the Paleolithic period, more than 2 million years ago. Oldowon stone tools (named after the archaeological site of Olduvai Gorge in Tanzania) have been found in South and East Africa and are associated with *Homo habilis*, who lived from about 2.2 to 1.6 million years ago. Such tools were "manufactured" in a relatively simple fashion by using one rock as a hammer to strike another, breaking it into a larger core and a smaller, detached fragment or flake. The exact purpose of these tools remains uncertain; they may have been used for nut-cracking, woodworking, the scraping of hides, or animal butchery (Schick & Toth, 1993). Approximately 1.4 million years ago, tools with greater standardization appear. These are circular or oval flakes that are shaped around their entire edge to form a bilaterally symmetrical hand-axe. This form of tool persisted for a very long time—it was being made by Neanderthals until 50,000 years ago (Mellars, 1996). In short, although there was not complete stasis, the development of stone tools was achingly slow. There was nothing like the cultural explosion that occurred at the beginning of the Upper Paleolithic, an explosion that is normally seen as marking the onset of a clear ratchet effect in human culture. Indeed, over the past 20 years or more, archaeologists have emphasized that the existence of such a long period in which stone tools underwent only minor and nonprogressive change is a striking phenomenon in itself, one that stands in need of explanation (Isaac, 1977; Binford, 1989; Mithen, 1999).

A possible explanation of that stasis is that humans either did not engage in, or were incapable of, genuine imitation until the start of the Upper Paleolithic. This argument is implausible, however. The production of symmetrical handaxes is a challenging task. It involves the appropriate choice of stones and the delivery of a series of hammer blows with the force and angle needed to achieve the symmetrical form. The complexity of the process and the very stability of the forms produced strongly suggest that tool manufacture depended on an ability to reproduce quite specific actions in order to manufacture a given form. More generally, as Mithen (1999) has pointed out, the archaeological record points to two distinct phases in the development of tool use by humans: an earlier phase, extending throughout much of the Paleolithic, in which tool manufacture was guided by imitation but nevertheless remained static, and a later phase, starting at the onset of the Upper Paleolithic, in which tool use was increasingly subject to a ratchet effect, with later, more complex forms elaborating on and displacing earlier forms.

Under what conditions might a ratchet effect have emerged with respect to tool use? One possibility is that our ancestors became more creative or planful in tool design. Certainly, many of the artifacts of the Upper Paleolithic—for example, the emergence of cave art and burial practices—attest to some emerging imaginative capacity (Harris, 2000). However, it is also worth considering the possibility that the shift occurred, not in the way that tools were conceived or invented, but rather in the particular way that tool use was passed on from one generation to the next. As we have just noted, it is unlikely that the shift can be attributed to the emergence of imitation as such. Moreover, the field observation of nonhuman primates strongly suggests that a capacity for imitative tool use can exist without leading to any clear-cut ratchet effect in tool culture (de Waal, 2001a; Nagell et al., 1993; Whiten et al., 1999). Still, in the case of early humans, it is possible that a capacity for imitative tool use was supplemented or honed in some important way so that cross-generational transmission took on a new and more dynamic form. In the next section we discuss the possibility that this new dynamism emerged with the advent of selective as opposed to nonselective imitation.

6.3   Nonselective and Selective Imitation

Broadly speaking, we can distinguish between two different types of transmission via imitation: nonselective and selective imitation. Suppose that a learner watches a model use different variants of a particular tool. When given a chance to imitate, the learner might use the several variants in a nonselective and indiscriminate fashion. Alternatively, the learner might discriminate among them, favoring one variant over another. By way of concrete illustration, consider an example from the literature on tool use by chimpanzees. An adult female might, on different occasions, probe a termite mound with varying lengths of stick, depending on the size of the mound. Her offspring, watching her performance on any given occasion, might reproduce her behavior in a loose fashion by probing a mound with a stick, but without adjusting the length of the stick to the height of the mound. Alternatively, they might reproduce her behavior in a more selective fashion, choosing a longer stick for a bigger mound.

Under what circumstances might selectivity be optimized? Suppose an infant chimpanzee watches two adults. One inserts a relatively short stick and retrieves no termites; the other inserts a longer stick and is duly rewarded with termites. Alternatively, suppose an infant watches her mother use a short stick, fail, and then succeed with a longer stick. In either of these two cases, an observing infant might find the successive modeling especially instructive because it shows the differential consequences of one choice rather than another. Still, for an observer who fails to grasp the relationship between stick length and termite retrieval, such modeling of one action and then another might fail to carry any useful information. In the next section we describe two experiments in which we ask whether young children display any signs of selective imitation. We focus on the case in which an adult model first uses a tool inappropriately and without success and then corrects himself.

6.4   Selective Imitation by Young Children

We tested 2- and 3-year-olds on the trap-tube task. This task was initially designed for nonhuman primates by Elisabetta Visalberghi and her colleagues (Modena & Visalberghi, 1998; Visalberghi & Limongelli, 1994,

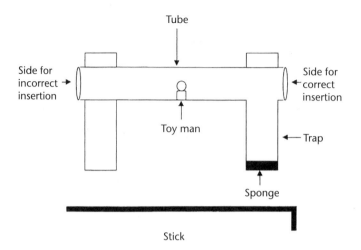

Figure 6.1

The trap-tube apparatus used in study 1. (Reprinted with permission, from Want & Harris, 2001.)

1996), but it can be easily adapted for young children. Figure 6.1 illustrates the apparatus. A toy man positioned in the center of the horizontal tube can be pushed out with the help of the stick. The task is complicated, however, by the presence of a trap. If the toy man is pushed toward the end of the tube where the trap is located, it will fall into the trap and be difficult to recover. On the other hand, if the toy man is pushed toward the opposite end, it can be extracted from the tube without hindrance.

In our first study, we initially presented the apparatus to children with no demonstration of how to use it. Thus, in phase 1, the children were encouraged to retrieve the toy man as best they could, with no demonstration of the way in which the stick could be employed as a tool. Very few of the children successfully extracted the toy; none of the 2-year-olds and only 12 percent of the 3-year-olds were successful. All those children who were unsuccessful then moved on to phase 2, in which they observed one of three different demonstrations. In the *correct* demonstration, the children watched as an adult inserted the stick into the correct side of the apparatus and pushed the toy man out of the tube. In the *incorrect + correct* demonstration, the children watched as the adult first inserted the stick into the incorrect side of the apparatus, pushed it toward the trap, said "Oops," and then inserted the stick into the correct side and obtained the toy. Finally, in the control demonstration, the children watched as the

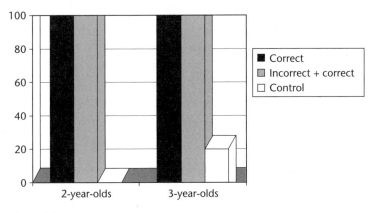

Figure 6.2
Percentage of children who used the stick by age and type of demonstration.

adult picked up the stick, but instead of inserting it into the tube, moved it along the outside of the tube in the same direction and in the same way as for the *correct* demonstration or the *incorrect + correct* demonstration. So in the control condition, the children saw the adult act on the stick, but not in a way that led to the recovery of the toy man. After seeing any given demonstration, the children were again invited to retrieve the toy man. They were given up to ten trials, with the apparatus rotated between trials to prevent reliance on a position habit.

The results can be described with two distinct questions in mind. First, we may ask if the children benefited from the demonstration in the sense that it prompted them to use the stick to try to extract the toy. Second, we may ask if the demonstration prompted the children, not just to use the stick, but also to carry out the appropriate type of insertion. Did they manage to extract the toy or did they end up pushing it into or toward the trap?

Figure 6.2 provides an answer to the first question. It illustrates the extent to which the children were prompted to use the stick following the three types of demonstration. The children were invariably prompted to use the stick once they had seen the experimenter do so. This was not simply because they had seen the experimenter act on the stick. Children in the control condition were much less likely to use the stick even though they had seen the experimenter pick it up and run it along the side of the tube. By implication, the experimenter's demonstration was effective insofar as it showed the children what to do with the stick and not because

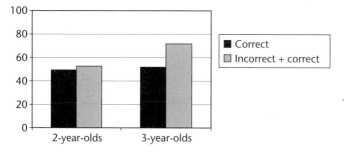

Figure 6.3
Percentage of trials in which children successfully extracted the toy.

it simply called their attention to it. Thus, the children's use of the stick cannot be explained in terms of so-called "local" or "stimulus" enhancement in which an observer's attention is attracted merely to the context or objects involved in a particular action.

Turning to the second question, figure 6.3 shows the percentage of trials on which children in the *correct* and *incorrect + correct* conditions successfully extracted the toy rather than trapping it. The figure shows that 2-year-olds extracted the toy on approximately half the trials following either type of demonstration. Effectively, they inserted the stick at random, trapping the toy on about half the trials and extracting it on the other half. Three-year-olds who saw the *correct* demonstration behaved in the same way; they trapped the toy on about half the trials and extracted it on the other half. By contrast, 3-year-olds who had seen the *incorrect + correct* demonstration were more selective. Although they too sometimes pushed the toy into the trap, they extracted it on about three-quarters of the trials. Statistical comparisons confirmed this overall conclusion. Overall, the 2-year-olds performed at chance in both conditions. The 3-year-olds were at chance in the *correct* condition but above chance in the *incorrect + correct* condition.

If we conceptualize these findings in light of the analysis presented earlier, we can conclude that the 2-year-olds are nonselective in their use of the stick. When they watch the adult demonstrate how to use it as a tool, they notice that it has to be inserted into the tube to extract the toy, but they are not sensitive to the differential consequences of a correct compared with an incorrect insertion, and no matter what they see, they produce one or the other indiscriminately. The 3-year-olds are also nonselective if they see only the *correct* demonstration. On the other hand, they are much more likely to be selective if they see both variants, as in the *incorrect + correct* demonstration.

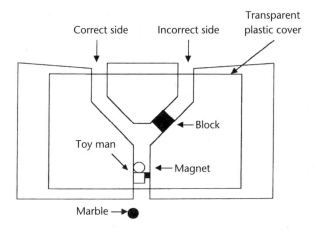

Figure 6.4
Apparatus used in study 2. (Reprinted with permission, from Want and Harris, 2001.)

These results raise various interesting questions. Why do 3-year-olds be-have differently from 2-year-olds and what specific aspect of the *incorrect +
correct* demonstration leads the 3-year-olds to be selective? We return to these questions later. For the moment, however, it is worth seeing whether the pattern of results that emerged in this first study is robust. In particular, does the same pattern emerge with a different apparatus and a different tool? To examine this question, we designed a new apparatus, illustrated in figure 6.4. It consisted of a Y-shaped transparent tube. A marble could be dropped in either arm with a view to dislodging a toy man held in place by a magnet fixed in the lower vertical section. Insertion of the marble into the correct arm would successfully dislodge the man; insertion of the marble into the incorrect arm would fail because the marble would be trapped by a block before reaching the man. Thus this apparatus retained certain features of the apparatus used in the first study: the use of a tool to extract a goal from a transparent tube and a choice between two places for insertion. In other respects, however, it was significantly different. First, it involved a projectile rather than a contact tool and second, the correct choice of side for the insertion of the tool was dictated by the fate of the tool (i.e., whether the marble was trapped or not) rather than by the fate of the goal object (i.e., whether the toy man was trapped or not).

As in study 1, the children were first shown the apparatus and, without being given any demonstration, they were invited to extract the toy man. No children in either age group managed to solve the task by themselves.

In the next phase, the children saw one of five demonstrations. In the *full correct* demonstration, they saw the experimenter drop the marble into the correct arm and thereby dislodge the toy man. In the *full incorrect* demonstration, they saw the experimenter drop the marble into the incorrect arm so that it was blocked in its descent toward the toy man. In the *full incorrect + correct* demonstration, they saw the experimenter drop a marble into the wrong arm, where it was visibly trapped by the block. The experimenter then said "Oops" and dropped a second marble into the correct arm. In the *partial incorrect + correct* demonstration, the experimenter inserted the marble about 1 inch into the wrong arm, said "Oops," removed it, and then released it into the correct arm. Finally, in the control condition, children saw the experimenter pick up the marble and move it from the top to the bottom of the apparatus without inserting it into either arm.

These various demonstrations were designed to answer several questions. First, would we obtain the same overall pattern as in study 1 despite the change of apparatus and tool? Second, do children need to see both an incorrect and a correct demonstration if they are to be selective? Alternatively, is selectivity prompted when they see only an incorrect demonstration? Third, if the combination of incorrect and correct is especially effective, is it because the children see the consequences of a wrong insertion (as in the *full incorrect + correct* but not the *partial incorrect + correct*) or is it because their attention is drawn to each arm of the apparatus (as in both these demonstrations)?

Figure 6.5 shows the percentage of children who inserted the marble at least once, whether into the correct or the incorrect arm, following the demonstration (the data are collapsed across the two age groups because

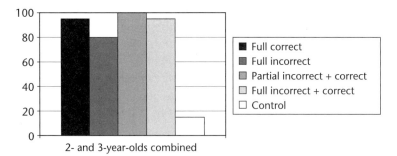

Figure 6.5
Percentage of children who inserted the marble at least once as a function of the demonstration.

they behaved in a similar fashion). Children in the control group rarely inserted the marble, but most of the remaining children managed to do so. This pattern is clearly similar to that observed in study 1. Before they saw any kind of demonstration, the children rarely solved the problem spontaneously. Having seen the experimenter insert the tool (the marble) into one of the tubes, the children typically did the same. If, on the other hand, they simply saw the experimenter manipulate the tool without inserting it, they rarely inserted it themselves.

Turning now to the accuracy of children's performance, figure 6.6 show the percentage of trials on which 2- and 3-year-olds successfully extracted the toy following each of the four informative demonstrations (i.e., excluding the control condition). Again the overall pattern resembles that found in study 1. Two-year-olds are nonselective; irrespective of the type of demonstration they saw, they only managed to extract the toy on about half the trials. On the remaining trials, they dropped the marble into the wrong arm so that it was trapped by the block. The 3-year-olds are also nonselective if they see either the *correct* or the *incorrect* demonstration, averaging about 50% correct. Their performance improves when the children are shown either of the two *incorrect + correct* demonstrations, and it is particularly accurate if the children are shown the *full incorrect + correct*. Again, statistical comparisons confirmed this overall conclusion. The 2-year-olds performed at chance across all four conditions. The 3-year-olds performed at chance in the *correct* and *incorrect* conditions, but above chance in both the *partial* and *full incorrect + correct* conditions.

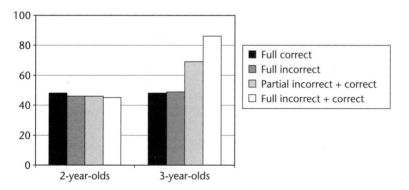

Figure 6.6
Percentage of trials in which children retrieved the toy as a function of age and type of demonstration.

In general, therefore, the findings from study 2 replicate and extend those from study 1. Two-year-olds are not selective in their imitation whichever demonstration they watch. Three-year-olds are not selective if they see an incorrect or a correct use of a tool demonstrated in isolation. On the other hand, they are selective if they see the experimenter use a tool in two different ways, once correctly and once incorrectly. They are especially accurate if they see the toy trapped by incorrect use of the tool and then see the tool used correctly.

We can now return to the two questions raised earlier. What accounts for the change with age? And what exactly leads 3-year-olds to be selective? Let us begin with the second question. One possibility is that 3-year-olds benefit from the opportunity to see the differential outcome of an incorrect versus a correct insertion. More specifically, what we may refer to as the two-sided demonstrations (i.e., the *partial incorrect + correct* and the *full incorrect + correct*) enabled children to observe that an incorrect insertion failed to extract the toy, whereas a correct insertion did extract it. At first sight, this emphasis on the role of differential observation offers a plausible account of the findings from both studies. There is, however, an objection. Recall that once they had seen the demonstrations, the children had an opportunity to retrieve the toy on up to ten trials. In the course of those trials—particularly when the children had observed only a correct or an incorrect demonstration in isolation—they typically performed at chance. Effectively, therefore, they had the opportunity to observe the results of both an incorrect and a correct insertion. If the opportunity to observe differential outcomes were instructive, we might expect the children to show considerable learning in the course of the ten trials. More specifically, we might expect them to show a greater proportion of successful insertions on later than on earlier trials. However, analysis of the trial data revealed only modest and inconsistent learning effects across studies 1 and 2. This contrasts with the systematic behavior displayed by 3-year-olds following a single demonstration of an incorrect plus a correct insertion. By implication, the 3-year-olds learned more rapidly and effectively from the model than they did from their own experience of trial and error.

Accordingly, we may consider an alternative interpretation—one that focuses on what the children may have learned from the adult's behavior. Suppose that the 3-year-olds engaged in a careful monitoring of the experimenter's expressive behavior. In particular, when the experimenter made a mistake, said "Oops," and then produced a correct action on the other side of the apparatus, the children may have taken note of the experimenter's exclamation. This explicit social marking that a mishap—or near mishap—

had occurred was clearly absent when the children themselves engaged in the series of test trials. Hence this account nicely explains why the children benefited systematically from the demonstration when it combined a single incorrect and incorrect action but showed only modest gains when they themselves produced a series of correct and incorrect actions in a haphazard fashion over trials.

However, this focus on social marking is probably too narrow to fully explain the 3-year-olds' behavior. Suppose that the children registered and understood the experimenter's exclamation of "Oops." They realized that the experimenter had in some sense made a mistake—a plausible assumption given that even 2-year-olds are sensitive to such verbal markers (Carpenter et al., 1998a). Such insight into the meaning of the experimenter's exclamation would not in itself have permitted the children to make much headway when it came to their own test trials; at that point, they had to choose one side of the apparatus or the other. Unless the children understood something about why one side was more effective than another, a simple registration of the experimenter's exclamation would not have helped them. A further weakness of this line of explanation is that it throws no light on the fact that the children benefited somewhat more from the *incorrect + correct* demonstration in its full than in its partial version. Yet in the course of both demonstrations the experimenter produced exactly the same exclamation.

We may therefore consider a third possible explanation, one that combines elements from each of the two possibilities considered so far. When the children saw the *incorrect + correct* demonstration (in either its full or partial version), they saw the experimenter make a mistake—or almost do so—and then proceed to correct himself. When they themselves were engaged in a series of trials and in the course of those trials happened to choose the wrong arm and thereby trap the toy (in study 1) or the marble (in study 2), there was no guarantee that their next action would be correct. Thus, the *incorrect + correct* demonstrations offered the children a relatively clear and immediate "lesson" in how an incorrect action might be improved upon; the experimenter made a mistake and then immediately demonstrated how to correct that mistake.

Although that lesson in self-correction was available in principle over the series of test trials carried out by the children themselves, it was present in a much more diffuse fashion. In the first place, a mistake by the child was not marked with an exclamation, and second, given the haphazard nature of the children's selection of a given side of the apparatus for insertion or release of the tool, there was no guarantee that it would be immediately succeeded by a correct action. Thus this hypothesis can explain why the children benefited from the experimenter's demonstration but not from their own series of failures and successes. It also suggests a plausible explanation of why the children were especially accurate following the *full incorrect + correct* demonstration. Given that the children saw the marble trapped by the block, this demonstration offered a clear and visible rationale for the experimenter's subsequent self-correction. By contrast, the *partial incorrect + correct* demonstration was less transparent in this respect. The children saw the marble inserted partway into the incorrect arm; they did not see it trapped by the block. Hence the experimenter's subsequent self-correction may not have been so easy for children to decipher.

How can we test this analysis in the future? In our analysis given here, we emphasized the critical importance of selective imitation for the ratchet effect. We proposed that the ratchet effect might emerge given two important preconditions: a set of action variants and a process of selective imitation. This analysis left open the possibility that selectivity could emerge when children observe a group of actions presented in any fashion, as long as there is an observable mix of more and less successful variants. For example, children might benefit from observing one model carry out a successful variant and another model an unsuccessful variant. The conclusions reached on the basis of the two experimental studies suggest, however, that selectivity might be especially likely under a more restrictive set of conditions—not when children see a random mix of more or less successful variants, but when they see deliberate and immediate self-correction by an experienced tool user. These different possibilities are obviously testable. For example, we can readily compare children who see one person produce the *full incorrect + correct* demonstration (as in studies 1 and 2) with children who see one person produce a *full incorrect* demonstration and a different person produce a *correct* demonstration. On the strength of the preceding analysis, we would predict that children would be more accurate following the former type of demonstration since it highlights what we take to be critical, namely deliberate self-correction on the part of the model. However, pending such experiments, we should acknowledge that although our studies so far demonstrate the emergence of selectivity, they offer for the moment a suggestive rather than a precise specification of the conditions that promote that selectivity.

Why did the 2-year-olds display no sign of selectivity? We may speculate about two possible reasons. First, it is possible that 2-year-olds are less adroit mind readers than 3-year-olds. More specifically, 2-year-olds may have difficulty in appreciating that the adult's production of an incorrect action, an exclamation, and a subsequent correct action, amount to a coherent action package—what we have referred to as a lesson in self-correction. Thus, even if 2-year-olds grasp that "Oops" typically marks a mistake or accident, they may not encode the model's next action as a deliberate repair of that mistake, one that needs to be noted and copied.

An alternative possibility is that the 2-year-olds had a less precise understanding of the causal mechanics of the two tasks than did the 3-year-olds. For example, the 2-year-olds may have understood that they needed to make contact with and displace the toy using the stick or the marble rather than their hand, but they may not have understood the constraints imposed by each apparatus on the direction from which that contact should be achieved. In this account, the 2-year-olds may have appreciated the fact that the experimenter corrected himself (in the *incorrect + correct* demonstration) but did not understand how insertion in the two sides yielded different outcomes.

These two accounts make different predictions about what would happen if the apparatus were simplified. Say, for example, the choice of arm was dictated not by the location of a trap or a block inside one of the tubes but instead by the diameter of the mouth of the tubes. Thus, if only one of the two tubes were large enough at its entry point to permit the stick or marble to be inserted, we could again present children with a demonstration in which the experimenter first approaches the wrong arm, and then corrects himself. Arguably, even 2-year-olds would understand the causal constraints dictated by the diameter of the tubes. If they showed selective imitation under these circumstances, the mind-reading interpretation would be ruled out. If they continued to show nonselective imitation, even in the face of such simple causal constraints, the mind-reading interpretation would be strengthened.

6.5 Conclusions

The results of the two studies that we have described show that the distinction between selective and nonselective imitation is valid and useful. Two-year-olds displayed nonselective imitation whereas 3-year-olds displayed selective imitation. For the time being, we do not have a full understanding of exactly when selective imitation occurs, but we can already identify in broad terms the conditions that facilitate it. The two studies converge in showing that there is a key difference between observation of a single action variant on the one hand and a combination of variants on the other. Moreover, post hoc analysis of children's performance across trials strongly suggests that the observation of a haphazard string of variants produced by the self is less instructive than an incorrect and correct variant produced in immediate succession by a model.

These developmental findings connect with two broader questions. We have already touched explicitly on one of these in the introduction. Tool use by early humans had a remarkably long period of stasis, a period in which imitation almost certainly occurred in the absence of any ratchet effect. Our admittedly speculative explanation of that stasis and its eventual disruption is that there was a shift from nonselective to selective imitation. Such a shift would have optimized tool use by speeding up the selective transmission of more effective variants from one generation to the next. The second question concerns the imitative competence of nonhuman primates. As we noted earlier, there is encouraging evidence that chimpanzees are capable of imitative tool use. At the same time, we know of no indications of any kind of ratchet effect in chimpanzee tool culture across successive generations. We interpret that conjunction as evidence that nonhuman primates engage in nonselective rather than selective imitation. It should be possible to test that prediction using the trap-tube task and its variants.[1]

Acknowledgments

We are grateful to the Society for Research in Child Development for permission to reprint figures 6.1 and 6.4, which appeared originally in S. Want & P. L. Harris (2001), Learning from other people's mistakes: causal understanding in learning to use a tool. *Child Development 72*, 431–433.

1. See the comments on this chapter by Comstock (vol. 2, ch. 8.8, p. 197). For relevant discussion, see especially Whiten et al., vol. 1, ch. 11; Donald, vol. 2, ch. 14; Gil-White, vol. 2, ch. 16; Greenberg, vol. 2, ch. 17; and Chater, vol. 2, ch. 18. ED.

7 Imitation as Entrainment: Brain Mechanisms and Social Consequences

Marcel Kinsbourne

7.1 Overt versus Covert Imitation

I address the following contradiction. On the one hand, action encoding is pervasive and is the basis of imitation. Indeed, imitation is so easy that even single neurons are thought to do it. On the other hand, people only infrequently imitate openly, and most animals hardly imitate at all. How can that be?

At the level of adaptive behavior, the answer is obvious. If organisms were to imitate habitually, they would be greatly at risk. We are all either predators or prey or both. The relationship between predator and prey is not imitative, it is reciprocal—the predator approaches, and the prey withdraws. If predators were to imitate their prey, the prey would have time to escape, and if prey were to imitate their predators, they would not survive the confrontation. So some way of encoding actions without overtly imitating, of suppressing the overt imitative response, would be adaptive for species in general, including even those that lack the inhibitory capacity of prefrontal cortex or have no cortex at all. Somehow the suppression is nonetheless accomplished in the course of evolution. However, under particular circumstances imitation does occur. What might those circumstances be?

Normal people imitate in certain conventional situations, such as in responsive recitation and during instruction. Were they to imitate outside conventional boundaries, their behavior would be seen as strange, and even provocative. The one who is imitated might feel mocked. However, people who are subject to certain disinhibitory brain dysfunctions are apt to imitate unintentionally under wider boundary conditions. This reveals that the imitative gesture is normally performed internally far more often than as overt behavior.

7.2   Enactive Coding

Underlying imitation is the far more general process of enactive, or action, encoding. It is persuasive that objects are encoded in part in terms of their affordances, that is, in terms of what one could possibly do with them or about them. When one perceives a person in action rather than a static object or scene, the obvious affordance is to imitate, to do the same thing, which is usually possible if the action is one performed by humans. So it is not surprising that animals, including humans, indeed encode perceived movements in terms of covert movements that imitate the model.

   As for infants, how could they ever learn the identity of anything if they did not encode it in terms of movements, distinct affordances that differentiate one thing from another? After all, infants can't give a thing a name and they can't flag its representation in their brain. Using perceptual representation alone, all they could do is differentiate and discriminate the object of interest from its contextual background. However, this would not enable them to establish a stable identity for the object because both contexts and perspectives constantly change. To identify things, infants would presumably have to resort to at least some coarse encoding in terms of affordances that differ for different objects. When they are older they will be able to bootstrap their earlier enactive encoding onto their emerging verbal capability for finer identification. The importance and pervasiveness of enactive encoding is unquestionable. How is it done?

7.3   Mirror Neurons

Imitation is studied at levels of organization from behavior through imaging to single-neuron recording demonstrating mirror neurons (see Rizzolatti, vol. 1, ch. 1). Mirror neurons would seem to be a minimal model for imitation. The neuron that fires when an organism perceives external action might, when it also fires during the organism's own action, (1) fire before the action is prepared, while intention is formed. That intention is perhaps instantiated in an image, an internal perceptual representation of what outcome is intended, of the goal. (2) It might fire while the movement is being prepared or (3) when it is being executed. (4) It might fire as reafference when the movement program is under way (Fogassi & Gallese, 2002; Hurley, vol. 1, ch. 7) or (5) after the movement is completed, as part of a signal that the goal has been achieved. Of course, it could be that it fires in more than one of these situations, and it could be that different mirror neurons fire under different sets of these circumstances. Since we cannot yet specify the exact role of mirror neurons, it remains possible that these mirror neurons are in fact perceptual in the strict sense, as in example (1). If so, they would be perceptual with respect to what is happening on the outside and also represent what is happening inside the mind itself, that is, an image. Many have suggested that the resonance at the level of neural representation between what is observed and what is intended enables certain feats of higher-level cognition, such as in theory of mind situations. It has even been speculated that people with autism who perform poorly on tests of theory of mind lack mirror neurons (J. Williams et al., 2001). But the forebrain is rich in neurons; it is highly interconnected and readily establishes correspondences. It could relate percepts to actions without needing to scrimp on how many neurons are involved by using the same neurons for both. As for autistic individuals, it seems more likely that they are not interested in imitating than that they are incapable of it (R. Mitchell, 1997). Also, a physical identity between the mechanisms for perceiving and performing actions would often tend to be maladaptive, as when an angry approach movement by another primes a similar approach by its target, who would actually be better off to turn away.

Mirror neurons may not have evolved specifically to tie together perceived and performed actions. A more parsimonious hypothesis is feasible. Perceptual representations are called upon (1) when the act is observed, (2) when the observer forms the intention to perform the act, (3) when the act is accompanied by an efference copy, (4) when the act is monitored upon completion. In each case the same movement is represented, and in each case mirror neurons may fire, indifferent to which one of these processes is occurring. Gallese's "shared manifold" would be a mental image of an action that is activated under multiple conditions. Perhaps it is also activated when the action is retrieved by episodic remembering.

7.4 Disinhibited Imitation

Organisms generally keep their enactive encodings to themselves for good adaptive reasons. How do they accomplish this, and under what circumstances do they fail? Mature adult humans fail to keep imitation covert when their prefrontal cortex is damaged or their caudate nucleus is overactive. A patient with prefrontal cortical lesions sometimes imitates unintentionally, without or even counter to instruction. Luria's three well-known tests for prefrontal deficits illustrate this. The tests are as simple as: "I tap once. You tap once. I tap twice. You don't tap." A patient with prefrontal lesions will have trouble not tapping twice when the clinician taps twice. It is not that the patient has forgotten the instruction; he or she can state what it is. Rather, the instruction's control over behavior is overcome by the salience of the directly perceived act (Luria, 1973, pp. 200–201). The lesion has disinhibited a latent but unwanted imitation, so that it becomes overt in the circumstances of clinical examination. Rarely, the imitation occurs outside the setting of an explicit task, as "echopraxia." The investigator casually does something that has nothing to do with the patient, and the patient does the same thing unbidden. The normally covert imitation makes a public appearance.

7.5   Boundary Conditions of Imitation

One should indicate not only when a phenomenon occurs, but also when it does not occur. Echopraxia is not pervasive. Echopraxics do not walk through the world twitching in response to every movement around them. They do not imitate the rustling of leaves and they do not imitate cars screeching to a halt. One elicits echopraxia by being a doctor, facing a patient, looking somber and purposeful, and giving the patient tasks. For echopraxia to occur, the pertinent lesion, although necessary, is not sufficient. One more thing is needed, which is arousal. I suggest that the face-to-face dyadic situation is intrinsically arousing for humans and that it is in this situation that one most readily observes unwanted imitation in people with malfunctioning brains. One type of neurologically incomplete organism is a person whose frontal lobes are lesioned and another is an infant. In my view, babies are actually the most perfect organisms of all, but for present purposes they are imperfect because they do not have functioning prefrontal lobes. Babies do imitate simple facial gestures (Meltzoff & Moore, 1989), but they also do not imitate every movement that happens around them. It depends not only on what the movement is but who or what is performing it, and in what relationship to the baby. Meltzoff (1995) presented a particular movement made by a person in one condition and by a mechanical device in the other. The babies did not imitate the action of the mechanical device, only that by the person. Again, a dyadic human interaction is required for imitation to occur.

Trevarthen and Aitken (2001) comprehensively review infant intersubjectivity. It is dyadic confrontation, with its arousing motivational property (Stern, 1993), that is needed to elicit the imitative behavior. Concurrent with that arousal, the baby experiences pleasure. Imitation is reinforcing. Babies love to imitate, either for its own sake or because imitating is a simple way within their limited repertoire to elicit further interaction from the caregiver and thus further attract welcome attention. If babies love to imitate, it is not because they think the caregiver has something to teach them, and want to learn, although some adults make that mistaken assumption. The point transcends imitation proper and applies to joint regard. For example, a baby points at something. The adult orients to the baby's locus of regard and tells the baby the name of the thing the baby is pointing at. I suggest that what the baby cares about is not the name, but the joint regard itself, the fact that the adult is doing what the baby is doing. Adult and child are now orienting to the same object. This of course is what generally happens when two adults engage in conversation. My argument is that babies love to entrain with adults and that imitation is more about affiliation or attachment than about learning, although it may be about learning too. If so, imitation would be a splinter instance of a much broader, more general behavior, which is entrainment—adopting shared rhythms of behavior.

7.6 Interactional Synchrony

Interactional synchrony is a dyadic state that was first described and named by Condon and Sander (1974), and documented in infants by Beebe et al. (1985) and others. Even newborn babies assume rhythms of orienting that are complementary to those of the adult who is speaking to them long before they begin to be able to understand speech. As a result, the speech rhythms of the caregiver are matched by the bodily rhythms of the baby. Crossmodal entrainment of speech movements still counts as imitation of the rhythmic component of the adult's actions. After all, imitation does not necessarily capture everything the other person is doing. One selectively imitates something about what the other person is doing, and the most basic attribute that can be imitated is the underlying rhythm. So interactional synchrony is imitation of rhythm. Humans are innately predisposed to adopt rhythms that accord with those of others.

The dyadic situation offers an opportunity to actualize this core predisposition, generates the needed arousal, and the entrainment then happens. It incorporates the basic property of communication, which is the following. Any communication, be it verbal or nonverbal, orients the recipient to the attentional focus of the initiator. It may be the focus of external attention or it may be the focus of the initiator's mental state to which the recipient orients. Either case begins with one person's attention having a particular focus and ends up with two people sharing that same focus. That is communication. If the initiator asks a question, then he or she intends to adopt the attentional focus of the other. This is still the same thing in its outcome: a shared orientation of mental or observational focus. The sharing may be between two people, or one person may enter into the orientation of many, or vice versa, in public speaking. I believe that there is a core predisposition of the human brain to entrain with conspecifics. As examples of this sort of thing, there is not only a baby's nonverbal behavior, but also his vocal behavior. You tell the baby something. The baby is really amused. The baby wants to hear it again. You tell it again. The baby wants to hear it again. My 20-month-old niece heard me sneeze and oriented to the sound with a major startle. Then she insisted that I continue to sneeze for a long time because she wanted to hear me sneeze over and over and over, and in turn imitate the sneeze. After all that, is she further informed about my sneezing capability? Surely not. Rather, she is affiliating. My niece and I are doing something together.

Even the great apes do not appear to interact in the manner described here. Indeed, although an infant ape orients to its mother's face, this orienting does not lead to confrontation and dyadic interaction (P. Wrangham, personal communication). In these primate species, mirror neurons must have a more modest role. If an infant with normal developmental potential is deprived of the opportunity to entrain, what is the consequence? "Hospitalism," the deprivation syndrome that results from prolonged hospital stays and confinement in understaffed orphanages largely derives from the lack of interactional entrainment. In its absence the child fails to build up the interpersonal affiliation that is integral to social and cognitive development.

Some children may lack the predisposition to entrain because of abnormal neurobiology. Among the brain anomalies that have been reported in autistic individuals is an underdeveloped cerebellum, especially vermis lobules VI and VII. The cerebellum is instrumental in tracking the trajectories of movements (Paulin, 1993), and the vermal structures coordinate auditory and visual signals. The cerebellar dysfunction in autism may compromise interactional entrainment. Entrainment in autism has been little studied. In a pilot study Feldstein et al. (1982) observed that autistic adolescents failed to achieve temporal synchrony in interactions with their parents.

7.7 Analysis by Synthesis

Discussions of simulation theory for empathy and theory of mind do not usually acknowledge that recognition by reconstruction is well known in an ostensibly quite different context. It is termed *analysis by synthesis*, when it is applied to the comprehension of speech. I suggest that the two situations have more in common than might at first appear (see Gordon, vol. 2, ch. 3).

During imitation, do the motor representations in prefrontal cortex simply resonate to the corresponding perceptual representations (Shepard, 1984), or does activation of the corresponding action actively assist the perceiving? The answer is not known. However, insofar as overt or covert motor responses to percepts play a role in direct perceiving (as distinct from priming, memorizing, or affiliating), they might do so by "analysis by synthesis" (K. Stevens & Halle, 1967). The listener analyzes the input by covertly simulating it. Analysis by synthesis has been broadly implicated in cognition and across species, for instance in sound localization and depth perception in humans, and between conspecifics in echolocation and birdsong (reviewed by Liberman & Mattingly, 1985). However, the prime application of the principle of analysis by synthesis is to the comprehension of speech. The motor theory of speech perception (Liberman & Mattingly, 1985) proposes that the listener decodes the auditory speech input by encoding it in terms of the articulatory gestures by which the speaker presumably constructed it, rather than more directly by the acoustic patterns of the speech. According to this influential view, the "generative" listener activates neural structures that counterintuitively do not correspond to particular patterns of perceived sounds, but to the vocal gestures that generated them. Listening, she covertly imitates the speaker's articulatory gestures and monitors her covert action for its meaning.

It is easy to see how speech analysis by synthesis might have evolved out of interactional synchrony. The infant resonates to a speaker's speech rhythms with her own bodily rhythms. With maturation, such overt resonance tends to become internalized. The internal "synthesis" might be put to work for purposes of comprehension.

Covert imitation in speech analysis by synthesis is subtler than "imitation" by mirror neurons, in that the actions that are imitated are not directly observable, but are inferred from the (auditory) output. In this respect it has more in common with the mechanism proposed by simulation theory for the genesis of empathy and mind reading, as exemplified in theory of mind experiments. The other's state of mind is also not directly observable. The observer simulates it based on an interpretation of the behavior that he observes. In the case of language, the listener imitates the spoken message. In the affective case, the observer "synthesizes" in himself the presumed subjective experience of the other person.

Conversing, irrespective of the topic, has a powerful affiliative effect that binds people together socially and gratifies them emotionally. This effect can perhaps be ascribed to the imitative turn-taking that is involved in a conversation during the analysis by synthesis. In order to comprehend, the listener constructs, and resonates with, the articulatory gestures of the speaker, entraining with them. In this view, entrainment in the dyadic situation, with its emotional and socializing consequences, derives not only from bodily interactional synchrony, it also derives from articulators that entrain, at least at the level of their representations in the forebrain. According to McNeilage et al. (1967), speech comprehension develops even in those who lack the ability to feel and control their articulators. In view of the generally earlier emergence of emotional than factual communication in phylogeny, it may be that the possible emotional role of entrained articulation even preceded its communicative function in human evolution. Perhaps traffic in speech sounds among individuals arose in the course of affiliation, and was adapted to communication when specific phonemic groupings later acquired symbolic meaning.

7.8 Entrainment and Social Control

The urge to entrain is by no means limited to babies. The caregiver just as happily entrains with his or her baby as the other way around. Entraining is compelling for people generally. I suggest that when one entrains in another's point of view, one is half persuaded simply by doing so. Being persuaded by the other is not just an exercise in assessing the merits of their case. Rather, being persuaded is as much emotional as it is cognitive, and the mere fact of entraining is a step toward accepting the other person's point of view. When we disagree vehemently with another's point of view, we often find that our disagreement softens when we finally meet the other person. This phenomenon is widely used in persuasion. Take prayer as an instance. In my Jewish religion, services include much chanting in unison. I suspect this is so in every religion; there are hymns, chants, responsive praying, all variants of entrainment, which is so persuasive. The worshipper feels elevated, inspired, influenced not only by the prayer's content, but also by the togetherness in praying. Consider marching songs, marching bands, drums, tom-toms, and ritualistic gestures made in unison. The faith healer works his routine on the crowd. The crowd is responsive. The emotional temperature goes up and up, and then the crowd is persuaded of the faith healer's powers, and logic has nothing to do with it.

And on the dark side, there is the goose step, the Heil Hitler cheer and salute, all serving to persuade people to do things that individually they would not dream of doing. It is as though entraining with the crowd suspends personal responsibility. Such is the potent effect of imitation on the behavior of our species.[1]

If there is something uniquely human about our intersubjectivity, it is unlikely to be due to a dedicated neural module, a gift from an arbitrary God. More likely, it would be due to a genetically fueled propensity to apply our prodigious computing capabilities to socially interacting with fellow humans. The subjective aspect would be a feeling of well-being when we do so, which in turn would serve as an incentive to repeat the experience. Functional imaging might reveal a characteristically human pattern of limbic system activation, even during interactions that on the surface are purely informational.

7.9   Self-Imitation

Finally, I turn to what I call self-imitation, in which the person learns from his or her own body. Infants are constantly on the move, perhaps for two reasons. One is that they are constantly thinking, and for babies, thinking is moving. There is no difference between the mental state and the bodily state of an infant because there is as yet no inhibitory barrier between computing and expressing. The brain state generates the corresponding bodily state without hindrance. One can read a child's mind from the child's body. A child expresses his states and his desires physically. It takes years and years of maturation before it becomes possible for a person to cloak their intentions and not reveal them through the body. In fact, in Italy this appears still not to have been accomplished, whereas in England a flutter of the eyelids may suffice to convey near-suicidal tendencies. So there is a cultural aspect.

The other reason babies move a lot is that by doing so they are learning about their bodies. They are basically discovering what entrains with what, which intention entrains with what motor consequence. One's notion of the body, the body image, individuates out of action. I think its origins are motoric and kinesthetic before vision enters the scene (Kinsbourne, 2002). Self-imitation, repeated over and over, builds up the body image. Evolution has determined that activities that are adaptively beneficial feel good

1. For relevant discussion, see especially Dijksterhuis, vol. 2, ch. 9; Eldridge, vol. 2, ch. 11; and Huesmann, vol. 2, ch. 12, ED.

subjectively. Babies love to kick their legs around, so they do it a lot, and thereby acquire the necessary information about their bodies.

Here is a final example of self-imitation: auditory hallucinations in schizophrenics. Chronic schizophrenics frequently have repetitive auditory hallucinations, so that they continually hear the same message, such as "Your body will rot. Your body will rot. Your body will rot," from morning to night, every day. Verbal hallucinations are subvocalized expressions of the individual (Green & Kinsbourne, 1990). The patients are vocalizing the hallucinated messages to themselves. In a few cases one can put a microphone to their mouth and capture some vibrations of that speech. However, it cannot be that simple, because schizophrenics do not report hearing their own voice, but another voice. Usually it is either the devil or their ex-husband, and often it is a voice of a different gender. They are subvocalizing and yet it is not their own voice that they hear. How can that be? My suggestion is the following. The hallucination arises from the thought-disordered person's intense expectation, anticipation, that she will hear a particular emotionally intense message originating from a particular source (person or spirit). What is an expectation? It is an image in the mind of what is expected, fashioned so that it can be matched efficiently to the input when it happens. So the person has in their mind a mental image of the expected voice saying the expected thing, and that image is so pathologically powerful that it overcomes inhibition and takes command of output mechanisms, and the subvocalizations occur (Kinsbourne, 1990). That is a self-imitation, in the sense that the individual perceives something and then responds imitatively in accordance to that which she perceived. In this case what is perceived happens to be endogenous rather than exogenous.

7.10 Concluding Comment

Imitation arises from disinhibition of enactive encoding, the visible tip of an action-coding iceberg. It is itself a splinter manifestation of a pervasive human propensity to entrain with other people. This rhythmic social entrainment is more innately compelling than reasoned argument in inducing two, or many, to adopt the same point of view. As Plato remarked in the *Republic*, volume III: "Rhythm and harmony find their way into the inward places of the soul." That concludes my hymn to imitation.[2]

2. See comments on this chapter by Claxton (vol. 2, ch. 8.9, p. 199) and by Brison (vol. 2, ch. 8.10, p. 202) ED.

8 Commentary and Discussion on Imitation and Human Development

8.1 Grasping Action
Paul L. Harris on Meltzoff

In a tightly argued chapter, Andrew Meltzoff not only lays out some influential findings concerning the development of imitation, he also seeks to answer a fundamental question about the origins of social cognition. How does the infant come to establish an equivalence between itself and others? His proposals echo a traditional philosophical argument about our knowledge of other minds—the argument from analogy—but he brings to that argument a wealth of empirical discoveries, many of them made in his own laboratory over the past quarter century. His thesis has ramifications for the infant's developing understanding of other people's attention, action, and emotion. In this brief set of comments, I focus on the action of reaching and grasping with a view to evaluating Meltzoff's argument.

Meltzoff's first claim is that there is an innate connection between the capacity to observe and encode the acts of another person and the capacity to execute those same acts. Developmental evidence for the existence of that innate connection comes from early imitation, by now a well-established phenomenon. As Meltzoff points out, there are many studies from different laboratories that testify to its existence. Moreover, it would be wrong to conclude that the phenomenon is very narrow in scope; it extends to a variety of gestures. However, I would insert one caveat. With one important exception that I discuss later, all of the findings on early imitation pertain to gestures that are not visible to the self. Neither a neonate nor I can see ourselves stick out our tongue, close our eyes, or purse our lips. Arguably, then, nature has provided the human species with an innate dictionary that specifies equivalences between facial gestures of the self and others because the construction of such a dictionary would be next to impossible on the basis of experience. So equipped, the human neonate enters the world ready to engage in the kind of expressive, face-to-face exchange with its caregivers that is so characteristic of our species.

In this account, it becomes plausible to speculate that such an innate dictionary is limited to invisible facial gestures and is not available for nonfacial gestures. We can, after all, observe our own hand movements. In principle, therefore, the neonate or young infant might come to link a given manual program with its visible result; for example, an infant might link the motor program for the opening and closing of his or her hand with the visible gesture that ensues. Then, on seeing a comparable visible gesture produced by another person, the infant might retrieve and execute the previously linked motor program. Indeed, to the extent that many manual gestures are directed at visible objects, and to the extent that the trajectory of the hand and the orientation of the fingers needs to be adjusted to the particular visible properties of the object, the capacity to visually monitor both grasping movements and the visible properties of the objects at which they are targeted is likely to be at a premium. Such fine-grained visual monitoring of the movements of the self might play a key role in establishing a larger repertoire of equivalences between the infant's own object-directed manual gestures and those produced by other people. In this view, the role of the innate dictionary of equivalence would be confined to a relatively narrow set of gestures, notably facial actions that cannot be subjected to visual guidance.

As Meltzoff points out, however, evidence is available suggesting that neonates not only imitate facial gestures, such as tongue protrusion and lip movements, they also imitate simple manual gestures such as opening and closing the hand (Meltzoff & Moore, 1977; Vinter, 1986). Consider the detailed report by Vinter (1986). She found that when 4-day-old infants watched an adult open and close her hand repeatedly, they were more likely to open and close their own hand—whether partially or fully—than in two control periods, one in which the model made a facial movement, namely tongue protrusion, or else remained still. Moreover, it was not the case that the infants became indiscriminately active when they saw the model open and close her hand—there was no comparable activation of tongue protrusion. Of course, we might insist that 4 days would be enough for neonates to pursue the alternative "visual monitoring" route that I sketched earlier, but that does not seem very plausible. Infants of this age are unlikely to spend time watching their manual gestures. In short, this study provides persuasive evidence that entries in an innate dictionary of self–other equivalence extend beyond invisible facial movements to include manual movements as well. The visual monitoring route may complement this innate foundation, but it is not its ultimate basis even for manual actions.

The next step in Meltzoff's argument is to propose that the child gradually builds up, on the basis of experience rather than an innate dictionary, links between the mental states that guide or accompany a given motor movement and the movements themselves. A couple of examples will be instructive. When a baby smiles, he or she presumably feels happy. That positive mental state will, by dint of repetition, come to be associated in memory with the facial expression that accompanies it. Subsequently, when a baby sees an adult smiling, the innate dictionary described earlier will provide a cross-reference to the baby's own facial expression; it will evoke a mental representation of that facial expression or trigger an actual, imitative movement. In either case, the associated mental state of feeling happy will be generated. Similarly, a baby who is able to make an accurate object-directed reach will come to associate the goal of grasping an object with the act of reaching. Seeing another person reach toward an object will evoke some mental representation of the infant's own object-directed reaches, or conceivably an actual reach, and that will in turn evoke a representation of the goal that guides such a movement.

Within this framework, Meltzoff describes the results of imitation experiments in which an infant watches an incomplete or unsuccessful action: a model reaches toward a target but fails to grasp it. Infants of 18 months and even 15 months appear to grasp the goal behind the action and instead of copying the failed gesture, execute it successfully. By implication, when an infant sees a model reach (albeit unsuccessfully) toward an object, that sight evokes some mental representation of the infant's own object-directed reaches, which in turn evokes a representation of the goal that guides such movements. Hence the infant imitates the model, not by slavishly copying the model's failed action, but by producing actions that do attain the model's apparent goal, including actions that the model did not even attempt.

What about younger infants? Meltzoff notes that results from two laboratories have shown that infants aged 12 months and younger do not produce this sophisticated goal-based pattern of imitation. In one study for example, 9-month-old infants imitated successful acts but not unsuccessful ones (Meltzoff, 1999b). How should we interpret the change in behavior from 9 to 18 months? Following Meltzoff's own analysis, it is tempting to conclude that 9-month-old infants have not yet established the appropriate connections between actions and goals that make such sophisticated imitation possible. More specifically, when they observe a model's unsuccessful action, they do not represent the goal of the action.

Other evidence, however, casts doubt on this interpretation. Consider recent findings by Woodward (1998). She reports that when infants of 6 and 9 months have seen an actor reach for a particular toy, they subsequently show greater dishabituation if the actor reached along the same path for a new toy than they do if the actor reached along a different path for the same toy. By implication, when the infants watched the initial reaching, they were more likely to encode the goal object that it was directed toward rather than the precise trajectory of the reach. These findings would lead us to expect that infants of 6 or 9 months would also attend to the goal of an action when they imitate, contrary to Meltzoff's findings.

How might we explain this inconsistency? One explanation might run as follows. An infant of 6 or 9 months can reach for objects. Therefore, in line with Meltzoff's proposals about the role of experience, an infant of this age will have established connections between its actions and its goals. Those connections help the young infant to interpret the actor's reaching as goal directed in Woodward's experiment. However, while the connections can serve interpretations of others' actions, they are not yet able to support the sophisticated imitative actions produced by 18-month-olds. Unfortunately, this defense of Meltzoff's account is weak at best. If his account is correct, essentially the same mental machinery is recruited whether the infant perceives the act of a model in terms of its goal or imitates the act of a model in terms of its goal. More generally, it is one of the strong predictions of Meltzoff's account that there is a tight link in development between the perception and interpretation of another's action and the imitation of another's action. Any developmental separation between perception and imitation causes trouble for the theory.

Here, then, is another line of defense. Arguably, it is simply harder to figure out the goal of a failed action—such as a reach that over- or undershoots the goal object—than to figure out the goal of an action that is brought to a successful completion. Meltzoff effectively asked whether infants could figure out the goal of unsuccessful actions, whereas Woodward asked whether infants could figure out the goal of a successfully completed action. Nine-month-olds can manage the latter but not the former, whereas 18-month-olds can manage both.

This account leads to a simple, testable prediction that is based on a merger of the methods introduced by Meltzoff and Woodward. The infant sees a model facing two toys, a toy bear positioned on a higher shelf and a cup positioned beneath it on a lower shelf. The model reaches up for the toy bear and grasps it. We then switch the positions of the two toys and give the infant an opportunity to imitate the model. The infant can either reproduce the model's movement by reaching up for the cup, or the infant can reproduce the model's goal by reaching down for the bear. If the same machinery serves action perception and action imitation, the pattern of imitation produced in this setup should parallel the pattern of habituation observed by Woodward (1998); it should reflect the goal rather than the movement by the actor.

Finally, we may consider a persuasive piece of evidence reported by Meltzoff. In the normal course of development, several things may happen concurrently, but it is difficult to infer any causal relationship from such concurrence. Training experiments are especially helpful in analyzing causal mechanisms. Brooks and Meltzoff (2002) have found that in the absence of any special training, infants are insensitive to whether or not an actor is blindfolded. So when an adult wearing a headband turned to look at something, 12-month-old infants turned to look in the same direction. Yet they also turned to follow the actor's "gaze" when the headband was replaced by a blindfold. By implication, they did not realize that the blindfolded adult could not see anything.

The preliminary results of a follow-up study by Meltzoff and Brooks indicate that when infants have experienced a blindfold themselves they behave differently. They no longer turn to follow a blindfolded adult. This is a compelling demonstration of the way in which a particular first-person experience can be attributed—by analogy with the self—to another person. Still, we can ask how general this analogical route is. To understand the mental experience that ensues from a blindfold, extrapolation from first-person experience with the blindfold seems the most direct route. True, one might slowly infer that restricted mental experience simply from observing the limited behavioral repertoire of an actor wearing a blindfold— first-person experience of wearing a blindfold is not critical. Still, that route into what the other is or is not experiencing seems tortuous, at best.

The advantages of analogizing from first-person experience is less clear-cut if we return to consider the act of reaching. Woodward has observed that 3-month-old infants do not show the type of goal encoding that is apparent with older infants. However, infants of this age are quite poor at reaching out to grasp an object themselves. Hence, their lack of goal encoding is just what one might expect in Meltzoff's account. Indeed, studies in progress at Woodward's laboratory underline the potentially didactic role of first-person experience. When the infants were fitted out with Velcro mittens that enabled them to "grasp" objects more successfully, they were subsequently able to encode the goal structure of an actor's reaching and grasping action (Woodward, 2002).

So, should we conclude that infants are attributing goals on the basis of their own goal-directed actions with the Velcro mittens? Possibly but not necessarily; when the infants wore the mittens, they had the experience of being an agent. However, they could also watch themselves—spectatorlike—as they made their successful reaches. If Meltzoff is right, the experience of being an agent is critical. Yet it is also possible that sustained visual monitoring of reaching is sufficient to teach infants to encode that action in terms of its goal. Experiments currently in progress at Woodward's laboratory should give us an answer. More generally, the simple act of reaching appears to be a wonderful vehicle for answering in some detail the question of whether our ability to execute a given action is inextricably woven into the way that we perceive it.

8.2   Do Babies Know What They Look Like? *Doppelgängers* and the Phenomenology of Infancy
Nicholas Humphrey on Meltzoff

When an infant imitates a face, is it possible that he can *see* the resemblance between his own face and the model's; that is to say, see it as a visual image, so he can compare what the two faces *look* like? To be able to picture oneself in any such literal sense is surely beyond the capacity even of most adults. So the suggestion that a baby might be doing it may seem absurd. Yet extraordinary data, of the kind Andrew Meltzoff has reported over the past 25 years, invite extraordinary hypotheses. And it is in this spirit that I want to introduce into the discussion a singular phenomenon: the illusion of the *doppelgänger*, or autoscopic hallucination, where a person does indeed *see* his or her own double.

The phenomenon, as it occurs in adults, is quite rare. It is sometimes experienced by healthy individuals, but is more common in those with epilepsy, and appears to be linked to right-hemisphere parietal lobe malfunction (Blanke et al., 2002; Krizek, 2000). Graham Reed has described the typical manifestation:

Usually the *doppelgänger* apparition appears without warning and takes the form of a mirror-image of the viewer, facing him and just beyond arm's reach. It is life-sized, but very often only the face or the head and trunk are "seen." Details are very clear, but colors are either dull or absent. Generally the image is transparent; some people have described it as being "jelly-like" or as though projected onto glass. In most cases the double imitates the subject's movements and facial expressions in mirror-imagery, as though it were his reflection in a glass. (Reed, 1972, p. 54)

Sometimes, however, the subject may have a more detached perspective, as in this case:

At first "B" usually "saw" his double only sideways, i.e. his profile, "but now I can see him from any possible position, from behind as well as from his front, just as if I was walking round him and choosing the position from which to look at him. He is absolutely identical with me in every detail of his features, expression of his face, his dress and movements." The "double" does everything the patient does in the given moment. (Lukianowicz, 1960, p. 985; see also 1958)

The fact that the human mind can create illusions of this kind, albeit when in a pathological state, would seem to imply that there must exist a "normal" capacity for modeling the body of a remarkable kind. Reed relates it to Sir Henry Head's notion of the "multimodal body schema"—"a plastic and isomorphic representation of one's body which must be incorporated in our nervous system if we are to account for our constant awareness of our posture and position in space"—and suggests that perhaps "the *doppelgänger* experience may be a displacement or projection of that internal model" (Reed, 1972, p. 55).

In volume 2, chapter 1 Meltzoff proposes an idea similar to Head's to explain normal infant imitation: his notion of "active intermodal mapping" (AIM). Thus he suggests that a baby, when imitating another person, maps a visual representation of the other person's body onto a proprioceptive representation of his own.

Now, it is surely possible that just the reverse of this could be happening in the case of the *doppelgänger*, so that the subject maps a proprioceptive representation of his own body onto a visual representation of another as-if person (although, in this case, it's himself!).

In the context of this book it hardly needs saying that mirror neurons might be just the ticket for creating such intermodal equivalences (and the suggestion of right-parietal involvement in creating the *doppelgänger* phenomenon fits nicely with the brain-imaging data reported by Decety and Chaminade vol. 1, ch. 4).

However, what interests me more than the mechanism of the *doppelgänger* is the question of what such a sophisticated mental construction might be good for. Does the *doppelgänger* have any functional utility? And if so, what and when?

It is true that in adulthood the *doppelgänger* is seemingly not good for anything (and in fact it is generally regarded by those experiencing it as a nuisance); moreover, it is experienced only by the very few. But could it be that the *doppelgänger* is primarily a phenomenon of early infancy? Could it even be that most babies experience their own bodies projected as an external visual image most of the time? *Doppelgänger*s as *near-birth* experiences? I think the *doppelgänger* might in this case be a remarkably useful "teaching aid." Meltzoff writes: "Infants can imitate and recognize equivalences between observed and executed acts" (2002a, p. 35). My proposal is that a baby's experience of his visual double would give him a relatively easy means of doing just this. But more than this, his capacity to see himself, not so much as others see him, but *as he sees others*, would be an invaluable tool for entering other people's minds (as many, from Nietzsche on, have pointed out).[1] For it would mean that when, for example, a baby feels sad, angry, happy, and so on, he would be able to know just how he himself looks and so have a basis for inferring what other people are feeling when they look the same way (see Humphrey, 2002, pp. 94–99).

We live in interesting times for the understanding of cognitive development. I suspect we have only just begun to discover how strange—but wonderfully designed by nature—the phenomenology of infancy may be.

8.3 Construing Selves from Others
Wolfgang Prinz on Goldman

In volume 2, chapter 2 Goldman discusses two major competing accounts of mind reading, that is, theory theory and simulation theory, and examines the possible role of imitation in both of them. Different as they may be, the two accounts do share one crucial, common belief. They both believe that access to one's own mental states is easier and in a way more direct than access to knowledge about the mental states of others. This is

1. Nietzsche not only advanced a "simulation theory" of mind reading, but explicitly linked simulation to bodily imitation. "To understand another person, that is *to imitate his feelings in ourselves*, we ... produce the feeling in ourselves after the *effects* it exerts and displays on the other person by imitating with our own body the expression of his eyes, his voice, his walk, his bearing. Then a similar feeling arises in us in consequence of an ancient association between movement and sensation. We have brought our skill in understanding the feelings of others to a high state of perfection and in the presence of another person we are always almost involuntarily practicing this skill" (Nietzsche, 1881/1977, p. 156).

particularly true of simulation theory, but as Goldman points out, it also applies to some brands of theory theory, particularly the version defended by Meltzoff and his colleagues, (e.g., Meltzoff & Moore, 1995; Meltzoff, 1999a; see also Meltzoff, vol. 2, ch. 1). The common question here is, how do we understand other people's minds—and how do young infants come to develop such understanding? The common answer is that we do it by resorting to our own minds—and young infants come to do it that way, also. To our own mental states, it is believed, we have direct or privileged, access. Hence, when we set about understanding others' minds, we use our own mentality to either infer or simulate the mentality of others, proceeding thereby from intrapersonal to interpersonal understanding (Meltzoff, 1999a). This is what researchers sometimes call the "you-like-me" perspective; I understand you as being like me (both a being of the same kind and being in the same state as I am in).

The notion of privileged access to first-person knowledge is deeply rooted in both philosophy and folk psychology, and to many researchers it appears to be a self-evident intuition. However, as it is often the case, there are good reasons to distrust such intuitions. In fact, I find it difficult to believe in privileged access to first-person knowledge. I believe that organisms are made for understanding the world surrounding them, rather than for understanding themselves; that is, how their own bodies and their own minds work. For instance, it has long been known that veridical perception relies on mechanisms that subtract, from the total information available, any contributions that are due to the perceiver/actor. Perceivers cancel the proximal information related to themselves in order to perceive the distal world surrounding them (cf., e.g., Woodworth, 1938; Epstein, 1973). In a way, then, we are made to know the world at the expense of knowing ourselves. The mere fact that we use certain cognitive tools for understanding the world neither requires nor implies that we understand how these tools work, or, as Millikan puts it so elegantly in the next section, "merely having a mind is not the same as knowing about minds" (p. 185).

Hence, if there is any privilege at all, it lies in the access to knowledge about things and persons in the world, but not about one's own mental states. In other words, privileged access refers to knowledge about third-person events, not about first-person states.

If this is true, we should think of reversing the question. The problem now is how we understand our own minds and how young infants come to develop such understanding. As in theory theory, the answer might be that we do it by resorting to the categories folk psychology offers us for understanding other minds—categories that gradually develop in young infants.

However, unlike in theory theory, these categories are first applied to others and then to oneself.

Accordingly, rather than understanding others as like ourselves (i.e., passing the "like-me" test), we may perhaps come to understand ourselves as like others (passing the "like-you" test, as it were). This is what I suggest calling the me-like-you perspective; I understand myself as being like you (again, both a being of the same kind and being in the same state as you).

Is there a role for imitation in this perspective? There is, but not surprisingly the functions of imitation are quite different from those discussed by Goldman in the you-like-me perspective. The question now is how young infants come to construe themselves as agents in exactly the same way as they construe other people. Imitation games offer an obvious tool to support such construal of subjectivity and agency. In these games, the infant may from time to time copy the adult's actions, but the infant's actions are mirrored by the adult as well. As a consequence of being mirrored by somebody else, the infant comes to perceive her own actions through the other. It may be such attending to one's own actions through the mirror of somebody else that may counteract and eventually help to overcome the inbuilt mechanisms for canceling the perceiver/actor and her contributions to the world she is perceiving and acting upon. In a way, then, the infant is in the situation of a portrait painter, who can easily see and paint a portrait of other people, but needs a mirror to see and portray herself.

To conclude, let me mention two issues, both of which require further elaboration in the you-like-me perspective. First, there is of course still a long way to go from perceiving one's actions mirrored through someone else to construing oneself as an agent like the other. For instance, one needs to explain how an infant can distinguish between the other mirroring the infant and the other acting on his own account. Second, how do infants come to understand other minds in the first place? The categories offered by folk psychology may be part of the answer, but some other part will certainly have to be derived from basic mechanisms of perceiving actions and events.

8.4   Some Reflections on the Theory Theory–Simulation Theory Debate
Ruth Garrett Millikan on Goldman

Goldman tells us that the theory theory and the simulation theory are different theories concerning "how ordinary people go about the business of attributing mental states" (vol. 2, ch. 2, p. 80). This phrase is ambiguous in ways that may make a difference, I think, both to the controversy between the theory theorists and the simulation theorists, and to the question of what imitation might have to do with mind reading.

First, the question might be taken to concern the natural ontology of beliefs about mental states. What kind of structure does a belief about a mental state have? Supposing that having a belief about a mental state requires one to have a concept or thought of that kind of mental state, what sort of thing is a thought of a mental state? Is it just like the thought of any other sort of state, say, the state of being old, or the state of being sick, or the state of being wet? Suppose that the mental state to be thought about is an intentional state, and suppose that intentional states are mental representations. Is a representation of a representation *as* a representation (not just as a vehicle) just another ordinary representation but one that happens to have a representation as its object? Or does it require a completely different sort of mental act?

Second, the question might be taken to concern the ontogeny of the ability to have beliefs about mental states. What are the steps in the normal developmental process that lead to the capacity to think about mental states? Was there perhaps a certain cultural or historical process that resulted in humans acquiring the ability to think about their mental states, as there was a cultural or historical process that resulted in humans acquiring the ability to think about numbers or, at least, say, about negative numbers? Or does each child acquire the ability to think about mental states all on its own, a strong disposition to this having been built in, perhaps, by natural selection?

Third, the question might be taken to concern the natural epistemology of beliefs about mental states. How do people discover what mental states other people are in, or discover what states they themselves are in? Besides knowing what states other people are in, sometimes we can predict what states they will soon be in. And sometimes we can retrodict what states they must have been in previously to account for the emergence of their current states. Sometimes we can predict what states we ourselves will be in given certain future conditions. And sometimes we know something of the etiology of the states we are currently in or have been in the past.

Now the origin of the "theory theory" was a story about the first of these three matters. It was a story about what is involved in having any sort of thought or concept at all, not a story specifically about thoughts or concepts of mental states. What kind of structure does a belief about anything have? The story was that beliefs are mental representations, indeed were originally mental sentences (e.g., Sellars, 1963, ch. 5; Quine, 1960, ch. 1) and that they acquire their content, they get to be about what they are about, because of their inference relations to one another plus their connections to perceptual input and, some philosophers thought, also to motor output. The concept of a kind of mental state was the concept of that state and not another for the same reason any other concept was about whatever it was about—namely, because of its role in inference. This sort of theory of what a thought is was aptly called a "theory theory" of the nature of thought because it was exactly the same as the theory developed in the second two-fifths of the twentieth century concerning the meanings of theoretical terms in a scientific theory. As was forcefully pointed out by Hempel (1950, 1951), Sellars (1963) , Quine (1960, ch. 2) and others, having a concept and having a theory came to much the same thing in this analysis. Or, putting this differently, the difference between changing your beliefs and changing what your thoughts were about (changing your meanings) became moot, or at any rate highly problematic.

Goldman objects to the theory theory as applied to thoughts of mental states partly on the grounds that if it were true, no account could be given of the second problem mentioned earlier, which concerns the ontogeny of the ability to have beliefs about mental states. Goldman claims that a child could not discover a set of laws concerning mental states by observing the origins and progression of its own mental states because in the theory theory, to be able to think about its own mental states, it must already know what the psychological laws are that define those states. Note, however, that in the theory theory of concepts, this sort of problem is perfectly general, having nothing to do with the theory theory of thoughts of mental states in particular. If the laws of a theory define the concepts in the theory, it seems one could not reach any theory by performing simple inductions in order to derive its associated laws. The criticism, if valid, would challenge the whole of the most characteristic twentieth-century theory of what thoughts are.

Sellars and Quine had a way out of this dilemma. They assumed that we learn to think by being taught to speak. We are taught connections between sentences by our elders and we internalize them. Ordinary people do not develop theories of their own, but slowly learn traditional methods of thought handed down through the generations. The formation of genuinely new theories was another matter. Many, including Sellars—the original theory theorist about thoughts of mental states—were explicit about the use of models and analogy in the development of theories. Sellars (1963, ch. 5) thought the original model for the ordinary theory of thought was language, and suggested that the development of this new theory took place originally during the history of ideas, not during evolutionary history. However, he thought individual children learned about the existence of mental states by being taught correct sentence connections and the conditions for uttering sentences about mental states by their elders and then internalizing these sentences and connections.

Sellars was also explicit about how a person introspects their own current beliefs and desires, and about how they learn to do this. That is, he also had a theory about part of the third question noted earlier. How do people discover what mental states they are in? It is not done (as Goldman suggests the theory theorist must hold) by observing one's behavior, but by catching oneself in the state of being disposed candidly to express a certain thought and then prefacing that expression with "I believe" or "I want" or whatever (Sellars, 1975). The fact that an entity is first discovered merely as a theoretical entity does not preclude the possibility that one can later learn how to observe it directly, how to make judgments about it directly from experience without inference. In contrast to this, no simulation theorist has, to my knowledge, developed a clear theory of how one knows what one's own thoughts are, whether they are really one's own, or merely thoughts that one has simulated in the pretend guise of another. What the theory theorist clearly has on his side concerning questions two and three above is the clear understanding that merely having a mind is not the same as knowing about minds, nor is having mental states the same as knowing one has mental states. The general capacity to think of mental states needs to be explained, including the capacity to know what particular mental states one is currently in.

Now I am not disposed to accept the classical theory theorist's view either of the nature of thoughts generally or of the nature of thoughts about thoughts. Nor, of course, am I disposed to accept their view of how children learn to think about thoughts. But it seems to me that a critique of the classical theory theory needs to go considerably deeper than Goldman's current analysis. Most important, to oppose the theory theorist on his original ground, one would need to develop a different theory than the classical twentieth-century theory theory, either of what it is to think about or have a concept of anything—say, of dogs, or of the state of being old, and so forth—or, alternatively, one would need to explain exactly why it is that mental states cannot be thought about in the same sort of way as any other states, and of how they are thought of instead. I myself think that the theory theory of thoughts and concepts is mistaken quite generally (for this, see Millikan, 2000). But moving closer to Goldman's view, there might also be a reason to suppose that there is something peculiar about concepts, not of mental states in general, but at least of *intentional* mental states, states that seem to be like inner representations.

Sellars assumed that our model for thoughts was words and sentences, not words and sentences classified by vehicle types, but rather as classified by "roles"; later terminology would have said by functional roles or inferential roles. He did not explain what it is to have a thought of a role, however. What would it be to think of a thought as being a mental sentence that plays a certain role in inference and as typically stimulated by such and such sensory input? Would a full-blooded theory theorist have to say that this would involve having a mental name for the sentence, say, "Tobermory," and then believing a whole host of psychological laws about which other mental sentences, such as those named, "Samantha" and "Melissa" and "Xavier," when these are believed, generally lead to belief in the sentence Tobermory, and which mental sentences, when believed along with Tobermory, generally produce in their wake still further sentences, for example, those named "Tobias" and "Melek" and "Dildar," and so forth? One way or another, it seems to me, the theory theorist would need to concede that our ability to think of the inferential role a mental sentence plays must ride piggyback on our own dispositions to make inferences with just such a mental sentence, not on an entirely independent and prior knowledge of what these dispositions are.

Putting this differently, suppose that thinking that someone holds a mental sentence, *p*, to be true involves thinking that they are likely to believe whatever *p* immediately implies. This supposition is definitional of the theory theory of what thought is if we spell out the theory theory assumption that believing that someone holds *p* true involves having a more or less correct theory of what it actually is to hold *p* true. Now ask what is it like to know what *p* immediately implies? The obvious answer would seem to be that this knowledge must somehow rest quite immediately on one's having *oneself* a set of inference dispositions with regard to the thought that *p*—not, in the first instance, a set of beliefs about laws of thought, but a set of dispositions to obey laws of thought.

Something like this principle would seem to generalize to any theory of what it is to have a thought of a thought if it is assumed that thoughts are mental representations. In order to believe that John plays the trumpet, I certainly don't need to be able to play the trumpet myself. But in order to believe that John believes that it is raining, I do need to be able, if not to believe that it is raining, at least to entertain the thought that it is raining. Surely, thinking of a representation, not just as a vehicle, but as something having a known intentional content, requires that I be able to think of or entertain that intentional content myself.

Returning to simulation, if we suppose that merely thinking about a certain content or entertaining it involves harboring a representation of that content that is processed offline, that is, it is not connected with dispositions to act, as in the case of online beliefs, and if we refer to this sort of offline processing as simulation of belief, then it seems to follow that any mental representation theorist will have to agree that the ability to simulate beliefs one does not have oneself must lie behind the ability to attribute beliefs to others.

Note, however, that it does not follow that one might not also simply remember from experience what kind of conclusions one has usually reached from what kinds of experiences or from what kinds of prior beliefs, or remember having been told what kinds of conclusions another has reached, thus concluding what another may think without currently engaging in simulation. Nor does it follow that the ability to know what kinds of nonintentional mental states tend to have what kinds of outcomes, or what kinds of situations tend to cause what kinds of nonintentional states, depends on concurrent simulation of these states. Only thoughts of intentional mental states succumb to this argument.

Concerning predictions of future intentional states, I think it is important to recognize that prediction of people's future intentions often works backward by prediction first of their future actions. That is, regularity in actions is what we notice first about people, perhaps including ourselves. We know what people generally do in specific situations, or what people of a certain culture or class are likely to do, or what a certain individual is likely to do, all by simple induction. If we then think about these people's intentions, it is likely to be in order to explain the behavior we expect rather than to predict their behavior by first knowing their intentions. Thus we are disconcerted when we find certain people "unpredictable," for most people are quite predictable in many broad ways (although not usually in the details of exactly *how* they will do this or that). The idea that we use mind reading primarily to predict behavior seems to me quite mistaken. Mostly we use it only to explain behavior after the fact, or to explain behavior that has been predicted by simple induction from previous behavior patterns.

My suggestion, then, is that thinking about intentional mental states probably requires the capacity, at least, to entertain mental representations offline. But so does imagining of all kinds, and so does hypothetical thinking, and so does considering possibilities and hypotheses and so forth. Do all of these derive somehow from the ability to imitate? That seems doubtful. Does the ability to imitate require the ability to think off-line? Well, that might depend, as Goldman seems to agree, on how you define imitation. In neither case, however, it seems to me, is there evidence of any but the most indirect connections between imitation and mind reading *specifically*.

I feel compelled to add one more skeptical comment. I do not know where it has been shown that the phenomenon of mirror neurons, mentioned in Goldman's chapter and in many of the talks at the Royaumont Abbey meeting on imitation, needs to be interpreted as any different from the well-known phenomenon of efferent copy. To interpret it as a phenomenon of efferent copy, all one needs to do is to assume that efferent copy can predict perceptions of object-centered or aperspectival happenings as well as perspectival happenings. If so, efferent copy could predict, say, that a hand is seen in an object-centered way grasping a nut, disregarding how the hand is related to the subject's own body. Another part of efferent copy, connected, say, with the "where" (the dorsal) rather than the "what" (the ventral) system, might predict the relation of the grasping to the subject's body. If that were so, there would be no potential causation between seeing another grasping a nut and grasping it oneself. The causation would only be between intending to grasp a nut and the firing of neurons anticipating the seeing of the grasping of a nut. However, it may be that the neurologists have their own careful reasons for thinking that is not the way it happens, and I just have not heard them yet.[2]

2. Here is a response to this paragraph from neuroscientist Marco Iacoboni: "An efferent copy can occur only when an agent does an action. It is a carbon copy of a motor plan. If the individual is only observing, there is no efferent copy. Mirror neurons may represent the input of the forward model if their activity during action observation is the expression of a simulation of an efferent copy. But their activity during observation can't be the expression of a real efferent copy, because the observer is not moving.

Now, even if mirror neuron activity during action observation is a simulation of an efferent copy, and during execution is a real efferent copy, it seems to me that the most parsimonious account of this machinery is to link seeing and doing for the purpose of imitating (and other things too, of course). To postulate that in fact this neural activity is only useful for linking the intention to grasp (during execution) with anticipating the seeing of a grasping (during observation) seems to me unnecessarily complicated" (personal communication). ED.

8.5   Who Can Imitate Depends on How We Define Imitation
Thomas R. Zentall on Anisfeld

Anisfeld systematically reviews the literature on infant imitation and proposes that (1) the evidence for imitation in infants younger than 11 months involves behavior either that is not novel or that can be attributed to other causes (i.e., to an increase in general arousal or "priming"), (2) many studies have not included the appropriate no-demonstration (baseline) control, and (3) the best evidence for the representation of an observed behavior is deferred imitation.

With regard to the first point, Anisfeld does not accept as evidence of imitation the copying of any response that may have been previously made by the observer. Instead, he views such behavioral matching as priming (a more automatic, reflexive behavior), in which the observed behavior primes the memory for the earlier action or elicits a "recognition response." However, there is no practical way to ensure that a similar behavior has never occurred before. All behavior, including behavioral sequences, are likely to be similar to some previous behavior or behavioral sequence, and thus it is impossible to rule out response generalization. Furthermore, although imitation sounds more cognitive than priming, there is no objective way to distinguish between imitation and behavior that is primed by the memory of observing that behavior demonstrated by another.

On the other hand, why should it be necessary that copied behavior be novel? We tend to think of the value of imitation in terms of the acquisition of new behaviors. But observers may imitate a familiar functional behavior in a context in which it would not otherwise be as likely to occur. Such imitation would also have adaptive value.[3] The theoretical importance of imitative behavior is not its novelty but the fact that the behavior is often "invisible" to the one imitating. That is, for the observer, there is often the absence of a sensory match (often referred to as the problem of correspondence) between the behavior of the model and the self.

Rather than insisting that the imitated behavior be novel, a more useful means of assessing the behavior is to compare its probability of occurrence with that found under suitable control conditions. Anisfeld seems to agree because he proposes that an appropriate control is a baseline condition in which the target behavior is assessed in the absence of its observation. However, he challenges Meltzoff's (1988b; Heimann & Meltzoff, 1996) use

---

3. See also Byrne, vol. 1, ch. 9. ED.

of the observation of an alternative activity as an appropriate control and suggests that a baseline period of no demonstration is more appropriate. Anisfeld argues that in Meltzoff's experiments, the observation of different actions suppressed the observer's spontaneous inclination to perform the target actions. But in the absence of imitation why should observation of a different response suppress spontaneous behavior? The suppression of target behavior suggests that the observer recognizes that the observed and target behavior do not match. And the recognition that they do not match implies that the observer would also have the ability to recognize that they do match.

In fact, the two-action method, in which whatever behavior is demonstrated is considered the target behavior and the nonobserved behavior is considered the comparison or control behavior, has become a standard method for assessing imitation in animals (see Zentall, 2001). For example, when Japanese quail observe a demonstrator quail step on a treadle (a small, flat, elevated, platformlike device), and then the observers are given access to the treadle, they show a strong tendency to step on it. However, when a different group of quail observe a demonstrator peck at the treadle, and they are given access to the treadle, they show a strong tendency to peck at it (Akins & Zentall, 1996). Furthermore, although the quail have certainly pecked and stepped before participating in this experiment, we can affirm that prior to this experiment they have never stepped on or pecked at a treadle.

The version of the two-action method used by Akins and Zentall (1996) also controls for two important nonimitative factors that might affect copying a response. First, observation of the manipulation of an object may result in stimulus enhancement (attention drawn to the object by its movement). In the case of the two-action method, however, each of the two actions results in similar movement of the treadle. Second, it is also possible for the observer to learn through observation *how* the treadle moves (downward, with a spring that brings it back up) without regard to how that movement was accomplished by the demonstrator. Such a phenomenon, often referred to as object-movement reenactment or learning of affordances (see Akins et al., 2002) is controlled for using this two-action method because the treadle moves in the same manner regardless of the behavior (stepping or pecking) that moves it. Anisfeld notes that if the imitation condition is not significantly different from a baseline (no demonstration) condition, the demonstration of an alternative behavior is not needed. However, a baseline control does not allow for the possibility that the presence of demonstrator may actually distract the observer from the demonstrated response (a negative "mere presence" effect resulting perhaps from competition with or attraction to the demonstrator; see Zentall & Levine, 1972).

Anisfeld notes that in most of the neonatal imitation studies, evidence for an increase in tongue protrusion has been found but not for an increase in mouth opening. This result allows for the possibility that the increase in tongue protrusion was mediated by an increase in general arousal. Furthermore, if the tongue protrusion by the adult model was the cause of the increased arousal, imitation need not be involved. Studies with older children (Meltzoff, 1988b; Heimann & Meltzoff, 1996) used only one target behavior, shaking a plastic egg, and various other controls (e.g., spinning an egg). Again, although it is perhaps less likely in this case, the asymmetry of the methodology (only one target behavior) allows for the possibility that an increase in general arousal could have produced this result. Use of the two-action method would have allowed them to rule out this possibility.

Finally, Anisfeld suggests that when the opportunity to perform an observed response is deferred but imitation still occurs, it suggests that the observer must have developed a representation that has been constructed mentally and retained over time. Perhaps this is true; however, Dorrance and Zentall (2001) included a group of quail that were tested 30 minutes after they observed either stepping or pecking, and the quail tested for deferred imitation showed levels of response copying similar to quail tested in the immediate imitation condition. If imitation, and even deferred imitation, can be demonstrated in Japanese quail, there is no reason why infants below the age of 11 months should not be able to imitate as well. Thus it may be that when imitation deficits are found in young infants, the deficits may reflect sensory and especially motor limitations rather than the inability to imitate.

8.6 What Does Infant Imitation Tell Us about the Underlying Representations?
Birgit Elsner on Anisfeld

In reminding us of Piaget's (1951/1962) original ideas, Anisfeld sheds new light on the discussion about imitation in infants and its underlying representations. Apparently some of Piaget's conclusions have been misinterpreted in the experimental investigation of infant imitation and are thus worth rethinking. Nevertheless, I believe that Anisfeld is too skeptical about the experimental data obtained so far. As to newborns' performance of facial gestures, he is right in stating that thus far it is not clear whether this is imitation or not. Even if it is not imitation, it tells us something about the "inner life" of newborns—what they find exciting and how they react to arousing stimuli. As for deferred imitation, I think the reviewed studies show that 6- to 12-month-old infants represent observed actions on objects and that they remember these actions for some time. These representations may not be symbolic, but still, the studies highlight some aspects that Piaget neglected. Prior to their first birthday, infants are able to acquire sensorimotor knowledge without immediate practice, and they are able to represent that knowledge over some time.

8.6.1 Imitation of Facial Gestures in Newborns

Ever since Meltzoff and Moore's (1977) seminal paper appeared 27 years ago, researchers have discussed whether the fact that newborns stick out their tongues at adults who just did so is an indicator of imitation or not. Some consistently claim that this behavior is indeed imitative (Meltzoff & Moore, 1999b), while others contend that it is not, but rather represents some reflexive arousal (Anisfeld et al., 2001) or exploration response (Jones, 1996).

Following this discussion, one wonders whether it would be possible at all to design experiments with appropriate control conditions that may help to resolve this fundamental issue. Meltzoff's attempts to show differential imitation in several modeling conditions are steps in the right direction. If tongue protrusion occurs more often in tongue-protrusion than in mouth-opening displays, and mouth-opening occurs more often in mouth-opening than in tongue-protrusion displays (Meltzoff & Moore, 1983a), this is strong evidence for neonatal imitation of facial gestures. Also, if young infants are able to shape their tongue protrusion to match a model's tongue protrusion to one corner of the mouth (Meltzoff & Moore, 1994), this speaks against a reflexive mechanism.

It certainly is often possible to question experimental evidence for methodological problems, and Anisfeld is right in pointing out the particular importance of meticulous experimental controls in research on infants. However, his statement that tongue-protrusion effects can be accounted for by arousal is a post hoc interpretation and needs separate experimental clarification. To test the arousal hypothesis, one should define in advance stimuli that arouse the newborn to different degrees and show that tongue protrusion varies as a function of these conditions. Jones (1996) used this more constructive approach and obtained evidence that tongue protrusion occurs in nonimitative contexts, for example, when newborns see blinking lights. However, such evidence does not rule out that in tongue-protrusion modeling situations, tongue protrusion may still be driven by imitative processes.

Leaving aside the question of whether neonatal tongue protrusion is imitation, what can we basically say about the underlying representations? Meltzoff and Moore (1994) speculate that an innate active intermodal mapping (AIM) mechanism drives imitation over the life-span. If this is true, however, why does the ability to imitate apparently disappear after the first weeks of life and then reappear several months later, around 6 to 9 months? This time course resembles that of neonatal reflexes. Some reflexive behaviors are present in newborns, disappear after several weeks, and reappear some months later when the behavior is subject to more voluntary control (e.g., the stepping reflex reappears in walking, the grasping reflex in goal-directed reaching). Thus, the developmental time course suggests that neonatal tongue protrusion is driven by reflexive mechanisms, be it automatic AIM, arousal, or exploration. However, the flexibility of later imitation implies that it is based on different representations than the neonatal behavior.

8.6.2   Deferred Imitation in the First Year

In his review of experimental studies on deferred imitation, Anisfeld concludes that the results do not prove the existence of deferred imitation before 11–12 months. However, in my reading of Piaget, and contrary to Anisfeld, I did not discern that Piaget-assumed deferred imitation to occur earlier than 18 months: "Hitherto [i.e., before stage VI], the child has only been able to imitate immediately movements and sounds" (Piaget, 1951/1962, p. 66). Therefore the evidence for deferred imitation beginning at 11–12 months, which Anisfeld accepts, is one of the reasons to dispute Piaget's timetable of the development of representational imitation in infancy.

Moreover, in my opinion, the reviewed studies provide evidence for deferred imitation in even younger infants. The studies use deferred imitation as a nonverbal test of infant memory, and they show that infants younger than 12 months reproduce part of an observed action sequence and can reproduce an observed familiar action with a novel object after a significant delay. Thus, the studies add to Piaget's work the supposition that babies prior to their first birthday acquire sensorimotor knowledge, not only by performing actions on their own, but also by observing others. Because Piaget concentrated on acquiring cognition by self-performing actions, he may have underestimated infants' ability to learn by observation. More important, the studies show that 6- and 9-month-olds represent the observed actions for some time without immediate practice. Anisfeld rejects this evidence because he considers the infants' reproductions to be recognition responses; the sight of the object activates the target action. Remembering a specific observed object-action association, however, requires some form of representation. It may not be symbolic, but at least it exists.

Taken together, the reviewed studies provide evidence to dispute Piaget's (1951/1962) theorizing about a qualitative, stagelike development of imitation. Evidence points to a quantitative, continuous development, which may be dependent on the emerging memory capacity. Hence, imitation starts before the first birthday with the application of known actions in new situations, and moves forward to combining actions sequentially without immediate practice. Therefore we should accept the reviewed studies on deferred imitation as what they were designed to be: nonverbal tests of infant memory.

8.7 Joining the Intentional Dance
Guy Claxton on Tomasello and Carpenter

I remember when I was about 5 years old standing watching my father doing something or other at his workbench in the garage, and after a while, saying to him innocently, "Dad, what are you trying to do?" Unfortunately he took this amiss; he thought I was questioning his competence. "I'm not trying to, I'm doing," he said, crossly. But I didn't mean that. I wanted to know what the goal was, so I could make better sense of his physical actions. Without some knowledge of where he was heading, I was having a hard time learning anything. I take it that the main aim of Tomasello and Carpenter's chapter is to validate this youthful concern of mine, and to show how early it develops.

I am a lapsed experimental psychologist turned educator. So although I am fascinated by Tomasello and Carpenter's delicate research designs, my main interest is in the implications of their ideas about imitation for real-life teaching and learning beyond early childhood. In this context, their findings about the ontogenesis of "intention reading" are powerful indeed. It makes good sense to me that as we grow up, our social learning draws on all the different aspects of imitation that Tomasello and Carpenter are at pains to distinguish. Of course it is useful to be able to mimic someone else's skilled action—to see exactly how a more accomplished piano player or arguer or teaser produces their effects. Of course it is useful to be able to watch other people getting objects, situations, and third parties to reveal their dispositions and affordances. Watching an elder sibling teasing the dog, I learn more about the art of teasing, *and* about the dog. And, most important, I get to infer what teasing is *for*, by observing what outcomes seem to please my big sister (what Tomasello and Carpenter signify by "There!"), and what misses the mark ("Whoops!"). It is indeed useful to have these conceptually distinguished so carefully, and interesting to have some clues about their developmental sequence. In practice, though, I wonder, for people of school age and beyond, how much these distinctions matter. Would a teacher want to break down his or her modeling into separate demonstrations of action, goal, and result? Probably not. If she wants her students to be able to perform a mathematical operation, she is more likely to be effective, I think, if she treats the operations she is using, where she is heading, and what the equation looks like when it has been solved as a single unit.

Likewise, in practice, it doesn't seem too important to worry about whether the learner is imitating directly or reciprocally. As Tomasello and Carpenter rightly point out (along with several other contributors), the young child's underlying goal is not to be an accurate imitator, but to join the social dance—what Bruner called, a long time ago, the "web of social reciprocity" (Bruner, 1960). Whether I do just what you do, or whether I do something complementary (as in playing peek-a-boo, or seesawing), is probably less important most of the time than getting that delicious feeling of entrainment; of being part of the action and having a part to play in making it happen. With different kinds of partners, you learn different kinds of dances, and sociocultural theorists such as Jay Lemke (2001) conceive of growing up as the introjection of an increasing variety of dances, dancing partners, and things to do when someone treads on your toes. It seems that infants will happily join a whole range of different kinds of dances. For example, mothers and babies, one of whom is deaf, dance in a very different way from normally hearing mothers and babies, but development is jeopardized only when the dance—any dance—breaks down, as it does with mothers suffering postpartum depression.

This leads me to a major question that Tomasello and Carpenter's chapter leaves hanging: why and how intention reading itself develops. They are content to sketch out a developmental timetable, and leave the mechanisms unexplored for the moment. Yet it seems to me that intentionality—acting as if you have a purpose in mind—may itself be learned through imitative processes. Western caregivers, through both their comments and their reactions, love to engage children in the particular dance called "you meant to," obsessively attributing intention to acts that may have had no goal at all. Yet in order to join this dance fully, especially at a linguistic level, children have to learn to impute intentional states to themselves. They come to seem to want, and to talk as if they wanted, what their partner responded to in their earlier behavior *as if* they wanted. The "intentional stance" (Dennett, 1987) (or perhaps better, the "intentional trance") does not just automatically mature during the second year of life; it is systematically and diligently modeled, coached, and elicited by adults who have, in their turn, been enculturated into an intentional folk psychology. I would love to know more about how the intentional stance arises out of the intentional dance, as I am sure it must.

I have two final caveats. The first concerns mentalistic language. It is very hard to talk about intention reading without inadvertently implying that children are in some way conscious of the intentions they are reading (and transmitting). When we say a child "understands what the actor intends," or "has a theory of other minds," it is hard not to begin to slide into the Cartesian trap of assuming that there must be "something going on" in their consciousness. But there need be nothing. All kinds of systems, many of them nonbiological, display intentionality, and Rodney Brooks' robot Kismet, at Massachusetts Institute of Technology, even seems to read it, up to a point (Brooks, 2003), but there is no reason—other than ingrained Cartesian habit—to assume that intentionality entails conscious reason. I suspect children remain small zombies long after they have learned to talk and act as if they were dealing with genuine mental entities called hopes and plans. It would be interesting to know Tomasello and Carpenter's thoughts about that.

Finally, the experimental caveat. One of the reasons I am no longer a card-carrying experimental psychologist is because the "myth of presumed universality," or the "assumption of content (and context) irrelevance," seem quite untenable, even for small children and primates. To assume that you can extrapolate to basic mechanisms from a subject's performance in one task is neat, convenient, productive, always unjustified, and frequently wrong. I would like to see a wider, more ingenious array of tasks being used in research programs like those of Tomasello and Carpenter, and greater use made of sociocultural and activity theory paradigms. Indeed, imitation, broadly conceived, is one of the core processes presumed by the growing army of neo-Vygotskean researchers, and I think their methods could illuminate the work of the cognitive scientists, just as much as approaches such as those of Tomasello and Carpenter could bring some much-needed rigor to the sociocultural camp.

8.8 Two Elegant Experiments
George Comstock on Harris and Want

The two elegant experiments by Paul Harris and Stephen Want reported in volume 2, chapter 6 (1) provide convincing evidence that the age of three is a critical threshold for the appearance of selective imitation that makes use of errors in acquiring tool-using skills by observing models, (2) are given interesting and insightful interpretations that rest on the rejection of plausible but inadequate alternatives, (3) lead to the formation of hypotheses and suggested designs for future research, and (4) encourage speculation on the emergence of the ratchet effect in the Upper Paleolithic, when the development and adoption of tools changed progressively and comparatively rapidly. In effect, they constitute a very satisfying paradigm for experimental research.

The key finding is that it is only by the age of three that children become able to learn from errors made by a model in imitating the model's use of tools. At an earlier age, the observation of errors fails to enhance performance. Thus, selective imitation in which responses that achieve a goal are favored appears only after some particular stage of cognitive development is reached. It is not solely a function of the ability to imitate. The authors advance an interpretation that rests on the entire sequence of a verbally signaled complete or partial error in tool use followed by a correct example. They reject the notion that stimulus enhancement had a major role in the selective imitation because the children did not improve by merely seeing use of the objects that achieved the goal of freeing a toy man from the Visalberghi tube trap or the authors' own Y-tube. They also reject reinforcement—the observation or experience of success—because performance did not improve as a function of the number of trials. Instead, they argue that what was required for learning what not to do was the combination of an observable partial or full error, a verbal signal ("Oops!") calling attention to the error, and observation of the correct response. The first two factors apparently make the correct response more identifiable as the means to achieve the goal. This interpretation assigns importance to two elements in achieving improved tool use—one cognitive and dependent on reaching a developmental threshold, and the other social and dependent on observing error and success.

The children evidently were quite motivated to free the toy man. The authors rightly recognize this as a common characteristic of tool use because the use of a tool ordinarily achieves or makes easier the achievement of a goal, and therefore this characteristic is properly part of a paradigm for studying acquisition of tool-using skills. Nevertheless, the presence of strong motive raises the question of when in a child's development tool use may be learned simply because a tool is at hand. Such serendipitous learning, attributable in part to stimulus enhancement as well as expectations about future utility, is quite useful to everyday life. A good example is knowing how to use a fire extinguisher before it is needed in one's kitchen. The question raised is at what age do curiosity and the demand features of the tool begin to have a role. The authors' paradigm similarly invites consideration of transfer effects. Whether learning one skill improves performance of another skill has been the subject of debate since the beginnings of the discipline of psychology. The tasks employed here seem well suited to investigating this issue, and the sequential pairing of the Visalberghi trap tube and the authors' Y-tube would be an excellent vehicle for such inquiry.

The experiments do not directly address the question of what happens when children observe only the error. The implication of the authors' reasoning is that children would simply imitate the error, with no improvement in the success rate. This raises a much larger question about the social transmission of behavior. Under what conditions (other than the circumstances represented by these two experiments), if any, is it effective for a model to display errors, in short, what not to do. Although it is a big leap from the authors' data to public information campaigns in the mass media, such a "what not to do" approach was the basis of the now notoriously ineffective antidrug "Just say no" campaign.

Four obvious hypotheses are that modeling what not to do would increase in effectiveness (1) with the direness of the consequences of the error, (2) with the clarity of the portrayal of the error (a hypothesis supported in the present instance by the modest disparity between the partial and full incorrect conditions), (3) when there are few rewards or none associated with the error, and (4) when the credibility or likelihood of the undesired outcome is high. Even so, with threat appeals there remains the possibility of denial to avoid the anxiety associated with thoughts of the risk. In the case of "Just say no," all four hypothesized factors may have been weak, while denial may have been courted. Theory and experience thus suggest that the positive, rewarded outcome is particularly effective in stimulating imitation, and examples of what not to do should be accompanied by correct responses.

At first reading, the context of the broad historical sweep of human tool use seemed a literary device to stir interest rather than a topic to which the behavior of young children at the present time would be pertinent. Upon reflection, however, the data seem insistently informative about the emergence of the ratchet effect. Reward or success seems an inadequate explanation for this effect, although perhaps the level of achievement became sufficiently enhanced to increase significantly the motive to develop tools. Another possibility is that population growth and increased contact among people made social transmission more likely. Although it may be wild speculation, the present data hint at an evolutionary factor: the development of cognitive skills analogous to those displayed at age three but not at age two, which would represent an improvement in the capacity of humans to learn from each other about the use of tools.

8.9 Against Copying: Learning When (and Whom) Not to Ape
Guy Claxton on Kinsbourne

Academic cognitive psychologists, neuroscientists, and so on are folk psychologists too. They may subscribe just as fully as lay people do to the "commonsense" psychological assumptions of their culture. They may do so just as unwittingly. And in doing so, invisible constraints are placed on the kinds of psychological approaches and ideas they are willing to countenance professionally. It takes a great deal of effort to escape from the unconscious gravitational field of these enculturated presuppositions.

This may be one reason why the "motocentric theory of perception," as Patricia Churchland calls it, keeps being forgotten and rediscovered (Churchland et al., 1994). It is countercultural in at least two senses. It refuses to place "perception" at the front of a sequence of cognitive operations, and in doing so it refuses to divide the brain into boxes with textbook labels, with "vision" here, "motor programming" over there, and "motivation" somewhere else. The motocentric view is harder to think about than the commonsense view because it is messier and more "holistic," as well as being culturally "strange." However, it is undoubtedly a more accurate representation of human cognition (and animal cognition, come to that).

Perception is not the extraction of a (more or less) accurate representation of the external world, upon which cognition proper then works. It is imbued with the selective influences of desire and capability right from the start. Perception, emotion, motivation, and action are functionally so tightly intertwined that it is misleading to think of them as separable systems at all. Jakob von Uexküll's delightful essay "A stroll through the worlds of animals and men," demonstrated this vividly in the 1950s (von Uexküll, 1957). James J. Gibson got part of the way there in the 1960s with his notion of "affordances" (Gibson, 1966). In the past few years such scholars as Andrew Clark, Patricia Churchland, Susan Hurley, Francisco Varela, and George Lakoff and Mark Johnson in their *Philosophy in the Flesh* have been having another go at formulating the motocentric view (Clark, 1997; Churchland, 2002; Hurley, 1998; Varela et al., 1991; Lakoff & Johnson, 1999). And now Marcel Kinsbourne's elegant ruminations in chapter 7 are designed to convince us that the renewed study of imitation, mirror neurons and all, does more than merely show that perceptual and motor "systems" are more tightly coupled than commonsense Cartesianism would have it. He reminds us that sensing, doing, feeling, and wanting are simultaneous facets of one rapidly unfolding, complex, neurodynamic process. The perceptual ends of the neural net are continually being affected by evanescent patterns of priming that reflect the momentary senses of capability, feeling, arousal, and need. Max Clowes used to say "There's no seeing, only seeing *as*" (personal communication); but it's worse than that: there's only seeing *for*.

Some of these sources of bias in perception are built in. I am inclined to agree with Kinsbourne, Trevarthen (1999), and others that the desire for "interactional synchrony" is innate; that babies will unearth and do whatever it takes to achieve entrainment (even if it risks damaging other aspects of their development); and that the "joint attention" that ensues forms the basis for the learning of language and much else. However, the part of the story that particularly intrigues me is the development of the inhibitory mechanisms that make this tendency to entrainment both more covert and more selective. Instead of entraining through simple forms of copying or reciprocating, we learn to keep it inside, and turn public imitation into private imagination. [There is neuroimaging evidence that "mental rehearsal" of, for example, piano scales, produces very nearly as much neuronal growth as actual practice (Pascual-Leone, 2001).]

We also learn to seek entrainment with a restricted circle of family, friends, and acquaintances—to inhibit the imitative impulse in the presence of some (kinds of) people, and to release it (albeit increasingly covertly) in the presence of others. Kinsbourne explains that privacy and selectivity are useful options if for no other reason than that imitation entails learning, and you cannot learn "everything." It seems as if we have two kinds or levels of inhibition at work here: one that curtails the external concomitants of mirror neuron activation but leaves cortical activation patterns relatively unaffected (and unattentuated), and another that prevents even these cortical patterns from forming (and thus blocks learning).

It seems likely that these developments of inhibitory sophistication continue well beyond infancy and thus may be of consequence in educational as well as familial settings. Though it is an enormous inferential leap from the laboratory to the classroom, one cannot help but be struck by the intense imitative selectivity of the average adolescent (as well as by the prevalence of those forms of covert identification that constitute the majority of daydreams). If it is true that mental rehearsal influences the development of the brain, then time spent "being Madonna" in the private theatre of your imagination will have a direct effect on the development of Madonna-like traits and habits. At the same time, the circuitry corresponding to the mathematical operations that Mr. Chips is trying to get you to learn will have lost the neural competition and been dampened down—as will the residual inclination to pick up Mr. Chips-like traits and habits, also.

In the context of sociocultural approaches to education, the latter is an important issue, for education is not only about the development of bodies of knowledge, skill, and understanding; it is (if Vygotsky, 1978, is right) about the progressive enculturation of a set of attitudes and values. These beliefs are communicated by a whole variety of means: the curriculum (mathematics is a different subject from physics), the timetable (learning can be turned on and off at will), assessment (what you know is what you can recall and write down under pressure), and so on. However, the most powerful, perhaps the determining force, is the mien of the teacher. Or it is unless the "interactional synchrony" of the student-teacher relationship has been blocked. Kinsbourne's approach invites us to explore when and how these acquired barriers to interpersonal transfer develop and are raised, but disappointingly, he fails to pursue the question himself.

Being face-to-face is neither a necessary nor a sufficient condition for imitational transfer to take place. It is not necessary because internalized models of other people can be used as the basis for imitation, as in daydreams, and it is not sufficient because Mr. Chips so often fails in his efforts to communicate his love of math. (Indeed, there may be some students in his class who resolve that he is exactly how they do *not* want to turn out.) There has to be a certain quality of relationship, we must suppose; call it respect, admiration, possibly just affection (which creates positive affect, and allows the pores in the "osmotic membrane" between brain and brain to open and each to be affected by the other.)

In sum, I found Kinsbourne's chapter philosophically congenial and practically stimulating. My main regret is that he sprays out fruitful ideas in a way that varies from the terse to the cryptic. I do hope that he finds the time to spell out all the interesting ramifications of his approach at greater length, before too long.

8.10   Imitating Violence
Susan Brison on Kinsbourn

According to Marcel Kinsbourne (in vol. 2, ch. 7), imitation is a form of entrainment, or "adopting shared rhythms of behavior" (p. 167), which is "more innately compelling than reasoned argument in inducing two, or many [persons], to adopt the same point of view" (p. 172). As a philosopher interested in theories of freedom of expression (Brison, 1998a,b) and in the effects of violence on the self (Brison, 2002), I find this view both refreshing and disturbing. It is refreshing in contrast with the overly rationalist, indeed Cartesian, view of free-speech theorists who assume that we are all rational, autonomous, and conscious information processors and decision makers. It is disturbing because if it is true, it indicates that we are naturally more prone to imitate media violence than free-speech theorists and public policy makers have so far been willing to acknowledge.

On April 4, 2002, I drove to the Grafton County courthouse in North Haverhill, New Hampshire, to attend the sentencing hearings of Robert Tulloch and James Parker, the two teenage boys who had pleaded guilty to the murders of my friends and colleagues, Half and Susanne Zantop. We heard, from the assistant attorney general, about the gruesome stabbings and about the state's case against the defendants. One of the things we learned was that the boys possessed—and had enjoyed playing for hours on end—a particularly violent and realistic interactive video game in which the player stabs his victims and watches them as they bleed to death.

That afternoon, I picked up my 7-year-old son from school and noticed that his school librarian had sent home a recent article from a local Vermont paper, the *Times-Argus*, entitled "Video game violence: harmful to society or just harmless fun?" It began with a quote from *Electronic Gaming Monthly*: "If you've ever wanted to run through a crowded mall while mowing down innocent shoppers with an M-16, or take a grenade launcher to storefronts and parked cars, [State of Emergency] is your game. [It] offers violent, vicarious thrills that are socially unacceptable, brazenly immoral and a helluva lot of fun."

What are the effects on children of violent video games and other forms of media violence as entertainment? What are their effects on adults? No one supposes that every child or adult who plays with or watches violent entertainment goes on to commit criminal acts, or even becomes more likely to do so. And many violent criminals (most of them, presumably, at least until very recently) have had no exposure to such violent entertainment. But this does not mean that there is *no* probabilistic causal connection between exposure to such media and the commission of violent crimes (just as the fact that not all smokers get lung cancer and some people who get lung cancer never smoked does not indicate the absence of a causal connection between smoking and lung cancer).

Not only are violent interactive video games cause for concern, given the desensitizing and disinhibiting effects they may have on those who play them, but there is evidence that even passive viewing of representations of violence can, in some contexts, have disinhibiting effects on some viewers' tendencies to imitate what they see. Kinsbourne's chapter indicates that the phenomenon of imitation is more pervasive and complex—and more central to human behavior—than we previously realized. His research suggests that the human drive to imitate others' behavior can undermine our autonomous decision-making processes—a finding that has important implications for a defense of free speech based on the view that citizens, as autonomous agents, have a right to unfettered freedom of expression and to unrestricted access to others' speech.

Even if media violence can be shown to have harmful societal effects, that finding by itself is not enough to warrant the governmental restriction of such speech, in the United States, anyway, since the free speech principle embedded in the First Amendment of the U.S. Constitution indicates that even *harmful* speech is worthy of special protection against government interference. As I have argued (Brison, 1998a), if speech is harmless, then there is no need to give it special protection, since a background assumption of our constitutional democracy is a general principle of liberty stating that the government may justifiably interfere with individual liberties only to prevent people from harming others.

What can be the reason for protecting even harmful speech? Numerous defenses of a special free-speech principle have been given, including the argument from truth, the argument from democracy, and the argument from autonomy. All of them presuppose that speech (which, under First Amendment doctrine, includes such things as graphically realistic violent films and video games) has no (or merely negligible) effects that are not under the conscious control of the audience. So, even if it can be shown that watching violent films and video games leads to an increased tendency to violence in the viewers, it is argued that the *viewers*, not the media, are entirely responsible for the violence because they consciously and autonomously choose to be influenced by what they see (and what they do, in the case of interactive video games). The violence is considered to be entirely due to the mental intermediation of the viewer—a conscious intervention that is assumed to break the chain of causality from the viewing of violent scenes to the committing of violent acts.

As Susan Hurley has argued, however, the research by Kinsbourne and others suggests that the imitation of others' behavior, including others' violent acts, is not always a consciously mediated process that is under the autonomous control of the viewers or imitators.[4] It might be argued that if we consider violent media to be even partially responsible for the violent behavior perpetrated by its consumers, then we must consider the perpetrators *not* responsible. In conversation, the assistant attorney general in the Zantop killings case told me that had the case gone to trial, the killers' frequent playing of this particular violent video game would have been used as evidence, not by the prosecution, but by the *defense*, as part of an insanity plea, in an attempt to show that the killers were not responsible for their actions. However, it does not follow from the claim that violent media cause people to be violent that the perpetrators are not 100% responsible for their violent acts. Two or more people can each be 100% responsible for the same crime, as in the case of multiple snipers who simultaneously fire many shots, fatally wounding their victim. If people are entrained, to use Kinsbourne's term, in violent behavior by their ever-greater exposure to increasingly violent media in our society, then we, as citizens, have to start taking responsibility for the violence that results.

4. Susan L. Hurley makes this argument in her excellent article "Imitation, media violence, and freedom of speech" (2004).

II Imitation and Culture

9 Why We Are Social Animals: The High Road to Imitation as Social Glue

Ap Dijksterhuis

Man is by nature a social animal
—Aristotle

9.1 Introduction

No one will deny that humans are indeed social animals. This has been said for such a long time and by so many great thinkers that it is treated as self-evident. It is simply true, and there is no arguing about it. Because it so evident that humans are social animals, the idea does not elicit much thought. It is a truism. In a way, the notion that humans are social animals falls in the same psychological category as the notion that New York is a large city or that tulips are beautiful. Hearing or reading such statements does not elicit more than a psychological shrug of the shoulders. Is New York large? Sure. Are tulips beautiful? Obviously. Are humans social? But of course.

Self-evident as it may be, it is much less clear *why* we are so social. What is the *essence* of being social? Or, more specifically, why is it that we see humans as very social animals? Is it because we live in groups? Well, it is true that humans are part of several groups, such as a family or a group of colleagues. On the other hand, we are certainly not the most group oriented of species. A lot of animals (female lions, female elephants, wolves, many fish, etc.) spend every hour of their lives in the same group. Is it because we communicate so effectively and elaborately? This is certainly important, but it does not make us stand out. Some animals that are seen as much less social than us (cats come to mind) have rather complex and intricate ways of communication. Other animals, which we do find social because they live in groups, do not communicate all that much.

Is it the enormous human capacity to imitate? We do know that humans have the capacity to automatically and unconsciously bring their behavior in line with their social environment. We imitate facial expressions (e.g., Meltzoff & Moore, 1977), postures, and gestures (e.g., Chartrand & Bargh, 1999), as well as accents, tone of voice, and other speech-related variables (e.g., Neumann & Strack, 2000). However, this in itself does not make us stand out either. Fish living in shoals copy the behavior of their fellow fish all the time (Breder, 1976; Pitcher, 1979). What does make humans special, though, is the wide range of behavior and even entire behavioral patterns that they imitate. As we will see later in this chapter, we not only imitate the observable behavior of others (such as a facial expression or a gesture), but we adopt multiple, sometimes rather complex aspects of others' psychological functioning (see Dijksterhuis & Bargh, 2001). Humans, in a way, can take on the role of other humans.

In this chapter, I would like to argue that imitation, and especially imitation of complex behavioral patterns, constitutes the "social glue" that makes us successful social animals. In various parts of the chapter I will stress the social benefits of imitation. Furthermore, I will argue that imitation is of such importance because it can be conceived of as default social behavior. Imitation is not something we only occasionally engage in. Instead, we *usually* imitate—automatically—and not doing it is the exception. In the next section, I briefly review some findings that show that people imitate the observable behavior of others and I emphasize the evidence for the social benefits of imitation. A more elaborate discussion of the imitation of entire behavioral patterns follows. Finally, I review some evidence showing that when people do not engage in imitation, the moderators causing this state of "nonimitation" can be tied directly to the social function of imitation.

9.2 Mirror Neurons and the Relation between Perception and Action

Our ability to imitate is not something we learn. Although it is certainly true that our ability to imitate evolves over time, the basics are already there when we are born. Some decades ago, most theorists assumed that for an infant to be able to imitate, it needed to have had at least some rudimentary associative experience between the observation and execution of actions. This in turn led to the assumption that infants would not be able to imitate until they were about 1 year old. The research by Meltzoff and Moore among infants dramatically changed this view. They convincingly showed that children can imitate hand movements in the first months of their life (Meltzoff & Moore, 1977, 1997). Moreover, imitation of facial expression was demonstrated to be possible only a few weeks after birth. In later work (Meltzoff & Moore, 1983a, 1989) they even obtained evidence for imitation of facial acts among newborns. In a study where the subjects were on average 32 hours old (the youngest being only 42 minutes old!) they showed evidence for imitation of facial acts.

The findings obtained by Meltzoff and Moore strongly suggested that humans have a shared neural system for perceiving and performing an action (see also W. Prinz, 1990). As Meltzoff recently noted, "Newborn imitation provides the 'existence proof' for a neural mapping between observed and executed movements in human infants" (2002a, p. 23). More recent research indeed demonstrated such neural mapping. Rizzolatti, Gallese, and colleagues demonstrated the existence of mirror neurons in the premotor cortex (Gallese et al., 1996; Rizzolatti et al., 1996a). These mirror neurons discharge both when an action is observed and when it is executed. Whereas these mirror neurons were first discovered in research on monkeys, other research has demonstrated that common brain regions for perceiving and executing an action can also be found in human subjects (e.g., Decety et al., 1997; Fadiga et al., 1995; Iacoboni et al., 1999).

A shared representational system for perceiving and executing actions was also demonstrated by Müsseler and Hommel (1997) with a very elegant experimental paradigm. They reasoned that if perception and execution depend on the same neural systems, and thus on the same resources, it could well be that execution of an action disrupts perception of this same action. After all, the system is already "busy" doing the action. This was indeed shown. If participants are instructed to press one of two arrow keys (< or >) and at exactly the time of execution are presented with another arrow key on the screen, their memory for the presented arrow key is dependent on whether the presented key is the same or the opposite of the one they pressed. When the keys are the same, perception is less accurate because the system responsible for perception of this key is already working on performance of the action.[1] The conclusion that can be drawn on the basis of the work discussed here is clear. We are wired to imitate.

9.3 Imitation as Social Glue

Imitation is beneficial for various reasons (e.g., it enables people to learn certain skills), but one consequence of imitation is of paramount importance for humans in the social realm; imitation leads to liking. Social interactions in which the participants imitate more than usual are

1. See also W. Prinz, vol. 1, ch. 5. ED.

characterized by more rapport. Gordon Allport (1968; see Chartrand & Bargh, 1999) pointed out that the original meaning of empathy was "objective motor mimicry." Only in the second half of the past century did the use of the term shift toward the more general meaning it has today.

The strong relation between imitation and liking was demonstrated quite a while ago (see Chartrand et al., in press; Dijksterhuis & Bargh, 2001), but the early demonstrations (Bernieri, 1988; Charney, 1966; LaFrance, 1979; LaFrance & Broadbent, 1976) merely showed correlations between imitation and rapport, thereby obscuring the direction of causality. It was not clear, in other words, whether imitation led to more liking or whether liking led to more imitation. Still, some effects were impressive and emphasized the importance and strength of the relation between imitation and liking. Bernieri (1988) observed interactions and obtained a correlation of 0.74 between the degree of posture mirroring and positive affect experienced during the interaction. LaFrance (1979) reported a correlation of 0.63 between posture mirroring and rapport.

Chartrand and Bargh (1999) aimed to shed light on the directionality of the relation between imitation and liking. Rather than investigating mirroring of postures, they manipulated actions such as foot shaking or nose rubbing. In a first experiment, a confederate either rubbed her nose or shook her foot while working with a participant on a task. Their first hypothesis, that the participants would imitate the behavior of the confederate, was confirmed. Under conditions where the confederate rubbed her nose, the participants engaged more in nose rubbing than in foot shaking, whereas the opposite was true when the participants interacted with the confederate who shook her foot.

Chartrand and Bargh (1999) replicated and extended this finding in a second study in which the confederate purposefully imitated the body posture of the participant. This study obtained clear evidence that imitation leads to increased liking of interaction partners. The participants who were surreptitiously imitated by the confederate liked the confederate more than the to participants who were not imitated. In addition, the participants who were imitated indicated that the interaction proceeded more smoothly.

Recently, Lakin and Chartrand (2003) showed that when people have the goal to affiliate, they imitate more. It is important to note that the degree of imitation was not the result of a strategic, conscious choice. The goal to affiliate was activated among participants without their awareness (cf. e.g., Bargh et al., 2001; Chartrand & Bargh, 1996). All that was done was that participants were presented subliminally with words related to affiliation (such as affiliate, friend, together), whereas control participants were not presented with these words. In a subsequent interaction with a confederate, the participants with the subliminally activated goal to affiliate imitated more. The confederate touched his or her face repeatedly, and the participants with the subliminally activated goal to affiliate did so too. These findings are particularly interesting because they clearly emphasize the social function of imitation. If we want to be liked, we imitate more, without being aware of it.

Research on mood contagion (e.g., Hatfield et al., 1994; Neumann & Strack, 2000) also sheds light on the important relation between imitation and liking. In experiments conducted by Neumann and Strack (2000), the participants listened to an audiotaped speech given by a stranger. While they were listening, the participants were asked to repeat what they heard and were audiotaped themselves. It was found that the participants adopted the tone of voice of the person on the tape they listened to. A sad tone of voice on the tape elicited a sad tone of voice in the participant, whereas a happy voice led to a happy voice in the participant. It is important to note that the participants changed their moods to agree with the mood of the person on the tape. In other words, imitation led to mood contagion.

The beneficial effects of mood contagion or mood sharing have been documented extensively. Bavelas et al. (1986, 1987) have shown that mood sharing led to greater liking (on various different measures) in a large series of studies. Zajonc et al. (1987) extended this work in an intriguing way. They reasoned that couples who had lived together for a period of time should have experienced the same emotions at the same times very often, and because frequent facial expressions eventually lead to changes in facial lines, they hypothesized that partners should start to look more like each other the longer they are together. In their experiment, they gave participants twenty-four photographs. These photographs were those of the partners of twelve married couples. Some photographs were made at the wedding, whereas others were made 25 years later. The task of the participants was to assess the degree of resemblance of various pairs of photographs. As predicted, partners who were together for 25 years resembled each other more than random pairs of the same age and than newly wed couples.

In a follow-up study, they demonstrated the importance of this resemblance. They had observed large variations in the degree of resemblance of life partners. This led to the intriguing hypothesis that partners who have grown to look like each other more may actually be happier together than those who have not, because their resemblance is due to a greater history of shared emotions. And, in general at least, shared emotions lead to a stronger bond between partners. A questionnaire study indeed confirmed this hypothesis, with the effects being impressive in size (with a correlation of .49 between resemblance and self-reported happiness).

Finally, van Baaren et al. (2003) demonstrated a more mundane but nonetheless spectacular benefit of imitation. Based on the research by Chartrand and Bargh (1999) that clearly shows that imitation leads to liking, they conducted a field experiment in a restaurant. They first established the average tip that waitresses received during a normal evening. They then instructed the waitresses to imitate the verbal behavior of their customers. That is, they were instructed to literally repeat the order for each customer. On other days, they were instructed to avoid literal imitation. In two separate studies, it was shown that exact verbal mimicry significantly enhanced the tips, whereas avoidance of mimicry reduced tipping compared to the baseline.

To summarize, the "social glue" function of imitation is well documented. Imitation of postures, speech, and facial expression leads to greater rapport and liking, to smoother interactions, to mood contagion (which can lead to a more satisfactory relationship), and even to a higher income.

9.4   The High Road to Imitation

In the research on imitation discussed in the preceding section, imitation pertained only to behavior that can be observed literally and directly. We perceive facial expressions, postures, gestures, and various speech-related variables such as accents and tone of voice. These observables lead to imitation in a very direct way. All that is needed is a shared representational system. An act is perceived and the perceiver acts correspondingly. We could call this the low road to imitation.[2]

The human perceptual repertoire, however, is very rich. We "see" much more than what can be literally perceived (see Dijksterhuis & Bargh, 2001). Twenty years of research in the social cognition domain have revealed two

2. The use of the terms "low road" and "high road" is taken from the work by LeDoux (1996). He used these terms to describe two different ways in which fearful stimuli are processed. The low road describes a rather direct process in which a stimulus is processed in the amygdala, whereas the high road describes a more elaborate process in which cognitions play a role as well. My use of the terms follows from roughly the same distinction. The low road describes a more direct lower-order process, whereas the high road represents a more complex series of psychological processes. For more details on how imitation through the high road proceeds, see Dijksterhuis and Bargh (2001).

important psychological processes that are central to our understanding of social perception. First, we generate *trait inferences* on the basis of the behavior of others. Such inferences can of course not be perceived literally, but are made upon the perception of behavior that is present and observed in the current environment. Importantly, inferences are made automatically upon perception of the observable act (e.g., Gilbert, 1989; Winter & Uleman, 1984). Upon hearing that "Nick volunteered to read the paper of someone who could not show up at the conference," we automatically translate this concrete behavior into an abstract personality trait. We draw the conclusion that Nick is a helpful person. We make such trait inferences spontaneously, unconsciously, and continuously, making them an integral part of everyday social perception (Dijksterhuis & Bargh, 2001; Higgins, 1989; Higgins & Bargh, 1987).

Second, in social perceptions, *social stereotypes* are automatically activated (Brewer, 1988; Devine, 1989). When we see a person, we automatically categorize that person as a member of his or her group, and we usually activate the stereotypes associated with that group (Devine, 1989; Greenwald & Banaji, 1995; Lepore & Brown, 1997). Seeing an African American, for instance, is sufficient to activate the stereotype of African Americans, such as "musical" or "aggressive" (Bargh et al., 1996; Chen & Bargh, 1997; Devine, 1989), whereas seeing an elderly person leads to the activation of stereotypes such as "slow" and "forgetful" (e.g., Dijksterhuis et al., 2000a). Stereotype activation occurs as a natural and automatic part of the process of everyday social perception.

These activated traits and stereotypes lead to imitation as well (see Dijksterhuis & Bargh, 2001, for a review). Traits and stereotypes do not evoke imitation in the sense that a perceiver exactly copies the behavior of the person observed. Rather, a process of behavioral adjustment ensues, in which behavior or behavioral patterns are, often subtly, brought more in line with the behavior of another person. This form of imitation is less direct than imitation of observables in that more mechanisms than a shared representational system play a role. The process is decidedly more complex (see Dijksterhuis & Bargh, 2001). We could call this the high road to imitation.

9.5 A Peek at the High Road

The effects of trait activation or stereotype activation on overt behavior have traditionally been investigated with priming manipulations. This work has recently been reviewed extensively (Dijksterhuis & Bargh, 2001), so rather than discussing all the relevant experiments published, here I list only a limited number of telling examples.

C. Carver et al. (1983) primed the concept of hostility among half of their participants by incidentally exposing them to words related to this concept (hostile, aggressive, etc.). The remaining half of the participants were not primed. Later, participants played the role of a teacher in a learning task based on the classic experiment of Milgram (1963). The participants were asked to administer electrical shocks to a second participant (actually a confederate, of course) whenever this second participant gave an incorrect answer to a question. The participants, however, were free to choose the intensity of the shocks. The results showed that the participants primed with hostility delivered more intense shocks than did the control participants. In other words, priming hostility indeed led to more hostile behavior.

Bargh et al. (1996, experiment 1) primed their participants with either rudeness or politeness. They presented their participants with a scrambled sentence task in which they were to construct grammatically correct sentences out of a random ordering of words (see Srull & Wyer, 1979), as a purported test of language ability. In one condition, the scrambled sentences contained some words related to rudeness (e.g., aggressively, bold, rude) whereas in a second condition the scrambled sentences contained some words related to politeness (e.g., respect, patiently, polite). In a third condition, the scrambled sentence task did not contain words related to either rudeness or politeness. After the participants had been given the instruction necessary to complete the scrambled sentence task, the experimenter left the room. The participants were asked to meet the experimenter in a different office when they finished the scrambled sentence task. When the participants approached the experimenter, the experimenter was talking to a confederate. The confederate surreptitiously measured the time it took for the participants to interrupt the conversation. The participants who were primed with rudeness were more likely to interrupt (63%) than were the control participants (38%), whereas the participants primed with politeness were least likely to interrupt (17%).

Macrae and Johnston (1998) investigated the consequences of activation of the trait "helpful." In their experiments, half of the participants were primed with the concept of helpfulness with the use of a scrambled sentence task, whereas the remaining participants were not primed. After finishing the priming task, the experimenter picked up her possessions from a desk (books, a paper, a bag, pens) and asked the participants to follow her to another experimenter. As she approached the door, she "accidentally" dropped the items she was carrying. As expected, the participants primed with helpfulness picked up more items from the floor (that is, they were more helpful) than did the control participants.

Bargh et al. (1996) were the first to report the effects of stereotype activation on actual motor behavior. In their second experiment, some participants were primed with a stereotype of the elderly, whereas others were not. The participants in the experimental condition were primed by exposing them to words related to the elderly (i.e., gray, bingo, Florida) in the context of a scrambled sentence language task. After the participants finished the priming task, they were told that the experiment was over. A confederate, however, recorded the time it took the participants to walk from the experimental room to the nearest elevator. The data from two separate experiments showed that the participants primed with the elderly stereotype walked significantly slower than the control participants. In other words, people displayed behavior corresponding to the activated stereotype. The elderly are associated with slowness, and activating the stereotype of the elderly indeed led to slowness among the participants.

It is also known that stereotypes and traits lead to corresponding behavior in the domain of intellectual (or mental) performance. Dijksterhuis and van Knippenberg (1998) improved people's intellectual performance in a series of experiments. In their first experiment, some of the participants were primed with the stereotype of professors. These participants were asked to think about college professors and to write down everything that came to mind regarding the typical behaviors and attributes of professors. The remaining participants were not given this task. In an ostensibly unrelated second experiment, the participants were asked to answer forty-two general-knowledge questions that were taken from the game Trivial Pursuit (such as "Who painted La Guernica?" a. Dali, b. Velasquez, c. Picasso, d. Miro). In line with the prevailing stereotype of professors as being rather intelligent, the primed participants answered more questions correctly than did the other participants. In another experiment by Dijksterhuis and van Knippenberg (1998), it was shown that participants could also be led to perform worse on a general-knowledge task by having them think previously about soccer hooligans, a social group that is associated with stupidity.

Also, various people have shown that activation of a stereotype can affect the performance of memory (Dijksterhuis et al., 2000a,b; Levy, 1996). Dijksterhuis et al. (2000b), for instance, obtained evidence showing that activation of the elderly stereotype affects memory performance among college students (i.e., participants for whom the stereotype is not self-relevant). In their experiment, the participants were seated at a desk on which fifteen objects were placed (e.g., a book, a pencil, a bag, an Ajax Amsterdam poster). Some participants were asked to answer questions about elderly people ("How often do you meet elderly people? Do you think elderly people are conservative?"), whereas others were asked to answer questions about college students. After answering questions for 3 minutes, the participants were placed in a different experimental room and asked to recall as many objects present in the previous room as possible. As expected, the participants primed with the elderly stereotype recalled fewer objects than the other participants. The deteriorating effects of activation of the elderly stereotype on memory have been replicated and extended by Dijksterhuis et al. (2000a), who used subliminal priming procedures and several different memory paradigms.

Finally, recent research shows that stereotype activation can lead to converging attitudes (Kawakami et al., 2003). In the domain of attitudes, the social glue function of imitation is especially evident. It is well known that people like other people more when they share their attitudes (D. Byrne, 1971). Children know this too. A 14-year-old child somehow knows that if he or she is angling for parental financial help to buy a new stereo set or a fancy new bicycle, it helps temporarily to feign an interest in Mozart or Bach and to downplay the achievements of the Sex Pistols or Eminem. In the experiments by Kawakami and colleagues, half of the participants were primed with the stereotype of the elderly. In different experiments, different priming methods were used, ranging from rather bold, conscious manipulations to subtle subliminal manipulations. In a second task, participants were asked to what extent they agreed with attitude statements such as "There is too much sex and nudity on TV these days" and "More people should go to church these days." Based on the prevailing stereotype of the elderly as being somewhat conservative, it was predicted that the primed participants would become more conservative in their attitudes. The results showed that this was indeed the case. The participants primed with the elderly stereotype were suddenly worried about the amount of sex on television and about the decreasing number of churchgoers in the Netherlands, relative to control participants who were not primed.

In a follow-up study, a more worrisome consequence of such stereotype-induced changes in attitude was found. Priming the stereotype of skinheads (associated with racism) led people to express more discriminatory attitudes. When asked to evaluate statements such as "The Netherlands should accept more immigrants from poor countries" or "I think that minorities ask too much in their demands for equal rights," the participants primed with skinhead stereotypes adopted more negative attitudes toward foreigners than the control participants who were not primed.

In sum, there is an abundance of evidence showing that trait activation or stereotype activation leads to convergence in a range of behaviors. Motor behavior, various forms of interpersonal behavior, intellectual performance, and attitudes are all changed in the direction of the behavior or attitudes in our social environment.

9.6 Characteristics of the High Road

One should note that in discussing imitation by the high road, the term "imitation" is used rather loosely. In the experiments discussed earlier, the participants did not literally imitate behavior. Instead, they adjusted their behavior to bring it more in line with their social environment. In addition, it should also be noted that traits and stereotypes do not evoke new behavior. The participants in the second experiment by Bargh et al. (1996) did not walk to the elevator because they were primed. Rather, they walked to the elevator because they wanted to go to a different floor, and they did this slowly because they were primed. Likewise, the participants in the experiments by Dijksterhuis and van Knippenberg (1998) did not of course spontaneously start to work on a general-knowledge test. They did this because the experimenter asked them to. Only the way they did it (very well or rather poorly) was affected by the prime. This all may seem obvious, but it is nonetheless important. The activation of traits and stereotypes does not so much elicit behavior as affect the parameters (slow versus fast, elaborate versus sloppy, etc.) of ongoing behavior.

Throughout this chapter, it was emphasized that imitation functions as social glue, making us like each other more, and in general leading to more smooth and pleasant social encounters. This is true not only for the low road but also for the high road. Adjusting the parameters of behavior in a social context is important because the effects permeate social encounters continuously and intensely. First of all, as should have become evident in the preceding section, the high road leads to imitation in a very broad domain of behavior. We adjust motor behavior and a range of interpersonal behaviors such as helpfulness or aggression; it affects mental performance in different ways; and it affects our attitudes. More concretely, relevant research has shown by now that imitation can make us slow, fast, smart, stupid, good at math, bad at math, helpful, rude, polite, long-winded, hostile, aggressive, cooperative, competitive, conforming, nonconforming, conservative, forgetful, careful, careless, neat, and sloppy.

Second, imitation as a result of stereotype activation is not limited to one aspect of behavior. Upon meeting an elderly person, multiple stereotypes are activated, such as slow, forgetful, and conservative. All these stereotypes can lead to the corresponding behaviors simultaneously. Although it has never been tested, we have every reason to assume that activation of these stereotypes leads to slowness, forgetfulness, and conservatism concurrently. In other words, such activation affects our entire psychological functioning.

Third, the high road is fast; we can even imitate in anticipation. After all, the activation of a trait or stereotype is enough, and this does not necessarily have to be mediated by actual perception. Merely thinking about a person also puts these imitative processes in motion. An undergraduate student waiting outside the office of a professor for a meeting is already adjusting his or her behavior. When we walk, cycle, or drive to see our parents or grandparents, we start to adjust our behavior as soon as we start to think about them (of course, leading to the fact that we arrive a little late because we traveled so slowly).

Notwithstanding the importance of the high road, there are also limitations. First, whereas traits are activated on the basis of relatively objective characterizations of observable behavior (again, Nick is seen as helpful after he reads the paper of someone who cannot make it to the meeting), stereotypes are truly examples of "going beyond the information given." Not all elderly are forgetful, and not all soccer fans are stupid. Some stereotypes (such as the association between African Americans and aggression) are formed because of various cultural forces and indeed describe social reality very poorly. This makes imitation through stereotyping very crude. Second, whereas imitation will lead to more liking and more pleasant interactions in general, this is obviously not true for each case. It is hard to see how imitation of hostile or aggressive behavior would lead people to like each other more. In other words, the high road functions as social glue usually, but certainly not always. The high road is functional from a social perspective, but not all its individual manifestations are functional in and of themselves.

9.7 Blocking the High Road

An intriguing question is, *When* exactly do we imitate? Previously it has been argued that imitation is default social behavior (Dijksterhuis & Bargh, 2001). We do not choose to imitate at some times and not others. Rather, we are wired to imitate and we do it all the time, except when other psychological processes inhibit imitation. In concrete terms, activation of the stereotype of the elderly causes us to be slow, except when other psychological processes deem this inappropriate. The conscious need to hurry, for instance, can override the imitative tendency to be slow.

By now, various moderators of the tendency to imitate have been investigated (see Dijksterhuis & Bargh, 2001, for a review), but the one investigated most extensively is especially important for appreciating the social glue function of imitation. This moderator was based on research on self-focus (C. Carver & Scheier, 1981; Duval & Wicklund, 1972). In this work, it is argued that people can focus their attention on the self or on the (social) environment, depending on the circumstances. One could say that people are on some occasions socially oriented, while on other occasions they are much more self-oriented. Whether one is self-focused or not has a variety of psychological and behavioral consequences (see e.g., C. Carver & Scheier, 1981; Duval & Wicklund, 1972; Gibbons, 1990). For instance, under conditions of self-focus, people behave more in line with their norms, goals, or attitudes, and are less susceptible to environmental influences on their behavior. The effects are usually investigated by comparing a control group with a group that is made to focus on the self. A very effective method—and indeed the manipulation used most often—is to put people in front of a mirror.

Given the important social function of imitation, one could assume that under conditions of heightened self-focus people would imitate less or not at all. After all, imitation may be inhibited under conditions of high self-focus because people are more concerned about their norms or their needs than about their social environment. That is, "social glue" may not be more than a secondary concern under conditions of self-focus. This hypothesis was tested in various experiments by Dijksterhuis and van Knippenberg (2000). In their first experiment, the participants were primed with the stereotype of politicians or were not primed. In addition, they were seated in front of a mirror or were not. Later, the participants were asked to write a short essay about the French nuclear testing program. Based on the stereotype of politicians as long-winded, it was hypothesized that the primed participants would write longer essays. This was indeed the case. It is important to note that, in line with the second hypothesis, this only happened among the participants who were not seated in front of a mirror. The participants with heightened self-focus did not show any imitation effects.

This finding was replicated in a second experiment. Here the participants were primed either with the stereotype of professors or with that of soccer hooligans. Again, self-focus was manipulated by seating half of the participants in front of a mirror. After being primed, the participants received a general-knowledge test. As expected, under conditions of no self-focus, the participants primed with the stereotype of professors outperformed those primed with the soccer hooligan stereotype, while no imitation effects were apparent under self-focus conditions.

Later, van Baaren et al. (submitted) obtained evidence showing that self-focus also obstructs imitation of observables. In their experiment, they closely followed the procedure used by Chartrand and Bargh (1999). A participant and a confederate worked together on a task, while the confederate engaged in either foot shaking or nose rubbing. When the participants worked on a task that did not alter their self-focus, they imitated the confederate's behavior, thereby replicating the results of Chartrand and Bargh (1999). In a different condition, however, the task the participant and the confederate engaged in was specifically designed to enhance self-focus. They were presented with a text in a foreign language (which neither the confederate nor the participants knew well) with omissions. The task was to guess which words were omitted, and the participants could choose among "I," "me," or "mine." This manipulation enhanced self-focus and, as predicted, no sign of imitation was evident under these conditions.

These studies emphasize the important social aspects of imitation. We do imitate under normal circumstances. However, when for some reason our attentional resources are used to focus on the self rather than on our social environment, imitation no longer occurs.

9.8 Conclusion

In this chapter, I have postulated and discussed two ideas. The first is that imitation is important in that it heavily permeates social life, and it does so more or less continuously. The second idea is that imitation is so incredibly important for us because it functions as the social glue that holds us together. It leads us to like each other, and it is the essence of our "socialness," so to speak. So if one asks why we walk slower in the presence of the elderly, or why we become smart in the presence of professors, or why cycling fans pedal faster during the 3 weeks every year that the Tour de France is on television, the answer is straightforward. We do all this because we want to be liked.[3]

---

3. See comments on this chapter by Brison (vol. 2, ch. 19.1, p. 363) and by Litman (vol. 2, ch. 19.2, p. 365). ED.

10 Deceptive Mimicry in Humans

Diego Gambetta

falsificando sé in altrui forma

—Dante, *Inferno*

10.1 Introduction

Passing oneself off either as a different individual or as a member of a group to which one does not belong is a common deceptive strategy. Adopting the term used in biology, I will call it deceptive *mimicry*.[1] Mimicry is employed in order to achieve aggressive or defensive goals. Most species, viruses and plants included, are either victims of it, perpetrators, or both. Humans are second to none. Unlike other organisms, they can

---

1. In common parlance, the terms *mimicry* or *mimicking* cover a wider range of behaviors than that covered by the notion of mimicry employed here. In biology itself (including in other chapters of this volume) the term is used as synonymous with imitation. Mimicking can also refer to a way of *entertaining* (e.g., cross-dressing, masking for fun, acting); in this case the receiver knows she is watching an act of mimicry, or her ignorance is inconsequential. It can also consist of *improving our image* by adopting the style, looks, or mannerisms of people we admire (as when people name their children after heroes or celebrities, an act that is not meant to cause identity confusion). Mimicry can take the form of *blending in* by adapting to local conventions (e.g., switching from British to American spelling and terminology when in the United States; wearing a tie or a skirt where everyone else is wearing one to avoid attracting attention; joining in activities one normally finds disagreeable during field or missionary work). Mimicry can also of course be a form of *insanity* (the classic "I am Napoleon"). Or a subconscious *by-product* of learning something else; while we learn, say, a language, we also absorb ancillary features such as accent or pitch (a phenomenon that generates, for instance, local conformities, not just of accent, but of voice pitch or handwriting). For another variety of nondeceptive mimicry studied by biologists, see note 4.

play the game intentionally and strategically rather than through natural selection. They do not just play it with other species as most other animals do, but against each other. And the vast range of signs on which humans can rely to identify themselves as individuals or as group members, and thereby transmit reputational information efficiently, gives them equally vast opportunities for mimetic manipulations. The study of mimicry is crucial for answering a fundamental question in the social sciences: How can human communication remain viable in spite of the ever-present threat of deception?

Mimicry abounds in the gray area of everyday acts by which people work their way into obtaining small prerogatives or avoiding petty nuisances. Everyone I tell about my project volunteers some personal episode. A distinguished member of the Columbia University faculty admitted passing himself off as a medical doctor in order to jump restaurant lines. A friend who worked for the British civil service and was barred from engaging in public controversies concerning his responsibilities wrote letters to the *Times* under an assumed name when the policies he advocated came under attack. Youths regularly try to pass as being over 18 to buy alcohol, cigarettes, adult magazines, or go to war, while older people try to pass as younger to qualify for student discounts.

There are of course far less venial episodes of mimicry. For instance, circumventing norms of fairness based on category is a common practice. A notorious example is the man who as the *Titanic* was sinking dressed up as a woman to get on a lifeboat; healthy people pose as disabled to qualify for benefits, to avoid military service, or to occupy parking spaces for the handicapped.

Criminals pass themselves off as someone else both to avoid detection and to trap their victims, and not a day goes by without a case of mimicry in the news. Consider a casual selection from New York City over 2 months of 1996. In November, local television channels broadcast two warnings, one concerned a phony Santa Claus expected to descend on midtown Manhattan during the Christmas period to beg for donations on behalf of nonexistent charities; the other concerned thieves impersonating Con Edison (the electric power company) employees in order to gain access to people's homes. Viewers were encouraged to ask for proof of their affiliation. In December, in Queens, five men wearing caps and windbreakers bearing the initials DEA (Drug Enforcement Agency) broke into a house searching for drugs. They roughed up the residents until a neighbor called the real police. In the same month two men rang the doorbell of an apartment on the upper West Side claiming to be from United Parcel Service

(UPS); one of them was wearing the UPS uniform. They shot and killed one man and wounded another in a robbery attempt. They must have heeded the warning given to television viewers and switched to impersonate UPS rather than Con Edison employees.

Defensive rather than predatory mimicry is also popular. There are many recorded cases of blacks passing as whites, Jews as Christian Poles, women as men, and gays as straight to avoid discrimination or persecution; and of Nazis passing as Jews to avoid arrest, straight men passing as gays to avoid conscription, and men passing as women to avoid detection. (In 1943 my father fled from German-occupied Turin arm-in-arm with his elder brother, wearing makeup and my mother's clothes.) If we include counterfeited goods and Internet-based commerce and communications, the list of mimicry episodes becomes endless.

Here I give some indications of how we might study this phenomenon. It is a programmatic essay without a punch line. Given the scope of this book and the scant scholarly attention devoted to mimicry, I chose to provide a broad-brush introduction to the concept, rather than analyze any particular example. First, I deal with the basic concepts and theory needed to understand how deceptive mimicry works. This part draws heavily on Bacharach and Gambetta (2001). I then discuss the links between mimicry and imitation. Finally, I describe some mimicry systems by way of examples, drawing on work in progress. My aim is no greater than to scratch the surface of the phenomenon and put it on the scholarly agenda.

10.2 Definition

In biology, the standard mimicry case has two phases. First, there emerges a mutant of some k-possessing type of organism that bears a clearly perceivable sign, m. k is any unobservable quality of the mutant, for example toxicity, and m is, say, a bright marking or distinctive odor. If a predator of that mutant learns to associate k with m and refrains from attacking it when perceiving m, this gives the mutant a selective advantage over other k possessors without m. This mutant is called a *model*. The discerning predator also has an advantage over a predator that does not perceive m or associate it with k.

In a second phase, there emerges a mutant without the k property (say, nontoxic) but also bearing m. Observing m, a predator refrains from attacking the nontoxic mutant because it takes it to be toxic. This second mutant also becomes selectively advantaged, in this case over other non-k-bearing organisms without m. This mutant is called a *mimic*, and the action by which a mimic "persuades" the predator that it has *k* and induces it to respond accordingly, is called *mimicry*. The receiver of the signal, in this example a predator, is often called a *dupe* (even though it may not be duped all the time by the mimic). In zoology, mimicry studies focus mostly on the mechanics of the second phase and on the population dynamics among model, mimic, and dupe, which ensues from it.

Camouflage can be conceptualized as a case of *negative mimicry*. There are often signs that are likely to be interpreted by the signal receiver, rightly or wrongly, as indicating not-*k*. Both an honest signaler with *k* who expects to be unjustly perceived if he displays an *m*, and an opportunist non-*k* who is afraid of being detected if he does, have a reason to camouflage. That is, they take steps *not* to show *m*. Camouflaging can be considered as a special case of mimicking, since the strategy of camouflaging non-*k*-ness by suppressing *m* is just that of mimicking *k* through displaying the notional sign "*no m.*"

10.3 Cognitive Skills

In simple biological models, the only creature that needs some cognitive ability is, paradoxically, the dupe. For in order to identify *m* and thus *k* possessors, the dupe has to be bright enough to memorize *m*, to discriminate it from other signs, and to associate *m* with *k*. The relation between model and dupe, more precisely between *k* and *m* in the mind of the dupe, must precede the mimicry of *k* through *m*.

For mimicry to succeed, the dupe must thus be smart, although not so smart as to detect the mimicry. If a species becomes too exposed to mimicry, however, the dupe's survival may be threatened. As mimics multiply, one of the dupe's possible evolutionary responses lies in refining its perceptive abilities, either by screening more identifying signs, including some that the model displays but the mimic does not, or by detecting the finer differences between a genuine *m* and a copy of it. At the same time, one of the model's possible responses is to evolve new signs that make it easier for the dupe to discriminate *m* and for model-dupe communication to continue to be viable. Mimicry thus exerts pressure on both the selection of more refined perceptive skills and on increasing diversification of perceivable traits. Mimicry is a force of evolution, the full extent of which is still to be established.

Unlike other species, humans can count on greater cognitive skills, which make them able both to perform mimicry and to defend themselves from it, intentionally and strategically. We can learn how to mimic without waiting for a lucky mutation. We can observe the relation between model and dupe, record how the latter responds to the former, and decide whether the same response would be beneficial for us. As would-be mimics we have the ability to work out by which *m* a dupe identifies a model and to devise ways to copy it and persuade a dupe to treat us as it would treat the genuine *k* possessor. We can exploit, not just the perceptive abilities of the dupe, but also the contingent constraints under which the dupe's perception operates and *the medium* through which it occurs. It is easier to pass as someone else in the dark or over the telephone.

Both models and dupes of course can also participate intelligently in mimicry situations. They can fight, together or separately, to protect themselves from mimics, and mimics can fight back. Among humans, the relentless struggle between mimics and their victims is not played out through natural selection, but through cultural and technological evolution. What the three protagonists aim to do and how, depends on their goals and the relations among them, which give rise to a variety of mimicry systems, some of which I mention later. What they can do depends on the nature of the signs they display, about which I will also say something later, as well as on the technology available for creating and manipulating signs, about which I will not say anything here.

10.4 Signs and Signals

The difference between signs and signals, which is unimportant for the "unconscious mimicry" of other species, becomes relevant when intentionality can govern communication. A sign is just a piece of perceptible evidence that informs a receiver that a state of affairs exists. A sign, unlike a signal, is not conveyed as the result of a decision. A sign is unintentionally emitted by an agent even if, like a signal, it can induce a certain response in another agent. My accent in Italian is a sign that I am from Piemonte, but only sometimes is it a signal that I deliberately use. In spite of the difference between them, signs can turn into signals and, once established, signals may live on as mere signs. Signs are dormant potential signals—the raw material of signals.

The basic form of sign-signal transformation is that a signaler takes steps to produce or display a preexisting sign. It is often taken for granted that signs are noticed, but this is not always the case. A dueling scar may not be on the face, but on the thigh or chest. One way of signaling is to take steps to make apparent a sign that would not be observed; to bare the chest to display a tattoo to signal, say, that one belongs to Yakuza, the Japanese Mafia.

One trigger of the transformation of signs into signals is the bearer's realization of their effect. I may be unaware that my accent or name is informing others of my ethnic identity until some observer acts in a way that makes me aware of this. Qualities of the signaler valued by the receiver trigger the mutation of signs into signals, while qualities of the signaler disliked by the receiver trigger measures to conceal the signs.

10.5 Signaling and Mimicking via Identity

Humans can deceitfully pretend to possess an unobservable property k, e.g., honesty or meekness, by adopting an m that is associated with k, e.g., looking people in the eyes to persuade them of one's honesty. Or they can feign certain dispositions—curiosity, excitement—or physical and emotional states—headaches, grief, orgasm—by imitating the looks, postures, words, or level of activity *directly* associated with these states. The model in these cases is not a specific agent or group of agents, but a generic state and its manifestations. This is not, however, the type of deceptive mimicry that concerns me here.

A great deal of human signaling takes place indirectly by signaling one's identity both as a specific individual and as a member of a group or category.[2] After we encounter an individual or group member and experience dealing with them, we form and retain an idea of whether this person or group has or lacks the k property that interests us. Identity signaling enables the signaler to exploit (or suffer from) a reputation.[3] In identity signaling, instead of using a two-layered inferential structure ($m \rightarrow k$), we use a three-layered structure, $g \rightarrow i \rightarrow k$, where, i denotes identity and g denotes a sign of identity, or *signature*. If persons or group members are re-identifiable by some signature, the next time we meet them we infer the presence or absence of k.

The re-identification of a signature, however, can itself be problematic. This is because frequently the fact that someone has a certain reputation

---

2. For a full description of identity signaling in connection with signaling theory, see Bacharach (1997) and Bacharach and Gambetta (2001).

3. This in turn exploits two beliefs in "trait laws" that we have about others. For individuals it exploits the belief that once a k always a k, and for groups it exploits the belief that if a member of a group has k, all other members also will have k. For a discussion of this point, see Bacharach and Gambetta (2001).

is an unobservable property of that person. For example, Armani has a reputation for selling well-designed clothes, but to exploit this reputation, the seller must convince customers that he is Armani. Islamic jihad has a reputation for carrying out its threats against hostages, but to exploit this reputation a group of kidnappers must convince governments that they belong to Islamic jihad. When a model signals his qualities via his identity, the threat of mimicry of k through m is replaced by the threat of mimicry of i through g. Much of human deceptive mimicry does precisely that; it exploits signaling via identity, and my interest is in this case.[4]

10.6 Mimicry and Imitation

The core cognitive dispositions that we have to imitate others generally, and which we deploy and develop from infancy, might be the same we use to mimic others as adults, and, more surprisingly, the same that we employ to protect ourselves from the mistaken identification and the mimicry of others.[5] "One of the psychological functions that early imitation subserves is to identify people. Infants use nonverbal behavior of people as an iden-

4. There is a type of nondeceptive identity mimicry worth mentioning, known as Müllerian mimicry after Fritz Müller, who discovered it in 1878: "Two or more equally uneatable species that look alike benefit from less predation each than if they looked different" (Pasteur, 1982, p. 193). Both species more efficiently convey *true* information to receivers. Signalers gain by sharing the same signature because receivers learn more quickly. It is a case of signal standardization. If red means "stop" everywhere, receivers learn faster and make fewer mistakes. Everyone gains. In the original example, both species act as mimic and model of each other and converge on a common signature by progressive mutual adjustments. Real gangsters and movie gangsters who mimic one another (Gambetta, 2005, ch. 4) are a human example of this type. They have something in common; they both make money by making people afraid and gain by converging on the same identification signs of a scary reputation. Other examples, however, are sequential. First an agent dons m, then another with the same property chooses to don m also. The adoption of gothic-style Oxbridge architecture by American universities is one such case; the standard attire of businessmen and women all over the world may be another. Note, however, that the nondeceptive variety of mimicry often joins the deceptive variety: "A species B can be equally uneatable as species A for a given predator, and much easier to eat for another predator. If the two species look alike, B will be a Müllerian model-mimic for the first predator and a Batesian mimic for the second. In fact the very existence of the pure Müllerian situation in nature has been at least once doubted" (Pasteur, 1982, pp. 193–194).

5. I am grateful to Andrew Meltzoff for bringing this link to my attention.

tifier of who they are and use imitation as a means of verifying this identity" (Meltzoff & Moore, 1992, p. 479). "Infants re-enact the behavior of an
adult in part to test the identity of the adult and differentiate them from
other particular ones" (Meltzoff & Moore, 1995, p. 55). "By 6 weeks of age,
distinctive human behaviors serve as *gestural signatures*, aiding the infant to
differentiate individuals within the general class of people: to distinguish
one individual from another and to re-identify [a] particular individual on
subsequent encounters" (Meltzoff & Moore, 1995, p. 58).

In spite of that cognitive link and even though mimicry and mimicking
are often treated as synonymous with imitation, the notion of mimicry is
not coextensive with that of imitation. What is mimicked is a k or an i, an
unobservable property of the model that the mimic does not possess. What
is imitated is an m or a g, a perceivable object or behavior, associated with k
or with the identity i of a k possessor. Mimicry is an act aimed at persuasion, which the mimic executes by copying or somehow displaying those
features of the model that can persuade the dupe of the mimic's k-ness.

To understand how the two concepts differ, consider that mimicry can
simply rely on lying, which is not an act of imitation. If I reply "yes" to the
question, "Are you Napoleon?" I am not imitating Napoleon, but am still
trying to mimic being Napoleon. Also, mimicry does not always require
an imitative effort on the part of mimic. Lucky mimics can exploit preexisting signs that they happen to share with models. All they need to do is
to display them and refrain from correcting the dupe's mistaken identification. A friend who has the same surname as a well-known mobster used to
get preferential treatment in hotels and restaurants because people assumed
she was a member of the mobster's family. Instances of this kind occur
when the signs of identity do not uniquely identify a person or group.

Still, very often mimics execute mimicry by imitating g. Imitation is
achieved through a variety of techniques—from wearing the model's apparel to undergoing plastic surgery; from using makeup to imitating body
movements, from faking or forging signs to stealing them. If I mimic a de-
vout person by wearing a skullcap, I do not fake the skullcap, I can just buy
one and put it on. If, however, I mimic a rich man by wearing what looks
like but is not a genuine Rolex watch, then I employ fakery to execute
mimicry. If I write your name on a check so that it is assumed to be yours, I
forge something to execute mimicry. The choice of imitative technique
depends on the nature of the relevant signs, and, as we will see later, on the
cost of reproducing them.

There are, however, differences between the type of imitative actions
that involve learning new or better practices from the example of others,

and the type of imitative actions that sustain mimicry. When by imitating someone a person learns how to improve his performance of something, the higher-quality action that the model performs and that the imitator copies could in principle be discovered by the imitator through other means, e.g., by trial and error. The ways in which an action can be performed has an objective distribution of quality, and one can move upward independently of the model's performance. The model simply offers the imitator an opportunity to move up more cheaply by imitation.

In mimicry episodes, by contrast, the model is not of contingent relevance. The relation between the model and the dupe defines what g is to be imitated by the mimic. If a rapist wants to imitate a cab driver to lure women into his car, the signs that he needs to copy are those that real cab drivers use to identify themselves and that passengers look for. To be successful, mimicry-driven imitation needs to be only as precise as the dupe's psychology demands. There is no such thing as an abstractly good or a bad imitation of g.[6] The quality of the imitation is in the eyes of the dupe. If a dupe decides on the basis of the model's contour that it is the model, copying that contour is sufficient for an act of mimicry to succeed.

10.7 Studying Mimicry: I. Signaling Theory

The best, perhaps the only candidate to serve as a general theory of deceptive mimicry is the theory of signaling games. It is a well-developed part of game theory, and the understanding of such games, as developed both in biology and in economics, can provide general predictions about the conditions under which mimicry can occur and how much of it we can expect.[7]

The main objective of the theory is to specify the equilibrium conditions in which truth is perfectly transmitted, even when the signalers

6. Mimicking that looks to us—members of a species gifted with but also bound by given perceptual abilities—as relying on good or poor resemblance, may fail or succeed with the intended dupe. The tendency to overlook this point seems to be the reason humans have been generally more alert to mimicry among invertebrates than among vertebrates. Since human perception is closer to the latter than to the former, we have underestimated the duping potency that rough copies can have in eyes different from ours; correspondingly, we have overestimated the duping potency of, say, insects with which we share little perceptual wiring.

7. For signaling theory, see A. Spence (1974), A. Zahavi and Zahavi (1997), and Bacharach and Gambetta (2001). Game theory textbooks normally carry a technical illustration of a signaling game, e.g., Fudenberg and Tirole (1992, pp. 446–460).

have an interest in deception. The main condition is that among the possible signals there is at least one that is cheap enough to emit, relative to the benefit, for signalers who have k, but costly enough to emit, relative to the benefit, for the would-be mimics who do not have k. If the cost relationships are such that all and only ks can afford to emit that signal, the equilibrium in which they do so is called separating or sorting. In such an equilibrium, signals are unambiguous, and the receiver is perfectly informed. When signals have such a perfect discriminating property, mimicry cannot occur, for no mimic can afford it. No poisoner seeks to demonstrate his honesty by drinking from the poisoned cup.

However, the differential cost condition may also give rise to weaker equilibria, so-called "semisorting" ones. In a semisorting equilibrium, there is a signal that is emitted by all ks, but not only by ks; a certain proportion of non-ks can just about afford to emit it also. Here, observing that signal is not conclusive evidence of truth; it makes it more likely that the signaler has k but does not imply that he does. Mimicry is possible. The higher the frequency of mimicry, that is, the proportion of non-ks who display a signal, the less conclusive is the evidence. Empirically, we know that most cases of signaling in animal life are not sorting but only semisorting equilibria (Guilford & Dawkins, 1991). The same appears true of human life. We seldom encounter such a thing as a fully mimic-proof signal. Virtually everyone who boards a plane gives a sign, most of the times unthinkingly, that he is not intending to cause it to crash. But as we know only too well from recent events, some terrorists may be prepared to do just that and can afford to mimic a normal passenger by boarding. They drink from the poisoned cup.

10.8   Studying Mimicry: II. Semiotic Distinctions

Signaling theory is abstract and does not arm us with the fine tentacles we need to grasp and organize the large variety of signs that can be emitted and processed. There is scope in humans for creating new signs, for discovering latent ones, and for protecting signs from mimics. Protective measures are in turn threatened by mimics' stratagems to get around them, giving rise to a relentless semiotic warfare in which technology plays a major part. This warfare depends on the nature of the relevant signs, which establish whether and how mimics can imitate them.

Despite lacking a concrete semiotic structure, signaling theory offers us a robust criterion by which to establish such a structure and classify signs. This criterion is simply how closely different types of signs meet the key condition of the theory—the existence of differential costs, which make it cheaper for a model than for a mimic to emit the model's signatures. In the following sections I summarize the results of our work on "semiotic" definitions of signs (Bacharach & Gambetta, 2001).

10.8.1 Cues

A cue of k is a sign whose display is costless for k possessors.[8] An example is an honest look for an honest person, or, in identity signaling, one's handwriting or voice.[9] The cost of showing that it is you, if it *is* you, is generally negligible. Cues tend to be favorable to models and unfavorable to mimics, for mimics will typically incur some cost in displaying them. Evolution has equipped us with many cues that are naturally protected from mimicry. These may be categorial, such as signs of gender, or individual, such as the face. Cues of this kind are often costly, sometimes impossible, to mimic. Some, like the face, could have evolved, together with our remarkable ability to discriminate among different faces, because they sustain cooperation by making identity signaling cheap and mimic-proof. A look-alike can succeed under certain conditions to pass as someone else—for example, appearing only at a distance or filtered by flattening media such as photography, or by carefully choosing dupes with a dim recollection of the model's face. Still, reproducing someone else's face well enough to stand scrutiny is close to impossible.

Other biological cues of identity, some of which are still being discovered, may have evolved for reasons unrelated to cooperation, or may be just random individual differences that become observable with the right technology. Insofar as they are heteronymous—each signature differs from all other signatures of the same type, avoiding the possibility of mistaken identity—these signatures can be employed for re-identification. Fingerprints and DNA are both unique to individuals. At best one can cover one's fingerprints with super glue but cannot implant someone else's fingerprints or DNA (so far).

8. It is the marginal cost of display, which is zero, not necessarily the historic cost of developing the capacity to display it.

9. This sense of "cue" resembles Hauser's (1996). Although k possessors who display an m may do so as a signal of k, they may also display m for some other reason, and indeed in some cases without any purpose. Rich people often wear expensive clothes with no thought of conveying anything about their wealth, but merely to make a *bella figura*; they give evidence of their wealth as an unintended by-product. In such cases m is a cue of k even though it is costly to produce, because it is not a costly input into the activity of inducing a belief in k-ness.

10.8.2 Marks

The next best mimic-proof signs after cues are marks acquired as by-products of the life that each individual lives. As people grow up in given cultural settings, they absorb social features such as language, accent, and mannerisms, or undergo common experiences that cannot be acquired in any other way and are therefore mimic-proof. Ethnic signatures are often of this kind. They come at no extra cost to those who have had the experiences, while they are very costly for anyone else to copy.

During World War II many Polish Jews considered passing themselves off as Polish Christians to save their lives. This was hard to do, however. The models could easily detect them and turn the mimics over to the Nazi dupes. Nechama Tec located 308 Polish Jews who either considered or tried that strategy:

[A] Jew had to sound and behave like a Pole. For most Polish Jews this was impossible. Poles and Jews lived apart, in different world. Their differences permeated all aspects of life.... According to a 1931 census only 12% of the Jewish population gave Polish as their native tongue, 9% mentioned Hebrew and the overwhelming majority Yiddish (79%).... Jews using the language in a grammatically correct way could still be recognized by their speech. Special phrases or expressions, even if grammatically sound, could be traced to the Jewish origins of the speaker.... In addition special intonations, a stress on special syllables could also become identifying signs. And while most of the Jews were unaware of their peculiar use of the language, the listening Poles were sensitive to all such nuances.... Another pressing condition was familiarity with the Catholic religion.... Those suspected of being Jewish were subjected to cross-examinations. Failure to pass such tests often led to death. In addition the existing cultural differences managed to penetrate into all aspects of life including dressing, eating and drinking habits. Thus, for example, onion and garlic were defined as Jewish foods. It was therefore safer to profess a dislike for each. Also, any man unable to hold hard liquor could be suspected of being Jewish. (Tec, 1984, p. 116)

This case shows how mimicking membership in a different ethnic group is connected as much with the difficulty of mimicking the signs of another group as with that of camouflaging those of one's own. It also shows that ethnic groups with a long common history are robust to mimicry because they are identified by a *constellation* of signatures. A mimic must concoct a large number of imitative acts to succeed. Yet, although estimates vary widely, thousands of Jews succeeded in saving their lives by mimicry (women seemed to be more successful than men, partly because they bore fewer *marks* of "Jewishness" than most men did; see Weitzman, 1999, ch. 11).

10.8.3 Symbolic Signs

Art Spiegelman reports that during the German occupation of Poland, his father used to travel to town by tram. Trams had two cars: "One was only Germans and officials. The second, it was only the Poles. He always went straight to the official car" where a simple salute, "Heil Hitler," was enough not to call attention, whereas "in the Polish car they could smell if a Polish Jew came in" (Spiegelman, 1991, p. 142). It was harder for a Jew to mimic the nuanced multiple signs of a Polish gentile than the fewer superficial signs of a pro-Nazi.

Nazi signs are not marks but symbols. These are configurations of characters or gestures, however physically realized, exemplified by names, logos, and Nazi salutes. What makes them open to mimicry is that among the physical realizations there are usually some that are very cheap for anyone, non-*k*s included, to produce. The efficient production cost of a Nazi salute is zero. Symbolic signs are attractive for signalers because they are cheap, but since they violate the cost differential condition, their evidential value is weak. The expansion of the scope for ultra-cheap transmission of symbol strings is indeed a major cause of the growth of mimicry in our time. Symbolic signatures, individual or categorial, abound, and are vulnerable to mimics. However, the cost of producing a signature may not be the only cost of displaying it. Even though the cost condition fails to be satisfied on the production side, there are ways in other respects in which models and dupes can often raise the cost of mimicry.[10]

10. "Stealing somebody's identity is to be made a specific criminal offence under plans to combat the growing fraud industry now believed to cost Britons at least £1.2bn a year.... A recent Cabinet Office report said that the move to internet and telephone transactions meant that existing systems of identification and authentication were no longer sufficiently robust. A passport could not be verified online and criminals were increasingly hijacking somebody else's identity, for example by obtaining a credit card in their name. The government is considering ways of making it much harder to obtain a driving license or passport by deception, by improving the security of the documents. The passport service is looking at issuing a plastic card using a microchip alongside the current passport book. The consultation paper will also outline a scheme to set up a database of 'stolen identities' so that electronic checks can be carried out online. Home Office ministers want to set up a police database of known and suspected fraudsters against which applications for government services could be cross-checked.... the home secretary, David Blunkett, has made clear his support for the introduction of a 'citizenship entitlement card', saying it would enable people to prove their identity more easily and also provide a simple way to access a range of public services" (*The Guardian*, "Plan to make identity theft a criminal offence", p. 2. May 6, 2002).

10.8.4   Fakeable Signs

A second important category of signs exposed to mimicry occurs when the signature is an object that can be faked. If g is a sign, by definition the receiver can tell by looking (smelling, hearing) whether the signaler is displaying a g of i. But if a thing can be faked, then ipso facto the receiver cannot tell whether what is displayed is really g. A fakeable object is one that can be simulated by another, a g'. For faking to be successful, the mimic must cause an observer to mistake g' for g. An important class of cases in which mimicry by faking occurs is that in which displaying a real g is harder than faking it. If you prove that you are who you are, then you are given a passport. To obtain a passport, a mimic could try to pass as you. But for someone who is not you, proving to be you is often costlier than forging the passport. Displaying g is prohibitively costly for a non-k; displaying a fake g' is not, because k possessors have no particular advantage in producing g', the manifest component of g.

10.9   Studying Mimicry: III. Mimicry Systems

The key principle of signaling theory and the semiotic distinctions derived from it are essential elements in understanding how mimicry works. However, even in the simplest mimicry episode, these elements come together in a triangular structure in which the dupe, the mimic, and the model interact in some way. These structures or *mimicry systems* are the proper unit of analysis for this phenomenon. The most exhaustive taxonomy of mimicry systems created in biology is the work of Pasteur (1982), who explicitly refers to "unconscious mimicry" only. Pasteur distinguishes mainly between models that are agreeable, forbidding, or indifferent to the dupe, and further, between aggressive and protective mimicry.

No taxonomic work has been attempted for "conscious" human mimicry. The distinctions one draws ultimately depend on one's analytical models and what these aim to explain. Still, a heuristic taxonomy might indeed be a precondition for investigating the large class of mimicry events. Here I offer a preliminary description of two important systems and a variant of one of them. It is merely meant to illustrate the kind of work that would be needed to classify mimicry and the kind of dynamic analysis that could be pursued by building on a classification of mimicry systems. My main criterion of distinction is simply the most general relationship between the three protagonists: who is doing what to whom.

All examples refer to *conjunct* mimicry cases (so called by Vane Wright and quoted in Pasteur, 1982), in which the three protagonists belong to the same species, ours. I also confine myself to cases in which the model is another human or group of humans rather than an inanimate entity. Woody Allen's suggested method of civil disobedience, "pretend to be an artichoke but punching people as they pass" (Allen, 1994, p. 72), will therefore not be considered here. Finally, I do not consider impersonation and consider only cases in which the model is a group or category of agents rather than an individual. The mimic, by contrast, whether he mimics an individual or a member of a group, is almost always an individual whose act of mimicry does not depend on others. There are cases, however, of so-called *joint* mimicry, in which succeeding in the mimicry takes more than one individual—passing as lovers, as wrestlers, or as an entire betting office requires two or more mimics.

10.9.1 Mimic versus Dupe via the Model

This system, probably the most common, includes those instances in which the mimic has no dispute with the model, but uses the model's semblance to manipulate the dupe. The mimic does not aim at damaging the model's interest. The mimic aims either to prevent the dupe from doing something harmful to him (defensive case) or to encourage the dupe to do something good for him (aggressive case), when the dupe would act otherwise if he knew that the mimic was a mimic. If successful, the mimic gains, the dupe loses, and the model at best gains nothing; more often it loses something.[11]

After the assassination of Rajiv Ghandi, Sikh taxi drivers took off their turbans to look like Hindus and avoid being slaughtered by them (even though the Tamil Tigers, not Sikhs, were probably responsible for the assassination). Hindu taxi drivers did not lose anything as a result of being mimicked. However, typically the model does lose by being mimicked. There are two ways in which a model can lose. In one case it can lose if the allocation of a resource is altered as a result of a mimic's actions, and in the other case by the corruption of the quality of communication between the model and the dupe.

First, if a resource becomes scarcer because of mimicry, the dupe loses and as a result he may change his actions toward the model, even if the dupe is not aware of the mimicry. If the mimics multiply, a "starved"

11. An instance of this case is the most common, or at least the most commonly studied, form of mimicry in animals, known as Batesian mimicry. The name derives from Henry Bates, who discovered it in 1861 (in fact he discussed many other variants, but this is the one that bears his name). It is a type of protective categorial mimicry in which one species takes on the appearance of another species that the dupes find repulsive, because, say, it is nasty-tasting or poisonous.

duped predator, for instance, may lower his tastes and begin to "eat" semi-toxic prey. Or he may turn nastier and attack all models, true or mimicked, with greater frequency to find out their real quality, albeit at a greater risk. If everyone in a dangerous city looks menacingly tough, whether they are or not, muggers may start attacking people indiscriminately. The real model tough guys lose out since they are more likely to be attacked. This effect can be caused by both protective and aggressive mimicry. If there is some scarce resource that a dupe bestows on the mimic instead of the model, the model suffers by getting less of it. If one buys counterfeited goods, one will not buy the real thing, and genuine producers suffer.

Consider now the second way in which model can lose. Suppose a dupe finds out that there are mimics around. The dupe becomes wary of the model's signatures and loses trust in them. The signatures become corrupt and stop sorting for the same beneficial effect. When the model and the dupe benefit from an on-going relation, mimicry inflicts new costs on both of them, for the dupe becomes less inclined to accept the same old signatures as evidence of the model's identity. Following the robbery in which a criminal posed as a UPS delivery man in New York, a real UPS man interviewed on television put it starkly: "This is real bad for people are not gonna believe us now, they are not going to believe me now." After 9/11, all air passengers lost because now they have to endure more elaborate probing of their identity. To avoid detection, the terrorists took deliberate steps to look like normal passengers, shaving their beards, carrying presents, and wearing business suits and apparel. Suddenly all those signs that we previously did not even think about have become of lesser use. Mimicry tends to destroy the value of a model's signatures.

Notice that as a result of mimicry, corrupt signals lose their value not just for the models but also for the additional mimics. In theory this dynamics must reach a semisorting equilibrium in which for an extra mimic it is no longer worth the mimicry, given the benefit, while for a model it still is advantageous to emit the signal, even though this is now only weakly semisorting. This obtains if the cost of displaying m is higher for the mimic than for the model. However, the weakness of a corrupt signature can reach a point at which the dupe and the model must endure additional costs to improve the model's identity signals or their perception, in order to keep their relation afloat. They can raise the hurdles that the mimic has to jump by better policing or by introducing new hard-to-fake signatures. They can do so independently of each other or cooperatively, for instance by informing each other or by agreeing on new conventional signals that are able to withstand the mimic's stratagems. Yet, mimicry can fatally corrupt a signal and make it impossible for a model to afford new convincing signs of his identity. Can an honest Middle Eastern man intent on becoming a pilot now find an affordable separating signal to persuade a U.S. flying school of his bona fides?

10.9.2 Mimic versus Model via a Dupe ("Kennedian" Mimicry)

In this system, the mimic's ultimate target is the model. The dupe here is just a means. The mimic is in competition with the model for a scarce resource that the dupe can dispense. The mimic confuses the dupe, who then dispenses his good to the mimic rather than to the model. The Kennedys, after which this mimicry system should perhaps be named, resorted to this ruse for electoral purposes:

> To insure that Jack won the primary campaign [in 1946], Joe paid Joseph Russo, janitor, to enter the race. This split the votes cast for Joe Russo, a legitimate politician who was already on the ballot, confusing voters.... Even the aunt of the real candidate voted for the janitor, recalled Joseph A. Russo, the real candidate's son. (Kessler, 1996, p. 293)

There are also cases of this system in which the model is a corporate entity. In the early 1990s in Rumania, President Iliescu's party—the National Salvation Front, which was then in power—feared they might lose the election. They created bogus opposition parties that had names and logos similar to those of the real opposition parties. Whether propelled by imagination or by imitating the Kennedy ways of mimicking, they hoped to confuse voters and divert their votes (T. Gallagher, 1996, pp. 155–156).

10.9.3 Mimic versus Dupe-Model

This type of mimicry system is a variant of the case in section 10.9.1, in which the model and the dupe are the same agents. I say "agents" because it is unlikely that anyone can pull off this type of mimicry with an individual. If someone rings your doorbell claiming to be you, you may think it a nightmare or a farce, but are unlikely to be fooled. This is the stuff of literature or madness, a form of which has the insane person haunted by the belief that there is a copy of himself around. In view of recent developments in cloning technology, this may turn out to be a rather prophetic insanity, but it is not yet part of everyday life.

It is, however, possible to dupe *collective* models,[12] posing, say, as an aristocrat among other aristocrats. To succeed at this, the mimic must

---

12. Here is an example from the animal world: "In New Guinea, a dolichopodid fly that visually mimics a psychodid species attracts males of this species by mimicking the sexual behavior of a receptive female, and catches them while they are enthralled in sexual display" (Pasteur, 1982, p. 188).

overcome a detection mechanism that works against him—agents are better at spotting a mimic posing as their sort than a mimic of a different sort. It is easier to pretend to be a Mafioso with non-Mafiosi than with the real guys, or a bogus doctor with patients than with colleagues. Still, many cases of this sort are recorded, and reveal mimicry's subtle ways.

Gunter Wallraff (1985), a German journalist, posed as a Turk to find out how badly Turkish immigrants were treated by Germans. He kept up his act for months, not just with Germans, but with Turks too, although he could barely speak Turkish. Crucial for his success was that no German, or Turk, expected anyone to feel the urge to pass as a Turk in Germany, and they did not bother to check on him.[13]

There is another case in which the dupe did not expect mimicry, although not quite for the same reason. Bryan Riggs (2002; La Stampa, "Nazisti, ufficiali del Fuhrer ed ebrei," p. 10, December 3, 1996) has documented 1200 cases of Jews who disguised their ethnicity to fight in the German army during World War II. Among them he found two generals, eight lieutenant generals, five major generals, and twenty-three colonels. One was Helmut Schmidt, the former German chancellor, who had a Jewish grandfather and according to the Nazi definition was "Jewish." And he found one Joseph Hamburger, who not only managed to hide the fact that both his parents were Jewish, but "went native" and is still today a Nazi sympathizer. Nazi dupes did not expect such chutzpah. It must have been unthinkable to them that any one could have the audacity to pull off such a feat. There is a twist in the story though. Seventy-seven of the 1200 Nazi Jews, all of them high-ranking officers, were discovered by the Nazi nazis, but Hitler himself decided by fiat that they were Aryans, and their genealogy was remanufactured accordingly. Maybe the model-dupe could not bear to be the victim of such spectacular duping. Shame may indeed be a frequent reason that prevents the duped from disclosing the mimicry. From these examples we learn that mimics can succeed when they defy the dupe's expectations by engaging in a deception that is either too odd or too daring for the dupe to conceive of it as probable enough to probe the signals.

I could introduce further mimicry systems, as, for instance, the case in which the model and the mimic assist each other in fooling the dupe, known as cooperative mimicry (the use of look-alikes, in which the model hires a mimic to pass as himself, is an instance of this system,). However,

13. Given that in the end the research was meant to help the Turks, they may have been quite glad to be "duped," unlike the Germans.

for reasons of space, I prefer to give an example of the kind of dynamic analysis that one can construct from the elementary mimicry systems, which shows how mimicry failures can be as interesting as successes.

Consider the case in which several mimics unbeknown to each other, but for the same purpose, simultaneously assume roles with the same model-dupe. G. K. Chesterton gives us the fictional classic case. In *The Man Who Was Thursday*, Syme is a policeman trying to infiltrate a group of anarchists by posing as one of them. He is eventually elected as one of the seven members of the "Anarchist Council" who take the name of the days of the week. Syme becomes Thursday. He meets the other seven members and slowly, in a hilarious crescendo, he finds out that all other six members are also policemen hidden under various disguises. They spy on each other, only to discover that There never was any Supreme Anarchist Council. "We are a lot of silly policemen looking at each other" Syme concludes (Chesterton, 1908, p. 156).

A real case happened during the campaign launched by Greenpeace against McDonald's, which ended in a trial in 1997 in the United Kingdom. In 1989, McDonald's decided to take legal action against London Greenpeace. To do so, the company needed to find out the names and addresses of Greenpeace members, and they hired two investigative firms. Seven spies infiltrated the group. They followed people home, took letters sent to the group, and got fully involved in the activities (including giving out anti-McDonald's leaflets). According to the account of this activity, at some London Greenpeace meetings there were as many spies as campaigners present and since McDonald's didn't tell each investigative firm about the other, the spies were busily spying on each other (the court later heard how Allan Claire had noted the behavior of Brian Bishop, another spy, as "suspicious").[14] The mimics ended up duping each other.

10.10 Conclusions

Mimicry in other species was observed and conceptualized in the middle of the nineteenth century by Henry Bates and other zoologists, and has been studied ever since. Still, despite its ubiquity, human mimicry has not been studied very much at all. Descriptions of countless acts of mimicry are narrated in studies of crime, espionage, business, war, class, political conflict,

---

14. Fran Tiller, a spy, defected and eventually became a witness for the defense. Another spy (Michelle Hooker) had a 6-month love affair with one of the activists. The source for this account can be found at www.mcspotlight.org/case/trial/story.html.

gender, religious conversion, and ethnic assimilation. Classical mythology, literature, fairy stories, and films thrive on mimicry episodes. Yet these acts are not theorized and examined as instances of a generalized sui generis behavior worth studying as such, as, for instance, cooperation is. The recognition of mimicry as a social phenomenon shows some sign of life in semiotics (e.g., Nöth, 1990; Maran, 2001). Umberto Eco defined semiotics as the study of "everything that can be used in order to lie"; "a 'theory of the lie'"—he added—"should be taken as a pretty comprehensive program for a general semiotics" (Eco, 1979, p. 7). This program, however, has remained *lettera morta*, and semiotics is now an atheoretical field that is strong on elaborate conceptualizations but weak on behavioral models.

An exception is represented by the literature in economics that originates from signaling theory, variously identified as "asymmetric information," "screening," or "incentive compatibility." It deals with the cost-benefit differential conditions that can make it impossible or nearly so for a dishonest signaler to cheat, and with the policies a rational receiver needs to implement to make sure that these conditions obtain. Although the term "mimicry" has not been used—a more common term is "dishonest signals"—and the range covered by this literature concerns forms of deception other than mimicry, several applications can be effortlessly classified as a study of the conditions under which mimicry can, and above all *cannot* occur. Unlike the literature in semiotics, the behavioral fundamentals are here clear, robust, and generalizable.

Still, much remains to be done. For instance, the standard version of the theory includes only the production costs of signals rather than also the display and protection costs of them, which are so often involved in mimicry and its detection. It also does not cover identity signaling (and a consequence of this is that most economic models of reputation are oblivious to the mimicry threat and treat re-identification as unproblematic). These issues are only briefly addressed in this essay. As for the empirical side, the economic applications confine themselves, naturally enough, mostly to business-related instances, whereas mimicry, as my examples suggest, occurs in a much broader range of domains. The theory's potential for novel applications to these other domains is vast, but in order to be effectively developed, it needs, as I argue, to be supported both by semiotic distinctions and by a taxonomy of mimicry systems, of the kind summarily sketched in this essay.

Finally, the economics literature has focused more on the honest rather than on the dishonest signals, and on separating rather than weaker equilibria.[15] As a result, mimics and the myriad strategies that they employ, while understood in their broad outline, have remained in the shadow, for if the incentives work against them, mimics do not have a chance and we do not need to bother with them. Yet, when one leaves the abstractions of modeling and delves into the wealth of empirical instances, one discovers that in real life the separating equilibria that screen mimicry out entirely, or nearly so, are not so frequent or stable. Often mimics succeed, and even if they fail, they can do so in interesting ways. Mimics' strategies are thus well worth a systematic empirical examination that compares them across different domains, and this can have an effect on the theory itself. For in so doing we are most likely to uncover other social and psychological mechanisms that govern the acts of the protagonists, and which cannot be subsumed by rationality alone, but to be properly understood require theoretical injections other than signaling theory. As was the case in the recent past for the study of trust, which was also an undertheorized and underresearched notion until the 1980s, the study of mimicry has the capacity to develop into a proper interdisciplinary field, and my prediction is that it will.[16]

Acknowledgments

The theoretical framework presented in this essay was developed in collaboration with my friend and colleague Michael Bacharach, who died in August 2002. He never read the essay, and he is thus not responsible for the form in which our ideas are presented here. I gratefully acknowledge a British Academy Readership, which supported my work.

15. In an essay on cheating signals in the animal behavior literature, Hasson reports a similar bias toward an honest signal. His "survey of the definition of signals or communication shows ... that many do not allow for any kind of cheating" (1994, p. 223).
16. See comments on this chapter by Litman (vol. 2, ch. 19.3, p. 368) and Seabright (vol. 2, ch. 19.10, p. 398). ED.

11 What Effects Does the Treatment of Violence in the Mass Media Have on People's Conduct? A Controversy Reconsidered

John Eldridge

Under the headline "Teenage girl torturers shock nation," the (London) *Observer* reporter Paul Webster wrote:

An abandoned old people's home where a 14-year-old high school girl was tortured by two of her school mates in a crime that has shocked France looks like a setting for a horror film. Dilapidated shutters hang from a peeling wall and the front door gives on to stairs leading to a cellar where the victim was disfigured and left for dead because she was considered too pretty.

After learning that the knife used to torture the adolescent resembled the one used in the film Scream, newspapers have competed to find exotic pseudonyms to add a Hollywood touch to a story tainted by scare videos and devil worship. (*The Observer*, March 24, 2002)

This story is accompanied by a picture captioned "the house of horror in a quiet part of provincial France." In the course of the story we are told that the two alleged torturers come from stable middle-class families and study at a private Catholic school. They had no previous reputation for violence, but "the older girl had just seen *Scream* and the younger one had taken part in Satanic practices with skinheads in the local cemetery." According to a local official (Jean-Francois Peretti), "they have both been subject to damaging cultural influences." The victim's father said his daughter could not explain why their usual games had taken such a horrifying turn and commented: "It seems to be a mixture of all sorts of things. Television, films, drink, Satan worship and madness."

Such stories, even when it is acknowledged that they are rare events, can be used to raise questions about youth culture and youth violence. Politicians are aware of this. In this case the Interior Minister, Daniel Valliant, is quoted: "The state cannot be held responsible for this crime. We are totally bewildered by this violent behavior, which contains an element of insanity."

We can see that a wretched event such as this creates all sorts of problems for those who want to explain it. In this case there is a perceived anomaly of their class position, gender, and schooling; a general reference to damaging cultural influences and the designation of insanity. Embedded in this is a reference to the media and its possible effects. Out of this a more general moral panic might be constructed, "the problem of youth violence," with political, legal, and social policy implications.

In 1993, in Liverpool, England, a 2-year-old boy, Jamie Bulger, was led away from a shopping mall by two 10-year-old boys and murdered. At the end of the trial the judge said, "I suspect that the killers' exposure to violent video films may in part be an explanation." (*The Guardian*, November 25, 1993). The video in question was *Child's Play 3*. This video had indeed been rented by the parents of one of the boys shortly before the murder, but there was no evidence that either of the children had actually seen the video, and the police did not introduce it as evidence in court. In this case the connection was clearly not established, yet the judge and the tabloid press treated it as an irresistible inference. This indeed was one of the elements that led to the media creation of a moral panic about video nasties and the problem of juvenile crime. So it was that the *Sun*, with a visual image from *Child's Play 3*, gave us the headline: "For the sake of ALL our kids ... BURN YOUR VIDEO NASTY" (*The Sun*, November 11, 1993).

The Bulger murder gave pause for thought to Anthony Burgess, author of the book, *A Clockwork Orange,* a novel about teenage violence. The novel was published in 1962 and a decade later was made into a film directed by Stanley Kubrick. The book and even more, the film, were the subject of much controversy and remain so. Burgess saw the book as a moral tale, a reflection on the nature of good and evil and on the problem of choice and human responsibility. For a number of reasons, mainly aesthetic, and with a sense that the film had not been faithful to the moral core of the book, he was not happy with the film. He came to think that whatever impact the book had had, it was much less than that of the film. Yet, because the film had come from the book, he felt that he was responsible for what some had called its malign influence on the young. He was particularly concerned that because of the way Kubrick had adapted the book it could be seen as an incentive to violence by youths, particularly in the United States. He commented on the report of a gang rape by four boys dressed in the droog style copied from the film. Even though the boys had not seen the film, some blame was pinned on him. Much later, in 1993, in the wake of the Bulger case, he wondered whether his novel might have contributed in some small way to a cult of violence among the young:

There are beliefs we cling to and will not let go ... it must be considered a kind of grace in my old age to abandon a conviction that was part of my blood and bone. I mean the conviction that the arts were sacrosanct, and that included the sub-arts, that they could never be accused of exerting either a moral or an immoral influence, that they were incorrupt, incorruptive, incorruptible. I have quite recently changed my mind about that. (Cited in Burgess, 2000, p. xxiv)

In 1994, Oliver Stone's film *Natural Born Killers* was released; in it a couple go on a killing spree across America. It led to a mixture of media speculation and assertion that criminals had copied this screen violence. Thus the *Sunday Mirror* produced the headline: "Two young men have murdered four people—including three pensioners—in a *real-life imitation* of a brutal, new Hollywood blockbuster" (*The Sunday Mirror*, November 9, 1994). As Victoria Harbord has pointed out, this led to the Board of British Film Classification (BBFC) withholding the film's certificate while they investigated the media claims that there were causal links between the film and real-life violence. Their conclusion was a salutary one for all who accept media claims at face value:

In all but one of the cases linked by the press with the title of the film, the accused or dominant member of an accused pair had been in prison and, in one case, also in a mental hospital, for serious acts of violence, including in three cases, murder. In the remaining case, an intention to commit the offence had been stated to a friend many months before the killing. In the two cases where a series of killings were attributed to an accused pair, the first killing had been committed before the film opened and there was no evidence that the accused had ever seen the film. On the other hand, drugs seem to have been involved in all the American cases. The one case in France is now known to have been politically motivated, the killers having formed their own anarchist group well in advance of the crime and having been supplied with a pump action shot gun by two other anarchists who have been imprisoned for complicity in the offence. There is no evidence in this case that either of the accused had ever seen the film in question. (BBFC press statement, December 12, 1994; cited in Harbord, 1997, p. 138)

When it comes to "media violence" there are so many agendas inscribed upon it that there seems to be some kind of overload. We can observe that much of this is not just a straightforward empirical matter. On the one hand there is a resistance to censorship from left-wing and some libertarian groups; on the other hand is the call for social control from the moral right, who express fears and anxieties concerning moral breakdown in modern societies. These represent distinct value positions. Their relationship to empirical research can be variable. Sometimes it can be dismissed in the name of common sense; we don't need to be told what we already know. Sometimes it may be endorsed (albeit selectively) if it agrees with a preexisting value position. Sometimes it may be criticized if it appears to throw doubt on existing convictions. So it is that the topic of media violence is inextricably enmeshed in controversy.

In the midst of complexity it would be psychologically satisfying to come up with a clear statement about effects, in terms, say, of "copycat" or imitative behavior. Yet the very concreteness of the term "media violence" is itself problematical. According to Barker, "There simply is no category 'media violence' which can be researched; that is why over seventy years of research into this supposed topic have produced nothing worthy of note. 'Media violence' is the witchcraft of our society. This is such an important point, yet its significance seems constantly to get lost" (Barker, 1997, p. 28).

Clearly, if there is such a basic problem with categorization, we can see why Barker logically challenges the proposition that media violence causes violence in society, despite the fact that as he notes, a large number of studies support this conclusion. He was therefore not impressed with the claim of a publisher's catalogue that there was a consensus among "psychologists, media theorists, sociologists and educators that there is a direct causal link between the excessive viewing of violence, or the playing of video games ... [and] acting violently or ... [becoming] desensitized to violence" (Barker, 1997, p. 24). We can expand a little on what is being alluded to.

In traditional approaches to media analysis, the causal relationship has often been treated in terms of the "magic bullet" approach, namely, that is what is seen on television (or films) has a direct impact on what people do. The extent of interest in the topic is well illustrated in American textbooks (Shoemaker & Reese, 1996; Wilson & Wilson, 1998; Grossberg et al., 1998). It predates the advent of television, going back to the arrival of film in the early days of the twentieth century. The magic bullet view of causality fits well with what has been described as the information-imitation theory, as noted by Wilson and Wilson: "The information-imitation theory contends that TV violence plays a prominent role in causing bizarre and violent behavior in society. It is believed that some people (usually mentally unbalanced individuals) observe information and activities in the media and then proceed to imitate what they see" (Wilson & Wilson, 1998, p. 411). It is on the strength of such concerns that arguments proceed for the censorship, licensing, or banning of films depicted as violent. The imitation is usually related to particular scenes: dousing someone with gasoline and setting them on fire, explicit rape scenes, or Russian roulette.

More generally the causal link between media violence and real-world violence is suggested by a number of American reports routinely cited in the textbooks. These include the National Commission on the Causes and Prevention of Violence (1968), the Surgeon General's Report (1972), the National Institute of Mental Health study (1982), and the U.S. Attorney General's Task Force on Family Violence (1996). According to an American Psychological Association report, "Big World Small Screen," which looked at 1000 reports and commentaries published since 1955, there was clear and cumulative evidence of a correlation between viewing violence and aggressive behavior (Wilson & Wilson, 1998, p. 418).

Another text reports the estimate that more than 3000 studies have been conducted since the 1950s to examine the effects of violence on audiences (Grossberg et al., 1998, p. 300). The authors conclude that there is strong evidence from survey research that "consistently shows that heavy viewers of violence on television are more likely to engage in aggressive behavior than are light viewers" (Grossberg et al., 1998, p. 301). But since the authors are careful to point out that these correlational studies do not provide sufficient evidence that media violence causes aggression, nor the direction of any causal relationship, "It might be that people inclined to act violently are more likely to watch television violence, and so it is their predisposition toward violence that leads to viewing violent TV, and not the other way round" (Grossberg et al., 1998, p. 301).

Nevertheless, Grossberg et al., despite the qualifications noted, do accept that the strongest argument of a causal relationship (if not the only one) between media violence and aggressive behavior is to be found in longitudinal and panel studies. Thus they cite Huesmann's (1986) study, which concluded that there was a clear relationship between the amount of violence children watched on television at the age of 8, the amount of aggressive behavior identified at the age of 18, and the seriousness of criminal acts committed by the same people at the age of 30. Among the processes going on that might account for this, they identify acting out an aggressive character's actions, the disinhibition of aggression among those already predisposed to be aggressive, and emotional desensitization of viewers to real-world violence as a result of prolonged viewing of media violence. These are somewhat different processes. The last-named does not imply that the viewer is stimulated to be violent in his or her own actions, but rather fails to act when the chance arises to help the victim of violence, or is apathetic about the presence of violence in the world. Bracketed out from this, because of the focus on particular causal imputations, is the possibility that the viewing of violence may have other consequences.

Since Aristotle we have been sensitive to the role of catharsis in viewing on the stage things that horrify and appall us. No one has seriously proposed that watching Shakespeare's *Timon of Athens* is an encouragement to participate in cannibalism, although that does not prevent the possibility of what technically are termed aberrant decodings. The contextualization and framing of episodes or actions defined as violent is important because that is how viewers come to them and interpret their significance and meaning. And we may remind ourselves that images of violence—the consequence, say, of war or famine—can move us to action and protest. The well-known instance of *Live Aid*, fronted by Bob Geldof, and subsequent events, are vivid examples of this.

We have begun to move onto other ground. There are questions of causality and there are questions of meaning. As we contemplate the great volume of studies that seek to establish the nature of causal links between media violence and real-life violence, we do have to recognize the difficulties, explicit or implicit, that we encounter. What is the definition of violence? It is presented in varying contexts, fiction and nonfiction, and in a great variety of genres and formats. It can range from foul play or a fist fight in a televised football match to scenes of carnage in a war zone; from the cartoon exploits of *Tom and Jerry* to "adult" films that contain scenes of killing, torture, or rape. What is it that is being counted as violence and what does it signify? A causal argument must rest on methodological decisions on what to include and why.

This is not only so, but if the causal case is situated within a model of multicausal connections, then we need to know whether, in the case of the media, we are working with intervening or primary variables. For example, we might find discriminating distinctions in age, gender, class, occupation, and ethnicity. If any of these are held to register as significant, then we have to embark on further studies as to why that is so, which necessarily will take us well away from the study of the media.

There remains the by no means simple matter of the explanation of violence among the subjects studied. Are we dealing with aggression in simulated laboratory situations? Are we making observations of actual aggression in real-life situations? Or are we simply relying on reported incidents? The basic questions of what we are counting and why remain crucial. So it is that, for my part, I have a considerable skepticism about the claims, given the problems of the formulation of the terms, the conceptualization of the issue, the methodological assumptions, and consequently, the evaluations that are based on them. Yet neither, I think, can I simply assert the null hypothesis in light of the methodological flaws I have identified. I return, therefore, to questions of meaning.

We live in a media-saturated world. Many media, many genres are available to us. Some of these media are dominant in the sense that they are available to millions of people. There are print media, film media, broadcast media. Words, images, music intermingle. New technologies have made possible the crossing of time and space in ways that would be unimaginable to earlier generations. New technologies have also generated new media. There is a multiplicity of cultural, linguistic, and visual codes. There are those who construct the messages and those who receive them. The purposes of those who construct the messages can be manifold—to entertain, to give pleasure, to educate and inform, to persuade and spread propaganda, to deceive and disinform. What we take from all this is a product of what is available, what we choose, and what we bring to it all: our interests, values, concerns, and perhaps intentions. Just as with other powerful institutions—education, the family, the state, religion—the mass media, which surround us, impinge upon us. They constitute part of the process of socialization and therefore of the formation of our consciousness (D. Miller & Philo, 1999).

Philo (1999b) in an exploratory study sought to amplify some of the issues involved in the socialization argument. He interviewed ten 12-year-old children at a Glasgow comprehensive school, all of whom had seen the film *Pulp Fiction*. The film is licensed as an "18" rated film, but is widely available on video and has been shown on television. This, incidentally, is a reminder that with new forms of media, the range and accessibility of media products is much greater, and it is much more difficult to control what children see. From the beginning there is a great deal of explicit violence in the film. Philo found that all the children were able to describe in writing violent episodes in the film, some of them with great accuracy. Moreover, when invited to say who they thought was "cool" or "uncool" in the film, it was the cool gangsters who killed the uncool victims. The killing, the obscene language, and the black humor that accompanied it were produced by people who were cool and would be looked up to. As one boy put it, "If the cool guy said shoot him, he'd shoot him, he'd do what he says to act cool to be in the cool gang."

Philo comments:

The children's ability to reproduce the film text, with such accuracy, does indicate the powerful interest which they have in it; and a fascination with its themes and language (which clearly impressed very strongly on them). It would be wrong to see the film as being merely chewing-gum for the eyes, or to assume that its meaning is lost among the mass of competing images from the media. (Philo, 1999b, p. 43)

It almost goes without saying that this does not imply that children who identify with the "cool" gangsters will become gangsters themselves. The argument rather is that media influence is part of "a matrix of other social relationships which affect the development and transfer of values. Children are influenced by families, peer groups and by their own direct experience. They negotiate situations, use processes of logic, make judgments and solve problems—they *act* in the world. They do not necessarily copy or identify completely with any single source of influence" (Philo, 1999b, p. 52). Part of Philo's argument is that the media are a site for the transmission of values. Since the values we adopt contribute to the kind of culture we have, then when there are value conflicts, a cultural struggle takes place. It is more fruitful to consider the implications of that than to "prove" whether a particular media product "causes" a single act of violence. These cultural struggles will take place in and outside the media.

There is a parallel set of considerations when we consider the question of pornography in relation to sexual violence. Proving the link is problematic in terms of causal models, but it still remains possible to consider the nature of media influence in terms of the ways in which pornography cultivates certain views of sexuality. Thus Jensen suggests that pornography can be considered as a stream of symbolic material that contributes to the process of socialization:

> Such a model can help us past the obsession with causation and point us towards questions about how the pornographic symbolic stream is produced, what it says about culture and how it shapes people's world views. So even if definitive judgments about causation are difficult to make, there is much to be said about the role of pornography in our culture. (Jensen, 1998, p. 5)

The intersections are difficult to identify in terms of the specifics. Given the way in which media "effects" tend to be associated with the magic bullet model, it may be helpful to think of these processes as "influences." We do not have to assume that the influences are all one way. It is common now in sociological accounts to refer to the ways in which media "texts" can be negotiated, resisted, or even rejected in terms of their intended meaning (assuming that concept is always unproblematic, which it is not) and consequently to refer to the concept of the "active" audience (Corner, 1998). We may infer that in many instances the meanings given to media texts by those who construct them are not always unidimensional and the meanings given by those who receive the texts are commonly variable. But this does not entail the view that the intended meanings or the decoded readings are infinite. Indeed this is so, even if we speak of media texts as "open." The existence of a text at all imposes constraints on its interpreters (Eco, 1990). As John Street has pointed out:

The capacity to deduce other interpretations is ... dependent on the capacity of the audience to offer an alternative account. Newspapers and broadcasters supply a resource—ideas, responses—out of which people fashion their view of the world. These resources are not supplied by news and current affairs alone; they are contained in the story lines of soap operas, in chart hits and Hollywood movies. Indeed, they are not confined to mass media. How these resources are used depends on the experiences and conditions that are brought to [their] reception. (Street, 2001, p. 97)

We can see that such an approach to the study of media influences takes account of the things people bring to their "reading" of the media and the things they take away from it (Eco, 1994). As my colleagues and I have argued elsewhere, this recognizes, for example, the pleasure people can get from the media, the social currency of different phrases or stories, and the ways in which media messages are incorporated into everyday conversation. Acknowledging these levels of complexity is not incompatible with theorizing about the influence of press, films, television, and radio. However, the complexity should not be allowed to obscure the realities of media power. Such power is not absolute nor does it exist in isolation (Eldridge et al., 1997).

We also live in a very violent world:

In the half century since the Second World War, some 25 million people have been killed, mostly civilians, and by their own governments, in internal conflicts and ethnic, nationalist or religious violence. Civilian fatalities have climbed from 5 percent of war related deaths at the turn of the (twentieth) century to more than 90 percent in the 1990s. About 50 million people were forced to leave their homes. In 1998 more than 2000 people every month were killed or maimed by land-mine explosions. It is impossible even to estimate the numbers injured and disabled, tortured and raped, during these conflicts. (S. Cohen, 2001, p. 287)

This prompts the question, How are the media implicated in many forms of violence? They certainly do not initiate it all. We can draw attention to some of the mechanisms and processes, not least to make it clear that imitation alone by no means accounts for the ways in which people relate to the media, either in terms of thought or action. But questions of social power—in the media and in society—do come into the reckoning.

Let us take the role of the media in relation to war and the violent conduct that war entails. There are, of course, a raft of considerations concerning propaganda. There is the propaganda that constructs an image of the enemy—inside the state in the case of civil war and when the state creates scapegoats—and in relation to other states. The anti-Semitic propaganda of the Nazi regime, with its horrific climax in the Holocaust, is an all too well-known example (Baumann, 1991). Such propaganda had as its deliberate purpose the dehumanizing of the "enemy" and the incitement to and justification of violence. In the case of the former Yugoslavia or the ethnic conflicts in Rwanda and surrounding states, the use of the broadcast media in actively encouraging violence is clear.

Through propaganda, citizens are encouraged to think of the moral rightness of their cause. War is portrayed as "necessary," as "inevitable" (even if regrettable) and therefore as "justifiable." These linguistic devices can be linked to recruitment campaigns—"Your country needs you" as in the case of the poster campaign featuring Field Marshall Lord Kitchener in World War I. The imitation being encouraged there was to join the army like all other patriotic young men. This campaign was later carried on along with compulsory conscription and the use of other sanctions and peer group pressures. The whole point of propaganda is that it is intended to have behavioral consequences in the lives of those to whom it is directed. The fact that it is not 100% effective or that forms of resistance to propaganda can sometimes be mobilized should not cause us to lose sight of this phenomenon. The attempt is made to socialize us or resocialize us into accepting certain values and, where considered appropriate, to encourage us to act on them. What is happening here is not the portrayal of violence, but the contextualizing of situations, which is designed to sanction and justify violence when it takes place.

Another facet of mediated violence is the treatment of war as spectacle. The Gulf War of 1991 was a very developed example of this (Baudrillard, 1995; Philo & McLaughlin, 1995). Much of this was in the presentation of the war, mainly through the filter of the military media machine, with its emphasis on sanitized war through the use of precision hi-tech "smart" bombs. The emphasis was on the damage inflicted on military targets. A great deal of this was transmitted to viewers through the use of video. The relationship between these computer-generated images and the reality of the war on the ground was highly questionable. The artificially constructed picture was one of the disciplined use of violence mainly on property rather than on people.

However, other pictures and accounts eventually emerged. There were pictures of the destruction visited on the retreating, fleeing Iraqi army on the road to Basra. What was not seen were the video films of the shooting of Iraqi soldiers by helicopter gun crews, who referred to what took place as a "turkey shoot" and which were later to become available on the black market. Only later did journalists such as Maggie O' Kane provide accounts about how many Iraqi soldiers had been buried alive as a result of the Allied assault. What is at issue is the representation of violence in times of war since that can influence the interpretations that are offered of the actions that take place. The question raised is, Who has the power to control these images of violence and to what extent can they be contested?

A further feature of media coverage of war is when actual wars become the occasion for fictional war films. They may take the form of American marines storming Pacific beaches, films about the Vietnam War, and more recently Stephen Spielberg's *Saving Private Ryan*, which included a depiction of the D-Day Normandy landings that was widely regarded as very "realistic." Such films, of course, will routinely have a story line with heroes and enemies, victims and victors, and deal with themes of love, courage, and death. The violence can be very bloody indeed, from deadly hand-to-hand fighting to the effects of bombing. These films are typically made for the purposes of entertainment. They commonly emanate from Hollywood and are intended for world-wide distribution. Essentially the violence that is portrayed is seen as justified and vindicated. In that respect it is being celebrated as an expression of what the victors had to endure to achieve success (including the loss of friends and allies in the conflicts). Essentially the audiences are being asked to endorse all this. We cannot assume that this routinely happens, but that is the way the stories are framed. Critiques of this genre may turn on the cultural values that are represented and the moral codes that are assumed, rather than on how these violent activities on screen are assimilated by audiences.

In the case of propaganda or to some extent war films, the intentions of the producers are usually decipherable, implicitly or explicitly, but there are other instances where events take place outside the intentions or wishes of the producers. When people saw on television the hijacked planes crashing into and destroying the World Trade Towers on September 11, 2001, many of them thought for the first moments that they were watching a disaster movie. Such movies specialize in that kind of format. There is so much we still do not know about that event, but we can recognize the way in which the perpetrators of this horror could draw on visual imagery, which, given their skills, resources, and ideological purpose, they were then able to activate. This is not only so, but by their awareness of the role of the mass media in the world of news, they were able to ensure that by the time the second plane crashed into the tower, the whole event would be filmed as it happened. One cannot say that the disaster movie genre "caused" the hijacking and subsequent crashes, but we can see the affinity between fiction and reality and the way in which the imagination of the perpetrators was or could be stimulated by the genre.

The relationship between fact (or actuality) and fiction, between fantasy and "reality" is often convoluted and intertwined. All of these elements are indeed, as Durkheim would insist, part of the social and what takes place in these processes has to be understood and explained at the level of the social (Durkheim, 1982). This is precisely because questions of interpretation and meaning and our understanding of symbols and practices in society can only be understood at the level of the social. What we choose to copy or not to copy, and the reasons we give for doing so or not doing so, as the case may be, is socially mediated. Reasons, that is to say, may be causes. The actions that spring from reasons may be regarded from particular points of view as foolish, misguided, or morally wrong by others. But whether or not that is so, they are part of the causal nexus. For actions to be put into practice, there has to be both a context and an opportunity structure as well as resources and organizing ability. We can see that this is another way of making the distinction between attitudes and conduct. While someone may be prejudiced against a particular ethnic group, they may not actually be in a position to exercise discrimination against members of that group.

We may be encouraged to think of such processes by some contemporary sociologists as part of the practice of reflexivity. Thus Giddens suggests, in his discussion of modernity, that "thought and action are constantly refracted back upon one another ... social practices are constantly examined and reformed in the light of incoming information about those very practices, thus constitutively altering their character" (Giddens, 1990, p. 38). This kind of reflexivity, which seeks to take account of the way an individual monitors and changes his or her conduct, bears upon the problem of motivation. In a sociological perspective this invites us to consider vocabularies of motive (Mills, 1963; Gerth & Mills, 1954). What is foregrounded here are the ways in which we account for our own or others' behavior. They are the ways in which we speak of what we do, are doing, or intend to do. We may use such vocabularies to account for particular modes of conduct in particular situations. Thus we may have a vocabulary of motives for being involved in academic work, in business, in criminal activity. These motives may seem to others as rationalizations for action, but to the person concerned they may be regarded as reasons. One person's rationalization is another person's reason. While such accounts may help us to explain behavior in particular situations—the person in business, for example, who acts according to the profit motive—in a complex societies we may find discrepant and competing vocabularies of motive. Thus C. Wright Mills commented:

Back of "mixed motives" and "motivational conflicts," are competing or discrepant situational patterns and their respective vocabularies of motive. With shifting and interstitial situations, each of several alternatives may belong to disparate systems of action which have different vocabularies of motives appropriate to them. Such conflicts manifest vocabulary patterns that have overlapped in a marginal individual and are not easily compartmentalized in clear-cut situations. (Mills, 1963, p. 450)

There are two comments I wish to make here. The first is that vocabularies of motive will be offered in particular social contexts. Thus the reasons for performing a particular action may relate to the presence of others who use and accept the same vocabulary. We see this in the behavior of gangs and soccer hooligans, just as we see it in other conventional social institutions. The vocabulary gives the participants a conceptual repertoire to account for, describe, and evaluate an action. Such a conceptual repertoire may shift and change and may in principle draw on many sources for practices that are then carried out. The conduct is social, whether or not it is carried out in the presence and with the help of others.

The second is that if we take reflexivity seriously, participants in conduct typically described as delinquent or deviant can also draw upon the vocabularies constructed by those wishing to explain "deviance" or "delinquency," such as psychologists and sociologists. This was amusingly illustrated in Stephen Sondheim's lyrics from *West Side Story:*

Dear kindly Sergeant Krupke you gotta understand
It's just our upbringing up-ke that gets us out of hand
Our mothers are all junkies, Our fathers are all drunks.
Golly Moses, natcherly we're punks
Officer Krupke, you're really a square
The boy don't need a judge, he needs an analyst's care!
It's just his neurosis that ought to be curbed.
He's pyshologic'ly disturbed.
Officer Krupke, you're really a slob.
This boy don't need a doctor, just a good honest job.
Society's played him a terrible trick
And sociologically he's sick.

I suppose we may call this a kind of imitation, but not as we usually think of it. It is the learning and reproducing of new vocabularies of motives to account for, explain, sometimes excuse, and sometimes justify conduct.[1]

---

1. See comments on this chapter by Comstock (vol. 2, ch. 19.4, p. 371) and a relevant discussion in the chapter by Huesmann (vol. 2, ch. 12, p. 257). ED.

12　Imitation and the Effects of Observing Media Violence on Behavior

L. Rowell Huesmann

12.1　Introduction

Anyone who attempts to make sense out of the 50 or more years of literature on the effects of media violence is faced with a daunting task. It is
a topic on which much has been written with passion, on which much
nonsense has been written, on which many outrageous claims have been
made, on which otherwise intelligent people seem to fall victim to the
worst kinds of wishful thinking, and yet on which an enormous body of
scientific research has accumulated. In other essays in this volume, some of
the key issues and controversies surrounding the potential effects of media
violence are outlined and discussed. However, it is important that such a
delineation of key issues be coupled with a review of the actual scientific
evidence that has been collected on the effects of media violence, the
psychological processes that have been identified as causing its effects,
and the exact role that imitation plays in the process. When this is done,
it becomes apparent that the recent research and thinking on imitation
reflected in many of the essays in this book increase one's confidence in the
conclusion that media violence is stimulating violent behavior.[1]

1. In this essay I will not deal with the several essays and books that have been
written by those who believe that the mass media cannot have a significant effect on
human behavior and on violent behavior in particular (e.g., Freedman, 1984, 2002; J.
Fowles, 1999). A number of carefully reasoned responses to these and other authors
have been published answering the critics and explaining why there is opposition
to believing that media violence could have an effect (Bushman & Anderson, 2001;
Hamilton, 1998; Huesmann et al., 1992a; Huesmann & Moise, 1996; Huesmann &
Taylor, 2003). The reader is referred to these for further information.

12.2   Processes Accounting for the Effects of Media Violence

To begin with, one must realize that different processes explain *short-term effects* and *long-term effects*. Short-term effects are due to (1) priming processes (2) excitation processes, and (3) the immediate imitation of specific behaviors (Bushman & Huesmann, 2001; Huesmann, 1988, 1998). Long-term effects will be discussed subsequently.

Briefly, priming is the process through which activation in the brain's neural network spreading from the locus representing an external observed stimulus excites another brain node representing aggressive cognitions or behaviors (Berkowitz, 1993). These excited nodes then are more likely to influence behavior. The external stimulus can be inherently aggressive, e.g., the sight of a gun (Berkowitz & LePage, 1967), or something neutral like a radio that has simply been nearby when a violent act was observed (Josephson, 1987). A provocation that follows a *priming* stimulus is more likely to stimulate aggression as a result of the priming. While this effect is short lived, the primed script, schema, or belief may have been acquired long ago and in a completely different context.

To the extent that the observation of violence (real-world or media) arouses the observer, aggressive behavior may also become more likely in the short run for two other possible reasons—excitation transfer (Zillmann, 1979, 1983) and general arousal (Berkowitz, 1993; Geen & O'Neal, 1969). First, a subsequent provocation may be perceived as more severe than it is because the emotional response stimulated by the observed violence is misattributed as being due to the provocation (Zillmann, 1979, 1983). Such excitation transfer could account for a more intense aggressive response in the short run. Alternatively, the increased general arousal stimulated by the observed violence may simply reach such a peak that the ability of inhibiting mechanisms such as normative beliefs to restrain aggression is reduced (Berkowitz, 1993).

The third short-term process is imitation of specific aggressive behaviors. As other essays in this book illustrate, in recent years the evidence has accumulated that human and some primate young have an innate tendency to imitate whomever they observe (Butterworth, 1999; Meltzoff & Moore, 2000; Rizzolatti et al., 1996a; Wyrwicka, 1996). Aggressive behaviors are no different than other observable motor behaviors in this regard. Thus, the hitting, grabbing, pushing behaviors that young children see around them or in the media are naturally tried out immediately afterward. The observation of specific aggressive behaviors around them increases the likelihood of children behaving exactly that way (Bandura, 1977; Bandura et al., 1963a,b).

Given these short-term effects, what process accounts for long-term effects? Long-term effects are also primarily a consequence of imitation, but of a more complex type of imitation that Bandura (1986) calls observational learning of cognitions. In recent theorizing (Huesmann, 1998; Huesmann et al., 2003), long-term relations have been ascribed foremost to the acquisition through *observational learning* of three social-cognitive structures: schemas about a hostile world, scripts for social problem solving that focus on aggression, and normative beliefs that aggression is acceptable (Bushman & Huesmann, 2001; Huesmann, 1988, 1998). World schemas affect the kinds of attributions one makes about others' intent; are they hostile or benign, for example. Scripts are cognitive programs (usually represented as "production systems" or "if-then" statements) that represent a coordinated sequence of behaviors to be used in a particular situation. Normative beliefs are the rules for appropriate behavior against which scripts are evaluated prior to use. The theory is that the observation of specific aggressive behaviors not only stimulates imitation of those behaviors in the short run but leads to the acquisition of more coordinated cognitive scripts, world schemas, and normative beliefs for social problem solving that emphasize aggression.

As the child grows older, the social scripts acquired though observation of family, peers, community, and mass media become more complex, abstracted, and automatic in their invocation (Huesmann, 1988, 1998). In addition, children's social cognitive schemas about the world around them begin to be elaborated. In particular, the extensive observation of violence around them biases children's world schemas toward attributing hostility to others' actions (Comstock & Paik, 1991; Gerbner et al., 1994). Such attributions in turn increase the likelihood of children behaving aggressively (Dodge, 1980a; Dodge et al., 1995). As children mature further, normative beliefs about what social behaviors are appropriate become crystallized and begin to act as filters to limit inappropriate social behaviors (Huesmann & Guerra, 1997). Children's own behaviors influence the normative beliefs that develop, but so does their observation of the behaviors of those around them, including behavior observed in the mass media (Guerra et al., 1995; Huesmann et al., 1992b; Huesmann, 1999). In summary, social-cognitive observational-learning theory postulates long-term effects of exposure to violence through its influence on the development of aggressive problem-solving scripts, hostile attributional biases, and normative beliefs that approve of aggression.

However, the kind of imitation called observational learning of cognitions is not the only process that causes the long-term effects of media violence. Long-term effects are also quite likely increased by the habituation process called desensitization. Most humans seem to have an innate negative emotional response to observing blood, gore, and violence. Increased heart rates, perspiration, and self-reports of discomfort often accompany such exposure (Cline et al., 1973; Moise-Titus, 1999). However, with repeated exposure to violence, this negative emotional response habituates, and the observer becomes desensitized. One can then think about and plan proactive aggressive acts without experiencing negative affect. Consequently, proactive aggression becomes more likely. This habituation process is not an imitation process, but it may exacerbate the effects of imitation by reducing emotion-related inhibitions against behaving aggressively.

12.3   Integration of Empirical Research Relating Media Violence to Aggression

Once these processes are understood, the wealth of empirical evidence implicating exposure to media violence as a cause of aggressive behavior does not seem so surprising. However, to understand how compelling the evidence really is, one needs to integrate the evidence from all the different empirical approaches that have been employed.

The methodologies used in studying the relation between media violence and aggression fall into three major classes: (1) experiments in which the researcher manipulates exposure to media violence; (2) correlational studies, or one-shot observational studies in which exposure to violence and concurrent aggressive behavior are measured with surveys or observations; and (3) longitudinal observational studies in which exposure and behavior are measured on the same sample repeatedly over long periods of time. It is critical to integrate the findings of all three bodies of research in reaching any conclusion.

Generally, experiments have consistently demonstrated that exposing children to violent behavior on film and television increases the likelihood that they will behave aggressively immediately afterward (see reviews by Bushman & Huesmann, 2001; Geen & Thomas, 1986; Paik & Comstock, 1994). The typical paradigm is that randomly selected children who are shown either a violent or nonviolent short film are then observed as they play with each other or with objects such as Bo-Bo dolls (1-meter-high plastic dolls weighted so they stand back up when knocked down). The consistent finding is that children who see the violent film clip behave more aggressively immediately afterward. They behave more aggressively toward persons (Bjorkqvist, 1985; Josephson, 1987) and toward inanimate objects (Bandura, 1977). These effects occur for all children from preschool to adolescence, for boys and girls, for black and white, and for normally aggressive or normally nonaggressive children. The average size of the immediate effect produced is about equivalent to a .4 correlation (Paik & Comstock, 1994). In these well-controlled laboratory studies, there can be no doubt that it is the children's observation of the violence that is *causing* the changes in behavior. As described earlier, the psychological mechanisms operating are priming, excitation transfer, and simple imitation (see also the discussion of priming by Dijksterhuis in volume 2, chapter 9).

The question then becomes whether these causal effects observed in the laboratory generalize to the real world. Do they have real significance in the world? Do they extend over time? Does real media violence cause real aggression in the real world, not just in the short run, but in the long run as well?

Empirical correlational studies of children and youth behaving and watching media in their natural environments have demonstrated that the answer to both these questions is "yes." The great majority of competently done one-shot survey studies have shown that children who watch more media violence day in and day out behave more aggressively day in and day out (Paik & Comstock, 1994). The correlations obtained are usually between .15 and .30. Such correlations are not large by the standards of variance explained, but they are moderate by the standards of children's personality measurement, and they can have real social significance (Rosenthal, 1986). In fact, as Rosenthal has pointed out, a correlation of .3 with aggression translates into a change in the odds of aggression from 50/50 to 65/35—not a trivial change when one is dealing with life-threatening behavior. Moreover, the relation is highly replicable even across researchers who disagree about the reasons (e.g., Huesmann et al., 1984; Milavsky et al., 1982) and across countries (Huesmann & Eron, 1986).

While these one-shot field studies showing a correlation between viewing media violence and aggression suggest that the causal conclusions of the experimental studies may well generalize to the real world, longitudinal studies with children can test the plausibility of long-term predisposing effects more directly. In perhaps the first longitudinal study on this topic, initiated in 1960 using 856 youths in New York State, Eron et al. (1972) found that boys' early childhood viewing of violence on television was statistically related to their aggressive and antisocial behavior 10 years later (after graduating from high school), even controlling for initial aggressiveness, social class, education, and other relevant variables (Lefkowitz et al., 1977). A 22-year follow-up of these same boys revealed that their early aggression predicted later criminality at age 30 and that early viewing of violence was also independently but weakly related to their adult criminality (Huesmann, 1986, 1995).

A more representative longitudinal study was initiated by Huesmann and his colleagues in 1977 (Huesmann & Eron, 1986; Huesmann et al., 1984). This 3-year longitudinal study of children in five countries (Australia, Finland, Israel, Poland, and the United States) also revealed that the television habits of children as young as first-graders also predicted subsequent childhood aggression, even controlling for initial level of aggression. In contrast to earlier longitudinal studies, this effect was obtained *for both boys and girls*, even in countries without large amounts of violent television programming, such as Israel, Finland, and Poland (Huesmann & Eron, 1986). In most countries the more aggressive children also watched more television, preferred more violent programs, identified more with aggressive characters, and perceived television violence as more like real life than did the less aggressive children. The combination of extensive exposure to violence coupled with identification with aggressive characters was a particularly potent predictor of subsequent aggression for many children. Still, there were differences among the countries. While the synchronous correlations were positive in all countries, the longitudinal effect of viewing violence on aggression was not significant for girls in Finland or for all children in Australia. In Israel, there were significant effects for children living in a city, but not for children raised on a kibbutz.

However, perhaps the most notable effect in this study stems from the just published 15-year follow-up of the American subjects (Huesmann et al., 2003). About 60% of these children were tracked down and reinterviewed when they were in their early twenties, 15 years later. The findings indicting effects of media violence are impressive. First, these children's exposure to media violence between age 6 and age 9 correlates significantly with a composite of eleven different kinds of measures of their aggression taken 15 years later when they were 21 to 25 years old. The correlation is .21 ($p < .01$) for males and .19 ($p < .01$) for females. Furthermore, the correlation is significant even if only physical aggression is used as the criterion. However, perhaps the impact of these findings is best conveyed by the results shown in table 12.1, where children who were in the top 20% on viewing violence in childhood are compared with those who watched

Table 12.1

Differences in frequency (%) of spouse abuse, serious physical aggression, and illegal behaviors "at least once" in past 12 months for high viewers of media violence in childhood compared with other children

Type of Behavior	Males			Females		
	High violence viewers (%)	Other viewers (%)	Chi-square Significance	High violence viewers (%)	Other viewers (%)	Chi-square Significance
Spouse abuse:						
Pushed, grabbed, or shoved your spouse	41.7	22.2	$p < .05$	34.6	21.2	n. s.
Thrown something at your spouse	20.8	14.8	n. s.	38.5	16.5	$p < .02$
Serious physical aggression:						
Respond by shoving the person	68.8	50.4	$p < .05$	68.6	43.2	$p < .01$
Punch, beat, or choke another adult	21.9	16.9	n. s.	17.1	3.6	$p < .01$
Criminal behavior:						
Self-reported any crime in last year	62.5	53.4	n. s.	48.6	25.9	$p < .01$
State-reported convictions	10.7	3.1	$p < .03$	00.0	00.0	n. s.
Driving behavior:						
Self-reported moving traffic violations	87.5	76.3	n. s.	80.0	57.6	$p < .01$
State-reported moving traffic violations	60.0	39.4	$p < .01$	28.9	28.4	n. s.

Source: Huesmenn et al. (2003).

[a] n.s., not significant.

less. The high viewers of violence were clearly more likely to engage in a whole variety of very serious aggressive acts, including criminal acts, spouse abuse, and assault.

Taken together with the many experiments that have unambiguously shown causation, these results certainly add credence to the conclusion that childhood exposure to violence in the media has lasting effects on behavior through a high-level process of imitation in which cognitions that control aggressive behavior are acquired. Moreover, with modern statistical techniques (structural modeling and multiple regression analysis), Huesmann et al. (2003) were able to show that these longitudinal relations could not be explained by more aggressive people simply liking to watch violence in the media, or as an artifact of social class or intelligence, or as an artifact of poor parenting or parental preferences for violent media; nor could they be explained by any of many other measured variables. None of these alternative models fit the data, but models in which exposure to media violence caused aggression do fit the data within statistically acceptable bounds of goodness of fit.

12.4   Public Understanding of Media Violence and Imitation

In conjunction with the theories described here, the results from these three kinds of research—experiments showing unambiguous causation, one-shot surveys showing that real aggression correlates with concurrent habitual exposure to violent media, and longitudinal studies showing that childhood exposure predicts increased adult aggression independent of childhood aggression—have led most objective scientists to conclude that exposure to media violence increases a child's risk for behaving aggressively in both the short run and the long run. In fact, despite what some write, there is a clear consensus of opinion among scholars who actually do research on the topic that exposure to media violence causes aggression. Surveys have shown that over 80% of those doing research on the topic have concluded from the evidence that media violence is causing aggression (Murray, 1984). Most major health professional groups have issued statements citing exposure to media violence as one cause of violence by youths. Two Surgeon Generals of the United States (in 1972 and 2001) have warned the public that media violence is a risk factor for aggression. For example, in March 1972, then Surgeon General Jesse Steinfeld told Congress:

it is clear to me that the causal relationship between [exposure to] televised violence and antisocial behavior is sufficient to warrant appropriate and immediate remedial action ... *there comes a time when the data are sufficient to justify action. That time has come.* (Steinfeld, 1972, pp. 25–27)

So who are the vocal minority that deny there can be any effects? The best-known social scientists who deny there are any effects (e.g., Cumberbatch, Fowles, Freedman, Jenks) generally have never done any empirical research on the topic. However, they are glib and compelling writers, and their opinions cannot simply be dismissed. Furthermore, there is a large body of other intellectuals who deny that there are any effects. They range from the president of the Motion Picture Association (Jack Valenti), to the president of the Interactive Digital Software Association (Doug Lowenstein); from movie directors (e.g., Rob Reiner) to comic book producers (e.g., Gerard Jones); from science writers (e.g., Richard Rhodes) to booksellers (e.g., Chris Finan, president of the American Booksellers Foundation), just to name a few.

Some of the reasons why many otherwise intelligent people refuse to accept the researchers' consensus are clear. None of us likes the idea that we could be affected simply by what we watch. Don't we have the free will to overcome such influences? Haven't we seen our own children watch violence and seemingly not be affected? And does not even the idea of bad effects suggest censorship, which we all find intolerable? However, in addition to these personal feelings that create biases, other important factors come into play with the research on media violence.

Enormous amounts of money are being made from media violence, and those whose profits are threatened by the idea that media violence could be very bad for some people have spent the past 50 years trying to deny the scientific evidence. It is easy for glib writers to pick apart statistical research on behavior. There are always studies showing no effects that they can focus upon. If one does not want to believe a truth about human behavior, one can always focus on exceptions. There are flaws in some of the research on media violence, and some people do overstate the results. No single study is ever perfect, particularly in the social sciences, and those whose agendas require opposition turn up every flaw. And often studies are misinterpreted by those who want to misinterpret them. A few longitudinal studies have been promoted as producing results at odds with the thesis that media violence causes aggression, but closer inspection of most of these studies reveals that their results are not discrepant, but simply not strongly supportive of the thesis (for a review, see Huesmann & Miller, 1994). For example, while NBC's longitudinal study of middle-childhood youths conducted in the 1970s (Milavsky et al., 1982) is usually reported as not finding significant longitudinal effects, 12 of the 15 critical coefficients for boys were positive and 10 of the 15 critical coefficients for girls were positive. Meta-analyses, which are the most statistically valid way to combine results, and which show average effect sizes of .2 for field studies (see Paik & Comstock, 1994), are usually ignored by the skeptics.

All of these explanations are important. However, I think the most important reason is something else. It is that most people do not really understand the power of imitation in molding every aspect of human behavior. They do not understand it as a process in the same way that they understand the role of poisons or carcinogens. In fact, as Bushman & Huesmann (2001) have shown, the size of the effect that media violence has on aggressive behavior is comparable or greater than that of many other biological public health threats that are generally accepted as serious. In the Huesmann et al. (2003) study, the size of the correlation between viewing media violence in childhood and later adult aggression was about .20. That is higher than the correlation between exposure to lead and IQ loss, between insufficient calcium intake and loss of bone mass, between exposure to asbestos and laryngeal cancer, and exposure to passive smoking in the workplace and lung cancer. Yet, most of the public is far more willing to recognize the latter as public health threats. The public accepts tobacco as causing lung cancer in part because they can imagine the physiological process through which tobacco starts tumors in the lungs. I am suggesting that the public is less willing to accept media violence as a major public health threat, as yet, because it does not understand the neurophysiological basis of imitation or the powerful role imitation plays in forming the adult self out of a child's experiences. It is hoped that, as this book and others like it advance knowledge about the important role that imitation plays, the public will become more accepting of the fact that long-term, habitual, violent behavior can be learned from observing others behaving violently in the media world as well as from observing others behaving violently in the real world.[2]

2. See the comments on this chapter by Hurley (vol. 2, ch. 19.5, p. 380). ED.

13   Imitation and Moral Development

Jesse J. Prinz

13.1   Introduction

Imitation is often investigated by those who want to understand how manual skills are learned, as in the case of mastery of tools. An imitator observes the behavior of another individual and then attempts to replicate that behavior. Manual skills are just the tip of the imitative iceberg. We certainly acquire forms of behavior by copying others, but imitation can also help us acquire forms of thinking. Aping others' reactions can be a valuable resource in acquiring cognitive as well as manual skills. In this chapter, I investigate a cognitive skill that is central to human interaction: moral comprehension. Our understanding of the moral domain is not exhausted by factual knowledge. It involves a range of emotional capacities. Acquiring these, I will argue, ordinarily depends on imitative learning. I first try to establish that ordinary moral competence has an affective dimension, and I then show how imitation comes in.

13.2   Psychopaths and Moral Concepts

Philosophers have a long-standing debate about the role of emotions in moral competence. Some authors argue that moral concepts necessarily involve emotional dispositions; otherwise they would not motivate us to act. In some versions of this view, distinguishing right from wrong would be impossible without emotional dispositions. Moral rationalists deny this, and claim that right and wrong can be distinguished by the power of reason. Moral reasoning can give us just grounds for action, even if we lack moral sentiments. Philosophers present this as a conceptual debate, but I want to recast it in empirical terms. Does our grasp of moral concepts ordinarily involve an emotional response? If moral emotions are not operative, can we nevertheless develop an understanding of the difference between right and wrong? Are there individuals who understand morality but have no emotional distaste for the bad and no inclination to do good? Philosophers call such individual amoralists.

The search for real-world amoralists leads immediately to the clinical condition of psychopathy. Psychopaths have been made infamous through fiction and film. They are portrayed as cunning, remorseless, and deviant personalities, who engage in atrocious acts of violence. They are bloodthirsty, predatory monsters. Hannibal Lector from the *Silence of the Lambs* is a paradigm example. Psychopathy is not a Hollywood creation, however. It is a real clinical syndrome, which is not uncommonly diagnosed. In reality, psychopaths are often less exotic. Psychopaths tend to be criminally versatile, running the full range from petty crimes to violent offenses. Rather than being driven by a desire for violence, their violent acts are more characteristically casual, dispassionate, and impulsive, often for some anticipated gain. Psychopaths seem to fit the description of amoralism because they have IQ levels within the normal range and seem to comprehend the difference between right and wrong. They can articulate the moral precepts embraced by the societies in which they live. A violent psychopath might acknowledge that his criminal actions were morally wrong without feeling bad about them.

Psychopathy does not appear as a main entry in the *Diagnostic and Statistical Manual for Mental Disorders, IV* (DSM IV, American Psychiatric Association, 1994), but it is listed as an alternative name for the antisocial personality disorder. The diagnostic criteria for this condition include impulsivity, restlessness, and a pattern of cunning, manipulativeness, cruelty, or other behaviors that could lead to arrest. As a rule, the DSM criteria are behavioral, not psychological. Robert Hare (1993) has argued that this leaves out the most essential features of psychopathy and fails to distinguish psychopaths from other individuals who engage in antisocial conduct. He has devised an alternative "psychopathy checklist," which is now a standard diagnostic tool (Hare, 1991). According to Hare (1991, 1998), psychopaths show a lack of guilt, remorse, and empathy, and tend to have shallow affective states quite generally. If moral concepts were emotion laden, this deficiency would have a profound impact on psychopaths' moral aptitude. But in fact psychopaths seem to grasp morality. Their problem lies not in moral comprehension, but in moral care.

This assessment should not be accepted too hastily. Psychopaths may not fully grasp moral concepts. Their lack of moral emotions may testify to a lack of moral comprehension. To support this claim, one would need to show that their understanding of moral concepts differs from our own. R. J.

R. Blair (1995) set out to do just that. He adopted a measure borrowed from Turiel (1983) and other defenders of "domain theory" in moral development. Turiel argues that moral maturity involves an ability to distinguish merely conventional transgressions from moral transgressions. He operationalizes this distinction by an appeal to revocability or dependence on authority. Suppose a school administrator announced that the school would no longer require its students to follow a dress code. Intuitively, it would no longer be wrong to dress casually for school. But now suppose the school administrator says that the school will allow students to hit each other. Hitting remains wrong. Imagine a culture where beating a spouse is encouraged. We may say that members of that culture judge spouse beating to be acceptable, but there is a deep sense in which it remains fundamentally wrong. Willful cruelty differs from violations of dress codes and table manners. Cruelty is wrong in a moral sense, whereas such things as dress and table manners are only wrong relative to the conventions operative in a social group. There are borderline cases between moral and conventional wrongs, but many cases fall clearly on one side of the divide. Recognition of this distinction comes easy to most people, and it is a basic part of our moral competence.

Blair (1995) had the excellent idea of testing whether psychopaths could draw the moral and conventional distinction. He presented a group of incarcerated criminal psychopaths with a series of scenarios involving misconduct in a school setting. In each case, the psychopaths were asked whether the conduct would continue to be wrong if the teacher said it was okay. Some of cases involved conventional transgressions (e.g., boys wearing skirts or talking in class), others were moral (e.g., hitting or hair pulling). Members of a nonpsychopathic incarcerated control group had no trouble distinguishing the two kinds of cases. They judged that talking in class would be okay if the teacher allowed it, but hair pulling would not be okay. Psychopaths were insensitive to the distinction. Blair interprets his findings as showing that psychopaths treat all wrongs as conventional. Their morality is borrowed. They recognize that members of their community regard things as wrong, and they try to convince others that they share this conviction, but their inability to distinguish moral and conventional wrongs suggests a serious deficiency. Psychopaths do not understand moral concepts the way that we do. They are blind to the idea that an action may be wrong even if there is no authority or social custom in place to discourage it.

Blair (1995) tries to explain the moral blindness of psychopaths by appeal to a deficit in what he terms the violence inhibition mechanism, or

VIM. The idea of a VIM is inspired by work in ethology. When one animal is aggressive toward another member of its species, the attacker will often stop when the victim makes a submission display. For example, Blair discusses a species-typical mechanism that causes one dog to stop aggressing when the victim dog offers its throat. The mechanism causes the aggressor to a have an aversive response to the distress of its victim. Blair thinks humans have VIMs as well. He suspects that the VIM is what causes us to experience distress when we encounter the suffering of others. Blair speculates that the VIM is deficient in psychopaths. As a result, psychopaths are not disturbed by the suffering of others. This prevents them from developing an empathetic capacity and moral emotions, such as guilt and shame.

Blair supports his hypothesis by showing that individuals with psychopathic tendencies are comparatively unperturbed by the sight of others in distress (Blair et al., 1997, Blair, 1999b; House & Milligan, 1976), but this is only weak support. There is no solid evidence showing that a VIM exists in humans. Even if it did, it would be very surprising if a VIM deficit were the *primary* cause of moral blindness in psychopaths. For one thing, psychopaths are not always violent. When they engage in antisocial behavior, it tends to take a variety of forms. One of the diagnostic criteria for psychopathy is criminal versatility. To explain nonviolent antisocial behavior in psychopaths, Blair relies on a developmental story. He believes that VIM dysfunction can lead to general deficits in moral emotions. Without developing a tendency to respond to the distress of others, a juvenile psychopath will not develop a healthy capacity for such emotions as shame and guilt. The diminished emotional capacity will then lead to a global deficiency in moral sensitivity.

Blair's developmental story does not explain enough. In addition to their deficit in moral emotions, psychopaths show a deficit in nonmoral emotions. Their emotions tend to be quite flat in general. There is no reason why a VIM deficit would cause a general reduction in, say, fear and sadness, because these arise in nonmoral contexts. Nonviolent criminal offenses by psychopaths may be due to a deficit in moral emotions, but this deficit seems to be symptomatic of a general emotional disorder, not a reduced inhibition of violence.

Blair's proposal also fails to explain other core symptoms of psychopathy. Most significantly, it sheds no light on the fact that psychopaths perform abnormally on some cognitive tasks. For example, they tend to make more errors than normal subjects when asked to complete mazes of increasing difficulty (Schalling & Rosen, 1968; Sutker et al., 1972). Psychopaths are tempted to go down blind alleys rather then eyeing the best route before beginning a maze. In addition, psychopaths have also been found to make perseverative errors in the Wisconsin card sorting task (e.g., Gorenstein, 1982). When an experimenter changes a sorting rule in the middle of the task, psychopaths find it harder than nonpsychopaths to discontinue following the initial rule that they were given.

Errors on mazes and card sorting perseveration can both be understood as involving impulsivity. In working through a maze, certain paths will seem promising at first glance, but one can quickly discover that they lead to dead ends by looking ahead. Psychopaths get stuck in the first glance. They act on the slightest hint of reward. In card sorting, an initially established rule will serve as a default. Once the rule is learned, it is easier to continue following it than to adopt a new form of behavior. Psychopaths get stuck on defaults. It is hard for them to change plans based on new information because they must inhibit an initial temptation to follow the default plan. This tendency can be compared to the behavior of a child who cannot help but take a cookie from the cookie jar despite admonitions not to. Once the temptation is experienced, psychopaths find it hard to resist. This is what it means to be impulsive. Impulsivity is a core symptom of psychopathy and a standard diagnostic criterion.

Neither mazes nor card sorting involve moral emotions, much less inhibition of violence. This suggests that a VIM deficit, even if it is found in psychopaths, could not be the root cause of the disorder. Fisher and Blair (1998) explain cognitive deficits in psychopaths by speculating that the VIM may be located in brain regions adjacent to those that are implicated in various cognitive tasks. They speculate that psychopathy may involve a brain abnormality that compromises several areas. This explanation is inelegant. If a more integrated explanation can explain the core symptoms of psychopathy, it should be preferred.

A more integrated explanation is available. The account I favor extends a proposal put forward by D. Fowles (1980). He argues that psychopathy derives from a deficit in a very rudimentary behavioral inhibition system (BIS) that underlies many aspects of emotion, motivation, and temperament. The BIS was first proposed by Jeffrey Gray (see Gray, 1987, for a review) in an influential theory of anxiety. In healthy individuals, the BIS allows us to stop and adjust our plans when we encounter a threat. In anxious individuals, the BIS is hyperactive, causing chronic inhibition under conditions that are perfectly safe. According to Gray (1993), BIS also plays a role in forms of inhibition that are unrelated to anxiety and fear. For example, it may allow us to stop a plan we are pursuing when another, better plan presents itself. An impairment in the BIS would make it more difficult to change plans. In a word, it would promote impulsivity. A person with a weak BIS would find it difficult to resist pursuing plans that ostensibly seem attractive, but that would be less attractive on further reflection. Such a person might even recognize that a given plan might lead to trouble, but would be incapable of using this knowledge to inhibit acting on the plan. A weak BIS explains impulsivity, and impulsivity explains cognitive deficits.

A weak BIS could also be used to explain some of the emotional abnormalities in psychopaths. Fowles emphasizes the fact that a weak BIS would result in a reduction of fear. This would explain why psychopaths show less galvanic response to scary pictures and show a lack of startle potentiation (Patrick et al., 1993). A weak BIS might explain other emotional abnormalities as well. It is the basic mechanism behind all inhibitory emotions in Gray's view, and one of the fundamental systems guiding our affective life. A BIS deficit could leave someone with a limited capacity for any emotion that involves inhibition. Sadness, for example, may involve just as much inhibition as fear. Sad people tend to withdraw and resist active pursuit of goals. A BIS deficit could lead to a sadness deficit.

Other emotions, such as happiness, may not involve BIS centrally, so we might expect to see a healthy capacity for happiness in psychopaths. But this will not always be the case. Someone profoundly deficient in fear and sadness may be unable to form many of the social ties that play a central role in human well-being. In addition, a weak BIS could lead to abnormal functioning in other rudimentary emotional systems. Gray postulates a counterpoint to the BIS, called the behavioral activation system, or BAS. This is the system that underlies arousal in positive emotional states. The BAS often functions in concert with the BIS. It is plausible that the two serve collectively to promote homeostasis. The BAS may tend to kick in when inhibition is lifted through nonpunishment. A BIS deficiency could lead, developmentally, to a BAS that responds less often and less vigorously than it would in healthy individuals. Ironically, a general deficiency in negative emotions could lead to a flattening of positive affect as well.

What is the source of moral blindness in this account? One possibility is that the fear deficit emphasized by Fowles prevents normal moral development. Fear of punishment is often induced by caregivers during moral training, and Rothbart et al. (1994) found that fear is correlated with dispositional empathy in infants. But fear is neither the only nor the best method of developing moral sensitivity. Fear can be negatively correlated with prosocial behavior (Caprara et al., 2001), and it gets mixed reviews from those who study moral development. Caregivers who try to promote good conduct by threatening punishment often find that the method is not completely effective. They can improve conduct in children more effectively by conveying disappointment or drawing a child's attention to the harm she has caused (see Hoffman, 2000 and later discussion). How might a BIS deficit explain these facts?

To see the answer, recall that other negative emotions are affected by a weak BIS. As remarked earlier, a weak BIS may reduce one's capacity for sadness. Sadness makes two crucial contributions to morality. First, moral sensitivity often involves recognition and response to the sadness of others, including the victims of transgressions and members of one's social group. Rothbart et al. (1994) found that sadness and empathy were correlated. It is interesting that Blair (1997) found that children with psychopathic tendencies tended to make more attributions of sadness than control subjects when they were presented with stories about people experiencing losses. The inflated response may reflect a compensatory strategy. Psychopathic children may infer that the events in the narrative are *supposed* to evoke sadness. This interpretation is plausible in light of other evidence, which suggests that psychopaths are deficient in sadness. Blair and collaborators have shown that children and adolescents with psychopathic tendencies have difficulty recognizing sad faces (Blair et al., 2001; Blair & Coles, 2000) and sad vocal tones (D. Stevens et al., 2001). Poor recognition of emotion is often associated with a deficiency in experiencing emotion. This would also make sense of the aforementioned fact that psychopaths show abnormally low electrodermal responses when viewing images of sad faces. Psychopaths show little vicarious sadness because it is difficult for them to experience sadness in the first place.

Second, sadness may be an ingredient in the primary moral emotions of guilt and shame. Many emotion researchers believe that some emotions are more basic than others. Basic emotions typically have a biological basis, analogues in other species, and characteristic facial expressions, and they appear early in development. Nonbasic emotions can be generated by blending basic emotions or by what I call "calibration" (J. Prinz, 2004). In calibration, an emotion that initially had one set of eliciting conditions is returned to a new set of eliciting conditions that is more specific than the initial set. For example, pride is joy calibrated to one's own accomplishments. I think that guilt and shame have sadness as an ingredient. Guilt is just sadness that has been calibrated to situations in which one has caused harm to someone that one cares about. Guilt leads to reparative behavior because reparation is seen as a way to make up for such harm and overcome the feeling of loss. Shame is a blend of sadness and aversive self-consciousness. (Aversive self-consciousness is a basic emotion that arises when one receives unwanted attention from others. It is also the root of embarrassment.) Shame is calibrated to situations in which one's reputation has been threatened by engaging in conduct that is discouraged by the members of one's community. If sadness does figure in these two emotions, then a deficiency in sadness will have moral consequences.

The claim that sadness figures in guilt and shame has not been systematically tested, but there is some suggestive evidence. Reparative behavior and sadness are highly correlated in childhood (Cole et al., 1992). There is also a direct correlation between sadness and emotions of guilt and shame (Zahn-Waxler & Robinson, 1995). Children who are often sad also experience these emotions frequently. In pilot studies, I have found that guilt is associated with the frowning expression that we associate with sadness. Such findings certainly do not prove that sadness is a constituent of guilt and shame, but they are suggestive. At this point, intuition provides the strongest evidence for a constituency relation. Intuitively, guilt and shame make us feel downtrodden, pained, and worthless. They weigh on us in much the same way that sadness does.

In summary, I am proposing that psychopathy derives from a general deficit in inhibition, and that this deficit results in impulsive behavior, owing to a lack of inhibition, and moral retardation, owing to a lack of inhibitory emotions, especially sadness. This proposal makes sense of the link between emotions and moral competence. But what, more exactly, does moral competence consist in? And why do psychopaths fail to comprehend the moral versus conventional distinction?

To answer these questions, I need to say something about moral development. I discuss several milestones in moral sensitivity that are characteristically seen in normally developing children. Each of these milestones, it turns out, ordinarily owes a debt to imitation.

13.3   Sentimental Education

The first milestone that I discuss is already exhibited in the first hours of life. Newborns try to mimic facial gestures that they see (Meltzoff & Moore, 1983a), including emotional expressions (Field et al., 1982). This tendency may be underwritten by mirror neurons (see Gallese, 2001). It requires an unlearned capacity to translate a visual experience into an action program. I believe that facial mimicry makes a contribution to moral development. For one thing, it can increase social interaction and attachment by capturing the attention of caregivers. This can promote bonding and instruction from caregivers. In addition, facial mimicry can lead to emotional contagion through facial feedback. When a person makes a characteristic emotional facial expression, the corresponding emotion may be experienced as a result (Zajonc et al., 1989). As infants and toddlers mimic perceived emotional expressions, they may "catch" the corresponding emotion. Some researchers have suggested that this process plays a role in developing the capacity to attribute mental states to others (Gordon, 1995a; Harris, 1992). More important for this context, it may help foster the development of concern. If an infant recognizes someone's distress by "catching" it, the infant will in effect be distressed by that person's distress. This vicarious distress eventually becomes metacognitive. At some point in development, we recognize that we are distressed *because* someone else is distressed, as when we instinctively feel tears well up in our eyes while watching the tears of an actor in a movie. But vicarious distress precedes mind-reading abilities. Before infants can attribute distress to others, they catch others' distress. This can be regarded as first-order concern. It is feeling bad because others feel bad, as opposed to feeling bad about others' feeling bad (second-order concern).

An early vicarious distress response is not always mediated by facial feedback. As Sagi and Hoffman (1976) have emphasized, one of the first indications of sensitivity to others is infantile crying contagion. Newborn infants cry when they hear the cries of other infants. The mechanisms behind crying contagion are not known. Unlike facial mimicry, there is little reason to think infants deliberately cry when they hear others crying; it is a spontaneous response. It may also be a phylogenetically ancient response. Rats, for example, become distressed when they experience the distress of other rats (G. Rice & Gainer, 1962).

Crying contagion diminishes in older infants, but other forms of emotional contagion remain. Older infants will show less vocal signs of sadness when they hear others cry, and very young children become sad when they see pictures of others crying. Even autistic children show this pattern of response, despite likely deficiencies in their understanding of other minds (Blair, 1999a). It is interesting that autistics also seem to understand the moral versus conventional distinction (Blair, 1996). This supports the idea that there may be a link between intact emotional response and moral development (contrast Kennett, 2002, who proposes that autists may deploy moral concepts of a more dispassionate variety).

Emotional contagion can be regarded as imitative in nature. As I use the term, imitation is a process by which one organism comes to exhibit a state or behavior exhibited by another organism through perceiving the other organism exhibit that state or behavior. Roughly speaking, imitation is mentally mediated replication. This broad definition offers considerable flexibility. One can imitate mere movements or more complex instrumental behaviors. One can also imitate internal states such as goals, attitudes, or affective states. In facial feedback and crying contagion, infants imitate both expressive behaviors and the underlying emotions. When young children become saddened by looking at photos of people expressing distress, they may imitate emotions without imitating expressions. As just remarked, this kind of imitation is intact in autistic children, despite some deficits in their ability to replicate manual skills (see S. Rogers, 1999).

Some researchers define imitation more narrowly. Tomasello (1999) restricts the term to cases in which the imitator duplicates both the means and the end of an instrumental behavior. He uses the term "emulation" for cases where an end state is replicated by means that differ from those of the model. This terminological fiat is permissible, of course, but I prefer the broader definition of imitation because it highlights a common thread running through ostensibly disparate methods of transmission. It may be useful to distinguish these methods for some purposes, but we should not obscure the similarities. We often learn by repeating what we have observed in others.

Even if one grants that emotional contagion is imitative, one might question whether it qualifies as a stage in *moral* development. First-order concern is quite selfish. Someone who feels bad as a result of others' distress may simply work to avoid others in distress rather than offering help or assistance. Ordinarily, however, this is not what happens. First-order concern takes on a more active and decidedly prosocial role in the second year of life. Toddlers engage in consolation. They come to the aid of those in distress. They initiate tender touches and other forms of soothing physical contact (Radke-Yarrow & Zahn-Waxler, 1984). They may offer a distressed person an object to provide comfort or distraction. Some of these behaviors may have a biological basis, but others may be copied from experience. A toddler who has found comfort in particular consolatory behaviors may attempt the same when confronted with another individual in distress (Hoffman, 2000).

Early consolation qualifies as imitative in two senses. First, the toddler is replicating the kind of consolatory behaviors that have brought relief to her in the past. Second, consolation is tied to emotional contagion. Seeing another individual in distress seems to trigger a consolatory routine in young children. Consolation is a way of coping with vicarious distress. This connection between perceiving the states of others and acting fits in with the emphasis on perception-action schemes found in the work of Wolfgang Prinz (1997a) and Preston and de Waal (2002). Seeing distress affords the offering of consolation.

At this second milestone of moral development, there is a shift from passive first-order concern to active first-order concern, but comprehension of the moral, as such, remains undeveloped. Children in the second year have moral responsiveness without moral competence. In early childhood, imitation begins to rely on mechanisms that are more reflective than reflexive. Children come to appreciate that behavior is governed by normative rules. Imitation may contribute here as well. Consider the methods by which moral rules are conveyed. When a child misbehaves, a caregiver can respond in several ways (Hoffman, 2000). One option is to assert power by displaying anger or threatening punishment. This can be effective with some children under some conditions, but other responses can be even more effective. A second option is withdrawal of love. One can refuse to show affection to a misbehaving child or display disappointment. Both anger and disappointment can threaten an attachment relation. A child who recognizes that her conduct has caused these responses in a caregiver may become concerned that her conduct will lead to a breach in that all-important relationship. That can lead to sadness about the action that led to the breach, and such sadness qualifies as regret—feeling bad about one's own actions. The capacity for regret owes something to imitation when love withdrawal is involved. Initially, a child feels bad because her caregivers have indicated that they feel bad. The bad feeling occurs because it is observed in others.

A third response to misconduct, known as induction, can also be regarded as imitative in the broad sense. A caregiver can draw a child's attention to the fact that her conduct has harmed someone else. After recognizing the harm, the child may come to feel bad and thereby recognize that her action was wrong. That bad feeling may stem, at least initially, from emotional contagion. If a child sees that her action has made another child sad, she may catch the sadness from her victim. A child with no capacity to catch emotions from others would find it difficult to learn through love withdrawal and induction. Such a child might recognize that her actions caused sadness in a caregiver or victim without becoming sad herself.

When love withdrawal is used, the potential threat to attachment can induce sadness in a child without the aid of emotional contagion, but even in this case, there is an imitative dimension. Attachment itself requires a relationship between caregiver and child that is reciprocal in nature. Both parties must be responsive to each other. As noted earlier, facial imitation can contribute to the development of attachment relations, but other forms of imitation may contribute as well. A child who responds to tender physical attention with similar behavior is likely to forge a more solid bond than a child who responds by withdrawing or becoming aggressive. A bad imitator is likely to form unstable attachments. If amenability to training through love withdrawal requires healthy attachment relations, it may work best with healthy imitators.

So far, I have mentioned three stages in moral development. In the first, infants simply experience the emotions of those around them. This stage allows for first-order concern and can contribute to the emergence of empathy. Concern and empathy can be understood as emotional responses to others' hedonic states. In the second stage, these feelings are put to work. Toddlers begin to engage in prosocial behavior. The third stage introduces sensitivity to moral rules. Moral rules tell us how to behave and when to praise and blame the behavior of others. The appreciation of moral rules depends on the earlier stages of emotional contagion and behavioral coping. By becoming aware of the emotions of caregivers and victims, young children can come to appreciate that certain forms of conduct should be avoided. This is achieved through sadness conditioning. Children come to recognize that actions can lead to sadness, and that sadness constitutes a simple form of regret. These actions associated with regret are subsequently avoided, and this avoidance constitutes an early appreciation of moral rules.

Sensitivity to moral rules has behavioral consequences. Children at this stage in development begin to engage in reparative behaviors when they transgress, and they may begin to condemn the transgressions of others. Both of these classes of behavior are likely to depend on skills acquired through imitation. While reparation may be a universal phenomenon, particular methods of reparation, such as verbal apologies, vary from culture to culture; likewise for condemnation. Children may learn these culturally specific behaviors by observing others. Imitation will also play a role in determining which forms of conduct a child will condemn. To condemn an action, a child must first come to dislike it, and this will often depend on picking up the attitudes of caregivers. For example, parents who frequently engage in acts of aggression may have children whose attitudes toward bullying are much more positive than those of children who come from less violent homes.

Children who are sensitive to moral rules do not necessarily recognize moral rules as such. They may not possess the concepts of moral right and wrong. To understand these concepts, one must pass through a further stage in moral development. This is where the moral versus conventional distinction comes in. Transgressions of conventional rules can have strong emotional consequences. A child who violates the prevailing rules of etiquette may incur anger and disappointment from caregivers. But by the time a child is 4 or 5 years old, she is likely to appreciate that transgressions of etiquette differ from transgressions of rules involving harm, fairness, religious values, and so on. As Turiel (1983) has shown, children at this age typically treat some transgressions as contingent on authorities and others as intrinsically and inalterably wrong. How do children arrive at this stage?

Much of the literature on the moral versus conventional distinction has focused on a difference in justificatory strategies. Conventional norms are said to depend on authorities, while moral norms depend more on ideals of welfare and justice that are independent of authority. How do children come to recognize that different rules lie on different sides of this explanatory divide? Both Blair and Turiel recognize that affect plays a role here. Moral and conventional norms have different emotional consequences. Five-year-olds recognize this fact. They have been found to associate moral transgression with strong bad feelings, while regarding conventional transgressions as affectively neutral (Arsenio & Ford, 1985). The real difference may be a bit more subtle. If one violates a purely conventional norm, such as the norm against wearing pajamas in public, one may feel embarrassment. And if someone else violates that norm, one might feel amused or smugly annoyed. If one violates a moral norm, in contrast, one is likely to feel guilt or shame. And if someone else violates that moral norm, one might feel anger, contempt, or disgust. These moral emotions can arise in the case of conventional transgressions, but only when one is focusing on an aspect of the transgression that is not contingent on social customs. If a child feels that wearing pajamas in public will disrespect those she cares about or lead those people to make negative judgments about her character, she will feel ashamed. This emotional response has nothing to do with the pajamas as such, but with the implications of the act. A conventional wrong (wearing pajamas in public) can also entail a moral wrong (disrespecting others). Emotions indicate which dimension of an action is under consideration. A person who is experiencing shame after a pajama episode is probably moralizing it.

These emotional differences arise in development because different kinds of transgressions have different kinds of effects. Those effects include reactions in caregivers and in those who are directly affected by our actions. When a child hits someone and sees that her victim has been hurt, it causes the child to feel bad by emotional contagion. This gives hurting a negative value that does not seem to depend on cultural conventions. In other cases, strong negative emotions are instilled by caregivers. Polluting the environment may be given moral standing by drawing a child's attention to the harm to future generations, and in older children, victimless transgressions such as masturbation may be moralized by convincing children that it will lead to disease, deviance, or divine censure (see Haidt et al., 1993). Contrast these cases with the that of wearing pajamas in public. If I wear pajamas in public, others may laugh at me. That makes me feel bad too, but there are two differences from the harm case. First, being laughed at may cause embarrassment rather than vicarious distress. Second, if the taboo against wearing pajamas in public is lifted, the emotional cost disappears because people would not laugh. This latter difference ultimately contributes to the development of distinct justificatory strategies, but the former difference is already sufficient for drawing a moral versus conventional distinction.

The acquisition of moral emotions may benefit from imitative learning. I suggested earlier that guilt and shame are simply forms of sadness that have been calibrated to special eliciting conditions—self-caused harm and a reduction in reputation, respectively. Roughly speaking, guilt is harm-sadness and shame is reproach-sadness (plus aversive self-consciousness). Notice that guilt and shame differ from vicarious distress and regret. The latter emotions constitute what I called first-order concern. They are negative emotions occasioned by the negative emotions of others, but not directed at the negative emotions of others. In their mature form, guilt and shame introduce a second-order component. Guilt draws our attention to the mental states of our victims. Shame draws our attention to the mental states of those who might judge us. But I believe that guilt and shame can also occur as first-order responses, which do not require metacognitive abilities. Suppose Sally hits Roger and Roger cries. If she catches Roger's sadness on that occasion, she may experience a negative feeling when she contemplates hitting someone on a future occasion. This would qualify as an early form of guilt about hitting. It can be explained by direct associative learning, with no need for anticipation or attribution of sadness to her victims. As Sally matures, she may attain the ability to attribute sadness to others, and when she does so, she will also experience sadness through emotional contagion. That metacognitive ability will cause her to feel guilty when contemplating potentially harmful actions that she has never performed in the past. In both mature and immature forms, the negative feelings of guilt depend on a tendency to catch the negative feelings of others. This is a form of imitation in my broad definition.

This is the last stage that I will consider in the developmental story. Moral responsiveness begins with emotional contagion in newborns. Then consolation behaviors emerge in toddlers. Soon after, children become sensitive to normative rules, and they start to engage in reparative behavior and in moral prescription and condemnation. Finally, different classes of norms are distinguished through the attainment of moral emotions, and these permit the development of various justificatory skills. Imitation makes contributions at each of these stages. It also contributes to moral development in other ways. For example, we often shape our moral attitudes and behaviors by following role models. These can be caregivers, peers, community leaders, or increasingly, celebrities and characters on film and television. The use of role models is an extension of the processes that I have been describing. It involves the attainment of attitudes and behaviors that conform to those that have been observed in others. If moral attitudes and conduct are acquired and shaped with the help of imitation, we should be somewhat concerned about the use of role models. If the media are providing children with role models that engage in antisocial behavior, there is a potential risk of destructive mimicry in action and attitudes (see Huesmann et al., 1997). We should also be concerned about antisocial parental and peer role models.

Bad role models are not the only source of bad conduct. If this developmental story is approximately right, healthy moral development depends on certain emotional capacities. Emotions figure in the picture from the very first stage. An emotionally impaired infant will have difficulty with emotional contagion. An emotionally impaired toddler may fail to develop tight links between perception of emotion and prosocial behavior. An emotionally impaired child may fail to understand the full consequences of transgressing norms. Without a normal emotional capacity, the distinction between moral and conventional rules can be missed. That difference begins with a subtle division in emotional responses. Violations of moral rules generate different emotions than violations of conventional rules. Violations of moral rules are also those where the emotional costs remain even if the rule is no longer enforced by authorities. Emotional deficiencies can engender insensitivity to these facts. Without healthy emotions, one has to identify norms by statistical regularities and social sanctions. An emotionally deficient individual learns that something is wrong because people discourage it and refrain from doing it. This does not distinguish moral from conventional rules. Thus, emotional deficits impede competence in the moral domain, which is precisely what we see in psychopaths. Psychopaths can imitate the behaviors of others to a reasonable degree, but they cannot imitate the emotional states of others, and this has serious implications for competence and conduct.

13.4 Conclusion

Psychopaths teach us that emotional deficiencies can impair moral competence. Psychopaths fail to distinguish moral and conventional transgressions because they never learn the appropriate emotional reactions to their conduct. For healthy moral development, sadness must be tuned to the impact that certain actions have on victims and caregivers. Imitation ordinarily plays a pivotal role in this tuning process.

Is imitation essential for moral development? Perhaps. "Good" and "bad" cannot be defined simply by pointing to examples. Caregivers tell children that some things are good and other things are bad, but they cannot point to goodness or badness. Moral concepts extend beyond the observable properties of situations and events. They involve our *reactions* to situations and events. A caregiver can draw a child's attention to some feature of an event with the hope that the child will have the appropriate reaction, but the reaction depends on the emotional dispositions of the child. Caregivers can cultivate emotional dispositions in children, but they cannot instill those dispositions by explicit instruction. Emotional dispositions are more readily established by imitation. If a child sees that her actions have upset others, she will become upset too through emotional contagion. Without this rudimentary imitative process, it would be very difficult to see the bad in things.[1]

1. See comments on this chapter by Huesmann (vol. 2, ch. 19.6, p. 386) and a relevant discussion by Sugden (vol. 2, ch. 15, p. 301). ED.

14 Imitation and Mimesis

Merlin Donald

14.1 Introduction

The only output of any nervous system is muscle movement. Therefore, the only way a nervous system can publicly display and transmit its perceptions of the world to another nervous system is to translate its perceptions into patterns of muscle movements. A mimetic act is basically a motor performance that reflects the perceived event structure of the world, and its motoric aspect makes its content a public, that is, a potentially cultural, expression.

Archaeological reconstructions of archaic hominid life suggest that the genus *Homo* evolved basic mimetic capacities about two million years ago, with mimetic behaviors appearing in some degree at that time, followed by a very slow cultural accumulation of knowledge. These archaic ancestors of modern humans discovered the uses of fire in opportunistic, single applications, and after hundreds of thousands of years eventually mastered its continual use on a single site. They also became better at the preprocessing of food and the locating of campsites. They improved their hunting of big game, which for a small, naked mammal implies that they had developed significantly better methods of social communication and cooperation. They took tool manufacture to a completely new level.

All this happened very slowly. The extraordinarily slow initial rate of change in hominid cultures makes it extremely unlikely that they had either language or protolanguage. Nevertheless, their capacity for group living and social coordination, as well as the accumulation of knowledge and custom, was so dramatically different from any of their predecessors that there is no alternative to postulating a major change in their communicative abilities very early in human evolution.[1]

1. For a relevant discussion, see Harris and Want (vol. 2, ch. 6). ED.

The most parsimonious hypothesis to explain the cognitive aspects of their survival strategy is a group survival strategy based on mimesis, that is, on nonsymbolic, analog communication skills that permitted better social coordination. Whereas the predecessors of *Homo* had lived a variant of the primate style of social life, the archaic members of genus *Homo* adopted a very different lifestyle that depended heavily on social coordination, shared knowledge, and the transmission of skill. From the start, *Homo* was able to master and refine skills and transmit them, to coordinate group life to some degree around a home base, and to develop a cooperative hunting and foraging strategy. The rudiments of these may conceivably have been present in ancestral primates and australopithecines, but they were suddenly much more in evidence once *Homo* emerged.

Mimesis endures in human life. As anyone who has played charades knows, mimesis is a frustratingly imprecise mode of expression that is based on analogy, association, and resemblance. Mimetic acts consist of continuous flows of action, neither segmented nor digitized (labeled). They are typically organized into events and episodes that resemble the events and episodes they represent. Thus, children may mime their parents having an argument by "playing back" the episode in tones of voice and gesticulations. Effectively, these actions are edited reenactments of the events they represent. The audience recognizes the significance of the reenactment with reference to similar episodes, or by recourse to mimetic imagination (which might be regarded as the true "Cartesian theater" of the human mind), in which the components of episodes are reviewed and recombined into variants of the original episode. A child may never have been beaten, but having seen another child subjected to a beating, it has no difficulty imagining what the experience must be like, and acting out the imagined event. This is a typical product of human mimetic imagination.

The mimetic mode is essentially theatrical and cinematic. It contrasts with the linear, digital, nature of speech and narrative storytelling. In the latter, episodes are never directly reenacted (except perhaps as a supplement to the story). Linguistic representations are not restricted by the rules of perceptual resemblance and thus escape the limitations of episodic representations. At the same time, they lose some of their evocative power. Linguistic representations break episodes into labeled components and recombine them into sentences that allow the speaker a virtual infinity of options in representing the same episode.

The contrasts between mimetic and linguistic representation find a useful metaphor in the recording of sound. A magnetic tape recording of a song is called "analog" when it directly reflects the physical energy it records, both in time and in space. This means it is a continuous, that is, nonsegmented, recording. While the singer performs, the analog recording tracks the physical energy in the room continuously, without breaking up the signal into labeled components. In contrast, a digital recording of the same song requires that the energy patterns of the song be sliced into discrete temporal chunks whose amplitude and frequency are quantified in numbers. In a digitized recording, every sound sequence is effectively translated into a series of numbers, with time on one axis, and another dimension, such as loudness or pitch, scaled on another axis. The digitizing process fragments the physical energy in the signal, converting a continuous stream of sound into a set of numbers, or symbols, that indicate relative values. Whereas an analog tape recording is completely nonsymbolic, a digitized recording is ultimately symbolic in nature because it uses a set of conventional symbols that encode the measured values of the performance.

In the same way, analog representations that are based on the brain's perception of animate motion (such as the event-enactments that determine the forms of a child's imaginative playacting) do not fragment the input. They "play back" perceived events in action, editing and compressing them without breaking down the sequence into a set of conventional labels. Event-reenactment is perhaps the clearest example of pure mimesis because it is a fairly literal reduplication of a perceived event in animate motion. Other reduplicative motor expressions, such as iconic or metaphoric gesture, or the rehearsal of skill, may be somewhat less literal and more abstract, but they are nevertheless analog in nature.

The most obvious arena of group mimetic cognitive activity is the refinement and ritualization of reciprocal emotional display, whereby one individual "mirrors" the emotional reactions of others. Humans are mimetic actors in this regard, or perhaps they are best seen as mirrors of one another's actions. Styles of group laughter, bullying, and rejection tend to have distinct characteristics in every human cultural group. Custom and ritual are thus basically mimetic and group specific. They rapidly relax into a standard pattern in any social group. Less obvious examples of mimetic cultural interaction are games of fantasy and play, which tend to acquire tribal significance in small groups. Craft and athletic prowess are also mimetic domains, with the creative process, as well as the dissemination of skills, both governed by mimetic capacity. The refinement of such skills is also achieved by mimetic means.

The mimetic behavior patterns that support human social interaction are just out of reach for most primates. Apes have some mimetic skill, but they are very poor at it. In contrast, mimetic competence is found in human children at an early age, reflecting a uniquely human capacity. As a result of this capacity, the human social world can publicly "model" its perceived universe in patterns of action, creating a virtual world within which more and more cultural interaction takes place. The stream of social mimetic action thus "mimes" the stream of perceived events in the individual members of a given culture. A human child's remarkable ability to playact within the context of its tiny social world allows it to rapidly assimilate the norms, customs, and skills of its culture at a rapid pace. This ability is the driving force underlying much of human social life. The absence of this capacity during development, which is characteristic of autism, can often hinder language development. Moreover, it is always a fatal impediment to successful social development.

14.2 Defining Mimetic Performance

Mimesis is sometimes confused with imitation and mimicry, which are also reduplicative behaviors. Mimesis is an umbrella term that includes imitation and mimicry. The scale of mimetic performance might be clarified in the following way.

Mimicry is the deliberate reduplication in action of a perceived event without careful attention to, or knowledge of, its purpose. The actor's attention is directed to the surface of the action, with varying degrees of success. Some examples are a young bird duplicating the song pattern of its conspecifics, a parrot mimicking speech, or a human mimicking an accent in an unreflective manner.

Imitation is a more flexible, abstract reduplication of an event with closer attention to its purpose. This implies varying degrees of success. It is common to discriminate between accurate means-ends imitation and what Tomasello (1999) calls "emulation," which involves achieving the result or goal of the observed action but not copying the observed means to this result. Primates and young children often emulate, without successfully imitating, an action.

Mimesis is the reduplication of an event for communicative purposes. Mimesis requires that the audience be taken into account. It also demands taking a third-person perspective on the actor's own behavior. Some examples are children's fantasy play, the iconic gestures used in a social context, and the simulation of a "heroic" death during a theatrical performance.

There are no discrete boundaries separating these levels of mimetic action. Rather, they form a scale of successively more abstract or "intelligent" versions of reduplicative action. This is a sliding, rather than a discrete, scale that varies with the depth of cognitive processing required by the kind of action-modeling involved. In the first case, mimicry, the action need only be captured accurately in its superficial aspect. In the second, imitation, the model is more complex; a purpose or goal must be understood, and as a result the performance must be subjected to a more rigorous metacognitive self-evaluation. In the third, mimesis, not only must the purpose of the action be understood, but its various social ramifications and interpretations must also be understood in context.

However, even this set of distinctions does not fully capture the subtleties of the mimetic continuum. In the end, it is really the intention of the actor and the evocativeness of a given performance that define where on the continuum a mimetic action can be placed. The very same physical action might be classified on one occasion as a naïve and literal reduplication (parroting); on another, where the purpose is clearer, as a sophisticated performance in which the purpose of the original act is clearly understood (imitation). And yet, in a third instance, an actor might use exactly the same reduplicated actions in a sophisticated ironic "commentary" on the original action, as, for instance, in a comedy, where someone's eccentricities are exaggerated. The latter is mimesis, not because the action itself is more complex, but because of the high level of social understanding and metacognition that enables its appropriate use.

Mimetic action constitutes a style of representation with different rules from language. It also forms the basis for evolving a basic level of cultural convention. There are four major manifestations of mimetic representation in human culture, each of which has a distinct operational definition: (1) reenactive *mime*, as in the flexible role-playing of children and adults; (2) precise means-end *imitation*, as in learning how to fry an egg or make a stone tool; (3) the systematic rehearsal and refinement of *skill*, where each rehearsal amounts to a reenactment of a previous performance, as in learning to throw a ball, drive a car, or develop a facial expression that elicits sympathy from others; (4) nonlinguistic *gesture*, as in learning how to dance or act in a theatrical production.

In each of these, the actions resemble the events they reenact by the principle of perceptual similarity. In this, mimetic representation can be said to follow an "analog" as opposed to a "symbolic" logic. Mimetic action involves a continuous playback of imagined events, in selective, edited actions that do not engage any of the characteristic elements of language, such as words or grammars. There are important methodological differences in how mime, imitation, skilled rehearsal, and gesture are measured. Each reflects the specific academic tradition in which it was first studied in detail. However, the underlying cognitive and neural mechanisms of mimetic action seem to overlap. At the top of the mimetic hierarchy there is reason to argue for a common underlying neural adaptation that started evolving in primates and culminated its evolution in human beings.

14.3   Some Properties of the Mimetic System

The ultimate source of mimetic representations is a mental model that is being expressed in action. The model is really a remembered event perception, or episode. The central questions for cognitive neuroscience are first, How are complex event perceptions resolved by the nervous system? and second, How are they mapped onto the motor regions of the brain so as to create an action-model of the episode?

Mimetic action can engage the actor's whole body. It is thus inherently amodal, although it can also play out in single modalities. But most often, mimesis involves the ability to integrate and match actions to perceptions in several sensorimotor channels at the same time. This involves a hypothetical entity that might be called the mimetic controller. This is a brain network that generates implementable motor maps of event perceptions.

In the human brain, mimetic capability has another important feature. It is metacognitive; that is, it is reflective and potentially self-supervisory in its uses. Mimesis is also recombinatory; that is, it is able to generate novel arrangements of a given mimetic action sequence. Thus, mimesis is also potentially creative, capable of generating novel action patterns. Finally, mimesis is imaginative; that is, it involves the active rearrangement of kinematic imagery.

Another key feature of mimesis is the mimetic controller's ability to offload its products to the automatic mode. Although mimetic learning initially requires conscious capacity, highly rehearsed actions can become so automatic that they make minimal demands on conscious capacity. This allows the actor, through repetitive skilled rehearsal, to weld together hierarchies of skills into very complex systems, such as those involved in playing a musical instrument or reading. Such skills are built essentially by imitating one's previous performances, reviewing them in mimetic imagination, and refining the motor model by matching it to a template of idealized action. Elaborate action systems involve installing in the nervous system a new functional architecture that governs each new skill hierarchy; thus, mimetic capacity redeploys the nervous system for novel ends by functional restructuring.

Presumably the so-called "mirror" neuron circuits are involved in mimesis, but the process itself is still not well understood. Mirror neuron circuits are found in large numbers in species, such as monkeys, that are very poor at imitation and gesture. It follows that the mere presence of a mirror neuron system in the brain is not sufficient for the emergence of mimetic skills or even of imitation. Mirror neuron systems, taken alone, lack some of the key cognitive components required for high-level mimetic action. The discovery of these neurons is nevertheless important because they provide investigators with a crucial clue as to where to look next. However, it is important to note that there are several important features of mimetic action that are missing from the paradigms used in our present definition of mirror neurons. First, these paradigms do not seem to provide the wide amodal framework that would be needed to explain the crossmodal flexibility and integrative power of mimesis; this point will be expanded later in this chapter.

Second, it is not clear how the nervous system generates the neural maps that combine and recombine perceptual and motor models on various levels of abstraction in a complex event-perceptual context. Nor is it clear how the brain can implement such mappings in specific motor command channels (for instance, in writing the letter "A" with the foot). Mirror neurons might indicate no more than the presence of powerful correspondence detectors in the motor control system (see Heyes, vol. 1, ch. 6), or they might indicate a more abstract process; only time, and many more experiments, will resolve this issue.

A capacity for mimetic action probably resides in higher-level integrative neural circuits that receive outputs from mirror neuron systems and feed them into a wider cognitive map of the social environment, and vice versa. The location and nature of these mimetic networks are still unknown, but they are almost certainly widely distributed. In many ways, this mimetic process, which binds event-percepts to action-patterns, represents the ultimate achievement of the mammalian nervous system. It can be regarded as a very advanced form of binding in which long, multiframe social events are perceived and remembered as unitary episodes. From the standpoint of information reduction, such percepts are incredibly complex achievements. Events unfold as patterns of physical energy presented in a series of frames, each of which is highly complex in the spatial configuration of the sensory energies that convey the event to the nervous system. This point will be expanded later.

14.4   The Evolutionary Road to Mimesis

Any evolutionary scenario is based on speculation, but there are not as many degrees of freedom in this regard as some may believe. Hypotheses about human origins must be based on sound axioms and assumptions, and these must take into account our best knowledge about both the nervous system and the mind. The major points of my evolutionary proposal for mimesis (Donald, 1991) are roughly as follows.

14.4.1   The Nonsymbolic Nature of Nervous Systems

Based on present evidence, we must assume that the mammalian nervous system (including the human central nervous system) is basically a nonsymbolic system, that is, similar in principle but much more complex and powerful than artificial neural nets. The latter are analog (as opposed to digital) in their internal modes of computation (this holds even when they are simulated on digital computers). Simulated neural nets function on the principle of impression-formation, without explicit symbolic programming. Living nervous systems seem to function along similar lines, and although they are much more powerful, there is no evidence for their having innate quasi-symbolic programming, and they do not seem to be born with explicit "operating systems" programmed into them. The human nervous system undoubtedly has complex innate architectures, especially in the sensory and motor regions, and innate capacities, but its modes of operation do not seem to be even quasi-symbolic. Rather, the brain is filled with many parallel analog impression-forming networks, each of which has a high degree of redundancy in design.

14.4.2   Emergence of Symbols

Language and all forms of symbol-mediated thought came very late in human evolution, and were preceded by earlier cognitive changes that set the stage for the evolution of symbolic processing. There is no reason to abandon the analog principle in constructing theories of language evolution. Symbols emerged from interacting groups of analog brains. They did not originate in the brain, but rather in distributed networks of brains wired for analog communication. Symbols thus have their origin in social interaction, even in modern humans. As Saussure observed long ago, languages emerge in the spaces between brains. Language, even in its most rudimentary forms, has never developed in an isolated human brain, and fully developed languages are always the product of group communicative interactions.

Languages and symbols can thus be regarded as the cultural products of interconnected cognitive systems. They exist at the level of the ecosystem, or "cognitive ecology," within which human beings exist, and the ecology always encompasses a population of brains rather than a single brain. We do not have to assume that single brains must have evolved all the necessary equipment to generate languages. They had only to evolve capacities that enabled the network to achieve this. Cognitive-cultural networks generated languages, and the first question to address is, What features of the brain allowed such networks to emerge in the first place? When juxtaposed with the first, this assumption imposes a strict discipline on any theory of the roots of language because the starting point must be a primate brain whose sole operating mode is something like the analog logic of neural net computation.

14.4.3   Need for Plasticity

The human brain evolved capacities that prepare it for the unpredictable nature of human culture. Our cultural environment is extremely variable, to a degree that has no parallel in any other species. Therefore the genome cannot "assume" very much about the specifics of its cultural adaptation. The hominid strategy was to build a more flexible brain. Cultures and languages must be assimilated easily by infants during development. Therefore the child's brain must be extremely plastic to optimize its adaptation to the unpredictable cultural environment. Given the importance of plasticity for adaptation to complex cultures, neurocognitive plasticity itself would have come under selection pressure during human evolution.

14.4.4   Zone of Proximal Evolution

Archaic hominid culture was shaped by its primate roots and had to fall within the primate "zone of proximal evolution" (Donald, 2001). This archaic adaptation determined a great deal about how language and symbolic thought emerged in the human species. The assumed generative sequence by which language evolved from mimetic skill was as follows. First, a form of protolanguage (perhaps one- and two-word utterances without complex grammars or inflectional rules) emerged in a simple cultural network, primarily to disambiguate mimetic gesticulations, which are inherently imprecise. This was achieved by negotiation, and the founding group agreed on a conventional mapping system that fixed the relationship between meaning and gesture.

The advantages of the vocal channel as a communication device have been discussed many times (see Donald, 1991, 2001) and will not be covered here. In the case of speech, a set of standard articulatory gestures emerged, not necessarily in an entirely vocal context. This rudimentary vocal-gestural system was disseminated selectively to those equipped to learn it, and these individuals had a fitness gain, putting selection pressure on the attentional, learning, and memory capacities needed to adapt to the changing linguistic demands of late hominid cultures. Since the properties of any specific human culture are indeterminate and highly unpredictable, this generated even more selection pressure in favor of increased plasticity.

14.4.5 Culture First

Most theories of cultural evolution have assumed that language must have been the catalyst for human culture. These are known as "language-first" theories, and they tend to place research emphasis on finding the specialized "language devices" of the brain. But this misses the point. Where could language have come from in the first place, if no symbolic system already existed? I have suggested a reversal of this conventional order (Donald, 1991, 1993), in a "culture-first" theory that places language second, not first, in cognitive evolution, and that scaffolds language on a series of mimetic cultural adaptations. A shared communicative culture, with sharing of mental representations to some degree, must have come first, before language, creating a social environment in which language would have been useful and adaptive. There is good reason to believe that such a culture was mimetic in its mode of representation. It would have provided the rudimentary gestural skills that allowed archaic hominids to share knowledge and memory in a limited way, and a physiological basis for evolving a rudimentary morphophonology. The adaptive value of improved mimetic skill is obvious. Hominids so equipped would have become better able to master skills, to develop a powerful system of social cognition, to perform coordinated work, and to express themselves in a nonverbal manner, long before the complex phenomenon we know as language came along, with its lexicons, grammars, and high-speed communicative capacity.

14.4.6 Mimetic Preadaptation

The suite of adaptations that made possible the development of a mimetic communicative culture was expressive in nature and primarily produced by changes in the motor systems of the brain, especially the more abstract aspects of motor control. Only motor outputs can create public displays of knowledge; that is, only action can move ideas out of the brain, into a public communicative space. Thus the first leap toward a distinctive hominid culture had to be a motoric one. Cultural expression took the form of whole-body action, incorporating facial expression, voice, attitude, posture, and movement. This led to a rudimentary expressive repertoire, enshrined in body language, custom, habit, group gesticulation, and ritual. This was and still is the basis of human "mimetic" culture, the first form of culture in which mental representations were truly shared, albeit in a vague and imprecise manner. This explains why human language remains amodal in its organization and can be expressed in a variety of modalities, unlike birdsong, which is restricted to the vocal channel.

14.4.7 Mimesis as a Social Adaptation
The evolution of imitation was embedded in a larger pattern of social and communicative evolution, rather than evolving along its own path. Under archaic hominid cultural conditions, imitation in various domains would have become a crucial survival skill in social life. The existing primate capacity for crude imitation, or emulation, was undoubtedly one of the starting points for this evolutionary change. But, judging from the uses of mimesis in modern human social life, it was not the only component that led to the evolution of mimetic skills. Mimesis is highly social. Its adaptive significance depends upon such phenomena as empathy, sympathy, social identification, role-playing, imagination (especially kinematic imagination), gesture, and mind reading, or the ability to track other minds and share attention with them. All these capacities are either present in primates in a limited degree or are well within the primate zone of proximal evolution. They would have evolved together, as a suite.

14.4.8 Persistence of Mimesis
The human mind and its cultures are still basically mimetic in their mode of organization. The earliest human cultures, and the sophisticated symbolic skills that came much later with language, retained a deep connection with primate cognition and culture. Despite the immense historical overlay of human enculturation that was imposed on an increasingly plastic brain, our minds are still basically primate on the deepest level of their operation. This has a social corollary. If mimesis was the adaptation that generated a distinctly human culture, it follows that the deepest communicative framework of human culture must still be mimetic. This follows from the scaffolding principle that applies in human cognitive development. New capacities are always scaffolded on existing ones. On this principle,

language was scaffolded on mimesis. Thus, mimetic rules of representation, based on perceptual resemblances and metaphors, continue to operate below the cognitive surface, obscured perhaps by the more spectacular human abilities that have succeeded them, but nevertheless indispensable. They continue to affect the way we use languages and symbols. Moreover, if we are to maintain continuity in our evolutionary accounts, this also implies that all distinctly hominid cognitive traits, including our highest symbolic processes, such as analytical thought and the semantics of language, are ultimately scaffolded on mimesis.

14.4.9   Language as a Network-Level Phenomenon

Human brains have evolved and are designed specifically to live in communities of minds. Mimetic skill was the cognitive foundation skill for our most distinctive human trait, the tendency to hook up, create, and live in, communities of minds. These communities are still dependent on a strong mimetic foundation for their stability. This idea has a major advantage for the continuity theorist. It establishes a platform on which the evolution of full-fledged language becomes feasible in a truly Darwinian sense (Donald, 1999). Language is a network-level phenomenon, and evolved more like an ecosystem than a single organism, as the negotiated product of interactions taking place in an established cognitive community.

The implications of this idea for brain research are profound. Cognitive neuroscientists are unlikely to find an innate language acquisition device, and should redirect their investigations toward the powerful analog processing systems out of which language can emerge in group interactions. Instead of looking for specific language genes, or dedicated grammar regions, we should be turning our attention to basic presymbolic capacities that create and stabilize the social networks within which languages and symbol systems are negotiated and disseminated. We should also be studying the executive brain systems that govern social learning and enable the brain to import language effortlessly from the social environment. These include such things as a much wider working memory system, multi-channel attention, and the capacity to keep several cognitive and behavioral systems active at the same time.

14.5   The Cognitive Starting Point for Mimetic Representation: Event Perception

Before the vertebrate brain could be expected to create pantomimes and reenactments of perceived events, it had to have the ability to perceive those events in the first place. This was no small evolutionary achievement. Event perception emerged in evolution very long ago, probably in reptiles, and possibly in some insects. Some existing species of reptiles, and most mammals and birds, are quite good at perceiving social events that are important to them. This includes such complex events as mating rituals, aggression displays, and hunting patterns. These patterns are highly variable and complex in social mammals, whereas they tend to be fairly fixed and simpler in nonmammalian species.

In social mammals, life is remembered and experienced as a series of events. This is evident in the ethological literature, where events may be regarded as the basic units of experience. Thus a dog tends to remember the specific details of such things as fights, rivalries, displays of aggression, attempts at mating, and patterns of socialization. In the memory system, this plays out as a time-marked series of events bound into discrete episodes. To the participants, the visual memory of a fight is arbitrarily broken up into a series of discrete frames, each of which has an internal event structure, whereas in real time, the action is continuous. The visual image is also interpreted in terms of other crucial information conveyed by other channels, such as sound, taste, smell, pain, balance, muscles, joints, tendons, and the sense of gravity. When all of these are taken into account, the event can be seen as a very complex pattern-recognition problem that requires large-scale amodal integration over time.

Amodal integration of complex social events is a fairly common capacity in mammals, and it is never a question of simply perceiving them, but also of selectively remembering them. Even though they are not cleanly separated from the events that precede and follow them, complex social events are parsed within the animal's stream of experience and remembered as discrete entities organized in terms of their social significance. In the case of a dogfight, the event is remembered by each protagonist as an encounter with a specific dog, in a specific place and time, with a specific outcome that affects all future interactions between them, and possibly with third-party observers as well.

The immense theoretical challenge such complex perceptions present becomes clearer when one considers the current precarious state of neural binding theory. We have enough difficulty explaining how the nervous system might bind color to form in shaping the static image of an object, or how the pattern of optical flow might relate to the control of locomotion. However, the perception of social events involves multiframe integration, that is, integration across time as well as modality. Such perceptions also involve instantaneous integration of inputs from several sensory modalities. Understanding an event as complex as a dogfight, from the viewpoint of either competitor, requires the integration of concurrent asynchronous inputs from vision, audition, olfaction, taste, and pain receptors, not to mention a number of internal channels conveying body sensations. The asynchrony in particular is difficult to explain, and large-scale neural integration on this scale is well beyond the explanatory power of any current version of binding theory. Yet it is commonplace among all higher vertebrates.

Incoming sensory channels are never perfectly synchronized in such events. What a dog sees may or may not coincide with what it hears or feels, and this is not a trivial problem. For such a complex event to be encoded by the brain as a unified episode, the brain must have computational powers that we cannot yet model with any degree of accuracy. We are only beginning to understand the computational challenges underlying the resolution of animate motion, and social events such as competitive mating or resolving conflict involve many simultaneous sources of animate motion acting in complex scenarios. Yet all mammalian species, and many species of birds and reptiles, seem able to perceive social events as a matter of routine.

Moreover, these event perceptions are almost never remembered as isolated events. They are batched into "episodes." One of the major problems in batching events is locating the boundaries of each event. The temporal boundaries of such episodes are rarely fixed or predictable, and their internal temporal and spatial structure is rarely constant across episodes. However, the boundaries of the event are crucial to its accurate storage in memory, and the brain must establish its beginning and termination time, as well as its relevance to the larger social scenarios that are under way. For instance, a dogfight might have long-term implications for the dominance hierarchy in a canine society, as well as a dog's relationships with every other dog in the pack. This must be realized immediately or there will be fatal consequences. Remarkably, these tremendous interpretative challenges are met routinely. The boundaries of the events are perceived instantly and clearly, and incidents preceding or following an event are rarely confused with the event itself.

Largely depending on its emotional valence and outcome, an event may or may not be stored in memory as an episode. The episode is the "atom" of experience for most social mammals. A social life is lived, and remembered, in terms of episodes. And despite the complex structure of episodes, many species with small brains can perform this kind of experiential sorting of the remembered past. They batch past events into small packets of experience, noticing and recording specific features of social events for future use.

This capacity plays out in social organization, generating hierarchies of social relationships that some ethologists compare to human culture. "Episodic" cultures based on a set of episode-by-episode reactions and interactions are often quite complex. The cultures of many social mammalian species, including especially canines and primates, reflect their ability to resolve social events (such as grooming episodes and changing alliances) accurately in memory. These remembered episodes form the basis of social life and are predictive of future social behavior.

Such animal societies are episodic in nature because despite the high resolving power of their social event perceptions, they live largely in the concrete present and are usually very poor at communicating with one another except through species-universal, stereotyped signals. This leaves most knowledge locked into the individual brain. Individual animals cannot convert their social perceptions into expressions that can capture and transfer specific information. They also lack voluntary recall from memory. Thus, they depend on the immediate environment to trigger memories of past episodes. While such species are often very good perceivers of social events in the moment, and can understand shifting alliances and changing hierarchies of dominance, they are poor at representing events.

This seems to be primarily due to a failure of action, not of perception. They know, but cannot express. This prevents the creation of transmissible social knowledge networks, even simple networks of very low fidelity. Judging from the archaeological record, such powers emerged only with archaic hominids, who were the first species to leave behind archaeological evidence of a cooperative, group-oriented cognitive strategy in which skills and knowledge could be accumulated and transmitted over many generations. Mimesis was the vehicle for this, the product of a change in the structure of motor control by which the primate apparatus of event perception was merged with the most abstract regions of the motor brain.

14.6 Conclusion

Imitation is a large subject, and yet from an evolutionary standpoint, perhaps it is not large enough to explain its own evolution. Broadly speaking, imitation is the deliberate copying, or reduplication, of behavior, especially the behavior of others, with an understanding of their intent. However, accurate reduplication is not necessarily a useful or adaptive trait. Evolution is driven by the conditions of life in specific ecologies, and function is an all-important consideration in the emergence of any new capacity in a species. Why would a species have evolved a capacity for the accurate re-duplication of another's behavior? What vital function would it serve for the species, and how would it enhance the reproductive fitness of individuals with such traits?

Accurate imitation is so highly developed in humans that it stands out as one of the defining characteristics of the human mind. Mimesis is a coherent social adaptation, and it makes sense in terms of an all-encompassing survival strategy for archaic hominids in the ecology in which they evolved. It also makes sense in terms of its vestiges in modern human life. According to the principle of conservation of gains, evolved traits tend to endure, provided that they still serve well in their niche. Mimesis endures in human life; language did not negate its value. Language came later and made mimetic communication far more exact. However, the evolution of mimetic cognition and culture before language is probably the best explanation for the underlying metaphoric "style" that governs both language and thought (Lakoff & Johnson, 1980; Fauconnier & Turner, 2002).

Mimesis is a more inclusive notion than imitation and speaks to the creative or generative aspect of human culture. It encompasses many forms of analog communication, skill, and social coordination, as well as accurate means-ends imitation. This does not necessarily imply that imitation, gesture, mime, and skill are all direct products of a novel hominid "mimetic module," or that all these capacities should emanate from the same brain regions. On the contrary, mimesis is complex and interconnected with many brain systems. Radical evolutionary adaptations, especially those that lead to new species, tend to occur simultaneously on many fronts and usually involve an entire "suite" of traits, including many aspects of anatomy and function. This was surely true of archaic hominids. They evolved on many fronts, including gross anatomy, cranial morphology, facial expression, posture and locomotion, body hair, heat dissipation, diet, energy distribution, and so on. The evolution of the brain also reflected this pattern. As hominids evolved, the primate brain changed in both size and connectivity on many concurrently changing fronts.

The cognitive aspects of hominid evolution were not independent of these physical changes, nor could they have occurred in a vacuum. Imitation and mimesis were products of complex evolutionary changes in both the brain and society, and it would be unrealistic to expect that these traits are highly developed in humans because of a straightforward change in brain anatomy or cognitive organization. These capacities emerged gradually out of a basically primate brain design, in an evolving cultural-cognitive network, and they occurred very high in the system. The most credible way to model such systems is to understand that any changes on this level took place within a larger functional context and were mostly focused on nonmodular, supramodal, and domain-general capacities of maximum flexibility.

It is doubtful whether our exceptional capacity for means-ends imitation is dissociable from mimesis in human evolution. Given the interconnectedness of communication and skill, the unique human capacity for accurate imitation must have evolved as an aspect of a wider adaptation for mimetic communication. The strongest evidence for this is that in primates the uses of emulation and imitation seem to be tied to emotionality and socialization, not just to toolmaking and problem solving. Where imitative capacity occurs in mammals, even in rudimentary form, it usually does so in the most social species. It shares some properties with social-cognitive phenomena such as emotional contagion, empathy, shared attention, and the rapid communication of group emotional reactions, such as panic or alarm. The common group dynamic is the spread of behavioral patterns through the group.

Mean-ends imitation is an effective mechanism for the transmission of simple skills. It can also account for the replication of local traditions and customs, to a degree. However, in its conventional definition it cannot account for the creativity or genesis of human culture, especially in its representational aspects. Yet there is reason to link the evolution of imitation with the emergence of gesture, mime, and skill. Human beings have a creative capacity that manifests itself in group cognition and that generates shared representational cultures. This includes body language, reciprocal emotional displays, and specific skill sets, such as athletic skills. These are all highly variable across cultures. The word "mimesis" captures this wider urge to generate culture, whereas the word "imitation" connotes the replication and transmission of existing patterns, not the creation of new ones, and leaves out the social dimension captured by gesture and role-playing. Mimesis places more emphasis on the expressive and social aspects of action and less on the accurate reproduction of means and ends, but it includes the latter.

Art and ritual are two of the continuing manifestations of mimesis in human society. Even in its daily uses, the human process of mimetic representation can come very close to art. In fact, this use of the term "mimesis" comes close to Eric Auerbach's use of the same term in the context of literary representation; this is no coincidence, since language has deep mimetic roots. All human beings represent reality through mimetic means, and language is scaffolded on mimesis in a child's development (Nelson, 1996). We are mimetic creatures. We identify mimetically with our tribal group and have an irresistible tendency to conform to its norms. Conformity, on all levels of overt behavior, is one of our signature traits, conferred by a universal mimetic tendency. We conform not only to the immediate patterns of our social group but also to the internalized ideals and archetypes of that group. And those archetypes shape the roles we tend to play during life, as actors in our own dramatic productions.[2]

2. See comments on this chapter by Christiansen (vol. 2, ch. 19.8, p. 391) and by Blackmore (vol. 2, ch. 19.9, p. 396). ED.

15 Imitation and Rationality

Robert Sugden

15.1 Introduction

Conventional economic theory depends heavily on assumptions about the rationality of economic agents. In this chapter, I appraise a theoretical strategy that has been offered as a justification of those assumptions. This strategy adapts Richard Dawkins's (1976, pp. 203–215) idea that human behavior is governed by "memes" that are transmitted from brain to brain through processes of imitation. It treats the rationality of individual agents, not as a property that is intrinsic to human psychology, but as one that emerges through the mutual adaptation of behavior among individuals who have certain tendencies to imitate one another. I argue that this strategy, in the form in which it has so far been used in economics, fails.

15.2 The Evolutionary Turn in Economic Theory

Economic theory has always been vulnerable to the criticism that human beings are not naturally rational in the ways that the theory assumes. Yet, for years, most economists brushed aside such criticisms, asserting that theories based on rationality assumptions generated successful predictions across a wide range of human behavior. There was an element of bluff in that response. Over the past two decades, this bluff has been called by the development of experimental tests of economic theories of decision making. These have revealed many ways in which human decision making deviates systematically from the predictions of conventional rational-choice theories.[1] One effect of these developments has been to prompt economists who favor rational-choice theories to seek reasons why such theories might predict well in the situations in which they are customarily applied, but not in the experimental environments in which they fail.

1. See Camerer (1995) for a survey of this evidence.

In the face of these concerns about the validity of rationality assumptions, many economists have been impressed by the apparent success of rational-choice models of animal behavior in biology. A body of work in theoretical biology, pioneered by John Maynard Smith and G. R. Price (1973), has modeled animal behavior as if it was the solution to the problem of maximizing each animal's reproductive success. Many of the situations studied are remarkably similar to decision problems analyzed in economics. For example, a bird that needs to find food each day for its young may have a range of alternative foraging strategies. If some areas in which food can be collected are richer in food while others are closer to the nest, the selection of the most fitness-enhancing strategy is a classic economic problem of optimization. Other problems animals face, such as when to escalate a conflict and when to back down, are analogous to strategic interaction games. In many such cases, animal behavior can be explained by assuming that each animal acts in the way that maximizes its own reproductive success, given the environment in which it is operating and the behavior that can be expected of other animals. The mechanism that induces these forms of maximizing behavior is natural selection.

What has all this to do with economics? In most of the situations in which economists use rational-choice theory, it is not credible to suppose that the rationality that is attributed to human behavior is a direct product of *biological* natural selection. Biologically, we human beings are adapted to respond to the environment that our ancestors faced in the distant past; but economics assumes that our behavior is a rational response to the problems we *now* face. For economists, evolutionary biology is attractive, not as a theory of economic behavior, but as a demonstration that apparent rationality can be the result of blind processes of selection. The thought is that the rationality of human actors, as represented in economic theory, might be the product of some process of cultural selection or trial-and-error learning, *analogous with* natural selection in biology.

If that could be shown, economists would be able to argue that rational-choice theory applies only in situations in which the relevant selection mechanisms are active. That might make it possible to define the domain of the theory in such a way as to include many forms of behavior in markets while excluding many laboratory experiments.[2] But if the use of evo-

---

2. Some leading experimental economists have used this line of reasoning to argue that economic theory is intended to predict the behavior in markets of *experienced* traders. Experimental tests of economic theory are accepted as valid only if subjects have been given adequate experience in the tasks they perform (see e.g., Plott, 1996).

lutionary models in economics is to be justified, we need to know which mechanisms in the world of human economic behavior are supposed to be analogous with which biological mechanisms. And we need to be convinced that there are the right kinds of isomorphism between the two sets of mechanisms. Economists have been much more ready to use evolutionary models than to consider, except at the most superficial level, what makes these models valid as representations of real human behavior.[3] Insofar as this issue has been addressed at all, one of the more common ways of justifying evolutionary modeling in economics has been to argue that the mechanism of selection is one of imitation.

15.3 Imitation as a Selection Mechanism

In this chapter I am concerned with a particular version of the argument that rationality is selected through imitation: the argument presented by Ken Binmore (1994, 1998). Binmore's approach is inspired by Dawkins's (1976) concept of a meme. The idea rests on a simple but radical analogy with biological natural selection. In biology, the apparent rationality of animal behavior is as if it was directed toward the objective of maximizing reproductive success, measured by the replication of genes. Why is the replication of genes the objective? Because an animal's behavior is governed by the genes it carries, and because natural selection *is* the differential replication of genes. So (the argument goes), if social evolution is to be understood through the analogy of biological evolution, we need to find what, in the social selection of behavior, plays the role of a gene. If selection takes place through imitation, what we are looking for is something that is transmitted by imitation—a meme. (The word was coined by Dawkins to suggest both imitation—the Greek root is *mimeomai*, to imitate—and an analogy with gene.) The closest Dawkins comes to a description of what a meme is is this:

Examples of memes are tunes, ideas, catch-phrases, clothes fashions, ways of making pots or of building arches. Just as genes propagate themselves in the gene pool by leaping from body to body via sperms or eggs, so memes propagate themselves in the meme pool by leaping from brain to brain via a process which, in the broad sense, can be called imitation. (Dawkins, 1976, p. 206)

In the analogy of biological natural selection, we should expect to find that social selection favors those forms of behavior that maximize the

3. I substantiate this criticism in Sugden (2001).

replication of their own memes. Binmore takes up Dawkins's idea and uses it to attempt to explain the supposed tendency for human beings to act as if they had consistent preferences of the kind assumed by rational-choice theory.

Binmore's argument is part of a massive treatise that offers a social evolutionary explanation of certain normative principles of justice. Binmore claims to offer a naturalistic account of why, as a matter of sociological fact, these principles are treated as having normative force in a wide range of human societies. The argument depends crucially on modes of analysis that are taken from rational-choice theory. It would be inconsistent for Binmore, as a philosophical naturalist, to appeal to the supposed normative force of rationality principles. Instead, he begins by declaring that if it is valid to model people as maximizers—as his own theory will do—this can only be because "evolutionary forces, biological, social, and economic, [are] responsible for getting things maximized" (Binmore, 1994, p. 20).

He then appeals to Dawkins's analysis of memes, arguing that there is a social evolutionary process that eliminates "inferior" memes:

In this story, people are reduced to ciphers. Their role is simply to carry memes in their heads, rather as we carry the virus for the common cold in the winter. However, to an observer, it will seem as though the infected agent is acting in his own self-interest, provided that the notion of self-interest is interpreted as being *whatever makes the bearer of a meme a locus for replication of the meme to other heads.* (Binmore, 1994, p. 20)

Thus, according to Binmore, there is a tendency for social selection to favor behavior that is as if it was motivated by consistent preferences:

the practical reasons for thinking consistency an important characteristic of a decision-maker cannot be lightly rejected. People who are inconsistent will necessarily sometimes be wrong and hence will be at a disadvantage compared to those who are always right. And evolution will not be kind to memes that inhibit their own replication. (Binmore, 1994, p. 27)

Notice that this argument does not presuppose any criterion of successful behavior which then directs imitation. The primitive concept in the theory is imitation itself. Whatever tends to be imitated thereby has a tendency to be replicated. When the process of selection has run its course, human behavior will be as if it was motivated by a criterion of success. But in this state of affairs, "successful" actions are not imitated because they are successful; *being imitated is what they are successful at.*

Binmore's meme-based argument should not be confused with other, less radical claims about the connections between imitation and rationality. In particular, it must be distinguished from claims about imitation that presuppose particular criteria of success. For example, if we assume that individuals are motivated by particular preferences, there may be circumstances in which imitation is effective as a rule of thumb for satisfying those preferences in an uncertain environment. (Consider the rule sometimes recommended to tourists, of choosing restaurants that appear to be well patronized by local people.) Imitation may also appear in evolutionary models as the mechanism by which selection works, given some criterion of success that is independent of imitation. For example, many applications of evolutionary game theory in economics presuppose that utility indices can be attached to the outcomes of games that are played recurrently in a population. Evolutionary selection in such models is simply a tendency for behavior to gravitate toward those strategies that maximize expected utility. Imitation—or more precisely, a tendency disproportionately to imitate the behavior of individuals who have been seen to be relatively successful in gaining utility—is often suggested as a mechanism that might lie behind this gravitation.[4]

Social evolutionary models that depend on assumed criteria of success have many applications, but no such model can provide a justification for the assumptions of rational-choice theory. The reason is simple. The most fundamental assumptions of rational-choice theory are *equivalent to* the assumption that there is a one-dimensional criterion of success for human action (that is, expected utility). In the absence of arguments from rationality, it is not clear what grounds we have for supposing there to be any such criterion. On the face of it, any human action can be described on many different dimensions. What makes all these different dimensions commensurable? The answer given by rational-choice theory is that commensurability is a product of rationality, and that the scale of measurement is that of subjective but rationally consistent preference. If we want an evolutionary *explanation* for the (supposed) fact that human beings are rational in the sense of rational-choice theory, we have to find a criterion of "success" that does not presuppose internally consistent preferences. We then have to show that selection tends to eliminate behavior that fails to maximize success, so defined. That is what Binmore claims to do.

4. Weibull (1995) presents a family of imitation models of this kind.

15.4 The Rational Replicator

According to Dawkins, genes are selfish. In his metaphor, animals are "survival machines" built by genes (1976/1989, p. 21). It is as if genes are the active agents in the biological world, each gene rationally seeking to replicate itself. Similarly, we are asked to think of memes as the active agents in the world of human culture, rationally seeking to replicate themselves in the medium of human minds. As a first step in analyzing Binmore's argument, it is useful to be clear about the sense in which genes and memes can be said to be (as if) rational.

Consider the following abstract model of replication. (Models of this kind are known in mathematical biology as Lotka-Volterra models.) Suppose there are things called *replicators*. At this stage, I do not specify what replicators are, but the concept is intended to encompass both genes and memes. These replicators come in m discrete *types*. There is a *population* made up of very large numbers of replicators of these various types. At any moment in time t, for each type i, there is a *frequency* $p_i[t]$, so that $\Sigma_i p_i[t] = 1$; this represents the proportion of the whole population of replicators that is of type i. The frequency distribution $(p_1[t], \ldots, p_m[t])$ is denoted by $p[t]$. Each replicator is capable of creating copies of itself (but not of other types of replicator). The *replication rate* of any type at any given time is defined as the average rate, per unit of time, at which each replicator of that type is creating copies of itself. (If replicators can "die," deaths are treated as negative copies.) Suppose that the replication rate of each type varies continuously with the distribution of types in the population, but otherwise is independent of time. Then, for each type i, we can define a continuous *replication function* $r_i(.)$ so that the replication rate of type i at time t is $r_i(p[t])$. We have now fully specified the dynamic process by which, starting from any arbitrary $p[0]$, the distribution of types in the population changes over time; this is the process of *replicator dynamics* (P. Taylor and Jonker, 1978).

A *rest point* in this process is a frequency distribution that persists indefinitely. A rest point p^* is *stable* if, starting from any frequency distribution sufficiently close to p^*, the dynamic process converges to p^*. Let us say that type k *survives* at a stable rest point p^* if $p_k^* > 0$. And let us say that type k *maximizes replication* at p if, for all i, $r_k(p) \geq r_i(p)$. It is easy to see that for any stable rest point p^*, any given type k survives at p^* only if it maximizes replication at p^*. (Once the path of $p[t]$ has come close to p^*, any type that maximizes replication will gradually increase its frequency relative to any type that does not.)

So, if the population of replicators is in a state of stable equilibrium, the replicators that survive in that population "act" in ways that maximize their own replication rates. In this special sense, replicators are acting as if they are rational. Thus, if behavior in some animal species is determined by genes, and if genes are replicators in the sense of the model I have set out, then in a state of equilibrium, *genes* are acting as if they are rational. This corresponds with Dawkins's picture of the "selfish gene." Similarly, if human actions in the domain of economics are determined by memes, and if memes are replicators in the sense of the model, then *memes* are acting as if they are rational. But what does the rationality of genes or memes tell us about the rationality of *actions*?

15.5 Replicators and Actors: The Simplest Model

In order to answer this question, we need a model that includes *actors* as well as replicators. In theories of animal behavior, the actors are individual animals; in Binmore's theory, they are individual human beings. The model has to represent both the mechanism by which replicators determine actors' choices among actions, and the mechanism by which the chosen actions determine the rates at which replicators replicate.

I present three alternative models of this causal loop. These models are offered as thought experiments, illustrating theoretical possibilities. I must emphasize that I am not proposing a theory of memes; I am examining claims that other theorists have made.

To keep things as simple as possible, the recurrent problems I consider are games against nature (that is, decision problems that do not involve strategic interaction between individuals). In all my models, I assume a finite set of *consequences*, X. A *decision problem* is a nonempty subset of X. A typical decision problem will be written as $\{x_1, \ldots, x_n\}$. The interpretation is that any actor who faces this problem has to choose one action from a set of n alternative actions; each action leads to a distinct consequence.

Conventional rational-choice theory requires that an individual's choices reveal a preference ordering among possible consequences. The issue to be investigated is whether selection at the level of replicators induces this form of rationality at the level of actors. In a model in which rationality is to have some chance of being induced by imitation, preference must be treated as a property of a population of actors, not as a property of any individual actor. So the idea to be tested is whether through mutual imitation within such a population, all the members of that population converge on a single pattern of choice that can be represented by a preference ordering.

Consider any fixed decision problem $\{x_1, \ldots, x_n\}$ faced recurrently by individual actors in a large population. At any time t, for each consequence x_j, there is a *decision probability* $P_j[t]$; this is the probability that in a randomly selected instance of the decision problem within the population of actors, that consequence will be chosen. Obviously, $\Sigma_j P_j[t] = 1$ at all t. Decision probabilities in the population of actors are assumed to be determined in some way by the relative frequencies of different types of replicators in a *replicator pool*. In turn, the replication rates of the different types of replicators are determined by the consequences that are chosen in the population of actors, and hence by the decision probabilities.

At this level of generality, the modeling framework can be interpreted either in terms of biological natural selection or in terms of imitation. If it is interpreted biologically, the replicators are genes, and each actor's actions are determined by the genes that it carries. If it is interpreted in terms of imitation, the actors are human beings, the replicators are memes, and each individual's actions are determined by the memes that he or she carries.

I begin with the simplest possible model. This can be interpreted as a highly simplified representation of how animal behavior is determined by biological natural selection.[5] It rests on two crucial (and unrealistic) assumptions.

The first assumption is that there is a one-to-one correspondence between genes and actions. The recurrent decision problem is a choice from an opportunity set of n consequences, $\{x_1, \ldots, x_n\}$. One piece of genetic code is responsible for determining which consequence is chosen in this problem, and is responsible for nothing else. There are exactly n alternative versions of this genetic code; each actor carries one and only one of these codes. I call these alternative codes "genes." (Biologists might prefer to call them alternative "alleles" of a single gene.) Each gene is associated with a distinct consequence in the decision problem, in such a way that an actor carrying the gene for some particular consequence invariably chooses the action that leads to that consequence.

The second assumption is that reproduction is asexual. When an actor reproduces, it produces offspring that are genetic copies of itself.

Given these assumptions, we can use the same indices $j = 1, \ldots, n$ for consequences and genes; the jth gene is defined as the gene that programs the choice of consequence x_j. Since each actor carries one and only one

5. I draw on Binmore's (1992, pp. 414–422) explanation of replicator dynamics as a representation of the life cycle of an imaginary (and biologically peculiar) species.

gene, and since each gene programs a distinct action, the frequency p_j of the jth gene in the gene pool is identically equal to the decision probability P_j for the consequence x_j. This requires that the dynamics of replication within the gene pool be reflected exactly in the dynamics of changes in decision probabilities.

Now consider how decision probabilities induce changes in the gene pool. For each consequence x_j, we can define a measure $R(x_j)$ of the *reproductive success* conferred on the actor by that consequence. Reproductive success is to be understood in terms of expected numbers of offspring. More precisely, averaging over all those actors that are genetically programmed to choose x_j, $R(x_j)$ is the rate at which these actors are producing genetic copies of themselves (with deaths counting as negative copies). I assume that for each x_j, the value of $R(x_j)$ is constant over time and independent of other consequences in the opportunity set.

In this model, reproductive success for an actor corresponds with replication of the gene that the actor carries, since reproduction is the creation of exact genetic copies. Thus, the replication rate of the jth gene is equal to $R(x_j)$. This rate is constant over time and is independent of the frequencies of the different types of gene in the gene pool. Clearly, genes with higher replication rates will increase in relative frequency in the gene pool at the expense of those with lower rates. Thus, if one consequence, say x_k, leads to strictly greater reproductive success than every other consequence, the relative frequency of the corresponding gene will increase continuously. So the dynamics of the gene pool will converge to a stable rest point at which only the kth gene survives. Correspondingly, the dynamics of decision probabilities will converge to a stable rest point at which x_k is chosen with a probability of 1. (If two or more consequences have equal reproductive success, and greater reproductive success than all other consequences, the sum of the decision probabilities for the consequences with greatest reproductive success will converge to 1.)

The implication is that after natural selection has run its course, actors behave as if they are rational in the sense of rational-choice theory. For each consequence x_j, there is an index $R(x_j)$ that is independent of the particular decision problem in which that consequence is located. In the long run, actors behave as if they are maximizing the value of this index. Thus, this index plays the role of a utility index in rational-choice theory; the ranking of consequences generated by this index plays the role of a preference ordering.

This model shows one way in which imitation could conceivably induce rationality. *If* the relationship between memes and actions in the real world was isomorphic with the relationship between genes and actions in this model, *then* selection operating on memes would induce rationality on the part of actors.

Here is a stylized example of how this could come about. Consider an artisan trade before the industrial revolution. The unit of organization is the workshop, owned by a master craftsman. Young men enter the trade by being apprenticed to a master, from whom they learn the skills of the craft; they then work on their own account. Let $\{x_1, \ldots, x_n\}$ be a set of alternative techniques. Suppose that each craftsman uses just one of these techniques; his apprentices learn this technique by imitation and then use it themselves. In this model, the master craftsmen are actors and the techniques are actions. "Reproductive success" for a master is measured by the number of his former apprentices who set up as masters. For each technique x_j, we can define an index $R(x_j)$ that measures the reproductive success (as just defined) of masters who use that technique, and hence also the replication rate for that technique. In the long run, the behavior of masters in choosing among techniques will be as if they are trying to maximize the value of the function $R(.)$. This pattern of behavior is rational in the sense of rational-choice theory (it maximizes *something*), even though it is not necessarily rational in the sense of maximizing each master's profits.

So this first model offers some support for the hypothesis that imitation induces rationality. However, the model represents a very simple relationship between replicators and actions. The relationship is one-to-one at both sides of the causal loop. Each replicator is the cause of one and only one action, and each action is capable of creating copies only of the replicator that causes it. In a model with this structure, "rationality" in the domain of replicators *does* induce rationality in the domain of actions. But what if the relationship between replicators and actions is not quite so simple?

15.6   Replicators and Actors: Sexual Reproduction

My second model, like the first, is based on biology. The only change I make to the model presented in section 15.5 is to introduce sexual reproduction.

In a sexually reproducing (diploid) species, each individual's genetic inheritance comes from two parents. Because of this fact, we must distinguish between *genes* (understood as the units of genetic material that are transmitted through reproduction) and *genotypes* (that is, alternative bundles of genes that an individual can inherit). To keep the model as simple as possible, I consider only one genetic "locus." Each actor inherits two genes, one from each parent. On the assumption that mating is random, each of these two genes can be thought of as resulting from a random draw from the same gene pool. The resulting *pair* of genes is the actor's genotype. I assume that each actor's behavior is uniquely determined by its genotype. As in the first model, each consequence has an associated measure of reproductive success, interpreted as the expected number of offspring for an actor who experiences it. However, to each of its offspring, each parent passes on only *one* of its pair of genes; which of the two is passed on is determined by a random process. In this model, selection does not necessarily eliminate behavior that fails to maximize reproductive success. The following example shows why.

Suppose there are just two genes: A and a. This gives three alternative genotypes: AA, Aa, and aa. (AA and aa are *homozygous*; Aa is *heterozygous*.) Consider the decision problem $\{x_1, x_2, x_3\}$. Suppose that actors with the AA genotype choose x_1, that Aa actors choose x_2, and that aa actors choose x_3. The decision probabilities for actions are uniquely determined by the relative frequencies of genes in the gene pool, but the link between the two probability distributions is more complicated than in the first model. Specifically, let q be the proportion of A genes in the gene pool. Then the decision probabilities for consequences x_1, x_2, x_3 are given by $P_1 = q^2$, $P_2 = 2q(1 - q)$, and $P_3 = (1 - q)^2$.

Now suppose that $R(x_2) > R(x_1) > R(x_3)$. Recall that $R(x_j)$ measures the contribution made by x_j to the reproductive success *of the actor who chooses it*. So the assumption is that x_2 is the consequence that maximizes reproductive success. But actors who choose x_2 carry the genotype Aa. When they reproduce, they create copies of *both* genes. Thus, both genes will survive in the gene pool and, as a consequence of this, all three genotypes will persist, and all three consequences will be chosen with positive probability. It is even possible that the consequence with the largest decision probability is not the one with the greatest reproductive success. For example, suppose that $R(x_1)/R(x_2) = 0.9$ and $R(x_3)/R(x_2) = 0.2$. It turns out that in equilibrium, $q = 0.89$,[6] which implies the decision probabilities $P_1 = 0.79$, $P_2 = 0.20$, $P_3 = 0.01$.

The implication of this model is that biological natural selection does not necessarily favor *actions* that maximize the reproductive success *of actors*. The evolution of decision probabilities can gravitate toward a stable rest point at which each of several actions is chosen with positive probability, even though these actions have very different degrees of reproductive

6. The general result is that $q/(1 - q) = [1 - R(x_3)/R(x_2)]/[1 - R(x_1)/R(x_2)]$. This is derived from the condition that copies of the genes A and a are made in the ratio $q : (1 - q)$, thus conserving the ratio in the gene pool.

success. The less successful actions survive, not because of *their* propensity to replicate the genes that cause them to be chosen, but because those genes are also replicated by other, more successful actions. This biological mechanism accounts for the genetic transmission of certain diseases, such as sickle-cell anemia. In this type of case, the aa genotype leads to the disease, but the Aa genotype gives its carriers some gain in fitness relative to those who carry AA.

This paradoxical result is entirely consistent with the idea of the "rational replicator." More precisely, the equilibrium I have described for the two-gene model is a stable rest point in the dynamics of the gene pool, at which both genes survive. At this rest point, the two genes have equal rates of replication. Thus, it is as if the surviving *genes* are maximizing their own replication. But rationality (in this sense) at the level of genes does not induce rationality at the level of actors. The source of the paradox is that the choice of an action is determined, not by a single gene, but by a combination of genes, and that each action has a tendency to replicate each of the genes in the combination that leads to its being chosen. Why should the same not be true of memes?

Seen in relation to the theoretical strategy of explaining economic rationality as the result of selection at the level of memes, this result is discouraging. That strategy treats both the concept of a meme and the process by which memes replicate as black boxes. All that is observed is the behavior of actors in response to decision problems. The objective of the theory is to explain that behavior. The theory depends on the hypothesis that meme selection mechanisms *in general* favor behavior that is rational at the level of actors. But it seems that that hypothesis is false.

15.7 Replicators and Actors: Mutual Imitation

In the second model—the model with sexual reproduction—the hypothesis that selection always induces rationality fails because the distribution of replicators in the replicator pool does not map in a straightforward way onto decision probabilities. My final model shows the effects of disrupting the other side of the simple causal loop of the model presented in section 15.5.

The model I now present is specifically intended to represent imitation among human beings.[7] The population of actors is taken to be fixed; actors

7. A more general form of the model discussed in this section, applying to choice under uncertainty and not formulated in the language of memes, is presented by Cubitt and Sugden (1998).

do not reproduce or die. As in the first model, there is a one-to-one correspondence between replicators and consequences. At any given time, each actor carries one and only one meme. Actors face the decision problem recurrently. For each consequence x_j there is a distinct meme such that, if an actor who is currently carrying that meme confronts the decision problem, she chooses x_j. Thus, the frequency distribution of memes in the meme pool corresponds exactly with the distribution of decision probabilities in the population of actors. The difference from the first model concerns the mechanism by which memes replicate. The replication mechanism in the present model is intended to represent a fundamental property of imitation—that imitation involves two actors, the actor who imitates and the actor who is imitated. It works as follows.

At random intervals, ordered pairs of actors drawn at random from the population meet one another. One actor is the *reviewer*, the other the *comparator*. The reviewer compares the consequence that she experiences, say x_j, with the consequence that the comparator experiences, say x_k. This comparison leads to one of two results. Either the reviewer imitates the comparator, or she does not. In terms of memes, either the reviewer comes to carry the meme for x_k, or she continues to carry the meme for x_j. In the former case, the comparator's meme has replicated itself (and the reviewer's original meme has been displaced).

In the biological models presented in sections 15.5 and 15.6, reproductive success is a property of consequences. In those models, each index of reproductive success $R(x_j)$ is a measure of the degree to which the occurrence of x_j produces offspring for the actor who experiences that consequence. Thus $R(x_j)$ also measures the degree to which the occurrence of x_j produces copies of the gene or genes carried by that actor. To find an analogue of $R(.)$ in the present model, we need to consider how the occurrence of particular consequences induces changes in the composition of the meme pool. The crucial feature of this model is that such changes are induced, not by the occurrence of single consequences, but by the occurrence of pairs of consequences.

For any ordered pair of consequences (x_j, x_k), we can define an *imitation probability* $M(x_j, x_k)$. This is the probability that, conditional on a meeting between a reviewer carrying the meme for x_j and a comparator carrying the meme for x_k, the reviewer comes to carry the comparator's meme (that is, the reviewer imitates the comparator's pattern of behavior). Note that because meetings are random, the probability of a meeting (in any given short period of time) between a reviewer carrying the jth meme and a comparator carrying the kth meme is equal to the probability of a meeting between a reviewer carrying the kth meme and a comparator carrying the jth meme. Thus, averaging over both types of meeting, we can treat $[M(x_k, x_j) - M(x_j, x_k)]/2$ as a measure of *net growth* in the numbers of carriers of the jth meme, per meeting between a carrier of one meme and a carrier of the other. To simplify the notation, I define a function $\varphi(.,.)$ so that $\varphi(x_j, x_k) = [M(x_k, x_j) - M(x_j, x_k)]/2$. Note that, by construction, this function is skew-symmetric; for all j and k, $\varphi(x_k, x_j) = -\varphi(x_j, x_k)$.

Clearly, if the decision problem contains only two consequences, x_1 and x_2, the process of imitation will favor whichever consequence has positive net growth in comparisons between the two of them. If, say, $\varphi(x_1, x_2) > 0$, P_1 will increase continuously at the expense of P_2; the dynamics will lead toward a stable rest point at which $P_1 = 1$. Thus, *in relation to any given binary decision problem*, this model implies that imitation selects behavior that is as if it was governed by a preference relation; that preference relation can be derived from $\varphi(.,.)$ by reading each $\varphi(x_j, x_k) > 0$ as "x_j is preferred to x_k."

However, this does not imply that behavior in decision problems *in general* has the properties postulated by rational-choice theory. The problem is that rational-choice theory requires the preference relation to be transitive. Nothing that I have said so far imposes the corresponding requirement on the process of imitation. For example, suppose there are three consequences x_1, x_2 and x_3 so that $\varphi(x_1, x_2) > 0$, $\varphi(x_2, x_3) > 0$ and $\varphi(x_3, x_1) > 0$. In words, comparisons between x_1 and x_2 induce a net growth in the number of actors choosing x_1; comparisons between x_2 and x_3 induce a net growth in the number of actors choosing x_2; and comparisons between x_3 and x_1 induce a net growth in the number of actors choosing x_3. When we bring together the implications of the model for the three binary decision problems $\{x_1, x_2\}$, $\{x_2, x_3\}$ and $\{x_3, x_1\}$, we find that these implications are not consistent with any preference ordering over the consequences x_1, x_2, x_3.

What happens if the decision problem is $\{x_1, x_2, x_3\}$? In this case, the dynamics of the model typically induce cycles in the values of the decision probabilities. These probabilities change continuously, but never converge to any rest point. From the viewpoint of rational-choice theory, such a pattern of behavior *at the level of actors* is inexplicable. At the level of memes, it might be said, these cycles make perfectly good sense. They reflect the fact that given the assumed properties of the imitation process, the rate of replication for any one meme depends on the relative frequencies of all three memes in the meme pool. But, in relation to the argument of this chapter, that is beside the point. The question at issue is whether selection acting on memes induces rationality at the level of actors—to which the answer must be "not necessarily."

To this, it might be objected that the cyclical pattern of imitation that I have hypothesized is incoherent or pathological, but this objection makes an implicit appeal to a criterion of "success" for actions other than imitation itself. Obviously, if we *presuppose* a one-dimensional measure of success for actions, and interpret imitation as the imitation *of success*, so defined, then cyclical patterns are not coherent. However, such a presupposition is incompatible with the theoretical strategy that I am appraising. It is an essential part of that strategy that no prior measure of success be assumed. So the implications to be drawn from this model are similar to those to be drawn from the model of sexual reproduction. Selection at the level of memes does not necessarily induce rationality at the level of actors.

15.8 Conclusion

Dawkins's original discussion of memes, written as a postscript to a book about natural selection in biology, is a heady mix of brilliant insight, imaginative speculation, and scientific hubris. (The hubris comes in the scarcely veiled suggestion that the investigation of memes is an intellectual greenfield site, ripe for development by biologists. There is no mention of the possibility that disciplines such as linguistics, art history, or economic history might be the various forms that the study of memes already takes.) The crucial thought is that within human populations, ways of thinking and patterns of decision making are not selected for the degree to which they serve the interests of human beings; they are selected for the degree to which they induce whatever conditions promote their own replication. On first reading, this is a startling claim, but I am convinced that it expresses an important truth. Nevertheless, social scientists need to be careful not to be carried away by Dawkins's rhetoric.

For mathematical theorists, I think, one of the seductive features of Dawkins's treatment of memes is its a priori character. It appears to be deriving significant conclusions about cultural transmission without any messy investigation of facts. Instead, it points to apparent analogies between cultural transmission and certain biological mechanisms that evolutionary game-theoretical models have already helped us to understand. The temptation is to think that we can arrive at a similar understanding of human imitation merely by importing those models into social science.

The truth is that biology is much more than evolutionary game theory. In particular, biological theories of natural selection depend on biologists' empirically grounded understanding of what genes are and the mechanisms by which they replicate. Without this kind of understanding, natural selection would not be the theory it is, but merely the tautology that in any pool of replicators, those replicators that are more successful at replicating will increase in frequency relative to those that are less successful. The "theory" of memes, as used in the arguments I have been appraising, *is* only that tautology. What is missing is an understanding of what memes actually are and how they in fact replicate. And that understanding is not possible without an investigation of the facts of cultural transmission.

Whether human decision-making behavior satisfies the rationality postulates of conventional choice theory is an empirical question. If it does, any explanation of that fact must depend on empirical propositions about how the world really is. Trying to find an explanation by manipulating tautologies about replicators is to attempt what is logically impossible.[8]

Acknowledgments

Many of the ideas in this paper were developed in collaboration with Robin Cubitt. I am grateful for comments from Mark Greenberg and Paul Seabright. My work has been supported by the Leverhulme Trust.

8. See comments on this chapter by Seabright (vol. 2, ch. 19.10, p. 398), and Greenberg (vol. 2, ch. 19.11, p. 402). ED.

16 Common Misunderstandings of Memes (and Genes): The Promise and the Limits of the Genetic Analogy to Cultural Transmission Processes

Francisco J. Gil-White

16.1 Introduction

There is now a vigorous debate on how Darwinism should be applied to culture (see Aunger, 2000). Following Dawkins (1976/1989), many now refer to units of cultural transmission and evolution as "memes," regard "replicators" as essential for a Darwinian process, assume "selfish memes," and adopt a "meme's-eye view."

Analogies and borrowed yardsticks are often useful for a new field, but may also cause misunderstanding. I will argue here that Dawkins's legacy for cultural Darwinism has not only given rise to confusion, but itself results from misconstruals of Darwinian theory.

I will not define a meme as a *selfish replicator*,[1] but adopt the broad *Oxford English Dictionary's* definition: "a cultural element or behavioural trait whose transmission ... [occurs] by non-genetic means."[2] Selfish replication, then, is a hypothesis about the behavior of the stuff that gets transmitted through nongenetic means. The relevant questions are

1. Nor do many others, including several authors in Aunger (2000, e.g., see chapters by Plotkin and Laland & Odling-Smee).
2. Unlike Sperber (2000, p. 163) I do not think this definition is trivial. Nor do I think that it corresponds to the way anthropologists have always thought about culture, as he claims. Implicit in this definition is the idea that memes are units, that they are materially stored, and that they are subject to selection. These intuitions open the way to a completely different form of cultural analysis from that which we anthropologists have traditionally contemplated. As Sperber (1996) has emphasized, anthropologists have tended to mystical approaches to culture that put it "out there" in the ether somewhere rather than in people's brains, and have failed to examine the processes of transmission in phenomenal and cognitive detail. By contrast, the idea of memes in any of its forms makes units of cultural transmission analogous to genes. This produces an entirely new perspective—a revolution of sorts.

1. Does this stuff behave like a selfish replicator?
2. If not, does this make Darwinian analyses of culture impossible?
3. Is it impossible to find the boundaries of memes?
4. Can we simply appropriate the selfish gene idea from biology?

I will answer "no" to each, but will nevertheless call memes that which is culturally transmitted.

16.2   What Is Required for Cumulative Genetic Evolution?

Darwinian processes are simple and blindly algorithmic, but they gradually accumulate purposeful design (often very complex). They have three main requirements: information must leave descendant copies (*inheritance*), new information should be routinely generated (*mutation*), and some items of information should reliably leave more descendants than others (*selection*).

Genes meet these requirements. They are inherited through reproduction; new genes are routinely created because of occasional copying mistakes, or mutations, during duplication of DNA; and a gene's effects on its carriers affect the probability that it will leave more copies. Thanks to selection and inheritance, genes that cause increased reproductive success in their average carrier leave more copies, and the gene's relative frequency in the population increases (if there are no frequency-dependent effects, eventually the whole population will have the gene). Thanks to mutation, new alternative genes are generated that occasionally amount to improvements, allowing the population to continue to evolve.

Cumulative genetic adaptations are possible because genetic mutations typically introduce incremental rather than massive changes and the mutation rate for genes is low. An overemphasis on these two properties of genetic transmission is responsible for the mistaken intuition that replication—perfect copying—is generally required for cumulative evolution in any of its imaginable manifestations. For this reason, I give it further attention.

We should expect organic evolution to consist of small incremental changes because the space of purposeful designs that are worse is vast relative to the space of better ones. Thus, random mutations are unlikely to improve any purposeful design. For example, if a monkey types a character at random as I write this essay, it is unlikely to improve it. But if a monkey presses a key that launches a program to rearrange at random all the letters in my essay, it is infinitely *less* likely to improve the essay. Given a selective force, a random novelty cannot maintain itself in a population longer than a geological instant unless it produces small changes. Thus, design improvements, which result from atypically lucky random changes, are incremental.

Mutations must also be infrequent because cumulative evolution is impossible without relative stability of design across time. If the offspring of A s are mostly non-A s, then even if A reproduces better than competitors B and C, this will not increase the frequency of A types, since the information in A is mostly lost after reproduction. When A s instead typically beget other A s, their higher reproductive success will soon make everybody in the population an A (if there are no frequency-dependent effects). Later, if a rare mutation generates a slight improvement in the A design—call it the A° design—these A° mutants will out-reproduce mere A s and the population will change again (but only slightly).

This covers the intuitive basics of genes. How similar are memes? Memes also show inheritance, mutation, and selection. We learn from each other through social interaction so, in a broad sense, my information can create a descendant copy in you (inheritance). People often make mistakes when copying, and they can also have stupid or bright novel ideas, generating modified items of information (mutation). And some ideas are copied more, stored longer, and rebroadcast more often, leaving more descendants than competing ideas (selection). The properties of human social-learning psychology make some ideas more popular than others.

Many critics have focused on how similar ancestor and descendant memes must be for the analogy with genes to hold. Some assert that selectionist approaches to culture cannot work because memes, unlike genes, are not true replicators, making cumulative evolution impossible (Sperber, 1996; Boyer, 1994). Others disagree, and have built models of cultural change with fundamental assumptions quite similar to those of evolutionary genetics, but adapted for the idiosyncrasies of culture (e.g., Boyd & Richerson, 1985; Lumsden & Wilson, 1981; Cavalli-Sforza & Feldman, 1981; Castro & Toro, 2002; for a review, see Feldman & Laland, 1996). To adjudicate, we must examine whether it matters that memes are poor replicators.

16.3   Do Memes Mutate Too Much?

Genes *replicate* because they almost never make copying errors during duplication. Since relative stability of design over time is a requirement of cumulative evolution, genetic replication allows organic evolution to be cumulative.

Dan Sperber compares memes ("representations") to viruses that infest brains in successive epidemics. But he sees an important difference:

whereas pathogenic agents such as viruses and bacteria reproduce in the process of transmission and undergo a mutation only occasionally, representations are transformed almost every time they are transmitted. . . .

. . . Memory and communication transform information. (Sperber 1996, pp. 25, 31)

For example, no one ever retells a story exactly, and this constant transformation, according to Sperber, makes cumulative evolution through meme transmission impossible.

In the case of genes, a typical rate of mutation might be one mutation per million replications. With such low rates of mutation, even a very small selection bias is enough to have, with time, major cumulative effects. If, on the other hand, in the case of culture there may be, as Dawkins (1989/1976) acknowledges, "a certain 'mutational' element in every copying event," then the very possibility of cumulative effects of selection is open to question. (Sperber, 1996, pp. 102–103)

G. C. Williams defines an evolutionary gene as "any hereditary information for which there is a favorable or unfavorable selection bias equal to several or many times its rate of endogenous change" (1966, p. 25). Dawkins's conception of memes applies the same standard, as stated clearly by Wilkins:

A meme is the least unit of sociocultural information relative to a selection process that has favorable or unfavorable selection bias that exceeds its endogenous tendency to change. (Wilkins, 1998, p. 8)

Sperber accepts this move by assuming that (1) replicators are the things to look for, (2) Williams's definition of an evolutionary gene gives the universal definition of a replicator, and (3) Darwinian analyses will apply to memes *only if* they can satisfy this definition. Sperber regards any other conceptualization of memes as trivial (Sperber, 2000, p. 163).

Since Sperber argues that memes mutate in every transmission event, he concludes that cultural selection cannot conceivably act fast enough; the meme's dizzying rate of endogenous change creates a ceiling effect (see also Atran, 2001). Thus, rather than selection, it is the cognitive processes of information storage and retrieval that will effect statisitical change by causing mutations in particular and systematic directions. By understanding how this happens, we can build models of directed mutation, as opposed to selectionist models of cumulative change (Sperber, 1996, pp. 52–53, 82–83; 110–112).

Hull cites Wilkins's definition approvingly for a science of memetics that he optimistically believes *possible*, despite expecting "howls of derision" from critics who find this definition insufficiently "operational" (Hull, 2000, p. 47). Ironically, the opposite has happened. Sperber, a prominent critic of selectionist approaches to culture, has accepted this definition and used it to argue that selectionist approaches to culture are *impossible*.

Hull and Sperber agree on the standard that Darwinian processes must meet, but disagree on whether culture satisfies it. Who is wrong? I suggest both are, since they have agreed on the wrong standard. Genetic replication is not necessary; rather, it is merely one way to get Darwinian processes going.

I accept Sperber's claims that memes mutate in every transmission event and in ways that are often systematically biased. But what matters, I will argue, is how large the mutations are, and how strongly biased they are in particular directions.

16.4   Terminological Clarification

Replication means producing copies "exact in all details."[3] Though Dawkins recognized that copying mistakes are essential to Darwinian evolution, he dubbed genes replicators because they are "astonishingly faithful" copiers that only "occasionally make mistakes" (Dawkins, 1976/1989, pp. 16–17). Only after rehearsing this point did he introduce memes as hitherto-unrecognized potential replicators (Dawkins, 1976/1989, pp. 191–192), arguing that cultural transmission is Darwinian, *only if* memes are replicators. Thus, if "meme transmission is subject to continuous mutation, and also to blending," (Dawkins, 1976/1989, p. 195) as seems to be the case, this was a problem for Dawkins. So he argued against it by saying "It is possible that this appearance [of constant mutation and blending] ... is illusory, and that the analogy with genes does not break down" (Dawkins, 1976/1989, p. 195).

In his introduction to Blackmore (1999), Dawkins now dispenses with these worries. Memes are definitely subject to Darwinian processes. This conclusion follows logically from his premises only if one decides (1) that memes are replicators, or else (2) that replication is not necessary for Darwinian processes. Dawkins, however, uses examples of *non*replicating memes and yet he keeps the replication standard, as if these memes had

3. *Oxford English Dictionary.*

met it.[4] Dennett (1995) and Blackmore do the same. "As long as we accept that ... information of *some* kind [my emphasis] is passed on ... then, by definition, memes exist," Blackmore says (2000a, p. 25). Since she also says that "memes are replicators" (p. 26), her definition of replication is that it happens when *any* information is passed on. Aunger likewise defines replication as "the recurrence of ... features" (2002, p. 3).

Meanings have been turned upside down. We started with replication—defined as near-perfect copying fidelity—as *the* requirement for Darwinian processes. But these writers now ask first whether a unit is Darwinian, and if it is, they call it a replicator, whatever its copying fidelity. As a result of this terminological switch, the view that replication is a requirement of Darwinian processes has become entrenched.

Aunger recognizes that replication is not necessary for Darwinian processes (2002), but he argues that (1) cultural replicators are rampant and, perhaps because both coinages originate with Dawkins, also that (2) replication entails a selfish-meme viral perspective on cultural change, with humans as mere hosts.

It is only when information *replicates* that an additional causal force becomes involved. This is the very essence of the meme hypothesis.... there is an information-bearing replicator underlying communication ... a puppeteer pulling invisible strings.... This puppeteer is the information packet itself, evolved to manipulate its carriers for its own ends. (Aunger, 2002, pp. 12–13; emphasis in original)

I argue, by contrast, that mapping the biases involved in social learning shows that only some rather specialized kinds of memes are really "selfish." We should avoid the direct analogizing from biology to culture. However, we can still view culture in Darwinian terms.

16.5 "Replication" Is a Red Herring

Sperber's argument, although intuitively appealing, fails. Even meme copying that is always imperfect can support cumulative adaptation. To explain why, I begin with a few preliminaries.

A genetic locus is the physical location on a chromosome where a gene is found. The eye color locus, for example, contains information that results

4. Dawkins's argument is that because humans keep trying to copy accurately, in the long developmental run meme copying is close enough to replication to justify the application of Darwinian tools of thought. However, this repeatedly refined copying is far from being replication. Even so, one can apply Darwinian tools to culture, as demonstrated in the text.

in the development of a brown or a blue eye. What is the memetic analogue? Imagine a locus for a tennis serve with whatever is necessary to produce a certain behavior when it is your turn to serve in tennis. Anything could be in it. Waving hello to your mom, or baking bread, would be ruled illegal by the judges, but in principle this information may be stored at the tennis serve locus (similarly, a useless sequence of nucleotides could, in principle, be stored at the eye color locus).

Cultural transmission does not require exactly duplicated neuronal structures, analogous to the duplication of exact nucleotide sequences in DNA, for Darwinian analyses to apply. Cognitively, the cultural locus is a *tag plus retrieval function*—a matter of categorization rather than physical location in the brain. What I retrieve as I begin a tennis point is information that is tagged "tennis serve." Waving to my mom or baking a cake have not been tagged this way (even though, in principle, they could be). The true alleles of my current serve, therefore, are other behaviors which I—and others— also tag as tennis serves because some individuals in the population perform them when beginning a point in tennis. I may choose to acquire one of these later, replacing what is currently at my tennis serve locus. This gives the cultural locus all the requisite functional similarity to the genetic case.

16.5.1 The Right Mix of Stability and Variation

Suppose Bob's tennis serve is the most attractive serve, and watching Bob induces people to modify the information in their own tennis serve loci. In principle, anything can result in the continuum bounded by the following two extremes:

1. Replication: people acquire information to reproduce Bob's serve exactly.
2. Random changes: people rewrite the information at their locus so that they produce behaviors typically bearing zero resemblance to Bob's serve.[5]

Consider first the causation of random changes. As implausible as it sounds, suppose that my admiration for Bob's top-spin serve motivates me

---

5. For a mathematical demonstration of the central argument of this section, see Henrich and Boyd (2002). Note that I am not here tracking information in the brain, although it is necessary for the process. Rather, I am tracking actual behaviors, and ignoring what particular information content in the brain may be causing them. The latter is not always unimportant (Gil-White, 2002a), but it is irrelevant to my present points. "Replication failure" here means failure of the copier to *perform* a serve that is identical to Bob's.

to put random information in my tennis serve locus, say, "wave at mom." You put randomly different, but typically equally dissimilar, information in your own tennis serve locus (say, "scratch the left knee").

What happens? We are assuming it is the *content* of Bob's serve (i.e., the specific sequence of motions, plus its relative success in winning points) that makes it attractive. But because the changes that observers make in their own loci are random, the tennis serves of copiers look nothing like Bob's, so they are not admired and cause no further changes in others. Bob's serve therefore does not become more common, nor does the mean serve in the population move in the direction of Bob's. Since evolution is about statistical changes in a population, and since Bob does not pull the population mean toward his serve, design improvements will not accumulate under these assumptions.

Now consider the other extreme assumption. This sounds implausible too. Here, watching Bob's serve produces information changes in the observers' loci so that the resulting behaviors are replicas—perfect copies—of Bob's. There are no mutations, of any size.

What happens? All those who copied Bob's serve in turn become models for other people, who in turn copy the serve. Bob's serve spreads until everybody serves identically. Again, selection cannot lead to cumulative design changes because the serves have all become identical to Bob's. Nobody ever makes mistakes, so the future will be a world where everyone serves exactly like Bob—forever.

Thus, neither the extreme of random changes nor that of replication (100% copying fidelity) allows accumulation of adaptive design. That occurs only in the middle, where descendant changes are relatively similar to the parent stimulus, but somewhat different. This can happen in two ways.

1. There are small copying mistakes, only once in a long while.   Descendant copies are replicas of parent serves, with a tiny probability of replication failure. Rare random modifications typically make Bob's serve less effective, because a tennis serve is a complex behavior in which many variables must be kept within narrow ranges to ensure success. Since only effective serves are attractive, most random changes produce less attractive serves. But very occasionally a random copying mistake begets a more effective—and therefore more attractive—serve, which then displaces Bob's serve as people begin replicating the improved version. Many iterations of this cycle lead to ever better serves.

This case is exactly parallel to genetics. Sperber (1996) claims that cultural transmission must be like this in order to allow cumulative adaptations. But let us take a look at a rather different process.

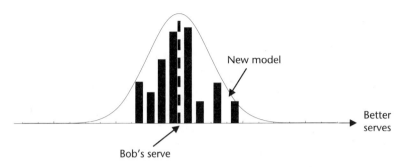

Figure 16.1
Copying with modest errors. Think of the units in the *x*-axis as being very small, so that the distance between the leftmost bar and the rightmost bar is not too great; that is, we are assuming that all serves produced are minor deviations from the target serve (which is Bob's).

2. Copying always involves mistakes, but closely follows an average of perfect accuracy (see figure 16.1).   Everybody's goal is to copy Bob's serve exactly, but there is always some error. However, the errors are relatively small, so that Bob's serve remains the template for all descendant serves. The population's mean serve is still Bob's serve, since errors cancel out around the mean. From the modest variations introduced by copying errors, a serve superior to Bob's emerges, and this becomes the new template for us all to imitate and thus the new mean of the population, with a cloud of error around it.

If we focus on the population mean, it is clear that despite the absence of replication, adaptive design accumulates under selective pressure. Moreover, the process is faster than natural selection because mutants are produced in every copying attempt.

The second case reflects the basic assumptions in many selectionist models pioneered by Boyd and Richerson (1985). Contrary to Sperber, cumulative cultural adaptation is possible under these assumptions. Replication itself is a red herring. Cumulative adaptation requires (1) sufficient copying inaccuracy that superior variants occasionally emerge and (2) sufficient accuracy that there is directional change at the population level (the mean) (cf. Boyd & Richerson, 2000).

16.5.2   Mutations May Have Consistent Biases
What about directed mutation? If a psychological bias creates an attractor, copying mistakes will be made in its direction. This is still not a problem, at

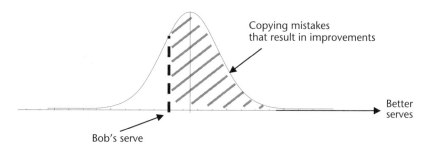

Figure 16.2
Adaptive mutation bias. In this case the population mean is closer to the optimum after copying, than is Bob's.

least not in principle. The attractor could be anywhere, but we can get our bearings by once again considering the two extremes.

1. The mutation attractor is the optimally effective serve (figure 16.2). Most of us try to copy Bob's serve exactly, but fail within a cloud of error with mean zero. A few, however, can see modifications that will make Bob's serve even better, and attempt these. This skews the mean "error" for the whole population in the direction of the optimal serve. Does this prevent cumulative adaptive design? No. Rather, it speeds up movement to the optimum, since mutations in this direction are slightly more likely. Design changes are cumulative because foresight does not extend to the optimal serve itself, merely to slight modifications of observable serves that take them in that direction.

2. The mutation attractor is in a direction opposite to the optimal serve (figure 16.3). If a good serve is a somewhat unnatural movement, errors will tend away from the optimal serve, so the mean copy is inferior to Bob's serve. However, as long as "errors" in the other direction (toward optimality) are not too unlikely, some descendant serves are better than Bob's and displace him as the model. The new distribution of copies again has a mean that lags the target serve, *but it is better than the previous population mean.* Hence, the population mean makes gradual progress toward the optimum despite always lagging its current target.

Only when variants better than Bob's are very unlikely, because the maladaptive attractor is too strong, will this prevent the emergence of cumulative design (figure 16.4). Therefore any plausible directed mutation effects should be modeled together with selection, and the algebraic sum of the forces will determine the direction of the system. We do not have to decide

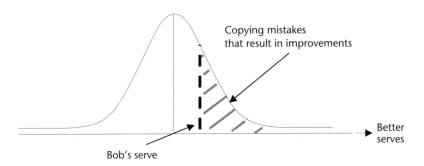

Figure 16.3
Maladaptive mutation bias. In this case the population mean is further away from the optimum after copying, than is Bob's serve. However, some copiers will make mistakes to the right of Bob, and since this yields a better serve, it will become the model for the next generation.

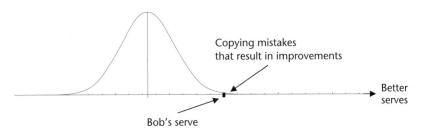

Figure 16.4
Overly strong maladaptive bias. Owing to a strong mutation attractor, the population mean is so far away from Bob's serve in a maladaptive direction that better serves will practically never appear.

between mutation and selection in our modeling exercises. Sperber is correct that constant directed mutation can prevent cumulative adaptation, but if and only if such mutation is (1) not toward the optimum and (2) of sufficient strength. Whether these conditions are met is an empirical question; they may be met for some domains and not for others. The answer will not be found from an armchair.

What is the evidence? Do we have empirical examples of cumulative cultural adaptations through selection? Yes. Consider technological items, such as tennis racquets; their design has accumulated gradually. Even with technology, Sperber's dictum that replication is a limiting case rather than the norm is correct (except in the case of very modern manufacturing techniques).

Or one could point to institutions, which are always imperfectly copied (consider that the Mexican political constitution is—on paper—almost a replica of the American constitution). And yet institutions accrete cumulative adaptive changes, as evidenced by the way that the institutions of complex societies have outcompeted those of simple ones (McNeill, 1963; Landes, 1998; Diamond, 1997; Wright, 2000).

Other examples could be given, but since technology and institutions include much of what is important in cultural evolution, it is already clear that selectionist approaches will be significant for historical explanations.

16.6 "Imitation" Is Another Red Herring

Blackmore regards imitation as the mechanism of memetic evolution. Yet she considers a narrative, which is not transmitted by imitation, a meme.

Dawkins said that memes jump from "brain to brain via a process which, in the broad sense, can be called imitation" (1976/1989, p. 192). I will also use the term "imitation" in the broad sense. So if, for example, a friend tells you a story and you remember the gist and pass it on to someone else then that counts as imitation. (Blackmore, 1999, p. 6)

This definition of imitation is much too loose. We need a handle on the social-learning cognitive mechanisms which, in combination with individual learning processes, are responsible for affecting the distribution of memes (cf. Plotkin, 2000; Laland & Odling-Smee, 2000). Imitation is important, but some domains depend on other processes.

The imitation of a motor act, the acquisition of a native language, and learning one's culture-specific social constructions have different developmental trajectories.... Each is based on different psychological mechanisms. It is almost certainly the case that the characteristics each displays in terms of fecundity, longevity, and fidelity of copying are also different in each case, and different precisely because each is based on different mechanisms. The suggestion that "we stick to defining the [sic] meme as that which is passed on by imitation" (Blackmore, 1998), if taken literally, is an impoverishment of memetics for reasons of wanting to maintain copying fidelity. (Plotkin, 2000, p. 76)

Blackmore apparently requires imitation because it suggests replication, which she regards as a requirement of Darwinian processes. Critics again agree with the standard but reach the opposite conclusion. In a section title, Atran says, "No Replication without Imitation; Therefore, No Replication" (because there is no real imitation), and hence no Darwinian processes in culture (2001, p. 364). But this is the wrong litmus test; proper advocacy or skepticism about a Darwinian approach does not turn on imitation.

True, some cultural transmission scholars have stressed the importance of imitation, but their concern is the human versus nonhuman comparison (Boyd & Richerson, 1985, 1996, 2000; Tomasello et al., 1993a). Although the appearance of imitation initially set humans along the path of cumulative cultural change, other tricks have since become possible. For example, I have recently argued that language became possible when imitation led to the emergence of prestige hierarchies (Gil-White, 2002b). Language now makes nonimitative processes possible, such as prestige-biased influence (Henrich & Gil-White, 2001). Here is another example: Narratives can accrue cumulative changes through selection but do not spread through imitation, even if the evolution of imitation was necessary for the emergence of language, which is indispensable for narrative. The phylogenetic indispensability of imitation should be distinguished from its current importance in cultural transmission.

16.7 Platonic Inferences

I have so far ignored an interesting problem. Individuals cannot replicate memes, although they do try. But what is their target? No two serves by Bob are ever replicas of each other; Bob's performance is itself a cloud of error around a mean. So copiers must be abstracting an "ideal Bob serve" from Bob's performances, which they try to copy. Sperber dismisses this as "a Platonist approach," claiming that formal properties cannot be causal (1996, p. 63).

I disagree. We must infer an ideal serve as Bob's goal and strive for that. Evolution could not design our social-learning psychology otherwise, given that the performances of the people we copy are statistical clouds (cf. Dennett, 1995, p. 358; Dawkins, 1999, pp. x–xii; Blackmore, 1999, pp. 51–52; Boyd & Richerson, 2000). Selectionist models may therefore define the meme as Bob's ideal goal, and track the population mean. Whether the simplification is legitimate depends on the problem being modeled.

However, there is no question that cognitive psychology and anthropology must study how the brain parses reality into important or irrelevant material. Understanding such cognitive filters will tell us what the memes are for a particular domain. Our present limited understanding of these filters is no obstacle to current selectionist models (*contra* Atran, 2002). These models concern the formal, emergent properties of Darwinian systems that, by assumption, are capable of cumulative adaptation, rather than the histories of specific memes (for a review, see Feldman & Laland, 1996). They teach us about the general properties of cultural evolutionary systems and the results that emerge from the interdependence between two systems of inheritance: genetic and cultural.

16.8   What Are the Boundaries of "A Meme"?

Memes have been criticized for lacking well-defined boundaries (Atran, 2001). Maurice Bloch writes:

> As I look at the work of meme enthusiasts, I find a ragbag of proposals for candidate memes.... At first, some seem convincing as discrete units: catchy tunes, folk tales, the taboo on shaving among Sikhs, Pythagoras's theorem, etc. However, on closer observation, even these more obvious "units" lose their boundaries. Is it the whole tune or only a part of it which is the meme? The Sikh taboo is meaningless unless it is seen as part of Sikh religion and identity. Pythagoras' theorem is a part of geometry and could be divided into smaller units such as the concept of a triangle, angle, equivalence, etc. (Bloch, 2000, p. 194)

But are the boundary problems any greater for memes than genes?

A Darwinian unit is of whatever size selection favors. For this reason, Dawkins (1982, pp. 87–89) is right not to view the gene as a *cistron* (from start codon to stop codon). Cistrons are more useful to molecular biologists. Is the meme the whole tune or only part of it? A tune, like a cistron, has a starting point and an ending point, which are a matter of mechanical performance, not selection; for the tune, a musical performance, and for the cistron, the construction of a polypeptide chain. In culture, our colloquial understandings tend to confuse the distinction between units of performance and units of information storage.

One cultural locus houses a finite number of competing beliefs about which piece should be played. Here, the meme "Beethoven's Fifth deserves to be played" has done well. A different locus houses competing beliefs about how much of a piece should be played. Here, the meme "play a piece from beginning to end" has fared well. Because these two memes are successful in their respective loci, Beethoven's Fifth symphony is played often and in its entirety—not because the whole symphony is encoded in the heads of listeners! What listeners remember of the piece is stored in yet another locus, where tune fragments compete to be remembered. For the most part, only the catchy opening theme of the Fifth is encoded.

These loci are related and yet independent. Very catchy but tiresome pop tune fragments are remembered so easily that the preference for the entire song *not* to be played will spread (at least after the song's initial success). So both the tune fragment and the *negative* preference for the song can occur simultaneously at high frequency (as in well-known tunes most people prefer not to hear). However, for a tune fragment to persist across generations, it must be enduringly popular (my grandchildren will know Beethoven's Fifth, but probably not contemporary popular tunes).

A meme cannot spread except in a favorable ecology of memes at other loci (for example, "Beethoven's Fifth deserves to be played"; the memes necessary to play a violin; the meme that violinists should be paid; and so on). Similarly, a gene prospers only when it is surrounded by a favorable ecology of genes at other loci in its own and other vehicles. If this does not undermine population analyses in biology, why is culture different? Yes, the Sikh shaving taboo will spread and stabilize if the existing religious memes are congruent, and yes, Pythagoras' theorem cannot be learned without first possessing the meme for triangles. But neither can a gene for reciprocity spread without genes for, say, living in proximity to one's conspecifics. There is no new difficulty here.

Finally, what is the appropriate level of abstraction? The details of a narrative, say, are apparently not stored in memory (Schank & Abelson, 1995). Critics may pounce: "Aha! No stability!" But at what level? If the narrative skeleton is stable, radical variation in the details is as worrisome to cultural Darwinian analyses as silent mutations in DNA are to evolutionary genetics (i.e., not at all). One must keep track of story skeletons, and changes there will be the real mutations (Gil-White, in preparation).

16.9 Meme "Content" Is Not Everything

Sperber (2000) makes a concession to the view that we make Platonic inferences, but he insists along Chomskian lines that these almost always depend on preexisting knowledge structures being triggered rather than new knowledge being bootstrapped; observation produces prepared "inferences" (see also Atran, 2002, 2001, 1998; and Boyer, 1998, 1994). For example, "language learners converge on similar meanings on the basis of weak evidence provided by words used in an endless diversity of contexts and with various degrees of literalness or figurativeness" (Sperber, 2000, pp. 171–172). There are no stable, discrete memes competing with each other under selective pressure. Rather, meme content is edited by successive directed mutations into the shape favored by the innately given content bias "attractors."

Sperber admits that at least some things are not merely triggered: "Learning to tap dance involves more copying than learning to walk." But, he insists, "For memetics to be a reasonable research program, it should be the case that copying [as opposed to triggering], and differential success in causing the multiplication of copies, overwhelmingly plays the major role in shaping all or at least most of the contents of culture" (Sperber, 2000, p. 172). In his view, this is not the case. Rather, "the acquisition of cultural knowledge and know-how is made possible and partly shaped by evolved domain-specific competencies" (Sperber, 2000, p. 172).

Sperber's requirement is not a proper test, for five reasons. First, he asks us to choose between complements rather than alternatives. Domain-specific competencies do not rule out selection-driven cumulative adaptations.

Second, for many domains, the way inferences are triggered supports a rather different point. Learning Bob's serve requires that we abstract his goal from the statistical cloud of his performances. This is an inference, but the preexisting knowledge it relies on concerns the purpose of a serve in a game of tennis, which does not derive from an innate, domain-specific module prepared to trigger "tennis." Because the rules of tennis need to be understood before Bob's goal can be inferred, this is a form of cumulative developmental bootstrapping that is not reducible to the triggering of innate and specialized content domains.

Third, Sperber's linguistic example is not even apt for his purposes. There is undoubtedly much innate knowledge dedicated to the bootstrapping of language, but a model that reduces historical linguistic processes to the triggering of innate knowledge cannot explain how Indo-European became Hindi in one place and Spanish in another.

Fourth, Sperber's requirement is asymmetrical. The mechanism he disfavors, the copying of knowledge, can only be significant if it is "overwhelmingly" dominant "in shaping all or at least most of the contents of culture," while his favored innate mechanism need only be partly responsible (2000, p. 172).

Finally, even granting Sperber's assumptions that there are innate attractors for everything, his conclusion does not follow. Henrich and Boyd (2002) show that as long as more than one attractor can exert influence over a given meme, and the attractors are strong relative to other selection pressures, the dynamics quickly becomes a contest between the discrete alternatives favored by each attractor, engaged in a selective contest. So even here we find something close to particulate selection rather than a fuzzy morphing into the attractor.

16.9.1   Noncontent Biases and Their Importance

Sperber might reply that even so, the contest is between innate attractors (core memes), so one cannot expect cumulative cultural evolution acting on arbitrarily varying memes (see also Atran, 1998; Boyer, 1998). A related view stresses that triggered inferences result mainly from local noncultural environments (e.g., Tooby & Cosmides, 1992), so cultural differences can be explained by the environmental conditions surrounding various local populations. By contrast, others argue—not instead but *in addition*—for the importance of *non*content biases allowing arbitrary variations to spread and remain stable (Boyd & Richerson, 1985; Henrich & Boyd, 1998; Henrich & Gil-White, 2001; Gil-White, 2001a,b). Our social-learning cognitive biases support the latter view.

Suppose Bob is your hero because he is a great tennis player. Bob likes a Wilson racquet. So you buy a Wilson racquet. Bob wears leather trousers; you buy leather trousers. Or, suppose everybody in your high school class is getting leather trousers. So you get leather trousers; you want to fit in. In these examples you acquire the meme, not because of its content, but because of contingently associated features: its source or its relative frequency. The tradition begun by Boyd and Richerson (1985)—with its roots in cultural anthropological questions—focuses on noncontent biases, such as conformity bias and prestige bias, which produce the accumulation of arbitrary differences among societies.

Research in social psychology suggests that humans have biases favoring memes that are common relative to competing memes at a particular cultural locus (D. Miller & McFarland, 1991; Kuran, 1995; Asch, 1956, 1963/ 1951). Boyd and Richerson (1985, ch. 7) and Henrich and Boyd (1998) explain the adaptiveness of informational conformism; it helps individuals acquire useful memes that others have already converged on. I (2001a) argue that interactional-norm conformism is adaptive because it maximizes the number of the conformist's potential interactants.

Boyd and Richerson, among others, have also speculated that prestigious individuals are copied more often than others. Henrich and Gil-White (2001) develop a lay model to explain the evolution of such a cognitive bias and review evidence for it in the social science literature. We argue that prestige bias is adaptive because successful individuals (i.e., those with better memes) tend to have prestige.

These two biases care nothing about content; conformity bias cares about relative frequency and prestige bias about source. As far as these biases are concerned, the memes could be about anything at all. Thus, in domains without strong content biases, we should see the following effects. First, the memes of prestigious individuals will tend to become more common. These will be unpredictably different for people in different communities given that every individual—including prestigious ones—has an idiosyncratic life history (e.g., I, but not you, may fall off a horse after washing my feet in a stream, and conclude superstitiously that the stream was somehow directly responsible). Second, such differences will be larger among members of different communities (even if we both fall off our horses after washing in the stream, I am more likely to blame the stream if my local community already believes that streams have supernatural powers). This sort of process will create arbitrary differences among societies, and a third effect—conformism—will keep the differences locally stable at high frequency. The fourth and last effect is historical. Such stable differences among societies produce acquired content biases that make future memes that are consistent with them more likely and other memes less likely. These effects set different societies on separate and distinct historical paths.

The conformist and prestige biases offer an appealing joint explanation for the different historical paths that result in dramatic variation among the world's cultures. They can explain why two populations living in the same environment can become quite different culturally—something that happens all the time.

16.9.2 Don't Reduce Everything to Content

Anthropologists are interested in cultural variability. This sometimes leads to the theoretical excess of cultural relativism, according to which human brains are blank slates upon which local cultures can inscribe anything. However, some anthropologists now overreact by claiming that nothing about culture approximates a blank slate.

The picture of the human mind/brain as a blank slate on which different cultures freely inscribe their own world-view ... [is] incompatible with our current understanding of biology and psychology.

... the brain contains many sub-mechanisms, or "modules," which evolved as adaptations to ... [ancestral] environmental opportunities and challenges (Cosmides & Tooby, 1987, 1994; Tooby & Cosmides, 1989, 1992) [and] ... are crucial factors in cultural attraction. They tend to fix a lot of cultural content in and around the cognitive domain the processing of which they specialize in. (Sperber, 1996, p. 113)

Other anthropologists in this tradition have expressed similar views in the course of explaining the widespread recurrence of certain memes—certain religious ideas (Boyer, 1994); concepts of living kinds (Atran, 1998);

ideas about so-called "races" (Hirschfeld, 1996)—in terms of universal and innate content biases. This approach is valuable, but these authors seem to think that such content biases refute the possibility of acquiring unconstrained memes (Boyer, 1998), and thus also refute the possibility of stable, arbitrary differences among cultures (Hirschfeld, 1996, pp. 21–22), which in turn implies that such nonexistent differences cannot support cultural group selection (Atran, 2002, ch. 10). However, the importance of content-driven versus arbitrary memes should be judged domain by domain. In some domains the assumption of a blank slate will be quite reasonable.

Blackmore (1999) and Dennett (1995) also argue for the primacy of content, but focus more on the meme as autonomous. Cultural evolution is viewed as a selective process that makes memes increasingly better propagators. As Dennett writes,

Dawkins (1976/1989, p. 214) points out that "a cultural trait may have evolved in the way it has simply because it is advantageous to itself." ...
... The first rule of memes, as for genes, is that replication is not necessarily for the good of anything; replicators flourish that are good at ... replicating—for whatever reason! (Dennett, 1995, p. 362)

For Dennett and Dawkins, the only thing affecting a meme's spread is whether *the meme itself* is good at proliferating. Selection will successively edit the meme's content, making it ever better at attracting human brains. This is the "meme's-eye" view. Memes with content that "looks" like what the brain "wants" will spread even if they lack the effects that the brain is adaptively "hoping for." The argument is valid for some memes, but not, I would argue, for most.

A meme can be lucky. Through no merit of its content, it can find itself in the head of a prestigious person, and thanks to prestige-bias bootstrapping (or even random drift processes), achieve stability at high frequency. Since content takes a back seat, memes may be favored despite what they are about. Prestige-biased and conformist transmissions are excellent explanations of why some maladaptive memes spread and stabilize, even when they are poorly designed for proliferetion. Dennett's "first rule of memes" is not a rule at all (cf. Conte, 2000, p. 88; Laland & Odling-Smee, 2000, p. 134; Boyd & Richerson, 2000).

Concessions from the content camp suggest that the controversy is resolvable. Atran acknowledges that from a cognitive standpoint, some cultural aspects are almost wholly arbitrary (2002, ch. 10). Boyer (1998) recognizes the importance of prestige bias, and Sperber (1996, pp. 90–91) explicitly recognizes its power to generate arbitrary differences among societies. Blackmore (1999, ch. 6) postulates source biases that I doubt exist, such as "imitate the good imitators," but which, as source biases, should undermine her view of meme selection as solely the result of meme content. Dawkins (1999, p. vii) introduces Blackmore's book by describing prestige bias. And Dennett and Dawkins are clearly aware of frequency-dependent effects such as conformism (Dennett, 1995, p. 352). The logical conclusions of these authors' own observations about noncontent biases are that arbitrary differences among cultures are not only possible but likely, and that to the extent they are widespread and stable, they generate selection pressures at the group level (Boyd & Richerson, 1985, ch. 7; Henrich & Boyd, 1998).

Susan Blackmore (1999, 2000a) has become an outspoken and pithy proponent of the view I criticize:

… replicators are the ultimate beneficiaries of any evolutionary process. Dennett (1995) urges us always to ask *cui bono?* or who benefits? And the answer is the replicators. (Blackmore, 2000a, p. 26)

Evolutionary processes do not need replicators (cf. Boyd & Richerson 2000, ch. 3; Henrich & Boyd, 2002). Neither is it true that memes, even if they were replicators, would be the ultimate beneficiaries of cultural evolutionary processes. However, this catchy argument is responsible for most of the attention given to the work of memeticists, and is the basis for Blackmore's arguments about brain evolution. I criticize these next.

16.10 Memetic Drive

According to the selfish-gene perspective, a chicken is an egg's way of making another egg. Blackmore adopts a parallel selfish-meme perspective, according to which a brain is just a meme's way of making another meme. "We humans … have become just the physical 'hosts' needed for the memes to get around" (Blackmore, 1999, p. 8). This leads to what some (Aunger, 2000, p. 11) regard as her most radical idea, that of memetic drive:

Memes are instructions for carrying out behavior, stored in brains (or other objects) and passed on by imitation. Their competition drives the evolution of the mind. (Blackmore, 1999, p. 17)

This claim is tautological if by "mind" Blackmore means the set of interconnections that end up instantiated in the brain as the result of development. The tautology is not useless because "meme" suggests Darwinian processes that have been hitherto neglected. The point is better put thus:

"Short-term cultural evolution results from competition among memes because a culture is a distribution of memes in people's heads." By the standards of cultural transmission theory, this is not a new or radical argument, notwithstanding Blackmore's view that she has advanced beyond it to a new, autonomous discipline (1999, pp. 15–17).

Blackmore means also to explain the evolution of the brain and argues that the "interests" of memes select for genes coding for brains that prefer those same memes (1999, ch. 6). Runaway processes of this sort, she says, have selected for our inordinately big brains.

This is radical, but wrong. A meme can select for a gene only if it is widespread (metapopulationally) and stable (intergenerationally), and there are only two ways for these conditions to arise. First, the meme could be selected by an innate content bias in the brain's design, making it widespread in the species and stable across time. However, this can't be Blackmore's memetic drive, because this meme fulfills the conditions necessary to select for a gene only because the gene evolved first—a catch-22.

Second, a process such as group selection through conformist transmission could make a meme widespread and stable, even though there was no innate content bias favoring it (Boyd & Richerson, 1985; Henrich & Boyd, 1998; Boyd et al., 2003). For example, suppose group selection makes the meme for group-welfare altruism spread when groups with high frequencies of this meme outcompete others. If some of these groups also have a meme that says "punish nonaltruists in your group," these groups will be the most competitive. Once such groups populate the world, it will become costly, everywhere, for individuals not to acquire the altruism meme quickly and reliably in early development. So genes coding for innate content biases favoring the acquisition of group-welfare memes will be favored, and memes will have indeed selected for brain structure in a Baldwinian process.

Such a process could work, but the suggestion is not radical or new. Such Baldwinian arguments are found in Boyd and Richerson (1985) and in subsequent work. Neither does this support Blackmore's claim that the interests of memes—in opposition to those of genes—are in the "driver's seat" in brain design.

The true claim that the replicative interests of memes affect *short-term* cultural evolution should not be confused with the false claim that the replicative interests of memes, as against those of genes, drive the *long-term* process of brain design. The brain cannot be designed against the interests of genes because this design must be coded for by genes, which cannot spread without differential reproductive success in their favor.

When memes select for genes, it will be only because the interests of memes and genes coincide. A culture-driven Baldwinian process is a very interesting way to generate this coincidence, but one still needs the coincidence. And a coincidence is just that—not, as Blackmore would have it, a radical turning of the tables on our understanding of what shapes brains.

16.11   Conclusion

The morals I draw are:

First, we should avoid narrowly genetic Darwinian thinking, and instead think in terms of the properties of statistical populations capable of inheritance and subject to selection. Despite its heuristic horsepower, the gene-meme analogy should not be a litmus test.

Second, if psychological biases are the main selective forces acting on memes, then the existence and importance of noncontent biases should be recognized. They do not detract from the importance of content biases, but merely add to the repertoire of relevant forces.

Third, psychologists and anthropologists should do more field and experimental work to trace the natural histories of particular memes in different domains and to explain the particular social learning biases responsible for such processes (see Gil-White, in preparation; Henrich & Gil-White, 2001). At this juncture, empirical work is sorely needed.[6]

6. See comments on this chapter by Blackmore (vol. 2, ch. 19.12, p. 406) and relevant discussion by Greenberg (vol. 2, ch. 17, p. 339) and Chater (vol. 2, ch. 18, p. 355). ED.

17 Goals versus Memes: Explanation in the Theory of Cultural Evolution

Mark Greenberg

17.1 Introduction

The Darwinian theory of biological evolution by natural selection is an extraordinarily fruitful explanatory paradigm. When Richard Dawkins (1976/ 1989) introduced the idea of a "meme"—a unit of cultural transmission— his suggestion was that Darwinian explanation might also prove fertile with respect to nongenetically based cultural development. There is, of course, an obvious and commonsensical competing account of cultural change that has a strong prima facie plausibility in a wide range of cases: According to this *goal-based* account, it is humans' deliberate pursuit of their conscious goals, rather than analogues of genetic mutations and natural selection, that explains why an idea or set of ideas comes into being and spreads. If a defender of a Darwinian theory of cultural evolution— *meme theory* for short—is to advance the idea that Darwinian theory is the best explanation of at least some aspects of cultural evolution, he or she must elucidate why meme theory offers explanatory advantages over competing theories, and, in particular, over a goal-based account.

What is the link to this volume's theme? Imitation holds a central place in Darwinian theories of culture. Dawkins, for example, suggests that memes are transmitted by imitation in a broad sense and that new memes are generated by copying mistakes. The goal-based account need not deny that imitation is an important mechanism for the transmission of ideas (although it is not plausible that it is the exclusive mechanism). But the goal-based account holds that it is our goals that determine which ideas are imitated (and which changes are introduced).

I want to emphasize that my purpose is not to argue against the explanatory potential of meme theory, but to focus attention on the need to address questions of explanation. There are numerous ways in which meme theory could offer explanatory benefits. As I will discuss, meme theorists could challenge goal-based explanations directly. For example, they could show that at least in some cases, the best explanation of the transmission of ideas is not human goals but selection in favor of "selfish" memes—ideas that are good at inducing their own replication. Or theorists could argue that even when each individual's decisions are explained by her goals, the long-term and large-scale consequences for the evolution of ideas are not what anyone wanted or intended. Thus, it might be that so-called "population-level" phenomena play a crucial role in the explanation of cultural evolution (see Boyd & Richerson, 1985, 2000). For example, the best explanation of why certain ideas are transmitted successfully from generation to generation might be that those ideas make a group more successful. A different possibility is that theorists could use meme theory to explain how human beings come to acquire their goals. Finally, once memes become an important part of the human environment, they can affect the selective pressures operating in genetic evolution; for example, genes might be selected for their effects on the transmission of memes. More generally, there is the possibility of gene-culture coevolutionary explanations.[1]

In this chapter, I elaborate on the importance of addressing meme theory's explanatory power, taking Francisco Gil-White's discussion in this volume as an illustration and point of departure. Gil-White is a proponent of a Darwinian theory of cultural evolution who wants to save meme theory by distancing it from the biological theory that is its inspiration. He defends meme theory against, on the one hand, proponents who (in his view) harm it by modeling it too closely on the biological case, and, on the other, detractors who think it cannot succeed because it is too unlike the biological case. I focus on two ways in which Gil-White argues that both proponents and critics of meme theory have adhered overly closely to the biological model. He argues first, that it is wrong to require that memes be capable of high-fidelity replication, and second, that it is misguided to try to extend Dawkins's "selfish-gene" perspective to cultural evolution.

I will show that these arguments neglect the explanatory role of meme theory. First, the argument against the need for high-fidelity copying is that cumulative directional change can occur even with an extremely high mu-

---

1. See Cavalli-Sforza and Feldman (1973, 1981), Boyd and Richerson (1985), Blackmore (1999; vol. 2, ch. 19.12, p. 406 and vol. 1, ch. 8.3, p. 203). Feldman and Laland (1996) provide further references.

tation rate. But even if there is a process that is, broadly speaking, Darwinian in the sense that there is accumulation of change by variation and differential reproduction, it doesn't follow that Darwinian theory has anything to add to the *explanation* of that change. It is not that I am restricting the term "Darwinian" to processes that do not involve goals; rather, the point is that to the extent that humans' pursuit of their goals accounts for the course of cultural change, an appeal to Darwin is idle.

Second, the criticism of a "selfish-meme" approach overlooks the explanatory point of that approach. It is true that there are reasons other than a meme's content that can explain its proliferation; for example, the prestige of those who display it. But the selfish-meme approach does not hold merely that a meme's content is what explains its proliferation. Rather, this approach offers a potentially powerful way of challenging the view that human goals are in the driver's seat. (Indeed, the noncontent biases that Gil-White emphasizes are important in part for the very same reason.)

Before turning to a detailed discussion of these points, I want briefly to elaborate my comments about explanation. If meme theory is to pull its weight, its claim cannot be merely that ideas are transmitted with variations, that the variations accumulate gradually over time, and that the ideas that are most common now are the ones that were transmitted the most. Even if all these propositions were true, it would not follow that the Darwinian model is a helpful, or the best, explanation of cultural evolution. In particular, even if a particular cultural feature has gradually accumulated variations, it could still be the case that *the best explanation* of why the idea has developed and spread is design—planful, foresighted decisions in pursuit of people's conscious goals. For example, the best explanation of a particular technology—refrigeration, say—may be design in the service of human purposes and needs, not accumulation of copying mistakes under selective pressure. At least prima facie, this seems a plausible and adequate explanation of much technological development—and much else in culture as well. A special case of this account is that the best explanation of the proliferation of some ideas may be the human goal of discovering the truth. Physics and mathematics may provide examples here. The point is *not* that it is false that ideas can change by accumulation of variation under selective pressure. Rather, *even when that proposition is true*, it may not be the best explanation of what is driving the change. In sum, what a defender of meme theory needs to do is to show that an appeal to an analogue of evolution by natural selection is the best explanation of cultural evolution.

17.2   Explaining Cumulative Change

A common objection to meme theory is that the mutation, or variation, rate in the transmission of memes is too high for Darwinian evolution to take place. I will argue that it is not enough for meme theory to show that cumulative adaptive change can occur, for example, because selective pressures are extremely strong. Meme theory must also show that Darwinian theory has something to add to the explanation of the cumulative change. For example, an obvious explanation of extremely strong selection is humans' deliberate selection of ideas because of their value with respect to some independent goal. To the extent that that is the source of the "selective pressures," our goals are doing the work.

Gil-White's defense of meme theory against the objection of a high mutation rate illustrates my point.[2] His main argument centers on his example of Bob's tennis serve (vol. 2, ch. 16, p. 323ff). Bob has "the most attractive" serve, and everyone tries to copy it. The point is that even with a mutation rate of 1, adaptive design can accumulate. To support this conclusion, Gil-White considers a version of the example in which small errors occur every time the serve is copied, but in which the mean serve is identical to Bob's (i.e., there is no directional bias to the errors).

From the *modest* variations introduced by copying errors, a serve superior to Bob's emerges, and *this becomes the new template for us all to imitate.* . . .

If we focus on the population mean, it is clear that despite the absence of replication, adaptive design accumulates under selective pressure. Moreover, the process is faster than natural selection because mutants are produced in every copying attempt. (my emphasis) (ch. 16.5.1, p. 325)

He next argues that even if there is a directional bias to the variations, design changes can still accumulate in the direction of the optimal serve. If the directional bias is toward the optimal serve, it will simply speed up evolution in that direction. If it is in the other direction, evolution toward the optimal serve can still occur as long as some variations improve on Bob's serve (again assuming everyone copies only the serve closest to the optimal serve, which displaces Bob's as the model).

I will make two points about the example. First, the example assumes what it needs to show. It is straightforward that a high mutation rate is

2. Gil-White attributes the objection primarily to Dan Sperber (1996). He does not adequately address Sperber's more important objection, based on the point that it is not true that each instance of an idea is even a low-fidelity copy of a particular ancestor idea.

consistent with cumulative directional change *if* (1) the selective pressures are strong enough and (2) the mutations are all relatively small. The tennis-serve example makes precisely these assumptions, however, and does nothing to support their plausibility. I will suggest that there is no reason to think that the corresponding assumptions will be true, or close enough to true, in a wide range of actual cases. Second, even when these assumptions are satisfied, more is needed to show that meme theory contributes much to the project of explaining the directional change. I discuss each of these points in turn.

17.2.1   The Assumptions of the Tennis-Serve Example

Two assumptions are crucial to the tennis-serve example. The first is that in any population of serves, there is always a unique most attractive serve, in the sense that everyone always chooses to copy it rather than any other serve in the population. All other serves are not copied at all. In other words, perfect selection is assumed.

The second is that variations from the model serve are always small. Even in the version of the example in which people are able to envision what a better serve would be, they can discover only small improvements since "foresight does not extend to the optimal serve itself, merely to slight modifications ... in that direction" (Gil-White, vol. 2, ch. 16.5.2, p. 326).

I consider the assumption of perfect selection first. It should be obvious how the tennis-serve example depends on this assumption. The basic argument is that despite the fact that every attempt to copy a target serve is imperfect, the population's mean serve will gradually improve. Why will it improve? As long as the copying errors sometimes produce improvements, there will at some point come into existence a new serve better than the original target serve. Thus, if, at every point in time, everyone is guaranteed to copy the then-optimal serve, the mean serve will improve (Gil-White, vol. 2, ch. 16, p. 324ff). Without the assumption that everyone will copy the optimal serve, however, it doesn't follow from the fact that copying errors sometimes produce improvements that the mean serve will gradually improve.

It is uncontroversial that a high rate of copying errors can result in cumulative directional change if selection pressures are strong enough. Gil-White (ch. 16, p. 320) cites G. C. Williams's definition of an "evolutionary gene" as "any hereditary information for which there is a favorable or unfavorable selection bias equal to several or many times its rate of endogenous change" (Williams, 1966), which implies that the acceptable rate of mutation is proportional to the strength of selection. So it should come as no surprise that if we assume the strongest possible selective pressure—only the best serve gets copied—a very high rate of error is consistent with cumulative directional change. After all, the various copying errors in directions other than the direction of optimal fitness (that is, optimal attractiveness) have no impact on future generations if only the best serve in each generation is copied.

In order for it to be plausible that even given an extremely high error rate, directional change will still occur in a wide range of cases, it must be plausible that selectional pressures will be strong enough. Since it is uncontroversial that sufficiently strong selection can allow for cumulative directional change even if the mutation rate is extremely high (at least assuming that the mutations are relatively small; see following discussion), and since the argument depends on assuming perfect selection, it becomes crucial to see just how problematic the assumption is. I will use the tennis example again to make the point.

Two ways of ranking tennis serves should be distinguished. First, serves can be ranked in terms of their attractiveness, where a serve is more attractive to the extent that people copy it in preference to other serves. Second, serves can be ranked in terms of their effectiveness—their contribution to winning tennis matches.

The existence of such an independent, objective standard of merit for tennis serves perhaps helps to lend surface plausibility to the idea that there is always a single serve that is most attractive to everyone; without an independent standard of merit that everyone is trying to meet, it is much less plausible that all people will always find one candidate meme ("allele") more attractive than all the other competitors in the population. The case of tennis is special; for many memes it is not the case that there is anything close to a unique standard of evaluation. Moreover, to the extent that selection is strong because everyone is trying to satisfy a unique standard, such as winning tennis matches, the explanation of the strong selection depends on everyone's sharing a goal, and meme theory thus does less explanatory work.

Yet even in the case of tennis serves, where there arguably is a clear, independent standard of evaluation,[3] it is not plausible that there is a unique serve that is most attractive to everyone. First, given the great differences in players' size and ability, different serves are more effective for different

---

3. Actually, it is not true that there is an unambiguous effectiveness standard for evaluating tennis serves. What if one serve is more likely to win a point, but is also more likely to injure your shoulder?

players. The serve that is best for a short, powerful man may be different from the serve that is best for a tall, slim woman. An excellent player with strong ground strokes and a weak net game may decide that it would be counterproductive to copy the big serve of someone with a serve-and-volley game.

Second, in playing tennis and choosing a tennis serve, people have motivations other than winning matches. They play to get exercise and for social reasons; they want to avoid injury, impress others, and so on. So even if there were a unique most effective serve (and everyone knew which it was), it would not be true that everyone would try to copy that serve.

Third, an implicit assumption that an effective serve is an attractive serve tends to obscure the point that as a general matter, how attractive a meme is to a person will depend on what other memes the person already has. The way I react to ideas depends on what ideas I am already committed to. This is another reason it cannot be assumed that in any population of competing memes there will tend to be a single meme that is most attractive to everyone.

More generally, which meme among competing candidate memes a person finds attractive may depend on circumstances other than the meme's content. This point illustrates the potential importance of noncontent biases. For example, a serve may be attractive, not because of its effectiveness, but because of the prestige of the person who displays it. We thus have additional factors that may affect the attractiveness of serves; it is an empirical question whether such factors will compete with factors such as effectiveness, thereby decreasing the strength of selection.

I want to emphasize that my concern is not whether tennis serves in particular develop by Darwinian evolution. As noted, whether Darwinian evolution will occur in circumstances where the rate of variation or mutation is extremely high depends on whether selection is strong enough (and whether variations are always relatively small). My present point is that the assumption that selection will be strong enough in a wide range of cases is problematic.

We have seen that even when there is a clear, independent standard of merit for competing memes, we cannot assume that there will be anything close to a unique most attractive meme. Things are presumably much worse when there is no single independent standard or goal that everyone is trying to meet. In such cases, it is often far less plausible that there will be a strong tendency for everyone to copy the same memes; consider men's ties, magazines, religious ideas, desserts, popular music, and so on. At least on the face of it, what we find is wide variation among different people with respect to what ideas are attractive.

In sum, it is true that given perfect selection, cumulative adaptation can occur even if small errors or variations occur every time an idea is transmitted. But this gives us no reason to be confident that extremely strong selection will be present in a wide range of cases. Moreover, when such selection is present because of humans' pursuit of a shared goal, the explanatory contribution of Darwinian theory is, to that extent, undermined.

I now turn to the second crucial assumption of the tennis-serve example: that variations from the model serve are always small. Without this assumption, there is no reason to think that there will be cumulative change in the direction of the optimal serve. For one thing, if single mutations or innovations can be very large, change need not be cumulative.

It is highly problematic to assume that every variation must be small (relative to the cultural development that is to be explained). The case of tennis serves again illustrates the point. When a weekend tennis player attempts to copy a professional's virtuoso serve, the results are likely to be very far from a good copy. More important, when people try to devise new serves, it cannot be assumed in general that the inventions will be marginal variations on a model. (It is not even true that inventions, in tennis or elsewhere, must be attempts to copy a model.) There is, perhaps, some plausibility to the idea that people won't suddenly come up with a very different tennis serve, but this likely has more to do with the limitations imposed by the human body and the rules of tennis than with a general truth that ideas change in small steps.

In general, ideas can be revolutionary, path-breaking. Scientists, inventors, and artists certainly build on the work of others, but there is no reason to think that large changes in ideas always come about by an accretion of small changes, beginning from a target idea and moving through a chain of descendants. Single developments need not be small. And the process of innovation need not be cumulative. An innovator may be influenced at once by many different ideas from widely disparate sources. These points will be important when I turn in the next section to the explanatory power of a Darwinian theory of cultural change.

17.2.2   What's the Best Explanation?

In the preceding section we saw that Gil-White's argument from the tennis-serve example depends on strong empirical assumptions. I suggested that those assumptions are not plausibly close to the truth in the case of tennis serves, and are much less plausible for memes in general. In this section I turn to my second, more fundamental point: Even when the necessary conditions are satisfied, so that cumulative change can occur, it does not follow that a Darwinian account is the best explanation of the change.

The tennis-serve example shows that a high error rate need not rule out cumulative directional change, but more is needed to defend meme theory successfully. Even when there is, broadly speaking, Darwinian evolution—differential survival of elements and cumulative change in the direction of complex apparent design—the best explanation of the change may be thinkers' deliberate innovation in pursuit of their conscious goals. If goals do all the work, appeal to Darwin is idle.

Suppose the meme theorist responds that whatever the explanation of the differential transmission of ideas, it is still true that the ideas that are around today are the descendants of the ones that succeeded in spreading the most. (Even this tautological-sounding claim may not be true since it may not be true that current ideas are the descendants, in any relevant sense, of earlier ideas.) According to this response, the fact that in some cases ideas spread because of our goals does not undermine meme theory any more than any other explanation of why some memes have greater fitness than others.

The problem with this imagined response is that if this were all that meme theory claimed—that the memes around today are the ones that spread the most—it would have nothing to offer. Meme theory needs to offer a distinctive explanation of why ideas spread, an explanation that competes with, or contributes something beyond, the goal-based account.

The tennis-serve example again illustrates the point. Rather than selection by blind forces, we have deliberate adoption of the most effective serve. And, in the more realistic version of the example, new serves are generated by self-conscious, successful innovation. Thus, the goal-based account of cultural change is a good candidate to explain the development of tennis serves. It therefore needs to be argued rather than assumed that Darwinian theory is a better explanation, or at least that it has something to add.

Gil-White suggests that the conclusions he draws from the tennis-serve example apply to technology in general, where "design has accumulated gradually," and thus that "selectionist approaches will be significant for historical explanations" (vol. 2, ch. 16, pp. 327–328). It is important to see why more argument is needed here.

First, although there is a weak sense in which technological change is cumulative (new technologies draw on existing knowledge), it is not clear that it is cumulative in the relevant sense (built up by successive additions). There can be sudden large breakthroughs because of one thinker's great idea (or because of an accident), as opposed to the accumulation of small variations through differential reproduction. Although researchers obviously draw on past ideas, each new idea need not be formed by making a change to a single past idea. And one can decide to scrap a whole project or design and begin from scratch.

Second, more importantly, in the case of technology there is a strong prima facie case that deliberate innovation is the best explanation of many developments. At least on the face of it, the reason that jet-engine technology has been invented and widely transmitted is that it satisfies human goals. If we contented ourselves with the thought that jet-engine memes are good at reproducing themselves in human minds (or have spread as the result of biases in the copying of ideas), we would miss a fundamental part of the explanation. (It is instructive to compare trying to predict the future course of technological development by considering, on the one hand, what goals humans have and, on the other, which memes are good at getting themselves reproduced by human minds and how human copying of ideas tends to be biased.)

It *could* be true that although people devote great time and energy to research and although they try to adopt the best models that research produces, a goal-based account of technological change is inadequate. How could this be? One way is that it could turn out that despite all efforts at deliberate innovation, the important steps forward tend to be the result of small copying errors—accidental mistakes in transmitting ideas. A different possibility is that even if the best explanation of each individual's decision is in terms of his or her goals, population-level phenomena, such as group selection, are crucial to the explanation of which technologies spread (Boyd & Richerson, 1985, 1989, 2000). A third possibility, which I take up in the next section, is that ideas could spread not because they serve our purposes, but because they are "catchy" (in a precise sense that I will explain). Again, it does not follow from the existence of cumulative change that Darwinian theory adds anything to the explanation of that change.

17.3   The Meme's-Eye Perspective

I now turn to the relevance of the "meme's-eye perspective" to the question of explanation. The idea is that the "interests" of memes explain the direction of cultural evolution—the analogue of the selfish-gene idea in biology. The important point here is that the selfish-meme approach[4] is a potentially important source of explanatory power for a Darwinian theory of culture; in particular, it is a main way in which meme theory may challenge goal-based explanation of cultural change.

I am not suggesting that Darwinian explanation must be adaptationist. As we will see, another possibility is that certain ideas spread because of social learning biases, for example, a human tendency to copy prestigious people. The point is rather that the explanatory payoff of Darwinian theory, whether adaptationist or not, cannot be taken for granted.

We have seen that meme theory needs to offer distinctive explanations for the spread of memes. To the extent that the fundamental explanation of the creation and transmission of memes is our pursuit of our goals, meme theory is doing no work. In the case of biology, Darwinian theory is an answer to the grand puzzle of how complex, apparent design has come about without any intelligence or design at all—a question that does not arise in the case of culture. Darwinian theory also provides answers to smaller-scale questions of why biological evolution takes particular directions. In the case of culture, there are analogous smaller-scale questions. For example, why does a particular idea take a long time to come about and then develop independently in many different places? Why do some ideas spread rapidly and persist for centuries? It is such questions of why cultural evolution proceeds in particular directions and at particular rates that meme theory must purport to answer.

In neo-Darwinian theory, one highly influential approach, made famous by Richard Dawkins (1976/1989), is to explain the course of biological evolution by taking the perspective of the gene, rather than that of the organism, group, or species. Roughly speaking, according to this "gene's-eye perspective," characteristics have evolved, not because they are in organisms' or species' interests, but because the genes for those characteristics were more successful than other genes at reproducing themselves in the local environment.

When Dawkins introduced the notion of the meme, his suggestion was that a meme's-eye perspective could offer explanatory power analogous to that of the gene's-eye perspective. The idea is that some features of culture are better explained by the memes' effectiveness at reproducing themselves than by what human creators of culture want or intend or have as goals. For example, we might better explain why some fad or prejudice or tune

4. I use "selfish-meme approach" and "meme's-eye perspective" interchangeably.

spreads by appealing to its "catchiness" than by appealing to human beings' intentions, goals, interests, and welfare. Just as a highly infectious virus may spread because it is good at taking advantage of features of our physiology rather than because we deliberately spread the virus to promote our goals, a highly infectious idea may spread because it is good at taking advantage of features of our psychology (other than our goals), rather than because we deliberately spread the idea to promote our goals.

Dawkins (1976/1989, pp. 196–200) suggested that since the memes that are good at reproducing themselves will tend to be the ones that are around today, we can think metaphorically of the memes as "trying" to reproduce themselves—as having an "interest" in doing so. Thus, the meme's-eye perspective explains the spread of ideas in terms of the interests of memes rather than of humans. Furthermore, meme theory might try to turn the tables on goal-based accounts, explaining why we have come to have our goals and intentions in terms of the interests of memes. (Of course, even if it is true that the meme's-eye perspective explains why we have certain goals, it doesn't follow that the goals are not what is now driving cultural change. Compare: biological evolution explains how memes came to be in the first place; it doesn't follow that memes are not now important in explaining cultural change, and possibly even in explaining which genes are selected for.)

It is dangerous to ignore the issue of meme theory's explanatory power. For example, Gil-White criticizes the meme's-eye perspective by emphasizing the importance of *noncontent biases*: whether and how frequently a meme gets transmitted can depend on features other than its content. It may be, as mentioned, that humans tend to adopt ideas that derive from prestigious members of the community. Or, how likely humans are to adopt an idea may depend on the frequency of the idea and of other ideas in the population. (As indicated earlier, such noncontent biases may conflict with the assumption that everyone will try to copy the most effective tennis serve.)

Why should the idea that memes can spread not just because of their content but also because of noncontent biases count as a criticism of the meme's-eye perspective? This would be an effective criticism if the gist of the perspective were the claim that only a meme's content is relevant to its spread. As I will elaborate, however, much of the importance of the perspective lies in its potential to challenge a goal-based account of the spread of ideas. Indeed, the significance of noncontent biases themselves cannot be understood without asking what explanatory payoff Darwinian theory provides over a goal-based account. Like the meme's-eye perspective, noncontent biases are potentially an important way to challenge goal-based explanations of cultural evolution.

Noncontent biases are explanations of the spread of ideas that do not appeal to the ideas' content. There is, however, an important distinction within the class of content-based explanations. On the one hand, as I have emphasized, ideas that are true or useful to humans can be spread because of humans' conscious goals.[5] On the other, ideas can spread because their content takes advantage of other features of human psychology—despite or regardless of humans' conscious goals or what is good for humans. That is, ideas may be catchy or infectious to human minds or brains.

We have to be careful to distinguish two senses of "catchy." In a broad sense, an idea is catchy if it has a tendency to spread. In this sense, the fact that a meme spreads as a result of its catchiness (as opposed to spreading as a result of noncontent biases) does not settle the question of the best explanation of the meme's spread. It might be that the best explanation of the meme's spread is our deliberate pursuit of our goals. Call this broad sense of "catchy" the *vacuous* sense.

In a narrow sense of "catchy"—the *interesting* sense—an idea is catchy if the idea's content makes it good at reproducing itself because of features of human psychology other than humans' deliberate pursuit of their goals. So advertising jingles, clichés, and religious cults are catchy in the interesting sense. In contrast, when people deliberately invent and spread an innovation—for example, the electric light—because it serves their interests, the explanation of why the innovation spreads is not its catchiness in the interesting sense, but our skillful and conscious pursuit of our interests. (In the vacuous sense of catchiness, the electric-light idea is catchy. But in this sense, catchiness is not the explanation of why the idea spreads. So notice that in neither the vacuous nor the interesting sense is catchiness the explanation of why the electric light spreads.)

Once we make the distinction between vacuous and interesting catchiness, we can see that the notion of interesting catchiness provides an important way in which Darwinian meme theory can compete with goal-based explanations of cultural evolution. Meme theory can try to show that the best explanation of why some ideas spread is not our conscious

5. It is an oversimplification to say that goal-based explanations must be content-based. Although goal-based explanations typically depend on features of ideas' contents, such as their truth or usefulness, goal-based explanations need not do so; in some circumstances, it will serve one's goals to adopt ideas for reasons other than their content.

goals, but the ideas' exploitation of other features of our psychology. Meme theory can even try to argue that our goals are themselves the product of our previous infection by catchy memes. The meme's-eye perspective is precisely the attempt to show that it is the meme's interests rather than ours that are in the driver's seat.

If we don't recognize the challenge that a goal-based explanation presents to other accounts of cultural development, we will not appreciate the importance of the meme's-eye perspective (as Gil-White's position illustrates). For the meme's-eye perspective, far from merely insisting on content-based explanations of the transmission of ideas, offers a way of challenging goal-based explanation, a central case of content-based explanation. Similarly, the importance of noncontent biases is better brought out by seeing them as another way of challenging goal-based explanations than by seeing them as a challenge to the meme's-eye perspective. Indeed, the reason it is appropriate to talk of *biases* in the transmission of ideas, as opposed to, say *methods*, *strategies*, or *policies*, is that it is implicit that an explanation in terms of biases is supposed to compete with an explanation in terms of deliberate choices. From this point of view, noncontent biases are an important ally, rather than a refutation, of the meme's-eye perspective.

17.4 Conclusion

Meme theory has the potential to challenge or complement other explanations of human cultural evolution, but it is crucial for theorists not to take the theory's explanatory power for granted. In order to defend meme theory successfully against the charge that the mutation rate is too high, it is not enough to show that if we assume perfect selection and relatively small variations, cumulative directional change can still occur. These assumptions themselves must be supported, and, more important, so must the substantive claim that Darwinian theory explains cultural change better than the commonsense goal-based account.

Noncontent-based explanations of cultural evolution are indeed important. The point of the meme's-eye perspective, however, is not to insist that explanations of cultural evolution must appeal only to the contents of ideas, but to oppose explanations in terms of our goals. Thus, noncontent-based explanations do not undermine the meme's-eye perspective. The meme's-eye perspective offers a possibly fruitful way for Darwinian theory to challenge the commonsense explanation of cultural change in terms of our skillful pursuit of conscious goals. In fact, the importance of noncontent-based explanations is better understood once we see them as another, complementary way of challenging goal-based explanations of culture.[6]

Acknowledgments

I am grateful to Andrea Ashworth, Francisco Gil-White, and Paul Seabright for helpful comments. I owe special thanks to Susan Hurley and Harry Litman for detailed suggestions and discussion.

6. See comments on this chapter by Blackmore (vol. 2, ch. 19.12, p. 406) and relevant discussion by Chater (vol. 2, ch. 18, p. 355). ED.

18 Mendelian and Darwinian Views of Memes and Cultural Change

Nick Chater

18.1 Introduction

One reason there is such interest in imitation in the study of cultural change is that imitation provides a mechanism for the replication of cultural phenomena, and this replication is a key notion in building what appears to be a deep and fruitful analogy between replication, variation, and selection in cultural change and replication, variation, and selection in biological change. This analogy, if it can established, is attractive because on the face of it at least, biological evolution appears to be much better understood than the evolution of culture, and there is therefore the hope of transferring insights from the biological to the cultural domain.

The understanding of biological evolution involves two deep but independent insights, one that is due to Mendel and one that is due to Darwin. Mendel's insight was that heritability between generations is mediated by discrete units of information that code for phenotypic outcomes and which are passed from parents to children. The spectacular breakthroughs in biology over the past 50 years have provided a rich, though still partial, understanding of the relevant molecular machinery (most notably, DNA): the chemical codes out of which genes are built, how they are transmitted from parents to children, and the processes by which they are translated in phenotypic traits.

Darwin, by contrast, assumed the existence of some mechanism of heredity but did not specify it. Darwin's insight was that heritability of traits, combined with processes of variation and selection, could provide an explanation of the origin of complexity. In Dawkins's (1986) elegant phrase, natural selection is the blind watchmaker: a nonpurposive process that is able to create creatures of such complexity that they would appear to be the work of an intelligent designer. A central analogy in Darwin's thinking, indicating how such a blind watchmaker might operate, concerned artificial selection in the breeding of plants and animals. Just as breeders could select from the naturally occurring variation in a species to breed faster racehorses, pug-nosed dogs, or high-yield wheat by processes of deliberate selection, so might processes of natural selection (i.e., arising from the differential reproductive prospects for different combinations of traits) lead to continual change in biological species. And where a variation involving some additional complexity arose that added to reproductive success, natural selection could lead incrementally to the emergence of complex, apparently designed, creatures, albeit with no input from a designer.

In attempting to draw parallels between explanations of biological and cultural change, theorists have considered possible cultural parallels of both Mendel's and Darwin's insights, but often without clearly distinguishing between the two. I suggest that the distinction is important because the analogy is much stronger in one case than in the other. Specifically, I suggest that mechanisms such as imitation do provide a notion of replication that might establish the potential utility of a notion of "meme" (see Blackmore, vol. 2, ch. 19.13; Dawkins, 1986; Gil-White, vol. 2, ch. 16): a transmittable unit of cultural information. But they do not suggest that cultural complexity should primarily be understood as generated by a blind watchmaker of selectional forces over such memes; that is, we need not see blind Darwinian processes as a universal explanation for the emergence of complexity (Blackmore, 1999, 2000a; Dawkins, 1986; Dennett, 1995). In a nutshell, the argument is that cultural change can be influenced by the collective insights and ideas of generations of intelligent and purposive agents. Cultural change operates in a world of sighted watchmakers, rather than through the blind watchmaker of Darwinian selection (see Greenberg, vol. 2, ch. 17).

18.2   Culture, Design, and the Blind Watchmaker

The Darwinian explanation of the emergence of biological complexity by natural selection makes two important assumptions. The first assumption is that the generation of variation is random. That is, it is not directed toward particular functional goals. This is crucial; if the generation of variation is itself directed, then the entire attraction of the Darwinian approach is lost because directing variation in a functionally appropriate way appears to require an intelligent designer to assess which variations are likely to be worth exploring. But then we have no understanding of where such a designer might come from. In practice, genetics reveals that the random processes of variation in the sequence of DNA are rather complex, but can be roughly summarized as involving recombination of genetic material from the parents (in sexually reproducing species) and a small amount of random mutation (although mutation rates are low; the copying fidelity of DNA replication is actually astonishingly high; Alberts et al., 1994).

The second assumption is that selection is global. Specifically, selectional forces are defined in terms of the reproductive success of whole organisms and hence, necessarily, operate over the entire genome of an organism. In particular, selectional forces cannot give particular positive or negative feedback signals concerning particular genes. Across a population, of course, one gene may prosper more than another because over a population of phenotypes, one gene may turn out to be associated with phenotypes that reproduce more successfully, on the whole, than another. Such systematic differences in the replication of genes may be due to the advantage that the gene confers on the reproductive powers of the phenotype to which it contributes. To the extent that this is true, then selectional processes will favor genes that are advantageous to the organism (or at least to its reproductive powers). Note that it is crucial to Darwin's account that there is no mechanism for applying selectional forces directly at the level of the individual gene. To do this would, again, require an intelligent designer (or perhaps more a scientist than a designer), to ascertain the relative contributions of specific genes to a particular organism's reproductive success. However, note that both these key assumptions appear to be violated in varying degrees in the case of the transmission of cultural information.

When cultural information is transmitted, the generation of variation is frequently, and one might assume typically, far from random. As Donald (vol. 2, ch. 14) notes in describing the breadth and subtlety of processes of mimesis in humans, we rarely merely "copy" the actions of another; rather, we reorganize, rearrange, and adapt what is being copied, to achieve our own functional purposes. This occurs in many different ways; in imitating another's actions, we adjust and recalibrate to our own body the patterns we observe. Moreover, we adjust the imitated process to the task in hand; for example, in imitating the laying out of cutlery, we make adjustments for the size of the table, plates, and number of people. We also deliberately select certain outcomes of "random" events as worthy of repetition; as folk wisdom has it, some cookery blunders lead to new recipes. In addition, processes of learning and conscious thought frequently lead to substantial and purposive modifications of what is being imitated (see Greenberg, vol. 2, ch. 19.11). Purposive human activity seems to fall into this category. We attempt to use existing methods to build a house, market a product, conduct an experiment, create a work of art, or make conversation, but our attention is engaged in selectively applying and adapting these existing methods to best achieve our current goals (Greenberg, vol. 2, ch. 17). The flexibility and speed of this purposive activity will, it seems, swamp any impact of slow, "blind" selectional forces.

Now consider the question of how far memes are selected globally, as in the biological case. Certainly, it seems plausible that memes that are part of entire systems of belief or practice (e.g., those associated with religion) may in some circumstances be replicated, roughly speaking, as wholes (e.g., either the whole set of practices and beliefs is transmitted from generation to generation, or none are). It is possible that there may be random variations in this transmission process, and that these might lead to selective modifications of the entire belief system, analogous to the biological case. However, it seems implausible that this type of mechanism plays a significant role in the development of cultural complexity. This is because any such effects will be so slow that they will be dwarfed by the power of local selectional forces; different aspects of cultural practices will be subject to very different patterns of selection. Certain beliefs will be unappealing or incomprehensible and may be winnowed out; other beliefs may be selectively amplified and modified. Moreover, note that these local processes of selection will themselves frequently be purposive. Indeed, different points of religious doctrine, aspects of artistic style, and scientific beliefs will often be the subject of active and overt debate. The outcomes of these debates will strongly influence the direction of cultural change.

18.3   Where Does the Blind Watchmaker Operate in Cultural Evolution?

In the theory of biological evolution, it has been pointed out that not every aspect of biological structure is an adaptation. Thus, to choose the cultural example used to make the biological point, the spandrels of the church of San Marco were not specifically "adapted" for any purpose; they were generated as side effects of structures that do have such a purpose (Gould & Lewontin, 1979). In both biology and culture, such structures can be subjected to positive selectional forces in the absence of any adaptive function.

In the cultural case, though, there is a further interesting class of cases; memes are "contagious" for some reason other than their success in achieving human purposes. To choose a much-discussed example, consider the now-spent craze for wearing baseball caps backward. This behavior is easily observed and easily copied (particularly given the high prior level of wearing baseball caps) and it had, perhaps, some high-prestige exponents. However, it does not have any particular purpose. Those who adopt this behavior are presumably acting purposively; their purposes may include modifying their social prestige in the eyes of certain groups, and adopting the behavior may achieve this successfully. But the particular cap orientation, or the fact that caps rather than, say, ties, are worn with unusual orientation, may not have any purposive explanation. Thus, the spread of such behavior may, in a real sense, not be the product of design. It spreads, not because people have decided that it is in any prior sense a good idea, but because it is "catchy" (see Greenberg, vol. 2, ch. 17, for a discussion of interesting and vacuous senses of "catchy").

Language change across generations may provide a further interesting example. For example, the regularization or contraction of phonological forms may be due to selectional forces affecting the learning and processing of language (regular forms are easier to learn; contracted forms are easier to say) (see Christiansen, vol. 2, ch. 19.8; Roberts et al., in press). Language change also involves powerful sociolinguistic factors concerning the relative prestige of different linguistic groups. These sorts of factors may explain aspects of language change and may even do so in a way that can be given an adaptive gloss (optimizing learnability, ease of production, social prestige), but these may not be purposes that are deliberately entertained by the speakers of those languages (although the influence of such deliberations cannot be completely ruled out). (Note, incidentally, that selectional forces on language appear to be highly local. In contrast to genomes, languages are replicated piecemeal from generation to generation, and selection operates directly on the pieces.)

In such cases, an evolutionary perspective seems to add substantially to our understanding of the selective transmission of cultural phenomena. In particular, it goes beyond what would be explained by deliberate, purposive selection by individual learners. As Greenberg (vol. 2, ch. 17) stresses, it is only where meme-based explanation goes beyond purposive explanation that it plays a substantial explanatory role.

Such selectional explanations appear to mirror the Mendelian aspect of biological evolution—at least in that we can understand the differential spread of memes in terms of the mechanism through which they are spread (the analogue of Mendel's heritability). This raises the interesting questions of whether the nature of the units of cultural selection are discrete or continuous, how exact replication needs to be, what error rates in replication can be tolerated, and so on (see the discussions in Gil-White, vol. 2, ch. 16, and Greenberg, vol. 2, ch. 17).

How far do meme-based explanations go in answering the question of the emergence of cultural complexity? That is, to what extent can cultural complexity be viewed as generated by the blind watchmaker of non-purposive selectional forces? It is not clear that there are any such cases. Cultural complexity appears, typically, to be the product of deliberate, purposive efforts that allow potentially extremely rapid change, whereas evolution by selection appears, at least in biological evolution and in computer simulations, to work very slowly. It seems natural to view the elaborateness of systems of religious or scientific beliefs; the structure of rituals; or the patterns of organizational, social, and moral structure as emerging from the application of generations of intelligence and creativity. "Mere" catchiness, driven by nonpurposive factors, may influence which complex cultural ideas survive and which die out. However, it is not clear that they contribute to explaining the origin of that complexity. It seems implausible to suggest that Ptolemaic astronomy, knitting, or Impressionist painting, were generated by blind processes of replication and selection. Surely such complex cultural forms were shaped by purposive selection and modification by successive generations of innovators. The historical record, taken at face value at least, seems to indicate that self-conscious, directed efforts by creative and intelligent individuals (scientists, garment makers, painters) are the source of cultural complexity, rather than blind selectional forces (a view also discussed by Greenberg in chapter 17).

18.4   Which Do We Understand Better—Culture or Biology?

The attempt to explain the emergence of cultural complexity using the machinery thought to underlie the emergence of biological complexity is a bold one, but it is worth reflecting on how strikingly counterintuitive it is. The metaphor of natural selection as a blind watchmaker is intended to explain how we can account for the complexity of biological structures without postulating a designer. The attempt to explain cultural complexity in Darwinian terms amounts to attempting to turn the tables and argue that even watches (as cultural artifacts) are really the product of blind selectional forces, rather than outcomes of the design of watchmakers! That is, it attempts to extend the metaphor of the blind watchmaker from biological evolution, where the existence of a relevant designer is a matter of debate, to cultural evolution, where the existence of designers is not in doubt. It seems rather startling to, in effect, attempt to explain cultural complexity as a product of blind watchmakers in a world of sighted, intelligent, and creative watchmakers who, moreover, appear to be vigorously engaged in designing watches.

One motive for attempting this startling reversal may be the intuition that the explanation of complexity is further advanced in biology than in the study of culture because of the existence of modern evolutionary theory. I suggest that this intuition is misleading. In the study of culture, our explanations of the creation of complexity, as products of the deliberate application of intelligence, are so routine that we hardly notice them. It is true that the specific processes that underlie the creation of a symphony, a theological doctrine, or a new style of dance are not well understood. However, large areas of academic enquiry, particularly in the humanities, are devoted to providing such explanation in informal terms, and there are subfields of cognitive psychology devoted to relevant processes of problem solving, reasoning, and creativity.

By contrast, the emergence of complexity in biological systems is little understood. Computer simulations of evolutionary processes and the use of genetic algorithms (Holland, 1992) and genetic programming (Koza, 1992) demonstrate the emergence of, at best, extremely modest levels of complexity. This has led some to speculate that natural principles of order in the environment that genes influence must be crucially involved in creating complex forms (e.g., Kauffman, 1993). However, in contrast to the cultural case, the data available to help guide accounts of how biological complexity emerges are woefully inadequate. In explaining the creation of a new cultural form, we typically have detailed historical records and can in some cases simply directly ask the relevant individuals about how the cultural form emerged. We may also be able to conduct controlled psychological studies of the processes underlying the creation of analogous cultural forms. Despite the biases inherent in any of these methods, they are far richer than the body of evidence available to the biologist, which consists of very partial historical information, either reconstructed from genes themselves or from extremely sketchy data in the fossil record.

The advocate of a Darwinian perspective on the origin of cultural complexity has another possible line of argument—suggesting that the purposive, intelligent behavior may itself result from Darwinian selectional processes *inside the head* (e.g., Edelman, 1989). That is, intelligent behavior itself may be a product of Darwinian forces. Yet this viewpoint seems to have little independent plausibility. Behaviorism proposed a selectionist viewpoint that was defined over observable behaviors; behaviors were presumed to be selected according to their level of reinforcement. A fundamental puzzle for this view is how behaviors can be planned and reorganized in creative, flexible ways (e.g., Chomsky, 1959). Just as Darwinian approaches to culture have difficulty explaining purposive design, so Darwinian approaches to mental processes have difficulty explaining purposive thought. Hence, it seems unpromising to attempt to save the thesis that cultural complexity arises from Darwinian processes merely by pushing Darwinian selection inside the individual.

I have argued that the analogy between biological and cultural evolution is only partial. The concept of a meme may explain the replication of cultural phenomena among individuals, just as Mendel's notion of discrete units of heredity explains the replication of biological structures across generations. Yet Darwin's deep insight that natural selection may act as a blind watchmaker, creating complex designs from the slow and grinding operation of blind processes of variation and selection, does not carry over to the cultural case. Cultural complexity works rapidly and flexibly because it *is* produced by design—through the cumulative and deliberate operation of human intelligence.[1]

1. See comments on this chapter by Blackmore (vol. 2, ch. 19.13, p. 409) and for relevant discussion see Gil-White (vol. 2, ch. 16, p. 317) and Greenberg (vol. 2, ch. 17, p. 339). ED.

19 Commentary and Discussion on Imitation and Culture

19.1 Not Waving but Drowning
Susan Brison on Dijksterhuis

Dijksterhuis claims that imitation of others' behavior "constitutes the 'social glue' that makes us successful social animals" and that imitation is "default social behavior," something we do automatically and frequently (vol. 2, ch. 9, p. 208). The research of Meltzoff and Moore (1977, 1997) is taken to support the claim that our capacity to imitate is innate, and the discovery of mirror neurons that discharge both when an action is perceived and when it is performed (Gallese et al., 1996; Rizzolatti et al., 1996a) is taken to provide the neurological explanation for this capacity.

The claim that in social perception we imitate what we perceive sounds straightforward enough. But *what* do we perceive? According to Dijksterhuis, we perceive three different classes of things, distinguished by three different methods by which we perceive them:

1. behaviors (or actions) "that can be observed literally and directly," including "facial expressions, postures, gestures, and . . . tone of voice" (p. 212).
2. traits that we perceive indirectly but automatically through inferences based on the observed behavior of others; and
3. stereotypes, or representations that are automatically activated because of the (perceived?) social group membership of the person(s) observed.

The perception of traits and stereotypes, while considered to be automatic (which I take to mean that they are not under the conscious control of the perceiver), is viewed as decidedly more complex than the simple perception of actions. However, the perception of actions is not as simple as Dijksterhuis suggests, and it is not clear that a strictly "literal" perception of an action is possible. Actions have meanings, just as words have meanings, and they are all subject to interpretation. Two (or more) actions can function as something like homonyms (they look exactly the same, but they have different meanings), as illustrated in the spare, evocative title of Stevie Smith's poem "Not Waving, but Drowning." In social perceptions, we frequently need to rely on inferences (about the inner states of the person observed, about the context) in order to know what behavior it is that we are perceiving—and in order to imitate it. If I wave back at a drowning person, have I imitated her? Perhaps, in a sense, but certainly not in a way that facilitates affiliation or empathy. In waving back, I am doing something similar to what I perceive her doing, but I am also doing something (disastrously) different. Suppose I realize that she's drowning and I either don't care or actually want her to drown and so I "wave back." This is now a different action and one in which I am intentionally *not* imitating the person I perceive to be drowning. In all of these cases, the drowning person and I are doing, physically, the same thing in flailing our arms, but we are performing actions with very different meanings—meanings that are not automatically or directly apparent to an observer.

Not only gestures, but also facial expressions, postures, and vocal inflections require contextualized interpretation. I am told that I look like I am frowning when I am not frowning, but concentrating. When I tell my husband, who is hunched over with his arms tightly crossed, that he looks clenched, he says he's not clenching, but freezing. Sometimes, when my son is on the verge of melting down, I think he is crying when in fact he is laughing (and vice versa).

One could imagine the case of a long-married couple whose facial expressions have come to resemble each other's, but not because they were experiencing the same emotions and literally imitating each other. One could develop the facial lines of a scowl as a result of a lifetime of "imitating" a myopic partner who was not scowling but squinting. Would it be correct to call what led to this facial resemblance "imitation"? Not if imitation implies empathy, as Dijksterhuis maintains. Just as actions, including gestures and expressions, are *intentional* only under some descriptions and not others, it seems actions are *imitative* only under some descriptions and not others. It is not clear to me how the research on mirror neurons might account for this.

None of this, however, undermines Dijksterhuis' main thesis that imitation functions as social glue, but it does suggest that the imitation of even simple behaviors is not as simple and automatic as he claims. What Dijksterhuis calls "the low road to imitation"—"literally and directly" observing an action and then imitating it (p. 212)—does not seem to be a busy thoroughfare, or even the road less traveled, but rather one that does not exist at all. What Dijksterhuis calls "the high road to imitation"—the complex, contextualized, and meaning-laden process by which we perceive and imitate "much more than what can be literally perceived" (p. 212) may be the only road there is.

19.2 The Imitation Superhighway
Harry Litman on Dijksterhuis

Dijksterhuis' chapter is surely one of the more provocative and synthetic (in the sense of bringing together different strains of thought) in this volume. At the Royaumont conference on imitation, the view was advanced, more or less axiomatically, that we could not function if we went around imitating everyone. Professor Dijksterhuis' chapter argues otherwise, suggesting that we not only can, but generally do, function in this way. Dijksterhuis marshals extensive evidence that imitation on many levels is our default mode of functioning and that it operates automatically unless it is countermanded.

As I read his chapter, Dijksterhuis' "high road" extends very well beyond discrete motor behaviors to "various forms of interpersonal behavior, intellectual performance, and attitudes" (vol. 2, ch. 9, p. 217). Thus, a slowed gait might arise from any of the following: seeing another's slow gait; seeing another's slow behavior other than a gait; seeing someone whom one knows to be a slow person; seeing a member of a slow group, such as the elderly (whether or not the observed group member in fact exhibits the trait stereotypically associated with the group); seeing or thinking of the word "slow"; thinking of words such as "molasses" that are associated with slowness; thinking of words that are associated with groups that are slow (for example, "geriatric" or "bingo," which are associated with the elderly); and subliminal associations with slowness. And that is just for one sort of behavior and one kind of priming input. As Dijksterhuis asserts in section 9.6 (p. 217), "relevant research has shown by now that imitation can make us slow, fast, smart, stupid, good at math, bad at math, helpful, rude, polite, long-winded, hostile, aggressive, cooperative, competitive, conforming, nonconforming, conservative, forgetful, careful, careless, neat, and sloppy." In other words, it affects our entire psychological functioning. We thus have the ideomotor idea writ enormous, applied not only to essentially all perception of the outside world, but also to all levels, conscious and subconscious, of human thought, feeling, and motivation. This is a high road with many, many lanes.

Much of this seems marvelous, and some of it perhaps seems dubious. Yet note that the effects or tendencies that Dijksterhuis reports are quite subtle and easily inhibited. (One possible criticism of Dijksterhuis's account is that he apparently does little to measure, or at least to relate, the magnitude of the priming effects he has observed in the clinic.) We plausibly are seeing here an account of a very low-level, ephemeral contribution of others to mood, a sort of intuitive registration (and, Dijksterhuis would posit, replication) of the behavior and likely behavior of those around us.

The implications for public policy of Dijksterhuis's imitation as "social glue" theory are immense (again, depending on the magnitude of the effects Dijksterhuis posits). Most obviously, his ideas about the prevalence of imitation provide strong ammunition to the proponents of regulating media violence. If Dijksterhuis is right, then each of the estimated six times in an hour of prime-time television that a violent act is portrayed, millions of viewers become somewhat more likely to commit violent acts, and some percentage of them will be caused to do so. (And that is not even to mention the countless references to or portrayals of violent behavior in news reports, music videos, football games, late-night movies, etc.) As he puts it, "We do not choose to imitate at some times and not others. Rather, we are wired to imitate and we do it all the time, except when other psychological processes inhibit imitation" (pp. 218–219). Dijksterhuis's theory that imitation occurs more or less automatically bolsters the case for regulation, notwithstanding free-speech concerns or constitutional protections.

In particular, the sort of research Dijksterhuis chronicles could support either of two kinds of arguments that are typically offered in response to free-speech challenges to regulation. The first is that the speech in question has an immediate and inexorable harmful impact.[1] Dijksterhuis suggests that given our hard-wired propensity to imitate, violence in the media will certainly, if subtly, increase the amount of violence in the community.[2] The second is that the regulation is in fact of concomitants of speech that arise through processes that are unrelated to the features of speech that justify its increased protection. Dijksterhuis' work provides a framework for arguing that depictions of violence in the media cause acts of violence in the real world through an extrarational, noncognitive process akin to a reflex. In other words, media violence does not persuade or influence so

---

1. See, e.g., *Abrams v. United States*, 250 U.S. 616, 630 (1919) (Holmes, J., dissenting) (articulating "clear and present danger" test for regulation of speech).
2. See Hurley, Imitation, media violence, and freedom of speech. *Philosophical Studies* (2004).

much as automatically catalyze or trigger antisocial acts.[3] In this fairly discouraging way of looking at things, the depictions of violence lose much of the value that generally justifies the protection of speech. Beethoven's Ninth Symphony is no doubt constitutionally protected expression, yet courts might well sanction its regulation if it demonstrably affected people at large the way it affects the reprogrammed Alex in *A Clockwork Orange*.

I doubt that at present either of these arguments would have much traction in the courts, which generally require far more concrete and individualized showings of injury, particularly where First Amendment interests are at stake. Moreover, it would, I think, require much more theoretical and empirical work to elaborate Dijksterhuis' theory before it could serve as the basis for policy. In general, his chapter is valuable and fascinating because it suggests the possibility of a hugely expanded inquiry into the phenomenon of imitation. As Dijksterhuis recognizes, in surveying the "high road" of imitation, he is using the term "imitation" rather loosely. It is quite a large move from the low road of imitating discrete physical actions (already a major achievement and apparently one that only higher primates and possibly some species of birds are capable of) to his high road of continuous activation of associated traits and stereotypes. Indeed one way to view Dijksterhuis's chapter is as a potential road map of the future of the study of imitation as a social phenomenon. For now, his account raises a number of rich and, it seems to me, challenging issues, and I note three of them here.

First, we need a better theoretical account of how and when a subject picks out, among myriad candidates, a certain behavior or stereotypical trait to imitate. It may be the case, as Dijksterhuis asserts, that soccer hooligans are "a social group that is associated with stupidity" (p. 215), but presumably they are also associated with athletic ability, or gregariousness, or beer drinking. Perhaps Dijksterhuis' view would be that being primed with pictures of soccer hooligans elicits behaviors consistent with all these associated traits and scores of others, but then the simplest stimulus would provoke an immediate cacophony of associated imitations.[4] It would be

---

3. Of course, notwithstanding the wealth of evidence Dijksterhuis marshals, this remains a controversial theory. For a general critical analysis of the studies, see Freedman (2002).

4. Similarly, at the level of base stereotype, the archetypal professor is not only intelligent, but, for example, absentminded and gentle; and a politician is not only long-winded, but well-groomed and ambitious. Which of these traits is essential to the imitating observer? And what role might the experimenter's preconceptions of the traits play?

very useful to explore how a particular observed or inferred trait comes to be the relevant candidate for imitation.

Second, we would benefit greatly from a more thorough account of the evolutionary origins and role of Dijksterhuis's notion of imitation. This presumably is what Dijksterhuis is adumbrating with his notion of "social glue" and his general conclusion that imitation is explained by the need to be liked. However, it is clear on brief reflection that such a motive would not itself account for a phenomenon of the breadth and impulsiveness that Dijksterhuis posits. For one thing, there are other strong and often conflicting agendas than the need to be liked, such as the needs to reproduce, to procure food, and to escape predators. And certainly there are many circumstances in which imitation would be decidedly counteradaptive. (Of course, that does not itself make it implausible—not all traits are adaptations—but Dijksterhuis's "social-glue" thesis does seem to presuppose an adaptive explanation.) Dijksterhuis suggests that the impulse to imitate is easily suppressed, but that does little to advance an evolutionary account of a phenomenon that is presented as both automatic and ubiquitous (and it raises a new issue of the adaptiveness of expending such extensive resources in continually priming and suppressing imitation).

Finally, and perhaps most daunting of all, is the challenge of constructing a neurophysiological account of the high road of imitation. It is fairly straightforward to conceptualize (and possible, although no mean achievement, to actually identify) the neural mechanisms that underlie the low road to imitation. Dijksterhuis in fact discusses the groundbreaking work on mirror neurons by Rizzolatti, Gallese, and others. This work, which has genuinely exciting implications for many fields of study, has located individual neurons of highly specialized function. It is fairly overwhelming to consider what would be required to expand that concept into the higher-order functions and locales involved in the far more conceptual stereotyping that takes place on Dijksterhuis's high road. Constructing an adequate neural description of the broad phenomenon that Dijksterhuis is describing would at a minimum be a Promethean task—a human genome project for imitation.

19.3   The Crimes of Proteus
Harry Litman on Gambetta

In a very interesting chapter that resonates in literature, film, dream theory, and true-crime yarns, Gambetta presents what he describes as a broad-based programmatic method to begin to study a phenomenon—mimicry—

that is widespread yet barely recognized. I will comment by offering a few points of practical connection between his ideas and the criminal law, followed by a few suggestions for ways in which his program might be carried forward if, as he predicts, the study of mimicry is to grow into a free-standing interdisciplinary field.

A brief prefatory point is that Gambetta's chapter illustrates the breadth and diversity of the phenomena grouped in these volumes under the umbrella term "imitation." The subpersonal and neural perspectives on imitation suggest two defining criteria—a discrete physical action and a defined goal—and neither is present here. Rather, Gambetta addresses a behavior, or set of behaviors, that is more abstract and considerably more broad in its manifestation than the behavior described by Rizzolatti (vol. 1, ch. 1) and Gallese (vol. 1, ch. 3).

Indeed, a possible criticism of Gambetta's concept is its potentially enormous span. For example, the concept arguably captures much of the psychological mechanics of the advertising industry, in which a behavior m—such as driving a Mercedes or wearing certain jeans—is used intentionally and often falsely to signal membership in, or pass oneself off to, a desired group k—such as the jet set.

As Gambetta writes, the world of crime is replete with instances of mimicry, and certainly it provides many of the genre's most flamboyant and consequential examples. Indeed, in keeping with Gambetta's suppositions, there is a crime that is widespread—it is in fact the fastest-growing crime in the United States—yet is only beginning to be recognized and classified in its own category.

This crime is identity theft. Several years ago, it was exotic enough to be unnamed; now it is an acknowledged epidemic. The U.S. government estimates that there were 27.3 million victims between 1998 and 2003, and 9.9 million in 2003 alone. The identity thief's modus operandi is to appropriate a critical piece of identifying information—Gambetta might say a "symbolic string"—and then to exploit the appropriated identity to commit fraud, for example, by securing loans or opening bank or credit card accounts in the victim's name.

One of the crime's more pernicious aspects is that most victims do not become aware for some time (on average, more than a year) that their identities have been stolen, and on average they wind up spending about 175 hours repairing the damage. Along with computer crime, identity theft is the crime par excellence of the Internet age, which has occasioned the widespread use and dissemination of more and more bits of identifying information.

It also is possible to draw parallels between, on the one hand, Gambetta's schema and terminology, and on the other, the policy responses to identity theft, which in main consist of what Gambetta might describe as various strategies to raise the production costs of mimicking signals. This is the shorthand explanation, for example, for requiring a government-issued photo ID to use an airline ticket. It is far more difficult and risky (among other reasons because it is a separate crime) to counterfeit some-one's driver's license than it is to ascertain that person's Social Security number.

We can further apply Gambetta's approach to a range of familiar be-haviors in crime and law enforcement, including instances in which the criminal can play model or dupe as well as mimic. Consider in this regard probably the most common and effective law enforcement strategy, the sting operation, in which an undercover agent, or even a cooperating crim-inal, feigns criminality to catch the target in a crime. It is interesting that in such high-stakes "communicative warfare," law enforcement is vulnerable in turn to a common counterstratagem, which is to ferret out the agent by making the differential costs of mimicry prohibitive to a law-abiding mimic. Thus, gang members who suspect that a confederate is a government agent may require him to carry out a killing or other violent crime, which, to use Gambetta's terms, raises the differential costs to a point that non-*k*s (i.e., noncriminals) cannot pay.

I close with a few suggestions for further study, particularly with respect to potential formulation of policy in the criminal law. Gambetta classifies mimicry systems according to the basic (and largely antagonistic) relation-ships between three protagonists—model, mimic, and dupe. Other taxon-omies could be helpful both as classification tools and as bases of policy. In the area of the criminal law, two additional criteria come to mind.[5] The first is the state of mind of the mimic. Gambetta looks at a range of behav-iors in which the mimic's motivation varies widely, from puffery to high wickedness. Placement along that spectrum will help determine whether behavior is criminal, as opposed to merely mischievous, and help assess the conduct's blameworthiness (which will largely determine the criminal penalty).

5. The classic and highly entertaining sociological study by the linguist David W. Maurer, *The Big Con* (1940), presented a fairly scientific breakdown of the confi-dence man's book of big-money grifts (i.e., the "wire," the "rag," and the "payoff") according to the elements of the individual scheme and its particular methods for "trimming" the "mark."

From the standpoint of criminal law policy, the second important criterion that Gambetta's work does not yet address is the kind and degree of the harm to the victim. The law is likely to draw distinctions according to whether the harm is tangible or intangible, and perhaps according to whether the victim is the dupe or the model. The criminal law is most easily adapted to redress tangible, economic harm to a dupe—the classic model of fraud and the typical pattern in the case of identify theft. But a full rendering of the harms occasioned by criminal mimicry would have to include intangible social harm, i.e., injury to the social interest in the security and relative mimic-proofness of signs. There is thus a separate crime for appropriation of another's Social Security number, even in the absence of any economic injury, which can be justified by the shared social interest in the reliability of the Social Security number as an identity signal.

Finally along these lines is the interesting case of intangible harm to the model as opposed to the dupe. Should we recognize, as we do in the law of defamation,[6] an intrinsic harm to the model separate and apart from any tangible loss? The mimic exploits and injures the model's recognizable identity, an essential aspect of trustworthy communication and productive exchange. To many victims of identify theft, it is this injury, more than the inconvenience and economic loss (which is often borne by commercial interests such as credit card companies) that is the most keen and fundamental.[7]

19.4   Media Violence and Aggression, Properly Considered
George Comstock on Eldridge

John Eldridge has produced a wide-ranging and interesting survey of issues raised by the topic of violence in the media. He explores a number of themes:

• the claims by some that the empirical research literature on media violence is incoherent and uninterpretable because media violence is too diffuse, complex, and varied for meaningful investigation;
• the tendency of the media and some public officials to leap to conclusions about media influence when more careful scrutiny of the events in question shows little or no evidence of media effects;

6. See Post (1986).
7. This is an interesting fact itself for further study. One can imagine an argument in evolutionary theory—akin to the evolutionary theory of literature on cheating—that addresses the nature of the injury inherent in being the victim of identity theft.

• the concern of an artist that the transfer of a work from one medium to another that is more popular and accessible may distort and obscure the original author's antipathy to violence, with the writer in this case Anthony Burgess, the filmmaker Stanley Kubrick, and the work *A Clockwork Orange*; and

• the use of the media in times of conflict to depict a nation's enemies as meriting punishment for the atrocious, violent acts they have committed

The first is an extraordinary case of myopia. Barker (1997) insists on seeing only the forest and doggedly averting his mind from identifying the various species contained therein. Plenty of meaningful research within the social and behavioral sciences has been done on media violence, although from a variety of perspectives. Two examples will suffice. One is the social cognitive paradigm of Albert Bandura (Bandura et al., 1963a,b). The other is the cultivation paradigm of George Gerbner (Gerbner & Gross, 1976; Gerbner et al., 1980). The first has examined the conditions under which children learn from models, some of whom may be vicarious—in entertainment, news, and sports—and who provide examples of aggressive and antisocial behavior. The second has examined how the emphases of media portrayals affect the public's perceptions, and violence—in entertainment, news, and sports—is a frequent emphasis.

Distortions of bizarre crimes by the tabloid press are probably a world-wide phenomenon. However, the examples also are probably more noticeable and nationally prominent in Great Britain than comparable coverage would be in the United States because the London press is a much larger presence on British newsstands than are the New York tabloids across the United States. In the United States, accounts emphasizing the harmful influence of the media have been the exception rather than the rule. In fact, in the United States the news media have been schizophrenic in their readiness to blame the media for violent occurences. The finger of blame has been readily pointed at the products and practices of popular culture in high profile cases, such as the car crash that killed Princess Diana, the murder committed in connection with the *Jenny Jones* show, and the Columbine High School shootings (Scharrer et al., 2003). In regard to an everyday link between television and film violence and aggressive and antisocial behavior, however, the news media have downplayed the possibility of a connection.

Bushman and Anderson (2001) document the latter pattern. They show that since 1975 the average correlation between exposure to violent portrayals and aggressive or antisocial behavior in experimental and non-experimental designs has increased in magnitude (a pattern attributable to the increase in the magnitude of the correlations in the nonexperimental designs), while the frequency of news reports that exposure to media violence and aggressive or antisocial behavior are correlated has decreased. The curve representing the correlation sweeps upward and the curve representing what the authors consider the accuracy of news reporting visibly declines. The two have followed quite different trajectories, with the media favoring accounts that downplay the possibility of media influence.

Anthony Burgess was probably justified in his concern. Movies (and television shows) never perfectly reproduce a novel (although some have come quite close), so the possibility of a change in emphasis or message is always present. In addition, while novels and written work in general certainly can influence behavior, movies (and television shows) have a number of properties that make them particularly likely to lead to imitation or emulation. The visual elements often clearly convey acts that otherwise would not be encountered, so there is both an easy-to-comprehend model and novel behavior. These are usually parsed in real time, with little critical reflection on the implications of content. Most of the thoughts that arise center on the qualities of the presentation as entertainment—plot, character, action, suspense, special effects—and whether it was worthy of attention. The models are typically very attractive and often antisocial acts are rewarded, with even villains in the short run (and sometimes in the long run, too) enjoying success. The perspective imposed by the director can easily (and sometimes does, as Burgess believed was the case with *A Clockwork Orange*) give a viewer quite different interpretations of what are concretely the same events, and can make antisocial or criminal behavior acceptable or at least not subject to the usual moral approbation.

The American crime epic *Heat* provides examples of several of these factors. The criminals successfully rob an armored truck using explosives available from any construction supplier. The truck's crew is wantonly killed by a psychopathic newcomer. Robert De Niro, the gang's leader, successfully maneuvers his men through a series of mishaps, including the repair of a marriage. A bank heist goes bad. Val Kilmer opens up on downtown Los Angeles with an automatic weapon. Cops die. Kilmer is a man of steel. He also has been among the most likeable of a very likeable bunch of crooks. We hope he will evade the trap using his wife as bait that is set for him by the lead detective in the case, Al Pacino. The hint of betrayal for this couple, even if forced, makes us uncomfortable. Kilmer evades the trap; De Niro is not so fortunate. Pacino kills him, but has the opportunity to do so only because De Niro pursues what he considers an act of honor. Thus a cold-hearted killer (Val Kilmer) and an accomplished criminal (De Niro) become sympathetic characters.

The role of the media in making harsh measures against members of an outgroup—whether defined by nation, religion, ethnicity, or social behavior, such as sexual preference—more acceptable is hardly trivial. This influence is particularly noticeable in international conflicts, where the media of each country typically portray its enemies as having committed atrocities or behaved in an infamous manner. This is the process, described by Albert Bandura in *Social Foundations of Thought and Action* (1986), by which categories are created that remove people from the human stream so that they can be treated inhumanely without public protest. This is a special case of desensitization—the inhibition of responses to the suffering of others.

The more general case is represented by the hypothesis that exposure to media violence reduces responses to everyday violence. In fact, there is not much evidence directly in support of desensitization to everyday violence as a result of media exposure. This is because the research has involved desensitization to mediated depictions—fictional or ostensibly factual—of violence. However, desensitization by the media to media depictions of violence is a socially important outcome. It is only through the media that we learn about what is transpiring beyond our immediate experience, including the behavior of other nations and people who are not like us. The news media become the basis in these cases for thoughts and feelings about what is just and right. They become the source for moral judgments. Thus, their role in desensitization to the violence they report has persistingly disturbing implications.

These are all important issues raised by the topic of violence in the media. However, one aspect of media violence not much addressed by Eldridge is the issue that is most central to the theme of this conference— imitation and emulation. The issue of the possible influence of violent television (and movie) portrayals on aggressive and antisocial behavior receives comparatively little attention. It is practically made to disappear under the unfurled flags of the other topics discussed.

The most useful introduction to the empirical evidence on television and film violence and aggressive and antisocial behavior at this point in time is through meta-analyses (Comstock and Scharrer, 2003). Using the standard deviation as a criterion, meta-analysis combines the results of as many studies as can be found to estimate the magnitude of the relationships among variables. It is a quantitative aggregation of study outcomes. The key element is a singular property of the standard deviation—it has the same relationship to every approximately normal curve regardless of the subject matter, metric, or distribution. Thus, about the same proportion of cases always falls within plus or minus 1 standard deviation of the mean. As a result, estimates of differences between those who receive and do not receive a particular treatment from both experimental and nonexperimental designs that represent their relationship to the standard deviation can be averaged. The method is analogous to the use of a percentile; a standing at a particular rank quantitatively always means the same thing regardless of the particular measure. These estimates, because they are based on many studies, are more reliable and more valid than those produced by a single study (M. Hunt, 1997). Meta-analysis thereby enhances the quality of evidence while also providing a quantitative survey of the outcomes in a particular area of inquiry.

Unhappily, meta-analysis is not a substitute for interpretation. Experimental designs must be evaluated for the generalizability of their outcomes to other, everyday circumstances. Nonexperimental designs similarly must be assessed for the meaning to be assigned to the everyday associations they record—correlation, causation, or essentially a null relationship.

In the present instance, there are seven quantitative aggregations of study outcomes. The first is simply a tabulation and did not employ the standard deviation as a criterion. Andison (1977) categorized the outcomes of sixty-seven experiments and surveys by the direction and size of the relationship between the viewing of violence and aggressive or antisocial behavior. The remaining six all employed the classic and now widely accepted meta-analytic paradigm. Hearold (1986) was the first to apply it to the literature on media and behavior. She was a student of Eugene Glass at the University of Colorado (who developed meta-analysis in the 1970s in an attempt to quantitatively discredit H. J. Eysenck's claims that psychotherapy was ineffective), and examined 1043 relationships (drawn from 168 studies) between exposure to anti- and prosocial portrayals and anti- and prosocial behavior. W. Wood et al. (1991) examined only experiments in which the dependent variable was "unconstrained interpersonal aggression" among children or teenagers, and analyzed the outcomes of twenty-three studies in and out of the laboratory that met these criteria. M. Allen et al. (1995) aggregated the data from thirty-three laboratory-type experiments in which the independent variable was exposure to sexually explicit video or film portrayals and the dependent variable was aggression. Hogben (1998) confined himself to fifty-six coefficients drawn from studies measuring everyday viewing, but included a wide variety of aggression-related responses, including hostile attitudes, personality variables, and in one case the content of invented news stories, as well as aggressive or antisocial behavior.

Bushman and Anderson (2001) calculated the correlations by 5-year intervals over a 25-year period (ending in 2000) in experimental and non-experimental designs between exposure to violent television or film portrayals and aggressive and antisocial behavior. Paik and Comstock (1994) comprehensively updated the portion of Hearold's analysis representing the relationship between exposure to television violence and aggressive and antisocial behavior (and ignored other portions, such as prosocial outcomes and portrayals and nonbehavioral antisocial outcomes), and included 82 new studies for a total of 217 that produced 1142 coefficients between the independent and dependent variables.

These analyses, representing the behavior of many thousands of persons of all ages, a wide range of independent and dependent variables representing the concepts of exposure to violence and aggressive or antisocial behavior, and a variety of methods, make it irrefutably clear that children and teenagers who view greater amounts of violent television and movie portrayals are more likely to behave in an aggressive or antisocial manner. This holds for the data from both experimental and nonexperimental designs. All seven of the quantitative aggregations support such a view, including the four not confined to a narrow focus in regard to aggression and antisocial behavior: Andison (1977), Hearold (1986), Bushman and Anderson (2001), and Paik and Comstock (1994).

The case for causation rests on the consistency of the outcomes for the experimental designs and the confirmation by the survey designs of the generalizability of the experimental findings. This is not simply a matter of agreement between different methods, but of different inferences making a stronger case than either would alone. The generalizability of the causal evidence from the experiments is supported by the positive correlations in the surveys between viewing violence on an everyday basis and everyday aggression and antisocial behavior that are not apparently explainable other than by some contribution from viewing violence.

The "reverse hypothesis," which holds that the correlations in everyday life are attributable to the preference for violent entertainment of those particularly likely to engage in aggressive or antisocial behavior, presents the strongest challenge and as a sufficient explanation fares quite badly. Two key datasets are Kang's (1990) reanalyses of the NBC 3.5-year repeated-measures panel data (Milavsky et al., 1982) on elementary schoolchildren and Belson's (1978) survey of about 1600 teenaged males in London. Most survey data must be confined to inferences of association rather than causation because variables are measured at only one point in time, thereby obscuring an answer to the question of which variable caused a change in the other. Kang evaded this particular obstacle by using data from the NBC survey design in which questionnaires were administered at multiple points in time. This permitted the inclusion of time order in the analyses, with either viewing or behavior preceding the other. He found twice as many significant coefficients, eight versus four, for a viewing-to-behavior effect than for a behavior-to-viewing outcome out of a total of fifteen pairings of earlier and later measurement (there were six waves of measurement; thus, a total of fifteen possible pairings).

Belson found in his very large sample that the reverse hypothesis did not supply an adequate explanation for a positive association between the viewing of violence and the committing of seriously harmful, illegal acts (such as attempted rape or the use of a tire iron or razor in a fight) among a subpopulation with a high likelihood of delinquent behavior. More specifically, he found by using various statistical manipulations that viewing violence predicted a substantial increase in antisocial behavior, while aggressive propensity predicted only a minute difference in viewing violence. Thus, behaving in an antisocial manner may sometimes predict the seeking out of violent entertainment, but it fails to fully explain the associations observed between exposure to television and film violence and aggressive and antisocial behavior.

The research, as one would expect, goes well beyond the question of whether the media influence antisocial and aggressive behavior. It also addresses two other issues—the psychological dynamics underlying effects and the various individual attributes that increase or decrease the likelihood of influence.

Although they have taken on a number of specific guises at the hands of different experimenters, the factors that psychologically govern responses to violent and antisocial portrayals fall into four broad categories (Comstock and Scharrer, 1999): efficacy, normativeness and pertinence in regard to the behavior in question, and susceptibility in regard to the readiness of the individual to act. Specifically, portrayals that present the behavior as rewarded (efficacy), socially approved (normativeness), and relevant to the viewer (pertinence) have been demonstrated to increase the likelihood of imitation or emulation. In turn, states of anger or frustration on the part of the viewer, particularly if a person responsible for the anger or frustration is a potential target for aggressive or antisocial behavior, increase the likelihood of imitation or emulation.

The evidence on behalf of these contingent conditions is quite strong because the data have all been collected by experimental designs in which causation in regard to the independent variable can be inferred. Thus,

individuals respond with apparent rationality to media portrayals, imitating or emulating when the behavior (1) is cast as likely to serve the ends
of the viewer, (2) is unlikely to arouse scorn and likely to enjoy the approval of others, (3) seems linked to the circumstances of the viewer, and
(4) there is some motivation to engage in the behavior. However, there is
some uncertainty over the process by which the first three of these factors
operates. Some authors emphasize cognitive elements, in which the media
alter attitudes, beliefs, and values (Eron & Huesmann, 1987). Others
(Comstock, 2004; Comstock & Scharrer, 2003) suggest that these factors
may operate by affecting the salience and accessibility of the behavior in
the repertoires of individuals without altering attitudes, beliefs, and values.
This is an issue yet to be resolved, and it is possible that both function under different circumstances or that the two operate simultaneously.

Three major attributes of individuals have been examined (Paik & Comstock, 1994; Comstock & Scharrer, 1999): gender, age, and predisposition.
Although the early experiments with Stanford nursery school children by
Bandura et al. (1963a,b) indicated that males would be affected more frequently, the overall pattern now shows that males and females are affected
about equally. There is some tendency for the size of effect to decline with
age, but a "medium" effect size among young adults of college age disrupts
the linearity of the trend, and the effect size for adults falls above "small"
although below "medium" (by the criteria of Cohen, 1988), so it cannot
be said the association between exposure and behavior vanishes among
those older. Predisposition is an important factor. There are plenty of datasets where the association between exposure and behavior is limited to or
greater among those registering as higher in earlier aggressiveness. However, this cannot be taken as a necessary condition. The consistent record
of positive outcomes for experiments recorded by the meta-analyses makes
a strong case that those not particularly predisposed also may be affected,
unless the definition of predisposed is made so broad as to cover large portions of the population. This should not be surprising. There is much that
those not familiar with aggressive and antisocial behavior might acquire—
in the sense of being better prepared to perform such acts by having seen
them performed with some success by others—from media portrayals.

Two issues remain. One is what meta-analysts call the "effect size": How
large is the association? The other is seriously harmful criminal behavior: Is
it affected?

Cohen (1988) advanced labels for effect sizes of $r = .10 = $ small; $r =$
$.30 = $ medium; and, $r = .50 = $ large (Rosenthal et al., 2000). By these criteria, the effect sizes recorded are usually modest (the plural is necessary

because the magnitude of associations will vary by such factors as type of aggression, method, television program characteristics, and age and gender of respondents or subjects), and vary from approaching or achieving the medium range to small and sometimes large. In the Paik and Comstock meta-analysis, a recent comprehensive endeavor, the effect sizes in the survey designs for interpersonal aggression approach medium ($r = .24$ for physical aggression against a person and $r = .27$ for verbal aggression). This represents a socially significant effect because the stealing, hitting, and name-calling involved would be quite unpleasant to most victims and could trigger retaliation. Interpersonal aggression is also the most examined in the surveys of all forms of aggressive or antisocial behavior, and thus enjoys substantial reliability as an outcome as well as a claim to validity as representing an unwanted, hurtful experience.

In a comparative approach, Bushman and colleagues (Bushman & Anderson, 2001; Bushman & Huesmann, 2001) assembled a number of effect sizes to compare with the overall effect size of $r = .31$ for television violence and aggression recorded by Paik and Comstock (1994), and found that it was exceeded in their collection only by that for smoking and lung cancer and was greater than that for passive smoking in the workplace and lung cancer or calcium intake and bone mass. By both quantitative standards (Cohen's criteria and Bushman and colleagues' comparisons), then, the magnitude of the association, while not large, has social importance.

The outcomes representing illegal activities are comparatively few—about one-twentieth of the total outcomes examined by Paik and Comstock (1994). Effect sizes are in the medium range for two categories of nonviolent crime (burglary and grand theft), but become miniscule for violence against a person, although all three coefficients achieve statistical significance. Belson (1978) in his survey of teenaged males in London recorded correlations between exposure to violent television entertainment and vicious behavior, such as rape, use of knives and guns in fights, and smashing up the interior of a house, which he concluded were best attributed to the causal influence of viewing violence. Thornton and Voigt (1984), although explicitly declining to venture into the realm of possible causation, in their large sample of several thousand children and teenagers of both genders in a large southern U.S. urban area found slightly stronger associations between media exposure and more serious forms of delinquency (including hurtful aggression using a weapon) than for less serious forms of delinquency (such as running away) after controlling for a variety of demographic and social variables. Kang's (1990) reanalysis of the NBC panel data makes a good case for a causal contribution of viewing violence to interpersonal aggression, and the scale employed has items that are certainly on the borderline of illegal or serious harmful activity—hitting and fighting.

J. Johnson et al. (2002), in their recent longitudinal survey ($N = 707$) and one widely publicized because of its appearance in the prestigious journal *Science*, found that "assault or physical fights resulting in injury" were more frequent among the males at the ages of 16 and 22 who had viewed greater amounts of television (and presumably greater amounts of violence) at the age of 14 when five important covariates of viewing and aggression were controlled: childhood neglect, an unsafe neighborhood, low income, low parental education level, and psychiatric disorder. Finally, the U.S. Surgeon General's recent report on violence by youth (U.S. Department of Health and Human Services, 2001), drawing on Paik and Comstock, concludes that viewing violent television entertainment between the ages of 6 and 11 is one of about twenty significant early risk factors for committing seriously harmful violent criminal acts between the ages of 15 and 18; while the effect size is small (by Cohen's criteria), it was as large as three-fourths of the other significant early risk factors. Despite the inevitable methodological issues that can always be raised about this comparatively small body of evidence on illegal and seriously harmful behavior, the data clearly support the view that such behavior, as well as less serious forms of antisocial behavior (for which the seven meta-analyses present a very strong case) are facilitated by exposure to violent television and film entertainment.

19.5   Applying the Science of Imitation to the Imitation of Violence
Susan Hurley on Huesmann

Since the Williams (1981) report,[8] many liberals have felt able to dismiss as unsubstantiated the thesis that exposure to media violence increases aggressive tendencies in viewers. This dismissal is now seriously dated. Huesmann surveys an impressive body of recent theoretical and empirical support for the thesis that exposure to media violence increases violence in viewers. To summarize his arguments: relevant short-term processes include priming, excitation transfer, and immediate imitation, while long-

8. While this report focused on pornography rather than media violence, since much pornography represents violence, issues about whether pornography and media violence have harmful effects are closely related. See Comstock and Scharrer (2003) on the increased effect sizes of stimuli with content that is erotic as well as violent.

term influences are theorized to operate through observational learning of cognitions (in particular, schemas for attributing hostile intentions to others, scripts that link situations to aggressive responses, and norms for evaluating such scripts), and desensitization. Moreover, repeated short-term processes can influence the acquisition of aggressive schemas, scripts, and norms in the longer term, as well as desensitization. Empirical support for these influences comes from various mutually supporting paradigms, which Huesmann integrates effectively.

Well-controlled experiments consistently support the thesis that exposure to media violence *causes* (not merely correlates with) immediate aggression. The generalization of this result from the laboratory to the real world, and across time, is supported by meta-analyses and by longitudinal studies. For example, exposure to media violence in childhood has been found to predict aggression post-high school and at age 30, where other possible explanations such as initial aggressiveness, taste for violent entertainment, class, education, and parenting are controlled for. The results stand up to regression analysis and cannot be explained other than by a causal thesis. There is a strong consensus among researchers on this topic that exposure to media violence increases violence in viewers in both the short and the long term. The effect sizes are comparable to those of other public health risks that are taken very seriously, such as the link between exposure to asbestos and cancer.

Why then does skepticism among the public and some commentators on this empirical work remain so strong?[9] Possible reasons spring readily to mind. These results may threaten our conception of ourselves as autonomous; we dislike any prospect of censorship; and powerful financial interests in the media industry are vested in violent entertainment (Hamilton, 1998). But I want to emphasize here a different (although compatible) reason, which is that the importance of imitation in general in molding human behavioral patterns has not been widely understood or its great social significance appreciated. In particular, the relevance of recent scientific work on imitation surveyed in these volumes to issues of media violence has not yet been assimilated by social science, jurisprudence, or social philosophy.

9. The strong consensus among researchers has not yet got across to the public or the media, who regard the issue as controversial to a degree belied by the actual consensus of opinion among researchers; see Bushman and Anderson (2001) on a disconnect between research results and public opinion on this topic so striking that it has become an object of research interest in its own right.

Responses to studies on the effects of media violence have often been highly politicized and have, unfortunately, ignored the lessons to be learned from the burgeoning work on imitation in general in the cognitive and neurosciences. This is a regrettable result of disciplinary boundaries and blinkers. We should view questions about the imitation of media violence in the context of scientific understanding of imitation in general. The imitation of violence does not have an a priori exemption from what is being learned about imitation at large, which suggests that a general tendency to imitate is fundamental to and distinctive of human nature.

What light does the scientific work on imitation in general throw on the imitation of media violence in particular? It is disturbing simply to rehearse what we have learned about imitation at large with application to violent behavior. Consider the distinctions between the priming of movements, the emulation of goals, and full-fledged imitation made by various contributors to these volumes. All are relevant here. Recall that human beings, along with various other animals, show significant tendencies toward both the priming of bodily movements and the emulation of goals (see R. Byrne, 1995; Heyes & Galef, 1996; Tomasello & Call, 1997; Fadiga et al., 1995). As far as I know, there is no reason to exempt violent action from these quite general tendencies. Thus, observing violent actions should tend to prime similar body movements in the short term, which may or may not be inhibited. When the goal of violent action is attractive, a tendency to emulate such goals, perhaps via trial-and-error learning, should be expected. However, if nonviolent means to the goal are more efficient than violent means, mere emulation of goals need not tend to produce violent behavior—*unless* the creature in question has a strong tendency not just to emulate, but to imitate.

That is just what we humans do have. Human beings have a distinctive and strong tendency to full-fledged imitation of intentional behavior, including novel means as well as novel goals (Tomasello, 1999; Meltzoff, vol. 2, ch. 1). Children tend to imitate, even when it is inefficient, not just to emulate—as do the children who imitate a model by using a rake inefficiently, prongs down, to obtain a treat, instead of simply turning it over to use the edge (see Nagell et al., 1993). If novel violent behavior is observed, human beings should be expected to have a greater tendency than other animals to imitate it. They will tend to copy the violent means as well as the goal, even when the violent means is not an efficient way to achieve the goal.

This underlying default tendency to imitate is poorly inhibited in children, whose frontal inhibitory function is weak (Kinsbourne, vol. 2, ch. 7), so children in particular should be expected to have difficulty in inhibiting the tendency to imitate violence they observe (see and cf. Philo, 1999a,b). According to ideomotor theories, the underlying tendency to imitate is the normal default tendency for adults all the time, needs specific inhibition, and has effects even when it remains covert (see Kinsbourne, vol. 2, ch. 7; Dijksterhuis, vol. 2, ch. 9; Prinz, vol. 2, ch. 13; and see Chartrand & Bargh, 1999). Thus, a tendency to imitate observed violence should be expected to be present in normal adults as well as children, and to have effects even when it does not result in immediate action. Watching or imagining violent behavior constitutes a kind of *practicing* for violence, a honing of the skills of violence, just as in sporting or musical activities (see Pascual-Leone, 2001; Jeannerod, 1997). Our automatic tendency to assimilate our behavior to our social environment has been called the *chameleon effect*: the mere perception of another's behavior increases, in ways subjects are not aware of, the likelihood that they will engage in similar behavior themselves; modeled personality traits and stereotypes automatically activate corresponding patterns of behavior in us (Bargh & Chartrand, 1999; Bargh et al., 1996; Chartrand & Bargh, 1999, 2002; Dijksterhuis & Bargh 2001; Dijksterhuis, vol. 2, ch. 9). The chameleon effect should lead us to expect that the mere perception of violent behavior will increase the likelihood of automatically engaging in similar behavior, in ways subjects are not aware of. Violent stereotypes or traits, like other stereotypes or traits, should be expected to prime unconscious automatic assimilation, mental as well as behavioral. The assimilation should be expected to apply to violent goals as well as violent means, and not to depend on the subject's volition or on any relevant independent goals the subject may have that would rationalize the resulting aggression or make it instrumentally efficient. If the chameleon effect is the underlying default tendency for normal human adults, then it needs to be specifically overridden and inhibited when violent action is observed, as much as when any other action is observed. If there is a direct link between perception and action, then observing violence should be expected to increase the likelihood of doing violence. The link between representations of violent behavior and similar actual behavior should be as strong and direct[10] as the link for other types of behavior, a

10. In *Ashcroft v. Free Speech Coalition* (2002), the U.S. Supreme Court struck down a statute banning virtual child pornography (produced without using actual children). The *Ashcroft* Court assumed without substantial argument that any causal links between images of child abuse and actual child abuse are "indirect" and "remote," not "strong," and that the criminal act "does not necessarily follow," but "depends upon

link on which powerful evidence from various disciplines converges, as described earlier.

These influences can and often do operate automatically and unconsciously. As a result, they may well bypass the processes of autonomous deliberation and control, in terms of which we normally understand our actions, and are least accessible to control when they are unacknowledged (see especially Bargh, in press; Bargh, 1999).[11] This bypass will be threatening in itself, so that these tendencies will tend to be denied by the subjects who demonstrate them (as Bargh has indeed found). We should expect such tendencies to be especially threatening to people's sense of rational autonomy and control when the influence could result in violent action. We should therefore expect that people will find it especially hard to accept that they might be influenced toward committing violence by watching violent acts (ironically, if Bargh is correct, thereby reducing their ability to inhibit such influences). Perhaps resistance to evidence of the effects of media violence can be explained, not just in terms of vested financial interests in the media industry, but also in terms of such vested interests in the public at large. That is, people have an interest in conceiving of themselves as autonomously rational, which this evidence appears to threaten. These results not only challenge us as individuals, but also challenge assumptions that may have deep roots in liberal political theory about human autonomy.

However, things are not quite as simple as this may imply. At one level our automatic tendency to imitate may threaten our autonomy, but at another level, this may not be so. Rational autonomy arguably depends on language and the ability to identify with and understand others, which in turn arguably depend, among other things, on the distinctively human capacity for imitation. Moreover, there are reasons to believe that the capacity and tendency to imitate is closely connected, both functionally and in terms of neural underpinnings, with other distinctively human

---

some unquantified potential for subsequent criminal acts." However, a robust causal link does not become indirect merely because it operates over a large population statistically rather than without exception. The Court in *Ashcroft* seems worryingly unaware of the scientific research presented in these volumes. First Amendment jurisprudence is in danger of wedding itself to the now-exploded myth that the content of external representations, words, or pictures does not normally have "direct" effects on behavior, but only effects that are under the actor's conscious control.

11. On the significance of this bypass for issues about freedom of speech, see comments by Brison (vol. 2, ch. 8.10, p. 202) and Litman (vol. 2, ch. 19.2, p. 365); see also Hurley (2004).

capacities—for language, for identifying with others and understanding other minds, and for counterfactual reasoning (see Iacoboni, vol. 1, ch. 2; Arbib, vol. 1, ch. 8.2; Gallese, vol. 1, ch. 3; Decety & Chaminade, vol. 1, ch. 4; Meltzoff, vol. 2, ch. 1; Gordon, vol. 2, ch. 3; and other chapters in volume 2; Arbib, 2002; Gallese & Goldman, 1998; Meltzoff & Moore, 1999a; Rizzolatti & Arbib, 1998; J. Williams et al., 2001; Whiten & Brown, 1998; Meltzoff & Decety, 2003). These capacities in turn are arguably fundamental to autonomous human rationality.

Thus it is not quite right to see our underlying imitative tendencies as simply threatening these distinctively human traits and capacities in general, even if they do so in particular cases. Although imitative processes may often be automatic and unconscious and bypass autonomous deliberation, they may nevertheless also contribute, both ontogenetically and phylogenetically, to our having these traits and capacities in the first place. It may not be true that we would be more rationally autonomous without these underlying imitative tendencies; they may well be a deep feature of human nature. We may only possess our distinctively human abilities to make up our own minds, in rationally autonomous ways, because of the distinctively imitative way in which our minds are made up. This rethinking of the nature of rational autonomy may have social and political implications. Different ways of understanding the nature and basis of our distinctively human rational autonomy may affect the roles this trait plays in political philosophy and practice, and the best ways to foster, protect, and respect it.

Finally, recall the standard objection that a correlation between exposure to media violence and aggressive behavior does not in itself show that such exposure causes violent behavior. As Huesmann explains in chapter 12, researchers have decisively rebutted this objection by demonstrating the convergent results of different research methods, including controlled experimental and cross-lagged longitudinal plus supporting statistical studies (see especially Huesmann & Miller, 1994; Huesmann, 1998; Huesmann et al., 2003; J. Johnson et al., 2002; Paik & Comstock, 1994; Anderson & Bushman, 2001). However, as with the correlation of smoking and lung cancer, understanding the causal mechanism in play contributes to establishing a causal connection. With the discovery of the mirror system and the current development of theories of its function, we may well be on track to understanding the causal mechanism that subserves human imitative tendencies at large, including the tendency to imitate observed violence. Perhaps when the role and mechanisms of imitation in general are more widely understood, so will be the risks associated with the imitation of media violence in particular.

19.6   Acquiring Morality by Imitating Emotions
L. Rowell Huesmann on J. Prinz

In volume 2, chapter 13, Jesse Prinz undertakes to explain how imitation plays an important role in humans' acquisition of morality. His broad-ranging chapter covers several different topics related to morality, including psychopathy, impulsivity, guilt, and shame, and he offers a variety of exciting and provocative ideas. However, here I want to focus specifically on the mechanisms he discusses that are most directly connected with acquiring what might be called "moral beliefs."

What do I mean by "moral beliefs?" Morality can be defined in terms of behavior, but that behavior may or may not be consistent with an individual's beliefs. By moral beliefs, I mean a person's cognitions about what is right and what is wrong for them to do. As I argue later, such beliefs are an important component of morality.

Now Prinz argues that it is through an infant's facial mimicry that imitation first begins to play a role in the acquisition of morality, and I completely agree. He suggests that both the social bonding produced by facial mimicry and the emotional contagion it produces are important. While not disputing that view, I think there is good reason to believe that the emotional contagion process is more important in the long run. Why? There is increasing evidence that there are innate connections between facial expressions and emotional responses (Ekman, 1993). As infants and toddlers imitate expressions, they therefore quite likely experience the corresponding emotion, which is the emotion that the model is experiencing. Essentially, the emotion is imitated and thus can be connected through conditioning with the external stimuli that produced the emotion in the model. As Prinz points out, emotional contagion can also occur without the mediation of facial expressions, but simply through auditory cues; e.g., crying is contagious for infants.

An interesting idea that is stimulated by the conclusion that emotions are imitated is that if one searched hard enough, one should find "mirror" neurons for emotions just as Gallese et al. (1996) have found mirror neurons for intended motor acts. The logic of that argument seems clear. Mirror neurons facilitate imitation by connecting to both the input and output systems. Emotions are imitated. Therefore, there must be mirror neurons for emotions.[12]

12. See discussions of emotional mirroring in Rizzolatti, vol. 1, ch. 1; Iacoboni, vol. 1, ch. 2; Gallese, vol. 1, ch. 3; and Decety and Chaminade, vol. 1, ch. 4. ED.

Let me turn now to the question of how the human child moves from a preliminary ability to imitate emotions to the acquisition of moral beliefs. Prinz concisely walks us through most of the process. By experiencing the emotions of those around them, the infant acquires what we would call empathy—the ability to feel what others feel. Prinz suggests that children then learn what behaviors are acceptable and not acceptable from perceiving what those around them feel in response to their behavior. The process outlined by Prinz is elaborate and undoubtedly correct as far as it goes. However, I think there is an additional imitative process that needs to be considered.

To understand the process I believe is important, one must understand the cognitive revolution that has taken place in social and developmental psychology over the past three decades. In that period social-cognitive and information-processing models have emerged as the dominant theories to explain how children's interactions with the environment lead to lasting behavioral and emotional dispositions (e.g., Anderson & Bushman, 2002; Crick & Dodge, 1994; Dodge, 1980b; Huesmann, 1988, 1998); Some studies focus more on the role of cognitive scripts, world and self-schemas, and normative beliefs (e.g., Huesmann, 1998), while others focus more on perceptions and attributions (e.g., Crick & Dodge, 1994). However, all of them hypothesize a similar core of information processing, and all draw heavily on the work of cognitive psychologists and information-processing theory; in particular they draw from Bandura's (1977, 1986) earlier formulations of cognitive processing in social learning as well as Berkowitz's (1990) neo-associationist thinking.

According to Bandura's (1986) social-cognitive formulations, social behavior is under the control of internal self-regulating processes. What is important is the cognitive evaluation of events taking place in the child's environment, how the child interprets these events, and how competent the child feels in responding in different ways. These cognitions provide a basis for stability of behavioral tendencies across a variety of situations. Internalized standards for behavior are developed from information conveyed by a variety of sources of social influence, including observing the behavior of others, e.g., parents, peers, and characters in the mass media. Berkowitz (1974, 1990), while not disputing the importance of internalized standards, has emphasized the importance of lasting conditioned associations among affect, cognition, and situational cues.

Building on this theorizing I (Huesmann, 1988, 1998; Huesmann & Guerra, 1997) have argued that a crucial phase of behavioral enactment is an evaluation phase in which the social scripts generated for behavior are evaluated against moral beliefs and rejected if they do not pass muster. These moral cognitions (denoted normative beliefs) are acquired though generalizations made from observing how others behave and the outcome of their behaviors, including the emotions they experience. This process clearly is a form of imitation, but it involves inferences and can only happen as the child becomes mature enough to make logical inferences. In fact I and my colleagues (Huesmann & Guerra, 1997) have shown that such beliefs only crystallize and begin to influence behavior during middle childhood.

In summary, the critical addition I would make to this excellent essay by Prinz is that moral beliefs are acquired, not only through the imitation of emotions and the development of empathy, but through the inferential acquisition of specific beliefs from the observation of others' behaviors and the observation of the emotional and the practical consequences of those behaviors.

19.7 Mirror Systems and Adam Smith's Theory of Sympathy
Robert Sugden

Almost 250 years ago, Adam Smith (1759/1976) proposed a "theory of moral sentiments," explaining human morality as a self-regulating equilibrium of affective responses to the stimuli generated in social life.[13] The basic building blocks of the theory are certain psychological hypotheses about sympathy, which Smith justifies by appeals to introspection and common human experience. I have long believed that Smith's naturalistic approach to the explanation of morality is more fruitful than the more rationalistic approaches that later economists have taken (see Sugden, 1986, 2002). It is exciting to discover just how far Smith's hypotheses about sympathy are consistent with the theories and experimental results of modern psychology and neuroscience.

Smith's *Theory of Moral Sentiments* begins with what I take to be his most fundamental hypothesis: that each of us, when vividly conscious that another human being is in a situation that would induce a particular affective state in us, tends to feel the same affect in a weaker form. Thus, in Smith's

13. This discussion reflects on what I learned about the psychology and neuroscience of sympathy by participating in the Royaumont conference on imitation, and by following up suggestions made to me by other participants, particularly Jean Decety, Robert Gordon, Mark Greenberg, Paul Harris, Stephanie Preston, Giacomo Rizzolatti, David Sally and Paul Seabright. My work has been supported by the Leverhulme Trust.

example of a typical human response to the sight of another person being tortured or beaten:

By the imagination we place ourselves in his situation, . . . and thence form some idea of his sensations, and even feel something which, though weaker in degree, is not altogether unlike them. . . . When we see a stroke aimed and just ready to fall upon the leg or arm of another person, we naturally shrink and draw back our own leg or our own arm; and when it does fall, we feel it in some measure, and are hurt by it as well as the sufferer. (A. Smith, 1759/1976, pp. 9–10)

In the literature on Smith, there has been much discussion about just what kind of imaginative identification he had in mind, and how far empathy or perspective-taking is involved. In my reading of Smith, perspective-taking supplements a more direct psychological mechanism, working below the level of reason or conscious control. As the example of the beating suggests, this mechanism induces in the observer, as an immediate and involuntary response to his consciousness of a stimulus operating on another person, an affective state similar to that which would be induced by the same stimulus operating on himself.

Many philosophers have dismissed this hypothesis as crude and mechanistic, thinking that a theory of sympathy ought to rest on assumptions more flattering to human reason. However, the mirror mechanisms that are being discovered by neuroscientists such as Jean Decety and Giacomo Rizzolatti seem to have many of the properties postulated by Smith. It seems that an observer's representation of a stimulus acting on another individual can have some of the same neural content as that of the observer's response to the same stimulus acting on him. Given what we now know (but Smith did not) about how brains work, the existence of such mechanisms should not be altogether surprising. In a system made up of a dense network of interconnections, we should expect that perceptions that have significant common features will be processed in overlapping ways, and thus have some tendency to activate similar affective states. Furthermore, as Stephanie Preston and Frans de Waal (2002) point out, this kind of overlap can have evolutionary advantages. Among animals that live in groups, the direct perception of some phenomenon (say, the approach of a predator) and the indirect perception that another individual has perceived it often call for the same action (say, escape). If this combination of perception and action is linked to an emotional response (say, fear), we have a rudimentary mechanism of sympathy.

However, as Smith realized, the idea that sympathy is merely emotional contagion does not seem to explain the *expression* of sympathy among social animals. If the consciousness of another person's pain is painful, why do we desire other people's sympathy when we experience pain? Why isn't our consciousness of their sympathetic pain also painful for us? And what motivates other people to express their sympathy for us if that merely enlivens their imaginative perception of our pain? Smith's response to this problem is to postulate an additional mechanism: "[the] correspondence of the sentiments of others with our own appears to be a cause of pleasure, and the want of it a cause of pain" (1759/1976, p. 14). According to Smith, whenever one person is conscious of a correspondence between his own affective response to some state of affairs and another person's response to it, that consciousness in itself has a positive affective quality; conversely, consciousness of dissonance of sentiment is painful. This hypothesis is crucial for Smith, since it motivates the mutual adaptation of sentiments that is the basis of morality.

This correspondence-of-sentiments mechanism has been overlooked by many commentators on Adam Smith, and does not seem to play much role in modern psychological theories of empathy. However, the modern literature contains clues which, I suggest, point toward the existence of Smith's mechanism. Particularly significant clues can be found in the comforting behavior that is characteristic of human infants and a range of social mammals. For example, an infant who believes that a parent is hurt will hug the parent, or offer a favorite toy that normally provides comfort to the infant; chimpanzees hug, pat, and groom fellow chimpanzees who are hurt (Batson, 1991; Zahn-Waxler et al., 1992; de Waal, 1996). Both human children and chimpanzees demand comfort when they are hurt, by pouting, crying, or throwing temper tantrums.

Such comforting is often classified as "helping" behavior in the literature of empathy, but it seems to consist primarily in the expression of an affective state of the comforter, which is aligned with that of the comforted. We can see it as helping only because we take for granted a desire on the part of the hurt individual for such a correspondence of affective states. Then, in explaining what motivates the comforter, it is simpler and more direct to suppose that the motive is a similar desire for the correspondence of affective states, rather than a desire to help. This Smithian interpretation of comforting is essentially that proposed by de Waal (1996) in relation to chimpanzees. Like Smith (to whom he refers with approval), de Waal sees the expression of corresponding affective states as a homeostatic mechanism that helps to stabilize social life among individuals with conflicting interests.

I have sometimes felt uneasy about advocating an eighteenth-century treatise as the starting point for current theorizing about the role of moral-

ity in economic behavior. I have always had the sense that Smith's intro-
spectively based hypotheses about human psychology were convincing,
but I was not sure whether they were supported by hard evidence. It seems
that they are.

19.8   The Relation between Language and (Mimetic) Culture
Morten H. Christiansen on Donald

Which came first, language or culture? On the one hand, language seems to
be woven into the very fabric of every human culture and to such an extent
that it is hard to imagine what human culture would be like without language. Indeed, most myths about the origin of humanity—whether religious or otherwise—seem to suggest that humans had language from the
very beginning. On the other hand, what use would humans have for language if they didn't have something to talk about? Living in groups governed by highly intricate social interactions would seem to provide an
endless amount of possible discussion material. Yet, many other primate
species also live in complex social groups, but notably without the benefit
of humanlike language. Some sort of shared culture would seem to be a
plausible additional component as a necessary prerequisite for language.[14]

Donald (vol. 2, ch. 14) argues for the latter scenario, proposing a
"culture-first" theory in which the prior emergence of a mimetic adaptation provides scaffolding for the subsequent evolution of language. A set
of domain-general cognitive skills is suggested to have evolved in early
hominids, allowing rudimentary knowledge to be shared across individuals in a nonverbal manner. The selective advantage of such information
exchange would then exert pressure toward improving communication,
leading to the emergence of language as an efficient system for sharing
cultural knowledge. Although this perspective provides suggestions regarding a possible origin of language, it tells us little about the subsequent evolution of language into its current form. Here I will seek to put Donald's
account in relief[15] by discussing possible cognitive constraints that may
help explain why language has evolved into the form it has today.

14. Thanks to Chris Conway, Rick Dale, and Gary Lupyan for their helpful comments on an earlier version of these comments.
15. It should be noted that the account of the *evolution* of language presented here is
not dependent for its validity on the merits of Donald's account of the *origin* of language. Rather, it is an independent account of language evolution that is compatible
with Donald's theory of language origin, but is not theoretically intertwined with it.

19.8.1 Mimesis and Language Evolution

The cornerstone of Donald's theory is *mimesis*, an evolved cognitive capacity unique to humans. The concept of mimesis is perhaps best understood when compared with the related notions of mimicry and imitation. Mimicry refers to a deliberate reduplication of a perceived action without attention to the possible purpose of the event, such as when a child parrots the speech of one of its parents. Imitation denotes a more abstract reduplication of action in which more attention is given to its purpose, such as when children imitate adult behavior and responses when playing "house." Finally, mimesis involves the reduplication of action sequences for the purpose of social communication, such as when a child stamps its foot to communicate its disagreement with some decision made by its parents. In this account, mimicry, imitation, and mimesis, rather than being categorical distinctions, correspond to points on a continuum of increasingly more abstract and socially informed reduplicative actions.

Whereas mimicry and to a limited extent imitation, can be found in nonhuman species, Donald argues that the capacity for mimesis has evolved only in the *Homo* lineage, starting some two million years ago. The emergence of mimesis is seen to have involved a series of adaptations primarily to the motor systems. This would have provided an expressive repertoire of motor actions upon which a nonverbal communicative culture could slowly emerge. This mimetic culture then formed the basis for the origin of language, first entering the evolutionary stage as a protolanguage encompassing one- and two-word utterances, and then gradually evolving into its current complexity through processes of cultural transmission.

19.8.2 Mimesis and Sequential Learning

An underlying assumption of Donald's view on the origin of language is that the first protolanguage must have relied on preexisting primate capabilities. Elsewhere he has thus suggested that "there might have been a dramatic discontinuity of *function* in the evolution of language, but there could not have been any discontinuities of *mechanism*" (Donald, 1998, p. 44). This continuity perspective becomes particularly important when it comes to explaining how various evolutionary changes in primate brain circuits may have affected the emergence and evolution of language.

A key component of the mimesis theory is the ability to memorize a social series of experienced events, or "episodes." As such, mimesis is crucially dependent on our ability for sequential learning; that is, the ability to encode and represent the order of discrete elements occurring in a temporal sequence. In line with the continuity perspective, hominid evolution does appear to have involved important refinements of sequential learning. A recent review by Conway and Christiansen (2001) of sequential learning in nonhuman primates indicates that these primates share with humans good abilities for learning fixed sequences (such as a fixed string of sounds making up a word) and simple statistically governed structures (for example, one can segment the strings "funny robot" into "funny" and "robot" because these two syllable sequences statistically occur more often together than does "nyro"). However, when it comes to the learning of hierarchical structure, monkeys and apes fall short of young children. Hierarchical learning appears to be crucial for syntactic processing, in which words are combined into phrases that can be combined with other words or phrases to form new phrases that in turn can be combined with yet other words or phrases, and so on. Not only would a preadaptation for hierarchical learning seem to be a precondition for Donald's nonverbal mimetic culture, but also—and perhaps more important—it would seem to be a prerequisite for the evolution of complex syntactic language.

19.8.3   Language Learning and Evolution

Donald suggests that the human brain has evolved to be maximally flexible and plastic so as to better be able to acquire the intricacies of human culture. As for language itself, he has suggested that "much of the replicative information needed to perpetuate language is stored in culture, not in the genes" (Donald, 1998, p. 50). However, if culture were the only constraint on language, this perspective would suggest that we should find few commonalities among languages (and cultures). Yet the languages of the world, despite their many differences, also share many systematic similarities in their structure and usage, which are sometimes referred to as linguistic universals. Although the space of logically possible ways in which languages could be structured and used is vast, the world's languages occupy only a small fraction of this space. For example, of the world's languages, more than 50% have a subject-object-verb word order whereas only 0.25% at most have an object-subject-verb word order (Dryer, 1989).

Donald's perspective does not allow us to explain the existence of such universal linguistic patterns; it cannot tell us why language is structured the way it is or why language is so readily learned. To answer these questions we need to go beyond the mimesis perspective (or at least augment it). Instead of asking why the human brain is so well suited for learning language, we need to ask why language is so well suited to being learned by the human brain. By turning what is often a standard question about the language evolution on its head, it becomes obvious that languages exist only because humans can learn, produce, and process them. Without humans there would be no language (in the narrow sense of *human* language). This suggests that cultural transmission has shaped language to be as learnable as possible by human learning mechanisms (Christiansen, 1994; Christiansen et al., 2002).

In order for languages to be passed on from generation to generation, they must adapt to the properties of the human learning and processing mechanisms. This is not to say that having a language does not confer a selective advantage on humans. It seems clear that humans with superior language abilities are likely to have a selective advantage over other humans (and other organisms) with lesser communicative powers. However, what is often overlooked is that the pressures working on language to adapt to humans are significantly stronger than the selection pressure on humans to be able to use language. In the case of the former, a language can survive *only* if it is learnable and processable by humans. On the other hand, adaptation toward language use is merely *one out of many* selective pressures working on humans (such as, for example, being able to avoid predators and find food). Whereas humans can survive without language, the opposite is not the case. Thus, language is more likely to have been shaped to fit the human brain than the other way around. Languages that are difficult for humans to learn simply die out or, more likely, do not come into existence at all.

This view of language as an adaptive system has a prominent historical pedigree. Indeed, nineteenth-century linguistics was dominated by an organistic view of language (for a review, see, e.g., McMahon, 1994). The evolution of language was generally seen in pre-Darwinian terms as a progressive growth toward attainment of perfection, followed by decay. In the twentieth century, the "biological" perspective on language evolution was resurrected within a modern Darwinian framework by Stevick (1963) and later by Nerlich (1989). Christiansen (1994) proposed that language be viewed as a kind of beneficial parasite—a *nonobligate symbiont*—that confers some selective advantage on its human hosts, without whom it cannot survive. Building on this work, Deacon (1997) further developed the metaphor by construing language as a virus.

The basic asymmetry in the relationship between language and the human brain is underscored by the fact that the rate of linguistic change is far greater than the rate of biological change. Whereas Danish and Hindi needed fewer than 5000 years to evolve from a common hypothesized proto-Indo-European ancestor into very different languages (McMahon,

1994), it took our remote ancestors approximately 100,000 to 200,000 years to evolve from the archaic form of *Homo sapiens* into the anatomically modern form, sometimes termed *Homo sapiens sapiens*. Consequently, it seems more plausible that the languages of the world have been closely tailored through cultural transmission to fit human learning, rather than the other way around. The fact that children are so successful at learning language is therefore best explained as a product of the adaptation of linguistic structures, and not as the adaptation of biological structures toward an innate endowment of linguistic knowledge (such as a Universal Grammar).

19.8.4   Constraints on Language Evolution

Although Donald acknowledges in his chapter that "cultures and languages must be assimilated easily by infants during development" (vol. 2, ch. 14, p. 291), it also seems clear that his account would suggest that the universal constraints on the acquisition and processing of language are essentially arbitrary. Given the emphasis on a cultural storage of the replicative aspects of language, linguistic universals appear arbitrary because it is possible to imagine a multitude of culturally useful, and equally adaptive, constraints on linguistic form. In the perspective on language evolution put forward here, linguistic universals are in most cases *not* arbitrary. Rather, they are determined predominantly by the properties of the human learning and processing mechanisms that underlie our capacity for language. The constraints on these learning mechanisms become embedded in the structure of language because linguistic forms that fit within these constraints will be more readily learned, and hence propagated more effectively from speaker to speaker.

This account of language evolution also has important implications for current theories of language acquisition and processing. It suggests that many of the cognitive constraints that have shaped the evolution of language are still at play in our current language ability. If this is correct, it should be possible to uncover the source of some of the universal constraints in human performance on sequential learning tasks. For example, in a series of studies that combined artificial neural network modeling and artificial language learning, we have shown how universal constraints on the way words are put together to form sentences, as well as the formation of complex questions across the world's languages, can be explained in terms of nonlinguistic constraints on the learning of complex sequential structure (for an overview, see Christiansen et al., 2002).

19.8.5   Conclusion

Donald proposes that the origin of language is rooted in a mimetic culture that evolved prior to the emergence of language. I have argued here that although mimesis may provide one possible explanation of the origin of language, it tells us little about its subsequent evolution, including why language looks the way it does today. I have suggested that we may obtain insights into these questions by asking why languages are so well suited for human learning, thus turning upside down the standard question of why human brains are so well adapted for learning language. From this perspective, language has been shaped by cultural transmission over many generations to be as learnable as possible by the learning mechanisms of human children. The specific cognitive constraints imposed on the process of learning through cultural transmission have then over time become "fossilized" in the languages of the world as linguistic universals.

Returning to the question of whether language or culture came first, it would seem that the linguistic adaptation account of language evolution is at least compatible with Donald's culture-first scenario. Nonetheless, the approach to language evolution presented here also suggests a possible third alternative, one in which language and culture evolved together in a spiral fashion, feeding on each other and constrained by the learning and processing mechanisms of early hominids. In this view, the issue of culture first or language first is of less importance. Instead, we can focus on the interplay between culture and language in hominid evolution, and how this interplay may have been constrained by the various cognitive mechanisms in the evolving hominid brain.

19.9   A Possible Confusion between Mimetic and Memetic
Susan Blackmore on Donald

The terms "meme" and "memetics" were used many times at the Royaumont conference on imitation, and they sound very similar to Donald's terms "mimesis" and "mimetic," so it may be helpful to distinguish between the two.

"Meme" was coined by Dawkins to give a name to a replicator that is copied by imitation. As examples of memes, he suggested "tunes, ideas, catch-phrases, clothes fashions, ways of making pots or of building arches" (Dawkins, 1976/1989, p. 192) and included scientific theories, poems, chain letters, and religious doctrines. He derived the term itself from the Greek word *mimeme* meaning "that which is imitated," abbreviating it to a monosyllable that sounds a bit like gene. This choice itself was, as we now know, a highly successful meme. So the core meaning of "meme" is that which is imitated.

By contrast, Donald's (1991) term "mimetic" is part of his three-stage account of the evolution of human brains, culture, and cognition. These three stages are (1) the acquisition of mimetic skill; (2) lexical invention—the creation of words, spoken language, and storytelling; and (3) the externalization of memory, including symbolic art and the technology of writing, both of which allowed humans to overcome the limitations of biological memory.

We can easily see that the terms are very different. Donald's "mimetic" is closer to "mime" than to imitation, and he includes "gesture, body language, and mime, any of which can communicate an intention quite effectively, without words or grammars." He also includes representing an event to oneself as a form of mimesis and describes mimesis as "a necessary preadaptation for the later evolution of language" (Donald, 2001, p. 263). So mimesis includes internal representations and excludes language, storytelling, and writing. In contrast, memes are anything that is copied from person to person; in the modern world, the vast majority of memes are words and combinations of words, both written and spoken.

These are the most obvious differences, but if we pursue them a bit further, we find that these two terms exemplify two fundamentally different approaches to human evolution. First, for Donald "mimesis rests on the ability to produce conscious, self-initiated, representational acts that are intentional but not linguistic" (1991, p. 168). This means that mimesis is essentially a symbolic or representational act. This is not implied in memetics. Memes are simply the actions, behaviors, or statements that people make, and the artifacts they build. If these memes can succeed in being copied, they will thrive, and there is no requirement for them to be symbolic or representational, let alone conscious.

A second difference concerns the origins of variation and creativity. Donald argues that, as a purely replicative skill, imitation cannot generate much cultural variation and plays a limited role in cultural evolution, that it is more a transmission device than a creative one. This more traditional view is completely reversed by the memetic view, which might be stated like this: Imitation is the copying mechanism that made cultural evolution possible. Errors in imitation provide one source of cultural variation, recombination of old memes to make new ones provides more, and selection from the variants completes the process. Memetic evolution is a creative process in exactly the same way that biological evolution is, and depends on imitation as its mechanism of heredity. In the memetic view, imitation is the key to all of human creativity.

Finally, the two approaches differ over the question, Who benefits? (Dennett, 1995). The main point of memetics, as conceived by Dawkins, was to illustrate that memes as well as genes can have replicator power. He argued that we should get out of the habit of always appealing to biological or genetic advantage because there may be other replicators that also drive evolution for their own advantage. Memetics is therefore the study of how the interests of memes affect human evolution and culture. By contrast, Donald sees mimesis as an adaptation, following the traditional view that the skill of copying gestures, actions, and mimes is of biological advantage to the people who acquired it, rather than being of advantage to the gestures, actions, and mimes themselves. We are far from knowing which theory, if either, is correct, but it may be helpful to realize how very different they are.

19.10   Imitation as a Tool of Cooperation and Manipulation
Paul Seabright on Sugden and on Gambetta

These two chapters explore in different ways the relevance of imitation for the social sciences. Gambetta asks about conscious, deliberate imitation, and specifically about the kind of imitation that involves deception, as opposed to the kind that transmits knowledge, skills, or forms of behavior from one person to another with the awareness or at least tacit consent of the former party. It is important to focus on the deceptive case precisely because much recent work on imitation stresses, for good reasons, its constructive and productive character. Indeed, imitation has increasingly come to be seen as the source of much of mankind's greatest creativity. Knowledge is, after all, typically expandable. When good ideas are imitated, they do not usually cease to be good ideas; on the contrary, they can thereby become accessible to many more people. Another way to put this is that knowledge is the kind of resource that is scarce only because of the costs of transmission, and a capacity for imitation (which lowers these costs) makes knowledge less scarce. However, this enthusiasm for imitation (which the chapters in this volume should do much to encourage) should not obscure the fact that imitation sometimes serves as a weapon in the struggle for *other* resources that may be very scarce indeed.

These are not inconsistent points of view. Over the long period of human history, the cumulative character of knowledge has irrevocably fashioned our culture; current knowledge builds on past knowledge in ways that only our remarkable capacity for imitation can explain. This complementarity often turns those who have knowledge into allies, since they have an interest in cooperating. The most sharp-witted survivors, though, have always realized that knowledge is also power, and that the scarce resources of food, military strength, and (for males) access to the favors of females could depend on knowing things that others do not. This predicament turns those who have knowledge into rivals, and Gambetta's chapter reminds us of the multiple baroque manipulations to which such rivalry can dispose us. These manipulations give color and energy to our social life, but they can also be deeply destructive of human cooperation. We already know that cooperation in general is central to human society, but that at the same time it is highly fragile; cooperation specifically in the sharing of knowledge illustrates this duality very well.

Sugden's chapter is about the kind of imitation that turns those who have knowledge into allies—the spread of good ideas through imitation, which may or may not be conscious. Specifically he asks whether rational behavior in the sense that an economist might recognize could be the product of memetic imitation. Could we have learned to be rational by imitating others—not in the sense that we have entered a deliberate and laborious apprenticeship with rationality as the outcome, for that would have required a strong commitment to rationality from the start—but rather in the sense that rationality could have invaded our brains by sheer force of charm? Perhaps this is a question that economists are likely to find more compelling than other people, since others may feel that rationality of a kind must have been the prerequisite for our capacity and compulsion to imitate in the first place (this is central to the arguments advanced by Michael Tomasello, 1999, for instance).

Sugden shows first that genetic evolution could not be guaranteed to produce a tendency for rational behavior, since genetic evolution selects combinations of genes rather than single genes, and some genes causing maladaptive behavior in the homozygotic form could cause relatively adaptive behavior in the heterozygotic form. Next he shows that memetic evolution could not be guaranteed to do so either, since if memetic evolution proceeds by bilateral imitation, the resulting behavior patterns may not display transitivity. Both of these conclusions are impeccably demonstrated, although they leave me wondering what exactly the evolutionary arguments under assault were supposed to show. We are not given reasons for thinking that irrational behavior is *in fact* favored by genes that have favorable consequences in the heterozygotic form, nor are we given reasons for thinking that intransitive behavior patterns are empirically likely because of inconsistencies induced by bilateral imitation. So Sugden's arguments appear to show that rationality was not guaranteed to develop by genetic or memetic evolution, but they are quite compatible with its having in fact developed by one of these means. Evolutionary explanations are rarely undermined by objections that there was nothing inevitable about the sequence of events to which they appeal.

What kind of factual considerations might we look for to help settle the argument? Memetic evolution could indeed display a strong tendency toward transitivity if the factors that made one meme more likely to replicate than another were not purely random but were linked to a widespread prior disposition to favor certain kinds of meme on the part of the brains between which they replicate. Such a prior disposition, to be sufficiently widespread, would have to have been favored by genetic and not just memetic evolution. Does this mean that the memes must have replicated merely in the interests of the genes, and that the memetic explanation is therefore redundant? Not in the least. An analogy with the logic of genetic evolution may help to explain why.

All interesting Darwinian explanations do more than just point out the truism that the most successful replicators become disproportionately represented in any population. They link certain identifiable environmental conditions to the evolution of replicators with identifiable characteristics that enable the replicators effectively to exploit those conditions for their replication. Thus polar bears evolved in the arctic and not in the temperate zones because of the adaptive value of white camouflage on snow and ice, and gray tree moths became disproportionately represented as the level of atmospheric soot rose during the industrial revolution. In both cases an identifiable environmental condition (the presence of snow or soot) is linked to some characteristic of the phenotype (white fur, gray wings). Similarly, an interesting explanation of some instance of meme evolution could not just confine itself to saying that since a particular meme is now widespread, it must therefore have successfully replicated. It would need to explain why the environment in which the meme had evolved was more favorable to that particular meme rather than some putative rival. This does not imply that the meme is evolving in the interests of that environment or indeed in any interest other than the meme itself. It just implies that the environment favors some memes over others, just as an ecological environment favors some genes over others. Thus an environment characterized by endemic malaria favors the evolution of sickle-cell anemia, although no one would suggest that this anemia evolves "in the interests of" malaria.

What is the environment in which memes have evolved? It is the brains, bodies, and behavior of *Homo sapiens sapiens*, initially as these had evolved prior to the invention of agriculture some 10,000 years ago. This environment has itself been subsequently evolving, mainly under the influence of memes. The purely genetic component of this environment has changed little, but this fact has clearly not constrained the evolution of memes very narrowly, because the behavior of modern *Homo sapiens sapiens*, interacting in a world of millions of strangers, is utterly different from our ancestors' behavior only 10,000 years ago. Nevertheless, genetically determined predispositions constrain the evolution of memes in recognizable ways. For instance, consider behavior that involves children leaving their mother to rush trustingly up to strangers. In a world in which strangers regularly do violent things to unrelated infants, which very probably characterized our hunter-gatherer ancestors, this would not be a successful meme (nor would a gene for this behavior be a successful gene, but that's a different point). The meme would not replicate successfully, for two distinct reasons. First, children who bear it would die, thereby limiting their ability to pass on the meme. Second, other children observing the fate of those who bear the meme would choose not to imitate this behavior (because of a highly adaptive genetic predisposition not to put their lives gratuitously at risk). In a world in which strangers do not regularly behave violently toward unrelated infants, the meme would stand more of a chance, although this might not be enough to favor it over a meme for more cautious behavior.

Put simply, the fact that people imitate opens the door to memetic evolution, but they do not imitate indiscriminately. Some of the behavior that thereby evolves could nevertheless be quite irrational. For instance, it seems likely that a tendency to accept (or at least to be favorably disposed toward) the opinions of the people who shout the loudest would have been quite adaptive during the Pleistocene era. The loudest shouter in the group most of the time would probably have been the person whose protection it was best to seek and whose opinion it was safest to follow. It is therefore plausible that memes are favored by characteristics (such as the loudness or more generally the conspicuousness with which they are expressed) that are unrelated to any other dimension of their "reasonableness." In the modern world, accepting the opinions of those who shout loudest may well be foolish in the extreme, both individually and collectively, but a tendency to do so may be part of our Pleistocene heritage it is now impossible to escape.

Whether in fact human beings have evolved to be economically rational is therefore an empirical question (the best answer going is probably "up to a point," as Evelyn Waugh might have put it). To the extent that they have, there has certainly been nothing inevitable about this, as Sugden's chapter convincingly demonstrates. And as Gambetta's chapter points out, such rationality can be deceptive and manipulative as well as cooperative. These two stimulating chapters remind us that human rationality underlies both our species' greatest triumphs and our most destructive excesses.

19.11   Proving Rationality
Mark Greenberg on Sugden

Conventional economic theory assumes that economic agents are rational decision makers in the sense that they act as if they were trying to maximize some one-dimensional criterion. A well-known body of experimental work has increasingly shed doubt on the assumption that human beings are rational in this sense, however. Recently, some economic theorists have tried to justify the assumption of rationality by appealing to a cultural analogue of natural selection. Robert Sugden's interesting chapter is highly critical of this strategy—*the evolutionary strategy*, for short. Indeed, some of Sugden's remarks might be read to suggest that Darwinian theorizing about cultural evolution is a sterile enterprise of "manipulating tautologies about replicators" (vol. 2, ch. 15, p. 316) that can have no relevance to the empirical question of whether human beings are rational. On this reading of Sugden's chapter, the evolutionary strategy is a failure, and, more generally, a Darwinian theory of cultural change—*meme theory*—can have no explanatory value. Sugden's arguments, however, do not warrant this dismissiveness toward the evolutionary strategy or toward meme theory. A better way to read his chapter, I suggest, is as a plea for empirical investigation *in addition to* relatively a priori theorizing. The larger interest of the chapter is less its criticism of a particular application of meme theory than its suggestiveness for further work in meme theory generally. Contrary to the implication of some of his remarks, Sugden's chapter itself illustrates that theoretical work on Darwinian theories of cultural change can fruitfully complement empirical investigation.[16]

19.11.1   The Evolutionary Strategy and Sugden's Response
Sugden focuses on a version of the evolutionary strategy, developed by Ken Binmore (1994, 1998), that relies on Richard Dawkins's (1976/1989) anal-

---

16. Sugden (2001), which I read after writing these remarks, suggests that, at least at that time, he would have been sympathetic to my preferred reading of his chapter. Sugden confirms that this reading is what he intends (personal communication).

ogy between cultural and biological evolution. Memes that are not good at influencing human behavior in a way that has the effect of propagating themselves will tend to be outcompeted by memes that are. Thus, according to the Dawkins-Binmore line of thought, in the long run, the memes found in our minds will tend to be ones that are very good at influencing their carriers to behave in a way that spreads those same memes. As a result, human beings will tend to act as if they are trying to spread the memes they carry—thus satisfying the assumption of conventional economic theory that economic agents act as if they are trying to maximize some one criterion (pp. 303–304).

Sugden's argument centers on two examples. The first involves a diploid species in which the action the agent chooses depends on the combination of genes the agent carries. Sugden shows, that under the right conditions, an action that does not have the greatest reproductive success can continue to be chosen at equilibrium (and can even continue to be chosen more often than actions with greater reproductive success). In the second example, a meme's likelihood of being replicated depends on the frequency of other memes in the population, with the result that there can be continuous cycling of the proportions of each meme and thus of the decision probabilities for each action. Sugden draws from his examples the conclusion that selection does not necessarily induce rationality *at the level of actors*. In equilibrium, Sugden argues, though *replicators* will behave as if they are trying to maximize their own reproduction, the consequence need not be behavior that appears rational from the perspective of the actors (pp. 310ff; 312ff).

19.11.2 How Well Do Sugden's Examples Address Binmore's Strategy?

In this section, I raise three questions about how well Sugden's examples are adapted for their purpose, and I also mention a concern about Binmore's strategy. First, Sugden's examples do not seem to squarely address the issue that is crucial to Binmore's evolutionary strategy—whether the consequence of Darwinian evolution will be that agents will act as if they are trying to maximize a single criterion—most relevantly, the reproduction of *the replicators they carry*. With respect to the diploid-species example, Sugden points out that although "it is as if the surviving *genes* are maximizing their own replication" (p. 312), "biological natural selection does not necessarily favor *actions* that maximize the reproductive success *of actors*" (p. 311). The relevant question, however, is whether agents maximize the reproduction of the genes or memes they carry, not whether they maximize their own reproductive success (in the sense of having the most descendants). Similarly, the second example shows that where the choices available to an agent are characterized in a way that is independent of the replication of the memes the agent carries, the result of an evolutionary process can be intransitive preferences among those choices (p. 314). Again, however, the relevant question is whether the result of evolution will be that agents will act as if they are maximizing the spread of the memes they carry. We cannot get a clear view of that question by looking at how agents behave with respect to choices that are characterized without regard to the replication of memes. Sugden's examples do not allow clear evaluation of the relevant question because it is not clear in the examples what would count as the agents acting so as to maximize the reproductive success of the replicators they carry.

Second, for a different reason, Sugden's examples are not well designed to address whether an analogue of natural selection will have the consequence that agents will behave as if they are maximizing the spread of the replicators they carry. As noted, Dawkins's idea is that given variation in replicators, there will be evolution in the direction of replicators that are better at inducing the conditions for their own copying. Thus, the memes that are around in the long run will be ones that are relatively good at getting themselves copied. Sugden's examples, however, exclude by stipulation the possibility of new genes or memes coming into existence. And the examples are constructed in such a way that none of the original genes or memes can, in the long run, be more successful at reproducing themselves than others.

Third, Sugden's examples assume that the structure of memetic reproduction, whatever it may be, is fixed for all time. But as Dawkins has argued, what is fixed in the short run may not be fixed in the longer run (1982, pp. 34–35). Thus, not only may new replicators emerge, but the fundamental mechanisms of replication can themselves be modified by evolution. The history of biological evolution includes many examples of this, including the development of multicellular organisms and sexual reproduction. We thus have very general empirical grounds for being cautious about the idea that the mechanisms by which replicators reproduce might happen to be fixed in a way that obstructs the operation of selective forces.

I also want to raise a concern about the Binmore strategy that Sugden does not mention. In normal cases, the actions we take cannot favor some of our genes over others. Our genes are all in the same boat—except for meiosis, over which we have no control. Matters are very different with our ideas. We can choose actions that will predictably spread some of our ideas more than others. (Also, the ideas we carry change from moment to moment.) Thus, even if cultural evolution operates in a way that is parallel to biological evolution, it is not clear that the consequence will be that humans will behave rationally in the relevant sense—i.e., as if they are trying to maximize a *one-dimensional* criterion of success.[17]

19.11.3 Empirical Questions and A Priori Theorizing

The most that Sugden's examples could show is that the evolutionary strategy depends on empirical assumptions; without an empirical showing that those conditions are not satisfied in the relevant cases, he could not hope to refute the evolutionary strategy. Now he is certainly correct that whether Darwinian evolution will occur (and whether it will have the claimed consequences for human rationality) depends on empirical conditions, in particular on "what memes actually are and how they in fact replicate" (p. 316). An important objective of theoretical work on Darwinian evolution, in both the biological and cultural domains, has been understanding the conditions needed for Darwinian evolution to occur or to take various directions (see, e.g., Gil-White, vol. 2, ch. 16). Indeed, as Sugden notes, economists who have appealed to an analogue of natural selection have hoped "to argue that rational-choice theory applies only in situations in which the relevant selection mechanisms are active. That might make it possible to define the domain of the theory in such a way as to include many forms of behavior in markets while excluding many laboratory experiments" (pp. 302–303).

Thus, it is actually important *to the evolutionary strategy* to claim that the relevant selection mechanisms operate only when certain empirical conditions are satisfied. It is therefore puzzling that Sugden thinks that his chapter argues "that this [evolutionary] strategy, in the form in which it has been used so far in economics, fails" (p. 301).

Some of Sugden's remarks seem to suggest that since it is an empirical question whether human beings are rational, it is pointless to engage in theorizing about cultural evolution. In the concluding words of his chapter:

Whether human decision-making behavior satisfies the rationality postulates of conventional choice theory is an empirical question. If it does, any explanation of that fact must depend on empirical propositions about how the world really is. Trying to find an explanation by manipulating tautologies about replicators is to attempt what is logically impossible. (p. 316)

Sugden is certainly right that empirical investigation is *necessary* to determine whether the conditions for the right kind of evolution are satisfied. It

---

17. Sugden (2001) makes a similar point.

does not follow, however, that empirical investigation is *sufficient* or that relatively a priori theoretical work cannot be helpful. After all, Sugden's chapter itself engages in a priori analysis that sheds light on the empirical conditions for Darwinian processes to take particular directions. Without such work, empirical investigators would not know what to look for.

19.11.4 Conclusion

Perhaps what Sugden should conclude is not that economists should give up the attempt to use the evolutionary approach. Instead, theorists have two tasks. They need to work out the conditions under which a Darwinian process would ensure rational behavior. And they need to investigate empirically whether those conditions are satisfied in the relevant cases. The first task is largely a nonempirical one. The second task is an empirical one, but it cannot be carried out without theorizing that identifies the conditions to be investigated.

Answering empirical questions tends to require empirical investigation. Darwinian explanations are no exception: they depend on empirical premises. It does not follow, however, that there is no explanatory work for a Darwinian theory of cultural evolution—that it is nothing but "the manipulation of tautologies." Sugden's chapter itself is an a priori exercise in meme theory that is suggestive of potential directions for empirical work.[18]

Acknowledgement

I am grateful to Harry Litman for valuable discussion and to Robert Sugden for helpful comments on the final draft of these remarks.

19.12 Even Deeper Misunderstandings of Memes
Susan Blackmore on Gil-White

Gil-White describes a memetics that I do not recognize. I will comment on just two of his main points.

First, he rejects three central concepts for memetics: replication, imitation, and selfish memes. He regards replication as a red herring, but he defines replication to mean copying with 100% fidelity and a replicator as something that is copied perfectly. This is not the usual definition of a replicator, and there could be no memetics if it were. In fact, the term

18. See relevant discussions in Gil-White, vol. 2, ch. 16; Greenberg, vol. 2, ch. 17; and Chater, vol. 2, ch. 18. ED.

"replicator" was coined by Dawkins (1976/1989) in terms of the very evolutionary process that Gil-White describes: universal Darwinism. Dennett (1995) refers to this general process as the evolutionary algorithm. If you have variation, selection, and heredity, you *must* get evolution. The information that is copied is called the replicator. Dawkins then invented the term "meme" to provide an example of a replicator other than the gene; one that is copied by the process of imitation. Gil-White claims that Dawkins insists on replication on the grounds that perfect copying is the only thing that can set Darwinian processes in motion. Not only is Gil-White wrong about Dawkins, but if replication is perfect, there is no variation and hence there can be no evolution—whether genetic, memetic, or any other kind.

Note that I prefer to use the original term "variation" here because variation is general to all evolutionary processes whereas "mutation" is a term specific to genes. I fear that Gil-White misleads us by talking about mutation in memes.

This highlights a major problem with Gil-White's analysis, which is that he relies heavily on analogies between memes and genes when these may not be warranted. He claims that insistence on a close genetic analogy reflects a misunderstanding of evolutionary genetics and regards Dawkins, Dennett, and myself as pushing the analogy too far. But it is he who insists on this analogy, not memeticists.

I want to make this point as clear as possible. Memetics starts, not from an analogy between memes and genes, but from the recognition that both are replicators (information copied with variation and selection). Beyond that, the two replicators work in very different ways. Genes have been evolving for several billion years and are now copied with extremely high fidelity. Memes have been evolving for only two or three million years at most, and are copied by all the messy, inaccurate, and variable processes of imitation that we have been learning about at this conference. This difference is crucial to understanding how memes work, and it does not undermine the point that both memes and genes are replicators. Understanding replication by imitation is the heart of memetics. Replication cannot be a red herring, for there can be no memetics without it.

Gil-White's second red herring is imitation. Again he defines imitating as making exact copies. From everything we have learned at this conference, it is clear that imitation rarely, if ever, produces exact copies of behaviors, and memetics must be based on this reality. Since memes are defined as the information that is copied by imitation, imitation cannot be a red herring for memetics.

Finally Gil-White rejects the notion of selfish memes. However, it might be helpful to point out that the concept of selfish replicators falls straight out of the idea of the evolutionary algorithm. Once you have a replicator being copied with variation and selection, then that information will get copied whenever it can, regardless of the consequences. So memes are selfish in exactly the same sense as genes are. This does not mean that they have selfish plans or intentions, but merely that they will spread whenever and however they can. This notion of selfishness is intrinsic to the idea of the meme as a replicator, and is the basis on which memetics can be used to make predictions different from those made on the basis of adaptations that favor genes. If this is a red herring, then there is nothing left of memetics.

I will skip now to the end of Gil-White's chapter. Here he claims (quite rightly) that meme content is not everything. The problem is that he accuses me of saying that meme selection occurs solely as the result of meme content, which I do not. Moreover, in arguing against what he takes to be my views on memetic drive, he quotes a section from my book that is not actually about memetic drive.

Let me be clear about memetic drive. I think that most memeticists would agree with what I have said so far in this commentary, but they may not agree that memetic drive occurs or that it can, as I have suggested previously, account for the rapid expansion of the human brain or our capacity for language. My hypothesis, put very briefly, is as follows. Once our ancestors were able to imitate, a new evolutionary process was let loose in which memes competed to be copied. The successful memes then changed the environment in which genes were selected, giving an advantage to genes for the ability to copy the currently successful memes. By this process, brains became successively better at copying the memes that had been successful in the memetic competition. In other words, genes were forced, to some extent, to track the direction of memetic evolution.

There are perfectly legitimate theoretical questions about whether this process could work, and empirical questions about whether it actually happened. The process has been successfully modeled, and also compared with better-known versions of gene-culture coevolution (Higgs, 2000; Kendal & Laland, 2000). However, what is important here is that memetic drive depends on heuristics such as copying, or mating with, the best imitators, which are related to those described by Gil-White. Without such bias memetic drive cannot work. The memetic drive hypothesis may be false, but it is not, and cannot be, based on the idea that only content determines which memes are selected. I hope these very brief comments may help to clear up some fundamental misunderstandings about memetics.

19.13 Can Memes Meet the Challenge?
Susan Blackmore on Greenberg and on Chater

Chater and Greenberg, in their different ways, describe the challenge faced by any memetic theory of cultural change. Chater points out how counterintuitive the idea is. Indeed it is. As he puts it, meme theory views cultural complexity as generated by the blind watchmaker of nonpurposive selectional forces rather than by the sighted watchmaker of conscious humans and their goals. Greenberg sets this up as goals versus memes, or as humans' deliberate pursuit of their conscious goals versus competition between memes.

The challenge to meme theory, then, is to show that at least in some instances, Darwinian forces with memes as the replicator can better explain cultural complexity than can intelligent, purposeful design by humans. It is important to stress at once that no meme theorist is likely to reject human goals as irrelevant to memetic evolution. The interesting question is what role they play. Are human goals the ultimate design force for culture (goal theory) or are they just one of many factors in a Darwinian design process acting on memes (meme theory)?

Analogies between genes and memes must be treated with caution, but we may usefully consider the role of animals' goals in biological evolution. Imagine a bird of prey whose goals include staying alive, guarding its territory, and feeding its chicks. These goals do not, on their own, design anything. Yet their pursuit has many design consequences, including the evolution of defenses or camouflage in the prey, improvements in the predator's hunting skills, and many unintended effects on genes in other organisms, such as the moss used for lining the predator's nest, the parasites that take up residence there, the food eaten by the prey, and so on. We can best understand the overall design of this bird by thinking of the ultimate driving force as a Darwinian process in which genes compete to be copied. In this process, the goals of the bird are relevant, but they are not the ultimate designer.

Consider now a favorite example of meme critics, the design of an aircraft. Surely, say the critics, this is completely different from the case of the bird, for the aircraft was designed by human intelligence and foresight in order to fulfill conscious goals. My response is that the goals are relevant, but that we get a better overall understanding of aircraft design by taking the meme's-eye view. In this view, memes such as wing shapes, engine types, seating plans, window construction, food storage, and safety features all compete to be copied. The numerous human designers are meme machines who, through their intelligence and education, are able to recombine memes to make new designs. Their many designs then compete to be brought to fruition, with many being dropped. The few that are finally built then compete in world markets and even fewer succeed for reasons that include fluctuations in the cost of oil, unexpected terrorist attacks that increase people's fear of flying, birds that accidentally get sucked into jet engines, the evolution of the bacteria that thrive in warm food, and the patriotism of people who want their national flag painted on the tail fins. In this process, the goals of the human designer are essential, but they cannot alone explain the final design of the plane.

The analogy is not close because genes and memes are copied and selected by such very different mechanisms, but I hope it is close enough to make this simple point—that in meme theory human goals are not treated as irrelevant, but are given the same status that the goals of plants and animals are given in biological evolution. That is, they are just one of many factors contributing to design by selection.

If we accept this role for human goals, can meme theory meet Greenberg's challenge and in his words, show that an appeal to an analogue of evolution by natural selection is the best explanation of cultural evolution? In the ambitious sense of providing a complete theory of cultural evolution, meme theory is very far from achieving this goal, but in limited domains it has already done so. A good example is the evolution of religions or, as Dawkins (1976/1989) calls them, "viruses of the mind."

In their adherence to religion, people invest precious resources in building temples and mosques. They spend time reciting scriptures and singing hymns. They burn offerings and pour away oils. They mutilate their children's genitals, causing them pain and disease. They wage wars in the name of religion and even kill themselves. And what is the role of humans' deliberate pursuit of their conscious goals in all this?

If asked, religious people might say that they wish to serve God; to enter into communion with spirit; to be a better Muslim, Jew, or Christian; or to attain life after death, but these goals are themselves derived from the religions and cannot explain the design of those religions. Meme theory takes the viewpoint of the religious memes themselves and investigates how and why they have succeeded in getting into people's behavioral repertoire and being passed on to others. The major religions are seen as memeplexes built around instructions to pass on those memes (teach your children, pass on the good news). Obedience is obtained by a mixture of immediate benefits (a sense of belonging, or aesthetic pleasure) and protected by untestable threats and promises (hell, heaven, and eternal damnation). These religions therefore out-compete other memes and so persist. Human goals were both exploited by those memes and redesigned by them. No sighted watch-maker was needed.

A more modern example is the design of the Internet, with its high-fidelity copying and massive storage capacity. From a memetic perspective, the whole system is a rapidly evolving product of coevolution between memes and their new copying machinery, with human goals being just one factor in selection.

Meme theory is a long way from fully meeting the challenges that Greenberg and Chater raise, but it has made a start. The implication is that human goals are part of the world in which memes compete and evolve, while the ultimate designer of culture is the Darwinian process of memetic selection.

Bibliography

Abravanel, E., & DeYong, N. (1991). Does object modeling elicit imitative-like gestures from young infants? *Journal of Experimental Child Psychology, 52*, 22–40.

Abravanel, E., & Sigafoos, A. (1984). Exploring the presence of imitation during early infancy. *Child Development, 55*, 381–392.

Adolphs, R. (1999). Social cognition and the human brain. *Trends in Cognitive Sciences, 3*, 469–479.

Adolphs, R., Damasio, H., Tranel, D., Cooper, G., & Damasio, A. (2000). A role for somatosensory cortices in the visual recognition of emotion as revealed by three-dimensional lesion mapping. *Journal of Neuroscience, 20*, 2683–2690.

Akhtar, N., & Tomasello, M. (1996). Twenty-four-month-old children learn words for absent objects and actions. *British Journal of Developmental Psychology, 14*, 79–93.

Akins, C., Klein, E., & Zentall, T. (2002). Imitative learning in Japanese quail (*Conturnix japonica*) using the bidirectional control procedure. *Animal Learning & Behavior, 30*, 275–281.

Akins, C., & Zentall, T. (1996). Imitative learning in male Japanese quail (*Conturnix japonica*) using the two-action method. *Journal of Comparative Psychology, 110*, 316–320.

Akins, C., & Zentall, T. (1998). Imitation in Japanese quail: The role of reinforcement of demonstrator responding. *Psychonomic Bulletin & Review, 5*, 694–697.

Alberts, B., Watson, J., & Bray, D. (1994). *Molecular biology of the cell* (3rd ed.). London: Taylor and Francis.

Aldridge, M., Stone, K., Sweeney, M., & Bower, T. (2000). Preverbal children with autism understand the intentions of others. *Developmental Science, 3*, 294–301.

Alissandrakis, A., Nehaniv, C., & Dautenhahn, K. (2002a). Do as I do: Correspondences across different robotic embodiments. In D. Polani, J. Kim, & T. Martinetz (Eds.), *Proceedings of the fifth German workshop on artificial life (GWAL5)* (pp. 143–152). Lübeck, Germany: IOS Press.

Alissandrakis, A., Nehaniv, C., & Dautenhahn, K. (2002b). Do as I do: Correspondences across different robotic embodiments. Poster presented at perspectives on imitation: From cognitive neuroscience to social science, Royaumont Abbey, France. Available at (http://www.warwick.ac.uk/fac/sci/Psychology/imitation)

Allen, M., D'Alessio, D., & Brezgel, K. (1995). A meta-analysis summarizing the effects of pornography II: Aggression after exposure. *Human Communication Research, 22*(2), 258–283.

Allen, W. (1994). *The complete prose of Woody Allen.* New York: Wings Books.

Allison, T., Puce, A., & McCarthy, G. (2000). Social perception from visual cues: Role of the STS region. *Trends in Cognitive Sciences, 4,* 267–278.

Allport, G. (1968). The historical background of modern social psychology. In G. Lindzey & E. Aronson (Eds.), *Handbook of social psychology.* (2nd ed., Vol. 1, pp. 1–80). Reading, Mass.: Addison-Wesley.

Amaral, D., Price, J., Pitkanen, A., & Carmichael, S. (1992). Anatomical organization of the primate amigdaloid complex. In J. Aggleton (Ed.), *The amygdala: Neurobiological aspects of emotion, memory, and mental disfunction* (pp. 1–66). New York: Wiley-Liss.

American Psychiatric Association. (1994). *Diagnostic and statistical manual of mental disorders* (4th ed.). Washington, D.C.: American Psychiatric Association.

Anderson, C., & Bushman, B. (2001). Effects of violent video games on aggressive behavior, aggressive cognition, aggressive affects, physiological arousal, and prosocial behavior: A meta-analytic review of the scientific literature. *Psychological Science 12*(5), 353–359. Available at (www.psychology.iastate.edu/faculty/caa/abstracts/2000-2004/01AB.html)

Anderson, C., & Bushman, B. (2002). Human aggression. *Annual Review of Psychology, 53,* 27–51.

Andison, F. (1977). TV violence and viewer aggression: A cumulation of study results. *Public Opinion Quarterly, 41*(3), 314–331.

Anisfeld, M. (1979). Interpreting "imitative" responses in early infancy. *Science, 205,* 214–215.

Anisfeld, M. (1984). *Language development from birth to three.* Hillsdale, N.J.: Erlbaum.

Anisfeld, M. (1991). Neonatal imitation. *Developmental Review, 11,* 60–97.

Anisfeld, M. (1996). Only tongue protrusion modeling is matched by neonates. *Developmental Review, 16,* 149–161.

Anisfeld, M., Turkewitz, G., Rose, S., Rosenberg, F., Sheiber, F., Couturier-Fagan, D., Ger, J., & Sommer, I. (2001). No compelling evidence that newborns imitate oral gestures. *Infancy, 2,* 111–122.

Arbib, M. (1987). Levels of modelling of visually guided behavior (with peer commentary and author's response). *Behavioral and Brain Sciences, 10,* 407–465.

Arbib, M. (1989). *The metaphorical brain 2: Neural networks and beyond.* New York: Wiley-Interscience.

Arbib, M. (2002). The mirror system, imitation, and the evolution of language. In C. Nehaniv & K. Dautenhahn (Eds.), *Imitation in animals and artifacts* (pp. 229–280). Cambridge, Mass.: MIT Press.

Arbib, M. (in press). From monkey-like action recognition to human language: An evolutionary framework for neurolinguistics. *Behavioral and Brain Sciences.*

Arbib, M., Billard, A., Iacoboni, M., & Oztop, E. (2000). Synthetic brain imaging: Grasping, mirror neurons and imitation. *Neural Networks, 13,* 975–997.

Arbib, M., & Rizzolatti, G. (1997). Neural expectations: A possible evolutionary path from manual skills to language. *Communication and Cognition, 29,* 393–424.

Arbib, M., & Rizzolatti, G. (1999). Neural expectations: A possible evolutionary path from manual skills to language. In Ph. Van Loocke (Ed.), *The nature of concepts. Evolution, structure, and representation* (pp. 128–154). London: Routledge.

Arrow, K. (1963). *Social choice and individual values* (2nd ed.). New Haven and London: Yale University Press.

Arsenio, W., & Ford, M. (1985). The role of affective information in social-cognitive development: Children's differentiation of moral and conventional events. *Merrill-Palmer Quarterly, 31,* 1–18.

Asch, S. (1956). Studies of independence and conformity: I. Minority of one against a unanimous majority. *Psychological Monographs, 70* (entire issue No. 416).

Asch, S. (1963/1951). Effects of group pressure upon the modification and distortion of judgments. In H. Guetzkow (Ed.), *Groups, leadership, and men.* New York: Russell & Russell.

Asendorpf, J. (2002). Self-awareness, other-awareness, and secondary representation. In A. Meltzoff & W. Prinz (Eds.), *The imitative mind: Development, evolution, and brain bases* (pp. 63–73). Cambridge, UK: Cambridge University Press.

Ashcroft v. Free Speech Coalition, 122 S. Ct. 1389 (2002).

Astington, J., & Gopnik, A. (1991). Theoretical explanations of children's understanding of the mind. *British Journal of Developmental Psychology, 9,* 7–31.

Astington, J., & Jenkins, J. (1995). Theory of mind development and social understanding. *Cognition and Emotion, 9,* 151–165.

Atran, S. (1998). Folk-biology and the anthropology of science: Cognitive universals and cultural particulars. *Behavioral and Brain Sciences, 21,* 547–609.

Atran, S. (2001). The trouble with memes: Inference versus imitation in cultural creation. *Human Nature, 12,* 351–381.

Atran, S. (2002). *In gods we trust: The evolutionary landscape of religion.* New York: Oxford University Press.

Atran, S., Medin, D., Ross, N., Lynch, E., Vapnarsky, V., Ucan Ek', E., Coley, J., Timura, C., & Baran, M. (2002). Folkecology, cultural epidemiology, and the spirit of the commons: A garden experiment in the Maya lowlands. *Current Anthropology, 43*, 421–450.

Augustine, J. (1996). Circuitry and functional aspects of the insular lobes in primates including humans. *Brain Research Reviews, 2*, 229–294.

Auerbach, E. (1953). *Mimesis.* New York: Doubleday.

Aunger, R. (2000). Introduction. In R. Aunger (Ed.), *Darwinizing culture: The status of memetics as a science* (pp. 1–25). Oxford & New York: Oxford University Press.

Aunger, R. (2002). *The electric meme.* New York: Free Press.

Avikainen, S., Forss, N., & Hari, R. (2002). Modulated activation of human SI and SII cortices during observation of hand actions. *NeuroImage, 15*, 640–646.

Baars, B. (1986). *The cognitive revolution in psychology.* New York: Guilford.

Bacharach, M. (1997). *Showing what you are by showing who you are.* Russell Sage Foundation Working Paper. New York: Russell Sage Foundation.

Bacharach, M. (1999). Interactive team reasoning: A contribution to the theory of co-operation. *Research in Economics, 53*, 117–147.

Bacharach, M., & Gambetta, D. (2001). Trust in signs. In K. Cook (Ed.), *Trust in society* (pp. 148–184). New York: Russell Sage Foundation.

Baldissera, F., Cavallari, P., Craighero, L., & Fadiga, L. (2001). Modulation of spinal excitability during observation of hand actions in humans. *European Journal of Neuroscience, 13*, 190–194.

Baldwin, D. (1991). Infants' contributions to the achievement of joint reference. *Child Development, 62*, 875–890.

Baldwin, D. (1995). Understanding the link between joint attention and language. In C. Moore & P. Dunham (Eds.), *Joint attention: Its origin and role in development* (pp. 131–158). Hillsdale, N.J.: Erlbaum.

Baldwin, D., & Baird, J. (2001). Discerning intentions in dynamic human action. *Trends in Cognitive Sciences, 5*, 171–178.

Baldwin, D., & Tomasello, M. (1998). Word learning: A window on early pragmatic understanding. In Eve V. Clark (Ed.), *Proceedings of the twenty-ninth annual child language research forum* (pp. 2–23). Chicago: Center for the Study of Language and Information.

Baldwin, J. (1906). *Mental development in the child and the race* (3rd ed.). New York: Augustus M. Kelley.

Bandura, A. (1969). Social learning theory of identificatory processes. In D. Goslin (Ed.), *Handbook of socialization theory and research* (pp. 213–262). Chicago: Rand-McNally.

Bandura, A. (1977). *Social learning theory.* Englewood Cliffs, N.J.: Prentice Hall.

Bandura, A. (1986). *Social foundations of thought and action: A social cognitive theory.* Englewood Cliffs, N.J.: Prentice Hall.

Bandura, A., Ross, D., & Ross, S. (1963a). Imitation of film-mediated aggressive models. *Journal of Abnormal and Social Psychology, 66,* 3–11.

Bandura, A., Ross, D., & Ross, S. (1963b). Vicarious reinforcement and imitative learning. *Journal of Abnormal and Social Psychology, 67,* 601–607.

Banta Lavenex, P. (1999). Vocal production mechanisms in the budgerigar (*Melopsittacus undulatus*): The presence and implications of amplitude modulation. *Journal of the Acoustical Society of America, 106,* 491–505.

Baptista, L., & Catchpole, C. (1989). Vocal mimicry and interspecific aggression in songbirds: Experiments using white-crowned sparrow imitation of song sparrow song. *Behaviour, 109,* 247–257.

Baptista, L., & Gaunt, S. (1994). Advances in studies of avian sound communication. *Condor, 96,* 817–830.

Bargh, J. (1989). Conditional automaticity: Varieties of automatic influence in social perception and cognition. In J. Uleman & J. Bargh (Eds.), *Unintended thought* (pp. 3–51) New York: Guilford.

Bargh, J. (1997). The automaticity of everyday life. In R. Wyer (Ed.), *Advances in social cognition* (Vol. 10, pp. 1–61). Mahwah, N.J.: Erlbaum.

Bargh, J. (1999). The most powerful manipulative messages are hiding in plain sight. *The Chronical of Higher Education* (January 29), B6.

Bargh, J. (in press). Bypassing the will: Towards demystifying the nonconscious control of social behavior. In R. Hassin, J. Uleman, & J. Bargh, (Eds.), *The new unconscious.* New York: Oxford University Press.

Bargh, J., & Chartrand, T. (1999). The unbearable automaticity of being. *American Psychologist,* July, 462–479.

Bargh, J., Chen, M., & Burrows, L. (1996). The automaticity of social behavior: Direct effects of trait concept and stereotype activation on action. *Journal of Personality and Social Psychology, 71,* 230–244.

Bargh, J., Gollwitzer, P., Lee-Chai, A., Barndollar, K., & Trötschel, R. (2001). The automated will: Nonconscious activation and pursuit of behavioral goals. *Journal of Personality and Social Psychology, 81,* 1014–1027.

Barker, M. (1997). The Newson report: A case study in "common sense." In M. Barker & J. Petley (Eds.), *Ill effects: The media/violence debate* (pp. 12–31). London: Routledge.

Baron-Cohen, S., Leslie, A., & Frith, U. (1985). Does the autistic child have a "theory of mind?" *Cognition, 21,* 37–46.

Baron-Cohen, S., Tager-Flusberg, H., & Cohen, D. (1993). *Understanding other minds: Perspectives from autism*. New York: Oxford University Press.

Baron-Cohen, S., Tager-Flusberg, H., & Cohen, D. (Eds.). (2000). *Understanding other minds: Perspectives from developmental cognitive neuroscience* (2nd ed.). Oxford, UK: Oxford University Press.

Barr, R., Dowden, A., & Hayne, H. (1996). Developmental changes in deferred imitation by 6- to 24-month-old infants. *Infant Behavior and Development, 19*, 159–170.

Barr, R., & Hayne, H. (1999). Developmental changes in imitation from television during infancy. *Child Development, 70*, 1067–1081.

Barr, R., Vieira, A., & Rovée-Collier, C. (2001). Mediated imitation in 6-month-olds: Remembering by association. *Journal of Experimental Child Psychology, 79*, 229–252.

Barresi, J., & Moore, C. (1996). Intentional relations and social understanding. *Behavioral and Brain Sciences, 19*, 107–154.

Batson, C. (1991). *The altruism question*. Hillsdale, N.J.: Erlbaum.

Baudrillard, J. (1995). *The Gulf War did not take place*. Sydney, NSW: Power Publications.

Bauer, P., & Mandler, J. (1989). One thing follows another: Effects of temporal structure on 1- to 2-year-olds' recall of events. *Developmental Psychology, 25*, 197–206.

Baumann, Z. (1991). *Modernity and the holocaust*. Cambridge, UK: Polity.

Bavelas, J., Black, A., Lemery, C., & Mullett, J. (1986). "I *show* how you feel": Motor mimicry as a communicative act. *Journal of Personality and Social Psychology, 50*, 322–329.

Bavelas, J., Black, A., Lemery, C., & Mullett, J. (1987). Motor mimicry as primitive empathy. In N. Eisenberg & J. Strayer (Eds.), *Empathy and its development* (pp. 317–338). Cambridge, UK: Cambridge University Press.

Beebe, B., Jaffe, J., Feldstein, S., Mays, K., & Alson, D. (1985). Interpersonal timing: The application of an adult dialogue model to mother-infant vocal and kinesic interactions. In T. Field & N. Fox (Eds.), *Social perception in infants* (pp. 217–246). Norwood, N.J.: Ablex.

Bekkering, H., & Prinz, W. (2002). Goal representations in imitative actions. In K. Dautenhahn & C. Nehaniv (Eds.), *Imitation in animals and artifacts* (pp. 555–572). Cambridge, Mass.: MIT Press.

Bekkering, H., & Wohlschläger, A. (2002). Action perception and imitation: A tutorial. In W. Prinz & B. Hommel (Eds.), *Attention and performance XIX. Common mechanisms in perception and action* (pp. 294–314). Oxford, UK: Oxford University Press.

Bekkering, H., Wohlschläger, A., & Gattis, M. (2000). Imitation of gestures in children is goal-directed. *Quarterly Journal of Experimental Psychology, 53A*, 153–164.

Bellagamba, F., & Tomasello, M. (1999). Re-enacting intended acts: Comparing 12- and 18-month-olds. *Infant Behavior & Development, 22*, 277–282.

Belson, W. (1978). *Television violence and the adolescent boy.* Westmead, UK: Saxon House Teakfield.

Berkowitz, L. (1974). Some determinants of impulsive aggression: The role of mediated associations with reinforcements for aggression. *Psychological Review, 81*, 165–176.

Berkowitz, L. (1990). On the formation and regulation of anger and aggression: A cognitive-neoassociationistic analysis. *American Psychologist, 45*, 494–503.

Berkowitz, L. (1993). *Aggression: Its causes, consequences, and control.* New York: McGraw-Hill.

Berkowitz, L., & LePage, A. (1967). Weapons as aggression-eliciting stimuli. *Journal of Personality and Social Psychology, 7*, 202–207.

Berlucchi, G., & Aglioti, S. (1997). The body in the brain: Neural bases of corporeal awareness. *Trends in Neuroscience, 20*, 560–564.

Bernieri, F. (1988). Coordinated movement and rapport in teacher-student interactions. *Journal of Nonverbal Behavior, 12*, 120–138.

Bernieri, F., Reznick, J., & Rosenthal, R. (1988). Synchrony, pseudo synchrony, and dissynchrony: Measuring the entrainment process in mother-infant interactions. *Journal of Personality and Social Psychology, 54*, 243–253.

Berthoz, A. (2000). *The brain sense of movement.* Cambridge, Mass.: Harvard University Press.

Binford, L. (1989). Isolating the transition to cultural adaptations: An organizational approach. In E. Trinkhaus (Ed.), *The emergence of modern humans: Biocultural adaptations in the later Pleistocene* (pp. 18–41). Cambridge, UK: Cambridge University Press.

Binkofski, F., Buccino, G., Posse, S., Seitz, R., Rizzolatti, G., & Freund, H. (1999a). A fronto-parietal circuit for object manipulation in man: Evidence from an fMRI-study. *European Journal of Neuroscience, 11*, 3276–3286.

Binkofski, F., Buccino, G., Stephan, K., Rizzolatti, G., Seitz, R., & Freund, H. (1999b). A parieto-premotor network for object manipulation: Evidence from neuroimaging. *Experimental Brain Research, 128*, 210–213.

Binmore, K. (1992). *Fun and games: A text on game theory.* Lexington, Mass.: Heath.

Binmore, K. (1994). *Game theory and the social contract.* Vol. 1: *Playing fair.* Cambridge, Mass.: MIT Press.

Binmore, K. (1998). *Game theory and the social contract.* Vol. 2: *Just playing.* Cambridge, Mass.: MIT Press.

Bjorkqvist, K. (1985). *Violent films, anxiety and aggression.* Helsinki: Finnish Society of Sciences and Letters.

Blackmore, S. (1998). Imitation and the definition of a meme. *Journal of Memetics–Evolutionary Models of Information Transmission, 2.* Available at (http://jom-emit. cfpm.org/1998/vol2/blackmore_s.html)

Blackmore, S. (1999). *The meme machine.* Oxford, UK: Oxford University Press.

Blackmore, S. (2000a). The meme's eye view. In R. Aunger (Ed.), *Darwinizing culture: The status of memetics as a science* (pp. 25–42). Oxford & New York: Oxford University Press.

Blackmore, S. (2000b). The power of memes. *Scientific American, 283*(4), 64–73.

Blackmore, S. (2001). Evolution and memes: The human brain as a selective imitation device. *Cybernetics and Systems, 32,* 225–255.

Blair, R. (1995). A cognitive developmental approach to morality: Investigating the psychopath. *Cognition, 57,* 1–29.

Blair, R. (1996). Brief report: Morality in the autistic child. *Journal of Autism and Developmental Disorders, 26,* 571–579.

Blair, R. (1997). Moral reasoning in the child with psychopathic tendencies. *Personality and Individual Differences, 22,* 731–739.

Blair, R. (1999a). Psychophysiological responsiveness to the distress of others in children with autism. *Personality and Individual Differences, 26,* 477–485.

Blair, R. (1999b). Responsiveness to distress cues in the child with psychopathic tendencies. *Personality and Individual Differences, 27,* 135–145.

Blair, R., & Coles, M. (2000). Expression recognition and behavioral problems in early adolescence. *Cognitive Development, 15,* 421–434.

Blair, R., Colledge, E., Murray, L., & Mitchell, D. (2001). A selective impairment in the processing of sad and fearful expressions in children with psychopathic tendencies. *Journal of Abnormal Child Psychology, 29,* 491–498.

Blair, R., Jones, L., Clark, F., & Smith, M. (1997). The psychopathic individual: A lack of responsiveness to distress cues? *Psychophysiology, 34,* 192–198.

Blakemore, S., & Decety, J. (2001). From the perception of action to the understanding of intention. *Nature Reviews Neuroscience, 2,* 561–567.

Blanke, O., Ortigue, S., Landis, T., & Seeck, M. (2002). Stimulating illusory own-body perceptions. *Nature, 419,* 269.

Bloch, M. (2000). A well-disposed anthropologist's problems with memes. In R. Aunger (Ed.), *Darwinizing culture: The status of memetics as a science* (pp. 189–204). Oxford & New York: Oxford University Press.

Bloom, L. (2000). The intentionality model: How to learn a word, any word. In R. Michnick Golinkoff, K. Hirsh-Pasek, L. Bloom, L. Smith, A. Woodward, N. Akhtar, M. Tomasello, & G. Hollich (Eds.), *Becoming a word learner: A debate on lexical acquisition* (pp. 124–135). New York: Oxford University Press.

Boesch, C., & Boesch, H. (1983). Optimisation of nut-cracking with natural hammers by wild chimpanzees. *Behaviour, 83*, 265–286.

Boesch, C., & Boesch, H. (1990). Tool use and tool making in wild chimpanzees. *Folia Primatologica, 54*, 86–99.

Boesch, C., & Tomasello, M. (1998). Chimpanzee and human cultures. *Current Anthropology, 39*, 591–694.

Borden, G., & Harris, K. (1984). *Speech science primer: Physiology, acoustics, and perception of speech.* Baltimore, Md.: Williams & Wilkins.

Boyd, R., Gintis, H., Bowles, S., & Richerson, P. (2003). The evolution of altruistic punishment. *Proceedings of the National Academy of Sciences U.S.A., 100*, 3531–3535.

Boyd, R., & Richerson, P. (1985). *Culture and the evolutionary process.* Chicago: University of Chicago Press.

Boyd, R., & Richerson, P. (1989). The evolution of indirect reciprocity. *Social Networks, 11*, 213–236.

Boyd, R., & Richerson, P. (1996). Why culture is common, but cultural evolution is rare. *Proceedings of the British Academy, 88*, 77–93.

Boyd, R., & Richerson, P. (2000). Memes: Universal acid or a better mousetrap? In R. Aunger (Ed.), *Darwinizing culture: The status of memetics as a science* (pp. 143–162). Oxford & New York: Oxford University Press.

Boyer, P. (1994). *The naturalness of religious ideas.* Berkeley: University of California Press.

Boyer, P. (1998). Cognitive tracks of cultural inheritance: How evolved intuitive ontology governs cultural transmission. *American Anthropologist, 100*, 876–889.

Bradley, L., & Bryant, P. (1983). Categorising sounds and learning to read—a causal connection. *Nature, 301*, 419–421.

Branigan, H., Pickering, M., & Cleland, A. (2000). Syntactic coordination in dialogue. *Cognition, 75*, B13–B25.

Branigan, H., Pickering, M., McLean, J., & Cleland, A. (Unpublished). Syntactic alignment and participant status in dialogue. University of Edinburgh.

Brass, M. (1999). Imitation and ideomotor compatibility. Unpublished dissertation, University of Munich, Germany.

Brass, M., Bekkering, H., & Prinz, W. (2001). Movement observation affects movement execution in a simple response task. *Acta Psychologica, 106*, 3–22.

Brass, M., Bekkering, H., Wohlschläger, A., & Prinz, W. (2000). Compatibility between observed and executed finger movements: Comparing symbolic, spatial and imitative cues. *Brain and Cognition, 44*, 124–143.

Braten, S. (1998). Infant learning by altercentric participation: The reverse of ego-centric observation in autism. In S. Braten (Ed.), *Intersubjective communication and emotion in early ontogeny* (pp. 105–124). New York: Cambridge University Press.

Brauth, S., Liang, W., & Roberts, T. (2001). Projections of the oval nucleus of the hyperstriatum ventrale in the budgerigar: Relationships with the auditory system. *Journal of Comparative Neurology, 432*, 481–511.

Breder, C. (1976). Fish schools as operational structures. *Fishery Bulletin, 74*, 471–502.

Brennan, S., & Clark, H. (1996). Conceptual pacts and lexical choice in conversation. *Journal of Experimental Psychology: Learning, Memory, and Cognition, 22*, 1482–1493.

Brewer, M. (1988). A dual process model of impression formation. In R. Wyer & T. Srull (Eds.), *Advances in social cognition* (Vol. 1, pp. 1–36). Hillsdale, N.J.: Erlbaum.

Brison, S. (1998a). The autonomy defense of free speech. *Ethics, 108*, 312–339.

Brison, S. (1998b). Speech, harm, and the mind-body problem in first amendment jurisprudence. *Legal Theory, 4*, 39–61.

Brison, S. (2002). *Aftermath: Violence and the remaking of a self*. Princeton, N.J.: Princeton University Press.

Brooks, R. (1999). *Cambrian intelligence*. Cambridge, Mass.: MIT Press.

Brooks, R. (2003). *Robots: The future of flesh and machines*. London: Penguin.

Brooks, R., & Meltzoff, A. (2002). The importance of eyes: How infants interpret adult looking behavior. *Developmental Psychology, 38*, 958–966.

Brooks, R., & Meltzoff, A. (2003). Gaze following at 9 and 12 months: A developmental shift from global head direction to gaze. Poster presented at the Society for Research in Child Development, Tampa, Fla., April 2003.

Brown, R. (1973). *A first language: The early stages*. Cambridge, Mass.: Harvard University Press.

Bruner, J. (1960). *The relevance of education*. Cambridge, Mass.: Harvard University Press.

Bruner, J. (1990). *Act of meaning*. Cambridge, Mass.: Harvard University Press.

Bruner, J. (1999). The intentionality of referring. In P. Zelazo, J. Astington, & D. Olson (Eds.), *Developing theories of intention: Social understanding and self-control* (pp. 329–339). Mahwah, N.J.: Erlbaum.

Bryant, P., MacLean, M., Bradley, L., & Crossland, J. (1990). Rhyme and alliteration, phoneme detection and learning to read. *Developmental Psychology, 26*, 429–438.

Buccino, G., Binkofski, F., Fink, G., Fadiga, L., Fogassi, L., Gallese, V., Seitz, R., Zilles, K., Rizzolatti, G., & Freund, H. (2001). Action observation activates premotor and parietal areas in a somatotopic manner: An fMRI study. *European Journal of Neuroscience, 13*, 400–404.

Buck, R. (1980). Nonverbal behavior and the theory of emotion: The facial feedback hypothesis. *Journal of Personality and Social Psychology, 38,* 811–824.

Bugnyar, T., & Huber, L. (1997). Push or pull: An experimental study of imitation in marmosets. *Animal Behaviour, 54,* 817–831.

Bull, L., Holland, O., & Blackmore, S. (2000). On meme-gene coevolution. *Artificial Life, 6,* 227–235.

Burgess, A. (2000). *A clockwork orange.* London: Penguin.

Bushman, B., & Anderson, C. (2001). Media violence and the American public: Scientific facts versus media misinformation. *American Psychologist, 56*(6–7), 477–489. Available at (www.psychology.iastate.edu/faculty/caa/abstracts/2000-2004/01BAA.a)

Bushman, B., & Huesmann, L. (2001). Effects of television violence on aggression. In D. Singer & J. Singer (Eds.), *Handbook of children and the media* (pp. 223–254). Thousand Oaks, Calif.: Sage.

Butterworth, G. (1999). Neonatal imitation: Existence, mechanisms, and motives. In J. Nadel & G. Butterworth (Eds.), *Imitation in infancy* (pp. 63–88), Cambridge, UK: Cambridge University Press.

Byrne, D. (1971). *The attraction paradigm.* New York: Academic Press.

Byrne, R. (1993). Hierarchical levels of imitation. Commentary on M. Tomasello, A. Kruger & H. Ratner, Cultural learning. *Behavioral and Brain Sciences, 16,* 516–517.

Byrne, R. (1994). The evolution of intelligence. In P. Slater & T. Halliday (Eds.), *Behaviour and evolution* (pp. 223–265). Cambridge, UK: Cambridge University Press.

Byrne, R. (1995). *The thinking ape: Evolutionary origins of intelligence.* Oxford, UK: Oxford University Press.

Byrne, R. (1997). The technical intelligence hypothesis: An additional evolutionary stimulus to intelligence? In A. Whiten & R. W. Byrne (Eds.), *Machiavellian intelligence II: Extensions and evaluations* (pp. 289–311). Cambridge, UK: Cambridge University Press.

Byrne, R. (1998a). Comments on C. Boesch and M. Tomasello "Chimpanzee and human cultures." *Current Anthropology, 39,* 604–605.

Byrne, R. (1998b). Imitation: The contributions of priming and program-level copying. In S. Braten (Ed.), *Intersubjective communication and emotion in early ontogeny* (pp. 228–244). Cambridge, UK: Cambridge University Press.

Byrne, R. (1999). Imitation without intentionality. Using string parsing to copy the organization of behaviour. *Animal Cognition, 2,* 63–72.

Byrne, R. (2002a). Imitation of complex novel actions: What does the evidence from animals mean? *Advances in the Study of Behavior, 31,* 77–105.

Byrne, R. (2002b). Emulation in apes: Verdict "not proven." *Developmental Science, 5,* 20–22.

Byrne, R. (2002c). Seeing actions as hierarchically organized structures: Great ape manual skills. In A. N. Meltzoff & W. Prinz (Eds.), *The imitative mind. Development, evolution and brain bases* (pp. 122–140). Cambridge, UK: Cambridge University Press.

Byrne, R., & Byrne, J. (1991). Hand preferences in the skilled gathering tasks of mountain gorillas (*Gorilla g. beringei*). *Cortex, 27*, 521–546.

Byrne, R., & Byrne, J. (1993). Complex leaf-gathering skills of mountain gorillas (*Gorilla g. beringei*): Variability and standardization. *American Journal of Primatology, 31*, 241–261.

Byrne, R., Corp, N., & Byrne, J. (2001a). Manual dexterity in the gorilla: Bimanual and digit role differentiation in a natural task. *Animal Cognition, 4*, 347–361.

Byrne, R., Corp, N., & Byrne, J. (2001b). Estimating the complexity of animal behaviour: How mountain gorillas eat thistles. *Behaviour, 138*, 525–557.

Byrne, R., & Russon, A. (1998). Learning by imitation: A hierarchical approach. *Behavioral and Brain Sciences, 21*, 667–721.

Byrne, R., & Stokes, E. (2002). Effects of manual disability on feeding skills in gorillas and chimpanzees: A cognitive analysis. *International Journal of Primatology, 23*, 539–554.

Byrne, R., & Tomasello, M. (1995). Do rats ape? *Animal Behaviour, 50*, 1417–1420.

Calder, A., Keane, J., Manes, F., Antoun, N., & Young, A. (2000). Impaired recognition and experience of disgust following brain injury. *Nature Neuroscience, 3*, 1077–1078.

Caldwell, C., & Whiten, A. (2002). Evolutionary perspectives on imitation: Is a comparative psychology of social learning possible? *Animal Cognition, 5*, 193–208.

Call, J. (2001). Body imitation in an enculturated orangutan (*Pongo pygmaeus*). *Cybernetics and Systems: An International Journal, 32*, 97–119.

Call, J., & Carpenter, M. (2002). Three sources of information in social learning. In K. Dautenhahn & C. Nehaniv (Eds.), *Imitation in animals and artifacts* (pp. 211–228). Cambridge, Mass.: MIT Press.

Call, J., Carpenter, M., & Tomasello, M. (submitted). Focusing on outcomes and focusing on actions in the process of social learning: Chimpanzees (*Pan troglodytes*) and human children (*Homo sapiens*).

Call, J., & Tomasello, M. (1994). The social learning of tool use by orangutans (*Pongo pygmaeus*). *Human Evolution, 9*, 297–313.

Call, J., & Tomasello, M. (1995). The use of social information in the problem-solving of orangutans (*Pongo pygmaeus*) and human children (*Homo sapiens*). *Journal of Comparative Psychology, 109*, 308–320.

Camerer, C. (1995). Individual decision making. In J. Kagel & A. Roth (Eds.), *Handbook of experimental economics* (pp. 587–703). Princeton, N.J.: Princeton University Press.

Campbell, D. (1954). Operational delineation of "what is learned" via the transposition experiment. *Psychological Review, 6*, 167–174.

Campbell, D. (1974). Evolutionary epistemology. In P. A. Schilpp (Ed.), *The philosophy of Karl Popper* (pp. 413–463). La Salle, Ill.: Open Court.

Campbell, F., Heyes, C., & Goldsmith, A. (1999). Stimulus learning and response learning by observation in the European starling, in a two-object/two-action test. *Animal Behaviour, 58*, 151–158.

Caprara, G., Barbaranelli, C., Pastorelli, C., Cermak, I., & Rosza, S. (2001). Facing guilt: Role of negative affectivity, need for reparation, and fear of punishment in leading to prosocial behaviour and aggression. *European Journal of Personality, 15*, 219–237.

Carpenter, M., Akhtar, N., & Tomasello, M. (1998a). Fourteen- through 18-month-old infants differentially imitate intentional and accidental actions. *Infant Behavior and Development, 21*, 315–330.

Carpenter, M., Call, J., & Tomasello, M. (2002). Understanding "prior intentions" enables 2-year-olds to imitatively learn a complex task. *Child Development, 73*, 1431–1442.

Carpenter, M., Nagell, K., & Tomasello, M. (1998b). Social cognition, joint attention, and communicative competence from 9 to 15 months of age. *Monograph of the Society for Research in Child Development, 63*(4), serial no. 255.

Carpenter, M., Pennington, B., & Rogers, S. (2001). Understanding of others' intentions in children with autism and children with developmental delays. *Journal of Autism and Developmental Disorders, 31*, 589–599.

Carpenter, M., Pennington, B., & Rogers, S. (2002). Interrelations among social-cognitive skills in young children with autism and developmental delays. *Journal of Autism and Developmental Disorders, 32*, 91–106.

Carpenter, M., Tomasello, M., & Savage-Rumbaugh, S. (1995). Joint attention and imitative learning in children, chimpanzees, and enculturated chimpanzees. *Social Development, 4*, 217–237.

Carpenter, M., Tomasello, M., & Striano, T. (submitted). Role reversal imitation and language in typically-developing infants and children with autism.

Carr, L., Iacoboni, M., Dubeau, M., Mazziotta, J., & Lenzi, G. (2001). Observing and imitating emotion: Implications for the neurological correlates of empathy. Paper presented at the first international conference of social cognitive neuroscience, Los Angeles, April 2001.

Carr, L., Iacoboni, M., Dubeau, M., Mazziotta, J., & Lenzi, G. (2003). Neural mechanisms of empathy in humans: A relay from neural systems for action representation to limbic areas. *Proceedings of the National Academy of Sciences, U.S.A., 100*, 5497–5502.

Carruthers, P., & Smith, P. (1996). *Theories of theories of mind*. Cambridge, UK: Cambridge University Press.

Carver, C., & Scheier, M. (1981). *Attention and self-regulation: A control-theory approach to human behavior*. New York: Springer-Verlag.

Carver, C., Ganellen, R., Froming, W., & Chambers, W. (1983). Modeling: An analysis in terms of category accessibility. *Journal of Experimental Social Psychology, 19*, 403–421.

Carver, L., & Bauer, P. (1999). When the event is more than the sum of its parts: 9-month-olds' long-term ordered recall. *Memory, 7*, 147–174.

Castiello, U., Lusher, D., Mari, M., Edwards, M., & Humphreys, G. (2002). Observing a human or a robotic hand grasping an object: Differential motor priming effects. In W. Prinz & B. Hommel (Eds.), *Common mechanisms in perception and action* (pp. 315–333). New York: Oxford University Press.

Castro, L., & Toro, M. (2002). Cultural transmission and the capacity to approve or disapprove of offspring's behaviour. *Journal of Memetics—Evolutionary Models of Information Transmission, 6*. Available at (http://jom-emit.cfpm.org/2002/vol6/castro_l&toro_ma.html)

Cavalli-Sforza, L., & Feldman, M. (1973). Cultural versus biological inheritance: Phenotypic transmission from parent to children (a theory of the effect of parental phenotypes on children's phenotype). *American Journal of Human Genetics, 25*, 618–637.

Cavalli-Sforza, L., & Feldman M. (1981). *Cultural transmission and evolution*. Princeton, N.J.: Princeton University Press.

Chaffee, S. (1972). Television and adolescent aggressiveness (overview). In G. Comstock & E. Rubinstein (Eds.), *Television and social behaviour*. Vol. 3: *Television and adolescent aggressiveness* (pp. 1–34). Washington, D.C.: U.S. Government Printing Office.

Chaminade, T., & Decety, J. (2002). Leader or follower? Involvement of the inferior parietal lobule in agency. *NeuroReport, 13*, 1975–1978.

Chaminade, T., Meary, D., Orliaguet, J., & Decety, J. (2001a). Is perceptual anticipation a motor simulation. *NeuroReport, 12*, 3669–3674.

Chaminade, T., Meary, D., Orliaguet, J., & Decety, J. (2001b). Is perceptual anticipation a motor simulation? A PET study. *Brain Imaging, 12*, 3669–3674.

Chaminade, T., Meltzoff, A., & Decety, J. (2002). Does the end justify the means? A PET exploration of the mechanisms involved in human imitation. *NeuroImage, 15*, 318–328.

Changeux, J., & Danchin, A. (1976). Selective stabilization of developing synapses as a mechanisms for the specification of neuronal networks. *Nature, 264*, 705–721.

Charman, T., & Baron-Cohen, S. (1994). Another look at imitation in autism. *Development and Psychopathology, 6*, 403–413.

Charney, E. (1966). Psychosomatic manifestations of rapport in psychotherapy. *Psychosomatic Medicine, 28*, 305–315.

Chartrand, T., & Bargh, J. (1996). Automatic activation of impression formation and memorization goals: Nonconscious goal priming reproduces effects of explicit task instructions. *Journal of Personality and Social Psychology, 71*, 464–478.

Chartrand, T., & Bargh, J. (1999). The chameleon effect: The perception-behavior link and social interaction. *Journal of Personality and Social Psychology, 76*, 893–910.

Chartrand, T., & Bargh, J. (2002). Nonconscious motivations: Their activation, operation, and consequences. In A. Tesser, D. Stapel, & J. Wood (Eds.), *Self and motivation: Emerging psychological perspectives* (pp. 13–41). Washington D.C.: American Psychological Association.

Chartrand, T., Maddux, W., & Lakin, J. (in press). Beyond the perception-behavior link: The ubiquitous utility and motivational moderators of nonconscious mimicry. In R. Hassin, J. Uleman, & J. Bargh (Eds.), *The new unconscious*. New York: Oxford University Press.

Chein, J., Fissell, K., Jacobs, S., & Fiez, J. (2002). Functional heterogeneity within Broca's area during verbal working memory. *Physiology and Behavior, 77*, 635–639.

Chen, M., & Bargh, J. (1997). Nonconscious behavioral confirmation processes: The self-fulfilling nature of automatically activated stereotypes. *Journal of Experimental Social Psychology, 33*, 541–560.

Cheney, D., & Seyfarth, R. (1990). *How monkeys see the world.* Chicago: University of Chicago Press.

Chesterton, G. (1908). *The man who was thursday.* London: Ameron House.

Chevreul, M. (1833). Lettre à M. Ampère sur une classe particulière de mouvements musculaires. *Revue des Deux Mondes, Série II*, 258–266.

Chomsky, N. (1959). A review of B. F. Skinner's verbal behavior. *Language, 35*, 26–58.

Chomsky, N. (1966). *Current issues in linguistic theory.* The Hague: Mouton.

Chomsky, N. (1981). Knowledge of language: Its elements and origins. *Philosophical Transactions of the Royal Society of London 295*, 223–234.

Chomsky, N. (1986a). *Knowledge of language.* New York: Praeger.

Chomsky, N. (1986b). Changing perspectives on knowledge and use of language. In M. Brand & R. Harnish (Eds.), *The representation of knowledge and belief* (pp. 1–58). Tucson: University of Arizona Press.

Chomsky, N. (1990). Language and mind. In D. Mellor (Ed.), *Ways of communicating* (pp. 56–80). New York: Cambridge University Press.

Chomsky, N. (1997). Language and cognition. In D. Johnson & C. Erneling (Eds.), *The future of the cognitive revolution* (pp. 15–31). New York: Oxford University Press.

Chomsky, N. (1999). On the nature, use, and acquisition of language. In W. Ritchie & T. Bhatia (Eds.), *Handbook of child language acquisition* (pp. 33–54). San Diego: Academic Press.

Christiansen, M. (1994). Infinite languages, finite minds: Connectionism, learning and linguistic structure. Unpublished PhD dissertation, University of Edinburgh.

Christiansen, M., Dale, R., Ellefson, M., & Conway, C. (2002). The role of sequential learning in language evolution: Computational and experimental studies. In A. Cangelosi & D. Parisi (Eds.), *Simulating the evolution of language* (pp. 165–187). London: Springer-Verlag.

Chugani, H. (1999). Metabolic imaging: A window on brain development and plasticity. *Neuroscientist, 5,* 29–40.

Churchland, P., Ramachandran, V., & Sejnowski, T. (1994). A critique of pure reason. In C. Koch & J. Davis (Eds.), *Large-scale neuronal theories of the brain* (pp. 23–60). Cambridge, Mass.: MIT Press.

Churchland, P. (2002). *Brain-wise: Studies in neurophilosophy.* Cambridge, Mass.: MIT Press.

Clark, A. (1997). *Being there: Putting brain, body and world together again.* Cambridge, Mass.: MIT Press.

Cline, V., Croft, R., & Courier, S. (1973). Desensitization of children to television violence. *Journal of Personality and Social Psychology, 27,* 360–365.

Cochin, S., Barthelemy, C., Roux, S., & Martineau, J. (1999). Observation and execution of movement: Similarities demonstrated by quantified electroencephalography. *European Journal of Neuroscience, 11,* 1839–1842.

Cohen, J. (1988). *Statistical power analysis for the behavioral sciences* (2nd ed.). Hillsdale, N.J.: Lawrence Erlbaum Associates.

Cohen, S. (2001). *States of denial: Knowing about atrocities and suffering.* Cambridge, UK: Polity.

Cole, P., Barrett, K., & Zahn-Waxler, C. (1992). Emotion displays in two-year-olds during mishaps. *Child Development, 63,* 314–324.

Collie, R., & Hayne, H. (1999). Deferred imitation by 6- and 9-month-old infants: More evidence for declarative memory. *Developmental Psychobiology, 35,* 83–90.

Comstock, G. (2004). Paths from television violence to aggression: Reinterpreting the evidence. In L. Shrum (Ed.), *Blurring the lines: The psychology of entertainment media* (pp. 193–211). Mahwah, N.J.: Erlbaum.

Comstock, G., & Paik, H. (1991). *Television and the American child.* San Diego: Academic Press.

Comstock, G., & Scharrer, E. (1999). *Television: What's on, who's watching, and what it means.* San Diego: Academic Press.

Comstock, G., & Scharrer, E. (2003). Meta-analyzing the controversy over television violence and aggression. In D. Gentile (Ed.), *Media violence and children* (pp. 205–226). Westport, Conn.: Praeger.

Condon, W., & Sander, L. (1974). Neonate movement is synchronized with adult speech: Interactional participation and language acquisition. *Science, 183,* 99–101.

Conte, R. (2000). Memes through social minds. In R. Aunger (Ed.), *Darwinizing culture: The status of memetics as a science* (pp. 83–120). Oxford & New York: Oxford University Press.

Conway, C., & Christiansen, M. (2001). Sequential learning in non-human primates. *Trends in Cognitive Sciences, 5,* 539–546.

Corkum, V., & Moore, C. (1995). Development of joint visual attention in infants. In C. Moore & P. Dunham (Eds.), *Joint attention: Its origins and role in development* (pp. 61–83). Hillsdale, N.J.: Erlbaum.

Corner, J. (1998). *Studying media: Problems of theory and method.* Edinburgh: Edinburgh University Press.

Corp, N., & Byrne, R. (2002). Leaf processing of wild chimpanzees: Physically defended leaves reveal complex manual skills. *Ethology, 108,* 1–24.

Cosmides, L., & Tooby, J. (1987). From evolution to behavior: Evolutionary psychology as the missing link. In J. Dupré (Ed.), *The latest on the best: Essays on evolution and optimality* (pp. 277–306). Cambridge, Mass.: MIT Press.

Cosmides, L., & Tooby, J. (1994). Origins of domain-specificity: The evolution of functional organization. In L. Hirschfeld & S. Gelman (Eds.), *Mapping the mind: Domain-specificity in cognition and culture* (pp. 85–116). New York: Cambridge University Press.

Couturier-Fagan, D. (1996). Neonatal responses to tongue protrusion and mouth opening modeling. *Dissertation Abstracts International: Section B: The Sciences and Engineering, 57*(3-B), 2173.

Craighero, L., Buccino, G., & Rizzolatti, G. (2002). Speech listening specifically modulates the excitability of tongue muscles: A TMS study. *European Journal of Neuroscience, 15,* 399–402.

Crick, N., & Dodge, K. (1994). A review and reformulation of social information processing mechanisms in children's adjustment. *Psychological Bulletin, 115,* 74–101.

Cronin, H. (1991). *The ant and the peacock.* Cambridge, UK: Cambridge University Press.

Cubitt, R., & Sugden, R. (1998). The selection of preferences through imitation. *Review of Economic Studies, 65,* 761–771.

Custance, D., Whiten, A., & Bard, K. (1995). Can young chimpanzees (*Pan troglodytes*) imitate arbitrary actions? Hayes & Hayes (1952) revisited. *Behaviour, 132,* 11–12.

Custance, D., Whiten, A., & Fredman, T. (1999). Social learning of an artificial fruit task in capuchin monkeys (*Cebus apella*). *Journal of Comparative Psychology, 113*, 1–11.

Cutting, J., & Kozlowski, L. (1977). Recognizing friends by their walk: Gait perception without familiarity cues. *Bulletin of the Psychonomic Society, 9*, 353–356.

Damasio, A. (1994). *Descartes' error: Emotion, reason and the human brain*. New York: Putnam.

Damasio A. (1999). *The feeling of what happens: Body and emotion in the making of consciousness*. New York & San Diego: Harcourt.

Darwin, C. (1871). *The descent of man*. London: Murray.

Dave, A., & Margoliash, D. (2000). Song replay during sleep and computational rules for sensorimotor vocal learning. *Science, 290*, 812–816.

Davidson, D. (1982). *Essays on actions and events*. Oxford, UK: Clarendon Press.

Davidson, D. (1984). *Inquiries into truth and interpretation*. Oxford, UK: Clarendon Press.

Davies, M., & Stone, T. (1995a). *Mental simulation*. Oxford, UK: Blackwell.

Davies, M., & Stone, T. (1995b). *Folk psychology*. Oxford, UK: Blackwell.

Dawkins, R. (1976). Hierarchical organisation: A candidate principle for ethology. In P. Bateson & R. Hinde (Eds.), *Growing points in ethology* (pp. 7–54). Cambridge, UK: Cambridge University Press.

Dawkins, R. (1976/1989). *The selfish gene*. Oxford, UK: Oxford University Press.

Dawkins, R. (1982). *The extended phenotype*. Oxford, UK: Oxford University Press.

Dawkins, R. (1986). *The blind watchmaker*. Harmondsworth, UK: Penguin.

Dawkins, R. (1999). Foreword. In S. Blackmore (Ed.), *The meme machine*. Oxford, UK: Oxford University Press.

Dawson, B., & Foss, B. (1965). Observational learning in budgerigars. *Animal Behaviour, 13*, 470–474.

Dawson, G., Meltzoff, A., Osterling, J., & Rinaldi, J. (1998). Neuropsychological correlates of early symptoms of autism. *Child Development, 69*, 1276–1285.

De Maeght, S. (2001). New insights in ideomotor action: Investigating the influence of perception, motor, and intention representation. Unpublished dissertation, University of Munich, Germany.

De Maeght, S., & Prinz, W. (2004). Action induction through action observation. Special Issue of *Psychological Research*. Available at: http://springerlink.com.

de Villiers, J., & de Villiers, P. (1978). *Language acquisition*. Cambridge, Mass.: Harvard University Press.

de Villers, P., & de Villiers, J. (1979). *Early language.* Cambridge, Mass.: Harvard University Press.

de Waal, F. (1996). *Good natured: The origins of right and wrong in humans and other animals.* Cambridge, Mass.: Harvard University Press.

de Waal, F. (2001a). *The ape and the sushi master.* New York: Basic Books.

de Waal, F. (2001b). *Tree of origin.* Cambridge, Mass.: Harvard University Press.

Deacon, T. (1997). *The symbolic species: The co-evolution of language and the brain.* New York: Norton.

Decety, J. (2002a). Neurophysiological evidence for simulation of action. In J. Dokic & J. Proust (Eds.), *Simulation and knowledge of action* (pp. 53–72). Philadelphia: John Benjamins.

Decety, J. (2002b). Naturaliser l'empathie [Empathy naturalized]. *L'Encéphale, 28,* 9–20.

Decety, J. (2002c). Is there such a thing as functional equivalence between imagined, observed, and executed action? In A. Meltzoff & W. Prinz (Eds.), *The imitative mind: Development, evolution, and brain bases* (pp. 291–310). Cambridge, UK: Cambridge University Press.

Decety, J., & Chaminade, T. (2003). Neural correlates of feeling sympathy. *Neuropsychologia, 41*(2), 127–138.

Decety, J., Chaminade, T., Grèzes, J., & Meltzoff, A. (2002). A PET exploration of the neural mechanisms involved in reciprocal imitation. *NeuroImage, 15,* 265–272.

Decety, J., & Grèzes, J. (1999). Neural mechanisms subserving the perception of human actions. *Trends in Cognitive Sciences, 3,* 172–178.

Decety, J., Grèzes, J., Costes, N., Perani, D., Jeannerod, M. Procyk, E., Grassi, F., & Fazio, F. (1997). Brain activity during observation of action. Influence of action content and subject's strategy. *Brain, 120,* 1763–1777.

Decety, J., & Ingvar, D. (1990). Brain structures participating in mental simulation of motor behavior: A neuropsychological interpretation. *Acta Psychologica, 73,* 13–34.

Decety, J., Perani, D., Jeannerod, M., Bettinardi, V., Woods, R., Mazziotta, J., & Fazio, F. (1994). Mapping motor representations with positron emission tomography. *Nature, 371,* 600–602.

Decety, J., & Sommerville, J. (2003). Shared representations between self and others: A Social cognitive neuroscience view. *Trends in Cognitive Science, 7,* 527–533.

DeMyer, M., Alpern, G., Barton, S., DeMyer, W., Churchill, D., Hingtgen, J., Bryson, C., Pontius, W., & Kimberlin, C. (1972). Imitation in autistic, early schizophrenic and non-psychotic subnormal children. *Journal of Autism and Childhood Schizophrenia, 2,* 264–287.

Dennett, D. (1983). Intentional systems in cognitive ethology: The "Panglossian paradigm" defended. *Behavioral and Brain Sciences, 6,* 343–390.

Dennett, D. (1987). *The intentional stance.* Cambridge, Mass.: MIT Press.

Dennett, D. (1995). *Darwin's dangerous idea: Evolution and the meanings of life.* New York: Simon & Schuster. Also London: Penguin.

Desimone, R. (1991). Face-selective cells in the temporal cortex of monkeys. *Journal of Cognitive Neuroscience, 3,* 1–8.

Devine, P. (1989). Stereotypes and prejudice: Their automatic and controlled components. *Journal of Personality and Social Psychology, 56,* 5–18.

deVoogd, T., Krebs, J., Healy, S., & Purvis, A. (1993). Relations between song repertoire size and the volume of brain nuclei related to song: Comparative evolutionary analyses amongst oscine birds. *Proceedings of the Royal Society of London Series B, 254,* 75–82.

di Pellegrino, G., Fadiga, L., Fogassi, L., Gallese, V., & Rizzolatti, G. (1992). Understanding motor events: A neurophysiological study. *Experimental Brain Research, 91,* 176–180.

Diamond, J. (1997). *Guns, germs, and steel: The fates of human societies.* New York: Norton.

Dickinson, A., & Balleine, B. (2000). Causal cognition and goal-directed action. In C. Heyes & L. Huber (Eds.), *The evolution of cognition* (pp. 185–204). Cambridge, Mass.: MIT Press.

Dijksterhuis, A., Aarts, H., Bargh, J., & van Knippenberg, A. (2000a). On the relation between associative strength and automatic behavior. *Journal of Experimental Social Psychology, 36,* 531–544.

Dijksterhuis, A., & Bargh, J. (2001). The perception-behavior expressway: Automatic effects of social perception and social behavior. In M. Zanna (Ed.), *Advances in experimental social psychology* (Vol. 30, pp. 1–40). New York: Academic Press.

Dijksterhuis, A., Bargh, J., & Miedema, J. (2000b). Of men and mackerels: Attention and automatic behavior. In H. Bless & J. P. Forgas (Eds.), *Subjective experience in social cognition and behavior* (pp. 36–51). Philadelphia, Pa.: Psychology Press.

Dijksterhuis, A., Spears, R., Postmes, T., Stapel, D., Koomen, W., van Knippenberg, A., & Scheepers, D. (1998). Seeing one thing and doing another: Contrast effects in automatic behavior. *Journal of Personality and Social Psychology, 75,* 862–871.

Dijksterhuis, A., & van Knippenberg, A. (1998). The relation between perception and behavior or how to win a game of Trivial Pursuit. *Journal of Personality and Social Psychology, 74,* 865–877.

Dijksterhuis, A., & van Knippenberg, A. (2000). Behavioral indecision: Effects of self-focus on automatic behavior. *Social Cognition, 18,* 55–74.

Dimberg, U., Thunberg, M., & Elmehed, K. (2000). Unconscious facial reactions to emotional facial expressions. *Psychological Science, 11,* 86–89.

Disbrow, E., Roberts, T., & Krubitzer, L. (2000). Somatotopic organization of cortical fields in the lateral sulcus of *Homo sapiens*: Evidence for SII and PV. *Journal of Comparative Neurology, 418,* 1–21.

Dodge, K. (1980a). Social cognition and children's aggressive behavior. *Child Development, 51*(1), 162–170.

Dodge, K. (1980b). Social cognition and children's aggressive behavior. *Child Development, 53,* 620–635.

Dodge, K., Pettit, G., Bates, J., & Valente, E. (1995). Social information processing patterns partially mediate the effect of early physical abuse on later conduct problems. *Journal of Abnormal Psychology, 104,* 632–643.

Donald, M. (1991). *Origins of the modern mind: Three stages in the evolution of culture and cognition.* Cambridge, Mass.: Harvard University Press.

Donald, M. (1993). Précis of *Origins of the modern mind* with multiple reviews and author's response. *Behavioral and Brain Sciences, 16,* 737–791.

Donald, M. (1998). Mimesis and the executive suite: Missing links in language evolution. In J. Hurford, M. Studdert-Kennedy, & C. Knight (Eds.), *Approaches to the evolution of language* (pp. 44–67). Cambridge, UK: Cambridge University Press.

Donald, M. (1999). Preconditions for the evolution of protolanguages. In M. Corballis & I. Lea (Eds.), *Evolution of the hominid mind* (pp. 138–154). Oxford, UK: Oxford University Press.

Donald, M. (2001). *A mind so rare: The evolution of human consciousness.* New York: Norton.

Dorrance, B., & Zentall, T. (2001). Imitative learning in Japanese quail (*Conturnix japonica*) depends on the motivational state of the observer quail at the time of observation. *Journal of Comparative Psychology, 115,* 62–67.

Dorrance, B., & Zentall, T. (2002). Imitation of conditional discriminations in pigeons. *Journal of Comparative Psychology, 116,* 277–285.

Downing, P., Jiang, Y., Shuman, M., & Kanwisher, N. (2001). A cortical area selective for visual processing of the human body. *Science, 293,* 2405–2407.

Dryer, M. (1989). Large linguistic areas and language sampling. *Studies of Language, 13,* 257–292.

Dubeau, M., Iacoboni, M., Koski, L., Markovac, J., & Mazziotta, J. (2001). Topography for body parts motion in the STS region. *Society for Neuroscience Abstracts, 27,* program number 165.34.

Durkheim, E. (1982). *The rules of sociological method.* London: Macmillan.

Duval, S., & Wicklund, R. (1972). *A theory of objective self-awareness*. San Diego: Academic Press.

Eco, U. (1979). *A theory of semiotics*. Bloomington: Indiana University Press.

Eco, U. (1990). *The limits of interpretation*. Bloomington: Indiana University Press.

Eco, U. (1994). Does the audience have bad effects on television? In U. Eco, *Apocalypse postponed* (pp. 87–107). Bloomington: Indiana University Press.

Edelman, G. (1989). *Neural Darwinism: The theory of neuronal group selection*. Oxford, UK: Oxford University Press.

Ehrsson, H., Fagergren, A., Jonsson, T., Westling, G., Johansson, R., & Forssberg, H. (2000). Cortical activity in precision- versus power-grip tasks: An fMRI study. *Journal of Neurophysiology, 83*, 528–536.

Eidelberg, D., & Galaburda, A. (1984). Inferior parietal lobule. *Archives of Neurology, 41*, 843–852.

Eidelberg, L. (1929). Experimenteller Beitrag zum Mechanismus der Imitationsbewegung [An experimental contribution to the mechanism of imitation movements]. *Jahresbücher für Psychiatrie und Neurologie, 45*, 170–173.

Ekman, P. (1973). *Darwin and facial expression: A century of research in review*. New York: Academic Press.

Ekman, P. (1993). Facial expression and emotion. *American Psychologist, 48*, 384–392.

Ekman, P. (1999). Facial expressions. In T. Dalgleish & M. J. Power (Eds.), *Handbook of cognition and emotion* (pp. 301–320). Chichester, UK: Wiley.

Eldridge, J., Kitzinger, J., & Williams, K. (1997). *The mass media and power in modern Britain*. Oxford, UK: Oxford University Press.

Elman, J., Bates, E., Johnson, M., Karmiloff-Smith, A., Parisi, D., & Plunkett, K. (1999). *Rethinking innateness: A connectionist perspective on development*. Cambridge, Mass.: MIT Press.

Elsner, B., & Aschersleben, G. (2003). Infants' imitation of action sequences: Not only a memory problem! Paper presented at 2003 biennial meeting of the Society for Research in Child Development. Tampa, Fla.

Elsner, B., & Hommel, B. (2004). Contiguity and contingency in the acquisition of action effects. *Psychological Research, 68*, 138–154.

Elsner, B., & Hommel, B. (2001). Effect anticipation and action control. *Journal of Experimental Psychology: Human Perception and Performance, 27*(1), 229–240.

Elsner, B., Hommel, B., Mentschel, C., Drzezga, A., Prinz, W., Conrad, B., & Siebner, H. (2002). Linking actions and their perceivable consequences in the human brain. *NeuroImage, 17*, 364–372.

Epstein, W. (1973). The process of "taking-into-account" in visual perception. *Perception, 2*, 267–285.

Eron, L., & Huesmann, L. (1987). Television as a source of maltreatment of children. *School Psychology Review, 16*(2), 195–202.

Eron, L., Huesmann, L., Lefkowitz, M., & Walder, L. (1972). Does television violence cause aggression? *American Psychologist, 27,* 253–263.

Fadiga, L., Craighero, L., Buccino, G., Rizzolatti, G. (2002). Speech listening specifically modulates the excitability of tongue muscles: A TMS study. *European Journal of Neuroscience, 15,* 399–402.

Fadiga, L., Fogassi, L., Pavesi, G., & Rizzolatti, G. (1995). Motor facilitation during action observation: A magnetic stimulation study. *Journal of Neurophysiology, 73,* 2608–2611.

Farrer, C., & Frith, C. (2002). Experiencing oneself vs. another person as being the cause of an action: The neural correlates of the experience of agency. *NeuroImage, 15,* 596–603.

Farrer, C., Franck, N., Georgieff, N., Frith, C., Decety, J., & Jeannerod, M. (2003). Modulating the experience of agency: A PET study. *NeuroImage, 18,* 324–333.

Fauconnier, G., & Turner, M. (2002). *The way we think: Conceptual blending and the mind's hidden complexities.* New York: Basic Books.

Feldman, M., & Laland, K. (1996). Gene-culture coevolutionary theory. *Trends in Ecology and Evolution, 11,* 453–457.

Feldstein, S., Konstantareas, M., Oxman, J., & Webster, C. (1982). The chronography of interactions with autistic speakers: An initial report. *Journal of Communication Disorders, 15,* 451–460.

Ferguson, G. (1965). *Nonparametric trend analysis.* Montreal: McGill University Press.

Fey, M. (1986). *Language intervention with young children.* San Diego: College-Hill Press.

Field, T., Goldstein, S., Vaga-Lahr, N., & Porter, K. (1986). Changes in imitative behavior during early infancy. *Infant Behavior and Development, 9,* 415–421.

Field, T., Guy, L., & Umbel, V. (1985). Infants' responses to mothers' imitative behaviors. *Infant Mental Health Journal, 6,* 40–44.

Field, T., Woodson, R., Cohen, D., Greenberg, R., Garcia, R., & Collins, E. (1983). Discrimination and imitation of facial expressions by term and preterm neonates. *Infant Behavior and Development, 6,* 485–489.

Field, T., Woodson, R., Greenberg, R., & Cohen, D. (1982). Discrimination and imitation of facial expression by neonates. *Science, 218,* 179–181.

Fillmore, C. (1966). The case for case. In E. Bach & R. Harms (Eds.), *Universals in linguistic theory* (pp. 1–88). New York: Holt, Rinehart & Winston.

Fink, G., Marshall, J., Halligan, P., Frith, C., Driver, J., Frackowiak, R., & Dolan, R. (1999). The neural consequences of conflict between intention and the senses. *Brain*, *122*, 497–512.

Fisher, L., & Blair, R. (1998). Cognitive impairment and its relationship to psychopathic tendencies in children with emotional and behavioral difficulties. *Journal of Abnormal Child Psychology*, *26*, 511–519.

Flanagan, J., Vetter, P., Johnson, R., & Wolpert, D. (2003). Prediction precedes control in motor learning. *Current Biology*, *13*, 146–150.

Flavell, J. (1999). Cognitive development: Children's knowledge about the mind. *Annual Review of Psychology*, *50*, 21–45.

Fodor, J. (1983). *Modularity of mind*. Cambridge, Mass.: MIT Press.

Fodor, J. (1987). *Psychosemantics: The problem of meaning in the philosophy of mind*. Cambridge, Mass.: MIT Press.

Fodor, J. (1998). *Concepts: Where cognitive science went wrong* (Oxford Cognitive Science Series). Oxford, UK: Clarendon Press.

Fogassi, L. (2000). Mirror neurons and language origin. Paper presented at the international conference on the development of mind, Tokyo, Japan, August 2000.

Fogassi, L., & Gallese, V. (2002), The neural correlates of action understanding in non-human primates. In M. Stamenov & V. Gallese (Eds.), *Mirror neurons and the evolution of brain and language* (pp. 13–36). Amsterdam: Benjamins.

Fogassi, L., Gallese, V., Fadiga, L., & Rizzolatti, G. (1998). Neurons responding to the sight of goal directed hand/arm actions in the parietal area PF (7b) of the macaque monkey. *Society for Neuroscience Abstracts*, *24*, 257.5.

Fontaine, R. (1984). Imitative skills between birth and six months. *Infant Behavior and Development*, *7*, 323–333.

Fowles, D. (1980). The three arousal models: Implications of Gray's two-factor learning theory for heart rate, electrodermal activity, and psychopathy. *Psychophysiology*, *17*, 87–104.

Fowles, J. (1999). *The case for television violence*. Thousand Oaks, Calif.: Sage.

Fox, P., Huang, A., Parsons, L., Xiong, J., Zamarippa, F., Rainey, L., & Lancaster, J. (2001). Location-probability profiles for the mouth region of human primary motor-sensory cortex: Model and validation. *NeuroImage*, *13*, 196–209.

Fragaszy, D., & Visalberghi, E. (2001). Recognizing a swan: Socially biased learning. *Psychologica*, *44*, 82–98.

Freedman, J. (1984). Effects of television violence on aggressiveness. *Psychological Bulletin*, *96*, 227–246.

Freedman, J. (2002). *Media violence and its effect on aggression: Assessing the evidence*. Toronto: University of Toronto Press.

Frith, C., Blakemore, S., & Wolpert, D. (2000). Abnormalities in the awareness and control of action. *Philosophical Transactions of the Royal Society of London Series B, 355*, 1771–1788.

Frith, C., & Frith, U. (1999). Interacting minds: A biological basis. *Science, 286*, 1692–1695.

Frith, U. (2001). Mind blindness and the brain in autism. *Neuron, 32*, 969–979.

Fritz, J., & Kotrschal, K. (1999, April). Social constraints and profitability of social learning. In K. Dautenhahn & C. Nehaniv (Eds.), *Proceedings of the AISB '99 symposium on imitation in animals and artifacts* (pp. 20–26). Brighton, UK: The Society for the Study of Artificial Intelligence and Simulation of Behaviour.

Fritz, J., Bisenberger, A., & Kotrschal, K. (1999). Social mediated learning of an operant task in greylag geese: Field observation and experimental evidence. *Advances in Ethology, 34*, 51.

Fudenberg, D., & Tirole, J. (1992). *Game theory.* Cambridge Mass.: MIT Press.

Galef, B. (1988). Imitation in animals: History, definition and interpretation of data from the psychological laboratory. In T. Zentall & B. Galef (Eds.), *Social learning: Psychological and biological perspectives* (pp. 3–28). Hillsdale, N.J.: Erlbaum.

Galef, B. (1992). The question of animal culture. *Human Nature, 3*, 157–178.

Galef, B. (1998). Recent progress in the study of imitation and social learning in animals. In M. Sabourin, F. Craik, & M. Roberts (Eds.), *Advances in psychological science.* Vol. 2: *Biological and cognitive aspects* (pp. 275–279). Hove, UK: Psychological Press.

Galef, B., Manzig, L., & Field, R. (1986). Imitation learning in budgerigars: Dawson and Foss (1965) revisited. *Behavioral Processes, 13*, 191–202.

Gallagher, S. (2000). Philosophical conceptions of the self: Implications for cognitive science. *Trends in Cognitive Sciences, 4*, 14–21.

Gallagher, T. (1996). A feeble embrace: Romania's engagement with democracy, 1989–1994. *Journal of Communist Studies and Transition Politics, 12*(2), 145–172.

Gallese, V. (2000a). The acting subject: Towards the neural basis of social cognition. In T. Metzinger (Ed.), *Neural correlates of consciousness. Empirical and conceptual questions* (pp. 325–333). Cambridge, Mass.: MIT Press.

Gallese, V. (2000b). The inner sense of action: Agency and motor representations. *Journal of Consciousness Studies, 7*, 23–40.

Gallese, V. (2001). The "shared manifold" hypothesis: From mirror neurons to empathy. *Journal of Consciousness Studies, 8*, 33–50.

Gallese, V. (2003a). A neuroscientific grasp of concepts: From control to representation. *Philosophical Transactions of the Royal Society of London Series B, 358*, 1231–1240.

Gallese, V. (2003b). The manifold nature of interpersonal relations: The quest for a common mechanism. *Philosophical Transactions of the Royal Society of London Series B, 358,* 517–528.

Gallese, V., Fadiga, L., Fogassi, L., & Rizzolatti, G. (1996). Action recognition in the premotor cortex. *Brain, 119,* 593–609.

Gallese, V., Fadiga, L., Fogassi, L., & Rizzolatti, G. (2002). Action representation and the inferior parietal lobule. In W. Prinz & B. Hommel (Eds.), *Common mechanisms in perception and action* (pp. 334–355). New York: Oxford University Press.

Gallese, V., & Goldman, A. (1998). Mirror neurons and the simulation theory of mind-reading. *Trends in Cognitive Sciences, 2,* 493–501.

Gambetta, D. (2005). *Crimes and signs: Cracking the codes of the underworld.* Princeton, N.J.: Princeton University Press.

Gangitano, M., Mottaghy, F., & Pascual-Leone, A. (2001). Phase-specific modulation of cortical motor output during movement observation. *NeuroReport, 12,* 1489–1492.

Garrod, S., & Anderson, A. (1987). Saying what you mean in dialogue: A study in conceptual and semantic co-ordination. *Cognition, 27,* 181–218.

Gattis, M., Bekkering, H., & Wohlschläger, A. (2002). Goal-directed imitation. In A. Meltzoff & W. Prinz (Eds.), *The imitative mind: Development, evolution, and brain bases* (183–205). Cambridge, UK: Cambridge University Press.

Gaunt, A., & Gaunt, S. (1985). Electromyographic studies of the syrinx in parrots (Aves: Psittacidae). *Zoomorphology, 105,* 1–11.

Geen, R., & O'Neal, E. (1969). Activation of cue-elicited aggression by general arousal. *Journal of Personality and Social Psychology, 11,* 289–292.

Geen, R., & Thomas, S. (1986). The immediate effects of media violence on behaviour. *Journal of Social Issues, 42,* 7–28.

Gentilucci, M., & Rizzolatti, G. (1990). Cortical motor control of arm and hand movements. In M. Goodale (Ed.), *Vision and action: The control of grasping* (pp. 147–162). Norwood, N.J.: Ablex.

Gerardin, E., Sirigu, A., Lehericy, S., Poline, J., Gaymard, B., Marsault, C., Agid, Y., & Le Bihan, D. (2000). Partially overlapping neural networks for real and imagined hand movements. *Cerebral Cortex, 10,* 1093–1104.

Gerbner, G., & Gross, L. (1976). Living with television: The violence profile. *Journal of Communication, 26,* 171–180.

Gerbner, G., Gross, L., Morgan, M., & Signorielli, N. (1980). The "mainstreaming" of America. *Journal of Communication, 30,* 10–29.

Gerbner, G., Gross, L., Morgan, M., & Signorielli, N. (1994). Growing up with television: The cultivation perspective. In J. Bryant & D. Zillmann (Eds.), *Media effects* (pp. 17–41). Hillsdale, N.J.: Erlbaum.

Gergely, G., Bekkering, H., & Király, I. (2002). Rational imitation in preverbal infants. *Nature, 415,* 755.

Gerrans, P. (forthcoming). *The measure of madness: Philosophy and cognitive neuropsychiatry.* Cambridge, Mass.: MIT Press.

Gerth, H., & Mills, C. (1954). *Character and social structure.* London: Routledge and Kegan Paul.

Geyer, S., Matelli, M., Luppino, G., & Zilles, K. (2000). Functional neuroanatomy of the primate isocortical motor system. *Anatomy and Embryology (Berlin), 202,* 443–474.

Gibbons, F. (1990). Self-attention and behavior: A review and theoretical update. In L. Berkowitz (Ed.), *Advances in experimental social psychology, 23,* 249–303.

Gibson, J. (1966). *The senses considered as perceptual systems.* Boston: Houghton-Mifflin.

Gibson, J. (1986). *The ecological approach to visual perception.* Hillsdale, N.J.: Erlbaum.

Giddens, A. (1990). *The consequences of modernity.* Cambridge, UK: Polity Press.

Gilbert, D. (1989). Thinking lightly about others: Automatic components of the social inference process. In J. Uleman & J. Bargh (Eds.), *Unintended thought* (pp. 189–211). New York: Guilford.

Gil-White, F. (2001a). Are ethnic groups biological "species" to the human brain? Essentialism in our cognition of some social categories. *Current Anthropology, 42,* 515–554.

Gil-White, F. (2001b). L'évolution culturelle a-t-elle des règles? *La recherché, Hors-Série 5,* 92–97.

Gil-White, F. (2002a). Comment on Atran et al. (2002). *Current Anthropology, 43,* 441–442.

Gil-White, F. (2002b). The evolution of prestige explains the evolution of reference. Paper delivered at the fourth international conference on the evolution of language, Harvard University.

Gil-White, F. (in preparation). I killed a one-eyed marmot: Why some narrative memes spread better than others, and how they maintain beliefs.

Gleissner, B., Meltzoff, A., & Bekkering, H. (2000). Children's coding of human action: Cognitive factors influencing imitation in 3-year-olds. *Developmental Science, 3,* 405–414.

Godfrey-Smith, P. (2000). The replicator in retrospect. *Biology and Philosophy, 15,* 403–423.

Goldenberg, G., & Hermsdörfer, J. (2002). Imitation, apraxia and hemispheric dominance. In A. Meltzoff & W. Prinz (Eds.), *The imitative mind* (pp. 331–346). Cambridge, UK: Cambridge University Press.

Goldman, A. (1989). Interpretation psychologized. *Mind and Language, 4,* 161–185.

Goldman, A. (1992a). In defense of the simulation theory. *Mind and Language, 7,* 104–119.

Goldman, A. (1992b). Empathy, mind, and morals: Presidential address. *Proceedings and Addresses of the American Philosophical Association, 66,* 17–41.

Goldman, A. (2000). The mentalizing folk. In D. Sperber (Ed.), *Metarepresentations: A multidisciplinary perspective* (pp. 171–196). New York: Oxford University Press.

Goldman, A. (2001). Desire, intention, and the simulation theory. In B. Malle, L. Moses, & D. Baldwin (Eds.), *Intentions and intentionality: Foundations of social cognition* (pp. 207–224). Cambridge, Mass.: MIT Press.

Goldman, A. (2002). Simulation theory and mental concepts. In J. Dokic & J. Proust (Eds.), *Simulation and knowledge of action* (pp. 2–19). Philadelphia Pa.: John Benjamins.

Goldman, A., & Gallese, V. (2000). Reply to Schulkin. *Trends in Cognitive Sciences, 4,* 255–256.

Goldstein, H. (1984). The effects of modeling and corrected practice on generative language and learning of preschool children. *Journal of Speech and Hearing Disorders, 49,* 389–398.

Goodall, J. (1973). Cultural elements in a chimpanzee community. In E. Menzel (Ed.), *Precultural primate behaviour* (pp. 144–184). Basel: S. Karger.

Goodall, J. (1986). *The chimpanzees of Gombe: Patterns of behavior.* Cambridge, Mass.: Harvard University Press.

Goodwin, C. (2000). Action and embodiment within situated human interaction. *Journal of Pragmatics, 32,* 1489–1522.

Goodwin, M., & Goodwin, C. (2000). Emotion within situated activity. In M. Budwig & I. Uzgiris (Eds.), *Communication: An arena of development* (pp. 33–53). Stamford, Conn.: Ablex.

Goodwin, C., & Heritage, J. (1990). Conversation analysis. *Annual Review of Anthropology, 19,* 283–307.

Gopnik, A. (1993). How we know our minds: The illusion of first-person knowledge of intentionality. *Behavioral and Brain Sciences, 16,* 1–14.

Gopnik, A., & Meltzoff, A. (1986). Relations between semantic and cognitive development in the one-word stage: The specificity hypothesis. *Child Development, 57,* 1040–1053.

Gopnik, A., & Meltzoff, A. (1997). *Words, thoughts, and theories.* Cambridge, Mass.: MIT Press.

Gordon, R. (1986). Folk psychology as simulation. *Mind and Language, 1,* 159–171.

Gordon, R. (1995a). Sympathy, simulation and the impartial spectator. *Ethics*, *105*, 727–742.

Gordon, R. (1995b). Simulation without introspection or inference from me to you. In M. Davies & T. Stone (Eds.), *Mental simulation* (pp. 53–67). Oxford, UK: Blackwell.

Gordon, R. (1996). "Radical" simulationism. In P. Carruthers & P. Smith (Eds.), *Theories of theories of mind* (pp. 11–21). Cambridge, UK: Cambridge University Press.

Gordon, R. (2000). Sellar's Ryleans revisited. *Protosociology*, *14*, 102–114.

Gordon, R. (2002). Simulation and reason explanation: The radical view. Special Issue of *Philosophical Topics*, *29*, Nos. 1 & 2.

Gorenstein, E. (1982). Frontal lobe functions in psychopaths. *Journal of Abnormal Psychology*, *91*, 368–379.

Gould, S., & Lewontin, R. (1979). The spandrals of San Marco and the Panglossian paradigm: A critique of the adaptationist programme. *Proceedings of the Royal Society of London Series B*, *205*, 581–598.

Gould, S., & Vrba, E. (1982). Exaptation: A missing term in the science of form. *Paleobiology*, *8*, 4–15.

Grafton, S., Arbib, M., Fadiga, L., Rizzolatti, G. (1996). Localisation of grasp representations in humans by positron emission tomography: 2. Observation compared with imagination. *Experimental Brain Research*, *112*, 103–111.

Gray, J. (1987). *The psychology of fear and stress*. New York: Cambridge University Press.

Gray, J. (1993). The neuropsychology of the emotions: Framework for a taxonomy of psychiatric disorders. In S. van Gooze (Ed.), *Emotions: Essays on emotion theory* (pp. 29–59). Hillsdale, N.J.: Erlbaum.

Graziano, M., Taylor, C., Moore, T., & Cooke, D. (2002). The cortical control of movement revisited. *Neuron*, *36*, 349–362.

Green, M., & Kinsbourne, M. (1990). Subvocal activity and auditory hallucinations: Clues for behavioral treatments. *Schizophrenia Bulletin*, *16*, 617–626.

Greenewalt, C. (1968). *Bird song: Acoustics and physiology*. Washington, D.C.: Smithsonian Institution Press.

Greenwald, A. (1970). Sensory feedback mechanisms in performance control: With special reference to the ideo-motor mechanism. *Psychological Review*, *77*, 73–99.

Greenwald, A. (1972). On doing two things at once: Time sharing as a function of ideomotor compatibility. *Journal of Experimental Psychology*, *94*, 52–57.

Greenwald, A., & Banaji, M. (1995). Implicit social cognition: Attitudes, self-esteem and stereotypes. *Psychological Review*, *102*, 4–27.

Grèzes, J., Costes, N., & Decety, J. (1998). Top-down effect of strategy on the perception of human biological motion: A PET investigation. *Cognitive Neuropsychology, 15*, 553–582.

Grèzes, J., Costes, N., & Decety, J. (1999). The effect of learning and intention on the neural network involved in the perception of meaningless actions. *Brain, 122*, 1875–1887.

Grèzes, J., & Decety, J. (2001). Functional anatomy of execution, mental simulation, observation and verb generation of actions: A meta-analysis. *Human Brain Mapping, 12*, 1–19.

Grèzes, J., Fonlupt, P., Bertenthal, B., Delon, C., Segebarth, C., & Decety, J. (2001). Does perception of biological motion rely on specific brain regions? *NeuroImage, 13*, 775–785.

Griffiths, T., Rees, G., Green, G., Witton, C., Rowe, D., Büchel, C., Turner, R., & Frackowiak, R. (1998). Right parietal cortex is involved in the perception of sound movement in humans. *Nature Neuroscience, 1*, 74–79.

Grill-Spector, K., Kourtzi, Z., & Kanwisher, N. (2001). The lateral occipital complex and its role in object recognition. *Vision Research, 41*, 1409–1422.

Gross, C. (1992). Representation of visual stimuli in inferior temporal cortex. In V. Bruce, A. Cowey, & A. Ellis (Eds.), *Processing the facial image* (pp. 3–10). New York: Oxford University Press.

Gross, C., & Sergent, J. (1992). Face recognition. *Current Opinion in Neurobiology, 2*, 156–161.

Grossberg, L., Wartella, E., & Whitney, D. (1998). *Media making: Mass media in popular culture.* London: Sage.

Grush, R. (1995). Emulation and cogntion. PhD dissertation, University of California at San Diego.

Guerra, N., Huesmann, L., Tolan, P., Van Acker, R., & Eron, L. (1995). Stressful events and individual beliefs as correlates of economic disadvantage and aggression among urban children. *Journal of Consulting and Clinical Psychology, 63*, 518–528.

Guilford, T., & Dawkins, M. (1991). Receiver psychology and the evolution of animal signals. *Animal Behavior, 42*, 1–14.

Haidt, J., Koller, S., & Dias, M. (1993). Affect, culture, and morality, or is it wrong to eat your dog? *Journal of Personality and Social Psychology, 65*, 613–628.

Hall, G. (1994). Pavlovian conditioning: Laws of association. In N. Mackintosh (Ed.), *Animal learning and cognition* (pp. 15–43). San Diego: Academic Press.

Hall, G. (1996). Learning about associatively activated stimulus representations: Implications for acquired equivalence and perceptual learning. *Animal Learning and Behavior, 24*, 233–255.

Halsband, U. (1998). Brain mechanisms of apraxia. In A. D. Milner (Ed.), *Comparative neuropsychology* (pp. 184–212). Oxford, UK: Oxford University Press.

Hamilton, J. (1998). *Channelling violence: The economic market for violent programming.* Princeton, N.J.: Princeton University Press.

Hanna, E., & Meltzoff, A. (1993). Peer imitation by toddlers in laboratory, home, and day-care contexts: Implications for social learning and memory. *Developmental Psychology, 29,* 701–710.

Happé, F., Brownell, H., & Winner, E. (1999). Acquired theory of mind impairments following stroke. *Cognition, 70,* 211–240.

Harbord, V. (1997). Natural born killers: Violence, film and anxiety . In C. Sumner (Ed.), *Violence, culture and censure* (pp. 137–158). London: Taylor and Francis.

Hare, R. (1991): *The hare psychopathy checklist—revised.* Toronto: Multi-Health Systems.

Hare, R. (1993): *Without conscience: The disturbing world of the psychopaths among us.* New York: Pocket Books.

Hare, R. (1998). Psychopathy, affect and behavior. In D. J. Cooke, R. D. Hare, & A. E. Forth (Eds.), *Psychopathy: Theory, research, and implications for society* (pp. 105–137). Dordrecht, Netherlands: Kluwer.

Hari, R., Forss, N., Avikainen, S., Kirveskari, E., Salenius, S., & Rizzolatti, G. (1998). Activation of human primary motor cortex during action observation: A neuromagnetic study. *Proceedings of the National Academy of Sciences, U.S.A., 95,* 15061–15065.

Harris, P. (1989). *Children and emotion: The development of psychological understanding.* Oxford, UK: Basil Blackwell.

Harris, P. (1992). From simulation to folk psychology: The case for development. *Mind and Language, 7,* 120–144.

Harris, P. (2000). *The work of the imagination.* Oxford, UK: Blackwell.

Haruno, M., Wolpert, D., & Kawato, M. (2001). Mosaic model for sensorimotor learning and control. *Neural Computation, 13,* 2201–2220.

Hasson, O. (1994). Cheating signals. *Journal of Theoretical Biology, 167,* 223–238.

Hatfield, E., Cacioppo, J., & Rapson, R. (1994). *Emotional contagion.* Cambridge, UK: Cambridge University Press.

Hauser, M. (1996). *The evolution of communication.* Cambridge, Mass.: MIT Press.

Hayes, K., & Hayes, C. (1952). Imitation in a home-raised chimpanzee. *Journal of Comparative and Physiological Psychology, 45,* 450–459.

Hayne, H., Boniface, J., & Barr, R. (2000). The development of declarative memory in human infants: Age-related changes in deferred imitation. *Behavioral Neuroscience, 114,* 77–83.

Hayne, H., MacDonald, S., & Barr, R. (1997). Developmental changes in the specificity of memory over the second year of life. *Infant Behavior and Development, 20*, 233–245.

Heal, J. (1986). Replication and functionalism. In J. Butterfield (Ed.), *Language, mind, and logic* (pp. 135–150). Cambridge, UK: Cambridge University Press.

Hearold, S. (1986). A synthesis of 1043 effects of television on social behavior. In G. Comstock (Ed.), *Public communication and behavior* (Vol. 1, pp. 65–133). New York: Academic Press.

Heilman, K., Barrett, A., & Adair, J. (1998). Possible mechanisms of anosognosia: A defect in self-awareness. *Philosophical Transactions of the Royal Society of London Series B, 353*, 1903–1909.

Heimann, M. (1989). Neonatal imitation, gaze aversion, and mother-infant interaction. *Infant Behavior and Development, 12*, 495–505.

Heimann, M. (2002). Notes on individual differences and the assumed elusiveness of neonatal imitation. In A. N. Meltzoff & W. Prinz (Eds.), *The imitative mind* (pp. 74–84). Cambridge, UK: Cambridge University Press.

Heimann, M., & Meltzoff, A. (1996). Deferred imitation in 9- and 14-month-old infants: A longitudinal study of a Swedish sample. *British Journal of Developmental Psychology, 14*, 55–64.

Heimann, M., Nelson, K., & Schaller, J. (1989). Neonatal imitation of tongue protrusion and mouth opening: Methodological aspects and evidence of early individual differences. *Scandinavian Journal of Psychology, 30*, 90–101.

Heimann, M., & Schaller, J. (1985). Imitative reactions among 14–21-day-old infants. *Infant Mental Health Journal, 6*, 31–39.

Heimann, M., & Ullstadius, E. (1999). Neonatal imitation and imitation among children with autism and Down's syndrome. In J. Nadel & G. Butterworth (Eds.), *Imitation in infancy* (pp. 235–253). Cambridge, UK: Cambridge University Press.

Heiser, M., Iacoboni, M., Maeda, F., Marcus, J., & Mazziotta, J. C. (2003). The essential role of Broca's area in imitation. *European Journal of Neuroscience, 17*, 1123–1128.

Hempel, C. (1950). Problems and changes in the empiricist criterion of meaning. *Revenue Internationale de Philosophie, 11*, 41–63.

Hempel, C. (1951). The concept of cognitive significance: A reconsideration. *Proceedings of the American Academy of Arts and Sciences, 80*, 61–77. Combined with Hempel, 1950, with some omissions and changes, in Empiricist criteria of cognitive significance: Problems and changes. In A. Martinich (Ed.), *The philosophy of language* (4th ed., pp. 34–60). Oxford, UK: Oxford University Press.

Henrich, J., & Boyd, R. (1998). The evolution of conformist transmission and the emergence of between-group differences. *Evolution and Human Behavior, 19*, 215–241.

Henrich, J., & Boyd, R. (2002). On modeling cognition and culture: How formal models of social learning can inform our understanding of cultural evolution. *Journal of Cognition and Culture*, 2, 87–112.

Henrich, J., & Gil-White, F. (2001). The evolution of prestige: Freely conferred status as a mechanism for enhancing the benefits of cultural transmission. *Evolution and Human Behavior*, 22, 165–196.

Hepp-Reymond, M., Hüsler, E., Maier, M., & Qi, H. (1994). Force-related neuronal activity in two regions of the primate ventral premotor cortex. *Canadian Journal of Physiology and Pharmacology*, 72, 571–579.

Heritage, J. (1989). Current developments in conversation analysis. In D. Roger & P. Bull (Eds.), *Conversation: An interdisciplinary perspective* (pp. 21–24). Clevedon, UK: Multilingual Matters.

Heritage, J., & Roth, A. (1995). Grammar and institution: Questions and questioning in the broadcast news interview. *Research on Language and Social Interaction*, 28, 1–60.

Herman, L. (2002). Vocal, social, and self-imitation by bottlenosed dolphins. In K. Dautenhahn & C. Nehaniv (Eds.), *Imitation in animals and artifacts* (pp. 63–106). Cambridge, Mass.: MIT Press.

Hesslow, G. (2002). Conscious thought as simulation of behaviour and perception. *Trends in Cognitive Sciences*, 6, 242–247.

Heyes, C. (1993). Imitation, culture and cognition. *Animal Behaviour*, 46, 999–1010.

Heyes, C. (1996). Genuine imitation? In C. Heyes & B. Galef Jr. (Eds.), *Social learning in animals: The roots of culture* (pp. 371–389). San Diego: Academic Press.

Heyes, C. (2000). We're all nativists now. Review of J. Nadel and G. Butterworth, Imitation in infancy. *Contemporary Psychology: The APA Review of Books*, 45, 398–400.

Heyes, C. (2001a). Causes and consequences of imitation. *Trends in Cognitive Sciences*, 5, 253–261.

Heyes, C. (2001b). Evolutionary psychology in the round. In C. Heyes & L. Huber (Eds.), *Evolution of cognition* (pp. 1–21). Cambridge, Mass.: MIT Press.

Heyes, C. (2002). Transformational and associative theories of imitation. In K. Dautenhahn & C. Nehaniv (Eds.), *Imitation in animals and artifacts* (pp. 501–523). Cambridge, Mass.: MIT Press.

Heyes, C. (2003). Four routes of cognitive evolution. *Psychological Review*, 110, 713–727.

Heyes, C., Dawson, G., & Nokes, T. (1992). Imitation in rats: Initial responding and transfer evidence from a bidirectional control procedure. *Quarterly Journal of Experimental Psychology*, 42B, 59–71.

Heyes, C., & Foster, C. (2002). Motor learning by observation: Evidence from a serial reaction time task. *Quarterly Journal of Experimental Psychology*, 55A, 593–607.

Heyes, C., & Galef, B. (1996). *Social learning in animals: The roots of culture*. San Diego: Academic Press.

Heyes, C., & Ray, E. (2000). What is the significance of imitation in animals? *Advances in the Study of Behavior, 29*, 215–245.

Heyes, C., & Saggerson, A. (2002). Testing for imitative and non-imitative social learning in the budgerigar using a two-object/two-action test. *Animal Behaviour, 64*, 851–859.

Higgins, E. (1989). Knowledge accessibility and activation: Subjectivity and suffering from unconscious sources. In J. Uleman & J. Bargh (Eds.), *Unintended thought* (pp. 75–123). New York: Guilford.

Higgins, E., & Bargh, J. (1987). Social cognition and social perception. In M. Rosenzweig & L. Porter (Eds.), *Annual review of psychology* (Vol. 38, pp. 369–425). Palo Alto, Calif.: Annual Reviews.

Higgs, P. (2000). The mimetic transition: A simulation study of the evolution of learning by imitation. *Proceedings of the Royal Society of London Series B, 267*, 1355–1361.

Hikosaka, O., Rand, M., Miyachi, S., & Miyashita, K. (1995). Learning of sequential movements in the monkey-process of learning and retention of memory, *Journal of Neurophysiology, 74*, 1652–1661.

Hikosaka, O., Sakai, K., Nakahara, H., Lu, X., Miyachi, S., Nakamura, K., & Rand, M. K. (2000). Neural mechanisms for learning of sequential procedures. In M. Gazzaniga (Ed.), *The cognitive neurosciences* (2nd ed., pp. 553–572). Cambridge, Mass.: MIT Press.

Hirschfeld, L. (1988). On acquiring social categories: Cognitive development and anthropological wisdom. *Man, 23*, 611–638.

Hirschfeld, L. (1996). *Race in the making: Cognition, culture, and the child's construction of human kinds*. Cambridge Mass.: MIT Press.

Hirsh-Pasek, K., Golinkoff, R., & Hollich, G. (2000). An emergentist coalition model for word learning. In R. Michnick, R. Golinkoff, K. Hirsh-Pasek, L. Bloom, L. Smith, A. Woodward, N. Akhtar, M. Tomasello, & G. Hollich (Eds.), *Becoming a word learner: A debate on lexical acquisition* (pp. 136–164). New York: Oxford University Press.

Hobson, R. (1989). On sharing experiences. *Development and Psychopathology, 1*, 197–203.

Hobson, R. (2002). *The cradle of thought*. London: Macmillan.

Hobson, R., & Lee, A. (1999). Imitation and identification in autism. *Journal of Child Psychology and Psychiatry, 4*, 649–659.

Hodges, S., & Klein, K. (2001). Regulating the cost of empathy: The price of being human. *Journal of Socio-Economics, 30*, 437–452.

Hodges, S., & Wegner, D. (1997). Automatic and controlled empathy. In W. Ickes (Ed.), *Empathic accuracy* (pp. 311–339). New York: Guilford.

Hoffman, M. (2000). *Empathy and moral development: Implications for caring and justice.* New York: Cambridge University Press.

Hogben, M. (1998). Factors moderating the effect of television aggression on viewer behavior. *Communication Research, 25,* 220–247.

Holland, J. (1992). *Adaptation in natural and artificial systems* (2nd ed.). Cambridge, Mass.: MIT Press.

Hollich, G., Hirsh-Pasek, K., & Golinkoff, R. (2000). Breaking the language barrier: An emergentist coalition model for the origins of word learning. *Monographs of the Society for Research in Child Development, 262,* 1–138.

Hommel, B. (2000). The prepared reflex: Automaticity and control in stimulus-response translation. In S. Monsell & J. Driver (Eds.), *Control of cognitive processes: Attention and performance* (Vol. XVIII, pp. 247–273). Cambridge, Mass.: MIT Press.

Hommel, B., Müsseler, J., Aschersleben, G., & Prinz, W. (2001). The theory of event coding (TEC): A framework for perception and action. *Behavorial and Brain Sciences, 24,* 849–937.

Hoppitt, W., & Laland, K. (2002). Neural network models of imitation. Poster presented at perspectives on imitation: From cognitive neuroscience to social science, Royaumont Abbey, France, May 24–26, 2002. Available at ⟨http://www.warwick.ac.uk/fac/sci/Psychology/imitation⟩

Horner, V., & Whiten, A. (2004). Causal knowledge and imitation/emulation switching in chimpanzees (*Pan troglodytes*) and children (*Homo sapiens*). *Animal Cognition,* in press.

Horowitz, L. (1963). *Power, politics and people: The collected essays of C. Wright Mills* (pp. 439–452). New York: Oxford University Press.

House, T., & Milligan, W. (1976). Autonomic responses to modeled distress in prison psychopaths. *Journal of Personality and Social Psychology, 34,* 556–560.

Huang, C., Heyes, C., & Charman, T. (2002). Infants' behavioral re-enactment of "failed attempts": Exploring the roles of emulation learning, stimulus enhancement, and understanding of intentions. *Developmental Psychology, 38,* 840–855.

Huesmann, L. (1986). Psychological processes promoting the relation between exposure to media violence and aggressive behaviour by the viewer. *Journal of Social Issues, 42,* 125–139.

Huesmann, L. (1988). An information-processing model for the development of aggression. *Aggressive Behavior, 14,* 13–24.

Huesmann, L. (1995). *Screen violence and real violence: Understanding the link* (brochure). Auckland, NZ: Media Aware.

Huesmann, L. (1998). The role of social information processing and cognitive schemas in the acquisition and maintenance of habitual aggressive behavior. In R. Geen & E. Donnerstein (Eds.), *Human aggression: Theories, research, and implications for policy* (pp. 73–109). New York: Academic Press.

Huesmann, L. (1999). The effects of childhood aggression and exposure to media violence on adult behaviors, attitudes, and mood: Evidence from a 15-year cross-national longitudinal study. *Aggressive Behavior, 25,* 18–29.

Huesmann, L., & Eron, L. (1986). *Television and the aggressive child: A cross-national comparison.* Hillsdale, N.J.: Erlbaum.

Huesmann, L., Eron, L., Berkowitz, L., & Chaffee, S. (1992a). The effects of television violence on aggression: A reply to a skeptic. In P. Suedfeld & P. Tetlock (Eds.), *Psychology and social policy* (pp. 191–200). New York: Hemisphere.

Huesmann, L., & Guerra, N. (1997). Children's normative beliefs about aggression and aggressive behavior. *Journal of Personality and Social Psychology, 72,* 408–419.

Huesmann, L., Guerra, N., Zelli, A., & Miller, L. (1992b). Differing cognitions relating to TV viewing and aggression among boys and girls. In K. Bjorkqvist & P. Niemela (Eds.), *Of mice and women* (pp. 77–87). New York: Academic Press.

Huesmann, L., Lagerspetz, K., & Eron, L. (1984). Intervening variables in the TV violence-aggression relation: Evidence from two countries. *Developmental Psychology, 20,* 746–775.

Huesmann, L., & Miller, L. (1994). Long-term effects of repeated exposure to media violence in childhood. In L. Huesmann (Ed.), *Aggressive behavior: Current perspectives* (pp. 153–186). New York: Plenum.

Huesmann, L., & Moise, J. (1996). Media violence: A demonstrated public threat to children. *Harvard Mental Health Letter, 12,* 5–7.

Huesmann, L., Moise, J., & Podolski, C. (1997). The effects of media violence on the development of antisocial behavior. In D. Stoff, J. Breiling, & J. Maser (Eds.), *Handbook of antisocial behavior* (pp. 181–193). New York: Wiley.

Huesmann, L., Moise, J., Podolski, C., & Eron, L. (2003). Longitudinal relations between childhood exposure to media violence and adult aggression and violence: 1977–1992. *Developmental Psychology, 39,* 201–221.

Huesmann, L., & Taylor, L. (2003). The case against the case against media violence. In D. Gentile (Ed.), *Media violence and children* (pp. 107–130). Westport, Conn.: Greenwood Press.

Hull, D. (2000). Taking memetics seriously: Memetics will be what we make it. In R. Aunger (Ed.), *Darwinizing culture: The status of memetics as a science* (pp. 43–68). Oxford & New York: Oxford University Press.

Hume, D. (1740/1984). *A treatise on human nature*. New York: Penguin Books. Earlier editions (1739–1740), London: Millar (1888) (L. Selby-Bigge, Ed.), Oxford, UK: Clarendon Press.

Humphrey, N. (1980). Nature's psychologists. In B. Josephson & V. Ramachandran (Eds.), *Consciousness and the physical world* (pp. 57–75). Oxford: Pergamon Press.

Humphrey, N. (1982). Consciousness: A just-so story. *New Scientist, 19*, 474–477.

Humphrey, N. (2000). The privatization of sensation. In C. Heyes & L. Huber (Eds.), *The evolution of cognition* (pp. 241–252). Cambridge, Mass.: MIT Press.

Humphrey, N. (2002). *The inner eye*. Oxford, UK: Oxford University Press. Earlier edition (1986), London: Faber & Faber.

Hunt, G., & Gray, R. (2003). Diversification and cumulative evolution in New Caledonian crow tool manufacture. *Proceedings of the Royal Society of London Series B, 270*, 867–874.

Hunt, M. (1997). *How science takes stock*. New York: Russell Sage.

Hurford, J. (2002). Language beyond our grasp: What mirror neurons can and cannot, do for language evolution. Paper presented at the fourth international conference on the evolution of language, Cambridge, Mass., March 2002.

Hurley, S. (1989). *Natural reasons*. New York: Oxford University Press.

Hurley, S. (1998). *Consciousness in action*. Cambridge, Mass.: Harvard University Press.

Hurley, S. (2001). Perception and action: Alternative views. *Synthese, 291*, 3–40.

Hurley, S. (2003). Animal action in the space of reasons. *Mind and Language, 18*(3), 231–256.

Hurley, S. (2004). Imitation, media violence, and freedom of speech. *Philosophical Studies, 117*, 165–218.

Hurley, S. (in press). Rational agency, cooperation, and mind-reading. In N. Gold, (Ed.), *Teamwork: A Multidisciplinary Perspective*. London: Palgrave.

Husserl, E. (1973). Cartesianische meditationen und Pariser Vorträge [Cartesian meditations and Paris lectures]. In E. Husserl & S. Strasser (Eds.), *Husserliana* (Vol. I). The Hague, Netherlands: Martinus Nijhoff.

Husserl, E. (1953/1977). *Cartesian meditations: An introduction to phenomenology*. (D. Cairns, translator). Dordrecht, Netherlands: Kluwer. Earlier edition (1960), The Hague, Netherlands: Martinus Nijhoff.

Husserl, E. (1989). *Ideas pertaining to a pure phenomenology and to a phenomenological philosophy, Second book: Studies in the phenomenology of constitution*. Dordrecht, Netherlands: Kluwer. (Cited as *Ideen II*).

Hutchison, W., Davis, K., Lozano, A., Tasker, R., & Dostrovsky, J. (1999). Pain-related neurons in the human cingulate cortex. *Nature Neuroscience, 2*, 403–405.

Hyvarinen, J. (1982). Posterior parietal lobe of the primate brain. *Physiological Review*, *62*, 1060–1129.

Iacoboni, M., Koski, L., Brass, M., Bekkering, H., Woods, R., Dubeau, M., Mazziotta, J., & Rizzolatti, G. (2001). Reafferent copies of imitated actions in the right superior temporal cortex. *Proceedings of the National Academy of Sciences U.S.A.*, *98*, 13995–13999.

Iacoboni, M., Woods, R., Brass, M., Bekkering, H., Mazziotta, J., & Rizzolatti, G. (1999). Cortical mechanisms of human imitation. *Science*, *286*, 2526–2528.

Ikebuchi, M., & Okanoya, K. (1999). Male zebra finches and Bengalese finches emit directed songs to the video images of conspecific females projected onto a TFT display. *Zoological Science*, *16*, 63–70.

Isaac, G. (1977). *Olorgesailie*. Chicago: Chicago University Press.

Ishikura, T., & Inomata, K. (1995). Effects of angle of model demonstration on learning of motor skill. *Perceptual and Motor Skills*, *80*, 651–658.

Jacobson, S. (1979). Matching behavior in the young infant. *Child Development*, *50*, 425–430.

Jaffe, J., Beebe, B., Feldstein, S., Crown, C., & Jasnow, M. (2001). Rhythms of dialogue in infancy. In W. Overton (Ed.), *Monographs of the Society for Research in Child Development*, *265*, vol. 66, 2.

James, W. (1890). *Principles of psychology*. New York: Holt.

Janik, V., & Slater, P. (2000). The different roles of social learning in vocal communication. *Animal Behavior*, *60*, 1–11.

Jarvis, E., & Mello, C. (2000). Molecular mapping of brain areas involved in parrot vocal communication. *Journal of Comparative Neurology*, *419*, 1–31.

Jarvis, E., Ribeiro, S., da Silva, M., Ventura, D., Vielliard, J., & Mello, C. (2000). Behaviourally driven gene expression reveals song nuclei in hummingbird brain. *Nature*, *406*, 628–632.

Jeannerod, M. (1997). *The cognitive neuroscience of action*. Oxford, UK: Blackwell.

Jeannerod, M. (1999). To act or not to act: Perspectives on the representation of actions. *Quarterly Journal of Experimental Psychology*, *52A*, 1–29.

Jeannerod, M. (2001). Neural simulation of action: A unifying mechanism for motor cognition. *NeuroImage*, *14*, S103–S109.

Jeannerod, M., Arbib, M., Rizzolatti, G., & Sakata, H. (1995). Grasping objects: The cortical mechanisms of visuomotor transformation. *Trends in Neuroscience*, *18*, 314–320.

Jellema, T., & Perrett, D. (2002). Coding of visible and hidden actions. In W. Prinz & B. Hommel (Eds.), *Attention and performance XIX. Common mechanisms in perception and action* (pp. 267–290). Oxford, UK: Oxford University Press.

Jellema, T., Baker, C., Oram, M., & Perrett, D. (2002). Cell populations in the banks of the superior temporal sulcus of the macaque monkey and imitation. In A. Meltzoff & W. Prinz (Eds.), *The imitative mind. Development, evolution and brain bases* (pp. 143–162). Cambridge, UK: Cambridge University Press.

Jellema, T., Baker, C., Wicker, B., & Perrett, D. (2000). Neural representation for the perception of intentionality of actions. *Brain and Cognition, 44,* 280–302.

Jensen, R. (1998). Pornographic dodges and distortions. In G. Dines, R. Jensen, & A. Russo, *Pornography. The production and consumption of inequality* (pp. 1–7). New York: Routledge.

Johnson, J., Cohen, P., Smailes, E., Kasen, S., & Brook, J. (2002). Television viewing and aggressive behavior during adolescence and adulthood. *Science, 295,* 2468–2471.

Johnson, S. (2000). The recognition of mentalistic agents in infancy. *Trends in Cognitive Sciences, 4,* 22–28.

Johnson-Pynn, J., Fragaszy, D., Hirsh, E., Brakke, K., & Greenfield, P. (1999). Strategies used to combine seriated cups by chimpanzees (*Pan troglodytes*), bonobos (*Pan paniscus*), and capuchins (*Cebus apella*). *Journal of Comparative Psychology, 113,* 137–148.

Jones, S. (1996). Imitation or exploration: Young infants' matching of adults' oral gestures. *Child Development, 67,* 1952–1969.

Jones, S. (2001). Four-week-old infants protrude their tongues to music. Paper presented to the biannual meeting of the Society for Research in Child Development, Minneapolis, April 2001.

Jones, S. (2002). Do neonates imitate? In M. West (chair). The proximate (and ultimate) infant. Invited symposium presented to the Annual Meeting of the Animal Behavior Society, Bloomington, Indiana.

Jordan, M., & Rumelhart, D. (1992). Forward models: Supervised learning with a distal teacher. *Cognitive Science, 16,* 307–354.

Josephson, W. (1987). Television violence and children's aggression: Testing the priming, social script, and disinhibition predictions. *Journal of Personality and Social Psychology, 53,* 882–890.

Kalaska, J., Caminiti, R., & Georgopoulos, A. (1983). Cortical mechanisms related to the direction of two-dimensional arm movements: Relations in parietal area 5 and comparison with motor cortex. *Experimental Brain Research, 51,* 247–260.

Kalaska, J., Cohen, D., Prud'homme, M., & Hyde, M. (1990). Parietal area 5 neuronal activity encodes movement kinematics, not movement dynamics. *Experimental Brain Research, 80,* 351–364.

Kang, N. (1990). A critique and secondary analysis of the NBC study on television and aggression. Unpublished PhD dissertation, Syracuse University, Syracuse, NY.

Kauffman, S. (1993). *The origins of order: Self-organization and selection in evolution.* Oxford, UK: Oxford University Press.

Kawakami, K., Dovidio, J., & Dijksterhuis, A. (2003). The effects of social category priming on specific attitudes: A clear and present danger. *Psychological Science, 14,* 315–319.

Kawato, M. (1999). Internal models for motor control and trajectory planning. *Current Opinion in Neurobiology, 9,* 718–727.

Kaye, K., & Marcus, J. (1978). Imitation over a series of trials without feedback: Age six months. *Infant Behavior and Development, 1,* 141–155.

Kaye, K., & Marcus, J. (1981). Infant imitation: The sensory-motor agenda. *Infant Behavior and Development, 17,* 258–265.

Keenan, J., Wheeler, M., Gallup, G. G., & Pascual-Leone, A. (2000). Self-recognition and the right prefrontal cortex. *Trends in Cognitive Sciences, 4,* 338–344.

Kendal, J., & Laland, K. (2000). Mathematical models for memetics. *Journal of Memetics 4*(1). Available at (jom-emit.cfpm.org/2000/vol4/kendal_jr&laland_kn.html)

Kennett, J. (2002). Autism, empathy, and moral agency. *Philosophical Quarterly, 52,* 340–357.

Kessler, R. (1996). *The sins of the father: Joseph P. Kennedy and the dynasty he founded.* New York: Warner Books.

Kinsbourne, M. (1989). A model of adaptive behavior related to cerebral participation in emotional control. In G. Gainotti & C. Caltigirone (Eds.), *Emotions and the dual brain* (pp. 248–260). New York: Springer-Verlag.

Kinsbourne, M. (1990). Voiced images. Imagined voices. *Biological Psychiatry, 27,* 811–812.

Kinsbourne, M. (2002). The role of imitation in body ownership and mental growth. In A. Meltzoff & W. Prinz (Eds.), *The imitative mind, evolution, development and brain bases* (pp. 311–330). Cambridge, UK: Cambridge University Press.

Klatt, D., & Stefanski, R. (1974). How does a mynah bird imitate human speech? *Journal of the Acoustical Society of America, 55,* 822–832.

Klein, P., & Meltzoff, A. (1999). Long-term memory, forgetting and deferred imitation in 12-month-old infants. *Developmental Science, 2,* 102–113.

Knoblich, G., & Flach, R. (2001). Predicting the effects of actions: Interactions of perception and action. *Psychological Science, 12,* 467–472.

Knuf, L. (1998). *Ideomotorische Phänomene: Neue Fakten für ein altes Problem. Entwicklung eines Paradigmas zur kinematischen Analyse induzierter Mitbewegungen. [Ideomotor phenomena: New facts for an old problem. Development of a paradigm for the kinematic analysis of induced ideomotor movements.]* Aachen, Germany: Shaker.

Knuf, L., Aschersleben, G., & Prinz, W. (2001). An analysis of ideomotor action. *Journal of Experimental Psychology: General, 130,* 779–798.

Kohler, E., Keysers, Ch., Umiltà, M., Fogassi, L., Gallese, V., & Rizzolatti, G. (2002). Hearing sounds, understanding actions: Action representation in mirror neurons. *Science, 297,* 846–848.

Kohler, E., Umiltà, M., Keysers, C., Gallese, V., Fogassi, L., & Rizzolatti, G. (2001). Auditory mirror neurons in the ventral premotor cortex of the monkey. *Society for Neuroscience Abstracts.* Vol. XXVII, 129.9.

Kohut, H. (1971). *The analysis of the self.* New York: International University Press.

Kokkinaki, T., & Kugiumutzakis, G. (2000). Basic aspects of vocal imitation in infant-parent interaction during the first 6 months. *Journal of Reproductive and Infant Psychology, 18,* 173–187.

Kornblum, S., & Stevens, G. (2002). Sequential effects of dimensional overlap: Findings and issues. In W. Prinz & B. Hommel (Eds.), *Common mechanisms in perception and action. Attention and performance* (Vol. XIX, pp. 9–54). Oxford, UK: Oxford University Press.

Kornblum, S., Hasbroucq, T., & Osman, A. (1990). Dimensional overlap: Cognitive basis for stimulus-response compatibility—A model and taxonomy. *Psychological Review, 97,* 253–270.

Koski, L., Iacoboni, M., Dubeau, M., Woods, R., & Mazziotta, J. (2000). Imitation of actions observed in mirror or anatomic configurations. *Society for Neuroscience Abstracts, 26,* 688.683.

Koski, L., Iacoboni, M., Dubeau, M., Woods, R., & Mazziotta, J. (2003). Modulation of cortical activity during different imitative behaviors. *Journal of Neurophysiology, 89,* 460–471.

Koski, L., Wohlschläger, A., Bekkering, H., Woods, R., Dubeau, M., Mazziotta, J., & Iacoboni, M. (2002). Modulation of motor and premotor activity during imitation of target-directed actions. *Cerebral Cortex, 12,* 847–855.

Koza, J. (1992). *Genetic programming: On the programming of computers by means of natural selection.* Cambridge, Mass.: MIT Press.

Krams, M., Rushworth, M., Deiber, M., Frackowiak, R., & Passingham, R. (1998). The preparation, execution and suppression of copied movements in the human brain. *Experimental Brain Research, 120,* 386–398.

Krauss, R., & Fussell, S. (1991). Perspective-taking in communication: Representations of others' knowledge in reference. *Social Cognition, 9,* 2–24.

Krizek, G. (2000). Is doppelgänger phenomenon a result of right-hemisphere brain injury? *Psychiatric Times, 17*(10). Available at (www.psychiatrictimes.com)

Kroodsma, D. (1996). Ecology of passerine song development. In D. Kroodsma & E. Miller (Eds.), *Ecology and evolution of acoustic communication in birds* (pp. 3–19). Ithaca, N.Y.: Cornell University Press.

Krubitzer, L., Clarey, J., Tweedale, R., Elston, G., & Calford, M. (1995). A redefinition of somatosensory areas in the lateral sulcus of Macaque monkeys. *Journal of Neuroscience, 15*, 3821–3839.

Kugiumutzakis, G. (1999). Genesis and development of early infant mimesis to facial and vocal models. In J. Nadel & G. Butterworth (Eds.), *Imitation in infancy* (pp. 36–59). New York: Cambridge University Press.

Kunde, W. (2001). Response-effect compatibility in manual choice-reaction tasks. *Journal of Experimental Psychology: Human Perception and Performance, 27*, 387–394.

Kunde, W., Koch, I., & Hoffmann, J. (2004). Anticipated action effects affect the selection, initiation, and execution of actions. *Quarterly Journal of Experimental Psychology. Section A: Human Experimental Psychology, 57*, 87–106.

Kuran, T. (1995). *Private truths, public lies: The social consequences of preference falsification.* Cambridge, Mass.: Harvard University Press.

Kurata, K., & Tanji, J. (1986). Premotor cortex neurons in macaques: Activity before distal and proximal forelimb movements. *Journal of Neuroscience, 6*, 403–411.

Lachlan, R., & Slater, P. (1999). The maintenance of vocal learning by gene-culture interaction: The cultural trap hypothesis. *Proceedings of the Royal Society of London Series B, 266*, 701–706.

Lacquaniti, F., Guigon, E., Bianchi, L., Ferraina, S., & Caminiti, R. (1995). Representing spatial information for limb movement: Role of area 5 in the monkey. *Cerebral Cortex, 5*, 391–409.

Ladefoged, P. (1982). *A course in phonetics.* San Diego: Harcourt Brace Jovanovitch.

LaFrance, M. (1979). Nonverbal synchrony and rapport: Analysis by the cross-lag panel technique. *Social Psychology Quarterly, 42*, 66–70.

LaFrance, M., & Broadbent, M. (1976). Group rapport: Posture sharing as a nonverbal indicator. *Group and Organization Studies, 1*, 328–333.

Lakin, J., & Chartrand, T. (2003). Using nonconscious mimicry to create affiliation and rapport. *Psychological Science, 14*, 334–339.

Lakoff, G., & Johnson, M. (1980). *Metaphors we live by.* Chicago: University of Chicago Press.

Lakoff, G., & Johnson, M. (1999). *Philosophy in the flesh: The embodied mind and its challenge to western thought.* New York: Basic Books.

Laland, K., & Bateson, P. (2001). The mechanisms of imitation. *Cybernetics and Systems: An International Journal, 32*, 195–224.

Laland, K., & Odling-Smee, J. (2000). The evolution of the meme. In R. Aunger (Ed.), *Darwinizing culture: The status of memetics as a science* (pp. 25–42). Oxford & New York: Oxford University Press.

Landes, D. (1998). *The wealth and poverty of nations: Why some are so rich and some so poor.* New York: Norton.

Lang, W., Petit, L., Höllinger, P., Pietrzyk, U., Tzourio, N., Mazoyer, B., & Berthoz, A. (1994). A positron emission tomography study of oculomotor imagery. *NeuroReport, 5,* 921–924.

Lashley, K. (1951). The problem of serial order in behavior. In L. Jeffress (Ed.), *Cerebral mechanisms in behavior: The Hixon symposium* (pp. 112–136). New York: Wiley.

LeDoux, J. (1996). *The emotional brain.* New York: Simon and Schuster.

Lefebvre, L. (2000). Feeding innovations and their cultural transmission in birds. In C. Heyes & L. Huber (Eds.), *The evolution of cognition* (pp. 311–332). Cambridge, Mass.: MIT Press.

Lefkowitz, M., Eron, L., Walder, L., & Huesmann, L. (1977). *Growing up to be violent: A longitudinal study of the development of aggression.* New York: Pergamon.

Legerstee, M. (1991). The role of person and object in eliciting early imitation. *Journal of Experimental Child Psychology, 51,* 423–433.

Leinonen, L., & Nyman, G. II. (1979). Functional properties of cells in anterolateral part of area 7 associative face area of awake monkeys. *Experimental Brain Research, 34,* 321–333.

Lemke, J. (2001). Becoming the village: Education across lives. In G. Wells and G. Claxton (Eds.), *Learning for life in the 21st century: Sociocultural perspectives on the future of education.* Oxford and New York: Blackwell.

Lepore, L., & Brown, R. (1997). Category and stereotype activation: Is prejudice inevitable? *Journal of Personality and Social Psychology, 72,* 275–287.

Levy, B. (1996). Improving memory in old age through implicit self-stereotyping. *Journal of Personality and Social Psychology, 71,* 1092–1107.

Lewis, M., & Sullivan, M. (1985). Imitation in the first six months of life. *Merrill-Palmer Quarterly, 31,* 315–333.

Lhermitte, F. (1983). "Utilization behaviour" and its relation to lesions of the frontal lobes. *Brain, 106,* 237–255.

Lhermitte, F. (1986). Human autonomy and the frontal lobes, Part II. *Annals of Neurology, 19,* 335–343.

Lhermitte, F., Pillon, B., & Serdaru, M. (1986). Human autonomy and the frontal lobes, Part I. *Annals of Neurology, 19,* 326–334.

Liberman, A., & Mattingly, I. (1985). The motor theory of speech perception revised. *Cognition, 21,* 1–36.

Liberman, A., & Whalen, D. (2000). On the relation of speech to language. *Trends in Cognitive Sciences, 4*, 187–196.

Lieberman, P. (1984). *The biology and evolution of language.* Cambridge, Mass.: Harvard University Press.

Lieberman, P. (1991). *Uniquely human: The evolution of speech, thought, and selfless behavior.* Cambridge, Mass.: Harvard University Press.

Lipps, T. (1903a). *Grundlegung der Ästhetik.* Bamburg and Leipzig: W. Engelmann.

Lipps, T. (1903b). *Einfüllung, innere Nachahmung und Organenempfindung* (Archiv für die Gesamte Psychologie, vol. I, part 2). Leipzig: W. Engelmann.

Lock, A. (1980). *The guided reinvention of language.* London: Academic Press.

Locke, J. (2001). First communication: The emergence of vocal relationships. *Social Development, 10*, 294–308.

LoLordo, V., & Jacobs, W. (1983). Constraints on aversive conditioning in the rat: Some theoretical accounts. In M. Zeiler & P. Harzem (Eds.), *Advances in analysis of behaviour* (Vol. 3, pp. 325–350). Chichester, UK: Wiley.

Lotze, M., Montoya, P., Erb, M., Hülsmann, E., Flor, H., Klose, U., Birbaumer, N., & Grodd, W. (1999). Activation of cortical and cerebellar motor areas during executed and imagined hand movements: An fMRI study. *Journal of Cognitive Neuroscience, 11*, 491–501.

Lotze, R. (1852). *Medicinische Psychologie oder Physiologie der Seele* [Medical psychology or the physiology of the soul]. Leipzig: Weidmann'sche Buchhandlung.

Lotze, R. (1858/1923). Mikrokosmos. Ideen zur Naturgeschichte und Geschichte der Menschheit. In R. Schmidt (Ed.), *Versuch einer Anthropologie* [Attempting an anthropology] (Vol. 2). Leipzig: Meiner, 1923, 6th ed.

Lovaas, O. (1987). Behavioral treatment and normal educational and intellectual functioning in young autistic children. *Journal of Consulting and Clinical Psychology, 55*, 3–9.

Lovaas, O., & Buch, G. (1997). Intensive behavioral intervention with young children with autism. In N. N. Singh (Ed.), *Prevention and treatment of severe behavior problems: Models and methods in developmental disabilities* (pp. 61–86). Pacific Grove, Calif.: Brooks/Cole.

Lukianowicz, N. (1958). Autoscopic phenomena. *Archives of Neurology and Psychiatry, 80*, 199–220.

Lukianowicz, N. (1960). Visual thinking and similar phenomena. *Journal of Mental Science, 106*, 979–101.

Lumsden, C., & Wilson, E. (1981). *Genes, mind, and culture: The coevolutionary process.* Cambridge, Mass., & London: Harvard University Press.

Luria, A. (1973). *The working brain.* Harmondsworth, UK: Penguin.

McCowan, B., & Reiss, D. (1997). Vocal learning in captive bottlenose dolphins: A comparison with human and nonhuman animals. In C. Snowdon & M. Hausberger (Eds.), *Social influences on vocal development* (pp. 178–207). Cambridge, UK: Cambridge University Press.

McDonough, L., & Mandler, J. (1998). Inductive generalization in 9- and 11-month-olds. *Developmental Science, 1,* 227–232.

McGrew, W. (1974). Tool use by wild chimpanzees feeding on driver ants. *Journal of Human Evolution, 3,* 501–508.

McGrew, W., Tutin, C., & Baldwin, P. (1979). Chimpanzees, tools, and termites: Cross-cultural comparison of Senegal, Tanzania, and Rio Muni. *Man, 14,* 185–214.

MacKay, D. (1987). *The organization of perception and action: A theory for language and other cognitive skills.* New York: Springer-Verlag.

McMahon, A. (1994). *Understanding language change.* Cambridge, UK: Cambridge University Press.

McNeilage, P., Rootes, T., & Chase, R. (1967). Speech production and perception in a patient with severe impairment of somesthetic perception and motor control. *Science, 219,* 1347–1349.

McNeill, W. (1963). *The rise of the West: A history of the human community.* Chicago: University of Chicago Press.

Macrae, C., & Johnston, L. (1998). Help, I need somebody: Automatic action and inaction. *Social Cognition, 16,* 400–417.

Maeda, F., Kleiner-Fisman, G., & Pascual-Leone, A. (2002). Motor facilitation while observing hand actions: Specificity of the effect and role of observer's orientation. *Journal of Neurophysiology, 87,* 1329–1335.

Mahler, M., Pine, F., & Bergman, A. (1975). *The psychological birth of the human infant.* New York: Basic Books.

Malach, R., Levy, I., & Hasson, U. (2002). The topography of high-order human object areas. *Trends in Cognitive Sciences, 6,* 176–184.

Mandler, J., & McDonough, L. (1995). Long-term recall of event sequences in infancy. *Journal of Experimental Child Psychology, 59,* 457–474.

Maran, T. (2001). Mimicry: Towards a semiotic understanding of nature. *Sign Systems Studies, 29*(1), 325–339.

Maratos, O. (1982). Trends in the development of imitation in early infancy. In T. Bever (Ed.), *Regressions in mental development: Basic phenomena and theories* (pp. 81–101). Hillsdale, N.J.: Erlbaum.

Marler, P. (1970). A comparative approach to vocal learning: Song development in white-crowned sparrows. *Journal of Comparative and Physiological Psychology, 71,* 1–25.

Marshall-Pescini, S., & Whiten, A. (unpublished). Social learning of a hierarchically organised artificial foraging task by infant and juvenile chimpanzees. Unpublished manuscript, University of St. Andrews, Fife, Scotland.

Martin, A., & Chao, L. (2001). Semantic memory and the brain: Structure and processes. *Current Opinion in Neurobiology, 11*, 194–201.

Matelli, M., Luppino, G., & Rizzolatti, G. (1985). Patterns of cytochrome oxidase activity in the frontal agranular cortex of the macaque monkey. *Behavioral Brain Research, 18*, 125–137.

Maynard Smith, J., & Price, G. (1973). The logic of animal conflicts. *Nature, 246*, 15–18.

Mazziotta, J., Toga, A., Evans, A., Fox, P., Lancaster, J., Zilles, K., Woods, R., Paus, T., Simpson, G., Pike, B., Holmes, C., Collins, L., Thompson, P., MacDonald, D., Iacoboni, M., Schormann, T., Amunts, K., Palomero-Gallagher, N., Geyer, S., Parsons, L., Narr, K., Kabani, N., Le Goualher, G., Boomsma, D., Cannon, T., Kawashima, R., & Mazoyer, B. (2001a). A probabilistic atlas and reference system for the human brain: International consortium for brain mapping (ICBM). *Philosophical Transactions of the Royal Society London Series B, 356*, 1293–1322.

Mazziotta, J., Toga, A., Evans, A., Fox, P., Lancaster, J., Zilles, K., Woods, R., Paus, T., Simpson, G., Pike, B., Holmes, C., Collins, L., Thompson, P., MacDonald, D., Iacoboni, M., Schormann, T., Amunts, K., Palomero-Gallagher, N., Geyer, S., Parsons, L., Narr, K., Kabani, N., Le Goualher, G., Feidler, J., Smith, K., Boomsma, D., Hulshoff Pol, H., Cannon, T., Kawashima, R., & Mazoyer, B. (2001b). A four-dimensional probabilistic atlas of the human brain. *Journal of the American Medical Informatics Association, 8*, 401–430.

Medina, L., & Reiner, A. (2000). Do birds possess homologues of mammalian primary visual, somatosensory and motor cortices? *Trends in Neurosciences, 23*, 1–12.

Mellars, P. (1996). *The Neanderthal legacy*. Princeton, N.J.: Princeton University Press.

Meltzoff, A. (1988a). Infant imitation after a one-week delay: Long-term memory for novel acts and multiple stimuli. *Developmental Psychology, 24*, 470–476.

Meltzoff, A. (1988b). Infant imitation and memory: Nine-month-olds in immediate and deferred tests. *Child Development, 59*, 217–225.

Meltzoff, A. (1990a). Towards a developmental cognitive science: The implications of cross-modal matching and imitation for the development of representation and memory in infancy. *Annals of the New York Academy of Science, 608*, 1–37.

Meltzoff, A. (1990b). Foundations for developing a concept of self: The role of imitation in relating self to other and the value of social mirroring, social modeling, and self practice in infancy. In D. Cicchetti & M. Beeghly (Eds.), *The self in transition: Infancy to childhood* (pp. 139–164). Chicago: University of Chicago Press.

Meltzoff, A. (1995). Understanding the intentions of others: Re-enactment of intended acts by 18-month-old children. *Developmental Psychology, 31*, 838–850.

Meltzoff, A. (1996). The human infant as imitative generalist: A 20-year progress report on infant imitation with implications for comparative psychology. In C. Heyes & B. Galef (Eds.), *Social learning in animals: The roots of culture* (pp. 347–370). New York: Academic Press.

Meltzoff, A. (1999a). Imitation. In R. Wilson & F. Keil (Eds.), *MIT encyclopedia of the cognitive sciences* (pp. 389–391). Cambridge, Mass.: MIT Press.

Meltzoff, A. (1999b). Origins of theory of mind, cognition, and communication. *Journal of Communication Disorders, 32*, 251–269.

Meltzoff, A. (2002a). Elements of a developmental theory of imitation. In A. Meltzoff & W. Prinz (Eds.), *The imitative mind: Development, evolution and brain bases* (pp. 19–41). Cambridge, UK: Cambridge University Press.

Meltzoff, A. (2002b). Imitation as a mechanism of social cognition: Origins of empathy, theory of mind, and the representation of action. In U. Goswami (Ed.), *Handbook of childhood cognitive development* (pp. 6–25). Oxford, UK: Blackwell.

Meltzoff, A., & Brooks, R. (2001). "Like me" as a building block for understanding other minds: Bodily acts, attention, and intention. In B. Malle, L. Moses, & D. Baldwin (Eds.), *Intentions and intentionality: Foundations of social cognition* (pp. 171–191). Cambridge, Mass.: MIT Press.

Meltzoff, A. N., & Brooks, R. (2004). Developmental changes in social cognition with an eye towards gaze following. Paper presented at the biennial meeting of the International Conference on Infant Studies, Chicago, IL, May, 2004.

Meltzoff, A., & Decety, J. (2003). What imitation tells us about social cognition: A rapprochment between developmental psychology and cognitive neuroscience. *Philosophical Transactions of the Royal Society of London Series B, 358*, 491–500.

Meltzoff, A., & Gopnik, A. (1993). The role of imitation in understanding persons and developing a theory of mind. In S. Baron-Cohen, H. Tager-Flusberg, & D. Cohen (Eds.), *Understanding other minds, perspectives from autism* (pp. 335–366). Oxford, UK: Oxford University Press.

Meltzoff, A., Gopnik, A., & Repacholi, B. (1999). Toddlers' understanding of intentions, desires and emotions: Explorations of the dark ages. In P. Zelazo, J. Astington, & D. Olson (Eds.), *Developing theories of intention: Social understanding and self-control* (pp. 17–41). Mahwah, N.J.: Erlbaum.

Meltzoff, A., & Moore, M. (1977). Imitation of facial and manual gestures by human neonates. *Science, 198*, 75–78.

Meltzoff, A., & Moore, M. (1979). Interpreting "imitative" responses in early infancy. *Science, 205*, 217–219.

Meltzoff, A., & Moore, M. (1983a). Newborn infants imitate adult facial gestures. *Child Development, 54*, 702–709.

Meltzoff, A., & Moore, M. (1983b). The origins of imitation in infancy: Paradigm, phenomena, and theories. In L. Lipsitt & C. Rovée-Collier (Eds.), *Advances in infancy research* (Vol. 2, pp. 265–301). Norwood, N.J.: Ablex.

Meltzoff, A., & Moore, M. (1989). Imitation in newborn infants: Exploring the range of gestures imitated and the underlying mechanisms. *Developmental Psychology, 25*, 954–962.

Meltzoff, A., & Moore, M. (1992). Early imitation within a functional framework: The importance of person identity, movement, and development. *Infant Behavior and Development, 15*, 479–505.

Meltzoff, A., & Moore, M. (1994). Imitation, memory, and the representation of persons. *Infant Behavior and Development, 17*, 83–99.

Meltzoff, A., & Moore, M. (1995). Infants' understanding of people and things: From body imitation to folk psychology. In J. Bermúdez, A. Marcel, & N. Eilan (Eds.), *The Body and the self* (pp. 43–69). Cambridge, Mass.: MIT Press.

Meltzoff, A., & Moore, M. (1997). Explaining facial imitation: A theoretical model. *Early Development and Parenting, 6*, 179–192.

Meltzoff, A., & Moore, M. (1998). Infant intersubjectivity: Broadening the dialogue to include imitation, identity and intention. In S. Braten (Ed.), *Intersubjective communication and emotion in early ontogeny* (pp. 47–62). Cambridge, UK: Cambridge University Press.

Meltzoff, A., & Moore, M. (1999a). Persons and representations: Why infant imitation is important for theories of human development. In J. Nadel & G. Butterworth (Eds.), *Imitation in infancy. Cambridge studies in cognitive and perceptual development* (pp. 9–35). Cambridge, UK: Cambridge University Press.

Meltzoff, A., & Moore, M. (1999b). Resolving the debate about early imitation. In A. Slater & D. Muir (Eds.), *The Blackwell reader in development psychology* (pp. 151–155). Malden, Mass.: Blackwell.

Meltzoff, A., & Moore, M. (2000). Resolving the debate about early imitation. In A. Slater & D. Muir (Eds.), *Infant development: The essential readings* (pp. 167–181). Malden, Mass.: Blackwell.

Merleau-Ponty, M. (1945/1962). *Phenomenology of perception.* (Translated from the French by C. Smith.) London: Routledge.

Metzinger, T. (1993). *Subjekt und Selbstmodell* [Subject and self-model]. Paderborn, Germany: Schoeningh.

Metzinger, T. (2000). The subjectivity of subjective experience: A representationalist analysis of the first-person perspective. In T. Metzinger (Ed.), *Neural correlates of con-*

sciousness. Empirical and conceptual questions (pp. 285–306). Cambridge, Mass.: MIT Press.

Milavsky, J., Kessler, R., Stipp, H., & Rubens, W. (1982). *Television and aggression: A panel study*. New York: Academic Press. Also published as Television and aggression: Results of a panel study In D. Pearl, L. Bouthilet, & J. Lazar (Eds.), *Television and behavior: Ten years of scientific progress and implications for the 80's* (Vol. 2, pp. 138–157). Technical reviews. Washington, D.C.: Government Printing Office.

Milgram, S. (1963). Behavioral study of obedience. *Journal of Abnormal and Social Psychology, 67,* 371–378.

Mill, J. (1843/1974). *System of logic.* Toronto: University of Toronto Press.

Miller, D. (1977). Two-voiced phenomenon in birds: Further evidence. *Auk, 94,* 567–572.

Miller, D., & McFarland, C. (1991). Why social comparison goes awry: The case of pluralistic ignorance. In J. Suls & T. Ashby (Eds.), *Social comparison: Contemporary theory and research.* Hillsdale, N.J.: Erlbaum.

Miller, D., & Philo, G. (1999). The effective media. In G. Philo (Ed.), *Message received* (pp. 21–32). London: Longman.

Miller, E. (2000). The prefrontal cortex and cognitive control. *Nature Review Neuroscience, 1,* 59–65.

Millikan, R. (1993). *White queen psychology and other essays for Alice.* Cambridge Mass.: MIT Press.

Millikan, R. (2000). *On clear and confused ideas.* Cambridge, UK: Cambridge University Press.

Mills, C. (1963). Situated actions and vocabularies of motive. In I. Horowitz, *Power, politics and people* (439–452). New York: Oxford University Press.

Milner, A. (1997). Neglect, extinction, and the cortical streams of visual processing. In P. Thier & H. Karnath (Eds.), *Parietal lobe contributions to orientation in 3D space* (pp. 3–22). Heidelberg: Spinger-Verlag.

Milner, A. (1998). Streams and consciousness: Visual awareness and the brain. *Trends in Cognitive Sciences, 2,* 25–30.

Mitchell, C., Heyes, C., Dawson, G., & Gardner, M. (1999). Limitations of a bidirectional control procedure for the investigation of imitation in rats: Odour cues on the manipulandum. *Quarterly Journal of Experimental Psychology, 52B,* 193–202.

Mitchell, J., Heatherton, T., & Macrae, C. (2002). Distinct neural systems subserve person and object knowledge. *Proceedings of the National Academy of Sciences U.S.A., 99,* 15238–15243.

Mitchell, R. (1987). A comparative developmental approach to understanding imitation. *Perspectives in Ethology, 7,* 183–215.

Mitchell, R. (1997). A comparison of the self-awareness and kinesthetic-visual matching theories of self-recognition: Autistic children and others. *New York Academy of Science, 818,* 39–62.

Mithen, S. (1999). Imitation and cultural change: A view from the Stone Age, with specific reference to the manufacture of handaxes. In H. O. Box & K. R. Gibson (Eds.), *Mammalian social learning* (pp. 389–399). Cambridge, UK: Cambridge University Press.

Modena, I., & Visalberghi, E. (1998). Imitazione e uso di strumenti in bambini nel secondo anno di vita: Comparazione con altre specie di primati non-umani [Imitation and tool use in two-year-old children: Comparison with various species of non-human primates]. *Età Evolutiva, 59,* 11–20.

Moise-Titus, J. (1999). The role of negative emotions in the media violence-aggression relation. Unpublished PhD dissertation, University of Michigan, Ann Arbor.

Molnar-Szakacs, I., Iacoboni, M., Koski, L., Maeda, F., Dubeau, M., Aziz-Zadeh, L., & Mazziotta, J. (2002). Action observation in the pars opercularis: Evidence from 58 subjects studied with FMRI. *Journal of Cognitive Neuroscience,* Suppl. S, F118.

Montague, P., Berns, G., Cohen, J., McClure, S., Pagnoni, G., Dhamala, M., Wiest, M., Karpov, I., King, R., Apple, N., & Fisher, R. (2002). Hyperscanning: Simultaneous fMRI during linked social interactions. *Neuroimage, 16,* 1159.

Moore, B. (1992). Avian movement imitation and a new form of mimicry: Tracing the evolution of a complex form of learning. *Behaviour, 122,* 231–263.

Morgan, C. (1896). *Habit and instinct.* London: Edward Arnold.

Morgan, M. (1989). Cultivation analysis. In E. Barnouw (Ed.), *International encyclopedia of communication* (Vol. 3, pp. 430–433). New York: Oxford University Press.

Mountcastle, V., Lynch, J., Georgopoulos, A., Sakata, H., & Acuna, C. (1975). Posterior parietal association cortex of the monkey: Command functions for operations within extrapersonal space. *Journal of Neurophysiology, 38,* 871–908.

Mowrer, O. (1960). *Learning theory and the symbolic processes.* New York: Wiley.

Murata, A., Fadiga, L., Fogassi, L., Gallese, V., Raos, V., & Rizzolatti, G. (1997). Object representation in the ventral premotor cortex (area F5) of the monkey. *Journal of Neurophysiology, 78,* 2226–2230.

Murray, J. (1984). Results of an informal poll of knowledgeable persons concerning the impact of television violence. *Newsletter of the American Psychological Association Division of Child, Youth and Family Services, 7*(1), 2.

Müsseler, J., & Hommel, B. (1997). Blindness to response-compatible stimuli. *Journal of Experimental Psychology: Human Perception and Performance, 23,* 861–872.

Myowa-Yamakoshi, M. (2001). Evolutionary foundation and development of imitation. In T. Matsuzawa (Ed.), *Primate origins of human cognition of behaviour* (pp. 349–367). Tokyo: Springer-Verlag.

Myowa-Yamakoshi, M., & Matsuzawa, T. (2000). Imitation of intentional manipulatory actions in chimpanzees (*Pan troglodytes*). *Journal of Comparative Psychology, 114*, 381–391.

Nadel, J. (2002). Imitation and imitation recognition: Functional use in preverbal infants and nonverbal children with autism. In A. Meltzoff & W. Prinz (Eds.), *The imitative mind: Development, evolution, and brain bases* (pp. 42–62). Cambridge, UK: Cambridge University Press.

Nadel, J., & Baudonnière, P. (1982). The social function of reciprocal imitation in 2-year-old peers. *International Journal of Behavioral Development, 5*, 95–109.

Nadel, J., & Butterworth, G. (1999). *Imitation in infancy*. Cambridge, UK: Cambridge University Press.

Nadel, J., Guérini, C., Pezé, A., & Rivet, C. (1999). The evolving nature of imitation as a format for communication. In J. Nadel & G. Butterworth (Eds.), *Imitation in infancy* (pp. 209–234). Cambridge, UK: Cambridge University Press.

Nagell, K., Olguin, R., & Tomasello, M. (1993). Processes of social learning in the tool use of chimpanzees (*Pan troglodytes*) and human children (*Homo sapiens*). *Journal of Comparative Psychology, 107*, 174–186.

Nehaniv, C., & Dautenhahn, K. (2002a). The correspondence problem. In K. Dautenhahn & C. Nehaniv (Eds.), *Imitation in animals and artifacts* (pp. 42–61). Boston, Mass.: MIT Press.

Nehaniv, C., & Dautenhahn, K. (2002b). The correspondence problem in social learning: What does it mean for behaviors to "match" anyway? Poster presented at perspectives on imitation: From cognitive neuroscience to social science, Royaumont Abbey, France, May 24–26, 2002. Available at ⟨http://www.warwick.ac.uk/fac/sci/Psychology/imitation⟩

Neisser, U. (1976). *Cognition and reality: Principles and implications of cognitive psychology*. San Francisco: W. H. Freeman.

Nelson, K. (1996). *Language in cognitive development: Emergence of the mediated mind*. Cambridge, UK: Cambridge University Press.

Nerlich, B. (1989). The evolution of the concept of "linguistic evolution" in the 19th and 20th century. *Lingua, 77*, 101–112.

Neumann, R., & Strack, F. (2000). "Mood contagion": The automatic transfer of mood between persons. *Journal of Personality and Social Psychology, 79*, 211–223.

Newell, A., & Simon, H. (1972). *Human problem solving*. Englewood Cliffs, N.J.: Prentice Hall.

Newell, K., & Molenaar, P. (Eds). (1998). *Applications of nonlinear dynamics to developmental process modeling*. Mahwah, N.J.: Erlbaum.

Nguyen, N. H., Klein, E. D., & Zentall, T. R. (in press). Imitation of two-action sequences by pigeons. *Psychonomic Bulletin & Review*.

Nichols, S. (2001). Mindreading and the cognitive architecture underlying altruistic motivation. *Mind and Language, 16*, 425–455.

Nietzsche, F. (1881/1977). Daybreak. In R. J. Hollingdale (Ed. and trans.), *A Nietzsche reader* (p. 156). Harmondsworth, UK: Penguin.

Nishida, T., Kano, T., Goodall, J., McGrew, W., & Nakamura, M. (1999). Ethogram and ethnography of Mahale chimpanzees. *Anthropological Science, 107*, 141–188.

Nishitani, N., & Hari, R. (2000). Temporal dynamics of cortical representation for action. *Proceedings of the National Academy of Sciences, U.S.A., 97*, 913–918.

Nissen, M., & Bullemer, P. (1987). Attentional requirements of learning: Evidence from performance measures. *Cognitive Psychology, 19*, 1–32.

Noë, A. (in press). *Action in perception.* Cambridge, Mass.: MIT Press.

Nöth, W. (1990). *Handbook of semiotics.* Bloomington: Indiana University Press.

Ohta, M. (1987). Cognitive disorders of infantile autism: A study employing the WISC, spatial relationship conceptualization, and gesture imitations. *Journal of Autism and Developmental Disorders, 17*, 45–62.

Olausson, H., Lamarre, Y., Backlund, H., Morin, C., Wallin, B., Starck, G., Ekholm, S., Strigo, I., Worsley, K., Vallbo, A., & Bushnell, M. (2002). Unmyelinated tactile afferents signal touch and project to insular cortex. *Nature Neuroscience, 5*, 900–904.

Orliaguet, J., Kandel, S., & Boë, L. (1997). Visual perception of cursive handwriting: Influence of spatial and kinematic information on the anticipation of forthcoming letters. *Perception, 26*, 905–912.

Oztop, E., & Arbib, M. (2002). Schema design and implementation of the grasp-related mirror neuron system. *Biological Cybernetics, 87*, 116–140.

Paik, H., & Comstock, G. (1994). The effects of television violence on antisocial behavior: A meta-analysis. *Communication Research, 21*, 516–546.

Palameta, B., & Lefebvre, L. (1985). The social transmission of a food-finding technique in pigeons: What is learned? *Animal Behaviour, 33*, 892–896.

Papousek, M., & Papousek, H. (1989). Forms and functions of vocal matching in interactions between mothers and their precanonical infants. *First Language, 9*, 137–157.

Parker, S. (1996). Apprenticeship in tool-mediated extractive foraging: The origins of imitation, teaching and self-awareness in great apes. In A. Russon, K. Bard, & S. Parker (Eds.), *Reaching into thought* (pp. 348–370). Cambridge, UK: Cambridge University Press.

Parsons, L. (1994). Temporal and kinematic properties of motor behavior reflected in mentally simulated action. *Journal of Experimental Psychology: Human Perception and Performance, 20*, 709–730.

Parsons, L., & Fox, P. (1998). The neural basis of implicit movement used in recognizing hand shape. *Cognitive Neuropsychology, 15*, 583–615.

Parton, D. (1976). Learning to imitate in infancy. *Child Development, 47*, 14–31.

Pascual-Leone, A. (2001). The brain that plays music and is changed by it. *Annals of the New York Academy of Sciences, 930*, 315–329.

Passingham, R. (1998). The specializations of the human neocortex. In A. Milner (Ed.), *Comparative Neuropsychology* (pp. 271–298). Oxford: Oxford University Press.

Pasteur, G. (1982). A classificatory review of mimicry systems. *Annual Review of Ecological Systems, 13*, 169–199.

Patrick, C., Bradley, M., & Lang, P. (1993). Emotion in the criminal psychopath: Startle reflex modulation. *Journal of Abnormal Psychology, 102*, 82–92.

Patterson, D., & Pepperberg, I. (1994). A comparative study of human and parrot phonation: Acoustic and articulatory correlates of vowels. *Journal of the Acoustical Society of America, 96*, 634–648.

Patterson, D., & Pepperberg, I. (1998). Acoustic and articulatory correlates of stop consonants in a parrot and a human subject. *Journal of the Acoustical Society of America, 106*, 491–505.

Paulin, M. (1993). The role of the cerebellum in motor control and perception. *Brain, Behavior Evolution, 41*, 39–50.

Pepperberg, I. (1981). Functional vocalizations by an African Grey parrot (*Psittacus erithacus*). *Zeitschrift für Tierpsychologie, 55*, 139–160.

Pepperberg, I. (1983). Cognition in the African Grey parrot: Preliminary evidence for auditory/vocal comprehension of the class concept. *Animal Learning & Behavior, 11*, 179–185.

Pepperberg, I. (1985). Social modeling theory: A possible framework for understanding avian vocal learning. *Auk, 102*, 854–864.

Pepperberg, I. (1986a). Acquisition of anomalous communicatory systems: Implications for studies on interspecies communication. In R. Schusterman, J. Thomas, & F. Wood (Eds.), *Dolphin behavior and cognition: Comparative and ecological aspects* (pp. 289–302). Hillsdale, N.J.: Erlbaum.

Pepperberg, I. (1986b). Sensitive periods, social interaction, and song acquisition: The dialectics of dialects? *Behavioral and Brain Sciences, 9*, 756–757.

Pepperberg, I. (1987a). Acquisition of the same/different concept by an African Grey parrot (*Psittacus erithacus*): Learning with respect to categories of color, shape, and material. *Animal Learning & Behavior, 15*, 423–432.

Pepperberg, I. (1987b). Evidence for conceptual quantitative abilities in the African Grey parrot: Labeling of cardinal sets. *Ethology, 75*, 37–61.

Pepperberg, I. (1987c). Interspecies communication: A tool for assessing conceptual abilities in the African Grey parrot (*Psittacus erithacus*). In G. Greenberg & E. Tobach (Eds.), *Cognition, language, and consciousness: Integrative levels* (pp. 31–56). Hillsdale, N.J.: Erlbaum.

Pepperberg, I. (1988a). An interactive modeling technique for acquisition of communication skills: Separation of "labeling" and "requesting" in a psittacine subject. *Applied Psycholinguistics, 9*, 59–76.

Pepperberg, I. (1988b). The importance of social interaction and observation in the acquisition of communicative competence: Possible parallels between avian and human learning. In T. Zentall & B. Galef (Eds.), *Social learning: Psychological and biological perspectives* (pp. 279–299). Hillsdale, N.J.: Erlbaum.

Pepperberg, I. (1990a). Cognition in an African Grey parrot (*Psittacus erithacus*): Further evidence for comprehension of categories and labels. *Journal of Comparative Psychology, 104*, 41–52.

Pepperberg, I. (1990b). Some cognitive capacities of an African Grey parrot (*Psittacus erithacus*). In P. Slater, J. Rosenblatt, & C. Beer (Eds.), *Advances in the study of behavior* (Vol. 19, pp. 357–409). New York: Academic Press.

Pepperberg, I. (1990c). Referential mapping: A technique for attaching functional significance to the innovative utterances of an African Grey parrot. *Applied Psycholinguistics, 11*, 23–44.

Pepperberg, I. (1991a). A communicative approach to animal cognition: A study of conceptual abilities of an African Grey parrot. In C. Ristau (Ed.), *Cognitive ethology: The minds of other animals* (pp. 153–186). Hillsdale, N.J.: Erlbaum.

Pepperberg, I. (1991b). Learning to communicate: The effects of social interaction. In P. Klopfer & P. Bateson (Eds.), *Perspectives in ethology* (pp. 119–162). New York: Plenum.

Pepperberg, I. (1992). Proficient performance of a conjunctive, recursive task by an African Grey parrot (*Psittacus erithacus*). *Journal of Comparative Psychology, 106*, 295–305.

Pepperberg, I. (1993). A review of the effects of social interaction on vocal learning in African Grey parrots (*Psittacus erithacus*). *Netherlands Journal of Zoology, 43*, 104–124.

Pepperberg, I. (1994a). Evidence for numerical competence in an African Grey parrot (*Psittacus erithacus*). *Journal of Comparative Psychology, 108*, 36–44.

Pepperberg, I. (1994b). Vocal learning in Grey parrots (*Psittacus erithacus*): Effects of social interaction, reference, and context. *Auk, 111*, 300–313.

Pepperberg, I. (1997). Social influences on the acquisition of human-based codes in parrots and nonhuman primates. In C. T. Snowdon & M. Hausberger (Eds.), *Social influences on vocal development* (pp. 157–177). Cambridge, UK: Cambridge University Press.

Pepperberg, I. (1999). *The Alex studies: Cognitive and communicative studies on Grey parrots.* Cambridge, Mass.: Harvard University Press.

Pepperberg, I. (2001). Lessons from cognitive ethology: Animal models for ethological computing. Lund, Sweden: *Proceedings of the First Conference on Epigenetic Robotics.*

Pepperberg, I. (2002). Allospecific referential speech acquisition in Grey parrots (*Psittacus erithacus*): Evidence for multiple levels of avian vocal imitation. In K. Dautenhahn & C. Nehaniv (Eds.), *Imitation in animals and artifacts* (pp. 109–131). Cambridge, Mass.: MIT Press.

Pepperberg, I., Brese, K., & Harris, B. (1991). Solitary sound play during acquisition of English vocalizations by an African Grey parrot (*Psittacus erithacus*): Possible parallels with children's monologue speech. *Applied Psycholinguistics, 12,* 151–178.

Pepperberg, I., & Brezinsky, M. (1991). Acquisition of a relative class concept by an African Grey parrot (*Psittacus erithacus*): Discriminations based on relative size. *Journal of Comparative Psychology, 105,* 286–294.

Pepperberg, I., Gardiner, L., & Luttrell, L. (1999). Limited contextual vocal learning in the Grey parrot (*Psittacus erithacus*): The effect of interactive co-viewers on videotaped instruction. *Journal of Comparative Psychology, 113,* 158–172.

Pepperberg, I., & McLaughlin, M. (1996). Effect of avian-human joint attention on allospecific vocal learning by Grey parrots (*Psittacus erithacus*). *Journal of Comparative Psychology, 110,* 286–297.

Pepperberg, I., Naughton, J., & Banta, P. (1998). Allospecific vocal learning by Grey parrots (*Psittacus erithacus*): A failure of videotaped instruction under certain conditions. *Behavioural Processes, 42,* 139–158.

Pepperberg, I., Sandefer, R., Noel, D., & Ellsworth, C. (2000). Vocal learning in the Grey parrot (*Psittacus erithacus*): Effect of species identity and number of trainers. *Journal of Comparative Psychology, 114,* 371–380.

Pepperberg, I., & Sherman, D. (2000). Proposed use of two-part interactive modeling as a means to increase functional skills in children with a variety of disabilities. *Teaching and Learning in Medicine, 12,* 213–220.

Pepperberg, I., & Sherman, D. (2002). Use of two-trainer interactive modeling as a potential means to engender social behavior in children with various disabilities. *International Journal of Comparative Psychology, 15,* 138–153.

Pepperberg, I., & Shive, H. (2001). Simultaneous development of vocal and physical object combinations by a Grey parrot (*Psittacus erithacus*): Bottle caps, lids, and labels. *Journal of Comparative Psychology, 115,* 376–384.

Pepperberg, I., & Wilcox, S. (2000). Evidence for a form of mutual exclusivity during label acquisition by Grey parrots (*Psittacus erithacus*)? *Journal of Comparative Psychology*, *114*, 219–231.

Pepperberg, I., & Wilkes, S. (2004). Lack of referential vocal learning from LCD video by Grey parrots (*Psittacus erithacus*). *Interaction Studies*, *5*, 75–97.

Perani, D., Fazio, F., Borghese, N., Tettamanti, M., Ferrari, S., Decety, J., & Gilardi, M. C. (2001). Different brain correlates for watching real and virtual hand actions. *NeuroImage*, *14*, 749–758.

Perner, J. (1991a). *Understanding the representational mind*. Cambridge, Mass.: MIT Press.

Perner, J. (1991b). On representing that: The asymmetry between belief and desire in children's theory of mind. In D. Frye & C. Moore (Eds.), *Children's theories of mind* (pp. 139–155). Hillsdale, N.J.: Erlbaum.

Perrett, D., & Emery, N. (1994). Understanding the intentions of others from visual signals: Neurophysiological evidence. *Current Psychological Cognition*, *13*, 683–694.

Perrett, D., Harries, M., Bevan, R., Thomas, S., Benson, P., Mistlin, A., Chitty, A., Hietanen, J., & Ortega, J. (1989). Frameworks of analysis for the neural representation of animate objects and actions. *Journal of Experimental Biology*, *146*, 87–113.

Perrett, D., Harries, M., Mistlin, A., Hietanen, J., Benson, P., Bevan, R., Thomas, S., Oram, M., Ortega, J., & Brierly, K. (1990a). Social signals analyzed at the single cell level: Someone is looking at me, something touched me, something moved! *International Journal of Comparative Psychology*, *4*, 25–55.

Perrett, D., Hietanen, J., Oram, M., & Benson, P. (1992). Organization and functions of cells responsive to faces in the temporal cortex. In V. Bruce, A. Cowey, & A. Ellis (Eds.), *Processing the facial image* (pp. 23–30). New York: Oxford University Press.

Perrett, D., Mistlin, A., Harries, M., & Chitty, A. (1990b). Understanding the visual appearance and consequence of hand actions. In M. Goodale (Ed.), *Vision and action: The control of grasping* (pp. 163–342). Norwood, N.J.: Ablex.

Peterson, G., & Barney, H. (1952). Control methods used in a study of the identification of vowels. *Journal of the Acoustical Society of America*, *24*, 175–184.

Peterson, G., & Trapold, M. (1982). Expectancy mediation of concurrent conditional discriminations. *American Journal of Psychology*, *95*, 571–580.

Petrides, M., & Pandya, D. (1994). Comparative architectonic analysis of the human and the macaque frontal cortex. In F. Boller & J. Grafman (Eds.), *Handbook of neuropsychology* (Vol. IX, pp. 17–58). New York: Elsevier.

Petrinovich, L. (1985). Factors influencing song development in white-crowned sparrows (*Zonotrichia leucophrys*). *Journal of Comparative Psychology*, *99*, 15–29.

Philo, G. (1999a). *Message received*. Harlow, UK: Longman.

Philo, G., ed. (1999b). Children and film/video/TV violence. In G. Philo (Ed.), *Message received*. London: Longman.

Philo, G., & McLaughlin, G. (1995). The British media and the Gulf War. In G. Philo (Ed.), *Glasgow media group reader* (Vol. 2, pp. 146–156). London: Routledge & Kegan Paul.

Piaget, J. (1951/1962). *Play, dreams and imitation in childhood*. London: Routledge & Kegan Paul, New York: Norton. (Translated from the French.)

Piaget, J. (1952/1963). *The origins of intelligence in children*. New York: Norton. (Translated from the French.)

Piaget, J. (1954). *The construction of reality in the child*. New York: Basic Books.

Picard, N., & Strick, P. (1996). Motor areas of the medial wall: A review of their location and functional activation. *Cerebral Cortex, 6*, 342–353.

Pickering, M., & Garrod, S. (in press). Toward a mechanistic psychology of dialogue. *Behavioral and Brain Sciences*.

Pitcher, T. (1979). Sensory information and the organization of behavior in a shoaling cyprinid fish, *Animal Behavior, 27*, 126–149.

Plotkin, H. (2000). Culture and psychological mechanisms. In R. Aunger (Ed.), *Darwinizing culture: The status of memetics as a science* (pp. 69–83). Oxford & New York: Oxford University Press.

Plotkin, H. (2002). *The imagined world made real*. New York: Penguin.

Plott, C. (1996). Rational individual behaviour in markets and social choice processes: The discovered preference hypothesis. In K. Arrow, E. Colombatto, M. Perlman, & C. Schmidt (Eds.), *The rational foundations of economic behaviour*. Basingstoke, UK: Macmillan.

Plumer, T., & Striedter, G. (1997). Auditory and vocalization related activity in the vocal control system of budgerigars. *Society for Neuroscience Abstracts, 100*, 10.

Plumer, T., & Striedter, G. (2000). Auditory responses in the vocal motor system of budgerigars. *Journal of Neurobiology, 42*, 79–94.

Pochon, J., Levy, R., Poline, J., Crozier, S., Lehericy, S., Pillon, B., Deweer, B., Le Bihan, D., & Dubois, B. (2001). The role of dorsolateral prefrontal cortex in the preparation of forthcoming actions: An fMRI study. *Cerebral Cortex, 11*, 260–266.

Porro, C., Francescato, M., Cettolo, V., Diamond, M., Baraldi, P., Zuiani, C., Bazzocchi, M., & di Prampero, P. (1996). Primary motor cortex activation during motor performance and motor imagery. *Journal of Neuroscience, 16*, 7688–7698.

Post, R. (1986). The social foundations of defamation law: Reputation and the Constitution. *California Law Review, 74*, 691.

Poulin-Dubois, D., & Forbes, J. (2002). Toddlers' attention to "intentions-in-action" in learning novel action words. *Developmental Psychology, 38*, 104–114.

Povinelli, D. (2000). *Folk physics for apes: The chimpanzee's theory of how the world works*. Oxford: Oxford University Press.

Povinelli, D., & Bering, J. (2002). The mentality of apes revisited. *Current Directions in Psychological Science, 11*, 115–119.

Povinelli, D., Bering, J., & Giambrone, S. (2000). Toward a science of other minds: Escaping the argument by analogy. *Cognitive Science, 24*, 509–541.

Povinelli, D., & Eddy, T. (1996). Factors influencing young chimpanzees' (*Pan troglodytes*) recognition of attention. *Journal of Comparative Psychology, 4*, 336–345.

Povinelli, D., & Giambrone, S. (1999). Inferring other minds: Failure of the argument by analogy. *Philosophical Topics, 27*, 167–201.

Povinelli, D., & Prince, C. (1998). When self met other. In M. Ferrari & R. Sternberg (Eds.), *Self-awareness* (pp. 37–107). New York: Guilford.

Preston, S., & de Waal, F. (2002). Empathy: Its ultimate and proximate bases. *Behavioral and Brain Sciences, 25*, 1–71.

Prigman, G. (1995). Freud and the history of empathy. *International Journal of Psycho-Analysis, 76*, 237–252.

Prinz, J. (2004). *Gut Reactions: An emotional theory of morals*. New York: Oxford University Press.

Prinz, W. (1984). Modes of linkage between perception and action. In W. Prinz & A. F. Sanders (Eds.), *Cognition and motor processes* (pp. 185–193). Berlin & Heidelberg: Springer-Verlag.

Prinz, W. (1987). Ideomotor action. In H. Heuer & A. Sanders (Eds.), *Perspectives on perception and action* (pp. 47–76). Hillsdale, N.J.: Erlbaum.

Prinz, W. (1990). A common-coding approach to perception and action. In O. Neumann & W. Prinz (Eds.), *Relationships between perception and action: Current approaches* (pp. 167–201). Berlin & New York: Springer-Verlag.

Prinz, W. (1997a). Perception and action planning. *European Journal of Cognitive Psychology, 9*, 129–154.

Prinz, W. (1997b). Why Donders has led us astray. In B. Hommel & W. Prinz (Eds.), *Theoretical issues in stimulus-response compatibility* (pp. 247–267). Amsterdam: North-Holland.

Prinz, W. (2002). Experimental approaches to imitation. In A. Meltzoff & W. Prinz (Eds.), *The imitative mind: Development, evolution, and brain bases* (pp. 143–162). Cambridge, UK: Cambridge University Press.

Prinz, W., & Meltzoff, A. (2002). An introduction to the imitative mind and brain. In A. Meltzoff & W. Prinz (Eds.), *The imitative mind: Development, evolution, and brain bases* (pp. 1–15). Cambridge, UK: Cambridge University Press.

Proust, J. (in press). Thinking of oneself as the same. *Consciousness and Cognition, 12.*

Quine, W. (1960). *Word and object.* Cambridge Mass.: MIT Press.

Radke-Yarrow, M., & Zahn-Waxler, C. (1984). Roots, motives, and patterns in children's prosocial behavior. In E. Staub, D. Bar-Tal, J. Karylowski, & J. Reykowski (Eds.), *Development and maintenance of prosocial behavior* (pp. 81–99). New York: Plenum.

Rakoczy, H., Tomasello, M., & Striano, T. (2004). Young children know that trying is not pretending—a test of the "acting-as-if" construal of children's early concept of "pretense." *Developmental Psychology, 40,* 388–399.

Ramachandran, V., & Rogers-Ramachandran, D. (1996). Denial of disabilities in anosognosia. *Nature, 382,* 501.

Reed, G. (1972). *The psychology of anomalous experience.* London: Hutchinson.

Reeve, T., & Proctor, R. (1990). The salient-features coding principle for spatial- and symbolic-compatibility effects. In R. Proctor & T. Reeve (Eds.), *Stimulus-response compatibility: An integrated perspective* (pp. 163–182). Amsterdam: North-Holland.

Reik, T. (1948). *Listening with the third ear: The inner experience of the psychoanalyst.* New York: Grove.

Reissland, N. (1988). Neonatal imitation in the first hour of life: Observations in rural Nepal. *Developmental Psychology, 24,* 464–469.

Remez, R., Rubin, P., Nygaard, L., & Howell, W. (1987). Perceptual normalization of vowels produced by sinusoidal voices. *Journal of Experimental Psychology: Human Perception and Performance, 13,* 40–61.

Rescorla, R., & Furrow, D. (1977). Stimulus similarity as a determinant of Pavlovian conditioning. *Journal of Experimental Psychology: Animal Behavior Processes, 3,* 203–215.

Ribeiro, S., Cecchi, G., Magnasco, M., & Mello, C. (1998). Toward a song code: Evidence for a syllabic representation in the canary brain. *Neuron, 21,* 359–371.

Rice, G., & Gainer, P. (1962). "Altruism" in the albino rat. *Journal of Comparative and Physiological Psychology, 55,* 123–125.

Rice, M. (1991). Children with specific language impairment: Toward a model of teachability. In N. Krasnegor, D. Rumbaugh, R. Schiefelbusch, & M. Studdert-Kennedy (Eds.), *Biological and behavioral determinants of language development* (pp. 447–480). Hillsdale, N.J.: Erlbaum.

Rice, M., Huston, A., Truglio, R., & Wright, J. (1990). Words from "Sesame Street": Learning vocabulary while viewing. *Developmental Psychology, 26,* 421–428.

Riggs, B. (2002). *Hitler's Jewish soldiers: The untold story of Nazi racial laws and men of Jewish descent in the German military.* Kansas City: University Press of Kansas.

Rilling, J., Gutman, D., Zeh, T., Pagnoni, G., Berns, G., & Kilts, C. (2002). A neural basis for social cooperation. *Neuron, 35,* 395–405.

Rizzolatti, G., & Arbib, M. (1998). Language within our grasp. *Trends in Neuroscience, 21,* 188–194.

Rizzolatti, G., & Arbib, M. (1999). From grasping to speech: Imitation might provide a missing link: Reply. *Trends in Neuroscience, 22,* 152.

Rizzolatti, G., Camarda, R., Fogassi, M., Gentilucci, M., Luppino, G., & Matelli, M. (1988). Functional organization of inferior area 6 in the macaque monkey: II. Area F5 and the control of distal movements. *Experimental Brain Research, 71,* 491–507.

Rizzolatti, G., & Fadiga, L. (1998). Grasping objects and grasping action meanings: The dual role of monkey rostroventral premotor cortex (area F5). In *Sensory guidance of movement* (pp. 81–103) (Novartis Foundation symposium 218). Chichester, UK: Wiley.

Rizzolatti, G., Fadiga, L., Fogassi, L., & Gallese, V. (2002). From mirror neurons to imitation: Facts and speculations. In A. Meltzoff & W. Prinz (Eds.), *The imitative mind: Development, evolution, and brain bases* (pp. 247–266). Cambridge, UK: Cambridge University Press.

Rizzolatti, G., Fadiga, L., Fogassi, L., & Gallese, V. (1996a). Premotor cortex and the recognition of motor actions. *Cognitive Brain Research, 3,* 131–141.

Rizzolatti, G., Fadiga, L., Matelli, M., Bettinardi, V., Paulesu, E., Perani, D., & Fazio, F. (1996b). Localization of grasp representations in humans by PET: 1. Observation versus execution. *Experimental Brain Research, 111,* 246–252.

Rizzolatti, G., Fogassi, L., & Gallese, V. (2000). Cortical mechanisms subserving object grasping and action recognition: A new view on the cortical motor functions. In M. Gazzaniga (Ed.), *The cognitive neurosciences* (2nd ed., pp. 539–552). Cambridge, Mass.: MIT Press.

Rizzolatti, G., Fogassi, L., & Gallese, V. (2001). Neurophysiological mechanisms underlying the understanding and imitation of action. *Nature Reviews Neuroscience, 2,* 661–670.

Rizzolatti, G., & Luppino, G. (2001). The cortical motor system. *Neuron, 31,* 889–901.

Rizzolatti, G., Luppino, G., & Matelli, M. (1998). The organization of the cortical motor system: New concepts. *EEG and Clinical Neurophysiology, 106,* 283–296.

Rizzolatti, G., Scandolara, C., Gentilucci, M., & Camarda, R. (1981). Response properties and behavioral modulation of "mouth" neurons of the postarcuate cortex (area 6) in macaque monkeys. *Brain Research, 255,* 421–424.

Roberts, M., Onnis, L., & Chater, N. (in press). Acquisition and evolution of quasi-regular languages: Two puzzles for the price of one. In M. Tallerman (Ed.), *Evolutionary prerequisites for language.* Oxford, UK: Oxford University Press.

Robinson, C., & Burton, H. (1980a). Somatotopographic organization in the second somatosensory area of M. fascicularis. *Journal of Comparative Neurology, 192,* 43–67.

Robinson, C., & Burton, H. (1980b). Organization of somatosensory receptive fields in cortical areas 7b, retroinsula, postauditory, and granular insula of M. fascicularis. *Journal of Comparative Neurology, 192,* 69–92.

Rochat, P. (1999). *Early social cognition: Understanding others in the first months of life.* Mahwah, N.J.: Erlbaum.

Rochat, P. (2002). *The infant's world.* Cambridge, Mass.: Harvard University Press.

Rochat, P., & Striano, T. (2000). Perceived self in infancy. *Infant Behavior and Development, 23,* 513–530.

Rogers, C. (1959). A theory of therapy, personality and interpersonal relationships as developed in the client-centered framework. In S. Koch (Ed.), *Psychology: A study of a science.* Vol. 3: *Formulations of the person in the social context* (pp. 184–256). New York: McGraw-Hill.

Rogers, S. (1999). An examination of the imitation deficit in autism. In J. Nadel & G. Butterworth (Eds.), *Imitation in infancy* (pp. 254–283). Cambridge, UK: Cambridge University Press.

Rogers, S., & Pennington, B. (1991). A theoretical approach to the deficits in infantile autism. *Development and Psychopathology, 3,* 137–162.

Rolls, E. (1992). Neurophysiological mechanisms underlying face processing within and beyond the temporal cortical visual areas. In V. Bruce, A. Cowey, & A. Ellis (Eds.), *Processing the facial image* (pp. 11–21). New York: Oxford University Press.

Romanes, G. (1884). *Mental evolution in animals.* New York: Appleton.

Roper, T. (1983). Learning as a biological phenomenon. In T. R. Halliday & P. J. B. Slater (Eds.), *Animal behaviour.* Vol. 3: *Genes, development and learning* (pp. 178–212). Oxford: Blackwell.

Rosenbaum, D., Meulenbroek, R., & Vaughan, J. (1996). Three approaches to the degrees of freedom problem in reaching. In A. Wing & P. Haggard (Eds.), *Hand and brain: The neurophysiology and psychology of hand movements* (pp. 169–185). San Diego: Academic Press.

Rosenthal, R. (1986). Media violence, antisocial behavior, and the social consequences of small effects. *Journal of Social Issues, 42,* 141–154.

Rosenthal, R., Rosnow, R., & Rubin, D. (2000). *Contrasts and effect sizes in behavioral research: A correlational approach.* New York: Cambridge University Press.

Roth, M., Decety, J., Raybaudi, M., Massarelli, R., Delon, C., Segebarth, C., Morand, S., Decorps, M., & Jeannerod, M. (1996). Possible involvement of primary motor cortex in mentally simulated movement: An fMRI study. *NeuroReport, 7,* 1280–1284.

Rothbart, M., Ahadi, S., & Hershey, K. (1994). Temperament and social behavior in childhood. *Merrill-Palmer Quarterly, 40,* 21–39.

Ruby, P., & Decety, J. (2001). Effect of subjective perspective taking during simulation of action: A PET investigation of agency. *Nature Neuroscience, 4,* 546–550.

Ruby, P., & Decety, J. (2002). Assessing the knowledge of others: A PET study of conceptual perspective-taking. Abstract B39, *Cognitive Neuroscience Society,* San Francisco.

Ruby, P., & Decety, J. (2003). What you believe versus what you think they believe: A neuroimaging study of conceptual perspective taking. *European Journal of Neuroscience, 17,* 2475–2480.

Rumiati, R., & Tessari, A. (2002). Imitation of novel and well-known actions. *Experimental Brain Research, 142,* 425–433.

Russon, A. (1996). Imitation in everyday use: Matching and rehearsal in the spontaneous imitation of rehabilitant orangutans (*Pongo pygmaeus*). In A. Russon, K. Bard, & S. Parker (Eds.), *Reaching into thought: The minds of the great apes* (pp. 152–176). Cambridge, UK: Cambridge University Press.

Russon, A. (1999). Orangutans' imitation of tool use: A cognitive interpretation. In S. Parker, H. Miles, & R. Mitchell (Eds.), *The mentalities of gorillas and orangutans* (pp. 117–146). Cambridge, UK: Cambridge University Press.

Russon, A., & Galdikas, B. (1993). Imitation in free-ranging rehabilitant orangutans. *Journal of Comparative Psychology, 107,* 147–161.

Russon, A., & Galdikas, B. (1995). Constraints on great ape imitation: Model and action selectivity in rehabilitant orangutan (*Pongo pymaeus*) imitation. *Journal of Comparative Psychology, 109,* 5–17.

Sacks, O. (1995). *An anthropologist on Mars.* New York: Vintage Books.

Sagi, A., & Hoffman, M. (1976). Empathic distress in the newborn. *Developmental Psychology, 12,* 175–176.

St. Peters, M., Huston, A., & Wright, J. (1989). Television and families: Parental co-viewing and young children's language development, social behavior, and television processing. Paper presented at the Society for Research in Child Development, Kansas City, Kan., April 1989.

Sakata, H., Takaoka, Y., Kawarasaki, A., & Shibutani, H. (1973). Somatosensory properties of neurons in the superior parietal cortex (area 5) of the rhesus monkey. *Brain Research, 64,* 85–102.

Scanlan, J. (1988). Analysis of avian "speech": Patterns and production. PhD dissertation, University College, London.

Schalling, D., & Rosen, A. (1968). Porteus maze differences between psychopathic and non-psychopathic criminals. *British Journal of Social and Clinical Psychology, 7,* 224–228.

Schank, R., & Abelson, R. (1995). Knowledge and memory: The real story. In R. Wyer (Ed.), *Knowledge and memory: The real story* (pp. 1–86). Hillsdale, N.J.: Erlbaum.

Scharrer, E., Weidman, L., & Bissell, K. (2003). Pointing the finger of blame: News media coverage of popular-culture culpability. *Journalism & Communication Monographs, 5*, 49–98.

Schick, K., & Toth, N. (1993). *Making silent stones speak.* New York: Simon & Schuster.

Schubotz, R., & von Cramon, D. (2001). Functional organization of the lateral premotor cortex: fMRI reveals different regions activated by anticipation of object properties, location, and speed. *Cognitive Brain Research, 11*, 97–112.

Schwebel, D., Rosen, C., & Singer, J. (1999). Preschoolers' pretend play and theory of mind: The role of jointly constructed pretense. *British Journal of Developmental Psychology, 17*, 333–348.

Sebanz, N., Knoblich, G., & Prinz, W. (2003). Representing others' actions: Just like one's own? *Cognition, 88*, B11–B21.

Sellars, W. (1963). *Science, perception and reality.* New York: Humanities Press.

Sellars, W. (1975). The structure of knowledge. Lecture II: Minds. In H. Castañeda (Ed.), *Action, knowledge, and reality: Critical studies in honor of Wilfrid Sellars* (pp. 318–331). Indianapolis: Bobbs-Merrill. Reprinted 1991 in D. Rosenthal (Ed.), *The nature of mind* (pp. 372–379). Oxford: Oxford University Press.

Seltzer, B., & Pandya, D. (1994). Parietal, temporal, and occipital projections to cortex of the superior temporal sulcus in the rhesus monkey: A retrograde tracer study. *Journal of Comparative Neurology, 343*, 445–463.

Seyfarth, R., & Cheney, D. (1986). Vocal development in vervet monkeys. *Animal Behavior, 34*, 1640–1658.

Shallice, T. (2001). "Theory of mind" and the prefrontal cortex. *Brain, 124*, 247–248.

Shepard, R. (1984). Ecological constraints on internal representation: Resonant kinematics of perceiving, imagining, thinking, and dreaming. *Psychological Review, 91*, 417–447.

Shettleworth, S. (1998). *Cognition, evolution and behaviour.* New York & Oxford: Oxford University Press.

Shiffrar, M., & Freyd, J. (1990). Apparent motion of the human body. *Psychological Science, 1*, 257–264.

Shiffrar, M., & Pinto, J. (2002). The visual analysis of bodily motion. In W. Prinz & B. Hommel (Eds.), *Attention and performance*, Vol. XIX: *Common mechanisms in perception and action* (pp. 381–399). New York: Oxford University Press.

Shima, K., & Tanji, J. (2000). Neuronal activity in the supplementary and presupplementary motor areas for temporal organization of multiple movements. *Journal of Neurophysiology, 84*, 2148–2160.

Shoemaker, P., & Reese, S. (1996). *Mediating the message: Theories of influence on mass media content.* London: Longman.

Shofield, W. (1976a). Do children find movements which cross the body midline difficult? *Quarterly Journal of Experimental Psychology, 28,* 571–582.

Shofield, W. (1976b). Hand movements which cross the body. Findings relating age differences to handedness. *Perceptual and Motor Skills, 42,* 643–646.

Siegal, M., & Varley, R. (2002). Neural systems involved in theory of mind. *Nature Reviews Neuroscience, 3,* 463–471.

Silverstone, J. (1989). Numerical abilities in the African Grey parrot: Sequential numerical tags. Unpublished senior honors thesis, Northwestern University, Evanston, Ill.

Smith, A. (1759/1976). *The theory of moral sentiments,* D. Raphael & A. Macfie (Eds.). Oxford, UK: Clarendon Press. Other edition: (1966), New York: Augustus M. Kelley.

Smith, I., & Bryson, S. (1994). Imitation and action in autism: A critical review. *Psychological Bulletin, 116,* 259–273.

Smith, W. (1991). Animal communication and the study of cognition. In C. Ristau (Ed.), *Cognitive ethology: The minds of other animals* (pp. 209–230). Hillsdale, N.J.: Erlbaum.

Sober, E., & Wilson, D. (1998). *Unto others.* Cambridge, Mass.: Harvard University Press.

Spence, A. (1974). *Market signaling: Informational transfer in hiring and related screening processes.* Cambridge, Mass.: Harvard University Press.

Spence, K. (1937). Experimental studies of learning and higher mental processes in infra-human primates. *Psychological Bulletin, 34,* 806–850.

Spence, S., Brooks, D., Hirsch, S., Liddle, P., Meehan, J., & Grasby, P. (1997). A PET study of voluntary movement in schizophrenic patients experiencing passivity phenomena (delusions of alien control). *Brain, 120,* 1997–2011.

Sperber, D. (1996). *Explaining culture: A naturalistic approach.* Oxford: Blackwell.

Sperber, D. (2000). An objection to the memetic approach to culture. In R. Aunger (Ed.), *Darwinizing culture: The status of memetics as a science* (pp. 163–175). Oxford & New York: Oxford University Press.

Spiegelman, A. (1991). *Maus. A survivor's tale.* New York: Pantheon.

Srull, T., & Wyer, R. (1979). The role of category accessibility in the interpretation of information about persons: Some determinants and implications. *Journal of Personality and Social Psychology, 37,* 1660–1672.

Srull, T., & Wyer, R. (1980). Category accessibility and social perception: Some implications for the study of person memory and interpersonal judgments. *Journal of Personality and Social Psychology, 38,* 841–856.

Stein, E. (1912/1964). *On the problem of empathy*. The Hague, Netherlands: Martinus Nijhoff. (English translation.)

Steinfeld, J. (1972). Statement in hearings before the Subcommittee on Communications of the Committee on Commerce (U.S. Senate, Serial #92-52, pp. 25–27). Washington, D.C.: United States Government.

Stephan, K., Fink, G., Passingham, R., Silbersweig, D., Ceballos-Baumann, O., Frith, C., & Frackowiak, R. (1995). Functional anatomy of the mental representation of upper extremity movements in health subjects. *Journal of Neurophysiology*, *73*, 373–386.

Stern, D. (1985). *The interpersonal world of the infant*. London: Karnac Books.

Stern, D. (1993). The role of feelings for an interpersonal self. In U. Neisser (Ed.), *The perceived self: Ecological and interpersonal sources of self-knowledge* (pp. 205–215). New York: Cambridge University Press.

Stevens, D., Charman, T., & Blair, R. (2001). Recognition of emotion in facial expressions and vocal tones in children with psychopathic tendencies. *Journal of Genetic Psychology*, *162*, 201–211.

Stevens, J., Fonlupt, P., Shiffrar, M., & Decety, J. (2000). New aspects of motion perception: Selective neural encoding of apparent human movements. *NeuroReport*, *11*, 109–115.

Stevens, K., & Halle, M. (1967). Remarks on analysis by synthesis and distinctive features. In W. Wathen-Dunn (Ed.), *Models for the perception of speech and visual form* (pp. 88–102). Cambridge, Mass.: MIT Press.

Stevick, R. (1963). The biological model and historical linguistics. *Language*, *39*, 159–169.

Stock, A., & Hoffmann, J. (2002). Intentional fixation of behavioural learning, or how R-O learning blocks S-R learning. *European Journal of Cognitive Psychology*, *14*, 127–153.

Stoinski, T., Wrate, J., Ure, N., & Whiten, A. (2001). Imitative learning by captive western lowland gorillas (*Gorilla gorilla gorilla*) in a simulated food-processing task. *Journal of Comparative Psychology*, *115*, 272–281.

Stokes, E., & Byrne, R. (2001). Cognitive capacities for behavioral flexibility in wild chimpanzees (*Pan troglodytes*): The effect of snare injury on complex manual food processing. *Animal Cognition*, *4*, 11–28.

Stokes, E., Quiatt, D., & Reynolds, V. (1999). Snare injuries to chimpanzees (*Pan troglodytes*) at 10 study sites in East and West Africa. *American Journal of Primatology*, *49*, 104–105.

Strafella, A., & Paus, T. (2000). Modulation of cortical excitability during action observation: A transcranial magnetic stimulation study. *NeuroReport*, *11*, 2289–2292.

Strawson, P. (1959). *Individuals*. London: Methuen.

Strawson, P. (1966). *The bounds of sense*. London: Methuen.

Street, J. (2001). *Mass media, politics and democracy*. Basingstoke, UK: Palgrave.

Striedter, G. (1994). The vocal control pathways in budgerigars differ from those in songbirds. *Journal of Comparative Neurology, 343*, 35–56.

Struhsaker, T. (1967). Behavior of vervet monkeys. *University of California Publications of Zoology, 82*, 1–74.

Stürmer, B., Aschersleben, G., & Prinz, W. (2000). Correspondence effects with manual gestures and postures: A study of imitation. *Journal of Experimental Psychology: Human Perception and Performance, 26*, 1746–1759.

Suddendorf, T., & Whiten, A. (2001). Mental evolution and development: Evidence for secondary representation in children, great apes and other animals. *Psychological Bulletin, 127*, 629–650.

Sugden, R. (1986). *The economics of rights, co-operation and welfare*. Oxford, UK: Blackwell.

Sugden, R. (2001). The evolutionary turn in game theory. *Journal of Economic Methodology, 8*, 113–130.

Sugden, R. (2002). Beyond sympathy and empathy: Adam Smith's theory of fellow-feeling. *Economics and Philosophy, 18*, 63–87.

Sugiyama, Y., Koman, J., & Bhoye Sow, M. (1988). Ant-catching wands of wild chimpanzees at Bossou, Guinea. *Folia Primatologica, 51*, 56–60.

Sutker, P., Moan, C., & Swanson, W. (1972). Porteus maze test qualitative performance in pure sociopaths, prison normals, and antisocial psychotics. *Journal of Clinical Psychology, 28*, 349–353.

Tager-Flusberg, H. (2000). Language and understanding minds: Connections in autism. In S. Baron-Cohen, H. Tager-Flusberg, & D. Cohen (Eds.), *Understanding other minds: Perspectives from developmental cognitive neuroscience* (pp. 124–149). Oxford, UK: Oxford University Press.

Tanji, J. (1994). The supplementary motor area in the cerebral cortex. *Neuroscience Research, 19*, 251–268.

Tanji, J. (1996). New concepts of the supplementary motor area. *Current Opinion in Neurobiology, 6*, 782–787.

Tanji, J., Shima, K., & Mushiake, H. (1996). Multiple cortical motor areas and temporal sequencing of movements. *Cognitive Brain Research, 5*, 117–122.

Tannen, D. (1989). *Talking voices: Repetition, dialogue, and imagery in conversational discourse*. Cambridge: Cambridge University Press.

Taylor, M. (1996). A theory of mind perspective on social cognitive development. In R. Gelman & T. Au (Eds.), *Handbook of perception and cognition* (Vol. 13, pp. 283–329). New York: Academic Press.

Taylor, M., & Carlson, S. (1997). The relation between individual differences in fantasy and theory of mind. *Child Development, 68,* 436–455.

Taylor, P., & Jonker, L. (1978). Evolutionarily stable strategies and game dynamics. *Mathematical Biosciences, 40,* 145–156.

Tec, N. (1984). Sex distinctions and passing as Christians during the Holocaust. *East European Quarterly, 18*(1), 113–123.

Terkel, J. (1994). Social transmission of pine cone feeding behaviour in the black rat. In B. Galef, M. Mainardi, & P. Valsecchi (Eds.), *Behavioural aspects of feeding* (pp. 229–256). London: Harwood Academic.

Tessari, A., & Rumiati, R. (2002). Strategies influencing action imitation. Poster presented at perspectives on imitation: From cognitive neuroscience to social science, Royaumont Abbey, France, May 24–26, 2002. Available at (http://www.warwick.ac.uk/fac/sci/Psychology/imitation)

Tessari, A., & Rumiati, R. (submitted). How endogenous and exogenous factors play tricks on human imitation. *Journal of Experimental Psychology: General.*

Thelen, E. (2001). Dynamic mechanisms of change in early perceptual-motor development. In J. McClelland & R. Siegler (Eds.), *Mechanisms of cognitive development: Behavioral and neural perspectives. Carnegie Mellon Symposia on Cognition* (pp. 161–184). Mahwah, N.J.: Erlbaum.

Thelen, E., Corbetta, D., Kamm, K., Spencer, J., Schneider, K., & Zernicke, R. (1993). The transition to reaching: Mapping intention and intrinsic dynamics. *Child Development, 64,* 1058–1098.

Thompson, D., & Russell, J. (in preparation). The observational learning of means actions in the second year: Imitation versus emulation.

Thorndike, E. (1898). Animal intelligence: An experimental study of the associative process in animals. *Psychological Review and Monograph, 2,* 551–553.

Thornton, W., & Voigt, L. (1984). Television and delinquency. *Youth and Society, 15*(4), 445–468.

Thorpe, W. (1956). *Learning and instinct in animals.* London: Methuen.

Thorpe, W. (1963). *Learning and instinct in animals* (2nd ed.). London: Methuen, and Cambridge, Mass.: Harvard University Press.

Tinbergen, N. (1953). *The herring gull's world.* London: Collins.

Titchener, E. (1909). *Lectures on the experimental psychology of thought processes.* New York: Macmillan.

Todt, D. (1975). Social learning of vocal patterns and modes of their applications in Grey parrots. *Zeitschrift für Tierpsychologie, 39,* 178–188.

Tomasello, M. (1990). Cultural transmission in the tool use and communicatory signalling of chimpanzees? In S. T. Parker & K. R. Gibson (Eds.), *"Language" and intelligence in monkeys and apes* (pp. 247–311). Cambridge, UK: Cambridge University Press.

Tomasello, M. (1994). The question of chimpanzee culture. In R. Wrangham, W. McGrew, F. de Waal, & P. Heltne (Eds.), *Chimpanzee cultures* (pp. 301–317). Cambridge, Mass.: Harvard University Press.

Tomasello, M. (1996). Do apes ape? In C. Heyes & B. Galef (Eds.), *Social learning in animals: The roots of culture* (pp. 319–346). San Diego: Academic Press.

Tomasello, M. (1998). Emulation learning and cultural learning. *Behavioral and Brain Sciences, 21,* 703–704.

Tomasello, M. (1999). *The cultural origins of human cognition.* Cambridge, Mass.: Harvard University Press.

Tomasello, M. (2001). Perceiving intentions and learning words in the second year of life. In M. Bowerman & S. Levinson (Eds.), *Language acquisition and conceptual development* (pp. 132–158). Cambridge, UK: Cambridge University Press.

Tomasello, M., & Barton, M. (1994). Learning words in non-ostensive contexts. *Developmental Psychology, 30,* 639–650.

Tomasello, M., & Call, J. (1997). *Primate cognition.* Oxford: Oxford University Press.

Tomasello, M., Davis-Dasilva, M., Camak, L., & Bard, K. (1987). Observational learning of tool-use by young chimpanzees. *Human Evolution, 2,* 175–183.

Tomasello, M., Kruger, A., & Ratner, H. (1993a). Cultural learning. *Behavioral and Brain Sciences, 16,* 495–552.

Tomasello, M., Savage-Rumbaugh, S., & Kruger, A. (1993b). Imitative learning of actions on objects by children, chimpanzees and enculturated chimpanzees. *Child Development, 64,* 1688–1705.

Tomasello, M., Strosberg, R., & Akhtar, N. (1996). Eighteen-month-old children learn words in non-ostensive contexts. *Journal of Child Language, 22,* 1–20.

Tooby, J., & Cosmides, L. (1989). Evolutionary psychology and the generation of culture, Part I: Theoretical considerations. *Ethology and Sociobiology, 10,* 29–49.

Tooby, J., & Cosmides, L. (1992). The psychological foundations of culture. In J. Barkow, L. Cosmides, & J. Tooby (Eds.), *The adapted mind: Evolutionary psychology and the generation of culture.* New York and Oxford: Oxford University Press.

Trevarthen, C. (1979). Communication and cooperation in early infancy. In M. Bullowa (Ed.), *Before speech: The beginning of human communication* (pp. 321–347). London: Cambridge University Press.

Trevarthen, C. (1999). Intersubjectivity. *MIT encyclopaedia of cognitive science* (pp. 415–417). Cambridge, Mass.: MIT Press.

Trevarthen, C., & Aitken, K. (2001). Intersubjectivity: Research, theory and clinical applications. *Journal of Child Psychology and Psychiatry, 42*, 3–48.

Turiel, E. (1983). *The development of social knowledge: Morality and convention.* Cambridge, UK: Cambridge University Press.

Turkewitz, G., Gardner, J., & Lewkowicz, D. (1984). Sensory/perceptual functioning during early infancy: The implications for a quantitative basis for responding. In G. Greenberg & E. Tobach (Eds.), *Behavioral evolution and integrative levels* (pp. 167–195). Hillsdale, N.J.: Erlbaum.

U.S. Department of Health & Human Services, (2001). *Youth violence: A report of the Surgeon General.* Rockville, Md.: U.S. Department of Health and Human Services. Centers for Disease Control and Prevention, National Center for Injury Prevention and Control; Substance Abuse and Mental Health Services Administration, Center for Mental Health Services; and National Institutes of Health, National Institute of Mental Health.

Uller, C., & Nichols, S. (2001). Goal attribution in chimpanzees. *Cognition, 76*, B27–34.

Ullstadius, E. (1998). Neonatal imitation in a mother-infant setting. *Early Development and Parenting, 7*, 1–8.

Umiltà, M., Kohler, E., Gallese, V., Fogassi, L., Fadiga, L., Keysers, C., & Rizzolatti, G. (2001). I know what you are doing: A neurophysiological study. *Neuron, 31*, 155–165.

van Baaren, R., Holland, R., Steenaert, B., & van Knippenberg, A. (2003). Mimicry for money: Behavioral consequences of imitation. *Journal of Experimental Social Psychology, 39*, 393–398.

van Baaren, R., de Bouter, C., & van Knippenberg, A. (submitted). *Self-focus and the chameleon effect.*

Van Schaik, C., & Knott, C. (2001). Geographic variation in tool use on *Neesia* fruit in orangutans. *American Journal of Physical Anthropology, 114*, 331–342.

Vanayan, M., Robertson, H., & Biederman, G. (1985). Observational learning in pigeons: The effects of model proficiency on observer performance. *Journal of General Psychology, 112*, 349–357.

Varela, F., Thompson, E., & Rosch, E. (1991). *The embodied mind: Cognitive science and human experience.* Cambridge, Mass.: MIT Press.

Vidal, J. (1997). *McLibel. Burger culture on trial.* London: Macmillan.

Vinter, A. (1986). The role of movement in eliciting early imitations. *Child Development, 57*, 66–71.

Visalberghi, E., & Fragaszy, D. (1990). Do monkeys ape? In S. Parker & K. Gibson (Eds.), *"Language" and intelligence in monkeys and apes* (pp. 247–273). Cambridge, UK: Cambridge University Press.

Visalberghi, E., & Fragaszy, D. (1996). Pedagogy and imitation in monkeys: Yes, no, or maybe? In D. Olson & N. Torrance (Eds.), *The handbook of education and human development* (pp. 277–301). Malden, Mass.: Blackwell.

Visalberghi, E., & Fragaszy, D. (2002). "Do monkeys ape?" Ten years after. In K. Dautenhahn & C. Nehaniv (Eds.), *Imitation in animals and artifacts* (pp. 471–499). Cambridge, Mass.: MIT Press.

Visalberghi, E., & Limongelli, L. (1994). A tool-using experiment on the comprehension of cause-effect relationships in capuchin monkeys (*Cebus apella*). *Journal of Comparative Psychology, 108*, 15–22.

Visalberghi, E., & Limongelli, L. (1996). Acting and understanding: Tool use revisited through the minds of capuchin monkeys. In A. E. Russon, K. A. Bard, & S. T. Parker (Eds.), *Reaching into thought. The minds of the great apes* (pp. 57–79). New York: Cambridge University Press.

Vischer, R. (1873). Über das optische Formgefühl: Ein beiträg zur Ästethik. In *Drei Schriften zum Ästetischen Formproblem* (pp. 1–44). Halle, Germany: Niemeyer.

Viviani, P. (2002). Motor competence in the perception of dynamic events: A tutorial. In W. Prinz & B. Hommel (Eds.), *Common mechanisms in perception and action* (pp. 406–442). Attention and Performance Vol. XIX. New York: Oxford University Press.

Voelkl, B., & Huber, L. (2000). True imitation in marmosets. *Animal Behavior, 60*, 195–202.

von Bonin, G., & Bailey, P. (1947). *The neocortex of Macaca mulatta*. Urbana: University of Illinois Press.

von Hoftsten, C., & Siddiqui, A. (1993). Using the mother's actions as a reference for object exploration in 6- and 12-month-old infants. *British Journal of Developmental Psychology, 11*, 61–74.

von Uexküll, J. (1957). A stroll through the worlds of animals and men. In C. Schiller (Ed. and transl.), *Instinctive behavior: The development of a modern concept* (pp. 5–80). (Introduction by K. Lashley.) New York: International Universities Press.

Vygotsky, L. (1978). *Mind and society*. Cambridge, Mass.: Harvard University Press.

Wallraff, G. (1985). *Ganz unten*. Cologne, Germany: Kiepenheuer & Witsch.

Walsh, V., & Cowey, A. (2000). Transcranial magnetic stimulation and cognitive neuroscience. *Nature Reviews Neuroscience, 1*, 73–79.

Want, S., & Harris, P. (2001). Learning from other people's mistakes: Causal understanding in learning to use a tool. *Child Development, 72*, 431–443.

Want, S., & Harris, P. (2002). How do children ape? Applying concepts from the study of non-human primates to the developmental study of "imitation" in children. *Developmental Science, 5,* 1–13.

Wapner, S., & Cirillo, L. (1968). Imitation of a model's hand movement: Age changes in transposition of left-right relations. *Child Development, 39,* 887–894.

Warren, D., Patterson, D., & Pepperberg, I. (1996). Mechanisms of American English vowel production in a Grey parrot (*Psittacus erithacus*). *Auk, 113,* 41–58.

Weeks, D., Hall, A., & Anderson, L. (1996). A comparison of imitation strategies in observational learning of action patterns. *Journal of Motor Behavior, 28,* 348–358.

Weibull, J. (1995). *Evolutionary game theory.* Cambridge, Mass.: MIT Press.

Weir, A., Chappell, J., & Kacelnik, A. (2002). Shaping of hooks in New Caledonian crows. *Science, 297,* 981.

Weitzman, L. (1999). Living on the Aryan side in Poland. Gender, passing and the nature of resistance. In D. Ofer & L. Weitzman (Eds.), *Women in the Holocaust* (pp. 187–222). New Haven & London: Yale University Press.

Wellman, H. (1990). *The child's theory of mind.* Cambridge, Mass.: MIT Press.

Wellman, H. (2002). Understanding the psychological world: Developing a theory of mind. In U. Goswami (Ed.), *Handbook of childhood cognitive development* (pp. 167–187). Oxford, UK: Blackwell.

Whiten, A. (1998). Imitation of the sequential structure of actions by chimpanzees (*Pan troglodytes*). *Journal of Comparative Psychology, 112,* 270–281.

Whiten, A. (2000). Primate culture and social learning. *Cognitive Science, 24,* 477–508.

Whiten, A. (2001). The roots of culture. *British Academy Review,* July–December, 57–61.

Whiten, A. (2002a). The imitator's representation of the imitated. In A. Meltzoff and W. Prinz (Eds.), *The imitative mind* (pp. 98–121). Cambridge, UK: Cambridge University Press.

Whiten, A. (2002b). Imitation of sequential and hierarchical structure in action: Experimental studies with children and chimpanzees. In K. Dautenhahn & C. Nehaniv (Eds.), *Imitation in animals and artifacts* (pp. 191–209). Cambridge, Mass.: MIT Press.

Whiten, A. (in press). The scope of "culture" in humans, chimpanzees and other animals: Nine contrasts. In F. Joulian (Ed.), *How the chimpanzee stole culture: Culture and meanings among apes, ancient hominids and modern humans.* Paris: Balland.

Whiten, A., & Brown, J. (1998). Imitation and the reading of other minds: Perspectives from the study of autism, normal children and non-human primates. In S. Braten (Ed.), *Intersubjective communication and emotion in early ontogeny* (pp. 260–280). New York: Cambridge University Press.

Whiten, A., & Custance, D. (1996). Studies of imitation in chimpanzees and children. In C. Heyes & B. Galef (Eds.), *Social learning in animals: The roots of culture* (pp. 291–318). San Diego: Academic Press.

Whiten, A., Custance, D., Gomez, J., Teixidor, P., & Bard, K. (1996). Imitative learning of artificial fruit processing in children (*Homo sapiens*) and chimpanzees (*Pan troglodytes*). *Journal of Comparative Psychology, 110*, 3–14.

Whiten, A., Goodall, J., McGrew, W., Nishida, T., Reynolds, V., Sugiyama, Y., Tutin, C., Wrangham, R., & Boesch, C. (1999). Cultures in chimpanzees. *Nature, 399*, 682–685.

Whiten, A., Goodall, J., McGrew, W., Nishida, T., Reynolds, V., Sugiyama, Y., Tutin, C., Wrangham, R., & Boesch, C. (2001). Charting cultural variation in chimpanzees. *Behaviour, 138*, 1489–1525.

Whiten, A., & Ham, R. (1992). On the nature and evolution of imitation in the animal kingdom: Reappraisal of a century of research. In P. Slater, J. Rosenblatt, C. Beer, & M. Milinski (Eds.), *Advances in the study of behavior* (pp. 239–283). San Diego: Academic Press.

Whiten, A., Horner, V., Litchfield, C., & Marshall-Pescini, S. (2004). How do apes ape? *Learning and Behaviour, 32*, 36–52.

Whiten, A., Horner, V., & Marshall-Pescini, S. (2003). Cultural panthropology. *Evolutionary Anthropology, 12*, 92–105.

Wicker, B., Keysers, C., Plailly, J., Royet, J.-P., Gallese, V., & Rizzolatti, G. (2003). Both of us disgusted in my insula: The common neural basis of seeing and feeling disgust. *Neuron, 40*, 655–664.

Wilkins, J. (1998). What's in a meme? Reflections from the perspective of the history and philosophy of evolutionary biology. *Journal of Memetics—Evolutionary Models of Information Transmission, 2*. Available at (http://jom-emit.cfpm.org/1998/vol2/wilkins_js.html)

Williams, B. (1981). *Obscenity and film censorship: An abridgement of the Williams Report*. Cambridge, UK: Cambridge University Press.

Williams, G. (1966). *Adaptation and natural selection*. Princeton, N.J.: Princeton University Press.

Williams, H. (1989). Multiple representations and auditory-motor interactions in the avian song system. *Annals of the New York Academy of Sciences, 563*, 148–164.

Williams, J., Whiten, A., Suddendorf, T., & Perrett, D. (2001). Imitation, mirror neurons and autism. *Neuroscience and Biobehavioral Reviews, 25*, 287–295.

Wilson, J., & Wilson, S. (1998). *Mass media/mass culture: An introduction*. London: McGraw-Hill.

Wimsatt, W. (1987). False models as means to truer theories. In M. Nitecki and A. Hoffman (Eds.), *Neutral models in biology* (pp. 23–55). London: Oxford University Press.

Winter, L., & Uleman, J. (1984). When are social judgments made? Evidence for the spontaneousness of trait inferences. *Journal of Personality and Social Psychology, 47,* 237–252.

Wise, S., di Pellegrino, G., & Boussaoud, D. (1998). The premotor cortex and non-standard sensorimotor mapping. *Canadian Journal of Physiology and Pharmacology, 74,* 469–482.

Wohlschläger, A., Gattis, M., & Bekkering, H. (2003). Action generation and action perception in imitation: An instantiation of the ideomotor principle. *Philosophical Transactions of the Royal Society of London Series B, 358,* 501–516.

Wolf, D. (1982). Understanding others: A longitudinal case study of the concept of independent agency. In G. Forman (Ed.), *Action and thought* (pp. 297–327). New York: Academic Press.

Wolff, P. (1987). *The development of behavioral states and the expression of emotions in early infancy: New proposals for investigation.* Chicago: University of Chicago Press.

Wolpert, D. (1997). Computational approaches to motor control. *Trends in Cognitive Sciences, 1,* 209–216.

Wolpert, D., Doya, K., & Kawato, M. (2003). A unifying computational framework for motor control and social interaction. *Philosophical Transactions of the Royal Society of London Series B, 358,* 593–602.

Wolpert, D., Ghahramani, Z., & Jordan, M. (1995). An internal model for sensori-motor integration. *Science, 269,* 1880–1882.

Wolpert, D., & Kawato, M. (1998). Multiple paired forward and inverse models for motor control. *Neural Networks, 11,* 1317–1329.

Wood, D. (1989). Social interaction as tutoring. In M. Bornstein & J. Bruner, (Eds.), *Interaction in human development* (pp. 59–80). Hillsdale, N.J.: Erlbaum.

Wood, W., Wong, F., & Chachere, J. (1991). Effects of media violence on viewers' aggression in unconstrained social interaction. *Psychological Bulletin, 109,* 371–383.

Woodward, A. (1998). Infants selectively encode the goal object of an actor's reach. *Cognition, 69,* 1–34.

Woodward, A. (2002). Infant representation of goal-directed action. Paper presented at the workshop on naive moral cognition, Cambridge, Mass., November 2002.

Woodworth, R. (1938). *Experimental psychology.* New York: Holt.

Wright, R. (2000). *NonZero: The logic of human destiny.* New York: Pantheon.

Wyrwicka, W. (1996). *Imitation in human and animal behavior.* New Brunswick, N.J.: Transaction Publishers.

Youngblade, L., & Dunn, J. (1995). Individual differences in young children's pretend play with mother and sibling: Links to relationships and understanding of other people's feelings and beliefs. *Child Development, 66,* 1472–1492.

Zahavi, A., & Zahavi, A. (1997). *The handicap principle*. Oxford, UK: Oxford University Press.

Zahavi, D. (2001). Beyond empathy. Phenomenological approaches to intersubjectivity. *Journal of Consciousness Studies, 8,* 151–167.

Zahn-Waxler, C., Radke-Yarrow, M., Wagner, E., & Chapman, M. (1992). Development of concern for others. *Developmental Psychology, 28,* 126–136.

Zahn-Waxler, C., & Robinson, J. (1995). Empathy and guilt: Early origins of feelings of responsibility. In J. Tangney & K. Fischer (Eds.), *Self-conscious emotions* (pp. 143–173). New York: Guilford.

Zajonc, R., Adelmann, K., Murphy, S., & Niedenthal, P. (1987). Convergence in the physical appearance of spouses. *Motivation and Emotion, 11,* 335–346.

Zajonc, R., Murphy, S., & Inglehart, M. (1989). Feeling and facial efference: Implications of the vascular theory of emotion. *Psychological Review, 96,* 395–416.

Zentall, T. (2001). Imitation and other forms of social learning in animals: Evidence, function, and mechanisms. *Cybernetics and Systems, 32,* 53–96.

Zentall, T., & Levine, J. (1972). Observational learning and social facilitation in the rat. *Science, 178,* 1220–1221.

Zentall, T., Sutton, J., & Sherburne, L. (1996). True imitative learning in pigeons. *Psychological Science, 7,* 343–346.

Zillmann, D. (1979). *Hostility and aggression*. Hillsdale, N.J.: Erlbaum.

Zillmann, D. (1983). Transfer of excitation in emotional behavior. In J. Cacioppo & R. Petty (Eds.), *Social psychophysiology: A sourcebook* (pp. 215–240). New York: Guilford.

Contributors

Editors

Susan Hurley PAIS and Philosophy, University of Warwick; All Souls College, Oxford

Nick Chater Psychology, University of Warwick

Contributors

Moshe Anisfeld Ferkauf Graduate School of Psychology, Yeshiva University, Bronx, New York

Michael Arbib Computer Science, Neuroscience, and USC Brain Project, University of Southern California

Susan Blackmore Psychology, University of the West of England

Susan Brison Philosophy, Dartmouth College, Hanover, New Hampshire

Richard W. Byrne Psychology, University of St. Andrews

Malinda Carpenter Max Planck Institute for Evolutionary Anthropology, Leipzig

Thierry Chaminade Institute for Learning and Brain Sciences, University of Washington, Seattle

Morten H. Christiansen Psychology, Cornell University

Guy Claxton Graduate School of Education, University of Bristol

George Comstock Newhouse School of Public Communications, Syracuse University

Jean Decety Institute for Learning and Brain Sciences, University of Washington, Seattle

Ap Dijksterhuis Psychology, University of Amsterdam

Merlin Donald Psychology, Queen's University, Kingston, Ontario

John Eldridge Sociology and Glasgow Media Project, University of Glasgow

Birgit Elsner Psychology, University of Heidelberg

Bennett Galef, Jr. Psychology, McMaster University, Hamilton, Ontario

Vittorio Gallese Department of Neuroscience, Section of Physiology, University of Parma

Diego Gambetta Sociology, Nuffield College, University of Oxford

Francisco J. Gil-White Psychology, University of Pennsylvania

Alvin I. Goldman Philosophy and Center for Cognitive Science, Rutgers University

Robert M. Gordon Philosophy, University of Missouri, St. Louis

Mark Greenberg Philosophy and Law, University of California, Los Angeles

Paul L. Harris Graduate School of Education, Harvard University

Cecilia Heyes Psychology, University College London

Victoria Horner Psychology, University of St. Andrews

L. Rowell Huesmann Institute for Social Research, The University of Michigan

Nicholas Humphrey Centre for Philosophy of Natural and Social Science, London School of Economics

Marco Iacoboni Ahmanson-Lovelace Brain Mapping Center, Department of Psychiatry and Biobehavioral Sciences, David Geffen School of Medicine, University of California at Los Angeles

Susan Jones Psychology, Indiana University

Marcel Kinsbourne Psychology, New School University

Harry Litman Center for Law and Public Affairs, Princeton University

Sarah Marshall-Pescini School of Psychology, University of St. Andrews

Andrew N. Meltzoff Institute for Learning and Brain Sciences, University of Washington, Seattle

Ruth Garrett Millikan Philosophy, University of Connecticut

Irene M. Pepperberg School of Architecture and Planning, Massachussetts Institute of Technology; Psychology, Brandeis University, Waltham, Massachusssetts

Martin J. Pickering Psychology, University of Edinburgh

Jesse J. Prinz Philosophy, University of North Carolina, Chapel Hill

Wolfgang Prinz Max Planck Institute for Human Cognitive and Brain Sciences, Department of Psychology, Munich

J. N. P. Rawlins Experimental Psychology, University of Oxford

Giacomo Rizzolatti Department of Neuroscience, University of Parma

Paul Seabright Institut d'Economie Industrielle, University of Toulouse

Robert Sugden Economic & Social Studies, University of East Anglia

Michael Tomasello Max Planck Institute for Evolutionary Anthropology, Leipzig

Stephen Want Department of Psychology, Sheffield University

Andrew Whiten Psychology, University of St. Andrews

Thomas Zentall Psychology, University of Kentucky

Index to Volume 1

Note: Page numbers followed by the letter f refer to figures.

Index to Volume 2

Note: Page numbers followed by the letter f refer to figures and t to tables.